DATE DUE

THE BOOK OF GIMP

THE BOOK OF GIMP

A Complete Guide to Nearly Everything

by Olivier Lecarme and Karine Delvare

**no starch
press**

San Francisco

THE BOOK OF GIMP

Authorized translation from the French language edition, *GIMP: Manuel de référence pour l'édition d'images en logiciel libre*, by Olivier Lecarme and Karine Delvare, published by Pearson Education France, Copyright © 2010 Pearson Education France.

English language edition published by No Starch Press, Copyright © 2013 by Olivier Lecarme and Karine Delvare.

First printing

Printed in China

15 14 13 12   1 2 3 4 5 6 7 8 9

ISBN-10: 1-59327-383-5
ISBN-13: 978-1-59327-383-5

Publisher: William Pollock
Production Editor: Serena Yang
Cover Illustration: Tina Salameh
Developmental Editor: Sondra Silverhawk
Copyeditor: LeeAnn Pickrell
Proofreaders: Paula L. Fleming and Riley Hoffman

For information on book distributors or translations, please contact No Starch Press, Inc. directly:
No Starch Press, Inc.
38 Ringold Street, San Francisco, CA 94103
phone: 415.863.9900; fax: 415.863.9950; info@nostarch.com; www.nostarch.com

Library of Congress Cataloging-in-Publication Data

```
Lecarme, Olivier.
  [GIMP. English]
  The book of GIMP : a complete guide to nearly everything / by Olivier Lecarme
  and Karine Delvare.
      pages cm
  Includes bibliographical references and index.
  ISBN 978-1-59327-383-5 -- ISBN 1-59327-383-5
  1. GIMP (Computer file) 2. Photography--Digital techniques. 3. Image
  processing--Digital techniques. I. Delvare, Karine. II. Title.
  TR267.5.G56L4313 2012
  621.36'7--dc23
                            2012020781
```

Brief Contents

Contents in Detail

Part III   Appendices

Introduction

GIMP stands for *GNU Image Manipulation Program*, and it is one of the most successful applications in the world of free software. The name *GNU* is a recursive acronym: *GNU's Not Unix*, coined in 1983 by the celebrated Richard M. Stallman as a name for his pet project—a free software, Unix-like operating system.

Free software is a term used to describe software that can be used, studied, modified, and redistributed by anyone with only one, very reasonable restriction: that other users enjoy the same freedom to use the software and to examine and modify the software's code. Free software is generally available without charge, but sometimes there is a fee.

The word *free* must be understood as in "free speech" rather than "free beer." The term *software libre* is gaining some popularity, as it negates this ambiguity. The French word *libre* means *free* in the sense of liberty, whereas the word *gratuit* means free of charge.

GIMP is freely distributed to (and by) anybody, and anybody can look at its contents and its source code and can add features or fix problems. The only restriction is that, if you make any change to GIMP and want to redistribute it to other people, you must do it in a way that grants the recipients exactly the same freedom that you enjoyed.

GIMP began in 1995 as the school project of two university students; now GIMP is a full-fledged application, available on all distributions of GNU/Linux and on recent versions of Microsoft Windows and Mac OS X. Installing GIMP is fairly easy, and if you haven't already done so, take a minute and install GIMP now (see Appendix E for installation instructions).

Compared to the dominant commercial image-manipulation application, which is developed by an army of well-paid programmers, GIMP is currently developed by a very small team of unpaid, but enthusiastic, volunteer programmers. Keep this in mind if (read: when) you run into glitches in the program or when a feature you'd like to have isn't available. Remember the GIMP credo: "If you want it so badly, make it, and share it with the rest of us!" Welcome to the world of free software!

This Book

When the idea for this book began to take form in the beginning of 2006, we imagined finishing it in 2010 and covering GIMP 3.0. The first goal was nearly met for the French edition—that was under our control—but GIMP 3.0 is still far off because volunteer developers can work only when they have time to do so. Still, GIMP 2.8 is a great leap forward compared to the previous version, GIMP 2.6. Some of the most noteworthy new features include a single-window interface; completely revised and more powerful brush dynamics; clarification of saving versus exporting images; improved handling of dockable dialogs; support for layer groups; the ability to lock pixels, channels, and paths; an improved

Free Select tool; support for selecting and tagging multiple objects in resource lists (brushes, gradients, and palettes); a new Text tool with on-canvas editing capabilities; a large set of new brushes, brush dynamics, and tool presets; and many other features that make the program easier and more enjoyable to use. GIMP still lacks nondestructive editing, CMYK native support, and 16-bit depth color handling. Some of these features will likely appear in the next version, with support from the Generic Graphic Library (GEGL).

This book aims to fulfill two different purposes: to provide hands-on, task-oriented GIMP tutorials and to provide a comprehensive reference manual. Because these two goals are distinct, we designed the book in two parts. In the first part, eight independent chapters will walk you through the main tasks you can perform using GIMP. Each chapter begins with a hands-on tutorial and ends with exercises that reinforce the concepts covered.

You might want to start with Appendix A, which explains the theory behind image representation, and Chapter 1, which helps you to start using GIMP, but you can read the other chapters in any order. For example, if you are mainly interested in photo manipulation, read Chapters 2 and 5. If you are more interested in graphic design, read Chapters 3 and 4. And if you read all the tutorial chapters in order, you'll have a solid grasp of most aspects of GIMP.

The final 14 chapters constitute a thorough GIMP reference manual. We tried to cover all aspects in a logical order, using as many examples and illustrations as possible. We also tried to avoid explaining the same thing several times. Of course, topics overlap between the two parts, but we tried to keep repetition to a minimum and, when it was unavoidable, to explain things in a new way.

The chapters in the second part are arranged in a logical order, but, because this part is intended as a reference manual, you certainly do not need to read the chapters in order. We've included cross-references to help you find what you need to move your project forward. Some of the chapters in the second part correspond directly with a chapter from the first part. In those cases, we recommend that you first read the tutorial chapter and then refer to the relevant chapter(s) in the second part of the book. These paired chapters include 3 and 15, and 6 and 18. Additionally, Chapters 9 to 14 present some basic concepts that are used regularly in later chapters.

We used a bleeding-edge, developmental version of GIMP to ensure that everything was up-to-date as of the book's completion, and we've covered every aspect of GIMP as thoroughly as possible, with the exception of the tools in the second half of the **Image: Create** menu and those in the **Image: Filters > Alpha to logo** menu. We chose not to cover those tools because they're self-explanatory and have only a few parameters.

We struggled with the decision of whether to cover the many plug-ins and scripts that users have added to GIMP. Many of them would require an entire long chapter of their own. We decided to cover only one addition, the plug-in set called GIMP Animation Package (GAP), because it adds a powerful capability that GIMP alone lacks. In Chapter 21, we mention a few additional plug-ins to give readers an idea of what's available.

The Authors

Karine Delvare contributed to this book project from the beginning. The concept, as well as the organization and early drafts of the chapters, were created by both authors. But after publishers were found (one for the French edition and one for the English edition) and the editing process began, Karine became pregnant and decided that motherhood was her first priority. Olivier offered her his full support and took over the majority of book-related responsibilities after that. In the end, Karine wrote Chapters 3 and 8, and Olivier wrote the rest. Karine gave birth to a healthy, happy girl named Lina, and one year later she gave birth to a second baby girl, Sophie.

Karine is a freelance consultant in web development and lives in Mérignac, near Bordeaux, France. She has a master's degree in computer science, with a specialization in image and sound, and she has collaborated on the GIMP development project in various ways.

Olivier is a professor emeritus in computer science at the University of Nice, France. He has a doctorate and a Thèse d'État in computer science. He has been a professor at the Universities of Grenoble, Montréal, Lausanne, and Nice and has taught many aspects of computer science, including algorithmics, programming, data structures, compiling, programming language fundamentals, and graphics processing. He lives in Grasse, a lovely town in the hills of the French Riviera, and several of the photographs used as examples in this book were taken from his house or in his garden.

Production Notes

This book was typeset using LaTeX, the document-preparation system developed by Leslie Lamport and based on the TeX typesetting system developed by Donald Knuth. Olivier wrote a specialized LaTeX class for this book.

All the figures used in Chapters 3 and 8 were created by Karine. All the figures used in the other chapters were created by Olivier, unless a copyright designation indicates otherwise. Appropriate authorizations were obtained from the people whose photographs were used in this book.

Most screen shots were created on computers running the Debian distribution of GNU/Linux with the Glossy preference theme. You may see minor differences in the appearance of windows on systems running other distributions or operating systems or using different preference themes.

Conventions

GIMP was used to crop the window decoration out of most screen shots to save space and highlight the relevant information.

The notation **Image: Colors > Curves** means that you should click the Colors menu in the window of the image you are working on and then click the entry called Curves. This type of notation can include more menu levels, of course. Similarly, **Layers: right-click > Add an Alpha channel** means that you should right-click in the Layers dialog and choose Add an Alpha channel from the menu that appears.

The notation U means you should press the corresponding key on the keyboard. CTRL+U means that you press and hold the Control key and then press the U key.

Small caps, as in FEATHER, are used to denote the name of an entry, a button, or a checkbox.

A monospace font like Abstract 1 is used to denote specific text that the user must type into an input field.

Acknowledgments

From the beginning, we wanted this book to be full color. We considered it a shame that most books published about GIMP contained color prints in a middle section only—or no color at all. We are very grateful to both our publishers for having agreed to print in full color, despite the additional costs.

Our debt to the GIMP developers is immense: The work they did and are still doing is tremendous. Moreover, we had the opportunity to ask them some questions, using the gimp-user and gimp-developer mailing lists and the #gimp IRC channel. They graciously responded to our questions with invaluable first-hand information about difficult aspects of GIMP. We'd especially like to thank Alexia Death, Michael Hammel, Ramón Miranda, Michael Natterer, Sven Neumann, Martin Nordholts, and Alexandre Prokoudine, but many others have also made a vital contribution to the project. Many thanks to everyone involved!

Several chapters of this book are based on an undergraduate course taught by Olivier from 2002 to 2008. Thus, many examples are inspired by tutorials or other sources dating from that time. We would like to acknowledge our debt to the many people who created these tutorials (especially in Chapters 4 and 6) but whose names we no longer remember.

We would also like to thank the LaTeX developers and especially Frank Mittelbach and Michel Goossens, authors of the *LaTeX Companion*, the bible for all LaTeX users. Olivier owes a special debt to Frank, who kindly helped him to discover an old bug in the core of LaTeX. He would also like to mention Yannis Haralambous, author of the definitive book about fonts and encoding, for his help in getting the proper quote in programming examples.

We are very grateful to No Starch Press for enthusiastically accepting our book proposal. It is always a pleasure to correspond with Bill Pollock and Tyler Ortman. We are also very, very grateful to Patricia Moncorgé, from Pearson France, who was the first to accept our book project, including simultaneous publication in French and English. Discussions with her have been long, lively, and very fruitful. Without Patricia, this book would probably not exist.

Thanks to Sondra Silverhawk, the developmental editor, and to Serena Yang, the production editor, at No Starch Press. Also, thank you to LeeAnn Pickrell, the copy editor of the English edition. The editors of the English edition spent innumerable hours correcting errors and language ambiguities in this thick book and improving its style. Special thanks to the two proofreaders, Paula L. Fleming and Riley Hoffman.

Karine would like to thank her husband Jean, who helped her stay motivated and clearly define her priorities so Olivier would not be kept in the dark, and Olivier for accepting the change of priorities so gracefully.

Olivier would like to thank his wife Jacqueline, who accepted the fact that for many years she could see her husband only sideways, facing a computer screen. He'd also like to thank his colleagues of the I3S Laboratory, who read drafts of most of the chapters and encouraged him in this long endeavor.

Part I
Learning GIMP

1

Getting Started

In this chapter you'll learn the basics that you need to know to get started with GIMP. You'll get the most out of this chapter if you work along, so read in front of a computer if possible.

GIMP doesn't have any fancy system requirements, like a high-end graphics card or a multicore processor. We do recommend at least 2GB of memory and a 20-inch monitor, although you can make do with less. We also suggest that you use a mouse rather than a touchpad or, better yet, invest in a graphics tablet.

1.1 GIMP Basics

If you need help installing GIMP, refer to Appendix E. From this point on, we assume that you have GIMP properly installed.

Tip: When you want to quit GIMP, use **Image: File > Quit** or CTRL+Q. If you try to quit by closing windows, you might lose a valuable dialog in the process.

The Screen Layout

When GIMP starts for the first time, three different windows pop up on your screen, as shown in Figure 1.1. These windows are the Toolbox, the Image window, and a dialog dock. By default they occupy the full width of the screen, regardless of the size of your monitor. This screen layout can be arranged to suit your taste, and one of the first actions that many GIMP users take is to rearrange the screen layout so that it's intuitive and pleasing to them. If you don't like the multi-window interface, GIMP now offers a single-window interface, which we introduce in "The Single-Window Interface" on page 6.

If you come up with a screen layout that suits you perfectly, you can save it so it will look the same the next time you start GIMP. To do this, select **Image: Edit > Preferences** and choose the WINDOW MANAGEMENT menu entry. You'll see the dialog shown in Figure 1.2. Click SAVE WINDOW POSITIONS NOW and then OK.

The WINDOW MANAGEMENT tab also contains a section called Window Manager Hints, which changes how the Toolbox and the dialog docks behave. In Figure 1.2 it's set to Utility window, which means that the Toolbox and the dialog docks will always remain above other windows and be visible when the Image window is active. In other words, you cannot minimize utility windows. You can also choose to treat the Toolbox and dialogs like normal windows or to simply keep them above other windows.

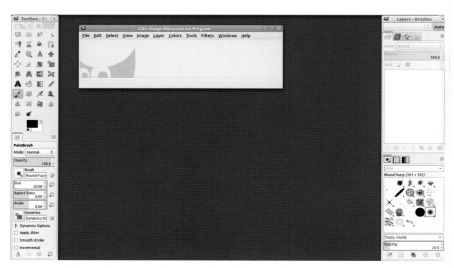

Figure 1.1 *The initial GIMP windows, multi-windows mode*

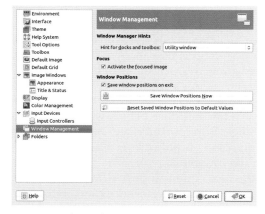

Figure 1.2 *The Preferences dialog, Window Management tab*

Dockable Dialogs

Figure 1.3 shows a common (although exaggerated) predicament that new GIMP users may find themselves in when working in multi-window mode. The screen is packed with windows: eleven of them in this case. Screen clutter can occur when you're using several different tools at once, when one tool has multiple windows associated with it, or when you're editing more than one image at a time.

When you add these extra windows to the standard dialogs for brushes, patterns, gradients, layers, and channels, you can easily wind up with a dozen or more open windows.

This is why GIMP uses *dockable dialogs*—small, interactive windows that can be grouped together into a multi-dialog window, as shown in Figure 1.4 (its two parts are laid out side by side). You can customize these windows to include any combination of the dockable dialogs, and you can have more than one open at a time.

Tip: If your screen gets too crowded, you can temporarily hide everything except the Image windows by pressing the TAB key. Pressing TAB again makes the hidden windows reappear in their original positions. This makes it very easy to optimize your screen space, even when working on a smaller monitor.

The window in Figure 1.4 contains two main sections. The left section contains four dockable dialogs: Layers, Channels, Paths, and Undo History. You can switch between them by clicking the tabs. The name of the current tab appears near the top of the dialog if there are one or two tabs, but it is replaced by an icon if there are three or more tabs. The right side of the

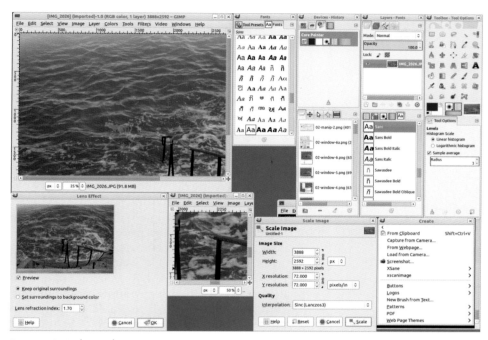

Figure 1.3 *A cluttered screen*

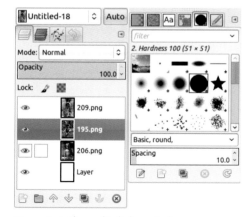

Figure 1.4 *The multi-dialog window*

Figure 1.5 *The Layers dialog menu*

window initially shows Brushes, Patterns, and Gradients, but we've added the Paint Dynamics and Fonts tabs. Each dialog tab has a main window, a row of buttons along the bottom of its window, and a small triangular button (to the right of the tabs). The buttons give you quick access to features like saving and loading

preferences, and the triangular button brings up a full menu of options specific to that dialog, as shown in Figure 1.5.

If you close a dockable dialog window, you can reopen it using **Image: Windows > Recently Closed Docks**. You can drag a dockable dialog out of the dock by clicking and dragging on its

Figure 1.6 *Moving a dialog between docks*

tab. You can then drop it anywhere on the desktop to make it an independent window, or you can drop it into another multi-dialog window as a new tab or as a new division at the bottom, top, or side of the window. Figure 1.6 shows the Channels dialog being moved to the bottom of the window.

The Toolbox

The Toolbox is split into two sections. The upper section of the Toolbox window is the Toolbox itself. By default, it contains icons for the most useful tools, though you can customize which are included and in what order. If you hover over any of these icons, GIMP displays the *tooltip*, which is the tool name, a brief description, and the keyboard shortcut. The current tool, if present in the Toolbox, is highlighted.

The lower half of the Toolbox window is actually a dockable dialog called Tool Options. It contains the Options dialog for the current tool. Although you can change this setup, it's best to leave it the way it is so that you can easily adjust the options of the tool you're working with.

The Single-Window Interface

Version 2.8 of GIMP includes a feature that has been anxiously anticipated by many of the GIMP users who work on Windows and Mac OS systems: the single-window interface. If you choose **Image: Windows > Single-Window mode**, all the current GIMP windows pack into a single window. If you start with the default multi-window arrangement, the single window will look like Figure 1.7. The Toolbox is a narrow column on the left, the multi-dialog window is on the right, and the center space is available to display an image. The single-window interface is designed to occupy the whole screen, but you can shrink it so as to view your desktop or other running programs at the same time.

Most components of this interface can be resized or moved, as we did using the multi-window interface. Figure 1.8 shows an example of the single-window interface in action. When there are two images open, or two views of the same image, you can switch between them using tabs, but you cannot view them at the same time. Figure 1.9 shows the same set of images and dialogs in the multi-window interface, for comparison.

As with multi-window mode, pressing TAB hides everything except the current image, but you can still access tools using menus or keyboard shortcuts.

Note that while in single-window mode the Toolbox cannot be moved or closed. It can be more difficult to adjust the size of the Image window, since it's constrained by all the docks and dialogs. Also, when you open a new dialog, it either extends to the full height of the window (and takes up a lot of space) or, sometimes,

Figure 1.7 *The initial GIMP windows, single-window mode*

Figure 1.8 *The single-window interface with two images open*

Figure 1.9 *The multi-window interface with two images open*

doesn't start out as a part of the main window, so you'll have to move it into place.

Although we recommend multi-window mode, you can use whichever mode you prefer while reading this book. Your choice of mode will rarely effect how the examples in this book work.

1.2 Image Handling Basics

In this section we'll show you how to open, scan, and save images, and we'll introduce you to the *Image window*. The Image window contains the image that's currently open in GIMP. If no image is currently open, closing the Image window quits GIMP. When GIMP begins, the Image window is empty.

Opening an Image

To open a saved image, select **Image: File > Open** or press CTRL+O. The window shown in Figure 1.10 will appear.

This window contains three panels: Places, Name, and Preview. You choose the folder where the image was saved in Places and select the image in Names. Thumbnails are shown in Preview. The left panel, Places, is divided into

three sections, as shown in Figure 1.10. The top section contains SEARCH, which searches for an image by name, and RECENTLY USED, which displays a list of the most recently used images. The middle section lists a fixed set of folders or devices, such as those that are visible on your desktop. The bottom section is a bookmark list. It's initially empty, but you can add folders by selecting them in the Names panel and clicking the +ADD button.

Clicking a folder in the left panel opens its contents in the middle panel. You can choose to list all images, images of a certain type, or all visible files. If the selected image is smaller than a certain threshold (defined in Preferences), a thumbnail preview automatically appears in the right panel. If it doesn't appear, you can manually display it by clicking on the file in the right panel.

The current path is displayed at the top of the window. You can type the image name directly into the LOCATION field, which can be toggled on and off using the button in the top-left corner of the window. The image type is normally determined automatically by GIMP, but it can also be manually selected.

Tip: You can drag an image thumbnail to the GIMP Toolbox to open it. This works with files

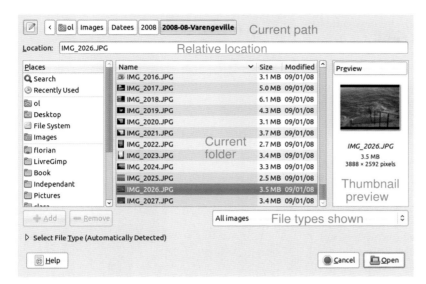

Figure 1.10 *Opening an image from a file*

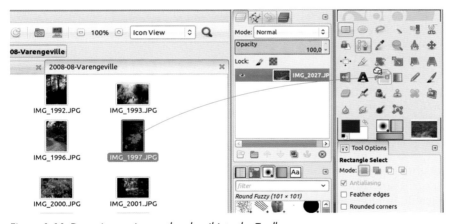

Figure 1.11 *Dragging an image thumbnail into the Toolbox*

on the computer, as shown in Figure 1.11, and with images from the Internet. Just drag the file from your browser to the GIMP Toolbox.

Maximizing an Image

If you're working on a small screen or working on a large, detailed image, you may want the image to fill the entire screen from time to time. We recommend that you use Fullscreen mode

via **Image: View > Fullscreen** or by pressing F11. This is *not* the same as maximizing the window with the window manager. When you use Fullscreen mode, all window decorations are removed, and you can even remove the menu bar, rulers, sliders, and status bar. You can even hide the Toolbox and dock windows (using TAB) to have the full screen at your disposal. The menus are still available by right-clicking in the image, and all the keyboard shortcuts are functional.

When you want to go back to the customary layout, just press F11 again (and TAB if the Toolbox is hidden).

The F11 command also works in single-window mode, but the image won't be as large, because some of the room on the screen will be taken up by the tab previews.

Scanning

You can digitalize old photos and drawings using a scanner. Many brands and models are available, from very cheap ones to expensive models for professional photographers. The most affordable option is often an all-in-one printer, which generally includes a printer, a simple photocopier, and a flatbed scanner. Most flatbed scanners can scan standard North American letter or international A4 format. More expensive scanners are sold separately, without a built-in printer, and often have a larger scanning bed. Larger beds are useful if you want to scan photographs mounted in a photo album.

The best software tool for scanning is XSane (*http://www.sane-project.org/*), a graphical front-end to SANE, which is an application programming interface (API) for scanning.

XSane works well on GNU/Linux, Mac OS, and many other operating systems but not on Windows, although this might change. The following discussion focuses on XSane, but much of the information is applicable to any scanning application.

You can use XSane from within GIMP by going to the **Image: File > Create > XSane** menu and choosing DEVICE DIALOG. You'll see a dialog that says "Scanning for devices," and once your scanner is recognized, two larger windows will appear. If this doesn't work, be sure to check that your scanner is plugged into your computer and powered up.

Figure 1.12 shows the Preview window, which will show you a preview of whatever you're scanning. There are a lot of buttons and menus, but

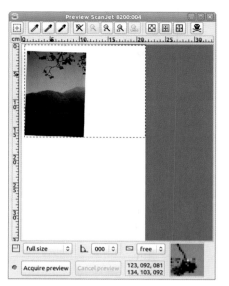

Figure 1.12 *Previewing a scanned photograph*

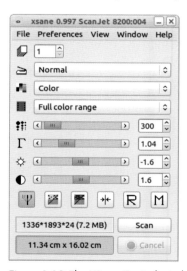

Figure 1.13 *The XSane Control window*

we'll just cover the basics that you need to know to get started.

Figure 1.13 shows the Control window. Two very important pieces of information that are shown here are the size of the scanned area (in pixels or your preferred units) and the size of the resulting file (in megabytes). Note how changes to the selected area in the Preview window, and to the scanning resolution in the Control window, affect the file size.

Previewing the Picture

Select a photo and place it facedown on the scanner glass. Don't place it right on the edge of the glass because many scanners don't scan all the way to the edge. In the Preview window, press the ACQUIRE PREVIEW button.

Eventually a preview of your photo appears, as in Figure 1.12. Sometimes the scan area is automatically adjusted to fit the image, but that was not the case in the figure. If you hover your mouse over the preview, you'll see a raw, zoomed representation of the section of the picture below the pointer and the values of the red, green, and blue (RGB) channels of the pixels in that section, in octal and in decimal notation, at the bottom of the dialog.

If your preview is upside down, you can flip it using the middle button in the second row from the bottom. You can choose from 12 rotations, including a vertical flip if the angle is followed by a vertical bar and a horizontal flip if the angle is followed by a minus sign.

Selecting and Scanning

To select the area you want to scan, click and drag the rectangular outline around your image in the preview area. Leave a little room around the image in case of parallax errors, which are caused by the thickness of the paper. See Figure 1.14. Don't worry if your photo is crooked. Getting it perfectly straight on the scanner glass can be tedious, and when you close the scanner, it can shift out of alignment again. You can easily rotate the image later in GIMP.

Once you've selected the scan area, adjust the parameters in the Control window. Select 1 for the number of pages, NORMAL for the source, COLOR, and then FULL COLOR RANGE. The ideal resolution depends on the photo's size and how

Figure 1.14 *Selecting the scan area*

you intend to use it. If you plan to print the image, choose a resolution that lets you print it at at least 300 ppi (pixels per inch). If you plan to touch up the image, or if you think you might want to print it larger than actual size, select a higher resolution. For this example, we chose 300 ppi for a selection area of 4.3 × 6.3 inches (11.3 × 16 cm), which will generate a file that's about 7MB before compression. Scanning at a higher resolution takes longer, and the file will be larger, but if you have the time and the hard drive space, choose a high resolution.

Choosing a high resolution allows you to make adjustments to improve the image without eroding the image quality. Later, if you want to send it in an email or post it on a web page, you can create a scaled-down copy.

Next, click the SCAN button. Scanning can take a while, and you can cancel the scan if you realize you made a mistake. First, the RGB data are received, and then the image is converted into a digital file. The image is also rotated if you selected a rotation in the Preview window. When the process is complete, the new digital image appears in the GIMP Image window.

Image Window Menus

Figure 1.15 shows the Image window with its main components labeled. You can toggle the visibility of the menu bar using **Image: View >**

Menu button   Menu bar   Window resize
                                                                     button

Rules

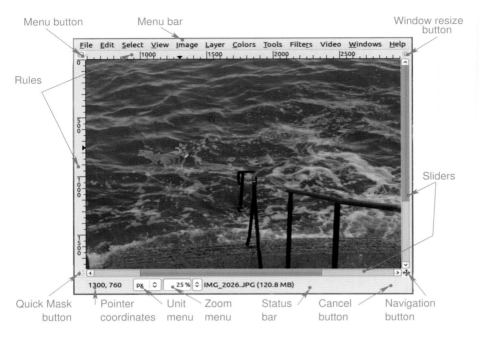

Sliders

Quick Mask   Pointer   Unit   Zoom   Status   Cancel   Navigation
   button   coordinates   menu   menu   bar   button   button

Figure 1.15 *The Image window*

Show Menubar. If you're using Mac OS X or the Ubuntu Unity interface, the menus will appear at the top of your screen instead, so Show Menubar won't do anything. You can also turn the visibility of the rules, sliders, and the status bar on or off via the **Image: View** menu.

The Image window can be used to access some very extensive menus, including the File menu and the Edit menu. There are three ways to access these:

- The menu bar, if it's displayed
- The menu button in the top left corner
- Right-clicking in the window

Therefore you always have a way to access the menus, even if only a small part of the Image window is visible.

When the menu is opened with the menu button or by right-clicking, it will have a dashed line at the top, as shown in Figure 1.16. If you click this line, the menu opens as a separate window.

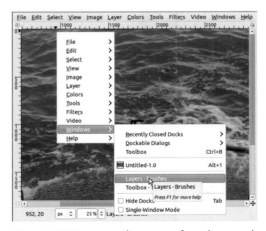

Figure 1.16 *Two cascading menus from the menu button*

Most of the remaining elements of the Image window are self-explanatory. Quick Mask is a selection-editing tool. The navigation button is a way to quickly change which part of the image is visible in the window, as shown in Figure 1.17.

Figure 1.17 *Using the navigation button*

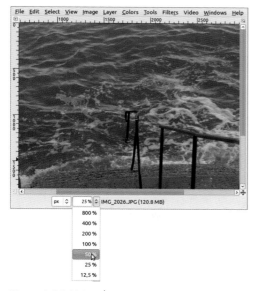

Figure 1.18 *Using the zoom menu*

Zooming

Zooming in on an image magnifies it on the screen without actually changing the image file. The level of magnification is expressed by the *zoom factor*. When you open an image, GIMP makes some automatic adjustments depending on the image size and the size of your screen. The zoom factor is 100% (actual size) for average sized images, less for really large files.

There are several ways to zoom in GIMP. One simple way is to use the window resize button in the top right of the Image window. By default it's unchecked, but if you check it, the image automatically zooms to fit the size of the window.

Alternatively, you can use the zoom menu shown in Figure 1.18. You can choose one of the predefined zoom factors from the drop-down menu, you can type one in, or you can use the mouse wheel while the pointer is in the field.

If you press and hold the CTRL key, you can zoom with the scroll wheel. Scrolling up zooms in, and scrolling down zooms out.

You can also use GIMP's Zoom tool, which can be selected by clicking the magnifying glass icon in the Toolbox or by pressing Z.

Tip: You can return an image to 100% zoom by pressing 1 on the keyboard when the Image window is active.

After adjusting the zoom factor of an image, you can use

Image: View > Shrink Wrap (or press CTRL+J), which resizes the window to fit the image. In single-window mode this can cut off dialogs, since the entire window shrinks.

Saving an Image

Once you've done work on an image in GIMP, you'll probably want to store the file so that you can come back to it later. GIMP's native format is XCF, and when you choose that format, all the components of your image (layers, transparency, etc.) will be retained. To save a new image as XCF, or to rename a previously saved XCF file, choose **Image: File > Save As** or SHIFT+CTRL+S. The dialog shown in Figure 1.19 will appear.

This window is similar to the Open Image dialog shown in Figure 1.10, but with the following differences:

- You can create a new folder with the CREATE FOLDER button.

- SELECT FILE TYPE (BY EXTENSION) allows you to choose the file type that your image will be

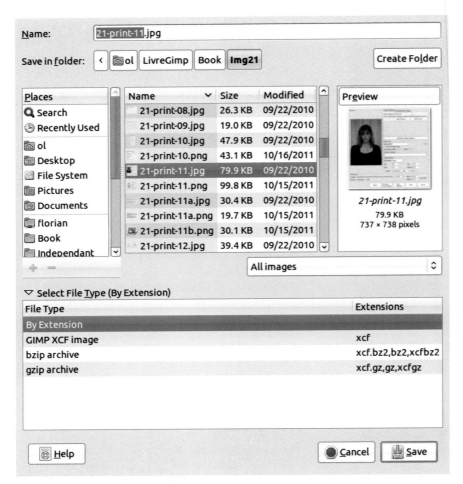

Figure 1.19 *The Save Image dialog*

saved as, but the choices are limited to XCF and compressed XCF.

You can store your image in a wide variety of other formats by exporting it via **Image: File > Export** or $\boxed{\text{SHIFT+CTRL+E}}$. The dialog that opens is identical to that in Figure 1.19, but lots of additional formats are available.

After you name your image, choose an extension, and click EXPORT, a dialog may pop up depending on the file type you chose. For example, when exporting to JPEG format for the first time, you'll be asked to set the quality rate and given the chance to adjust other parameters.

If you want to save an XCF image without changing its name or file type, select **Image: File > Save** or press $\boxed{\text{CTRL+S}}$. This does not open any dialog if the image is in the XCF format. If the image is in a different format, the Save dialog will open. If you want to export an image to replace a previous version, select **Image: File > Overwrite**.

The command **Image: File > Save a Copy** is similar to **Image: File > Save As**, but it creates a copy without altering or changing the name of the current image.

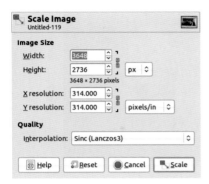

Figure 1.20 *The Scale Image dialog*

1.3 Working with Images

In this section, we'll help you get started working with your images. We'll show you some popular, easy-to-use tools that let you crop, resize, and sharpen your images, and then we'll introduce you to a couple of GIMP's many filters. We'll also show you the power of layers and demonstrate some basic drawing tools.

When you open a file in GIMP, it takes up more space than it did when it was sitting there on the hard drive. This is because GIMP lets you undo and redo actions. In order to let you return to a previous state, GIMP has to store that state, and the one before, and the one before that. To undo something, select **Image: Edit > Undo** or press CTRL+Z. If you change your mind and want to redo, select **Image: Edit > Redo** or press CTRL+Y.

Resizing an Image

If you want to put an image on a web page, send it in an email, or print it, you may want to change its size. You can resize an image in GIMP using **Image: Image > Scale Image**. This tool's dialog is shown in Figure 1.20. The most important parameters are the WIDTH and HEIGHT fields. You can change the units for these fields (by default they're set to pixels) or type in the new resolution. The little chain on the right determines whether the aspect ratio of the image should be preserved or not. It's connected by default, which is usually best, but it will disconnect if you click it.

Suppose you change the width of the image to 1024 pixels. When you press ENTER, the height is automatically changed to 683 pixels, though the image doesn't actually change size until you click the SCALE button. You may also want to set the INTERPOLATION to SINC (LANCZOS3), which is a rather processor-intensive algorithm that usually yields the best results.

If you choose to use units other than pixels (such as inches or centimeters), you'll need to pay attention to the X and Y resolution fields. The resolution is measured in pixels per inch, so an image that's 300 pixels wide would be one inch wide at 300 ppi. The default value, 72 ppi, is appropriate for a CRT screen. For an LCD screen it should be 98 or 100 ppi. For printing, it should be at least 300 ppi. If you use a lower resolution when printing, your image will look pixelated.

After scaling down an image, you should sharpen it, as scaling down can reduce the sharpness of an image. **Image: Filters > Enhance > Unsharp Mask** is the simplest way to do this. A dialog will appear—simply click OK.

Cropping an Image

Cropping an image permanently removes part of it, like cutting a photo with scissors. You might crop a photo to remove uninteresting areas, to emphasize the main subject, or to alter the composition. An image in which the main subject is exactly centered is often less lively than one in which the subject is a bit to one side.

Take, for example, the photograph shown in Figure 1.21. It's wider than most photos, and it's hard to tell what we're suppose to be looking at— is this a picture of the man dozing on left or of the contrasting light in the doorway on the right? You could crop the photo in two different ways to emphasize these potential subjects.

Figure 1.22 shows the Crop tool's icon selected in the Toolbox.

Figure 1.21 *A photo to crop*

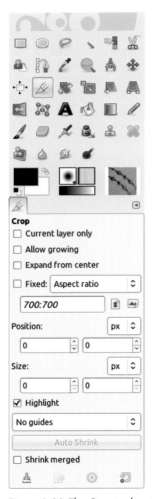

Figure 1.22 *The Crop tool and its options*

Figure 1.23 *Using the Crop tool*

Figure 1.24 *Changing the location of the area to be cropped*

The Crop tool has a lot of options, shown in Figure 1.22, but you can leave them as is for now. If the Crop tool is selected, the pointer becomes crosshairs with an icon of a blade next to it. Select the area to crop by clicking and dragging, as shown in Figure 1.23.

When you stop dragging, the area outside your selection is dimmed, and the outline of the selected area looks like the one in Figure 1.24. The pointer changes to a cross with four arrows, which is the icon of the Move tool in GIMP. You can move the cropping rectangle around in the image by dragging it.

When you hover the pointer over one side of your selection, the pointer's shape changes, as shown in Figure 1.25, and you can drag the side to change the size of the rectangle. You can also drag the corners of the selection to change the size of the area to be cropped

Figure 1.25 *Changing the dimensions of the area to be cropped*

Figure 1.27 *The Add Border dialog*

Figure 1.28 *The Color Selection dialog*

Figure 1.26 *Our masterpiece photo*

while maintaining the aspect ratio. Once you've selected the area to crop, click inside it or press ENTER to proceed. Clicking outside the selected area cancels the selection.

Adding a Frame with Filters

What do you do with the masterpiece you just created? You put it in a frame, of course. You can frame images digitally in GIMP using *filters*, which are a diverse collection of tools grouped together in the **Image: Filters** menu.

We've decided to frame the photo shown in Figure 1.26. To begin framing, select **Image:** **Filters > Decor > Add Border**, which brings up the dialog shown in Figure 1.27.

You can choose the width of the border, the color, and the characteristics of the shading that gives the frame depth. Our photo is 800×1200 pixels, so the default width of 12 pixels is too small. We changed it to 40 for both dimensions. A delta value of 25 is also rather small, so we changed it to 50. We didn't like the blue color, so we clicked the color button, which brings up the dialog shown in Figure 1.28.

The four tabs on the top left allow you to choose different methods of color selection. For now we'll use the leftmost tab, with an icon of Wilber's head on it. Wilber is the GIMP mascot.

The vertical strip in the center shows that blue is currently selected. You can click in the strip to select a different color. The large square on the left shows the shade of blue. You can click to choose a lighter or darker shade.

We want our frame to be brown, but there is no brown in the vertical color bar. We make one by choosing a red hue in a dark shade. By moving the hue cursor down to the red

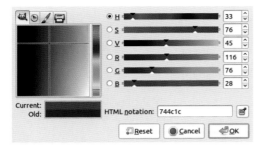

Figure 1.29 *Choosing the frame color*

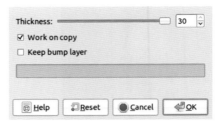

Figure 1.31 *The Add Bevel dialog*

Figure 1.30 *The frame has been added*

Figure 1.32 *The beveled frame*

section in the vertical strip, you get a mahogany color. By moving the cursor farther up, you get something closer to oak or chestnut. Our choice is shown in Figure 1.29. After you choose a color and click OK, GIMP will process for a while, and the dialog will disappear. And it looks like nothing changed!

Well, you may have seen the result if your Image window was larger than the image, but if it looked like nothing happened, the frame is just hidden. To reveal it, press CTRL+J to fit the Image window to the image. Now you can see the result, shown in Figure 1.30. It's not very realistic, so we'll improve it using a bevel filter.

Select **Image: Filters > Decor > Add Bevel**, and the dialog shown in Figure 1.31 appears.

Increase the THICKNESS to 30 and uncheck the WORK ON COPY checkbox. Click OK, and GIMP adds the bevel. If the result is too subtle, you can quickly run the same filter with the same parameters a second time by pressing CTRL+F. Our result is shown in Figure 1.32.

Using Layers

You may want to keep several sketches in one file, add a background to a painting, or make a composite image of several files. You can do all of these things using one of GIMP's most powerful features: *layers*.

The Layers dialog is located by default in the upper section of the multi-docks window. Figure 1.33 shows that our current image is composed of two layers. The lower layer, called

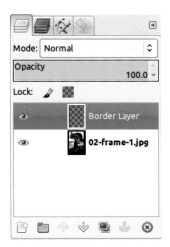

Figure 1.33 *The Layers dialog*

Create a New Layer
Untitled-127

Layer name: New Layer

Width: 824

Height: 1224 px

Layer Fill Type
○ Foreground color
○ Background color
○ White
● Transparency

Help   Cancel   OK

Figure 1.34 *Creating a new layer*

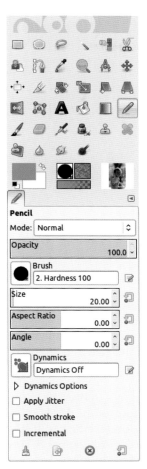

Figure 1.35 *Choosing the Pencil tool*

Background, is the original photograph. The upper layer, called Border Layer, was added by the Add Border filter and modified by the Add Bevel filter. This layer is currently active, so it's highlighted. The eye to the left of the layer's name tells you that the layer is visible. Click the eye to turn the visibility on or off.

You can create a new layer by clicking the button on the lower left. The dialog shown in Figure 1.34 will appear. You can choose the new layer's name, size, and fill type. The default fill type is Transparency. When you click OK, the new layer is created and becomes the current layer.

Drawing in GIMP

GIMP is a great program for making digital art, be it a quick sketch or a detailed painting. In this section we'll go over some of the basics that you'll need to know to start making your own digital art in GIMP.

GIMP offers a number of tools that you can use to draw or sketch. Each tool is modeled after a real drawing tool, such as a brush, pencil, or pen. To demonstrate some of these tools, we're

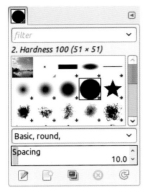

Figure 1.36 *The Brushes dialog*

Figure 1.37 *A signature made with the Pencil tool*

going to sign Wilber's name on some images. In Figure 1.35 we simulated a felt-tip pen using the Pencil tool. We did this by adjusting the *brush* option, which represents the size and shape of the pencil's tip. We chose the Hardness 100 brush and changed its size to 20. You can adjust the brush settings in the Pencil tool options or in the Brushes dialog, which is located in the bottom half of the multi-dock window (see Figure 1.36).

You can also choose the ink color. This doesn't appear in the Pencil options—the Pencil tool will use the current foreground color, which is displayed in the upper box in the bottom left of the Toolbox. The lower box shows background color. The double-pointed arrow between these two boxes switches the foreground and background colors, and the smaller black and white boxes to the left reset the foreground and background colors to black and white, respectively. We left the color on the default setting (black).

When we used a mouse and the Pencil tool to sign Wilber's name, the result was awkward, as shown in Figure 1.37. This is because the Pencil tool doesn't use *antialiasing* (smoothing the edges with semi-transparent pixels) and because it's difficult to draw with a mouse.

Figure 1.38 *A signature made with the Brush tool*

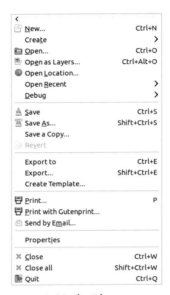

Figure 1.39 *The File menu*

Hide the pencil layer by clicking the eye next to its name in the Layers dialog, and then create another transparent layer. In the pop-up dialog, replace the layer name with Paintbrush. Select the Paintbrush tool by clicking its icon, which is next to the Pencil tool's icon, and again choose a round, size 20 brush. The signature, shown in Figure 1.38, looks a little better because of the antialiasing, but signing with a mouse is still awkward. We'll show you how to sign with a stylus in "Working with a Tablet in GIMP" on page 23.

Printing with GIMP

You can print your photos and drawings directly from GIMP once you've finished working on them. Figure 1.39 shows the File menu, where you'll find the print choices that are available.

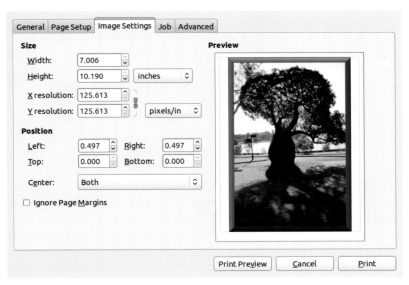

Figure 1.40 *The Print dialog, third tab*

Depending on the GIMP extensions installed on your computer, the menu may contain only some of the entries shown. Specifically, the entry PRINT WITH GUTENPRINT requires the Gutenprint package. This collection of free printer drivers is available only for GNU/Linux and Mac OS X systems.

If you're using GNU/Linux or Mac OS X, choose PRINT from the **Image: File** menu. The dialog that appears contains five to seven tabs, depending on which printer you choose in the first tab. In the second tab, you can choose a paper type and paper source from those that are defined for your printer, as well as the size and orientation of the paper. The third tab (shown in Figure 1.40) shows a print preview. Here you can change the resolution or dimensions of the printed image, as well as its position on the page. If your printer has more advanced settings, they will be listed on the tabs that follow. The last tabs allow you to change parameters that are useful only if you have several printers and several people trying to use them at the same time.

On Windows, the print dialog is very different. It contains only two tabs, but in the first one, where you select your printer, you can click the PREFERENCES button to open a new dialog. This dialog has several tabs and allows you to set the same parameters as the print dialog described above but presented differently and in a different order.

For all systems, once the parameters are set as you want, click PRINT to accept your selections and print your image.

1.4 Using a Tablet

In "Drawing in GIMP" on page 19, we saw how awkward it is to draw using a mouse—our signature was ugly and unnatural. A mouse is great for clicking, but the large pointer makes it difficult to select a single pixel, and it's virtually impossible to draw a straight line or a graceful curve. In the coming chapters, we'll often want to draw precise lines or smooth contours.

If you plan to do much work in GIMP, we highly recommend investing in a graphics tablet. Depending on the manufacturer, the tablet's

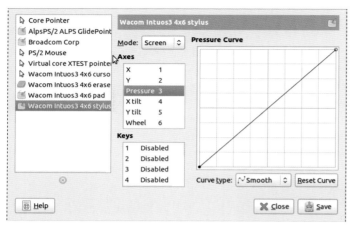

Figure 1.41 *The Configure Input Devices dialog*

size, and its capabilities, prices can range from $20 to more than $2000. You can find an excellent tablet with all the really useful features for about $350, though you can pick one up for less if you compromise on pressure and tilt sensitivity.

Installing a Tablet

Graphics tablets generally plug into a USB port. Depending on your operating system, you may have to install software from an accompanying CD or configure some system files to get your tablet working. On GNU/Linux systems, support is provided by the Linux Wacom project (*http://linuxwacom.sourceforge.net/*), and usually a tablet works as soon as it's plugged in.

Even though the official websites of tablet manufacturers often neglect to mention that their tablets are compatible with GIMP (or any free software), most tablets are. Once the tablet is installed and working, you just need to let GIMP know that its there. To do this, open the **Image: Edit > Preferences** dialog to the INPUT DEVICES section. Click CONFIGURE EXTENDED INPUT DEVICES, and the dialog shown in Figure 1.41 will appear. The same dialog can be opened from **Image: Edit > Input Devices**. For now, the only fields you need to pay attention to

are the device menu on the left and the MODE button.

If your tablet is properly installed, you should see four new devices in the device menu: Cursor, Pad, Eraser, and Stylus (or any other names chosen during the tablet's installation). Cursor corresponds to the tablet's mouse, and Stylus and Eraser correspond to the two ends of the tablet's pen. You can forget Pad for the moment. For these three new devices, set MODE to SCREEN. Now click CLOSE in this dialog and OK in the Preferences dialog, and your tablet is ready to go!

The Tablet Mouse and Stylus

Depending on your needs, you may decide to either put the tablet beside your keyboard like a mouse or move your keyboard to the side and place the tablet directly in front of your monitor. An artist or other professional will generally do the latter, while a more casual user may just leave the tablet to the side except when it's needed. You can experiment to see which arrangement is more comfortable for you.

The tablet mouse acts like a normal mouse, but with one difference. With a regular mouse, there is generally a component called *acceleration*. When you move the mouse a little, the pointer on the screen moves proportionally. If you move the mouse faster, the pointer moves more quickly and farther across the screen. This feature allows you to move the pointer across a screen 2000 pixels wide with only a slight gesture of the hand, while still allowing you to make very precise movements slowly.

The tablet mouse does not use acceleration. A position on the tablet corresponds to the equivalent position on the screen, which always remains constant. In other words, the top left corner of the tablet always corresponds to the top left corner of the screen. This means that you'll have to move your hand farther to move the pointer across the screen than you would with an ordinary mouse, especially if you have a larger tablet.

The tablet's stylus behaves in the same way. When the tip of the pen is close to the tablet's surface, the pointer moves to the corresponding position on the screen. Touching the pen to the tablet is equivalent to left-clicking with the mouse. You can click, double-click, and drag using the pen. You can also right-click by pressing a button on the pen.

The pen usually has two active ends: one for drawing and one for erasing. The drawing end often looks like a fine felt-tip pen. Sometimes the pen will come with more than one tip, and these tips resemble different drawing tools. The other end is usually shaped like a pencil's eraser. You can associate different tools with these ends and save your settings in GIMP. We associate the Paintbrush tool with the normal tip and the Eraser tool with the other end. Some tablets even allow you to have several different pens, which could be set up as a red brush, a yellow pen, and a black pencil, for example.

The amount of pressure that you apply when drawing with the pen is transmitted to the drawing application. In GIMP, most drawing tools use a feature called *paint dynamics*, which handles input from the tablet's pen. This will be covered in detail in "Paint Dynamics" on page 333.

Figure 1.42 *Using the tablet pen*

If you choose the Basic Dynamics, pen pressure is correlated to the brush opacity and pen velocity to the brush size.

Some tablets also sense the tilt of the pen and even its rotation. In GIMP, these properties are also handled by Paint Dynamics.

Working with a Tablet in GIMP

Figure 1.42 shows the correct way to hold a tablet pen. It can take a little time to learn to use it comfortably, especially if the tablet is placed beside the keyboard rather than directly in front of the screen.

Figure 1.43 shows three signatures made with the tablet pen, using three different GIMP tools. The first was made with the Pencil tool, with opacity controlled by pen pressure. The brush size is controlled by the pen's velocity, which you can see by looking at the underline—the pen was moving faster toward the left. The second signature was made with the Paintbrush tool, using the same dynamics. The third was made using the Ink tool, which is useful for simulating calligraphy.

Figure 1.44 shows the effect of changing the pressure parameters of the Paintbrush tool. The lines were drawn in the same way, increasing the pen pressure from left to right. The brush was also the same. For the first line, only opacity was controlled by the pen pressure. For the second line, only hardness, which means that the brush is less fuzzy when pressure increases. For the third line, only size changed. For the fourth line,

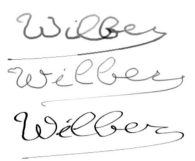

Figure 1.43 *Signatures made with the tablet pen*

Figure 1.44 *Changing the paint dynamics of the Paintbrush tool*

all three parameters (opacity, hardness, and size) were controlled by pen pressure.

A graphics tablet can come in handy when doing a variety of tasks in GIMP. In Chapter 2, we'll use one to make precise selections in a photograph. In Chapter 3 you'll see more examples of using a tablet with drawing tools. In the rest of the chapters, we'll note when using a tablet is beneficial.

One question often comes up when people install a new tablet: Once you've installed a graphics tablet, can you throw away your old mouse?

Well, it's up to you. Some people put a mouse pad on top of their tablet and use an ordinary mouse most of the time. When they use GIMP to draw or make a precise selection, they remove the pad and mouse and use the tablet pen.

Other people do throw away the old mouse and only use the tablet. They might alternate between using the tablet mouse for normal tasks and the pen for drawing and selecting, or they might use the pen for every task that most people use a mouse to do.

1.5 Exercises

Exercise 1.1. In the **Image: Windows** menu, open the Dockable Dialogs menu and build a new dock with the dialogs you think will be useful.

Exercise 1.2. Rearrange the screen layout to better suit your tastes. You can add or remove dockable dialogs, rearrange windows, or even switch to single-window mode. When you're done, save the layout so that GIMP remembers it next time you launch the program.

Exercise 1.3. If you have a digital camera, load some pictures onto your computer. You might plug the camera into your computer using a USB cable, or you might remove the memory card and insert it into a card reader on your computer. The memory card is seen as a new USB device, so you can find it and your photos with your file manager.

Exercise 1.4. Crop and resize one of your photos. Don't forget to use the Unsharp Mask filter afterward. When you're happy with the image, print it out.

Exercise 1.5. Bonus points: If you don't have a graphics tablet, go buy one! When you have it, connect it to your computer and make sure it's properly installed. Once GIMP recognizes it, practice signing your name using the different drawing tools.

Exercise 1.6. Pictures used in photo identification cards, like drivers licenses and passports, are notoriously unflattering. Find a good picture of yourself and use it to make a sheet of several ID photos, ready to be printed and cut out.

2 Photograph Retouching

For many people, GIMP is a program for processing photographs. GIMP is actually much more than that, but photo processing is, indeed, one of its most valuable uses. This is why the first manipulations we demonstrated in Section 1.3 dealt mainly with photographs and why we devote two chapters to the subject—this one and Chapter 5. The main difference between these two chapters is that in this chapter we process only one photograph at a time, whereas in Chapter 5 we'll process several simultaneously to create composite images.

2.1 Tutorial: Enhancing Badly Taken Photographs

Most photographs can be improved with digital processing, but finding a single photograph with every possible defect is difficult. Therefore, we'll have to demonstrate the many useful photo-correction techniques you can do with GIMP on several different sample photographs.

Cropping, Straightening, and Restoring Perspective

The photograph shown in Figure 2.1 needs to be cropped and straightened. We then need to restore the perspective. This image could also use some lighting correction to enhance visibility inside the church. First, however, we'll straighten out the picture. To do this, we determine the rotation angle and then use the Rotate tool to level the image.

The rotation angle can be measured with the Measure tool (SHIFT+M). In its options dialog, check the USE INFO WINDOW box. A good place to measure the angle is along the window frame. Zoom into the image and position it in the Image window so the top of the frame occupies the width of the Image window. To zoom, click the menu at the bottom of the Image window and select 100%. To reposition the image, use the crossed arrows in the bottom-right corner of the Image window. You can also reposition an image by holding down the SPACE key and moving the mouse or by using the scroll wheel on your mouse. The scroll wheel moves the image vertically, by default, or horizontally if you press SHIFT. Pressing CTRL while using the scroll wheel allows you to zoom in or out.

Once you have the image in view, using the Measure tool, click and hold on to the top-left corner of the frame. While pressing the mouse button, drag the cursor to the top-right corner of the frame. Figure 2.2 shows the two crosses

Figure 2.1 *The initial photograph*

Figure 2.2 *Measuring the rotation angle*

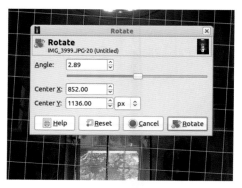

Figure 2.3 *Rotating the image*

Figure 2.4 *Applying the Perspective tool*

that mark the measured distance, as well as the measured angle, which is 2.89°.

Now we'll rotate the image so the frame is level. Choose the Rotate tool (SHIFT+R) and click the image. In the dialog that appears, set the angle to 2.89 (see Figure 2.3). The center of rotation appears as a circle in the bottom of the figure (the center of the image). In the options dialog for the Rotate tool, PREVIEW has been set to IMAGE+GRID. Click ROTATE: The frame should now be horizontal.

For the next transformation, we'll use the Perspective tool (SHIFT+P). Again, select the IMAGE+GRID PREVIEW option in the tool's options dialog, and then click anywhere on the image. You cannot set the angle or dimension directly. Instead, you must click and drag in the image to warp the perspective. The grid provides a helpful frame of reference. Figure 2.4 shows the warping process. When you're satisfied with the perspective, click TRANSFORM.

Next we'll crop the image. Because the doorway was our intended subject, we want to shear off the top of the picture. To do this, use the Crop tool (SHIFT+C). First, select the area that you want to keep, as shown in Figure 2.5. You can modify the area by clicking and dragging the sides or the corners of your selection. When you're satisfied, click in the selected area or press ENTER. The result appears in Figure 2.6.

Correcting Exposure

A good digital camera should always set a correct exposure. But what is the correct exposure for a scene with strong contrast? In Figure 2.7, for example, the photographer chose to point the camera at the sky, and thus the house is much too dark. Adjusting this in GIMP is fairly easy.

Figure 2.5 *Cropping the image*

Figure 2.6 *After cropping*

First select the sky. Because a disconnected bit of sky appears to the left of the building, the best tool to use is the Select by Color tool (SHIFT+O). Clicking anywhere on the sky selects part of it, which you see now inside the *marching ants* (i.e., the moving dashes that follow the border of the selected area). To augment this selection, press SHIFT and continue to click in areas of sky that are not selected, especially around the corners of the image and near the trees in the center of the photograph. Figure 2.8

Figure 2.7 *The initial image*

Figure 2.8 *Selecting the sky*

shows the sky correctly selected. In this case, you don't need to refine the selection. In more difficult cases, you can use Quick Mask to refine your selection (see "Making a Selection" on page 38).

You've selected the sky, but what you really want is to select everything *but* the sky. Therefore, invert the selection (CTRL+I). Hide the marching ants with CTRL+T to see the result more clearly, and then open the **Image: Colors > Levels** tool. Leave the color balance as it is, at least for now, and work only on the Value channel.

To better see the Input Levels histogram, select Logarithmic by clicking the button on the top right of the dialog, on the same line as CHANNEL. Move the rightmost white triangle under the histogram until it points to the first peak, as shown in Figure 2.9. The modification is too subtle, so also change the Gamma cursor. Move the middle, gray triangle to the left until you are satisfied with the result. The setting shown in

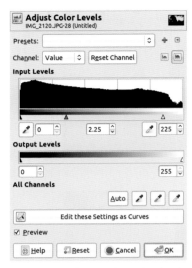

Figure 2.9 *Adjusting the Value levels*

Figure 2.10 *The final result*

Figure 2.11 *Using another method*

Figure 2.12 *A photograph with a blue cast*

- Select **Image: Layer > Duplicate Layer**.
- Press $\boxed{\text{SHIFT+CTRL+D}}$.
- Select **Layers: right-click > Duplicate Layer**.
- Click the fourth button from the left at the bottom of the Layers dialog.

Finally, at the top of the Layers dialog, change the MODE to Screen mode and adjust the opacity of this layer. The result appears in Figure 2.11. You can also combine the two methods if you aren't satisfied with the results of either one.

Correcting the Color Balance

As with exposure, even a very good digital camera may produce a photograph with a color cast. A number of factors, including user error, can lead to color cast in a photograph. Figure 2.12 shows a photograph with a blue cast. If you don't like how that looks, here's a tool you can use to correct it.

Figure 2.9 yields the result shown in Figure 2.10. In Chapters 7 and 12, we introduce techniques that you could use to further improve this photograph. Similarly, the edited image shown in Figure 2.6 could benefit from additional exposure correction, but the techniques required are beyond the scope of this tutorial.

You can use another, simpler method to brighten an underexposed photograph. This technique doesn't always work, but it may at least yield interesting results. Open the photograph from Figure 2.7 in GIMP, and immediately duplicate the only layer. You can do this in many ways:

Figure 2.13 *The Levels dialog*

Figure 2.14 *The final result*

To correct the color cast, use the Levels tool again. Click **Image: Colors > Levels** to get started. Figure 2.13 shows the Levels dialog. Select the Blue channel. To adjust the input levels, move the black (leftmost) triangle slightly to the right to extend the blue color range, and then move the gray (central) triangle to the right until you are satisfied with the color cast reduction. Leaving the PREVIEW box checked lets you see the effect of these changes without committing to them. If you're still not satisfied with the color balance, try making corrections in the other two channels. Figure 2.14 shows the photograph with color corrections applied.

Figure 2.15 *The initial image*

Removing an Object

So far we've focused on ways to improve the overall quality of an image without actually altering the content. In this section, we show you how to remove an eyesore, in this case, a garbage can that pollutes the entrance to the pergola shown in Figure 2.15. Removing the unwanted obstruction is easy, thanks to the Clone tool. Select it by pressing the letter C on your keyboard. In the tool's options dialog, reset all the options to their default values using the yellow arrow in the bottom-right corner of the dialog. Choose the Hardness 075 brush, and set its diameter to **76** pixels. Zoom in to enlarge the garbage container and place it in the center of the window. Now, "paint" over the unwanted container by cloning the surrounding scenery:

1. Press CTRL and click the part of the image you want to copy (the source point).

2. Release CTRL and "paint" the container (the target) with the scenery you have just selected.

Figure 2.16 shows this process. The source point isn't fixed; it's relative. As you paint, the source point moves in the same way that your brush moves, which allows you to paint over a large area with a single CTRL click. However,

Figure 2.16 *Erasing the garbage container*

Figure 2.17 *The final result after a lighting adjustment*

in this example, changing the source point from time to time is still necessary, especially when erasing the bin supports.

With GIMP's handy Clone tool, you are able to erase that ugly bin in a few seconds. Figure 2.17 shows the final image, after improving the lighting using the technique described in "Correcting Exposure" on page 26.

Improving Sharpness

You might assume that if you use the ideal settings and select a high resolution, then you'll be able to take sharp photographs with your

Figure 2.18 *The initial photograph*

digital camera. That's not always the case, however, for several reasons. One reason is that the resolution of files that the camera can store is actually larger than the resolution of its sensors. In this case, the image you get is the result of an interpolation. The same thing happens when you use a scanner to create a digital image from a print. Any digitalized image can, therefore, benefit from the adjustments that we show you in this section. It's important to note that you should make the following corrections during the final steps of image production, after you've made any adjustments to the image's resolution.

This phenomenon, motion blur, and the haze of smoke drifting across the landscape contribute to the fuzziness of our example image, shown in Figure 2.18.

Select the filter **Image: Filters > Enhance > Unsharp Mask**. Despite its name, this filter is an excellent tool for improving sharpness. The dialog shown in Figure 2.19 appears. Play around with the parameters. You can see the effect of your adjustments in the Preview window. When you're satisfied, click OK. Our sharpened image is shown in Figure 2.20.

Removing Red Eye

The red eye phenomenon is well known: When you take a portrait using a flash, the flash lights up the back of the eye, which appears red, at least for humans. This effect is most apparent when the subject is looking straight at the photographer and when the ambient light is dim,

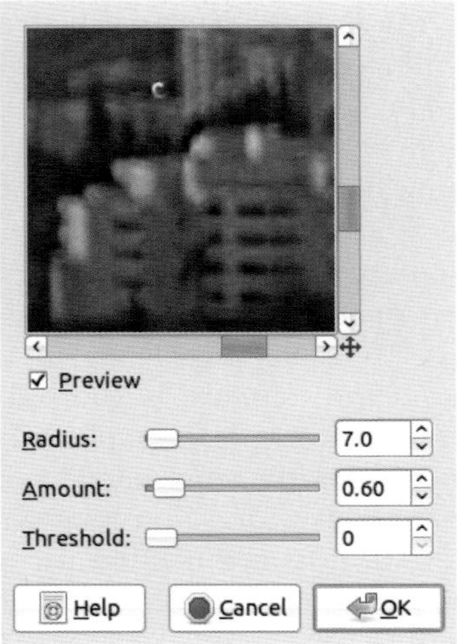

Figure 2.19 *The Unsharp Mask filter dialog*

Figure 2.20 *The final result*

Figure 2.22 *Selecting the eyes*

causing the pupils of the subject's eyes to widen. To avoid red eye, most cameras have a very short preflash, which dazzles the subject's eyes and causes her pupils to contract. If the pupil is small, the back of the eye is no longer visible. This doesn't always work, however. Moreover, narrow pupils can make the subject look less attractive. Correcting the problem with GIMP may, therefore, be a better solution. Figure 2.21 is a good example of the red eye phenomenon.

GIMP has several techniques that you can use to correct red eye. We describe some of them in "More Correction Methods for Red Eye" on page 47. Here, we use the simplest one—the specialized filter: Select **Image: Filters > Enhance > Red Eye Removal**. If you select this filter without any preparation, the dialog appears with this message: "Manually selecting the eyes may improve the results." If you ignore the message and click OK, the filter modifies the colors in places you didn't intend, such as the lips of the model.

To avoid unintended color modifications, you need to select the eyes before applying the filter. Do this with the Free Select tool ([F]). For the first eye, draw an imprecise outline that includes the whole iris. To include the second eye in the same selection, press and hold [SHIFT] as you roughly outline the other eye. You can see the completed selection in Figure 2.22.

Figure 2.21 *The initial photograph*

Figure 2.23 *The Red Eye Removal filter dialog*

Figure 2.24 *The final result*

Now select the Red Eye Removal filter, which brings up the dialog shown in Figure 2.23. You no longer see a warning, and the preview looks good with the current settings. Click OK. The final image is shown in Figure 2.24.

2.2 Global Transformations

In this section, we discuss global transformations, which affect an entire photograph.

Resizing an Image

GIMP offers five important tools for correcting photographs that are tilted, poorly framed, taken from an awkward point of view, and so on. Learning how to use these tools correctly is important. You already used the Rotation tool,

the Crop tool, and the Perspective tool in this chapter. We now demonstrate the Scale tool and how to resize an image.

When you scan an image or transfer a file from a digital camera, it may be too large to fit on the monitor. Recall that a 1024 × 768 image, which fills a small screen, will be only 3.4 inches (8.7 cm) wide when printed. This is because screen resolution is 72 or 96 pixels per inch (ppi), whereas in print the standard is 300 ppi. Thus if you want to print your photograph with a 6-inch (15-centimeter) width, your image file must be at least 1800 pixels wide. Note that on an inkjet printer several dots are needed for a pixel, and thus the resolution in dots per inch (dpi) is not equivalent to ppi.

As we reiterate several times in this book, whenever possible, you should take a photograph at the highest resolution available on the camera. The larger files take up more memory, but you'll use all that extra information when you process the image. If you reduce the file size of your image *after* you've completed the editing process, the final result will look a lot better. We recommend always exporting a photograph at its full original size, preferably in the lossless PNG format. When a smaller file is needed (i.e., for a website), resize a copy of the image to 1024 × 768 or even 800 × 600 and export it as a JPEG. To print a photograph at 300 ppi, compute its new width by multiplying the desired width (in inches) by 300 (or by 118 if the desired width is in centimeters). For example, a 10 × 15 cm print should be 1180 × 1770 pixels. Don't worry too much about the math, however. The software that controls your printer should be able to resize the print to whatever dimensions you want. Generally, you should adjust the dimensions of an image when printing it via the printing software. This leaves the image file unaltered, preventing the loss of quality that's inherent in resizing.

That being said, assuming you do want to resize a photograph using GIMP, how would you do it? GIMP has several ways to do this:

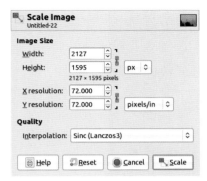

Figure 2.25 *The Scale Image dialog*

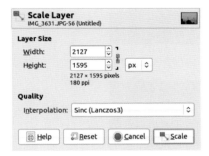

Figure 2.26 *The Scale Layer dialog*

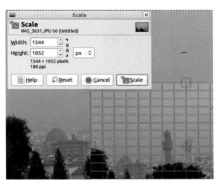

Figure 2.27 *Resizing a layer with the Scale tool*

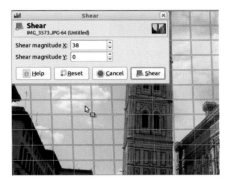

Figure 2.28 *Using the Shear tool*

- Resize the entire image using **Image: Image > Scale Image**. Figure 2.25 shows the dialog that appears. Adjust the WIDTH or the HEIGHT of the image. The chain linking width to height preserves the image's proportions, and leaving the chain intact is generally best. You can also change the X and Y RESOLUTION, but this does not have any effect on the image's size, and you generally only need to worry about resolution when you print the image. Even then, you can select the resolution using your printing software.

- If an image contains only one layer, resize the layer and then resize the canvas to fit. First, select **Image: Layer > Scale Layer**, which brings up the dialog shown in Figure 2.26. Once the layer has been resized, adjust the canvas size with **Image: Image > Fit Canvas to Layers**.

- You can also use the Scale tool ([SHIFT+T]) to resize layers. Select it and click anywhere

in the image. A small dialog appears, and the pointer icon changes. Click and drag the image to resize the layer. In Figure 2.27, we changed the PREVIEW option in the options dialog for the Scale tool to IMAGE+GRID.

Note that you can also change the dimensions directly in the dialog. Click SCALE to complete the scaling. Again, a linked chain preserves the proportions of width to height.

Shearing an Image

The last transformation tool that we'll mention is the Shear tool ([SHIFT+S]). Calling this tool brings up the dialog shown in Figure 2.28. Although you can input a value for both X and Y, only one coordinate (X or Y) can be modified at a time. The first value you adjust is retained, and the other is ignored. For example, if you adjust

Figure 2.29 *The initial photograph*

Figure 2.30 *Selecting the brighter areas*

SHEAR MAGNITUDE Y to 10 and then adjust SHEAR MAGNITUDE X to 10, the image will be sheared in the Y direction. When you apply the Shear tool, the image is tilted and deformed in the chosen direction. This tool is rarely useful, so don't worry if it's still a bit confusing.

Changing Brightness, Contrast, and Levels

In photography, lighting is vital. Adjustments to lighting can improve the look of an image dramatically. Lighting problems are especially common when you use a scanner to digitize an old photograph or 35mm film. But you might also want to adjust the lighting of a photograph taken with a good digital camera if the wrong settings were used or the subject was poorly or unevenly lit. Some of the most beautiful photographs are taken in difficult lighting conditions.

Consider the photograph shown in Figure 2.29. The area under the pergola is too dark, and the detail of the lianas overhead is completely lost. Since the lighting range is full, with a real black in the woman's clothes and a very clear white in the center of the picture, only some areas of the image need correction.

Use the Free Select tool ([F]) to select only the areas that need correction. In the options menu,

Figure 2.31 *First correction of lighting*

make sure the FEATHER EDGES box is checked and set the RADIUS to **10.0**. Trace around the brighter sections of the picture. In this example, there are two bright sections, one in front of the person and another to the right. Turn on Add to Selection by pressing the SHIFT key. You can make minor adjustments to the selection by using Quick Mask (see "Making a Selection" on page 38). The completed selection can be seen in Figure 2.30.

Figure 2.32 *Second correction of lighting*

Figure 2.33 *The initial photograph*

Figure 2.34 *Selecting the light areas*

Figure 2.35 *The final result*

Next invert the selection (CTRL+I) so you can adjust the lighting in the darker areas of the picture. Use the **Image: Colors > Levels** tool to brighten those dark areas. Once you've selected the Levels tool, simply click the AUTO button to get the results shown in Figure 2.31.

Although the auto adjustment helped a little, the top of the pergola is still much too dark. To lighten it further, repeat the same process. First, select the dark area using the Free Select tool (F). Don't invert the selection this time. Select the Levels tool, and click the AUTO button once more. You can see the results of this second adjustment in Figure 2.32.

GIMP has many other ways to improve the lighting of a photograph. Figure 2.33 shows a dim, hazy image. Because this image is so dark, simply using the Levels tool on the entire image wouldn't be effective: The sky and water would turn out too pale. To effectively brighten those areas, we need to select them first.

This time, call the Fuzzy Select tool to make your selection. Hold down the SHIFT key to select multiple areas. Outline all of the light areas in the photograph, as shown in Figure 2.34. Next, invert the selection (CTRL+I), hide it (CTRL+T), and select the Levels tool. Again, press the AUTO button, but this time also move the Gamma (gray) triangle slightly to the left with the Value channel selected and then to the right with the Blue channel selected. These additional adjustments will reduce the color cast.

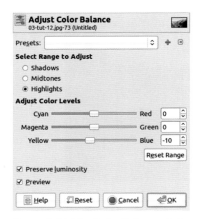

Figure 2.36 *The Color Balance dialog*

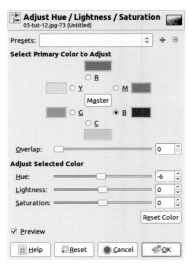

Figure 2.37 *The Hue-Saturation dialog*

After adjusting the Levels, we straightened the picture by rotating it and then cropped the image to clean up the edges. The final result appears in Figure 2.35.

Adjusting Colors

Adjusting colors across an entire photograph is occasionally appropriate, for example, when the use of a flash indoors results in a ubiquitous red cast. Figure 2.12 is a simple example of color correction in which we used the Levels tool to correct a blue cast. GIMP has other tools that you can also use for simple or more complex color correction.

One such tool is **Image: Colors > Color Balance**(Figure 2.36). To correct a blue cast, push the slider between Yellow and Blue to the left. Since Preview is checked, you can observe the result immediately. You can also adjust the color balance with the slider, the mouse wheel, or the small arrows beside the numbers on the right. Notice that this change is not made for the whole image but only for the selected subrange: shadows, midtones, or highlights. This tool is fairly powerful but not very easy to use.

Another color correction tool is **Image: Colors > Hue-Saturation**. In the dialog for this tool (Figure 2.37), you can choose one of six different color subranges, corresponding to the three

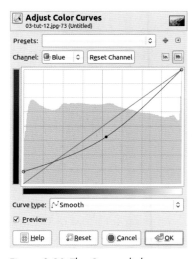

Figure 2.38 *The Curves dialog*

primary and the three complementary colors. You can also select the whole subrange by clicking Master. Moving the Hue cursor shifts all colors within the selected subrange. For Figure 2.12, we would want to select the blue subrange and shift the Hue cursor to the left.

The last tool, **Image: Colors > Curves**, allows you to make the same adjustments but gives you much more control. As shown in Figure 2.38,

Credit: Vincent Lecarme

Figure 2.39 *The initial photograph*

Figure 2.41 *The final result*

Figure 2.40 *After reducing the opacity of the top layer*

Figure 2.42 *The initial image*

you can deform the response curve of the Blue channel to remove a blue cast. Here, push the leftmost point higher, which is equivalent to moving the left black triangle to the right in the Levels tool. This brings out the color in the darkest parts of the image. Adjust the middle point so it's under the diagonal to reduce the blue cast throughout the image. The rightmost point is left unchanged, so the sky remains blue. You can deform the color curve in many ways, often with strange results.

Figure 2.39 shows a photograph with a different color balance issue. The difficult conditions (a very low temperature and early morning light at a high altitude) give this picture a strong blue cast, which isn't an accurate representation of what you would see if you were actually looking out over this snowy vista.

Duplicating an image layer and applying different transformations to the layers often leads to pleasant, or at least interesting, results. Try the following:

1. Duplicate the layer (SHIFT+CTRL+D).

2. Desaturate the lower (background) layer (**Image: Colors > Desaturate**).

3. Change the blending mode of the upper layer to Multiply.

4. Reduce the opacity of the upper layer to 60%.

The result is shown in Figure 2.40. Admittedly, the sky is now too dark. The solution is to again duplicate the upper layer, leaving the blending mode and opacity the same. See Figure 2.41.

The image shown in Figure 2.42 presents a different set of challenges and possibilities,

Figure 2.43 *Selecting the dark areas*

Figure 2.44 *The final result*

providing a good demonstration of GIMP's flexibility. This photograph was taken at night, without a tripod, which caused an obvious motion blur. The camera did assign a true white to the lights in the bottom center and a true black to portions of the sky. Because the whole value range is covered, a global change using the Levels tool would have no effect.

Instead, use the Levels tool to edit the dark areas and the light areas separately. This is easy:

1. Choose the Select by Color tool (SHIFT+O) and click anywhere in the sky. You get the complicated selection shown in Figure 2.43.

2. Hide this selection (CTRL+T) and select the Levels tool. Click the AUTO button.

3. Now invert the selection (CTRL+I) to select the unmodified areas. Select the Levels tool again and click the AUTO button.

The result, which appears in Figure 2.44, could be considered a creative interpretation of lights at night.

2.3   Local Transformations

The upcoming examples and techniques require the precise selection of a part of the image, so simply clicking anywhere in the photo with the Select by Color tool will not be sufficient. Now, you have to really dig in to make minor correc-

Figure 2.45 *Selection tools in the Toolbox*

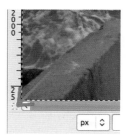

Figure 2.46 *The position of the Quick Mask button*

tions to your selections by hand. Do this using Quick Mask.

Making a Selection

GIMP has eight selection tools that are located in the top two rows of the Toolbox (Figure 2.45). Let's take a closer look at each one now.

The Selection Tools Options

Quick Mask, accessed by pressing the small button in the bottom-left corner of the Image window (see Figure 2.46), is an invaluable addition to these tools.

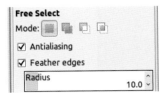

Figure 2.47 *The Free Select tool options*

All of the selection tools offer the options shown in Figure 2.47, but most also have additional, unique options. Generally, you should leave the ANTIALIASING option checked. Check FEATHER EDGES when you want a smooth outline around a selection. RADIUS specifies the width of the smoothing border. MODE determines how a new selection interacts with an already existing selection:

- In Replace mode, the existing selection is replaced by the new one.
- In Add mode (also set if you press SHIFT), the new selection augments the existing one.
- In Subtract mode (CTRL), the new selection is subtracted from the existing one.
- In Intersect mode (SHIFT+CTRL), the final selection contains only the areas common to both the existing and the new selections.

As you have already seen, often you need to add to or modify a selected area before making image adjustments. You can do this even after switching among selection tools.

In the next section, we discuss the selection tools that are useful for retouching photographs. The Rectangle and the Ellipse Select tools are rarely helpful because they can only make simple geometric selections. Additionally, the Rectangle tool is tricky to use unless the target rectangle's sides are exactly parallel to the image's sides. The Paths tool is an indirect and complex way to build selections, so we don't include it in this section.

Simple Selection Tools

Free Select (F) is a very handy tool. We've already used it several times in this chapter. Free

Figure 2.48 *Selecting a polygon with the Free Select tool*

Select is best used with a graphics tablet stylus. Draw around the area to be selected and accept the selection by finishing very near the start point or by pressing ENTER. See examples in Figures 2.22 or 2.30. Instead of drawing, you can also click several times around the outline of the shape you want to select. This builds a polygon around the target. Figure 2.48 shows a simple example where the Rectangle Select tool would not have worked.

The Fuzzy Select tool (U), also known as the Magic Wand, was used in Figure 2.34. Fuzzy Select selects all the pixels adjacent and similar to the clicked pixel, according to a given threshold. Change the threshold in the tool options if the area selected is too large or too small. Generally, make the selection by clicking in several places along the outline of the target while pressing the SHIFT key. This tool is especially useful when selecting an area with a complex shape.

The Select by Color tool (SHIFT+O) was used in Figure 2.43. It works in almost exactly the same way as the Fuzzy Select tool. The only difference is that the pixels need not be contiguous; this is an advantage if you want to select an area consisting of many small, separate parts that are all approximately the same color. Sometimes,

Figure 2.49 *Selecting with the Scissors Select tool*

Figure 2.50 *The final selection*

however, unwanted pixels are included in a selection simply because they are similar enough to the target color. Thus, each tool is useful in different circumstances.

The Scissors Select Tool

The Scissors Select tool ($\boxed{\text{SHIFT+I}}$) is also known as Intelligent Scissors. As with the Fuzzy Select tool, click along the outline of the target area to

Figure 2.51 *The initial image*

make a selection. If the target area is delimited by strong contrasts with the background, then Scissors Select automatically follows the outline, however complicated it may be. Figure 2.49 shows the selection being built. Note that some points may be placed far apart as the selection will follow obvious contours. Figure 2.50 shows the resulting selection, obtained after closing the path and clicking in the center of the selection. In the example selection, we cut off the feet and include the area between the legs of the statue, but we could easily fix that by continuing the initial selection to the base of the statue and then removing the area between the legs using Subtract mode.

The Foreground Select Tool

The Foreground Select tool is useful in a few specific situations; for instance, when you want to select a subject that's in the foreground of an image and clearly separate from the background, like in Figure 2.51. Select the Foreground Select tool from the Toolbox and draw an approximate outline around the target, just as you would with the Free Select tool. When the outline is closed, the selected area appears as shown in Figure 2.52.

Without changing the selection tool (or else work done so far will be lost), draw a continuous path within the selection that touches on

Figure 2.52 *After selecting the outline*

Figure 2.53 *Selecting the foreground colors*

Figure 2.54 *The future selection*

Figure 2.55 *Using Quick Mask*

all of the colors to be included, as shown in Figure 2.53. We used red for the path, but you can choose any color as long as it is different from the colors in the intended selection.

When you stop drawing the path, the selection appears as in Figure 2.54. As you can see, the image is not yet perfect. Some of the face, including the eyes, has been omitted. You can add more brushstrokes to capture the missing areas, or you can press ENTER to surround the selection with marching ants and then click the Quick Mask button to continue editing the selection.

The result is shown in Figure 2.55. The unselected areas appear in red. You can continue to edit the selection using the Brush tool. While Quick Mask is on, select the Brush tool from the Toolbox and set the colors to black and white. If we paint in black, the painted pixels are removed from the selection and become red. If we paint in white, the painted pixels are added to the selection. To switch between black and white, use the X key, which exchanges the foreground and background colors.

When you're satisfied, click the Quick Mask button again to reveal the selection, as shown in Figure 2.56.

Modifying Sharpness

As we already mentioned, scaling down a photograph, for example, to put it on a website or to print it, reduces sharpness. Therefore, we advise using the **Image: Filters > Enhance > Unsharp Mask** at the very end of any transformation process. Ideally, you should do this periodically throughout the transformation process.

Sometimes reducing the sharpness of areas in a photograph increases the appearance of

Figure 2.56 *The final selection*

Figure 2.58 *Selecting the cat*

Figure 2.57 *The initial photograph*

Figure 2.59 *The final result*

depth. Consider, for example, Figure 2.57. The cat blends into the background because its colors are similar to those of the rocks behind it, and at least some of the plants are as sharp as the cat itself, if not sharper. What we want to do is to make the background fuzzy so the cat stands out.

We first select the cat, which isn't easy. Although the cat is in the foreground, the Foreground Select tool doesn't work well because the lighter parts of the cat are almost the same color as the background and its dark ears are similar to the shadows in the bushes. To get the result seen in Figure 2.58, we carefully selected the cat using Quick Mask. We found it easiest to select the background, painting the cat in black with Quick Mask to remove it from the selection. The

result is not perfect, yet it's good enough to see the intended effect.

Making the selection was the hardest part. After that was done, we simply had to add a strong Gaussian blur using **Image: Filters > Blur**, with a radius of 20 pixels, to get the result shown in Figure 2.59. The background is now quite blurred, and the cat stands out.

Modifying Brightness

Modifying the brightness of specific areas in a photo is another way to alter the apparent depth of an image, and it may also increase visibility in a picture with strong contrasts. This is the case for Figure 2.60.

Again, building the selection is the most difficult part. You need to select the window and its contents as well as the parts of the wall that

Figure 2.60 *The initial photograph*

Figure 2.62 *The final result*

Figure 2.61 *Selecting the window*

Figure 2.63 *The initial photograph*

are directly lit by the sun. You can use the Free Select tool for an initial, approximate selection, but then you need to spend time refining it with the Quick Mask tool to get the selection shown in Figure 2.61.

Once we've made the selection, we choose the Levels tool. Clicking AUTO won't change much, but moving the Gamma triangle will accomplish what we want. The result is shown in Figure 2.62.

Our next example is a photograph with a number of major defects. As you can see in Figure 2.63, the image is tilted, the lighting is dim, the sky is hazy, and, in general, the image lacks contrast. We will not create a great picture out of this image, but we can at least make some improvements.

First, use the Rotate tool to straighten the image. Because you don't have an easy way to measure the angle needed, zoom in on the roof of the cathedral, which you know should be horizontal. Select the Rotate tool, and in the tool options, choose a CORRECTIVE direction. Then, align the grid with the roof and press ROTATE.

Figure 2.64 *After rotation and cropping*

Figure 2.67 *Adding some light to the foreground*

Figure 2.65 *Selecting the sky: first step*

Figure 2.68 *Building a sky*

Figure 2.66 *Selecting the sky: second step*

After cropping the resulting image, we get Figure 2.64.

Now let's select the sky so we can enhance its color. The Fuzzy Select tool is useful, but the boundary between the sky and the town is too blurry. When we make our selection, we get not only the sky but also a fair amount of land near the horizon (see Figure 2.65). Note that we've inverted the selection.

Correct the selection using Quick Mask. This process is finicky. The border between the sky and the town requires some care. The bell tower must also be selected by hand by painting in Quick Mask. Handling the scaffoldings on the side of the dome perfectly is virtually impossible. Our final selection is shown in Figure 2.66.

This selection allows us to add some light and color to the foreground, thanks to the Levels tool. Turn off Quick Mask and make sure the foreground, rather than the sky, is selected, and then adjust the levels until you're satisfied. Our lightened image appears in Figure 2.67. Note that the general contrast could be improved by separating the trees in the foreground from the rest of the picture. Later in this tutorial, we do just that. For now, the results are adequate.

Figure 2.69 *The final image*

Next you need to invert the selection so it contains the sky. Click the Blend tool and choose the Horizon 1 predefined gradient. Press the CTRL key to draw vertically (pressing this key ensures that the angle of the line is a multiple of 15°). Click in the middle of the sky, and draw downward, past the bottom of the image. If you don't draw far enough, part of the sky will appear brown. This process should result in Figure 2.68.

To complete the corrections and obtain Figure 2.69, do the following:

1. With the Select by Color tool, select the trees in the foreground.

2. Invert the selection and choose the Levels tool.

3. Click the AUTO button. The resulting image has a strong red cast.

4. Select the Red channel and move the Gamma triangle to the right until you're satisfied.

Using the Clone Tool

The Clone tool is one of the most powerful tools for changing details in a photograph. In this tutorial, we correct one photograph using features from another, more successful shot. Figure 2.70 shows the two images, open in our workspace. In one of the photographs, the red eye effect obscures the cat's eyes. In this case, the effect is so dramatic that the red eye removal filter didn't

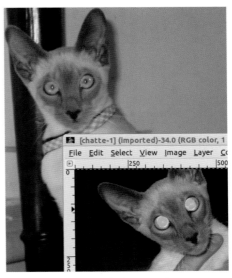

Figure 2.70 *The initial photographs*

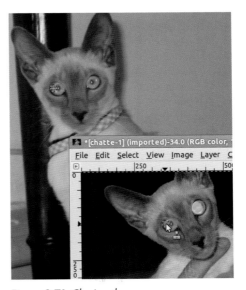

Figure 2.71 *Cloning the eyes*

work. To fix the problem, copy the eyes from the first photograph to the second one.

First, you must ensure that the eyes are the same size in both pictures. If this is not the case, change the scaling of the second image, using **Image: Image > Scale Image**.

Figure 2.72 *The final result*

Figure 2.74 *The initial image*

Figure 2.73 *Figure 2.24 after some healing*

Next, choose the Clone tool (C̄) with a Hardness 075 brush scaled to size **20**. C̄TRL-click on a blue source eye and then paint over a red eye with the Clone tool as in Figure 2.71. Figure 2.72 shows the result.

When taking a portrait, you often capture blemishes and spots that can detract from the subject's natural beauty. You can remove blemishes in GIMP using the Clone tool, but the Healing tool is generally better when working with portraits. It works exactly like the Clone tool, except that instead of simply replacing target pixels, it blends them, thus blending the source more smoothly with the target. Figure 2.24 is a good example. After using the Healing

tool on this portrait (tip and right side of the chin, bridge of the nose, lower lip, area over the eyebrows), we achieved the results shown in Figure 2.73.

Perspective Cloning

Sometimes you may want to clone an object in an image so it appears several times at different distances from the viewer. To get the perspective effect, you need to size the cloned objects appropriately.

The Perspective Clone tool is tailor-made for this effect. Although most people rarely need this particular effect, when you do, the Perspective Clone tool is extremely useful.

Take, for example, the photograph shown in Figure 2.74. We'll show you how to duplicate the small cobblestone gutter that crosses the walkway. Select the Perspective Clone tool in the Toolbox (no keyboard shortcut is available). Check MODIFY PERSPECTIVE in the options dialog. Then click in the image. Squares appear in the corners, which you can move to define the perspective of the object that you're about to clone. Move the squares so the guidelines align with the edges of the walkway.

Figure 2.75 *Cloning the gutter*

Figure 2.76 *The final result*

Once you've set the perspective, check PER-SPECTIVE CLONE in the options dialog. Now use the tool exactly as you would the Clone tool. First, CTRL-click on the gutter, or whatever you happen to be copying, and then use the Hardness 075 brush in a large size to paint the area where you want another gutter. Figure 2.75 shows the work in progress, and Figure 2.76 shows the final result. This tool doesn't work as well when the perspective angle is more dramatic.

Figure 2.77 *The initial photograph*

More Correction Methods for Red Eye

In "Removing Red Eye" on page 30, we demonstrated the simplest way to handle red eye: the red eye removal filter. However, other, less automated techniques can yield better results, depending on the image. In "Using the Clone Tool" on page 45, we used the Clone tool to correct red eye using a second image as a source. Here, we demonstrate a few more techniques.

First Method: Selecting the Red Channel

A rather challenging case of red eye can be seen in Figure 2.77. The red is very apparent, but not much contrast is available at the border between the gray iris and the red pupil. Zoom the image to 400% so the left eye is as large as possible. Use **Image: View > New View** to simultaneously view the same image at 100% zoom to better preview the final image as you work.

Select the Dodge/Burn tool (SHIFT+D) and press the BURN button. Choose the Hardness 075 brush and set its size to **12**. Finally, in the Channels dialog, click the Green and Blue channels to deselect them. All three channels remain visible, but the tool will change only the Red channel (see Figure 2.78).

Figure 2.78 *Deselecting the Green and Blue channels*

Figure 2.79 *Correcting the right eye*

Figure 2.80 *The final result*

Now burn away the red spot. Click and/or paint the pupil with the Burn tool, taking care to avoid the bright reflection in the center of each pupil. As Figure 2.79 shows, you can check your work on the image at 100% zoom. Adjust the EXPOSURE in the tool options if the effect is too strong or too weak. The final result appears in Figure 2.80.

Second Method: Selecting the Red Spots

As the heading indicates, this next method requires that you select the red areas in the eyes. You can do this with the Free Select tool if you zoom in far enough, but in this case, the Ellipse Select tool actually works best.

Select it by pressing (E). In the options, check the boxes EXPAND FROM CENTER and FIXED. Set the FIXED option to ASPECT RATIO, and check that the box below displays "1:1." Click and drag from the center of the red spot to build a circle around it. When you're satisfied with the selection, choose the Add mode under options and build a second circle for the other eye.

When you're finished, hide the selection (CTRL+T) and return the zoom to 100%. The

color adjustment is made with **Image: Colors > Hue-Saturation**. Move the Hue cursor until you like the result. After selecting the red in the eyes, you could also use **Image: Colors > Desaturate** to remove the color. This doesn't always work as well, but it did this time. If the image is too light, you may find it helpful to first use **Image: Colors > Invert**.

Next, we show you a safer way to handle red eye. Beginning with the red spots selected, try the following.

Duplicate the only layer. In the upper layer, create a layer mask: **Layers: right-click > Add Layer Mask**. Check SELECTION in the dialog that appears.

Select the upper layer by clicking the thumbnail. You should see a white border around the layer, rather than the mask, in the Layers dialog. With the mask in place, any change done to the upper layer will effect only the red spots. The lower layer will remain unchanged.

Now adjust the color of the red spots. Try **Image: Colors > Desaturate** and then **Image: Colors > Brightness-Contrast**. You may also find it useful to apply a slight Gaussian blur (**Image: Filters > Blur > Gaussian Blur** with a radius of 1 or 2 pixels).

Figure 2.81 *The initial photograph has a dull sky.*

Figure 2.82 *A photograph with an interesting sky*

Changing the Sky of a Landscape

In landscape photography, the appearance of the sky is very important. Unfortunately, capturing a beautiful sky can be challenging. In this chapter, you've seen several unsatisfying skies: one that was too pale (Figure 2.7), one that was too white (Figure 2.15), and one that was too hazy and gloomy (Figure 2.63). A dark blue sky over a mountain landscape on a clear, sunny day is a bit better, but a simple, uniform dark blue isn't very interesting. A dark blue sky with a few well-placed clouds, however, adds just the right effect.

We generally find it's impractical to wait around until the landscape that we want to

Figure 2.83 *Selecting and removing the sky*

capture has a perfect blue sky with fluffy white clouds. We show you how you can add a perfect sky to a landscape photograph that's lacking in that department. We already showed you one way to do this (see Figure 2.69), but using a predefined gradient is not really an ideal solution. Here, we try another technique, demonstrated on Figure 2.81 using the sky from Figure 2.82.

To begin, select the sky with the Select by Color tool ($\boxed{\text{SHIFT+O}}$). This requires just one click in the center of the sky, followed by one or two in the corners as you press the $\boxed{\text{SHIFT}}$ key. Next, add an Alpha channel to the only layer (**Layers: right-click > Add Alpha Channel**). Cut out the selection ($\boxed{\text{CTRL+X}}$) to get Figure 2.83.

In this figure, you can see that the selection made using the Select by Color tool isn't very precise. A blue halo remains around the cypress in the center of the image, as well as in the branches on the right. To correct this, undo the cut ($\boxed{\text{CTRL+Z}}$) and use **Image: Select > Grow**, which extends the selection by a fixed number of pixels. Choose **2** pixels. Next, use **Image: Select > Feather**, which smooths the selection outline, and again choose **2**. Now, add an Alpha channel to the layer if its name appears in

Figure 2.84 *Improving the selection*

Figure 2.85 *Two layers of the image*

boldface, and cut out the selection. The result is much better, as you can see in Figure 2.84.

Now you need to place the sky from Figure 2.82 as a bottom layer in the image. A simple solution is to open this image in GIMP and, while it is active, drag the thumbnail of its only layer from the Layers dialog to the image you are working on. Then drag this new layer to the bottom of the layer stack, as shown in Figure 2.85.

Once the sky layer is added, you can change the composition by repositioning the layer with

Figure 2.86 *The final result*

the move tool ($\boxed{\text{M}}$). This process works best when the sky image is larger than the landscape image, which gives you some latitude when choosing the composition. A possible final result appears in Figure 2.86. To further improve this landscape, we used the Eraser tool ($\boxed{\text{SHIFT+E}}$) to remove some spindly little branches from the tree on the right. You could also hide a few other unattractive details using the Clone tool.

2.4   Retouching a Scanned Photograph

Photographs deteriorate over time, so if you're digitalizing your old family photos, you may want to restore them to their original glory. Even if your photo is brand-new, your scanner may not capture the image exactly as it is. Although you can make adjustments to your images using your scanner's software, GIMP gives you greater control and is much more powerful.

Correcting Colors

Figure 2.87 shows a photo album page that was scanned at 300 ppi. The photos were developed in 1975 and have since deteriorated. A

Figure 2.87 *The original scan*

Figure 2.89 *The picture of interest*

Figure 2.88 *Selecting the picture of interest*

Figure 2.90 *Rotating and cropping the image*

transparent sheet is also stuck to the page and is visible in the bottom photograph. We would like to restore all of these photographs at some point, but here we focus on the top left photo.

First, use the Rectangle Select tool ($\boxed{\text{R}}$) and select the photograph you want to restore. Because the photo is slightly crooked, select an area larger than the picture, as shown in Figure 2.88. Create a new image with a copy of this selection:

1. Copy the selection by pressing $\boxed{\text{CTRL+C}}$.

2. Paste the copy as a new image by pressing $\boxed{\text{SHIFT+CTRL+V}}$.

You can also find these commands in the **Image: Edit** menu.

The new image is shown in Figure 2.89. Rotate it ($\boxed{\text{SHIFT+R}}$) and crop it ($\boxed{\text{SHIFT+C}}$) to straighten it and remove the remnants of the album page.

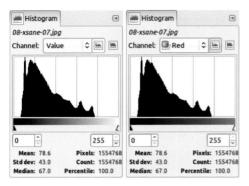

Figure 2.91 *The Value channel and Red channel histograms*

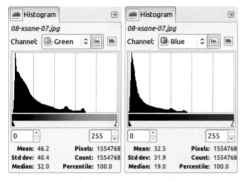

Figure 2.93 *Automatically adjusting the levels*

Figure 2.92 *The Green channel and Blue channel histograms*

The result appears in Figure 2.90. You can see how the colors have decayed by selecting the Histogram dialogs: **Image: Windows > Dockable Dialogs > Histogram**. In the small window that pops up, choose a channel to display. Figures 2.91 and 2.92 show the histograms for the Value, Red, Green, and Blue channels. Ideally, the histograms should be bell-shaped curves, but all of these histograms are skewed. They peak on the left, in the low values. The Value and Red channels' histograms also have a notch in the low values.

The value range in all channels should be extended so they span the full range. Select the Levels tool and press AUTO to get the result shown in Figure 2.93. This image is slightly better than the original image, and the histograms

Figure 2.94 *Adjusting the levels with the eyedroppers*

have changed a lot, especially for the Value and Red channels.

Now use the eyedroppers in the Levels tool to hand-select points in the image that are black, gray, and white. Using this tool well can be tricky, especially since the order matters. To get the result in Figure 2.94, we chose a black point on the cat's ear, a gray point in the cat's fur, and a white point in the lightest part of the sheepskin. The "best" result is a matter of personal

Figure 2.95 *Adjusting the curves*

Figure 2.96 *The initial image*

taste, so experiment with different selections until you find the one that you like.

The Curves tool can also be used to adjust color balance. Select it via **Image: Colors > Curves** and try adjusting the four curves. Move the end points of the curve in so they touch the edges of the histogram, which is similar to pressing AUTO in the Levels tool. Then move the middle of each curve slightly while watching the effect in the Preview window. Figure 2.95 shows the result, which is just one of an infinite number of possible results.

Correcting Scratches and Spots

Often, very old photographs are folded, scratched, or stained. In the past, the only way to repair such damage was to retouch the prints by hand with pencils and brushes. Now, you can retouch old photographs much more easily and safely using a scanner and GIMP.

Figure 2.96 shows a photograph taken more than a century ago. Although the sepia color is the result of degradation, it's pleasant, so leave it as it is. The low values are washed out, but this makes the portrait softer, so you won't change those either. But you do want to remove some blemishes. The print had been folded in the

Figure 2.97 *After retouching folds, scratches, and spots*

middle, and some stains or scratches appear at the top, especially on the left, and some tiny white spots are scattered around the image, for example, in the hair on the left.

Fortunately, the fold didn't leave a mark on the eyes and only left some light traces on the nose. To begin, zoom in to see the details.

Select the Smudge tool (S) and choose the Hardness 075 brush. Use short, sliding strokes on the face to smooth out imperfections. To

Figure 2.98 *Another folded print*

Figure 2.99 *Result after some corrections*

Figure 2.100 *A photograph from the early 20th century*

Figure 2.101 *Correcting the major defects*

Restoring Very Old Photographs

remove the fold marks, select a large brush size. For the small dots, choose a very small brush.

Next, select the Clone tool ([C]) to remove the scratches and the fold marks in the hair. Again, use the Hardness 075 brush in a size proportionate to the blemish you're removing. If you use the stylus of a graphic tablet with Basic Dynamics, you can simply vary the pressure to change the brush size, which is very intuitive and makes the task much easier. Although the stroke depends on what's being corrected, generally following the direction of the scratch is best. For a small white spot, a quick touch of the pen may be enough. The final result is shown in Figure 2.97.

Figures 2.98 and 2.99 show the result of applying these same methods to a different print, with less success. Since the damage is more severe, this image needs to be touched up by hand.

The photograph shown in Figure 2.100 is more than a century old, and it has deteriorated over the years. The sepia tone is actually a decayed grayscale. To return the image to grayscale, you could desaturate it, but the resulting image wouldn't look very good because a number of major defects would remain, so touch up the image first.

Begin by using the Clone tool to erase the large stain in front of the horse. CTRL-click on the area just to left of the stain and carefully paint over the stain to remove it. To get rid of the blue cast in the lower-right corner, select the area and use the Levels tool. Adjust the Gamma cursor in the Blue channel, and the cast is gone.

Cancel the selection (SHIFT+CTRL+A), and use the AUTO button in the Levels tool to improve the general value range. Finally, the time has come to desaturate the image and return it to the original grayscale. This should be your final step, but the result, as it appears in

Figure 2.102 *Final result*

Figure 2.101, looks rather flat despite the strong contrast. We're accustomed to seeing old photographs in sepia tones, so this image will look better if you change it back. You can simply select **Image: Edit > Undo**, but you can probably get a better result by recoloring the image:

1. Duplicate the layer.

2. Use the tool **Image: Colors > Colorize** on the top layer, and move the Hue cursor to the left until you're satisfied with the color.

3. Reduce the opacity of this layer to about 50%.

The final result appears in Figure 2.102. The front feet of the horse are faded and could use some retouching, but the work required is beyond the scope of this tutorial.

2.5   **Advanced Techniques**

In this section, we consider various techniques that are a bit more difficult and less frequently used.

Making a Photograph Look Older

GIMP is a great tool for cheating time. In a previous section, we updated an old photograph to look more recent. In an upcoming section, we try to make someone look younger. In this section, we make a modern photograph look like it was taken over 50 years ago.

One of the most efficient ways to age a photograph is to remove the color and to give the

Figure 2.103 *The initial photograph*

Figure 2.104 *Using the Old Photo filter*

photograph a sepia tone. We chose to age Figure 2.103, which lacks obvious modern features. If you're feeling lazy, you can just try the filter (**Image: Filters > Decor > Old Photo**). The filter doesn't have many adjustable parameters, so simply press OK. We got the result shown in Figure 2.104. The image does look old, but we can do better.

First, desaturate the image (**Image: Colors > Desaturate**). Select the whole image (CTRL+A) and copy it (CTRL+C). Make the

Figure 2.105 *After setting the Layer mask on the Sepia layer*

Figure 2.107 *After using the Round Corners filter*

Figure 2.106 *After inverting the Layer mask and changing to Color mode*

Figure 2.108 *Adding a coffee stain*

foreground color a sepia tone, for example, **a28a65** in HTML notation. Create a new layer (SHIFT+CTRL+N) and choose to fill it with the foreground color. Add a Layer mask to this layer (**Layers: right-click > Add Layer Mask**) and check SELECTION in the dialog that appears. Paste the copy you just made into the mask by pressing CTRL+V. Anchor the floating selection to the Layer mask (press the ANCHOR button at the bottom of the Layers dialog or press CTRL+H).

The result, which appears in Figure 2.105, is still not right. To improve it, check that the Layer mask is active (click the thumbnail if you're not sure), and then invert the color (**Image: Colors > Invert**). Change the Blending mode of the top layer to COLOR. The result (Figure 2.106) is much better, but you can tweak it further if you're still not satisfied. You can

Figure 2.109 *The initial photograph*

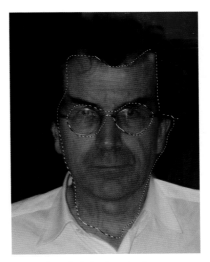

Figure 2.110 *Selecting the face*

try reducing the opacity of the top layer or try using the Curves tool (**Image: Colors > Curves**) on the layer itself (not on the layer mask). Select the Value channel and nudge the bottom of the curve up and the top of the curve down. This should improve the contrast.

You can use some of the filters in the **Image: Filters > Decor** submenu to complete the aging effect. For example, Figure 2.107 results from the application of the Round Corners filter with all parameters set to twice their default values.

In the same submenu, you'll find the Coffee Stain filter, which creates that realistic "Oh, that wasn't a coaster?" look (Figure 2.108).

Improving a Portrait

In magazines, your favorite actor or singer always looks wonderful, thanks to the magic of programs like GIMP. If you met him on the street, you might be surprised by the difference that photo retouching can make. These days hiding blemishes, removing wrinkles, and even changing the color of a person's eyes is very easy. Let's experiment with a portrait of a very unimportant person, one of the authors of this book. Figure 2.109 shows a rather unflattering portrait, which we'll improve.

First, select the Levels tool and improve the general lighting throughout the picture. Next, select the areas that you'll work on. Although we'd like to remove the glasses in this image, doing so would prove very difficult. You could try erasing them with the Clone tool, but removing the reflections completely would be a lot of work. Too much work. So leave the glasses intact. The clothes don't need any retouching, so concentrate only on the skin. Select the work area with the Free Select tool. First, draw a rough outline around the face, and then, with the CTRL key pressed, remove the glasses from the selection. Figure 2.110 shows the result.

GIMP offers a number of different ways to reverse-age our subject. We'll try the following:

1. Apply a very light Gaussian blur to the selection: A radius of 2 or 3 pixels is enough.

2. Use the Healing tool to erase blemishes and discolorations.

3. Finally, select the Smudge tool (S). Choose the Hardness 075 brush, set its size to **12**, and

Figure 2.111 *After blurring, healing, and smudging*

Figure 2.112 *After dodging the nose and adding a faint smile*

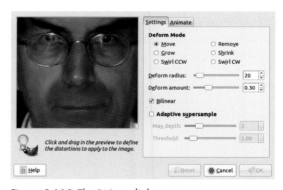

Figure 2.113 *The IWarp dialog*

paint over wrinkles or anywhere that you want to make the skin look smoother. This tool works by selecting a color from the starting point and blending it into the image as you draw—like a finger smudging wet paint.

After some work, we get Figure 2.111, which is much better. The selection that you made at the beginning helped you to avoid making unwanted changes to the glasses and the clothes.

This portrait can be enhanced further: The nose is too dark, and our subject looks too serious. To retouch the nose, use the Dodge/Burn tool (SHIFT+D) set to Dodge mode with the Hardness 075 brush in a large size. The result, which appears in Figure 2.112, isn't spectacularly different, but it's a bit better.

In this image, make another subtle modification: Brighten our serious subject's mood a little. Use the **Image: Filters > Distort > IWarp** tool, which brings up the dialog shown in Figure 2.113. Before calling IWarp, use the Rectangle select tool to select the center of the image to get a larger view of the target area in the IWarp dialog.

Then, with the default settings, which are shown in the figure, extend the corners of the lips out slightly, nudge the middle of the upper

lip up, and nudge the middle of the lower lip down. You can also move the lower eyelids up slightly. Now the subject, if not smiling, seems a little less serious.

Using Multiple Captures of the Same Scene

With today's digital cameras, taking several shots of the same scene is easy and costs nothing. As you've seen in several of the example photographs, choosing the proper exposure for scenes with strong contrast can be difficult, even impossible. Taking multiple shots of a

Figure 2.114 *First capture, normal exposure*

Figure 2.116 *Superposing the two photographs*

Figure 2.115 *Second capture, exaggerated exposure*

Figure 2.117 *Using the Color blending mode*

Figure 2.118 *Using the Overlay blending mode*

high-contrast scene at different exposures is one way to handle the challenge. Many digital cameras even offer a mode called "auto exposure bracketing," wherein the camera takes three shots at various exposures in quick succession around the optimal, automatic exposure.

Figures 2.114 and 2.115 show an example. The first image was taken using the automatic exposure, whereas the second was overexposed. Open both pictures in GIMP: the first one in the normal way, the second one by using **Image: File > Open as Layers** or CTRL+ALT+O. Reduce the opacity of the top layer to 50% to check whether the images superposed properly. These photographs were taken without a tripod, and you can see that the photographer has moved slightly between shots. Using the Move tool (M), align the layers as carefully as you can to get the image shown in Figure 2.116. If you look closely, you'll see that the alignment is still not quite perfect.

Finally, try to improve the result using blending modes. Figure 2.117 shows the Color blending mode, which works well for this image. Grain merge, Soft light, and Overlay (Figure 2.118) also work nicely.

2.6   Exercises

Exercise 2.1. The Levels tool has many features that we didn't use in this chapter. Experiment with some of these features on a photograph of your own. Try to figure out what each of the five eyedropper buttons do.

Exercise 2.2. In this chapter, we used the Perspective tool to insert objects at various distances from the viewer. This tool can also be used to correct perspective distortion. Take a picture of a skyscraper (or any tall building) from below, so the perspective is distorted, and then try to correct it using the Perspective tool. Be sure to save the unedited photograph for the next exercise.

Exercise 2.3. This time, add some new embellishments to your distorted skyscraper photograph using the Perspective Clone tool. You can add extra windows, doors, or anything else that appears on the building. Add embellishments to many different levels of the building.

Exercise 2.4. Usually, the most effective way to build a selection is with a combination of selection tools. Finicky corrections to a complex selections are generally done with the Quick Mask tool. Experiment with the selection tools to select complicated areas in a photograph. If you make a mistake, you can undo your work by pressing CTRL+Z or redo it by pressing CTRL+Y. Generally, Undo and Redo don't work on partially built selections, but they do work on selections that require successive steps. Experiment with the **Image: Edit > Undo** and **Image: Edit > Redo** commands to see when they're effective and when they're not.

Exercise 2.5. The **Image: Filters > Enhance** menu has several filters we didn't use. Experiment with some of them on your own photographs, especially the various Sharpen filters (other than Unsharp Mask).

3 Drawing and Illustration

Although most people don't think of GIMP when they think about digital illustration software, it's a surprisingly powerful tool for colorizing or personalizing images—or even creating original artwork from scratch. In this chapter, we'll show you how to add color to a drawing and give you an insider's look at how digital painting is done. We introduce a few basic tools and techniques, including paintbrushes, fill tools, and methods you can use in GIMP to draw simple shapes.

3.1 Tutorial: Colorizing a Drawing

Colorizing a drawing is a great way to learn many of the digital art techniques and tools available in GIMP. In this tutorial, we'll use paint tools like the Paintbrush and modifying tools like the Smudge tool. Colorizing is also a flexible process: As a beginner, you can add color to a small drawing reasonably quickly, while also exploring the techniques and tools, and once you're an experienced colorist, you can spend hours producing a fine work of art. And most importantly—colorizing is fun!

The Black and White Drawing

Before you start colorizing, you need something to color! A black and white line drawing works best, whether drawn by you or someone else. Finding black and white line art is pretty easy if you don't want to draw it yourself. Some artists enjoy drawing line art but lack the skill, time, or desire to add color, so they make their art available for anyone to colorize. Many comic artists pass their line art to professional colorists, who each have a unique personal style.

We're going to colorize the drawing of mushrooms shown in Figure 3.1. This drawing is composed of clean, solid lines, which is ideal if you're a beginner. If you find line art online, download the largest image you can find. A width and height of over 1000 pixels works best. Small errors disappear when the image is sized down, and GIMP can handle a large canvas size without a problem. For this tutorial, we'll use a canvas that's 1200 pixels wide and 1800 pixels tall.

Using Layers to Keep Outlines Visible

Layers are a great asset to a colorist, as they cut down on the time required for boring things like defining objects and leave more time for the fun

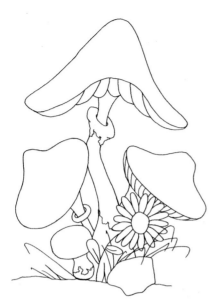

Figure 3.1 *Line art of mushrooms*

Figure 3.2 *The New Layer button in the Layers dialog*

Figure 3.3 *The foreground and background colors*

Figure 3.4 *A red stroke covers the lines*

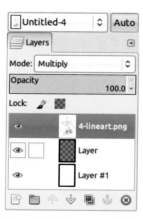

Figure 3.5 *The Layers dialog for Figure 3.6*

stuff like playing with different color combinations and adding shadows.

Keep an unaltered copy of the line art on a separate layer so you can always see the lines. If you put it at the bottom of the layer stack and start to add color, the lines will disappear! Try it for yourself: Once you've opened your line art image (**Image: File > Open** or CTRL+O), create a new transparent layer. You can do this in one of four ways: Select **Image: Layer > New Layer** or **Layer: right-click > New Layer**, or press SHIFT+CTRL+N or the Layers dialog button as seen in Figure 3.2. Then paint a red stroke on the image:

1. Select the Paintbrush tool in the Toolbox (or press P).

2. Click the Foreground Color box in the bottom-left corner of the Toolbox (top left in Figure 3.3). The foreground color is black by default.

3. In the Color chooser dialog that appears, choose a bright red and click OK.

4. In the Paintbrush tool options, check that the BRUSH is set to Hardness 075. If it's not, click in the left square and choose the correct brush.

5. Change the SIZE slider (in tool options) to **70**.

6. Scribble across the image.

Your result will probably look something like Figure 3.4.

To keep the line art visible while adding color, place the line art layer on top (**Image: Layer > Stack > Raise Layer**). The red stroke disappears behind the black and white drawing. To put it back on top, first create a new layer at the

Figure 3.6 *The red stroke shows through*

Figure 3.8 *A medium color*

Figure 3.7 *A grayish color*

Figure 3.9 *A vivid color*

bottom of the layer stack. This layer will be the background and can be any color that you like.

Next, select the top layer (with the line art) and set it to Multiply mode, as shown in Figure 3.5. The red stroke should reappear, as shown in Figure 3.6. From now on, anything you paint on the middle layers will show through the white without obscuring the lines.

Defining Objects and Base Colors

Before we get started, let's review some basic GIMP skills that you'll need to color a drawing. To choose new colors, open the Color chooser dialog by clicking the Foreground Color box.

Experiment with the six sliders (Hue, Saturation, Value, Red, Green, Blue) and the clickable areas on the left to make a selection. Your color selection appears in the Current color box in the bottom right.

Use the Saturation and Value cursors (Figures 3.7 and 3.8) to adjust the gray levels for more realistic colors. If you want a more cartoonish style, you could choose only vivid, fully saturated colors (Figure 3.9).

Figure 3.10 *The Bucket Fill tool icon*

Figure 3.11 *Filling with the Bucket Fill tool*

To add color, either use the Bucket fill tool to fill a region with one click (select **Image: Tools > Paint Tools > Bucket Fill**, press SHIFT+B, or click the Toolbox button shown in Figure 3.10) or paint the area with a mouse or tablet pen, which takes longer. If using the Bucket Fill tool, make sure you check SAMPLE MERGE so the black lines (which are on a separate layer) are taken into account. You may need to play around with the THRESHOLD until you fill the object and nothing else.

Although Bucket Fill is fast, it's generally not very accurate. Dark gray pixels often remain gray (see Figure 3.11). You can enhance the result by continuing to experiment with the THRESHOLD, but the result may never be perfect.

Figure 3.12 *The Paintbrush tool icon*

Figure 3.13 *Paint Dynamics*

Figure 3.14 *Painting with the Paintbrush tool*

Figure 3.15 *The Eraser tool icon*

The Paintbrush tool produces a more accurate, clearer result, but using it takes longer (although you'll get faster with experience). (Select **Image: Tools > Paint Tools > Paintbrush**, or press P, or click the Toolbox button shown in Figure 3.12 to access the Paintbrush tool.) If you use a tablet, apply full pressure when coloring the center of an object or you'll end up with partially transparent pixels. Alternatively, you can set the Paint Dynamics (Figure 3.13) to Dynamics Off to turn off the pressure sensitivity.

Be careful at the borders of an object. The color should go up to the darkest part of the line (over any dark gray pixels) but not beyond it. Figure 3.14 shows what happens when the borders aren't colored carefully: On the left, the colorist didn't go far enough, and on the right, the colorist went too far.

Figure 3.16 *A carefully painted border*

Figure 3.17 *Defining the mushroom stem*

If you are careful and take your time, meticulously adding color where paint is missing and using the Eraser tool (select **Image: Tools > Paint Tools > Eraser**, or press SHIFT+E, or click the Toolbox button shown in Figure 3.15) where you went too far, you can fill an object with color very accurately. You can see a carefully painted border in Figure 3.16. As you work, experiment with different brush sizes: Try a large brush size for painting the center of an object, and switch to a smaller size when you get near the border. Now, let's try coloring our simple cartoon.

Coloring the Mushrooms

The most efficient way to colorize in GIMP is to create a layer for each base color in an object and then add the color and the shading. This gives you more control and flexibility and actually makes shading a lot easier. If you choose too many different base colors, however, you'll spend all day switching among layers.

Start with the object that's farthest from the viewer. Create a new layer for that object, at the bottom of the stack, just above the background. In the advanced options, choose to fill the layer with transparency. In our mushroom cartoon, the farthest object is the mushroom stem, so

Figure 3.18 *Now coloring the mushroom cap*

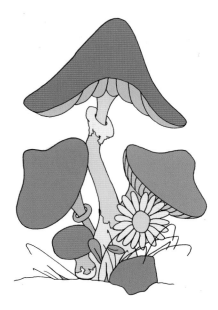

Figure 3.20 *After adding base colors*

Figure 3.19 *One layer per object*

we call this layer `Small mushroom stem`. Next, we choose a color and paint the mushroom stem, as shown in Figure 3.17.

Next, create another new, transparent layer, and choose any object one step closer: In this example, either the bottom of the stem or the mushroom cap will do. Note that you can paint well beyond the lines of any object that is above the current layer, as shown in Figure 3.18. The number of layers increases quickly, so give them meaningful names, as shown in Figure 3.19.

Continue creating layers and adding colors until every object is defined and you have a basic colored drawing like the one in Figure 3.20.

Now is a good time to step back and look at the drawing as a whole to make sure you like how the colors look together. If you want to change one, simply check the Lock alpha channel box of the corresponding layer (see Figure 3.21), choose a new color, and drag-and-

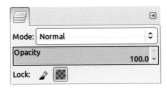

Figure 3.21 *Locking a layer's transparency*

drop it from the foreground color box into the image. The LOCK box keeps the transparency of each pixel unchanged, so you can fill just the area that you colored.

Shading

Now that every object has a color, let's add some shading. You'll need to decide which direction the light is coming from. It might come from above, from a lamp in the drawing, or from anywhere else you like.

Before adding any shading, merge all the layers of each individual object (**Image: Layer > Merge Down**) so the object is shaded consistently. For example, if you merge all the layers of one of the mushrooms and you decide to light

Figure 3.22 *The Dodge/Burn tool icon*

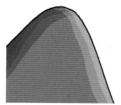

Figure 3.23 *Using Dodge/Burn to shade a mushroom*

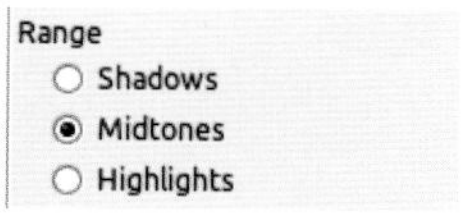

Range
○ Shadows
◉ Midtones
○ Highlights

Figure 3.24 *The Range option for the Dodge/Burn tool*

it from the right, then you can add shadow on the left and light on the right, all in one stroke.

Now we're ready to add shading. Choose the Dodge/Burn tool (select **Image: Tools > Paint Tools > Dodge/Burn**, or press SHIFT+D, or click the Toolbox button shown in Figure 3.22). In Dodge mode, this tool adds light, and in Burn mode, it adds shadow. This tool lightens or darkens the opaque areas without changing the colors.

Dodge each object along the side facing the light source, and burn the other side. Dodge a large area first, and then dodge over a smaller area, closer to the light source, to create a gradient as shown in Figure 3.23.

The Dodge/Burn tool acts on pixels differently depending on whether it classifies them as dark or light. The RANGE option (Figure 3.24) changes how pixels are classified. Figure 3.23 shows shading done with the RANGE option set to MIDTONES, whereas Figure 3.25 was done with the RANGE option set to HIGHLIGHTS.

The shading added so far is crude, and although it has improved the drawing considerably, you can make the result much better by smoothing the color transitions.

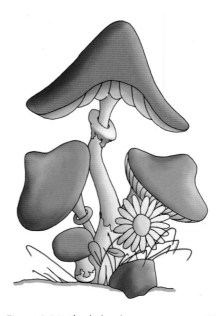

Figure 3.25 *Shaded with Range set to Highlights*

Figure 3.26 *The Smudge tool icon*

Figure 3.27 *Using the Smudge tool to smooth the gradients*

Choose the Smudge tool (select **Image: Tools > Paint Tools > Smudge**, or press S, or click the Toolbox button shown in Figure 3.26). This tool blends colors or transparencies, so if you smudge near the object's border, you'll get a fuzzy border. To keep the borders sharp, check the Lock alpha channelbox of the corresponding layer (Figure 3.21). After smudging, you should get a gradient like the one in Figure 3.27.

Tip: Start by smudging perpendicularly to the dodge lines and then in the same direction as the

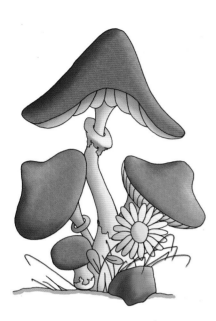

Figure 3.28 *Adding texture with a pattern*

Figure 3.29 *Adding polka dots*

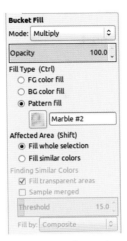

Figure 3.30 *The Bucket Fill tool options*

lines. Alternatively, use small circular strokes to create a more organic gradient.

Dodge, burn, and smudge each object in your drawing until you have a fully shaded drawing, like the one in Figure 3.25.

Finishing Touches

After you've finished shading, you can add some finishing touches, like a pattern (Figure 3.28), or hand-painted details, like the polka dots in Figure 3.29, or anything else that comes to mind.

To add texture, select the layer you want to modify and pick the Bucket Fill tool. Change its options to the ones shown in Figure 3.30: set MODE to MULTIPLY, set FILL TYPE to PATTERN FILL, choose a light pattern (a colorful pattern will change your colors too much), and set the AFFECTED AREA to FILL WHOLE SELECTION. Make sure Lock alpha channel is checked. Now click your image to see the result.

To add hand-painted polka dots, duplicate one of the mushroom cap layers by selecting **Image: Layer > Duplicate Layer** or **Layer: right-click > Duplicate Layer**, by pressing $\boxed{\text{SHIFT+}}$ $\boxed{\text{CTRL+D}}$, or by clicking the Layers dialog button, as shown in Figure 3.31). Add a layer mask to the new layer (**Image: Layer > Mask > Add Layer Mask**), and initialize the mask to LAYER'S

Figure 3.31 *The Duplicate Layer button in the Layers dialog*

Figure 3.32 *Initializing the layer mask*

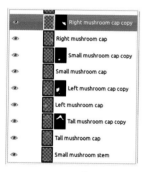

Figure 3.33 *Each mushroom cap has an additional layer with a layer mask.*

ALPHA CHANNEL (Figure 3.32). Next, clear the layer content (**Image: Edit > Clear** or DEL), and you have a new layer that will cover only that mushroom cap.

Set the layer's MODE to GRAIN MERGE, select the Paintbrush tool, and choose white as the foreground color. Make sure Lock alpha channel is *not* checked this time, and start painting dots on the mushroom cap. You can paint dots on the edge of the cap without painting on the background thanks to the layer mask, and the dots will be a lighter shade of the cap color thanks to Grain Merge Mode. Create a new layer for each of the remaining caps to paint

Figure 3.34 *Brushes*

polka dots on all of them (using a layer mask as shown in Figure 3.33). You've completed the mushroom colorizing tutorial.

3.2   Painting and Drawing

We are now going to explore some of the painting tools in more detail, but first, some remarks about brushes ...

Brushes

Brushes are used with every painting tool and work just like brushes in real life—a larger brush lays down more color at once, and a fuzzy brush results in softer edges. Figure 3.34 shows some of the simple effects that you can get by changing brushes. Because this is digital painting, however, you can also use brushes to create effects that you couldn't do so easily with real paint. The basic brushes, Hardness 100 and Hardness 075, are versatile and straightforward and are used frequently in this book.

Figure 3.35 shows some creative effects that you can achieve using just the Hardness 100 brush. We created a scalloped edge by adjusting the SIZE, ASPECT RATIO, and ANGLE parameters. To draw the ghostly line on the left, we played with the paint dynamics settings. For the striped line on the top, we used a gradient as the paint color and the Random Color paint dynamics to vary the color at random within that gradient.

Figure 3.35 *Creative effects with brushes*

The Pencil Tool

The Pencil tool (accessed via **Image: Tools > Paint Tools > Pencil**, N, or the Toolbox button shown in Figure 3.36) is draws freehand strokes with a hard edge, even when used with a fuzzy brush, as it doesn't include any antialiasing.

Antialiasing smooths edges, even at low resolutions, by taking advantage of how vision works. The Paintbrush tool uses antialiasing to produce soft strokes by generating semi-opaque pixels on the edges, whereas the Pencil tool generates only fully opaque pixels. Figure 3.37 shows spots drawn with the Paintbrush tool (left) and the Pencil tool (right). These spots were magnified to show the effect of antialiasing at the pixel level.

The Pencil tool is useful when you want to control exactly how a pixel changes. For example, pixel art is often done using the Pencil tool with a brush size of 1 pixel (SIZE option set to 1.00). The Pencil tool is also useful for drawing very small images like icons.

Drawing an Icon

Some icons are drawn in a vector graphics program and scaled down to their final size afterward. But small, simple icons often come out better when drawn at their intended size, pixel by pixel.

Icons, like those representing the tools in the GIMP Toolbox, are generally tiny images (around 16 × 16 pixels) and are drawn with a limited color palette in indexed mode. The limited palette gives an icon set a more uniform

Figure 3.36 *The Pencil tool icon*

Figure 3.37 *Paintbrush and Pencil spots*

look. Indexed mode can be selected via **Image: Image > Mode > Indexed**.

To work at the pixel level, zoom to 800% (**Image: View > Zoom > 8:1** or use the zoom drop-down list at the bottom of the Image window). When the image is magnified so dramatically, however, you might find it hard to see what the icon will look like at normal zoom.

To help with that, you can display a second view of the image (**Image: View > New View**) at 100% zoom. Because the second view is so small, hide the layer borders (**Image: View > Show layer boundary**) to gain clarity. An example of these two views is shown in Figure 3.38. Note that in single-window mode, you won't be able to view both at once; you'll have to tab back and forth.

Pixel Art

Pixel art is a form of digital art that's created on the pixel level. Graphics in old video games and many mobile phone games are pixel art.

Again, choosing a color palette, drawing at 800% zoom, and opening a second view at 100% is best. Pixel art comes in two major categories: isometric and nonisometric. *Isometric* pixel art is based on the isometric line, and the result is a 3D object that is viewed from above and to the side. *Nonisometric* pixel art deviates from this line, resulting in a 2D object that is shown from any other view, such as the top, bottom, side, or front. The isometric line is shown in Figure 3.39: 2 pixels across and 1 pixel up.

Drawing pixel art with a gray, 1 × 1 pixel grid is easier. To view this grid, select **Image: Image > Configure Grid** and change the

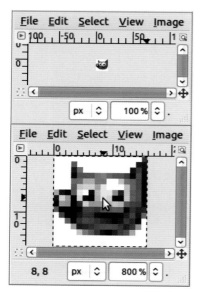

Figure 3.38 *Using two views to draw an icon*

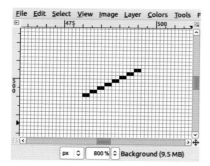

Figure 3.39 *An isometric line*

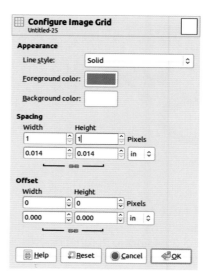

Figure 3.40 *Grid configuration*

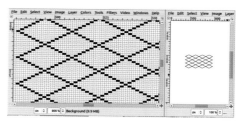

Figure 3.41 *An isometric grid*

Figure 3.42 *An isometric cube*

foreground color to gray and the width and height to 1 pixel, as shown in Figure 3.40. Then use **Image: View > Show Grid** to display it.

You can build an isometric grid (Figure 3.41) quickly by selecting the pixels of an isometric line. Use the Rectangle Select tool (**Image: Tools > Selection Tools > Rectangle Select** or R) to select specific lines or sections of the grid or the Select by Color tool (**Image: Tools > Selection Tools > By Color Select** or SHIFT+O) to select all the black pixels. Copy (**Image: Edit > Copy** or CTRL+C) the line, paste it (**Image: Edit > Paste** or CTRL+V), and flip it (**Image:**

Layer > Transform > Flip Horizontally). Move this copy to the proper place, and then use Paste and Flip Horizontally or Flip Vertically to add additional lines. You might need to practice, but once you have a nice grid, you can use it over and over. The length of the initial isometric line determines the grid's density.

For example, you can use the grid to make the isometric cube shown in Figure 3.42. Start with two isometric squares and link them with vertical lines. Erase the pixels that should be hidden, and enhance the three-dimensional effect by

Figure 3.43 *Creating a larger cube*

Figure 3.44 *A wall of bricks*

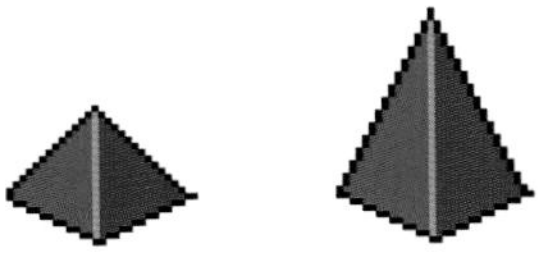

Figure 3.45 *Pyramids*

Figure 3.46 *A cylinder*

Figure 3.47 *A house*

Figure 3.48 *A tower*

Figure 3.49 *Cylinder detail*

Figure 3.50 *The Paintbrush tool icon*

filling each face with a different shade of the same color to suggest shadow and light.

You can create a larger cube with the same grid, as shown in Figure 3.43. Figure 3.44 shows a large cube that's been decorated to look like bricks. These bricks follow the same rules: The horizontal lines are isometric lines, and the vertical lines are parallel to the cube lines. We also added lighting to the individual bricks and shading to the cube faces.

You can rotate the isometric line to build other basic shapes like the pyramids in Figure 3.45 and the cylinder in Figure 3.46. These shapes can be combined to build things like the house in Figure 3.47 or the tower in

Figure 3.48. To add a shading gradient to round objects, use *dithering*. When pixels of similar color are interspersed, as shown in Figure 3.49, they blend into each other and look like an intermediate color to the eye. You can also add more detail and even build tiny towns with isometric cars, people, or trees. See, for example, *http://sparklette.net/art/navy-open-house-ad-impressive-pixel-art/*.

The Paintbrush Tool

The Paintbrush tool (press $\boxed{P}$ or click the Toolbox button shown in Figure 3.50) is used for freehand strokes with a soft edge. Even with a hard brush, it produces soft edges, and with a fuzzy brush, the edges are even fuzzier.

In digital painting, the Paintbrush tool is used for two main things: drawing lines and filling areas. Generally, the first step in digital painting is to sketch the objects. A black fuzzy brush works well for sketching. If the lines will remain as

Figure 3.51 *Painting outlines*

Figure 3.52 *Painting sketch lines*

Figure 3.53 *Filling outlines*

Figure 3.54 *Filling in a sketch*

Figure 3.55 *The Airbrush tool icon*

Figure 3.56 *Adding light with the Airbrush tool*

You can also use the Paintbrush tool to fill the objects with color, as shown in Figures 3.53 and 3.54. You might add individual objects to larger paintings like the landscape in Section 3.5.

The Airbrush Tool

The Airbrush tool (accessed via **Image: Tools > Paint Tools > Airbrush**, Ⓐ, or the Toolbox button shown in Figure 3.55) is used to paint soft areas of color. If you use a graphic tablet and Basic Dynamics, opacity will be linked to pen pressure, so when you press lightly, a fine mist of color is added. Each stroke adds color, regardless of whether you've lifted the pen off the tablet. Moreover, speed matters: The more slowly you move the pen, the more paint is left.

outlines around the object, they should be clean and done with a relatively small brush size, as shown in Figure 3.51. If the lines are just a sketch and will be erased, use a larger brush size with a looser style, as shown in Figure 3.52. Painting without permanent outlines is more challenging because you'll need to be much more careful when finishing the edges of objects.

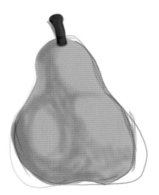

Figure 3.57 *Adding shadow with the Airbrush tool*

Figure 3.58 *The Ink tool icon*

Calligraphy

Figure 3.59 *Traditional European calligraphy*

Figure 3.60 *Japanese katakana*

Figure 3.61 *The Bucket Fill tool icon*

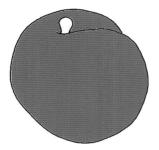

Figure 3.62 *Filling with a solid color*

You can use the Airbrush tool to add light (Figure 3.56) or shadow (Figure 3.57). The Airbrush tool lets you to choose colors for the light and the shadows, unlike the Dodge/Burn tool. To smooth transitions, see "The Smudge Tool" on page 76.

The Ink Tool

The Ink tool (accessed via **Image: Tools > Paint Tools > Ink**, K, or the Toolbox button shown in Figure 3.58) is used for calligraphy because it replicates the look of a quill, especially if you use a graphic tablet that handles pressure and tilt.

For calligraphy, adjust the Ink tool options (see Figure 15.53 on page 347) until they suit your style. In particular, adjust the ANGLE, TILT, and SPEED sensitivity until you get the result you want. Figure 3.59 is an example of traditional European calligraphy, and Figure 3.60 is an example of Japanese katakana.

3.3 Filling an Area

In this section, we introduce tools that are designed to fill an area with a color, pattern, or gradient.

The Bucket Fill Tool

Use the Bucket Fill tool (**Image: Tools > Paint Tools > Bucket Fill**, SHIFT+B, or the Toolbox button shown in Figure 3.61) to fill an area with a solid color or pattern either by clicking in the area that you want to fill or by dragging the foreground or background color and dropping it over the image.

When you click to fill, you fill only the contiguous space with that color or pattern. This means that a line drawing can act as a boundary. For example, we clicked in the line drawing of a peach to fill it with dark orange (Figure 3.62) and then a swirly pattern (Figure 3.63).

Figure 3.63 *Filling with a pattern*

Figure 3.64 *Using a gradient in a button*

Figure 3.65 *The original photograph, without color*

Figure 3.66 *A dramatic stormy sky*

Figure 3.67 *Mushroom A*

Figure 3.68 *Mushroom B*

Figure 3.69 *Mushroom C*

Gradients

Gradients work well in the background of buttons (Figure 3.64), banners, or drawings. They can also add simple shading effects or a unique touch to a photo.

For example, we added color to enhance the dramatic look of the stormy sky photo in Figure 3.65. The cloud front is diagonal to the horizon. We applied the gradient perpendicularly to the cloud front, so that areas with heavier cloud cover are darker, as shown in Figure 3.66.

You can also use gradients in layer masks to create smooth transitions between layers. This is how we combined the mushrooms from Figures 3.67 to 3.69 to create Figure 3.70. Gradients are used in layer masks to transition between black and white, as shown in Figure 3.71. White areas are visible, black areas are transparent, and gray areas create the transition.

Figure 3.70 *All mushrooms faded into one composition*

Figure 3.71 *The Layers dialog for Figure 3.70*

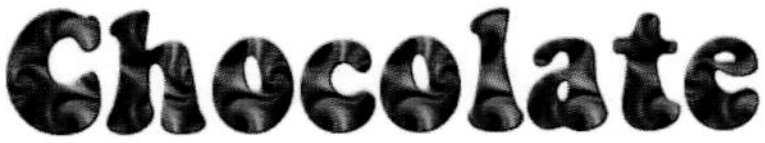

Figure 3.73 *First coat of burning*

Chocolate

Figure 3.72 *Using a pattern*

Patterns

Apply patterns to decorate a background, create text effects (as shown in Figure 3.72), or make the surface of an object look more organic. See "The Patterns Dialog" on page 337 and "Building New Patterns" on page 580 for more details.

Figure 3.74 *Second coat of burning*

Figure 3.75 *Third coat of burning*

3.4 Dodging, Burning, and Smudging

As you saw when we painted the peach and the pear, shading and smudging can greatly improve the look of digitally painted objects. Dodging, burning, and smudging are common ways to add finishing touches to elements in your digital art.

The Dodge/Burn Tool

As you saw in the tutorial, you can use dodging and burning to add shadows and highlights to a drawing.

Switch between dodging and burning with the TYPE option or the CTRL key. Remember that the Dodge tool lightens, and the Burn tool darkens. When you go over an area several times, each stroke increases the effect.

To create a shading gradient, you could burn a large area lightly and then reburn (darken) a smaller area, and so on. Alternatively, you can start by burning a small area that will be the darkest and then burn it again and enlarge the area, and so on, as shown in Figures 3.73 to 3.75.

Figures 3.76 and 3.77 show the last two steps: smudging and dodging.

You could apply just one coat of dodge or burn and then smudge it into the base color, but the result won't be as natural. The RANGE option changes how great an effect one coat has. Although painting on shadows gives you

Figure 3.76 *Smudging to soften the transitions*

Figure 3.77 *With dodging added*

Figure 3.78 *The original photograph*

Figure 3.79 *After burning the background*

greater control, the Dodge/Burn tool does a pretty good job without much time or effort.

You can also use dodging and burning to make a subject stand out in a photograph, as

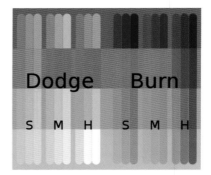

Figure 3.80 *An example of different range values*

shown in Figures 3.78 and 3.79. When you dodge or burn the background, the subject of the photo stands out. You can either select the subject with the Foreground Select tool (**Image: Tools > Selection Tools > Foreground Select**), invert the selection, and then burn it, or you can burn the background manually using a brush.

Figure 3.80 shows the effects of dodging and burning using the three different range settings: **S**hadows, **M**idtones, and **H**ighlights. We started with a vertical stripe comprised of four tones. From top to bottom, the tones were dark, bright and fully saturated, light, and very pale. We made 18 copies of the stripe, arranged into groups of 3. Within each group, from left to right, one, two, or three coats of dodge or burn were applied. As you can see in the figure, half of the groups were dodged, and the other half were burned, using each of the three range settings.

The Smudge Tool

Use the Smudge tool to soften transitions, hide objects, or even create textures. Earlier in this chapter, we used the Smudge tool to soften the color transitions after adding shading and highlights in "The Airbrush Tool" on page 72 and after shading with the Dodge/Burn tool in the previous section.

You can also use the Smudge tool to achieve subtle color transitions, applying drop strokes of different colors and smudging them as

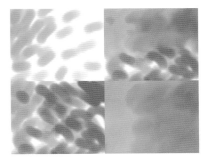

Figure 3.81 *Successive steps of smudging*

Figure 3.83 *A flashy monster with fur*

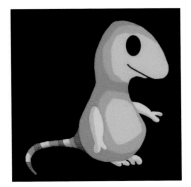

Figure 3.82 *A flashy monster*

Figure 3.84 *Smudging the peach*

traditional painters do. Start by covering an area with dense strokes of one color, which gradually thin, and then do the same with different colors in different areas so the colors bleed. Next, smudge in small circular strokes. Any white background that was showing through will blend in as well, lightening the area. Continue smudging until the whole image is done, and smudge again in larger circles to make the result smoother, but use caution. The final result in Figure 3.81 looks natural because some irregularities remain.

You can also use the Smudge tool to create fur, grass, or other similar textures. The little monster shown in Figure 3.82 has very sharp edges. If we smudge perpendicular to the edge, in swift, even strokes, we can make the little guy look furry, as shown in Figure 3.83.

Figure 3.85 *Smudging the pear*

Figure 3.86 *Starting with the sky color*

Figure 3.87 *Adding the clouds layer*

Figures 3.84 and 3.85 show how the Smudge tool can create smoother transitions in the images from Figures 3.56 and 3.57.

3.5 The Digital Painting Process

In this section, you get to look over the shoulder of a digital painter as she develops a complete landscape painting in GIMP. Although this isn't a follow-along tutorial, it shows you how a digital painter plans and executes a moderately complex piece, and you get to see a variety of practical techniques and tricks in action.

Composition

I'll begin by creating layers for each major aspect of the landscape, going from the most distant (the sky in Figure 3.86) to the closest

Figure 3.88 *Adding the mountains layer*

Figure 3.89 *Adding the hills layer*

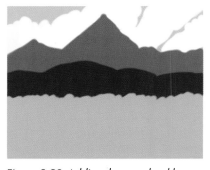

Figure 3.90 *Adding the grassland layer*

element (the river in Figure 3.92) in Figures 3.86 to 3.92. I initialize each layer with a transparent background, so the layers behind show through. At this stage, I just use basic paintbrush strokes to get a general idea of the composition. I don't spend much time on the colors—I pick whatever comes to mind because I can tweak them later. I also don't spend much time getting the shapes

Figure 3.91 *Adding the trees layer*

Figure 3.92 *Adding the river layer*

Figure 3.93 *Darkening the top of the sky*

Figure 3.94 *Smudging to get a richer sky*

Figure 3.95 *Adding shadows to the clouds*

exactly right: Mountains (Figure 3.88) are rough triangles, and trees (Figure 3.91) are scribbles.

Once all the layers are set up, I adjust colors by locking the Alpha channel and dropping new colors in (as we did in "Coloring the Mushrooms" on page 64). I try to capture a mood with the color combination. When you're first starting out, finding the right combination might seem difficult, but with more practice, you'll be able to envision what a piece will become even at this early stage.

Next I refine each layer. I use a graphics tablet with the Paint Dynamics set to Basic Dynamics so pressure controls opacity.

Sky and Clouds

I'll start with the sky. I make the sky richer using the techniques described in "The Smudge Tool" on page 76, dropping small paintbrush strokes (Figure 3.93) and smudging in a circular motion (Figure 3.94). This makes the flat, plain sky much more interesting.

Now I add volume to those flat white shapes to make them look more like clouds. I lock the Alpha channel, add gray paintbrush strokes to the bottom of the clouds (Figure 3.95), and smudge the shadows to create soft transitions (Figure 3.96). I then unlock the Alpha channel

Figure 3.96 *Smudging the clouds' shadows*

Figure 3.97 *Smudging the edges of the clouds into the sky*

Figure 3.98 *Snowy mountains*

Figure 3.99 *Exposed dirt and rocks*

Figure 3.100 *Smudged dark detailing*

Figure 3.101 *Adding a blueish tone*

and smudge the cloud edges a bit to get that fluffy feeling (Figure 3.97).

Mountains

The mountains layer is challenging because I want snowy mountains but need to distinguish the mountains from the clouds. Now that the bottoms of the clouds are shadowed, I can

add the snow without losing the mountains. I lock the Alpha channel again and add white paintbrush strokes, pressing harder where the sun makes the snow bright and lighter on the other side (Figure 3.98). This time, the brush strokes look nice, so I'm not going to smudge them. To make the mountains more interesting, I want to add some dark areas where the snow has melted or couldn't reach. I paint in

Figure 3.102 *Adding light to the hills*

Figure 3.103 *Softening*

MULTIPLY mode to maintain the lighting I just defined (Figure 3.99). I smudge these areas chaotically to give them a natural, artistic look (Figure 3.100). Finally, I add a slight blueish tone to the snow, giving it a more realistic feel (Figure 3.101).

Hills

The hills just need a nice texture so they look like grassy hills. I start by lighting them with the Dodge/Burn tool set to RANGE HIGHLIGHTS (Figure 3.102). The hills' color is rather dark, so I use several coats to get the result shown. I then smooth the result with the Smudge tool (Figure 3.103).

I'll add some noise to the hills to make them look less smooth and bare. I experimented with the filters in the **Image: Filters > Noise** menu and found that one of them, **Image: Filters > Noise > RGB Noise**, results in something close

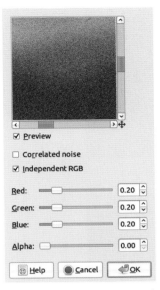

Figure 3.104 *The RGB Noise dialog*

Figure 3.105 *Adding noise*

to what I have in mind, so I apply it with the default parameters (Figure 3.104) and get the result shown in Figure 3.105.

Grassland

First I want to create a soft transition between the hills and the grassland. I start by choosing a vertical gradient ranging from the deep green of the hills to the middle green of the grass. With the Alpha channel locked, I apply the gradient from the top of the grassland to the middle of the grassland. Figure 3.106 shows the result.

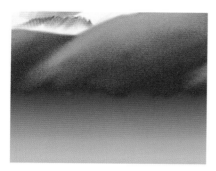

Figure 3.106 *Gradient transition*

Figure 3.107 *Smudging the gradient*

Figure 3.108 *Adding noise*

I then unlock the Alpha channel and improve the transition between the two layers with the Smudge tool. I also smooth any seams in the grassland that were created by the gradient. The smudged gradient is shown in Figure 3.107.

I decide to texture the grassland using the same filter that worked so well for the hills: **Image: Filters > Noise > RGB Noise**. The result, shown in Figure 3.108, is what I expected, but

Figure 3.109 *Marking the edge*

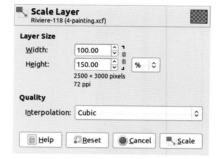

Figure 3.110 *The Scale Layer dialog*

the transition between hills and grassland is now too subtle. This time I want to sharpen a transition. I use the Eraser tool to remove some of the smudging done earlier to reveal more of the dark base of the hills. I stop when I'm happy with the transition (Figure 3.109).

Trees

While painting the background, something about the trees started to bug me. It's not just that they're ugly scribbles; they don't seem to fit in the composition. First I need to figure out what is making me uneasy, and then I can fix it. Is it the color (too dark for the mood of the painting)? Or the position? Maybe the size? Yes, that's it: The trees look too small compared to the rest of the landscape.

A quick layer transformation confirms my suspicion. I select **Image: Layer > Scale Layer**, unlock the chain, and choose 150% height and

Figure 3.111 *Making the trees grow*

Figure 3.112 *Bark and roots*

Figure 3.113 *A leaf*

Figure 3.114 *Rotated leaves*

Spacing (percent):	20
Description:	GIMP Brush Pipe
Cell size:	200 x 200 Pixels
Number of cells:	8
Display as:	1 Rows of 8 Columns on each layer
Dimension:	1
Ranks:	8 random
	1 random
	1 random
	1 random

| Help | Cancel | Export |

Figure 3.115 *Save as Brush Pipe*

100% width (see Figure 3.110) so the trees get taller but not wider. My intuition was good, and after erasing a bit of the bottommost trunk, I get Figure 3.111, which is a better composition.

Now, I want to make these trees look like something other than scribbles. I start with the trunks and leave the foliage for last because it lies on top of the trunks.

I add vertical strokes to the trunks to give the impression of tree bark. I use the Airbrush tool to get a natural effect, adding dark brown lines on the shady side and lighter lines on the sunny side. The trees in the front should have more contrast than those in the back, whose colors blend in the distance. Whenever I add shadows, I make sure the shady side is the same on the mountains, hills, and trees.

I use the Smudge tool to create roots, stroking vertically from the feet of the trees into the grass. The closest tree should have roots more detailed, whereas the distant trees only need a few strokes. The result is in Figure 3.112.

For the foliage, I create my own animated leaf brush. I start by drawing a leaf on a relatively large canvas (200 × 200 is fine) and fill it lightly. I draw the leaf in grayscale so the brush can pick the Foreground color. The result is shown in Figure 3.113.

I then create a new image for the animated brush (1600 × 200) and copy and rotate the leaf eight times, as shown in Figure 3.114. (Chapter 22 goes into more detail about animated brushes.) I remove white from the new brush and set it up so any color can replace black pixels (**Image: Colors > Colors to Alpha**), and then I export the brush in GIMP animated brush format with the options shown in Figure 3.115.

Figure 3.116 *Leaves*

Figure 3.118 *River bank*

Figure 3.117 *Leaves with depth*

Figure 3.119 *Waterline smoothed*

When I refresh the Brushes dialog, my new brush appears. I select it, pick the Paintbrush tool, and select the Random Color Paint Dynamics setting. I choose a greenish gradient (one called Greens is somewhere in the middle), change the brush spacing to get the full gradient potential, and start painting to experiment. Leaves that are 200 × 200 pixels are a bit too large for this drawing, so I adjust the SIZE to make the brush smaller. When I make it too small, I can't really make out the leaves anymore. A size of 100 × 100 works best. I cover the trees with foliage, as shown in Figure 3.116, letting some of the brown sketch show through as branches.

Next, I want to give the trees some depth to distinguish the foliage of the close trees from the distant ones. I paint over the leaves with the same brush and the same gradient, but with the mode set to LIGHTEN ONLY for highlights and to DARKEN ONLY for shadows (Figure 3.117).

River

Now on to the final element: the river. Currently, it lies flat on the grass, but I'll fix that by adding banks. I'll draw them on a new layer, using a color gradient to give it some detail. I do that by defining a new paint dynamics that correlates Color with Fade. I choose a FADE LENGTH by trial and error. The foreground and background colors that the gradient will span should be close to each other so the gradient isn't too hard on the eyes. I paint the banks in small vertical strokes, following the bends of the river, as shown in Figure 3.118.

The waterline should be flat, so I erase the bottom of the bank with a fuzzy brush, resulting in Figure 3.119.

I add volume by drawing a semitransparent gradient over the bank. I first lock the Alpha channel to keep the gradient on the bank. I pick a dark color, the Blend tool, and the FG to

Figure 3.120 *Bank gradient added*

Figure 3.122 *After adding a current*

Figure 3.121 *Grass blades extend over the bank*

Transparent gradient. I begin each stroke above the bank, cross over it, and end at the water line. Now that the bank is darker, some imperfections become evident, so I unlock the Alpha channel and fix them, using the Smudge tool to fill the holes and the Eraser tool to clean up the waterline. The current result is shown in Figure 3.120.

The grass should curve over the edge of the bank, so I draw blades of grass with the Smudge tool. I do the same thing on the other side of the river, as shown in Figure 3.121.

The river still looks pretty flat, so I'll add some details. I burn the far side of the river, to put it in shadow, and airbrush a current with long, soft strokes, as shown in Figure 3.122. The state of the Layers dialog once the painting is finished is shown in Figure 3.123. The final painting is shown at its full size in Figure 3.124.

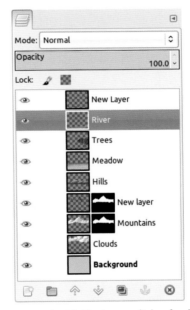

Figure 3.123 *The Layers dialog for the finished painting*

3.6 Drawing Shapes

GIMP does not have any shape-drawing tools: no rectangle tool, no circle tool, nothing. So does that mean drawing a clean rectangle in GIMP is impossible? Of course not! Drawing shapes is actually very easy.

Drawing a Straight Line

You can draw a straight line with any drawing tool by pressing SHIFT. You have to draw

Figure 3.124 *The finished painting*

something with the tool first (a little dot works). After you've drawn something, press SHIFT, and you'll see a segment extending from the dot (or whatever you drew) to the pointer (Figure 3.125). If you click, the line will be drawn.

Since you can use this method to draw a line with the Clone tool, the Erase tool, or any other drawing tool, you can get more than just plain lines. This is a very versatile technique.

Drawing Ellipses and Rectangles

If you want to draw a basic shape in GIMP but don't want to draw it line by line, you can use the selection tools. Several methods are available. To draw a circle, try one of these techniques:

- Draw a circular selection with the Ellipse Select tool (**Image: Tools > Selection Tools > Ellipse Select** or E). To make a solid circle, drop in a color or pattern or use the Bucket Fill tool. To make a ring, turn your selection into a 1- or 2-pixel border with **Image: Select > Border**, and then fill the resulting selection.

- Draw a circular selection and then stroke it with **Image: Edit > Stroke Selection**. The Stroke Selection dialog allows you to choose

Figure 3.125 *Drawing a straight line*

Figure 3.126 *A patterned circle with painted detail*

Figure 3.127 *A plain rectangle with a dashed border*

Figure 3.128 *A duck-shaped path*

Figure 3.129 *A line drawing of a duck*

among several drawing tools and emulate their paint dynamics, as explained in "Using a Path" on page 303.

- Draw a circular selection. Change your selection into a path (**Image: Select > To Path**), and then use **Paths: right-click > Stroke Path** to paint along this path. Stroke Path works in the same way as Stroke Selection, and you can make additional transformations to the path.

- Draw a circular selection. Make a new, transparent layer, and drop a color or pattern in it. Shrink the selection by 1 or 2 pixels, and delete the contents of the new selection (DELETE).

You can draw a rectangle in the same way by using the Rectangle Select tool (**Image: Tools > Selection Tools > Rectangle Select** or R) instead.

Figures 3.126 and 3.127 are examples of shapes drawn in GIMP using these methods.

Drawing a Complex Shape

You can use the Paths tool (**Image: Tools > Paths** or B) to draw more complicated shapes or to make line art (see Figure 3.128). You can then stroke the path using **Paths: right-click > Stroke Path**. If your drawing is made up of more than one path, you'll have to stroke them one by one, as we did when making Figure 3.129.

The Paths tool is also useful for tracing an existing image (see Figure 3.130). In Figure 3.131,

Figure 3.130 *Using the Paths tool to trace a photograph*

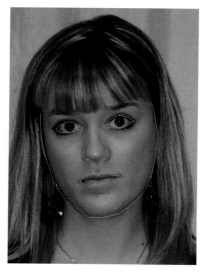

Figure 3.131 *The resulting paths with anchors hidden*

Figure 3.132 *The result of stroking the path with the Ink tool*

we hid the anchors to show the tracing more clearly. Figure 3.132 shows the result of stroking this path with the Ink tool.

You can also draw geometric shapes in GIMP using Gfig (**Image: Filters > Render > Gfig**), which is described in detail in Chapter 17.

3.7   Exercises

Exercise 3.1.   Draw a simple cartoon character with the Paintbrush tool. Use a tablet if you have one. Draw clean, solid lines.

Exercise 3.2.   Colorize your drawing (or find some clean line art if you skipped the first exercise). Refer to Section 3.1 for tips on where to place your line art layer and what mode it should be in. Add areas of solid color to your character.

Exercise 3.3.   Now try using the Dodge/Burn tool to add shading to one part of your character, and then use the Airbrush tool for a different part. Use whichever method you prefer to shade the rest of the cartoon character.

Exercise 3.4.   Use the Smudge tool to blend the shading. If your character has hair or fur, use the Smudge tool to add it.

Exercise 3.5.   Use the Ink tool to sign your work, and experiment with the options until your signature looks right.

4 Logos and Textures

The logo is an important part of any web page, advertisement, or letterhead. GIMP is an excellent tool for creating logos. In fact, many built-in logo plug-ins are available under **Image: File > Create > Logos**. They're self-explanatory, so we won't cover them in this book.

In addition to logos, we discuss textures in this chapter because textures are an important part of logo design. Many of the same techniques are effective for both logo design and texture creation. We demonstrate this in the upcoming tutorial, in which you'll build a texture and then use it as the basis for a logo.

4.1 Tutorial: Making a Luggage Tag

First, you're going to build a texture that simulates leather. You will then emboss it with text. The final product will be a luggage tag for "Mr. Gimp Junior."

Create a new image (**Image: File > New** or press $\boxed{\text{CTRL+N}}$). Choose 400×250 as the size and RGB as the image type, and use the default background color (i.e., white).

Fill this image with hurl noise. Select **Image: Filters > Noise > Hurl**, which opens the dialog in Figure 4.1. Push the RANDOMIZATION slider

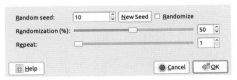

Figure 4.1 *The Hurl dialog*

Figure 4.2 *After applying the Hurl tool*

to 60% (try using the mouse wheel to do this). Leave the REPEAT slider at its default value of 1. Click OK. You get something like Figure 4.2.

Now select **Image: Filters > Distorts > Mosaic**. Choose the parameters shown in Figure 4.3 (i.e., OCTAGONS & SQUARES for TILING PRIMITIVES and 10.0 for TILE SIZE). Of course, you're welcome to experiment with other values later, but for now follow along with us.

The result, seen in Figure 4.4, bears a vague resemblance to leather, but the mosaic is too pronounced. Select the Hurl filter again, but

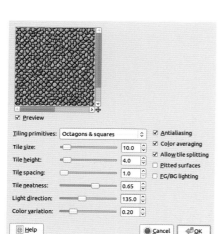

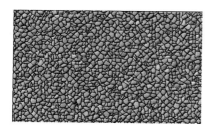

Figure 4.3 *The Mosaic dialog*

Figure 4.5 *After applying the Hurl filter again*

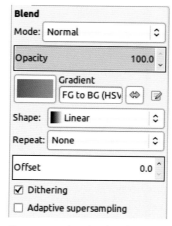

Figure 4.6 *The Blend tool options*

Figure 4.4 *After applying the Mosaic filter*

Figure 4.7 *After applying the Gradient Map tool*

this time set the RANDOMIZATION to 40%. In Figure 4.5 the mosaic is more subdued, but the colors still aren't realistic.

Choose two shades of brown—a darker shade as the foreground color and a lighter one as the background color. We chose 8c6434 and a29d89. Temporarily select the Blend tool (L) and check that the tool options are set as shown in Figure 4.6 (i.e., a linear gradient from foreground to background with no repetition).

Now apply the **Image: Colors > Map > Gradient Map** tool. This tool acts immediately without any dialog appearing. You already set the options in the Blend tool. The result appears in Figure 4.7. Note the foreground color is applied to sunken parts of the image, and the background color is applied to the bumps.

But the image lacks relief. The best tool for adding some is the **Image: Filters > Map > Bump**

Map filter. In the dialog shown in Figure 4.8, the relief is wrong because the channels appear as bumps and the bumps as depressions. This happens because the light comes from below due to the AZIMUTH value. This parameter assigns the direction of the light: 0 is from the right, 90 is from above, 180 is from the left, and 220 is from below. Choose 135 so the light comes from the top left. Set the other parameters as shown in

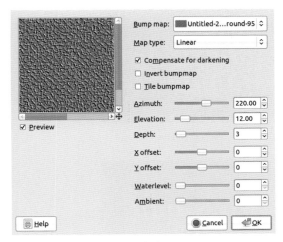

Figure 4.8 *The Bump Map dialog*

Figure 4.9 *After applying the Bump Map filter*

the figure. Click OK and you should see Figure 4.9.

The next tool we use is the Text tool (T). Its options appear in Figure 4.10. Set the foreground color to black, and choose a bold font and a large font size. We chose 50 pixels, which worked well for this example.

Once you've set the options, click in the upper-left corner of the leather texture that you just created. Type *Mr. Gimp Junior*—or your own name if you prefer. The text appears at the proper size in the image, in a new transparent layer above the background. In Figure 4.11, the limits of the new layer are visible.

Now duplicate the text layer. Note that the copy keeps the special property of being a text layer. Ensure the copy is selected and then select

Figure 4.10 *The Text tool options*

Figure 4.11 *After typing the text*

the **Image: Filters > Blur > Gaussian Blur** filter. In the dialog shown in Figure 4.12, choose 5.0 for both radii. The BLUR METHOD is irrelevant here. Click OK.

Now create a new layer filled with white (the left button at the bottom of the Layers dialog). Move this layer below the blurred text layer (the down arrow button in the Layers dialog). Merge the blurred text layer with the white layer (right-click the blurred text layer line in the Layers dialog, and choose MERGE DOWN). Hide both text layers (click the eye icons next

Figure 4.12 *The Gaussian Blur dialog*

Figure 4.13 *The Layers dialog*

Figure 4.14 *After embossing the text*

Figure 4.15 *After illuminating the text*

to their thumbnails in the Layers dialog). Select the background layer (click its thumbnail in the Layers dialog).

The Layers dialog should now look like Figure 4.13. Select **Image: Filters > Map > Bump Map**. From the Bump Map menu, choose the blurred text layer as the map. The Waterlevel must be about 80. Either leave the other parameter values as they are or play with them. Note that with an azimuth of 135, the text is embossed in the leather, while with an azimuth of 225, it is in relief. Click OK to get the image shown in Figure 4.14.

This result still needs some improvement. Select the initial text layer, and make it visible (click the eye in its line). Right-click this layer

line in the Layers dialog, and choose Alpha to Selection. Because this layer's background is transparent, you get a perfect selection around the text. Shrink this selection by 1 pixel (**Image: Select > Shrink**).

In the Layers dialog, hide the text layer and select the leathery background. Choose a bright red as the foreground color, and fill the selection using Ctrl+,. Finally, remove the selection with Shift+Ctrl+A. You'll get the final result shown in Figure 4.15.

You could complete the label by adding a bevel (**Image: Filters > Decor > Add Bevel**), reducing the amount of leather around the label, punching a hole in the corner, and so on. We leave these optional flourishes up to you.

4.2　Textures

As you saw in the preceding tutorial, building a logo often requires creating a texture first. The patterns provided by GIMP can be used as textures. You can browse through these in the Patterns dialog, initially located below the Layers dialog. But you have only a few patterns to choose from, and they're somewhat small. You can find more patterns and textures online, but building your own isn't very difficult, and you'll discover that creating the texture you want, exactly as you want it, is often faster.

In this section, we introduce you to tiling, which lets you fill an unlimited area seamlessly by repeating a smaller image and blending the edges together. We then present a short list of the tools available in GIMP for creating new textures. Finally, we demonstrate these tools, so you can use them to create your own textures quickly.

Tiling

A pattern is *tilable* if you can use it to fill an area of any size and shape. You should also not see any visible seams between the tiles of the pattern.

Many, but not all, of the predefined patterns in GIMP are tilable. For example, the Blue Squares pattern is tilable, but the Amethyst pattern is not. To see the pattern names, open the drop-down menu by clicking the triangle button in the top-right corner of the Patterns dialog. Select VIEW AS LIST.

Sometimes, even when a pattern is tilable and lacks a visible seam, the repetition is still very obvious. For example, the Chocolate Swirl pattern is clearly repetitive. This is partly because it's rather small at 50×50 pixels. Although the Blue Web pattern is only 64×64, it isn't as clearly repetitive because it doesn't have a simple geometrical form. The Nops pattern has no simple geometrical form and is 128×128, so it seamlessly fills a large area.

If you want to fill a large area with a texture, generally you don't want to build the texture as large as the intended area. This is especially true if you want to fill the background of a web page. Not only is the area large, but often you can't predict its size as that depends on the size of the browser window. Of course, if the texture is pavement, seeing the seams between tiles is

Figure 4.16 *The original pattern*

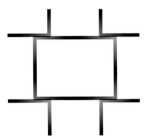

Figure 4.17 *After applying the Make Seamless filter*

fine. On the other hand, if the texture is a grassy field or water, you definitely don't want to see the seams.

The Make Seamless Filter

GIMP has a tool that allows us to build a tilable image with ease. We demonstrate it on a simple geometrical form. Create a new 400×400 image with a white background. Using the Rectangle select tool ([R]), select a 250×200 rectangle centered in the image. Using **Image: Select > Border**, create a border 5 pixels wide. Finally, fill this border with black, and remove the selection ([SHIFT+CTRL+A]). You can see the result in Figure 4.16.

This very simple tile wouldn't make a very good pattern. By applying the Make Seamless filter (**Image: Filters > Map > Make Seamless**) (which has no parameters and works immediately), you get Figure 4.17. The rectangle has been cut into four parts and copied into the corners of the image. A gradient has also been applied, although, in this case, it makes almost no difference because the background is white.

To check the result, call **Image: Filters > Map > Small Tiles**. The result appears in Figure 4.18. The original image has been reduced

Figure 4.18 *Checking that the result is seamlessly tilable*

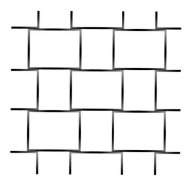

Figure 4.19 *Another seamlessly tilable image*

in size by half and duplicated four times. This image is clearly seamlessly tilable, and the pattern is surprisingly interesting.

In the previous example, the Make Seamless filter was effective. This isn't always the case if the original image is more complicated. The correct starting image can produce a reasonably good pattern, as in Figure 4.19, but that's the exception, not the rule. To create a pleasing pattern from a complex image, you first need to edit your image with some of the other tools available in GIMP.

Other Filters for Generating a Tilable Image

The HSV and RGB Noise filters (**Image: Filters > Noise**) automatically generate simple tilable patterns. Let's give it a try:

Figure 4.20 *The original image*

Figure 4.21 *The Tileable Blur dialog*

1. Create a new image of any size.

2. Select **Image: Filters > Noise > RGB Noise** and leave all parameters as set.

3. Call **Image: Filters > Map > Small Tiles** and observe the results.

You can also create a tilable image with the **Image: Filters > Render > Clouds > Solid Noise** filter. Check the TILABLE button, and you're done.

To create a tile from an existing image, you can use the **Image: Filters > Blur > Tileable Blur** filter, which merges and blurs the borders of the image, making it tilable. This filter also blurs the rest of the image, but you can fix that.

Let's try this with the image in Figure 4.20. Duplicate the layer and work on the copy. Select the Tileable Blur filter to open the dialog shown in Figure 4.21. Set the RADIUS value to 20 ("Radius" has the same meaning as in the Gaussian

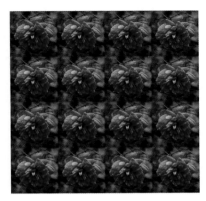

Figure 4.22 *The final texture*

Blur filter), and click OK. Use this blurred top layer to create a border:

1. Add an Alpha channel to this layer.

2. Select the full image ([CTRL+A]).

3. Shrink the selection by 200 pixels (**Image: Select > Shrink**).

4. Feather the selection by 100 pixels (**Image: Select > Feather**).

5. Cut the selection ([CTRL+X]), and discard it ([SHIFT+CTRL+A]).

6. Merge the two layers (**Layers: right-click > Merge Down**).

You get the final result, shown in Figure 4.22, by selecting the Small Tiles filter.

Creating Textures

In the following sections, we show you different ways to build textures. First, we demonstrate how to get started with a background, and then we briefly introduce a number of useful tools. Later, we walk you through creating a variety of patterns.

Building the Background

First, create the background. You can use an existing image, build one with the drawing tools introduced in Chapter 3, or automatically generate something with a filter. The **Image: Filters >** **Noise** menu offers several surface-filling filters: HSV NOISE, HURL, and RGB NOISE all make nice background textures. The other three filters in that menu will also work, but you have to start with an existing image. The **Image: Filters > Render** menu lists tools for generating more complicated backgrounds. Beginning with a new blank image, try the following:

- Apply **Clouds > Plasma** to generate a colorful texture.

- Apply **Clouds > Solid Noise** to generate a monochromatic bumpy texture that you can tile.

- Apply **Pattern > Checkerboard** to generate a black and white checkerboard.

- Apply **Pattern > Maze** to generate a maze that you can tile.

On the **Image: Filters > Artistic** menu, you'll find tools similar to those on the **Image: Filters > Render** menu. Three of these tools generate nice texture backgrounds. Experiment with these filters:

- Apply **> Apply Canvas** and **> Clothify**, which both generate a tilable, cloth-like texture.

- Apply **> Weave**, which adds a new layer in Multiply mode that contains a tilable texture similar to wickerwork.

Of course, you can use the filling tools to create a background. Use the Bucket Fill tool with an existing pattern or the Blend tool with one of the many available gradients, shapes, or repeat modes.

Transforming the Background

Once you have a background, the next step is to transform it. The **Image: Filters** menu is a gold mine.

One of the most useful submenus is **Image: Filters > Blur**. Generally, before you emboss or bump an image, you apply a blur to create the edges of the relief.

What if you want to distort the initial background? If you do, the **Image: Filters > Distort** submenu provides the necessary tools, including **Emboss**, **Mosaic**, **Ripple**, and **Whirl and Pinch**. We try some of them in the next sections.

The **Image: Filters > Light and Shadow** submenu contains some nifty tools, but only one is useful for creating textures: the **Glass Tile** filter. The tools in the **Image: Filters > Artistic** submenu are also handy for texture building. Experiment with the **Oilify** filter and what is often called the "texturing Swiss army knife": **GIMPressionist**. For more information on GIMPressionist, see "GIMPressionist" on page 434.

Embossing and bumping tools, which add relief to textures, are spread across several filter submenus:

- **Emboss** and **Engrave** are in **Image: Filters > Distorts**.
- **Lighting Effects** is in **Image: Filters > Light and Shadow**.
- **Bump Map** is in **Image: Filters > Map**.

Other Texture Tools

Several other GIMP tools can be used to improve a texture and give it a unique appearance:

- Create a texture with multiple layers, and use a blending mode other than NORMAL. You'll see this in action in several of the following examples.
- Adjust colors and color balance using the tools in **Image: Colors**. The **Auto** submenu contains tools for automatized adjustments without any parameters. The **Map** submenu contains several more powerful tools.
- In many cases, duplicating the current layer and making modifications is beneficial. For instance, you can add a Gaussian blur or some noise to the new layer and then merge the layers using a blending mode selected in the Layers dialog.
- The Fuzzy Select tool and the Select by Color tool can be used to generate wild patterns

from an automatically generated pattern such as Plasma. This is the basic idea behind the Scott effect, which is used to generate natural-looking aged surfaces.

- Finally, use ordinary tools in unusual ways to create some very special effects. For example, try applying a spiral gradient to an image 1 pixel wide and then enlarging the image.

Using the Blend Tool

The Blend tool is quite useful for easily creating textures.

You can change four main parameters: the blending mode, the gradient, its shape, and whether it repeats. You can also affect the result by changing the starting and stopping points of your stroke. This tool can generate innumerable textures—limited only by imagination!

We step you through some of the possible variations, and then we concentrate on one specific and spectacular effect. We begin each test with a new 400×250 image, but you can work at any size. Note that textures produced with the Blend tool are not tilable, so you can use the Blend tool only to fill an area as large as the image you begin with. But some parameter combinations require a lot of computing power, which increases with larger image sizes.

First, reset the foreground and background colors to their default values ([D]). Also reset the Blend tool options to their defaults using the yellow arrow button at the bottom right of the tool options: The gradient should be black to white, the shape should be linear, repeat should be set to none, and the mode should be NORMAL.

Some Simple Blending Effects

The spectacular effect in Figure 4.23 can be achieved in just two steps:

1. Change the Gradient Shape to Spiral.
2. Click in the center of the image and move the mouse as little as possible: just 1 pixel is ideal.

Figure 4.23 *A Spiral gradient with a very short mouse move*

Figure 4.24 *A repeating Triangular wave in Multiply blending mode*

Figure 4.25 *Triangular wave repetition mode with Darken only blending mode*

To make this easier, zoom the image to 400% or 800%.

If your result looks more like a spiral, you've moved the mouse too far. Zoom in further and try again.

This effect occurs because pixels provide only an approximation of the complicated shape that is built. You can produce variations on this effect by choosing other gradients or by changing the foreground and background colors if one of the FG to BG gradients is selected.

Create other interesting effects by changing the blending and repetition modes. To see the effect of changing the blending mode, apply the Blend tool several times. In normal blending mode, a new blend simply replaces the old one. The other blending modes allow you to blend layers to create new composite effects. The repetition mode changes the pattern in which the colors are repeated when you apply a gradient that's shorter than the canvas. To see the effect, create two new images. Choose the radial shape, set the gradient to something colorful such as one of the full saturation options, and draw a short gradient across each blank image using the Sawtooth wave for one and the Triangular wave for the other.

You can also use repetition modes to produce interesting grayscale patterns. We generated Figure 4.24 in the following way:

1. Beginning with the default settings, we changed the blending mode to Multiply.

2. We changed the repetition mode to Triangular wave.

3. We made two very short, perpendicular strokes on the image.

A surprising side effect is that, if you're lucky and have hit upon just the right combination of strokes, this texture is tilable!

Figure 4.25 shows the result of half a dozen strokes in random directions with the blending mode set to Darken only and the repetition mode set to Triangular wave.

The Difference Blending Mode

You can achieve interesting effects using the Difference blending mode. In this mode, every pixel painted by the Blend tool is mixed with the existing pixel. The value of the new pixel is the absolute value of the difference between both pixels. Thus, a dark pixel lightens, and a light pixel darkens.

This mode produces the most interesting results when you draw many crisscrossing strokes. Long strokes usually work better than short ones. Figure 4.26 was created using several long random strokes and the Triangular wave

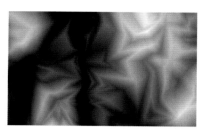

Figure 4.26 *Long strokes in Difference blending mode*

Figure 4.28 *After edge detection and colorizing*

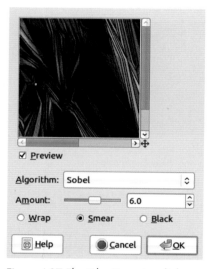

Figure 4.27 *The Edge Detection dialog*

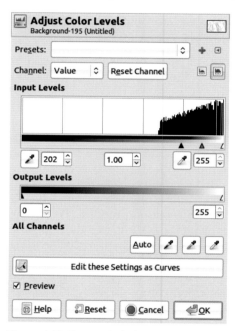

Figure 4.29 *The Levels dialog*

repetition mode. We use this pattern as the basis for the next two textures.

Using Edge Detection

Select **Image: Filters > Edge-Detect > Edge**. In the dialog that appears, select the options and value shown in Figure 4.27. Click OK, and finish the texture by using the **Image: Colors > Color Balance** tool to give it some color (Figure 4.28).

A Piece of Silk

The next texture is more complicated to generate. First, apply a Gaussian blur with a radius of 25 (**Image: Filters > Blur > Gaussian Blur**) to the texture from Figure 4.26. Then use the Edge filter, as in the last example, but with a value of 2.

The result is very dark, so invert it with **Image: Colors > Invert**.

To adjust the texture's contrast, select the **Image: Colors > Levels** tool and adjust the left triangle in the Input Levels area, as shown in Figure 4.29. Our result is shown in Figure 4.30.

We could stop here, but we'd like to make a few more subtle changes before calling this texture complete. Add a new layer in a medium gray, for example, 808080 in hexadecimal. Then select **Image: Filters > Noise > RGB Noise**, uncheck the INDEPENDENT RGB box, and set all three colors to 0.2. Next, apply **Image: Filters >**

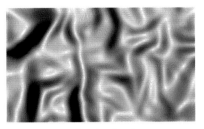

Figure 4.30 *After the first four operations*

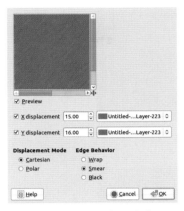

Figure 4.32 *The Displace dialog*

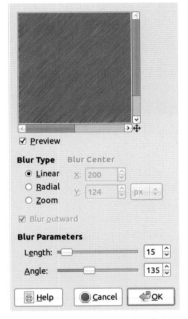

Figure 4.31 *The Motion Blur dialog*

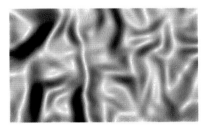

Figure 4.33 *After merging both layers*

Figure 4.34 *A new starting texture*

Blur > Motion Blur along with the parameters shown in Figure 4.31.

Apply **Image: Filters > Map > Displace** with the parameters shown in Figure 4.32 and then change the blending mode to Overlay. After you merge the layer, you get Figure 4.33. You can then colorize the texture by selecting, for example, **Image: Colors > Color Balance**.

Hanging Drapes

Build a new texture using the Blend tool with Difference blending mode and Triangular wave repetition mode (see Figure 4.34). Add a transparent layer, and select **Image: Filters > Render > Clouds > Plasma**. Set the Turbulence to its maximum of 7.0. Blur this layer with a Gaussian blur of radius of 10.0 (Figure 4.35).

Then select **Image: Filters > Distort > IWarp**. With the Deform radius set to 50, add some swirls using the SWIRL CCW and the SWIRL CW deform modes (Figure 4.36).

Now apply **Image: Filters > Artistic > Oilify** with mask size 15, then **Image: Filters > Artistic > Cubism** with tile size 10, and then Oilify

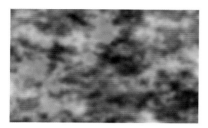

Figure 4.35 *After applying the Plasma and Gaussian Blur filters*

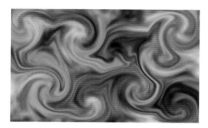

Figure 4.36 *After applying the IWarp filter*

Figure 4.37 *After applying the Oilify, Cubism, and Oilify filters*

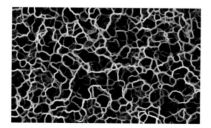

Figure 4.38 *After edge detection*

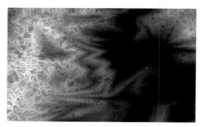

Figure 4.39 *After adjusting the Curves*

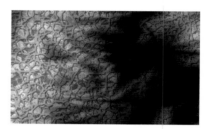

Figure 4.40 *After applying the Bump Map and Colorize filters*

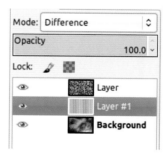

Figure 4.41 *The Layers dialog*

again (Figure 4.37). Applying **Image: Filters > Edge-Detect > Edge** with the amount set to 10 results in Figure 4.38.

Using the Select by Color tool ($\boxed{\text{SHIFT+O}}$), click a black area in the image, cut the selection

($\boxed{\text{CTRL+X}}$), and discard it. Set this layer's mode to Darken only and its opacity to 50%. Using the **Image: Colors > Curves** tool, adjust the value curve until your image resembles Figure 4.39.

Now apply Bump Map on the upper layer, using the layer itself as the map (**Image: Filters > Map > Bump Map**), and colorize it using **Image: Colors > Colorize**. See the results in Figure 4.40.

Finally, add a new, transparent layer just above the background. Select the Blend tool in normal blending mode with Triangular wave repetition mode. Draw a very short horizontal stroke in the intermediate layer, and place the layer in Difference mode. Figure 4.41 shows

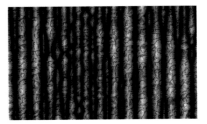

Figure 4.42 *The final texture*

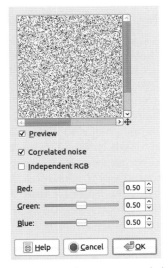

Figure 4.43 *The RGB Noise dialog*

Figure 4.44 *The Motion Blur dialog*

Figure 4.45 *After colorizing the result*

the Layers dialog at this point. The final result appears in Figure 4.42.

Of course, you could create an infinite variety of textures using this process.

Using the Noise Filters

The **Image: Filters > Noise** menu has six entries. Three of them create a more or less random pattern of pixels on the active layer. The other three change the active layer by moving the existing pixels. The general idea is to generate an unpredictable arrangement of pixels. HSV NOISE and RGB NOISE provide some control over the color of the pixels generated.

Let's generate noise and use it as the foundation for some fine-grained textures.

First Method: The Brushed Metal Effect

The simplest method produces a brushed metal effect. Because a metal is usually just one color, generate monochromatic noise. You can do this with the RGB Noise filter. In the dialog shown in Figure 4.43, uncheck the INDEPENDENT RGB box to get gray noise. Check the CORRELATED NOISE box to get stronger noise. Finally, push the three sliders (which are linked) to 0.5 to get a moderately coarse noise.

To turn the noise into brushed metal, select the **Image: Filters > Blur > Motion Blur** filter. In the dialog shown in Figure 4.44, set ANGLE to 0 to get a horizontal effect and set LENGTH to 100.

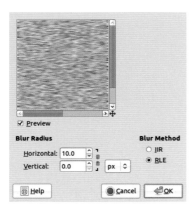

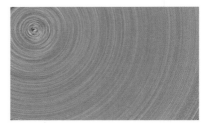

Figure 4.48 *A wood texture*

Figure 4.46 *The Gaussian Blur dialog*

Figure 4.47 *A canvas texture*

If you don't like the metallic look, changing the color is easy with the **Image: Colors > Colorize** tool. As you can see in Figure 4.45, the right side of the texture looks strange. To fix it, remove that edge with the Crop tool (SHIFT+C).

Second Method: A Canvas Texture

Next, we create a simple canvas texture. In a new image, generate some RGB Noise. Its strength determines the result's appearance. Choose 0.7. Duplicate the layer, and apply a Gaussian blur to each layer. Select a layer by clicking it in the Layers dialog. When you apply the blur, break the chain between the horizontal and the vertical radius (see Figure 4.46). For one of the layers, set the horizontal radius to 0 and the vertical radius to 10. For the other layer, reverse this: Set the horizontal radius to 10 and the vertical radius to 0 (as shown in the figure). Set the top layer to Multiply mode, and you get the canvas texture shown in Figure 4.47.

Third Method: A Wood Texture

The last example in this section simulates a piece of wood. As before, begin with a new 400×250 image. Fill the background with a neutral gray, such as 999999. Create an additional layer filled with the medium gray 7F7F7F (127 in the three RGB channels). Select Grain extract as the blending mode. Add some strong RGB Noise (**Image: Filters > Noise > RGB Noise**). Uncheck the INDEPENDENT RGB box, and move the three cursors to 1.00. To get the wood texture, add a motion blur: Apply **Image: Filters > Blur > Motion Blur** with a Radial blur type, an angle of 60, and the blur center set to about 50 for X and Y.

Since wood is rarely this shade of gray, colorize it. To do this, add a third layer, fill it with brown (8c6434 in our case), and set the blending mode to Color blending mode. See the result in Figure 4.48. Note this way of colorizing preserves the original, grayscale texture, unlike the Colorize or Color Balance tools.

Using the Embossing Filters

As stated previously, the embossing, or bumping, filters are scattered across three different filter menus.

First Example: A Realistic Canvas Texture

The simplest of these filters is **Image: Filters > Map > Bump Map**. Let's use this filter to improve the canvas texture from Figure 4.47. First, merge the two layers. Then select the filter.

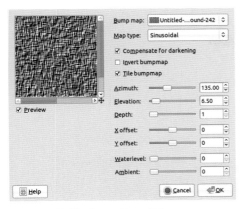

Figure 4.49 *The Bump Map dialog*

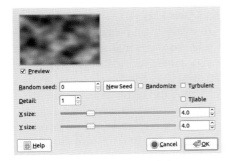

Figure 4.50 *A more realistic canvas texture*

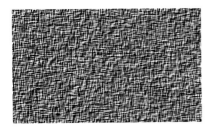

Figure 4.51 *The Solid Noise dialog*

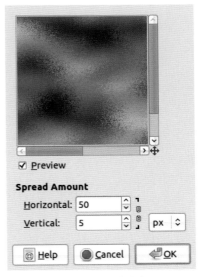

Figure 4.52 *The Spread dialog*

Figure 4.53 *After the first three filter applications*

Choose the parameters shown in Figure 4.49 and click OK. See the result in Figure 4.50.

Second Example: A Water-like Texture

In the next example, we use the same filter to build a water-like texture. Fill a new image with the **Image: Filters > Render > Clouds > Solid Noise** filter, using the parameters shown in Figure 4.51. Then apply the **Image: Filters >**

Noise > Spread filter with the parameters shown in Figure 4.52. Apply a Gaussian blur of 5 in both directions to get Figure 4.53.

Next, select the Bump Map filter, using the image itself as a map, as in the preceding example. To get ripples on the waves, set ELEVATION to 80 and DEPTH to 40. The AZIMUTH is set to 135, but this setting isn't very important. The aquatic appearance is enhanced by using the **Image: Colors > Curves** tool, as shown in Figure 4.54. Now the water, shown in Figure 4.55, just needs some color. We do this with Color Balance, Colorize, Levels, or even Curves, all of which are found in the **Image: Colors** menu. You could also add a new colored layer and set it to Color mode.

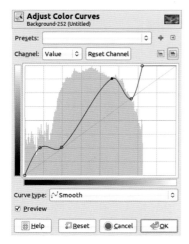

Figure 4.54 *The Curves dialog*

Figure 4.57 *Filling the selection with gray*

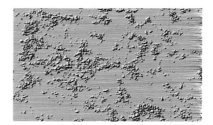

Figure 4.58 *Adding corrosion to the metal layer*

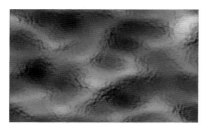

Figure 4.55 *After applying the Bump Map filter and adjusting the Curves*

Figure 4.56 *Making a selection*

Third Example: The Scott Effect

Next we demonstrate the Scott effect, used to create decayed or rusty textures. The idea is simple, but it can be used as the basis for some very nice, natural textures. Here, we give you a foundation to work from. First, create a new image, and fill it with **Image: Filters > Render >**

Clouds > Plasma. Choose a turbulence of 2.0. Select at random with the Select by Color tool (SHIFT+O). To build a larger selection, press the SHIFT key and continue to click randomly within the image. Build a selection similar to the one shown in Figure 4.56.

The purpose of the plasma layer is simply to generate the selection. Hide it and add a white layer and then a transparent layer. With the transparent layer active, fill the selection with a shade of gray. The result appears in Figure 4.57.

Hide the top layer, and discard the selection. Activate the middle layer, and build a brushed metal texture, using the RGB Noise filter and then Motion Blur, as we did in "First Method: The Brushed Metal Effect" on page 101. To complete the effect, select the Bump Map filter and use it to bump the metal layer, utilizing the top layer as a map. Play around with the parameters, especially Elevation and Depth. See one possible result in Figure 4.58.

The result can be bumped on another form or colorized in various ways. Retrieve the Select by Color tool selection by converting Alpha to Selection in the top layer and then cut it out or colorize it. Of course, these are just a few

Figure 4.59 *The Lighting Effects dialog*

Figure 4.60 *The final stone texture*

suggestions. You can continue to edit this texture using any of the effects available in GIMP.

Fourth Example: A Stone Texture

In our final example in this section, we use the **Image: Filters > Light and Shadow > Lighting Effect** filter to build a stone texture. First, create a new image, and fill the background layer using **Image: Filters > Render > Clouds > Solid Noise**. Add some RGB Noise with the three channels set to a low value.

Add a new layer and fill it with a moderately turbulent Plasma. This layer will be used as a bump map, so make it invisible and select the background. Select the Lighting Effects filter, and in the Lighting Effects filter dialog, shown in Figure 4.59, select the BUMP MAP tab and ENABLE BUMP MAPPING with the Plasma layer serving as a map. You can also change the light source, the light color, and a few other options. The final result, which appears in Figure 4.60, can be colorized using any of the methods we've demonstrated.

Figure 4.61 *A tilable texture built with a gradient brush*

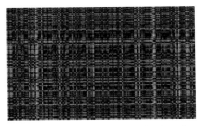

Figure 4.62 *A tilable texture built with a 1-pixel-wide layer*

More Ways to Create Textures

You can use and combine many other techniques to generate new textures.

Using a Gradient Brush

You can create the tilable texture in Figure 4.61 by doing the following:

1. Create a new white image.

2. Select the Paintbrush tool (P). Select the Random Color paint dynamics, the Caribbean Blues gradient, and the Animated Confetti brush, set to a size of 60.

3. Cover the background by painting on it with the brush.

4. Apply **Image: Filters > Map > Make Seamless**.

Using a 1-Pixel-Wide Layer

Another, somewhat surprising technique produces the interesting result shown in Figure 4.62. Try the following:

1. Create a new white 400 × 250 image.

2. Add a new 1 × 250 layer. Apply the Plasma filter. Using **Image: Layer > Scale Layer**, scale

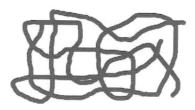

Figure 4.63 *The first strokes*

Figure 4.64 *The Offset Layer dialog*

Figure 4.65 *After all the strokes*

this layer to 400×250. Take care to break the chain between WIDTH and HEIGHT. With the Move tool ($\boxed{\text{M}}$), move this layer to occupy the whole image.

3. Repeat step 2 for a third layer, this time starting with a size of 400×1.

4. Put the top layer in Difference mode, and merge it down.

Note that this plaid texture is already tilable, without requiring any further action. Go ahead— try it out!

Constructing by Hand

Our last texture is built almost entirely by hand without using powerful tools. We build it step-by-step and provide some key illustrations to guide you.

Begin with your customary white 400×250 image. Draw a tilable texture, using only the Paintbrush tool ($\boxed{\text{P}}$). Select the Hardness 100 brush, and set it to size 10 using the Size option. Choose a bright color—red, for example—and draw some random curves, scattered across the image but not touching the edges, as shown in Figure 4.63.

Now select the **Image: Layer > Transform > Offset** tool (or $\boxed{\text{SHIFT+CTRL+O}}$). In the dialog shown in Figure 4.64, check WRAP AROUND and click OFFSET BY X/2, Y/2 and then OFFSET. Change the color of the Paintbrush tool, and draw more curves, especially over white space. Repeat this process twice more, changing color each time and also alternating between an offset of $[x/2, 0]$ and $[0, y/2]$. The result appears in

Figure 4.65. You can check that it's tilable if you wish.

Deform this image with **Image: Filters > Distorts > Whirl and Pinch**. Choose an angle of approximately 120 degrees. Next, apply the **Image: Filters > Map > Small Tiles** filter using the default parameters. Add a Gaussian blur with a radius of 20. Select **Image: Colors > Levels**, and adjust the input levels by moving the black triangle to the right and the white triangle to the left so the three triangles are close together. The result is shown in Figure 4.66.

Select **Image: Colors > Curves**, and change the shape of the curve so it resembles the letter M, with the high points near 64 and 192 and the low points at the origin, 128, and 256, respectively. The result appears in Figure 4.67. This texture is already interesting and tilable, and you might want to save a copy before you go on.

Next remove the color using **Image: Colors > Desaturate**, followed by **Image: Colors > Auto >**

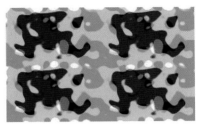

Figure 4.66 *After applying the Whirl and Pinch and Small Tiles filters and then adjusting the Levels*

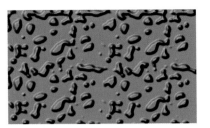

Figure 4.68 *After building the pattern and applying the Bump Map filter*

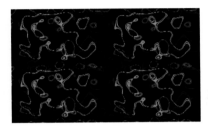

Figure 4.67 *After adjusting the Curves*

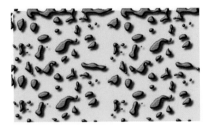

Figure 4.69 *The final texture, almost ready to tile*

Stretch Contrast. To add relief, first create a Gaussian blur with a radius of 10 and then duplicate the layer. Place the top layer in Subtract mode. The result is completely black, since you subtract each pixel from itself. Use the Move tool ([M]) to move the top layer a few pixels down and to the right. We recommend using the arrow keys for this minute adjustment. The result is a dark image with subtle swirls of light.

Merge the two layers, and adjust the levels again so the triangles are close together under the black area on the far left of the histogram. Add a Gaussian blur with a radius of 5. Create a new layer, and fill it with light gray. Bump map this layer, using the background as a map, and adjust the parameters until it resembles Figure 4.68. Note that, because you moved the top layer slightly, the image is no longer tilable. We'll fix that later.

To make this texture more interesting, do the following:

1. Select the bottom layer ([CTRL+A]), and copy it ([CTRL+C]).

2. Add a layer mask to the top layer.

3. Paste the copied layer into the top layer ([CTRL+V]), and anchor it to the layer mask ([CTRL+H]).

4. Use the Levels tool to make this mask sharper.

5. Hide the bottom layer, and add a layer above it filled with some light color.

6. Apply the mask to the top layer, and transform its Alpha channel to a selection.

7. With the middle layer active, fill this selection with some dark color. Remove the selection.

8. Apply a Gaussian blur to the middle layer, with a radius of 5, and move it a few pixels down and to the right. This creates the shadow cast by the texture in the top layer.

9. Colorize the top layer.

The result appears in Figure 4.69. To make it tilable, select a 200×125 rectangle from somewhere in the center of the image. Be sure to avoid the edges. Copy the selection, and create a new image with the copy ([SHIFT+CTRL+V]).

This new image is tilable. You could use the same process to make the texture from Figure 4.67 tilable.

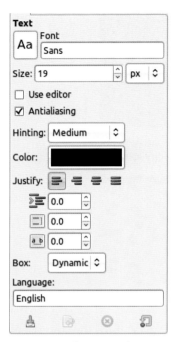

Figure 4.70 *The Text tool options*

4.3 Logos

In this last section of the chapter, we build a few logos using some of the techniques described for textures. Note, however, that the **File: Create > Logos** menu provides a lot of predefined logos.

The Text Tool

To build a logo, you need a way to add text to an image. Do this with the Text tool, which is accessible from the Toolbox or with T. Its options dialog appears in Figure 4.70.

The three most important parameters are the FONT, SIZE, and COLOR of the text. You can change the font by clicking the button that displays the letters "A" and "a" in the current font. You can also use the Fonts dialog, a dockable dialog generally found in the multi-dialog window.

GIMP doesn't ship with any fonts. It accesses the fonts that are available on your system. If you wish to add additional fonts, many are available for free online, but keep in mind that intricate fonts can decrease readability. Moreover, when transforming a logo to add relief, a bold or even ultra-bold font works best.

The default size of the Text tool is 18 pixels, which is much too small for a logo. Generally, logo text should range from 50 to 200 (or more) pixels. You can change the text size, as well as the other parameters, as you work and so can use some trial and error to home in on the perfect settings for your logo.

The Color button brings up the standard Color chooser. Once you've built the text, you can also drag a color from the Toolbox to the image.

When text is added to an image, it becomes a text layer. As long as it keeps this property, you can change the parameters or even the text itself. This new layer is the size of the text plus a small border, so it's generally smaller than the canvas. While the text layer property is active, you can change the dimensions of the layer using the corner handles customary for selections. The layer itself is transparent, and the text is printed on this transparency.

To add text to an image, click in the image wherever you want the upper-left corner of the text to appear. If you want to move the text, change to the Move tool, but you can still go back to the Text tool and edit the text itself.

Adding Relief

One of the simplest ways to make the text in a logo more prominent is to add relief. The best tool for this is the Blend tool, using any one of the three Shapes: angular, spherical, or dimpled. The effect of these shapes depends on the font used, so experiment and find the one you like.

To create the relief, first check the LOCK AL-PHA CHANNEL box in the Layers dialog (found just under the OPACITY slider). Now the Gradient tool will affect only the text, not the transparency behind it.

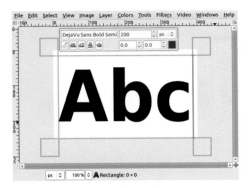

Figure 4.71 *Creating the text layer*

Figure 4.72 *After adding relief*

Next, choose the gradient. A simple gradient from the foreground color to the background color using RGB progression is generally the best choice. The gradient should progress from a light color to a dark one because the middle of the characters will be colored with the first color and the edges with the second one. If the foreground color is darker than the background color, which is usually the case, simply check the REVERSE box or the double arrow just to the right of the GRADIENT button.

To apply the gradient, just make a stroke in the image. The direction and length of the stroke don't matter when using a shaped gradient shape.

Figure 4.71 shows some meaningless text written using the Monospace Bold font at 200 pixels. Figure 4.72 shows the result after adding a shaped (spherical) gradient to this text. After the gradient is applied, the text layer no longer has the text property.

Figure 4.73 *Using the Emboss filter*

You can add relief to a logo using other methods. Here's one:

1. Begin with some simple text, as shown in Figure 4.71. Merge the text layer with the background.

2. Apply a Gaussian blur. The blur radius will determine the amount of relief: 8.0 in our case.

3. Apply the **Image: Filters > Distort > Emboss** filter. Check the EMBOSS button, leaving the three parameters in place.

The result appears in Figure 4.73. Our image is now grayscale, but you could colorize it after embossing. Or if you made a copy of the initial text layer, you could transform it to a selection and use it to colorize the background and the text in different colors.

Proper Shade vs. Cast Shadow

The terms *shade* and *shadow* can have similar meanings, but here we use them to refer to discrete effects, so we add some modifiers to further differentiate the terms. The *proper shade* is the shading on an object that's caused by the object itself; the *cast shadow* (also called the *drop shadow*) is the shadow cast by the object onto the object's environment. For example, in Figure 4.73, the object is supposed to be lit from the lower left, so the upper-right sides of the text are in proper shade. But the object is not high enough above the background to cast a shadow.

Figure 4.74 *Casting some shadow*

Figure 4.76 *Giving the text itself some relief*

Figure 4.75 *Tilting the shadow*

Figure 4.77 *Adding a reflection in front*

Generating a Cast Shadow

Generating a cast shadow is simple. Start with the text from Figure 4.71. Duplicate the text layer. The middle layer will be used for the cast shadow. Because the shadow shouldn't be completely black, change the color of the middle layer to a dark gray. With the Lock Alpha channel box unchecked, apply a Gaussian blur with a radius of 10 to the dark gray text. This blur gives the cast shadow a soft, natural look. Move this layer away from the intended light source. The more you move this layer, the higher above the background the text will appear to be. See the result in Figure 4.74.

In this example, the cast shadow is the same size and same orientation as the text, both of which give the illusion of a background parallel to the text. Use the Perspective tool (SHIFT+P) to change the perspective of the cast shadow, as shown in Figure 4.75. Now the background no longer appears to be parallel to the text.

If you add a gradient, as you did to create Figure 4.72, you get the image shown in Figure 4.76.

You can also add a reflection of the text. This is similar to a cast shadow, although it's usually lighter, more tilted, placed in front of the text, and flipped vertically. To add a reflection, follow these steps:

1. Enlarge the canvas to 400×280 pixels (**Image: Image > Canvas Size**). Enlarge the background layer to the same size (**Image: Layer > Layer to Image Size**).

2. Duplicate the top layer, which will eventually become the reflected text, and apply the **Image: Layer > Transform > Flip Vertically** tool.

3. Change its color to a light gray, and apply a Gaussian blur (with the Lock Alpha channel box unchecked).

4. Deform it with the Perspective tool and, again with the Lock Alpha channel box unchecked, move the reflection until you're satisfied with the result.

Our shadowed and reflected text appears in Figure 4.77.

Figure 4.78 *Generating relief and proper shade*

Figure 4.79 *After spreading and shifting*

Figure 4.80 *Using a gradient on a layer mask*

Adding Relief and Proper Shade

Now we demonstrate a way to add relief and proper shade simultaneously. Create a new image and add some text using the same parameters as before. But this time the text should be blue because what you are about to do will not work if the text is black.

Duplicate the text layer twice, and then do the following:

1. Apply a Gaussian blur with a radius of 8 to the bottom layer of text. Offset it (SHIFT+CTRL+O) by 3 in both X and Y.

2. Apply a Gaussian blur with a radius of 5 to the top layer of text. Offset it by −2 in both X and Y.

3. Deform the Value curve of the top layer (**Image: Colors > Curves**) to add relief. Depending on the curve's final form, several different effects are possible. We simply picked up the middle of the curve and dragged it toward the top-left corner.

4. Change the blending mode of the top layer. You might try Screen, Overlay, Lighten Only, or Addition. We used Difference mode to create Figure 4.78.

Applying a Texture

In this section, we show you how to change the material that the logo is made of. This is generally equivalent to changing its texture.

A Burning Logo

Begin by typing some text in white on a black background, and then merge the text layer with the background. Duplicate the layer, and apply the following effects to the new top layer:

1. **Image: Filters > Noise > Spread**: Break the chain, and set the horizontal parameter to 0 and the vertical parameter to 100.

2. **Image: Filters > Distorts > Shift**: Shift vertically by 25.

   The result appears in Figure 4.79.

   Then add a white layer mask (**Layers: right-click > Add Layer Mask**) to the top layer, and use the Blend tool (**L**) to apply the following gradient to this mask: black to white, linear, without repetition, using a vertical stroke spanning from the middle of the image toward, but not up to, the top border. Press the CTRL key to get a perfectly vertical stroke. The result is shown in Figure 4.80.

   Merge the layers, and apply the following effects:

1. **Image: Filters > Distorts > Ripple**: Set orientation horizontal, amplitude 1, period 20.

2. **Image: Filters > Distorts > Shift**: Shift horizontally by 5.

Figure 4.81 *The final logo*

Figure 4.82 *A radioactive logo*

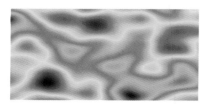

Figure 4.83 *The golden background*

3. **Image: Filters > Noise > Spread**: Amount equals 5 in both directions.

4. **Image: Filters > Blur > Gaussian Blur**: Use a radius of 5 in both directions.

Add some color to this image with the **Image: Colors > Curves** tool. In the Red channel, drag the middle point of the curve toward the top-left corner. In the Blue channel, drag the middle point toward the bottom-right corner. The result appears in Figure 4.81. Of course, you can (and should) experiment with different values for all the filter parameters to gain a better sense of what the filters can do.

A Radioactive Logo

In this example, the initial logo is written in black on a white background. Duplicate the text layer, and merge the middle layer with the background. Activate the bottom layer and apply the following effects:

1. Apply **Image: Colors > Invert**.

2. Apply a Gaussian blur of 5.

3. Apply **Image: Colors > Auto > Stretch Contrast**.

4. Open the **Image: Colors > Levels** tool and choose the Green channel. Push the gray triangle under INPUT LEVELS to the left until you're satisfied with the effect.

The result appears in Figure 4.82. By using a different channel, or even several channels at the same time, you can change the color of the glow. You could also colorize the top layer.

A Golden Logo

The next technique utilizes several powerful filters that we've used previously. The result will be interesting, but the process is rather complicated.

Begin with a new white 400×200 image. Apply the **Image: Filters > Render > Clouds > Solid Noise** filter with x and y sizes set to 2.8 and the other parameters set to the default values. Stretch the contrast (**Image: Colors > Auto > Stretch Contrast**) and apply a Gaussian blur of 5.

In the Blend tool options, choose the Golden gradient. Check that the shape is set to Linear and that there is no repetition set. Apply the **Image: Colors > Map > Gradient Map** tool, which bumps the gradient using the background as a map. The resulting texture is shown in Figure 4.83. If you had checked the TILABLE box in the Solid Noise filter dialog, this texture would be tilable.

Create a new image ($\boxed{\text{CTRL+N}}$) of the same size, and using the ADVANCED OPTIONS, choose GRAYSCALE color space and fill it with black. Add some white text in a large bold font. Merge the two layers and apply a Gaussian blur of 5.

Create a third image of the same size in the RGB color space and fill it with black. In this Im-

Figure 4.84 *The golden logo*

Figure 4.85 *Using the Bump Map filter to texturize the logo*

age window, select the **Image: Filters > Light and Shadow > Lighting Effects** filter. You already saw its dialog in Figure 4.59 on page 105.

On the OPTIONS tab, check CREATE NEW IMAGE and HIGH QUALITY PREVIEW.

On the BUMP MAP tab, check ENABLE BUMP MAPPING, choose the grayscale text image as the BUMPMAP IMAGE, set CURVE to LINEAR or SINUSOIDAL, and set MAXIMUM HEIGHT to 0.02.

On the ENVIRONMENT MAP tab, check ENABLE ENVIRONMENT MAPPING and choose the golden texture as the ENVIRONMENT IMAGE.

You can adjust the settings on the two remaining tabs or simply click OK. The result appears in Figure 4.84. You can personalize this logo in many ways, for example, by adjusting the remaining options in the Lighting Effects filter or by using the Curves or Levels tool to change the color.

A Textured Logo

Despite the title of this section, we haven't yet built a truly textured logo. It's time to correct that omission. First, create a new white 400×200 image and type our logo text in black. Duplicate the text layer, add a white layer under it, and merge the top layer with the white one. Finally, apply a Gaussian blur of 10 to this layer, which will be used as a bump map.

Now select a texture that you've made, for example, the one shown in Figure 4.50 on page 103, and open it as a new layer in your image (CTRL+ALT+O). Alternatively, you may open it in a new image and then drag its thumbnail from the Layers dialog to the text image. If the new layer is too large, use **Image: Layer > Layer to Image Size**.

Figure 4.86 *Cleaning up*

With the new layer active, select **Image: Filters > Map > Bump Map**. Choose the top text layer as a bump map, and modify the other parameters to get the effect you want. A low ELEVATION or a high DEPTH will add a cast shadow in addition to the proper shade.

Click OK and see that the texture occupies the whole layer (Figure 4.85). You want the textured text on a white background, which you can do fairly easily since you kept a copy of the initial text layer. In the Layers dialog, convert the Alpha channel of this text layer to a selection. Its outline follows the characters, not their relief, so select **Image: Select > Grow** and enlarge the selection by 5 pixels. Then activate the top layer, invert the selection (CTRL+I), and cut it (CTRL+X). The result appears in Figure 4.86.

4.4 Exercises

Exercise 4.1. One staple of the texture-building tutorials was the Mosaic filter. Look through the **Image: Filters** menu for other filters that you could use to build different textures in a similar way.

Exercise 4.2. Many steps were involved in creating the texture shown in Figure 4.42 on page 101. Try repeating or omitting some of the steps and see how many different results you can achieve.

Exercise 4.3. In the example shown in Figure 4.48 on page 102, we used a Radial blur. Try choosing a Linear blur or a Zoom blur and see how the result changes. Adjust other parameters or other steps of the process to improve the result.

Exercise 4.4. The example of the Scott effect was very simple. Use the basic principle to transform a photograph of a metal object. When you're finished, the object should appear to be rusted in places but still recognizable.

Exercise 4.5. We used the Lighting Effect filter in two different ways (see Figure 4.60 on page 105 and Figure 4.84 on the preceding page). Using what you understand about the function of this filter, try to re-create the texture of raw uncut gold.

Exercise 4.6. As seen in Figure 4.73 on page 109, the Emboss filter produces a grayscale result. Build a similar embossed logo in copper or gold.

Exercise 4.7. Automatically generate a logo using **Image: File > Create > Logos > Cool Metal**. Without looking at the way it's built, try to re-create the elements of the logo: relief letters, a color gradient, cast shadow, reflection. Hint: Try one effect at a time and then combine them.

Exercise 4.8. The textured logo shown in Figure 4.86 is rather minimal for a final product. Use a different texture for the lettering. Then add a textured background on which the logo casts a shadow bumped by the texture's relief.

5 Composite Photography

In Chapter 2, we retouched existing images. In this chapter, we show you how to create unique pictures, using multiple photographs to build composite images.

5.1 Tutorial: Building a Composite Portrait

A *composite portrait* is an image that combines several different portraits to build a new portrait. For example, you could merge several artists' renderings of eyewitness accounts to create the most accurate possible likeness of a dangerous criminal. You could also use these techniques to guess what the child of two people would look like or to invent a strange hybrid animal.

In this example, we create a composite of several young women who kindly agreed to let us use their pictures for this demonstration.

Each portrait was taken in front of the same neutral background, with the same lighting, and with the girls in approximately the same position. But differences in skin hue or in the tilt of their head will create some interesting challenges. Using photographs taken under disparate conditions would be much more difficult, though. Imagine trying to copy a nose lit from the left onto a face lit from the right. Of course, you could flip the first image vertically, but that could lead to undesirable effects elsewhere in the image. Scaling a feature because the source photograph is much larger—or much smaller—than the target one would lead to differences in sharpness. And putting the chin of a middle-age man on the face of a young woman, or vice versa, would, for many reasons, look odd. For this example, we chose conditions that make the project feasible and simple while still being instructive.

Begin with the four 900×1200 portraits shown in Figure 5.1. The four portraits are arranged as layers within a single image. Our composite will have the eyes from portrait 1, the hair from portrait 2, the nose from portrait 3, and the mouth and chin from portrait 4.

The first thing you need to do is correct the lighting so it's the same across all four portraits. Use the **Image: Colors > Levels** tool on each layer separately: Select the layer in the Layers dialog and then the Levels tool, and click AUTO. The result is shown in Figure 5.2. The skin hues still vary widely but less than they did before the adjustment.

Figure 5.1 *The four source portraits*

Figure 5.2 *After lighting correction*

Taking Features from Different Portraits

Of all the features, the girls' hair is the most difficult to copy. No selection tool could capture it precisely, and correcting it with the Quick Mask tool would be tedious—and extremely difficult. The best solution is, therefore, to copy the other features onto the face with the hair you want (for this example, portrait 2). The composite girl will be wearing the black shirt from this portrait, but all of the girls are dressed in black anyway, so the shirt doesn't make much of a difference.

To create the new image that will be the composite portrait, simply click and drag the layer of portrait 2 from the Layers dialog to the Toolbox. Immediately save this image (SHIFT+CTRL+S, and from time to time, save it again (CTRL+S), so you don't risk losing all your work.

Next, copy the features from the other portraits. You can do this in two ways:

- Select the feature in the source image, copy it, paste it into the target image, and create a new layer (SHIFT+CTRL+N) with the resulting floating selection.

- Use the Clone tool to copy from the source image to the target one, preferably into a new transparent layer.

Each technique has advantages and drawbacks, so we show you both techniques and let you decide which one works best for you. Creating a new layer for each new feature is important because it allows you to change one feature without having to rebuild the whole portrait. Containing the features in different layers also lets you make adjustments to the color,

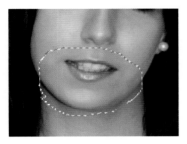

Figure 5.3 *Selecting the mouth and chin*

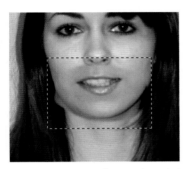

Figure 5.4 *Pasting the mouth and chin*

Figure 5.5 *Selecting the eyes*

Figure 5.6 *After pasting the eyes*

orientation, or size of one feature without changing the rest of the portrait.

Once you're satisfied with the placement, size, and coloration of the copied features, you can flatten the image and then do some minor retouching to better incorporate the new features into the face.

Zoom the initial portraits and your new portrait to the same zoom factor, for example 50%. Make sure portrait 4 is the active layer. Select the Free Select tool ($\boxed{\text{F}}$). Check the FEATHER EDGES box and choose a RADIUS of 10. Build a tight selection around the mouth and chin of portrait 4, as shown in Figure 5.3. If you copy too large an area, you might end up with discrepancies in skin color.

Copy the selection made in portrait 4, and paste it into the composite picture. Press $\boxed{\text{SHIFT+CTRL+N}}$ to create a new layer with the floating selection. The copy appears in the center of the image; move the copy to its proper place with the Move tool. Because the girl in

portrait 4 tilted her head, the new mouth and chin are crooked. To correct this, flip the new layer horizontally with **Image: Layer > Transform > Flip Horizontally** and then rotate it ($\boxed{\text{SHIFT+R}}$) into the proper position. The mouth and chin are now aligned, but the color is uneven, as shown in Figure 5.4. We'll correct this later. Double-click the new layer in the Layers dialog and change the name to mouth.

Make sure portrait 1 is visible and active and then copy the eyes, again using the Free Select tool. To avoid selecting the eyebrows and the bridge of the nose, build the selection in two parts. First, draw a circle around one eye, press and hold the $\boxed{\text{SHIFT}}$ key, and draw a second circle around the other eye. See Figure 5.5. You could also change the MODE in the tool's options, rather than pressing $\boxed{\text{SHIFT}}$.

Again, copy the selection, paste it into the composite picture, and create a new layer from the floating selection. Name this layer eyes. Move the layer into place, and rotate it slightly ($\boxed{\text{SHIFT+R}}$). The result, shown in Figure 5.6, isn't bad, although you could improve the skin color transition.

For the nose, use the Clone tool ($\boxed{\text{C}}$). Create a new transparent layer and call it nose. Select

Figure 5.7 *Copying the nose*

the Clone tool and select the Hardness 075 brush. Set the Clone tool's size option to 20, and select ALIGNED as your ALIGNMENT option. Using a tablet stylus if you have one, or the mouse if you don't, CTRL-click the tip of the nose in portrait 3 and then paint on the composite picture, beginning at the tip of the nose. The resulting image has two main problems: First, the skin color is inconsistent, and second, the tilt of the nose isn't quite right. The nose tilt can be corrected by rotating the new layer slightly. One possible result appears in Figure 5.7.

Smoothing Transitions

Next, smooth the features to create a more coherent composite portrait. Here, we demonstrate a few of the ways you can do this.

For the mouth and chin, use the Levels tool. Select it, and with the mouth layer active, move the right and middle triangles slightly for each of the three color channels. You should get a skin color similar to that of the original portrait. The area under the chin is still much too dark, however. Because the chin is on a separate layer, you can simply erase the part you don't need. Select the Eraser tool (SHIFT+E), and choose the brush and size that you used with the Clone tool. Zoom in to work more precisely, and if you have one, use a tablet pen. You'll still see a hue discrepancy between the chin and the neck, but don't worry about that.

Figure 5.8 *The final composite picture*

The main problem now is the color of the nose. Correct it using the Levels tool. Move the middle triangle in the Value channel liberally toward the left. Try somewhere near 1.8.

Now you've done all you can with a multilayer image. To complete the composite portrait, you need to flatten the image. As a precaution, save the multilayer image and then duplicate it (CTRL+D), and work on the copy. Merge all layers (**Layers: right-click > Flatten Image**), so you can use the Smudge, Dodge/Burn, or Clone tools on the image as a whole.

Several parts of the composite portrait require delicate touch-ups. Use the Smudge tool (S) to smooth the transitions between the various components of the final portrait, especially around the nose and on the upper part of the mouth and chin fragment copied from portrait 4. You can also use the Healing tool (H) to correct slight irregularities on the nose bridge or on the cheekbones.

Finally, select the whole face, but not the hair, and apply a very light Gaussian blur with a radius of 1 or 2 pixels. This makes the face smoother and helps to hide any visible borders that remain between the features and the face. Figure 5.8 shows the final result.

5.2 Selections, Overlaying, and Blending Modes

This chapter focuses on the construction of composite images using elements from several different photographs. The three main tools for this process are selections, overlaying, and blending modes.

Masks and Selections

As the preceding tutorial demonstrates, making selections is one of the most important, and trickiest, tasks involved in photo manipulation. So we'll spend some time clarifying the functionality of the selection tools available in GIMP.

When you build a selection with the Rectangle Select tool, you get an area bounded by a simple geometric form. The simplicity makes it easy to tell whether pixels are within the selection. If you choose to feather the edges of the selection, however, the boundary is less clear: Some pixels are clearly out of the selection and some are deep within it, but what about those pixels on the feathered border?

The situation is even more complicated when you use the Fuzzy Select tool or the Select by Color tool. The selections that these tools build are usually not defined by clear and simple outlines. This shortcoming is obvious when you turn on Quick Mask, which displays the unselected pixels in red (by default). If the selection is feathered, you see that some pixels are completely red (unselected); others aren't red at all (selected); and some pixels are, well, reddish. Figure 5.9 shows a feathered selection made with the Select by Color tool, whereas Figure 5.10 shows the same selection with the Quick Mask tool active. Both images are shown with a zoom factor of 800%.

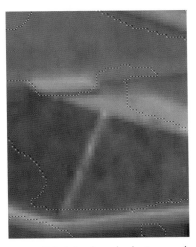

Figure 5.9 *A feathered selection made by the Select by Color tool*

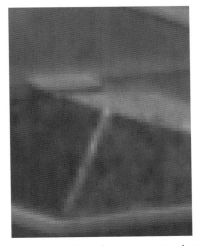

Figure 5.10 *The selection as a Quick Mask*

As you may have guessed, those reddish pixels are partially selected. A selection and a mask are actually the same thing. They are both grayscale images that specify to what degree each pixel is selected. If the pixel value of the mask is 0 (i.e., black), the corresponding pixel in the image is not selected at all. If this value is 255 (i.e., white), the corresponding pixel is fully selected. A partially selected pixel has a value somewhere between 0 and 255.

Figure 5.11 *A selection saved in the Channels dialog*

Figure 5.12 *The Edit Channel Attributes dialog*

Along the feathered edge of a selection, pixels are partially selected. All actions made to the selection affect these partially selected pixels to a lesser degree: Painting is semitransparent; burning is partial; cutting leaves some of the pixels in place; and so on. Partial selections are what make selections so useful in photo manipulation. They allow you to build composite pictures that don't look like clumsy collages.

Because a selection and a mask are the same thing, and a mask is a grayscale image, you can manipulate it with the same tools that you would use on an image. You can paint on it with the painting tools demonstrated in Chapter 3. You can select and edit specific areas. And you can save it and use it later with **Image: Select > Save to Channel**. The mask appears as an additional channel in the Channels dialog, as shown in Figure 5.11. In this figure, the channel is selected (its line is emphasized), so if you paint on the image now, you'll be painting on the mask. To paint on the image itself, switch to the Layers tab, select the layer you want to modify, and begin painting.

You can also use this property to change the mask in the same way we use the Quick Mask tool. To do this, open the Channels dialog and click the box to the left of the mask so the eye is visible. The mask now appears over the image (in gray by default). You can change the mask's display color by selecting **Channels: right-click >**

Edit Channel Attributes to open the dialog shown in Figure 5.12. You can change the channel's name and its opacity, as well as the color of the mask. Click the large button on the right to open the Color chooser, where you can pick any color you want. But keep in mind that using a color that contrasts with the image is generally best.

When a selection (a mask) is saved in a channel, you can use it again later by simply clicking the red square button at the bottom of the Channels dialog. If you hover the pointer over the button, you'll see that the standard key combinations allow you to activate different selection modes. You can save an unlimited number of selections as masks in the Channels dialog.

A mask used to determine the transparency of pixels in a layer is known as a *layer mask*. A layer mask is a part of a specific layer, and its pixels specify the transparency of the corresponding pixels in that layer. If a mask pixel is white, the corresponding layer pixel is opaque and thus visible in the image if not hidden by another pixel located in an upper layer. If a mask pixel is black, the corresponding layer pixel is transparent and thus invisible. Intermediate values for the mask pixels produce intermediate transparency levels for the layer pixels. Note, however, that the layer itself is unchanged.

You can add a layer mask by applying Add Layer Mask from the **Image: Layer > Mask** menu. Once added, you can access its options via the same menu. You can also add or manipulate a layer mask by right-clicking in the Layers dialog. When you add a mask to a layer, you can choose among several options: a completely

Figure 5.13 *The first photograph*

Figure 5.15 *Selecting the sky*

Figure 5.14 *The second photograph*

Figure 5.16 *The final result*

white or completely black mask, the current se-lection, a specified channel, and others. Once you've built the mask, you can change it by paint-ing on it, for example, with Quick Mask. You can change some of its properties, such as how it displays on the image. Finally, you can apply it to the layer, making its effect final.

We already demonstrated some of these op-tions in previous chapters, and we come back to them later in this chapter.

Overlaying Images

Simply overlaying opaque images isn't very inter-esting. Modifying the opacity of the top layer sometimes yields a satisfying result, but doing so doesn't give us much control over it. Once you build a selection, however, you can create your own unique and imaginative images.

For example, take the photographs shown in Figures 5.13 and 5.14. Open the first one, and add the second one as a layer ($\boxed{\text{CTRL+ALT+O}}$). Then, with the Fuzzy Select and Select by Color

tools, select the sky in the top layer, which re-quires about a dozen clicks in several areas of the sky. Recall that pressing $\boxed{\text{SHIFT}}$ allows you to add to the selection, whereas pressing $\boxed{\text{CTRL}}$ allows you to subtract from the selection. The completed selection is shown as a Quick Mask in Figure 5.15.

Our goal is to make the sky transparent so the building from the other photograph is visi-ble behind the tropical vegetation. If we simply cut the selection, however, the sky is replaced by opaque white because the layer doesn't con-tain any transparency (indicated by the boldface layer name) and so any cut pixels are replaced by the background color. To add transparency, add an Alpha channel to the top layer: **Layers: right-click > Add Alpha Channel**. Now if you cut the selection, you get Figure 5.16.

You can also use a selection to copy some-thing from one photograph and paste it into another one. You did this earlier on a smaller scale when you created the composite portrait at the beginning of the chapter. Moving larger

Figure 5.17 *The first photograph*

Figure 5.18 *The second photograph*

Credit: Vincent Lecarme

Figure 5.19 *Pasting the man*

objects from one photograph to another presents its own challenges, as you'll soon see.

As you saw previously, newly pasted objects are added to an image as a *floating selection*. They appear in the Layers dialog (which you should always keep visible in your workspace) and act somewhat like a layer located on the top of the stack. But as long as a floating selection exists, you can't change anything else in the image. The other layers are inactivated, just as the unselected regions of an image are inactive as long as a selection exists.

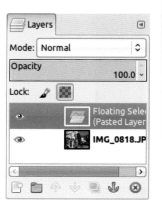

Figure 5.20 *The new layer as a floating selection*

Figure 5.21 *The final result*

With a floating selection, you can do the following:

- Create a new layer to contain the object you've just pasted.
- *Anchor* the pasted content to whatever was active just before you created the floating selection. This layer might be the active layer (highlighted in the Layers dialog) or the active layer mask (see the previous section), but not the active channel.

Let's say you want to combine elements from the photographs shown in Figures 5.17 and 5.18. You've decided to place an overdressed man in front of a sunny villa on the French Riviera. Select the man on the right, as shown in Figure 5.18. Make the selection with the Free Select tool and complete it by painting with Quick Mask. Don't very careful when selecting his legs, however, because they won't be visible.

Figure 5.22 *The upper layer and the lower layer*

Copy the selection from Figure 5.18 and paste it onto the image in Figure 5.17. The man appears in the center of the image, as shown in Figure 5.19, as a floating selection (see Figure 5.20).

Create a new layer for this floating selection and move the man to the bottom-right corner of the sunny scene. He's darker than his surroundings, so select the Levels tool and add some light and contrast. Also apply **Image: Layer > Transform > Flip Horizontally** to flip him around. You can see the result in Figure 5.21.

Using Blending Modes

GIMP has 21 blending modes, which you can select from the Layers dialog. The MODE option contains a drop-down menu with a list of blending modes that will act on the active layer. Each blending mode uses a different mathematical model to compute a new pixel value from the active layer and the layer below. Although we won't go into any detail regarding the mathematics of blending modes, we will introduce some of the modes most useful for overlaying images.

Begin with the photographs from Figure 5.22. Put them into the same image with the first one as the upper layer. The blending modes are arranged in a logical order, as explained in Chapter 12. In the following list, we briefly introduce

these modes, in a different order, so we can run through them more quickly.

- If the mode is set to Normal, the upper layer completely hides the lower one, except if its opacity is less than 100%. Figure 5.23 (left) shows an image with a top layer opacity of 50%. Each new pixel contains half of the upper pixel and half of the lower one.

- Dissolve mode looks the same as Normal mode until you reduce the opacity of the top layer. As you decrease the opacity of the top layer, the layers are blended using *dithering*, and the resulting pixels are a random mixture of the upper and lower pixels. Opacity corresponds to the likelihood that the new pixel value will be taken from the upper layer. Figure 5.23 (middle) shows the effect of Dissolve mode with the top layer at 50% opacity.

- In Multiply mode, the pixels' values are multiplied and then *normalized*. The resulting pixels are darker than those of the initial layers. Figure 5.23 (right) shows the result of Multiply mode: black pixels whenever one of the pixels is black and light pixels only when both pixels are light.

- Divide mode divides and normalizes the pixel values. The result depends largely on the upper pixel. If the upper pixel is black, the

Figure 5.23 *Normal mode and Dissolve mode, 50% opacity; Multiply mode*

Figure 5.24 *Divide mode, Screen mode, and Overlay mode*

result is almost white, as shown in Figure 5.24 (left).

- The mathematics of Screen mode are more complicated. As Figure 5.24 (middle) shows, the dark areas in the top layer are more transparent than the light ones. If you want to learn more about Screen mode, flip ahead to Chapter 12.

- Overlay mode combines Multiply and Screen modes and results in a washed-out upper layer. As Figure 5.24 (right) shows, the upper layer is no more than a ghost in the picture.

- Dodge and Burn are the traditional techniques used in analog photo development to make areas in a picture lighter or darker. As you can see in Figure 5.25 (left and middle), these modes operate according to the same principles: The upper layer is used to dodge or burn the lower one, and the intensity of the action corresponds to the value of the upper layer.

- Hard light and Soft light are similar combinations of Multiply and Screen. As shown in Figure 5.25 (right), Hard light mode isn't very

Figure 5.25 *Dodge mode, Burn mode, and Hard light mode*

Figure 5.26 *Soft light mode, Grain extract mode, and Grain merge mode*

useful in this example because the upper layer almost completely hides the lower one. As Figure 5.26 (left) shows, Soft light mode produces a more interesting result, although in this example, the result is very similar to Overlay mode (see Figure 5.24, right).

- Grain extract and Grain merge are another pair of sibling modes. Grain extract is similar to Difference mode, whereas Grain merge is similar to Addition mode (which we explain next). These modes are suppose to mimic film grain, but sometimes the similarity isn't

apparent. Figure 5.26 (middle) illustrates how Grain extract uses the light areas from the upper layer to exaggerate the light areas in the lower one. Figure 5.26 (right) shows the more subtle effects of Grain merge, which uses the texture of the upper layer to change the lower layer.

- Difference, Addition, and Subtract are also sibling modes. Difference mode, shown in Figure 5.27 (left), subtracts the lower pixel from the upper one and uses the absolute value of the result. The resulting image is

Figure 5.27 *Difference mode, Addition mode, and Subtract mode*

Figure 5.28 *Darken only mode, Lighten only mode, and Hue mode*

difficult to predict. Addition mode , shown in Figure 5.27 (middle), adds pixel values, and values greater than 255 appear white. The resulting image is much lighter. Subtract mode, shown in Figure 5.27 (right), subtracts the pixel values, and values that would be negative appear black.

- Darken only and Lighten only, shown in Figure 5.28 (left and middle), do what their names imply: The darkest or the lightest pixel is selected from the two layers.

- The last four modes are related: The new pixel gets some combination of HSV components from the initial layers. In Hue mode (Figure 5.28, right), the upper layer colorizes the lower one. Saturation mode (Figure 5.29, left) takes the hue and value components from the lower layer. Color mode (Figure 5.29, middle) takes only the value from the lower layer. Value mode (Figure 5.29, right) is the exact opposite: It takes only the value from the upper layer.

Figure 5.29 *Saturation mode, Color mode, and Value mode*

5.3 Building a Panorama

With a digital camera, you can easily take several pictures of the same subject and capture a view from multiple vantage points. You can also build *panoramic images* (i.e., wide pictures that cover a larger area than you can see at any one time).

Software tools that specialize in building panoramas are available. One of them is Hugin (see *http://hugin.sourceforge.net/*), which is free and works on GNU/Linux, Mac OS X, and Windows. It uses a powerful algorithm called *SIFT*, which was developed at the University of British Columbia. It builds the panorama in a completely automated way. The algorithm finds a collection of *control points* in the different photographs. The result is spectacular, but the algorithm is processor intensive, especially if the panorama is being built from a lot of large photographs.

We also use Pandora, a GIMP plug-in developed by Akkana Peck, at the end of this section. After you install it, Pandora is accessible in **Image: Filters > Combine**.

Taking the Pictures

Some digital cameras offer a panorama mode designed to ensure the images overlap sufficiently. Don't worry if your camera lacks that feature; taking the pictures you need for your panorama, using normal settings, is easy. Just follow this advice:

- Keep your feet firmly planted as you shoot. Rotate the top of your body to capture each successive shot, but try to keep the camera at the same height as you move across the landscape so each shot has the same amount of sky visible. Too much vertical motion can reduce your final panorama to a very narrow strip. If feasible, use a tripod for greater stability.

- Do not change the exposure as you move: The settings must be the same for all pictures, even if the lighting conditions are not the same. Choose the optimal settings for some part of the intended panorama (the center, for example), fix them, and then take all the pictures. If you're not sure how to do this, refer to your camera's manual.

- Take more pictures than necessary. To build a panorama, you need a lot of overlap. A camera's optical system generally distorts the corners, and sometimes the sides, of every image. Only the center of an image isn't distorted in any perceptible way. This is why you build your panorama using mainly the center of each picture.

Figure 5.30 *Adding the first photograph*

Perhaps your camera can take photos with a really high pixel count. For example, Olivier's camera has a maximum image size of 3888 × 2592. When loaded in GIMP, an image of that size occupies 90.9MB. If you load six of them, probably the minimum number for a panorama, they occupy 545.4MB, which is too much for most computers to handle. And as soon as you begin working on an image, its size increases because of the stored information that allows you to undo. Basically, unless your computer is an extraordinary beast with a huge amount of memory, building an enormous panorama causes it to crash.

Generally, really large panoramas are impractical anyway. A panorama intended for a web page shouldn't be much wider than 1000 pixels. If you want to print the image, a width of 4000 pixels results in a print size of 13.3 inches or 33.9 cm when printed at 300 ppi.

You can take the pictures for your panorama using the highest setting available on your camera and then scale them down to a usable size. Be careful not to scale down too much, however, or you'll lose precision and sharpness.

Superimposing the Pictures

Olivier took eight photographs of the view from his balcony, following the advice in the previous section. The images are 3888 × 2592, but we scaled them down to 1200 × 800. When scaling an image, choose the Sinc (Lanczos) algorithm, which, although somewhat processor intensive, does the best job. After scaling down, we applied the **Image: Filters > Enhance > Unsharp Mask** filter with its default parameters to compensate for the loss of sharpness caused by scaling.

Because these photographs overlapped a lot, as they should, the complete panorama will not be more than 2800 pixels wide. As keeping the camera at exactly the same height for all shots was difficult, we created a new image that was 2800 × 1000, which happened to give us some wiggle room. This image isn't extremely large, but it will have to be scaled down for a web page. On the other hand, this image is rather small

Figure 5.31 *Loading the second photograph*

for printing. Here's how we would build the panorama.

1. Load the first photograph into this new image with CTRL+ALT+O. The new layer appears in the center of the image; move it completely to the left, as shown in Figure 5.30.

2. Load the second photograph as a new layer and change its opacity to 50% so you can see whether it's positioned correctly. Move it so the overlapping areas of the two photographs align. Focus on superimposing the house in the middle so it's as sharp as possible. Use the arrow keys to tap it into place. As Figure 5.31 shows, a perfect superimposition is impossible because of the lens distortion. Here, we are able to get the house in sharp focus, but the surrounding hills are blurry and the electric pole on the left is doubled. We can tell from the horizon that the camera was slightly tilted when the second picture was taken.

3. To improve the transition from one photo to the other, add a white layer mask to the top layer. Select the Blend tool and choose a linear gradient from black to white without repetition. You want the top layer to transition from transparent on the left to opaque on the right. To create a perfectly horizontal gradient, press CTRL while dragging from left to right, beginning somewhat to the right of the left edge and ending at the house.

4. Once the gradient is built, click the layer thumbnail to select the layer itself. Set the opacity of this layer back to 100% and move it very slightly (with the arrow keys) so the house is as sharp as possible. You also need to rotate the top layer a tiny bit to compensate for the camera's tilt. This is tricky because partial transparency disappears while you are using the rotation tool. Figure 5.32 shows the result so far as well as the Layers dialog.

Touching Up the Panorama

Repeat this process for the remaining photographs: Load the photograph, set transparency to 50%, position it, remove the

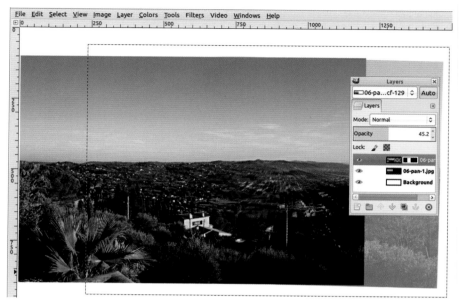

Figure 5.32 *Positioning the second photograph*

Figure 5.33 *All the photographs are positioned.*

transparency, add a layer mask, draw a gradient on this mask, and finish positioning the photograph. To avoid creating weird artifacts in the scenery, be careful not to make the gradient too wide and avoid placing it in an area with a lot of fine detail. As you add layers, the size of the image increases and, in this case, is 123.4MB after we've added all eight photographs.

Sometimes, if a detail from the lower layer appears out of place, changing the gradient is helpful. You can adjust the gradient by painting on the layer mask, or you can add another gradient over the problem area—above the existing gradient. Set the second gradient to Multiply mode (from the MODE menu in the tool options dialog). To see the layer mask itself, ALT-click its thumbnail or right-click in the Layers dialog.

The current result appears in Figure 5.33. The color of the sky is uneven at a couple of the junctions between photographs. Because the sky contains clouds and a light haze on the extreme right, replacing it completely with some

Figure 5.34 *The final panorama*

Figure 5.35 *The Pandora filter dialog*

gradient between two different shades of blue would detract from the image. We prefer to leave the panorama as is, although some careful (and tedious) work with the Dodge/Burn tool (in Dodge mode) or the Clone tool could improve the result.

With all the pictures in place, all that's left is to crop and flatten the image. Our final panorama appears in Figure 5.34.

The Pandora Plug-in

The Pandora plug-in, mentioned at the beginning of this section, can also be used to build a panorama. Here's how you use it:

1. Load all the photographs as layers in a new image. Do this quickly using CTRL+ALT+O.

2. Select the **Image: Filters > Combine > Spread out layers** filter. In the dialog that appears (Figure 5.35), select the OVERLAP quantity between images (in this case, 80 is better than 50) and decide whether the top layer is on the

Figure 5.36 *The original image*

left or right. Note that the last image loaded becomes the top layer.

3. The finishing touches are left up to you. Move the layers and fine-tune the layer masks to get a smooth panorama.

5.4 Image Overlaying

In the previous section, we considered a very specific application of image overlaying. Now, we show you techniques for more general use.

Digital Collage

Begin with the photograph shown in Figure 5.36. We want to replace the seascape, seen through the window, with Figure 5.37. To do this, you need to make the seascape transparent. You could try selecting it with the Select by Color tool or the Fuzzy Select tool, but this time try a brand new method instead.

Figure 5.37 *A new background*

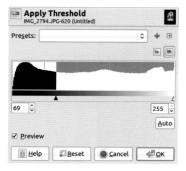

Figure 5.38 *The Apply Threshold dialog*

Duplicate the layer, and choose the **Image: Colors > Threshold** tool, which opens the dialog shown in Figure 5.38. Move the black triangle to the left until you see a silhouette of the window only. Invert it with **Image: Colors > Invert** to get the result in Figure 5.39. Use this as a mask to make the window fully transparent.

Now do the following:

1. Select the top layer and copy it.

2. Open the image shown in Figure 5.37 as a new layer by selecting **Image: File > Open as Layers** or pressing CTRL+ALT+O.

3. Duplicate the bottom layer, and move it to the top of the layer stack.

4. Add to it a layer mask (**Layers: right-click > Add Layer Mask**).

5. Paste the copy made earlier, and anchor it to the layer mask (CTRL+V and CTRL+H).

6. Arrange the layers as shown in Figure 5.40.

Figure 5.39 *Threshold result after inversion*

Figure 5.40 *The Layers dialog for Figure 5.41*

Figure 5.41 *With the new background added*

The resulting image appears in Figure 5.41. You could stop here. But the wall is so dark that its stones are almost invisible. Fortunately you can adjust this without altering the landscape seen through the window: In the Layers dialog, click the thumbnail in the top layer to select the layer and not the layer mask. Use the Levels tool (**Image: Colors > Levels**) to adjust the Gamma triangle until you're satisfied. Only the layer is affected, not the layer mask or the other layers in the stack. If, on the other hand, you want

Figure 5.42 *The final result*

Figure 5.43 *The frame*

Figure 5.44 *The portrait*

to adjust the layer mask, you could select its thumbnail and then use the Brush tool to add to or remove from the mask.

The final image appears in Figure 5.42. Note the initial image is still present and unchanged in the bottom layer.

Next, use the same principles to build an image that's slightly more complicated. The photograph shown in Figure 5.43 will serve as a frame for the portrait shown in Figure 5.44. You want this portrait to appear in the open French windows, larger than life, but with the landscape still visible behind her. You first need to remove the beige background that's currently behind the subject, which is easy enough. Once you've done that, however, you can't simply copy the portrait and paste it in because her shoulders would extend beyond the window frame.

To position the portrait properly in its unconventional frame, follow these steps:

1. Open the image shown in Figure 5.43. Add an Alpha channel (**Image: Layer > Transparency > Add an Alpha Channel** or **Layers: right-click > Add an Alpha Channel**).

2. Using the Free Select tool, make a selection by clicking the four corners of the French windows.

3. When the selection is complete, cut it and then paste it back into the image as a floating selection. Create a new layer from the floating selection (click the leftmost button at the bottom of the Layers dialog or press $\boxed{\text{SHIFT+CTRL+N}}$). Move the new layer to the bottom of the layer stack. The image looks the same, but it's divided into two different layers.

4. Open the photograph shown in Figure 5.44 as a new layer. Add an Alpha channel to this layer. Select the Fuzzy Select tool and select the beige background. Decrease the THRESHOLD in the tool options, and as usual, press

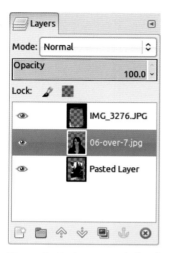

Figure 5.45 *The Layers dialog for Figure 5.46*

Figure 5.46 *The final result*

SHIFT to add to, or CTRL to remove from, the selection as you build. Take care when selecting the area around her hair. When you're finished, cut the selection (CTRL+X) and discard it (SHIFT+CTRL+A).

5. Select the Scale tool (SHIFT+T), choose NUMBER OF LINES in the GUIDES options, and click in the portrait layer. Enlarge the portrait, and move it into the window opening.

Credit: Vincent Lecarme

Figure 5.47 *The initial photograph*

Figure 5.48 *Self-compositing in Hard light mode*

Figure 5.49 *Duplicating the top layer twice more*

6. Finally, arrange the layers so the French window is on top, the portrait layer is in the middle, and the cutout landscape is at the bottom, as shown in Figure 5.45.

The final result should resemble Figure 5.46.

Self-Compositing

Here, begin with a photograph of a winter scene, shown in Figure 5.47, that is almost uniformly gray and flat. To transform this picture into the image shown in Figure 5.48, simply duplicate the

Figure 5.50 *The initial photograph*

Figure 5.52 *Selecting the light areas*

Figure 5.51 *Self-compositing in Screen mode*

Figure 5.53 *Adding a layer mask to shield the lighter parts*

layer and change the mode of the top layer to Hard light. By repeating this process, you can increase the contrast further, but this adds a strong blue cast to the image, as shown in Figure 5.49. Correct this effect using the Levels tool.

The photograph shown in Figure 5.50 (taken from an airplane) is much too dark. To lighten it, begin by duplicating the layer, as you did in the previous example, but this time use Screen mode.

Figure 5.51 shows the result after two duplications. Now the color and detail in the foreground are visible, but some details in the lighter areas of the background have been lost.

To bring back some of that background detail, select the light areas in the image (i.e., the sky and the clouds) with the Fuzzy Select tool, but this time, forget about pressing SHIFT or CTRL. Instead, click somewhere in the sky, and then drag the cursor down or to the right. As you do, the tool threshold increases, which increases the selected area. If you drag the cursor

up or to the left, the selected area decreases. The result appears in Figure 5.52.

Invert the selection (CTRL+I), add a layer mask to the top layer, and in the dialog that appears, choose to create the mask from the current selection. Do this for the top layer only, however, to avoid creating an unnatural effect on the lighter areas of the mountains. Figure 5.53 shows the result. The image could be improved more by adjusting the Gamma pointer in the Levels tool and by removing a few minor, age-related imperfections from the photograph, as you saw in Chapter 2.

Self-compositing photographs can also be used to create some artistic, filter-like effects. Open the photograph shown in Figure 5.54 and duplicate the layer. If you set the top layer's mode to Difference, the resulting image will be completely black because the difference between two equal quantities is always zero. But if you use the Move tool to move the top layer a few pixels up and to the left, you get the

Figure 5.54 *The initial photograph*

Figure 5.55 *Using Difference mode*

Figure 5.56 *Using Grain extract mode*

Figure 5.57 *Using Divide mode*

Figure 5.58 *The initial photograph*

image shown in Figure 5.55, which is a bit more interesting.

Change the top layer's mode to Grain extract to get Figure 5.56. Then change it to Divide mode to get Figure 5.57. You can create variations on these effects by changing the amount and direction of offset or the top layer's opacity or by adding new layers in different modes, and so on.

A Composite Photography Project

The photograph shown in Figure 5.58 was taken early in the morning when clouds partly filled in the valleys in front of Olivier's house. He planned to use that image in a composite photography project, but he snapped the photo in a rush and the image doesn't truly capture what he saw.

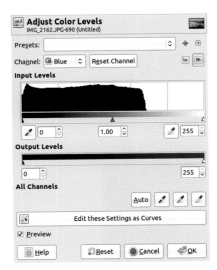

Figure 5.59 *The Blue channel's histogram*

Figure 5.60 *After extending the levels*

If you call the Levels tool and look at the color histograms, you see the Green and Blue channels are truncated on the right. The Blue channel, which appears in Figure 5.59, is the worst. Simply clicking the AUTO button corrects this, and you get the result shown in Figure 5.60. This landscape is now very much as Olivier remembers, so he decided to use it in the following creative project, shown in Figure 5.61.

Here's how to create this image:

1. Add the image shown in Figure 5.36 on page 131 to Olivier's landscape as a new layer.

2. Scale this layer to the same width as the underlying image (**Image: Layer > Scale Layer**).

3. Set the top layer to Darken only mode.

4. Crop the image.

Figure 5.61 *Compositing with another image in Darken only mode*

Figure 5.62 *Another image to be composited*

Figure 5.63 *Compositing with another image in Burn mode*

Similarly, add the photograph shown in Figure 5.62 to the image as another layer, and select Burn mode. You'll get the image shown in Figure 5.63.

In the following examples, we duplicated an image layer and then coupled various blending modes with a Gaussian blur of radius 10 that we applied to the top layer. Figure 5.64 shows the result when the top layer is set to Divide mode.

Figure 5.64 *A blurred layer in Divide mode*

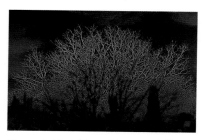

Figure 5.65 *A blurred layer in Difference mode*

Figure 5.66 *The top layer in Burn mode*

To create Figure 5.65, we chose Difference mode, and we also adjusted the Levels by moving the Gamma triangle to the left.

In Figure 5.66, we removed the Gaussian blur and set the layer to Burn mode. Note how this enhances the clouds in the foreground.

You can add depth by moving the top layer 10 pixels up and to the left. The offset images in Figures 5.67 and 5.68 were cropped to illustrate the effect.

Figure 5.67 *An offset layer in Divide mode*

Figure 5.68 *An offset layer in Difference mode*

5.5 Exercises

Exercise 5.1. Finding a single set of images that can be used to accurately demonstrate all blending modes is a difficult task. The choice made in "Using Blending Modes" on page 123 is not ideal. Find a better set of images for this demonstration.

Exercise 5.2. Creating a uniform sky is often the most difficult part of panorama construction. Explore solutions to the problems seen in Figure 5.34 on page 131. Adjust the layer mask before merging the layers or touch up the final result using the Smudge tool, for example.

Exercise 5.3. The photograph shown in Figure 5.43 on page 133 contains two potted plants with large leaves, which might look nice in front of the subject instead of behind her. Devise a method to do this.

Exercise 5.4. Using the concepts demonstrated in "Self-Compositing" on page 134, create a unique work of art with your own digital photos.

6 Animation

Although GIMP wasn't designed to build animations, it does have some video-editing capabilities that you can use to animate a logo, for instance, or decorate a web page. In this chapter, we first introduce some simple animations, and then, in subsequent sections of this chapter as well as in Chapter 18, we demonstrate more complex animations and show how to manipulate existing video sequences in GIMP.

6.1 Tutorial: Animated Text

Suppose, for the purposes of this tutorial, that your first name is Carol, a respectable, non-gender-specific name. Suppose you, Carol, want to decorate an online photo album with an animated logo of your first name. The letters of your name will appear progressively and then move into position. Once your entire name has appeared, the animation stops.

In Chapter 4, you learned how to build a complex logo. Because the focus of this tutorial is the animation, the logo will be very simple. If you like, you can combine these animation techniques with more advanced logo designs, but be advised that such combinations often result in an awkward mess.

As you'll see in Section 18.1, an animation is made from successive image frames. One of the ways to create an animation is to build a multi-layer image in which each layer is one frame.

Method One: Frame by Frame

The simplest way to create the frames is to build each one in turn by hand. Of course, this method is also the most cumbersome and feasible only for very simple animations.

In this tutorial, we use the background layer as the animation background and move only the letters of the name in successive image layers.

To begin, create a new 600 × 400 image (CTRL+N). Fill the background with the color of your choice. To do this, click the Color chooser in the Toolbox (see Figure 3.3 on page 62), choose your color, and then press CTRL+, to fill the layer with the foreground color. Alternatively, you could choose the Bucket Fill tool (SHIFT+B) and click to fill the area.

Now select the Text tool (T). Pick a bold font (in our case, we selected DejaVu Sans Bold Semicondensed), and set the size to 100. Select a text color that shows up clearly against your background color.

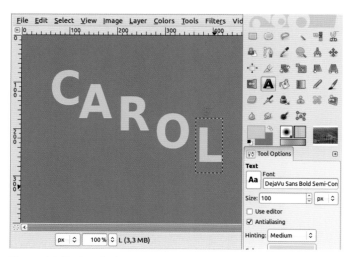

Figure 6.1 *Typing the letters*

The first click corresponds to the upper-left corner of the box containing the first letter. If you click elsewhere in the image after typing the first letter, a new layer is automatically created for the next letter, which is exactly what you want. After adding all the letters, your image should look like Figure 6.1. The colors we chose for the logo are 2f91dc and f6ee11 in HTML notation.

This image is already a simple animation. To test it, select **Image: Filters > Animation > Playback**. In the window that opens, simply click the PLAY button, and you see the animation playing.

Why does it work? When you click PLAY, GIMP reveals the layers one by one, and because text layers have transparent backgrounds, the letters don't cover up the background, or the rest of the logo, when they appear.

To complete this logo, press (SHIFT+CTRL+E) and export it as a GIF image. In the dialog that opens, check SAVE AS ANIMATION and uncheck LOOP FOREVER.

As explained in "Output Formats" on page 476, this produces a file that you can display in a browser. After exporting your logo as a GIF, you can use it at the top of your web page, for example.

Test your animation by opening it in your browser, generally by selecting **File > Open** or pressing CTRL+O. You can also include the animation in an HTML page with the <img src='...' /> tag.

Method Two: Filtering All Layers

The previous animation was simple. Suppose you want something more complicated. Building all the frames by hand would be time consuming and boring—especially if you want to create a smooth animation, which requires many frames. To make such animations in a practical way, you need a program that automatically generates frames from an initial image. The GIMP Animation Package (GAP) does just that. You install it separately from GIMP, but the process is simple (see Appendix E for help installing GAP).

When GAP is installed, a menu called VIDEO appears in the Image window, and two additional entries appear in the FILTERS menu: FILTER ALL LAYERS and FILTERMACRO. Another tool installed with GAP is **Image: Filters > Animation > Selection to AnimImage**, which is similar to Filter all Layers.

Create a new image that's the same size and background color as used in the last exercise. As

Figure 6.2 *The initial logo*

Figure 6.3 *The duplicate layer button*

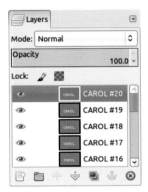

Figure 6.4 *The Layers dialog*

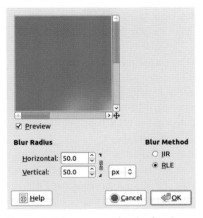

Figure 6.5 *Parameters for the first layer*

Figure 6.6 *Intermediary step*

Figure 6.7 *The final dialog*

before, use the Text tool to create the logo in the same color, size, and font, but this time type the name as a single layer. Our result is shown in Figure 6.2.

For this animation, the text layers must be opaque. Merge the text layer with the background by selecting **Image: Layer > Merge Down** or right-clicking on the text layer in the Layers dialog and selecting Merge Down.

The animation has 20 layers, which begin as identical copies of the initial logo image. After you've merged the text with the background, change the name of the layer, for example, to CAROL #1, by double-clicking in the layer name. Then click the DUPLICATE LAYER button 19 times (Figure 6.3) in the Layers dialog (see Figure 6.4).

Now select **Image: Filters > Filter all Layers**. This tool applies a filter to all the layers of an image. You choose the parameters of the filter for

the first and last layers, and the tool interpolates the values for the layers in between.

For our logo, we apply a blurring filter. Type the word blur in the Search field and click SEARCH BY BLURB.

Choose plug-in-gauss, and click APPLY. The numeric field and the small curve next to APPLY allow you to change the speed of the progression: It can be uniform or slow at the beginning and faster at the end (for this example, choose 4), or vice versa (a negative number would reverse the speed). When the next dialog appears, set a large blur radius, such as 50 pixels, as shown in Figure 6.5.

Click CONTINUE. The dialog shown in Figure 6.6 appears. Click CONTINUE again, and another dialog similar to Figure 6.5 appears.

This time, set the blur to 0 for the final frame. Click OK. Now the dialog shown in Figure 6.7 appears.

Next you need to name a temporary file where the animation will be stored. Choose a directory, type `caroltemp.xcf` (or any name you like), and then click CONTINUE once more. The process takes some time because GIMP is applying the Gaussian Blur filter to 20 layers.

Once this process finishes, the animation is ready. Test it by selecting **Image: Filters > Animation > Playback**. When the animation finishes playing, it returns to the beginning.

You can change this in several ways :

- Export the animation as a GIF image, and uncheck the LOOP FOREVER option.

- Change the duration of the last frame (i.e., the topmost layer); to do this, double-click the layer name in the Layers dialog and type (`1000ms`) after the name. Be sure to include the parentheses and a space between the name and the duration. The final frame now displays for a full second while the others last for only 100 milliseconds.

- Duplicate the top layer as many times as you'd like.

Method Three: Moving Along a Path

When using FILTER ALL LAYERS, you can only control what is done to the first and the last frame. Additionally, because frames are represented by layers, you can't have multilayer frames. GAP provides tools that you can use to build animations with much more control.

In the **Image: Video** menu that was added when you installed the GAP plug-in, you'll find tools for creating animations with frames stored as separate image files.

The names of these image files must be of the form *namexxxx*.xcf, where *name* is the name you give to the animation and *xxxx* is a number beginning with *0001* and increasing consecutively until the last frame. The number of digits can vary depending on the length of the animation.

Figure 6.8 *Model of the intended animation*

Make Duplicates of Frame Range

From Frame:	1
To Frame:	1
N times:	1

Help   Cancel   OK

Figure 6.9 *The Image: Video > Duplicate Frames dialog*

The first frame of a very short animation might be named *01*. Longer animations can have 6, or even 10, digits.

For this example, imagine you want to build a new animation, similar to the last two but a bit more complex. This time, the name CAROL will grow progressively larger and become increasingly opaque. Simultaneously, a rectangular frame will grow and become opaque and then rotate from a vertical position, perpendicular to the text, to its horizontal position, neatly framing the text.

First, build a model for the animation, which is a three-layer image. Create a new 300×150 image ($\boxed{\text{CTRL+N}}$) with the same blue background color. Once again, add the text layer with the name CAROL. Finally, build the frame in the same color as the text:

- Create a new transparent layer.

- Using the Rectangle Select tool, select the frame of the text layer.

- Apply **Image: Select > Border** to this selection; choose a width of 5 for the border.

- Fill the selection with the foreground color (for example, $\boxed{\text{CTRL+,}}$), and cancel the selection ($\boxed{\text{SHIFT+CTRL+A}}$).

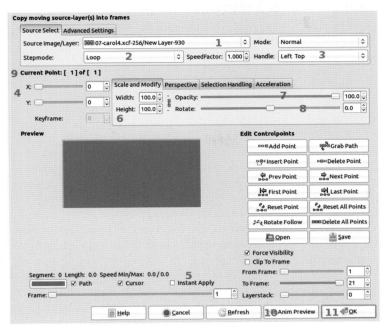

Figure 6.10 *The Move Path dialog*

The result is shown in Figure 6.8. Keep this image opened in GIMP.

To better organize your workspace, create a new folder called Carol in whatever directory you use to store images. You'll store all of the animation frames in that new folder.

Create the first frame by clicking and dragging the background layer thumbnail of your model image from the Layers dialog to the Toolbox. Save this image ([SHIFT+CTRL+S]) in the new folder, and name it carol-0001.xcf. This is the background of the first frame.

Next duplicate this frame. The simplest method is to use **Image: Video > Duplicate Frames**. The dialog shown in Figure 6.9 appears. Move the N TIMES slider to 20 and click OK. After GIMP finishes working, nothing seems to have happened, but if you check, you'll see the new frames are in the Carol folder. We'll be working on the first frame only, so ignore the new frames for now.

One of the most useful tools in the GAP plug-in is **Image: Video > Move Path**. Open the first frame, carol-0001.xcf, and then call the Move Path tool. As shown in Figure 6.10, the dialog that appears is quite large, but don't panic—in this tutorial, we focus on just a few of its features.

Use the MOVE PATH tool to add layers, which are taken from an open image (the model image in our case), to the animation frames. The move is applied along a path defined with points. At each point, you can apply transformations such as blending modes, scaling, opacity, rotation, and perspective to the added layer. If you add several layers at the same time, you can choose how they are taken from the model image.

We've added numbers to Figure 6.10 that correspond to numbers in the text to guide you through the following steps. Select the layer in the SOURCE IMAGE/LAYER menu from among those in the currently open images (1). First, choose the frame layer. Because there is only one layer, choose NONE from the STEPMODE menu (2).

The coordinates of the path's points are taken according to the origin selected in the HANDLE

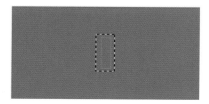

Figure 6.11 *After adding the rectangle to the first frame*

Figure 6.12 *The Anim Preview dialog*

menu. Choose CENTER (3), and then set the X and Y coordinates (4) to 150 and 75, respectively. A red crosshair appears in the background frame. To see the frame, check the INSTANT APPLY box (5) at the bottom of the dialog.

The original characteristics of the frame layer are 20.0% for scaling (6), 20.0% for opacity (7), and −90° for rotation (8).

Now you've set the first point, which applies to the first frame. Add another point by clicking the ADD POINT button. Note that the point number has changed (9). For this point, which will be the last frame, the layer's position and opacity change, but the point coordinates should remain the same. change WIDTH, HEIGHT, and OPACITY to 100% and ROTATE to 0.0. The first layer of the animation is now complete.

Click OK, and GIMP processes the frames. This process can take a while, depending on the size and number of frames. When GIMP finishes, you'll see the first frame with an additional layer: the logo's rectangular frame in its initial position, as seen in Figure 6.11.

To add the second layer (the text), use the MOVE PATH tool again. This time, select the text layer in the model image. Select the same values for STEPMODE, HANDLE, the X and Y coordinates, WIDTH and HEIGHT, and OPACITY, as you used for the previous layer. Check INSTANT APPLY to see the result.

Add a new point, and set WIDTH, HEIGHT, and OPACITY to 100%, but don't change the coordinates. The animation is finished! To check it before saving, click ANIM PREVIEW (10). The dialog shown in Figure 6.12 appears. Click OK. GIMP

builds a reduced version of the animation as a multilayer image, with the Playback window already open. Although previewing the new animation is exciting, it not only takes a while but also builds an unnecessary image that clutters up your workspace. We recommend skipping this feature and simply clicking OK (11) in the Move Path dialog.

Once GIMP finishes processing, all the frames of the animation contain the same three layers as the model image but with progressive changes to the frame and text layers. You can view this animation by selecting **Image: Video > VCR Navigator** and clicking the PLAYBACK button.

Suppose you want to export this video as a GIF animation. To do this, you need to transform this multi-image animation to a multilayer one and merge the layers in each frame. You can do this automatically using **Image: Video > Frames to Image**, which brings up the dialog shown in Figure 6.13. Leave everything as is and click OK. Once again, GIMP works for a while, eventually creating a new multilayer image. Change the duration of the last frame (the topmost layer) to 1000 ms by typing (1000ms) after the layer name. You can then check your animation with **Image: Filters > Animation > Playback** or export it as a GIF file.

6.2 Building an Animated GIF by Hand

At the beginning of this chapter, we built an animation frame by frame as layers in one image. Here is a general list of the steps to use as a guide for building similar animations:

Create Multilayer-Image from Frames

From Frame:	1
To Frame:	22
Layer Basename:	frame_[######] (1000ms)

Layer Mergemode:
- ○ Expand as necessary
- ◉ Clipped to image
- ○ Clipped to bottom layer
- ○ Flattened image

Exclude BG-Layer: ☐

Layer Selection:
- ○ Pattern is equal to layer name
- ○ Pattern is start of layer name
- ○ Pattern is end of layer name
- ○ Pattern is a part of layer name
- ○ Pattern is a list of layerstack numbers
- ○ Pattern is a list of reverse layerstack numbers
- ◉ All visible (ignore pattern)

Layer Pattern: 0

Case sensitive: ☑

Invert Layer Selection: ☐

Pixel Selection:
- ◉ Ignore
- ○ Initial frame
- ○ Frame specific

[Help] [Cancel] [OK]

Figure 6.13 *The Frames to Image dialog*

Figure 6.14 *The background image*

Figure 6.15 *Parameters for the first color*

1. Create a stationary background for the animation.

2. Create another layer with the object that will move; it may be cut from a photograph, drawn using paint tools, or typed in as text.

3. For each new position of the object, duplicate the preceding layer and apply some transformation to the new layer: Move, rotate, or deform the object, zoom in or out, and so on. Take care when doing this, or the animation will be choppy.

4. Because each new layer must replace the preceding one, duplicate the background layer once per object layer, intersperse these copies between the object layers, and then merge each object layer with a background layer.

5. The animation is finished!

You've just created a simple animation in which a single object moves along a fixed background. While you can use this technique to animate multiple objects, the process is awkward and repetitive. Remember that if you're doing a repetitive task on a computer, you're not using the computer in a clever way.

In the next section, we demonstrate some other ways to create simple animations.

Drawing a Rainbow Daisy

The first example is so simple that duplicating the background is not necessary: Layers are progressively added to draw the petals of the daisy.

Begin with the background image shown in Figure 6.14.

Then we draw the petals by hand with the Paintbrush tool. We draw one petal at a time, using different colors for each petal. To change the color, we change only the hue by a set amount from petal to petal. The background is rather dark, so we choose a bright, saturated color, beginning at one end of the hue scale, as shown in Figure 6.15.

Figure 6.16 *Workspace after the petals have been added*

Every petal has its own layer. First create a new layer. In the dialog that appears, add a number to the layer name. With the Hardness 100 brush set to a small size, draw the first petal in the upper-left corner of the image.

For the second petal, choose a color with the same saturation and value as the first one but with a different hue. To change the hue, set the new value in the field to the right of the radio button labeled H. The hue values range from 0 to 360. Because the daisy has seven petals, plus its stem, we need eight different hues. So we add 40 to the preceding hue value for each new petal, create the new layer, name it, and draw the petal in the proper place until the daisy is finished.

When the daisy is finished, we have nine layers, and the animation is almost complete. The animation will look better if it pauses at the beginning and at the end, so add an explicit duration of 1000 ms to the first and last layers by typing (1000ms) after the layer name.

To test the animation, go to **Image: Filters > Animation > Playback**. Figure 6.16 shows the final image with the Layers dialog.

Notice that the Playback window always displays the image at its actual size—this can be problematic if you build an animation with an image that's larger than your screen. When an animation takes up most of the screen, detach it from the Playback window by clicking the fourth button from the left at the top of the window.

When you're satisfied with the animation, you can export it as an animated GIF, as shown in "Method One: Frame by Frame" on page 139.

Zooming Toward the Viewer

The second animation is slightly more complicated to build. This time, we want to make a word zoom toward the viewer.

We begin with a new background image. Select the Text tool, choose your favorite font, in a

Figure 6.17 *Adding text to an image*

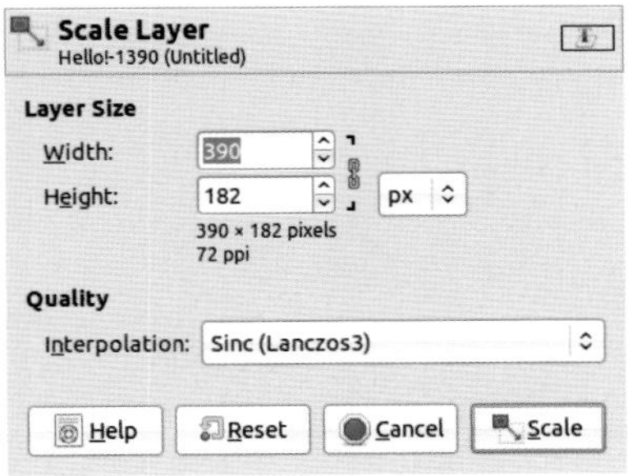

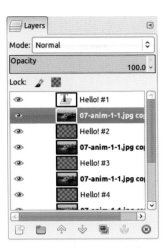

Figure 6.19 *The Layers dialog with text and background layers*

Figure 6.18 *Scaling the layer*

large size and a bright color, and write "Hello!" on the image. Figure 6.17 shows the result, with a FreeSans Bold font in size 140 in a bright red.

Next, we build several copies of this layer, each with a smaller and smaller zoom factor and an increasing blur. We build the layers in reverse order, so the last built is the first to display. To build a smooth animation, we change the height of the layer by the same amount each time, and we use the same blurring factor.

Duplicate the text layer, and work on the lower copy. Using **Image: Layer > Scale Layer**, reduce the layer height by 20 pixels (see Figure 6.18). Then select **Image: Filters > Blur > Gaussian Blur** and apply a blur with the default parameters. If you're not sure whether the parameters are set to their default values, reset all the filters via **Image: Filters > Reset all Filters**.

Repeat this process four more times, always working on the lower text layer (the one that has

just been transformed). You can speed up the process by pressing CTRL+F to repeat the last filter used.

At the end, you should have six text layers. As it stands now, however, you can't use this image as an animation because all the layers are visible. The solution is to duplicate the background layer so you have one background layer per text layer. By alternatively clicking the DUPLI-CATE button and the RAISE button at the bottom of the Layers dialog, you can quickly create the sequence of layers shown in Figure 6.19.

Then merge each text layer with the underlying background layer by selecting **Layer: right-click > Merge Down**. Keep one more version of the background at the bottom of the layer stack so the animation begins with the original background. The resulting sequence of layers is shown in Figure 6.20.

Our animation is almost ready. Because we duplicated the background layer so many times, the file is 12MB, which is quite large. But much of the background actually remains the same, creating redundancy, so we can reduce the size without losing valuable information.

GIMP provides a way to reduce the size: Apply **Image: Filters > Animation > Optimize (for**

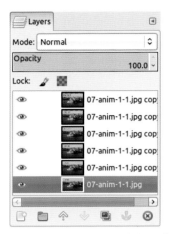

Figure 6.20 *The Layers dialog after merging text and background layers*

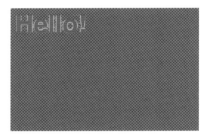

Figure 6.21 *The first layer after optimization for GIF*

Figure 6.22 *The initial image*

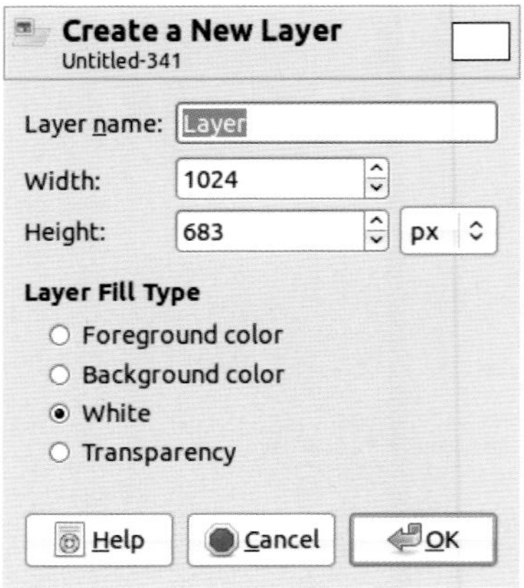

Figure 6.23 *Building the layer*

GIF). The filter has no dialog and does its job immediately. It generates another, smaller image file: In our case, the file is 362KB. The filter replaces parts of the image that don't change with transparency, as shown in Figure 6.21. Because the animated word doesn't move across the background, most of the background remains unchanged, and, as a result, the size is reduced significantly.

The optimization tool also adds the layer replacement mode (combine) to every layer except the bottom one. Therefore, the new layer does not replace the previous one but is *combined* with it. In the previous animation, we used the (replace) combination mode, which is the default.

We still need to do two things before this animation is complete. First, we need to change

the timing of the first and last frames (bottom and top layers) to make the animation smoother. Because the optimization process automatically added a duration of 100 ms, we have to change the timing already specified for these two layers by adding another zero to the duration, so it becomes (1000ms).

Finally, we export the completed animation as a GIF.

Adding Rain to a Landscape

This animation is easy to build and takes less than 10 minutes. Those of you with a little programming knowledge could even automate this process by creating a script.

As a background, we use the photograph in Figure 6.22, a sandy beach on the North Coast

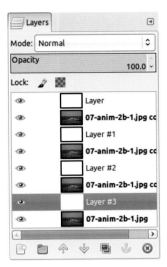

Figure 6.24 *The resulting Layers dialog*

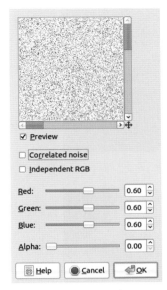

Figure 6.25 *Creating the rain: adding noise*

of New South Wales, Australia. We want to add some rain falling on this landscape.

Duplicate the background image three times. Now you have four layers. Next, add a new, white layer above each background layer (see Figure 6.23). The resulting Layers dialog is shown in Figure 6.24.

Use the white layers for the rain. First, add noise to the white layers with **Image: Filters > Noise > RGB Noise**, using the parameters shown in Figure 6.25. Do this for each white layer by selecting it and pressing CTRL+F. Change this noise into rain by applying **Image: Filters > Blur > Motion Blur**, using the parameters shown in Figure 6.26. Repeat this process for each white layer.

The animation is almost finished. Here are the remaining steps:

1. Change the blend mode of every rain layer to Multiply; note that other blend modes work too, for example, Screen or even Grain Merge.

2. Merge each rain layer with the underlying background layer (use **Layers: right-click > Merge Down**).

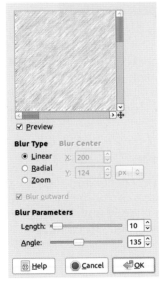

Figure 6.26 *Creating the rain: adding motion blur*

3. Test the animation with **Image: Filters > Animation > Playback**.

4. Optimize the animation for GIF, and export it as an animated GIF.

Figure 6.27 *The final image*

Figure 6.29 *Applying the noise filter*

Figure 6.28 *The initial image*

Figure 6.30 *Inverting the layer*

The final result appears in Figure 6.27. Of course, the actual animation is a lot more interesting than the still image shown. To see it, visit the book's website (*http://the-book-of-gimp.blogspot.com*).

Adding Snow to a Landscape

You can use a similar process to add snow to a picture. To demonstrate more of the tools available, in this example, we apply some alternative methods to arrive at the result. In GIMP, you'll generally discover many different ways to complete a given task.

We begin with the image shown in Figure 6.28, a photograph taken in the northern French Alps. We create snow by again applying **Image: Filters > Noise > RGB Noise** but this time on a new, transparent layer. To apply the noise to a transparent layer, make sure Correlated noise is unchecked and then move the ALPHA cursor to 100.

The snow is black, as shown in Figure 6.29. In the previous example, we adjusted the color of the rain when we changed the blending mode to Multiply. This time we use **Image: Color > Invert** to make the snow white, as it should be (see Figure 6.30).

Now we want to make the snow fall slowly over the landscape. First, duplicate the snow layer and then apply the Offset tool: Select **Image: Layer > Transform > Offset** or press SHIFT+CTRL+O. Set a small, positive Y offset—around 10. Check the WRAP AROUND box, or the snow will disappear from the top of the image (see Figure 6.31).

Duplicate this offset copy, and apply the tool again on the copy of the copy. Repeat this process several times.

As shown in "Method Two: Filtering All Layers" on page 140, duplicate the background, add copies under every snow layer, and merge each snow layer with the underlying background copy. The result is a working animation.

Figure 6.31 *The Offset dialog*

To make the snow fall gracefully, we have to generate many layers, and we have to apply the same Y offset relative to the preceding snow layer. A smooth animation would require at least 30 frames. In "Animating a Still Image" on page 151 and Section 18.4 we show you two different methods for generating these layers automatically, saving a lot of time.

6.3 Using Animation Tools

GIMP offers numerous tools and filters for creating animations. In this section, we show you some of those tools.

Interactive Deformation

With this tool and little work, you can create an impressive, or at least amusing, animation.

Basically, we'll warp an existing image and then automatically generate the intermediate layers of the animation. To do this, we need to introduce an additional capability of a tool used previously to distort still images.

We start with a picture of a rather serious girl, the first one in Figure 5.1 on page 116. Our animation will make her smile in a silly, exaggerated way. First, select the face with the Fuzzy Select tool.

Select the IWarp tool: **Image: Filters > Distorts > IWarp**. The dialog shown in Figure 6.32 pops up. Select the MOVE Deform Mode, and choose a small DEFORM RADIUS, such as 10 pixels. With the mouse pointer, or a tablet stylus if you have one, click and drag both sides of the mouth up and out with small, careful strokes. Increase the deform radius and move the lower lip down slightly and the upper lip up slightly. You can also move the lower eyelids down a little and pull the corners of the eyes out just a tiny bit. This tool has no real undo capability, but if you make a mistake, you can use the REMOVE Deform Mode to correct what you just did.

We could use this tool to change the still image. If we click the ANIMATE tab, however, we can automatically generate an animation. Set the NUMBER OF FRAMES to 20 and check the PING PONG box. The additional layers of the animation are built by GIMP after you click OK.

As with the preceding animations, adjust the timing of layers, optimize the image for GIF, and then export the image as a GIF.

Animating a Still Image

Earlier in this chapter, we used the Filter all Layers tool to make an animation from a multilayer image (see "Method Two: Filtering All Layers" on page 140). Filter all Layers can also be used to apply systematic changes to all the frames of an existing animation. The tool works by applying a filter to all the layers. You can set the initial and final values of the filter parameters, and if those values are different, the tool filters each layer by varying the parameters progressively from the beginning value to the final one.

Most of the filters available in GIMP can be applied progressively to the layers of an image. You can even use the Filter all Layers tool with several different filters, one after the other.

To demonstrate, we'll animate the image of Olivier's Siamese cat shown in Figure 6.33. Because her name is Aria, change the first layer name to Aria #1. Duplicate the layer 39

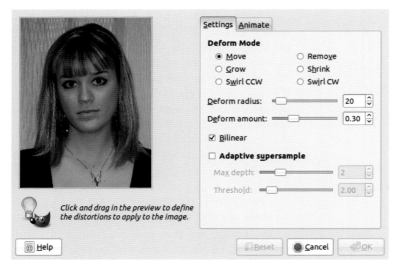

Figure 6.32 *The IWarp dialog*

Figure 6.33 *The initial image*

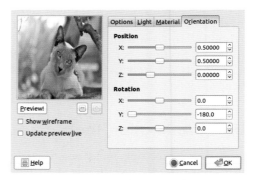

Figure 6.34 *Parameters for the first filter*

times, and the successive layers are automatically named and numbered from 1 to 40.

To choose among the mapping filters in the Filter all Layers tool, type the word map in the Search box and click SEARCH BY NAME. Choose the plug-in-map-object filter, and click APPLY.

Map the image on a plane and then change the Y value on the Orientation tab. We want the image to rotate on a vertical axis and make a full 360-degree rotation, so we change the value of Y to −180, as shown in Figure 6.34 (taken after we clicked PREVIEW!). Click OK, and after the first layer is transformed, a small dialog appears.

Click CONTINUE. As shown in Figure 6.35, change the Y rotation to +180. Click OK, type

some filename in the continuation dialog, and click CONTINUE. The process takes a long time to run because of the number of layers. In the resulting animation, Aria rotates around the vertical axis, as shown in Figure 6.36.

Now we want to apply a second filter to all of the layers. We apply the filter PLUG-IN-APPLYLENS, using the same parameters for every layer. Apply the filter via Filter all Layers and click the APPLY button to get Figure 6.37. Leave the parameters as they are and click OK. The same dialogs as shown previously appear, but this time leave the parameters unchanged. The result appears in Figure 6.38.

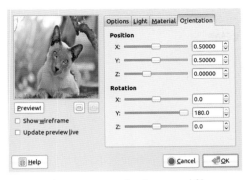

Figure 6.35 *Parameters for the second filter*

Figure 6.36 *The first animation*

Figure 6.37 *Parameters for the second global filter*

Figure 6.38 *The final animation*

You can use the Filter all Layers tool with more than a hundred filters. But the tool does have some limitations:

- Although the tool interface lists all the filters, from time to time, we encounter a filter that does not work correctly. A filter isn't working if you don't see the successive dialogs that usually appear. This discrepancy happens because each filter must be adapted by the programmer to work with Filter all Layers, and sometimes filters are released without the necessary adaptation. If you run into this problem, all you can do is be patient and hope for an update. In the meantime, you can probably find another, similar filter that does work with the tool.

- Although Filter all Layers can be used with a variety of filters, the tool itself is fairly straightforward and performs one basic function: It generates a smooth transition between the initial image and the filter-transformed image.

Morphing

The next tool is simple to use, but it produces a very interesting effect if the parameters are set correctly. The main function of the Morphing tool, found in the **Image: Video > Morph > Morph** menu, is to progressively transform a given image into another one. Generally, this works best if the images have something in common. Note that this tool is also a part of GAP, so you need to install this set of plug-ins to use it.

To demonstrate this tool, we'll morph one portrait into another. The two portraits were taken on the same day and under the same

Figure 6.39 *The first portrait*

Figure 6.40 *The second portrait*

Figure 6.41 *The portraits as layers*

align the shoulders and faces of the two girls. Crop the layers so they're the same size. Figure 6.41 shows the result, with the top layer still semitransparent.

Before you use the Morphing tool, both layers *must* have an alpha channel: **Layers: right-click > Add Alpha Channel**. After you add an Alpha channel, the layer name is no longer in boldface in the Layers dialog.

Now select the Morphing tool. Its large dialog has many components, but you need to use only a few of them. The purpose of the Morphing tool is to progressively transform the source image (which appears on the left side of the dialog) to the destination image (which appears on the right side of the dialog). Here the lower layer serves as the source, but you may change that if you prefer. Choose images of a moderate size, so they appear in the preview windows in a correct scale.

The morphing process uses points placed on the source image and corresponding points placed on the destination image. The source image is transformed by the animation to move each point, as well as its neighboring pixels, to the position of the corresponding point.

First, place *shapepoints* around the border of both images to prevent weird deformations of

conditions. As Figures 6.39 and 6.40 show, these girls are of the same age, both are blond with blue eyes, both are wearing black clothes, and both were photographed in front of the same background. But their faces, hair and clothing styles, and head tilts are different.

Open both images as layers in a new image, for example, by dragging the thumbnail of one portrait to the Toolbox to create a new image and then dragging the thumbnail of the second portrait into the new image you just created. Make the top layer semitransparent by adjusting the opacity and then move it slightly to the image frame. Leave the default number, 64, un changed, and click the SHAPE button. Now the outlines of the images correspond.

Next we add shapepoints to the source image and move the corresponding points on the destination image. Click some characteristic feature in the first image. A yellow point appears, and a corresponding yellow point appears on the destination image. We add points on the tip of the nose, at the corners of the eyes, around the mouth, along the chin and hair, and so on. You can experiment with the Edit modes while adding shapepoints. For example, you can move existing shapepoints or delete them or zoom in or out to place difficult shapepoints.

After adding the shapepoints, the only parameter we change from its default value is the number of steps. This value is the number of layers that will be built as intermediate layers between the source and the destination. We recommend at least 20 steps—or more if the two images being morphed are very different.

Finally, click OK. The large dialog disappears, and GIMP begins to create the new layers. This process may take a while, depending on the size of the images and on the number of steps. When GIMP is done, the image is ready to be tested with **Image: Filters > Animation > Playback**. We recommend you increase the duration of the first and last frames.

The best results are obtained when the images are fairly similar and the shapepoints have been carefully placed. Figures 6.42 and 6.43 show frames 7 and 14 of our 22-frame animation, respectively. Because the hair and clothing styles were different, the morphing is unnatural for these features, but the faces morphed smoothly.

To finish the animation, optimize for GIF, and then export the image as an animated GIF.

6.4 Using GAP

The two simple GAP examples demonstrated on pages 140 and 142 are only a brief introduction

Figure 6.42 *Frame 7 of the animation*

Figure 6.43 *Frame 14 of the animation*

to this complex and powerful plug-in. In fact, GAP isn't a plug-in at all, but rather a diverse collection of animation-related plug-ins. Most, but not all, are found in the **Image: Video** menu.

In this section, we consider only the plug-ins that are found on this menu. All of these plug-ins (except the ones in the Morph submenu) deal with multi-image animations rather than multi-layer animations, which we've created in all but one of the preceding examples (see "Method Three: Moving Along a Path" on page 142).

The multi-image format is ideal for building and manipulating large and complex animations. It allows you to convert to and from popular video formats like MPEG. When necessary, GAP also converts between multi-image and multilayer animation formats. All these benefits take this set of plug-ins a long way toward being a complete video manipulation tool embedded within GIMP.

The Move Path Tool

The Move Path tool (**Image: Video > Move Path**) is the main interface for GAP. As you learned in "Method Three: Moving Along a Path" on page 142, you first need to follow these steps:

1. Open at least one multilayered or multi-image animation in GIMP. This image will serve as the source of the layers you'll add to your animation; you may choose to open several images.

2. Create a new folder to contain the new animation.

3. Place a background image for the new animation in this folder. Call it something like `name-00001.xcf`.

4. Open this background image in GIMP, and duplicate it using **Image: Video > Duplicate Frames**. The number of copies should equal the desired number of frames.

5. Once you have the source and background files open, select the Move Path tool from the animation's source image.

If you haven't set up the environment properly before opening the Move Path tool, the tool complains and refuses to work. Note that you can use an existing multi-image animation as the background, rather than creating one as we've done. In this case, simply open the source animation (Step 1) and then open the background animation, and you're ready to open the Move Path tool.

The Move Path tool adds layers from the source image to a sequence of frames in the target animation. You define how layers are added to the frames by modifying several parameters. Basically, you define *positions* (i.e., relative

Figure 6.44 *The initial landscape*

locations) in the target animation; for each position, define these values for the following parameters:

- Position

- Orientation

- Scale in X and Y

- Opacity

- Perspective

If the source image has an active selection, however, you can choose to add just the selection to the new animation.

You can use the Move Path tool to build an animation with several scenes by building a complex path for the layers in the successive frames and applying changes to only a subset of the frames that correspond to a specific scene.

Finally, and this point is important, to add several layers to the target frames, apply the Move Path tool multiple times—once for each layer.

We'll walk you through two new examples to demonstrate some nifty things this tool can do.

Binocular Animation

First, we make an animation that simulates somebody looking at a scene through binoculars and moving the binoculars in search of a target. The scene is a village surrounded by mountains, as shown in Figure 6.44.

We add the binoculars as a new layer that's completely black except for two overlapping

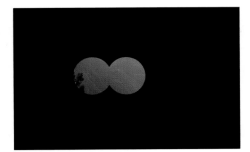

Figure 6.45 *Adding the binoculars*

Figure 6.46 *Moving the binoculars*

circles that are transparent. Here are the steps to create the binoculars:

1. Create a new transparent layer.

2. Build a circular selection.

3. Save it to a channel (**Image: Select > Save to Channel**) and then select the layer again.

4. Move the selection a horizontal distance equal to about two-thirds its diameter.

5. In the Channels dialog, add the saved channel to the current selection.

6. Save the new binocular selection as a channel.

7. Select the top layer on the Layers tab, invert the selection, and fill it with black.

The result should look like Figure 6.45.

In our animation, we move the binoculars around the landscape. But both layers are currently the same size, so as the binoculars move, the black won't fully cover the background, resulting in something like Figure 6.46. To avoid

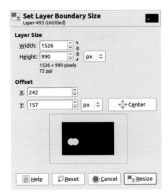

Figure 6.47 *Enlarging the upper layer*

this, we need to enlarge the top layer to cover the landscape.

Select **Image: Layer > Layer Boundary Size**, increase the size in both directions, and center the canvas around the enlarged layer, as shown in Figure 6.47. Then make this entire layer black, except for the binocular window. Because this layer is now larger than the canvas, this step is somewhat tricky. Here's one way to do it:

1. Save the binocular selection in a channel, if you haven't already, and then return to the layer and cancel the selection.

2. Select **Image: Image > Fit Canvas to Layers**.

3. Fill the layer with the foreground color (CTRL+,).

4. Restore the selection saved in a channel, return to the layer, and clear the selection contents (DELETE).

5. Cancel the selection.

Because we enlarged the image, we need to crop it at the end of the process.

Now create a new folder for the animation; call it Binoculars. Drag the background layer thumbnail from the Layers dialog to the Toolbox, and save the image as bin-0001.xcf in the new folder Binoculars.

Duplicate this frame 59 times, using **Image: Video > Duplicate Frames**. The animation now has 60 frames. We use a path to move the

Figure 6.48 *The binocular path across the landscape*

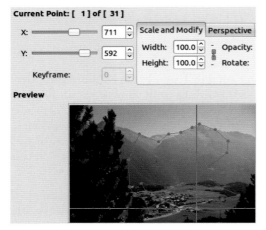

Figure 6.49 *Importing the path as a sequence of controlpoints*

binoculars around the landscape. Choose the Path tool in the Toolbox ([B]) and click to add points to the background image you just saved, as shown in Figure 6.48.

Select the Move Path tool (**Image: Video > Move Path...**). In the dialog, check that the selected layer is the top layer of the source image, which appears mostly black in the thumbnail. Choose None for the STEPMODE and Center for the HANDLE.

Click the GRAB PATH button in the EDIT CONTROLPOINTS area of the dialog to import the path we just built as a sequence of controlpoints, which are equally placed across the 60 frames. Then the dialog should look similar to Figure 6.49.

The GAP plug-ins lack the capability to undo, so check the animation you just built by clicking ANIM PREVIEW. If everything is correct, click OK to generate the final animation. Discard the multilayer image that was created for the preview.

Improving the Binocular Animation

Although it did serve as a basic introduction to using paths with the Move Path tool, the animation we just created isn't very realistic. If you are looking through binoculars, it's the landscape that appears to be moving, not you.

If you closed it, open the binocular animation that you just made. Create a new folder for the next version of the animation and then create a new blank image that's much smaller than the landscape in the source image. For this example, we create a 521×338 image, and our landscape image is 1042×676. Save this image into the new folder with name bin-0001.xcf, and duplicate it 59 times with **Image: Video > Duplicate Frames**.

Open the Move Path tool dialog (**Image: Video > Move Path**). Choose the landscape layer of the previous animation as the source layer (top left of the dialog), None for STEPMODE (below SOURCE IMAGE/LAYER), and Center for HANDLE (to the right of STEPMODE), and check INSTANT APPLY at the bottom of the dialog. This time, let's build the path within the Move Path tool dialog by clicking in the preview to place points. Click ADD POINT and then click in the preview to add a new point. If you click close to an existing point in the preview, you end up moving that point rather than adding a new one, so click the last point and drag it to add a new one instead. Note that the source image moves around as you place the points. Our result is shown in Figure 6.50.

Before finalizing this animation, check the CLIP TO FRAME checkbox and then click OK. GIMP processes for a while as it builds the first part of the animation, with the landscape moving in the smaller image. You can test the result

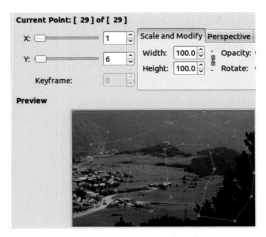

Figure 6.50 *Creating the path by hand*

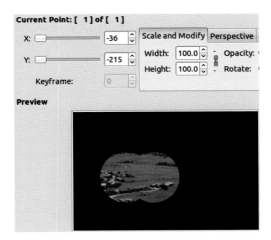

Figure 6.51 *Placing the second layer*

by selecting **Image: Video > Playback**.

Now place the binoculars above these landscape frames. Use a layer mask. Add the mask as a new layer to all the frames with the Move Path tool again. Figure 6.51 shows the settings we used. The binocular layer is chosen as source layer and placed in the center of the image.

Simply click OK to get the new animation. Each frame contains three layers—from top to bottom: the binocular image, the landscape, and a white background. We want to merge the topmost layer with the background and use the

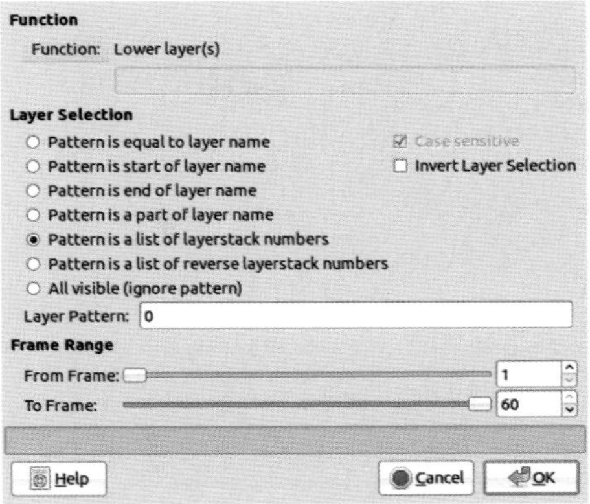

Figure 6.52 *Lowering the topmost layer*

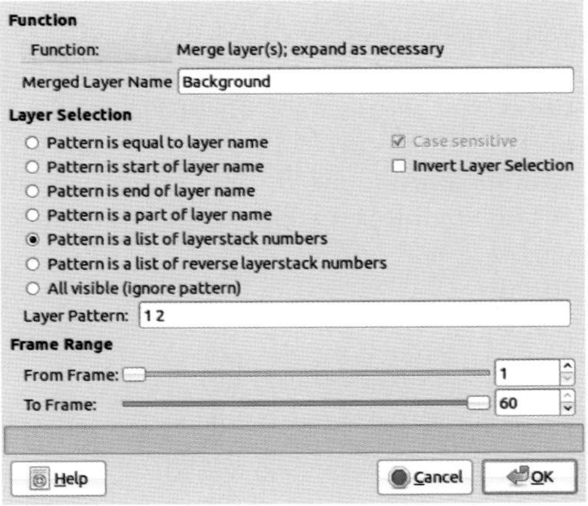

Figure 6.53 *Merging the two bottom layers*

resulting layer as a mask for the landscape layer. This reduces the number of layers and demonstrates the **Image: Video > Frames Modify** tool at the same time.

The Frames Modify tool is handy for modifying a set of layers across all the frames in a multi-image animation. The dialog appears in Figure 6.52, showing our first selections. Click the FUNCTION menu (at the top of the dialog) and select LAYER STACKPOSITION > LOWER LAYER(S). Leave PATTERN IS A LIST OF LAYER STACK NUMBERS checked, and enter 0 for LAYER PATTERN. Click OK.

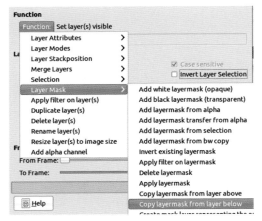

Figure 6.54 *Using the bottom layer as a layer mask*

Next we merge the two bottom layers. Select the Modify Frames tool again, and this time choose the settings shown in Figure 6.53. Because the layers are numbered from top to bottom beginning at 0, the layer pattern is "1 2." The resulting composite layer is named Background.

The final step is shown in Figure 6.54. The bottom layer acts as a mask for the landscape layer.

6.5 Exercises

Exercise 6.1. You know those exasperating advertisements that flash tirelessly on some web pages? Build one in which the logo progressively fades in and out. Do it entirely by hand.

Exercise 6.2. Make the same flashing logo as in the preceding exercise, but this time use the Filter all Layers tool.

Exercise 6.3. If you have two multilayer animations with the same background, creating an animation that combines all these layers is easy. Use this idea to build an animation in which the logo first appears progressively from the background and then flashes in the foreground. You can do it by hand or by using the Filter all Layers tool.

Exercise 6.4. Use the IWarp tool to animate a photographic portrait. You can get an aesthetic result, but more likely you'll get a funny result. So use the tool on the portrait of somebody you know extremely well, for example, yourself.

Exercise 6.5. Use the Morphing tool to build an animation in which a logo progressively changes to another one. Both logos should be the same size.

Exercise 6.6. Use the Move Path tool to build an animation in which a logo moves horizontally across the background.

Exercise 6.7. You can use the Move Path tool to add successive layers from a multilayer animation to an animation that you're building, in effect merging the contents of two different animations using LOOP as a Stepmode. Use this idea to create a logo that moves horizontally while flashing.

Exercise 6.8. Re-create the animation from the third exercise in this chapter, "Method Three: Moving Along a Path" on page 142, but this time use the tools found in the **Image: Video** menu. First, you must build the two multilayer animations, using the Filter all Layers tool, and then convert these animations from multilayer to multi-image. Edit them to produce the final animation.

7 Image Preprocessing

Preprocessing is most commonly used in scientific imaging to remove noise and distortions from an image prior to analyzing its meaningful content. Scientists preprocess satellite images, for example, to remove interference like atmospheric debris and clouds before using the images for research. Even if you're not a scientist, you may want to preprocess your images, since these techniques can help you correct distortions, improve color balance, and enhance visibility.

7.1 Tutorial: Extracting Information from a Picture

So, how do you separate noise from the meaningful elements in a picture? One way is to gather information about the image, via histograms, to see if there's distortion in any of the channels. The image we'll use in this tutorial isn't particularly interesting, but it is representative of the problems you may encounter when dealing with badly taken photographs. As you can see in Figure 7.1, the picture's quality is very poor. The photograph was taken through a closed window, in poor lighting, and with the camera's automatic settings.

Figure 7.1 *The initial photograph*

Dynamics Extension

Begin by gathering information on the image dynamics, such as the ratio between the smallest and largest values in various channels. The combined histograms shown in Figure 7.2 are a way to visualize the image dynamics. Open them via **Image: Colors > Info > Histogram**, and change the CHANNEL to RGB. The three channels—Red, Green, and Blue—are shown in the same graph in their corresponding colors. The colors in the areas where the histograms superimpose are additive. A position on the horizontal axis represents a specific value between 0 and 255. The height of the histogram (the vertical axis) represents the number of pixels with that value.

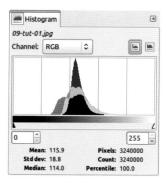

Figure 7.2 *The histogram for the initial photograph*

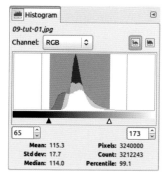

Figure 7.3 *The meaningful part of the histogram*

Figure 7.4 *After equalizing*

Move the small triangles under the horizontal grayscale bar to frame the meaningful interval of values. Figure 7.3 shows that almost no pixels have a value less than 65 or greater than 173. In fact, 99.1 percent of the pixels are in the framed interval, which explains why the image is dull and hazy.

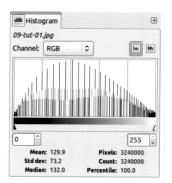

Figure 7.5 *The histogram after equalization*

Figure 7.6 *After stretching the contrast*

Extending the dynamic range is fairly easy with the tools available in GIMP. The simplest one is **Image: Colors > Auto > Equalize**, which automatically stretches the dynamic range in each channel to span the entire available range. Figure 7.4 shows the result, and Figure 7.5 shows the corresponding histogram. Because the image has only slightly more than a hundred different values, and the range has 255 values, extending the existing values over the full range leaves a lot of values unrepresented, which explains the strange "comb" shape.

In the resulting image (Figure 7.4), you see the squirrel is more visible, but the color distortions in the image have been exaggerated.

The same menu contains other automatic tools. For example, Figure 7.6 shows the image and its histograms after we used **Image: Colors > Auto > Stretch Contrast**. You could also

Figure 7.7 *After using Auto in the Levels tool*

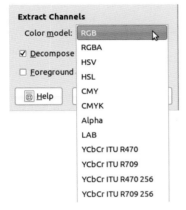

Figure 7.8 *Extracting the RGB channels*

Figure 7.9 *The red channel*

Figure 7.10 *The green channel*

Figure 7.11 *The blue channel*

try **Image: Colors > Auto > Normalize**, which gives a similar result.

Pressing the AUTO button in the Levels tool yields the image shown in Figure 7.7. You can get a similar result by using **Image: Colors > Curves** to manipulate the curves in each color channel and suppress high and low values, which are not present in this photograph.

Histogram Modification

The histograms you saw in the preceding section are not very useful because they are crammed into one window, and their significance is not obvious in the image. A better way to visualize the three channels is to use **Image: Colors > Components > Decompose**. In the dialog shown in Figure 7.8, choose RGB to decompose the image into its three RGB channels. A new image with three grayscale layers, one for each channel, is created. In the Histogram window, choose the Value channel, which is done automatically because the image has no color or transparency.

Figures 7.9 to 7.11 show the three channels, along with their respective histogram. Clearly the Blue channel contributes much less to the image than the other two channels. Let's see what happens if you stretch its histogram and leave the others unchanged.

Figure 7.12 *Stretching the dynamics of the Blue layer*

Figure 7.13 *After recomposing the image*

Select the Blue layer in the Layers dialog and apply **Image: Colors > Auto > Equalize**. The result, if you hide the other two layers, appears in Figure 7.12. Next, apply **Image: Colors > Components > Recompose**. The result, shown in Figure 7.13, is worse than the original. This image demonstrates that proper preprocessing requires an understanding of image dynamics that goes beyond being able to use the automatic tools.

Noise Reduction

Noise is a set of small fluctuations around the average value intensity in some region of an image. As you'll see later in this chapter, noise reduction is useful in many circumstances. But in the present case, the image is mostly noise, and no noise reduction process can really improve it. The only tool that's even slightly useful is **Image: Filters > Enhance > Unsharp Mask**, which brings up the dialog shown in Figure 7.14.

Figure 7.14 *The Unsharp Mask dialog*

Figure 7.15 *After using Unsharp Mask*

If you increase the RADIUS to more than 40, you improve the image a bit, as shown in Figure 7.15. The squirrel is more visible and has more relief, but identifying most of the plants in the background would still be very difficult.

Edge Detection

Generally, edge detection enhances the visibility of objects in a photograph. But when we applied the various filters in the **Image: Filters > Edge Detect** menu to our initial squirrel photograph, we didn't see any improvement. You can achieve a better result by successively applying several different tools.

For example, first select the Levels tool, and click AUTO. Next, apply the Unsharp Mask filter. Finally, choose the **Image: Filters > Edge-Detect > Edge** filter. Using the settings shown

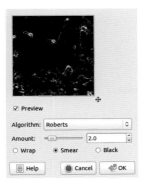

Figure 7.16 *The Edge filter dialog*

Figure 7.17 *After using the Roberts edge detection filter*

in Figure 7.16, you get the result shown in Figure 7.17. Admittedly, this version is not really an improvement if your goal is to create a realistic image of the squirrel in its habitat. You could try applying the last filter on a copy of the layer and then adjusting the blending mode to get a more natural result.

7.2 The Principles of Preprocessing

In this section, we introduce you to the general principles of preprocessing.

Subjective Aspects of Preprocessing

Image preprocessing enhances the visibility of the elements that we're interested in within an image. In other words, the aim is to restore the original information as faithfully as possible. Generally speaking, preprocessing methods make pixels in the same regions more similar or increase the differences among pixels in different regions. But defining exactly what makes up a "region" is difficult.

As mentioned at the beginning of this chapter, preprocessing is more commonly used in scientific imaging applications than when creating decorative imagery or photos for fun. If a photographer wants to touch up portraits he's taken of an actor, he'll probably use the techniques from Chapters 2 and 5, not the techniques in this chapter. Erasing wrinkles or blemishes doesn't require a lot of information, just a steady hand and a little time.

On the contrary, biologists often want to extract as much information as possible from a *micrograph*, a photo taken through a microscope. If they want to enhance the image quality, they can't use techniques that degrade the information contained in the image. This also holds true for an intelligence agent using a photo taken via satellite or for an astronomer using a photo taken through a telescope.

The techniques used in this chapter modify the look of an image so you can extract information from it more easily. They remove useless and detrimental information (i.e., noise) to reinforce the meaningful information.

The idea of improving an image is a highly subjective one. But the human eye is especially sensitive to high contrasts, so the techniques we present here are generally intended to increase an image's contrast, as it's is the best way to improve visibility within a scene.

Although this chapter's appeal is narrower than that of previous chapters, we think the techniques presented here can be useful to almost anyone who processes photographs with GIMP. In particular, the noise-reduction and edge-detection techniques have a variety of applications. Moreover, this information will help you to build a more thorough understanding of GIMP's capabilities, which might come in handy when you least expect it.

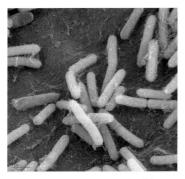

Figure 7.18 *A micrograph of bacteria*

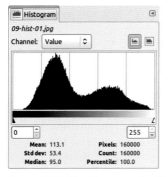

Figure 7.19 *The histogram for Figure 7.18*

Histograms and Decomposition into Channels

The main purpose of image preprocessing is to get information that helps make the image more readable. When you use the image histogram to make adjustments, you change the individual pixel intensities. This transformation does not change the shape of the regions, but it can change their texture, color, luminosity, or contrast with the surroundings.

Figure 7.18 is a grayscale photo of bacteria that was taken with a microscope. Figure 7.19 shows its corresponding histogram. Among the 160,000 pixels in this image, 1684 of them have a value of 77, in the interval from 0 to 255.

Choose the Levels tool and adjust the image's only level, as shown in Figure 7.20. The result appears in Figure 7.21 with its histogram. The histogram now spans the entire range, but not all values are represented because the total number

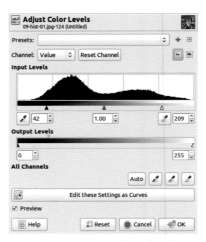

Figure 7.20 *Improving the value dynamics*

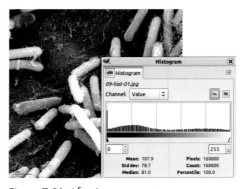

Figure 7.21 *After improvement*

of discrete colors is less than the length of the interval [0:255]. The contrast has been increased, and the resulting image is more readable.

Figure 7.22 shows a micrograph of human blood, this time in color. Figure 7.23 shows the combined histograms for this image. You see that these histograms each have two separated peaks of different heights and in different positions depending on the channel chosen. The Red channel extends further into the high values than the other two, but none of the channels extends all the way to 255.

You can get more information by decomposing the image into its three channels using **Image: Colors > Components > Decompose**. From

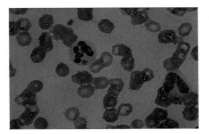

Figure 7.22 *A micrograph of human blood*

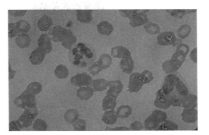

Figure 7.25 *The Red channel for Figure 7.22*

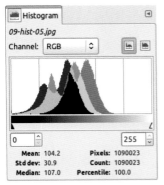

Figure 7.23 *The combined histograms for Figure 7.22*

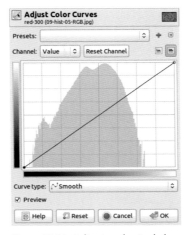

Figure 7.26 *Adjusting the Red channel*

Figure 7.24 *The Decompose tool dialog*

the dialog that appears (Figure 7.24), choose the first color model—RGB. Leave DECOMPOSE TO LAYERS checked, and click OK. A new image is created with a layer for each channel. Each layer is a grayscale representation of the corresponding channel. For example, Figure 7.25 shows the Red layer.

One useful tool for improving these channels separately is **Image: Colors > Curves**. When you apply it to the layer corresponding to the Red channel, you get Figure 7.26. Click the small button on the right, just above the curve, to get

a logarithmic histogram. In this histogram, the height of the vertical bars is not proportional to the number of pixels: The ratio between the height and the number decreases as the height increases. In many cases, this type of histogram is more readable.

Adjust the curve as shown in Figure 7.27 to keep only the interesting parts of the histogram. Figure 7.28 shows the result with the corresponding altered histogram. Note the white vertical bars that correspond to the unrepresented values.

Do the same thing with the other two channels: Select the corresponding layer, select the Curves tool, and adjust the curve. When you've done this for the three layers, choose **Image: Colors > Components > Recompose**, which

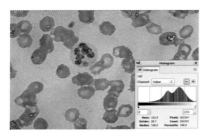

Figure 7.27 *Changing the curve*

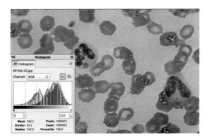

Figure 7.28 *The resulting Red channel*

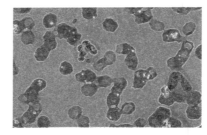

Figure 7.29 *After adjusting the three channels*

reconstitutes the original image using the values of the three channels in the decomposed layers. The result appears in Figure 7.29 with its combined RGB histograms. The image is much more readable, and the biologist can now see and interpret some details that weren't really visible before.

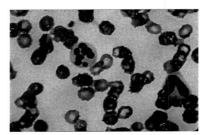

Figure 7.30 *After Image: Colors > Auto > Equalize*

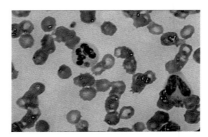

Figure 7.31 *After Image: Colors > Auto > White Balance*

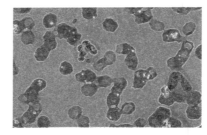

Figure 7.32 *After Image: Colors > Auto > Color Enhance*

Extracting Information through Dynamics Extension

In the previous tutorial, we used some automatic tools to extend an image's dynamics, but the results weren't very good. Although they can be useful in some cases, you clearly shouldn't depend on automatic tools to adjust an image's dynamics. In this section, we use several automatic tools on a micrograph of bacteria—with some interesting results.

Figures 7.30 to 7.35 show the result of using the six entries from the **Image: Colors > Auto** menu. In this case, the best choice is not a matter of taste but rather of utility. The biologist

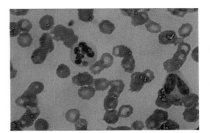

Figure 7.33 *After Image: Colors >
Auto > Normalize*

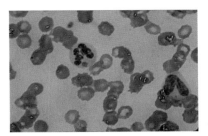

Figure 7.34 *After Image: Colors >
Auto > Stretch Contrast*

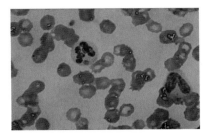

Figure 7.35 *After Image: Colors >
Auto > Stretch HSV*

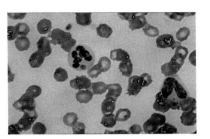

Figure 7.36 *After using Auto in the Levels tool*

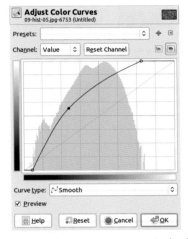

Figure 7.37 *Increasing gray pixel values (darkening)*

who will interpret this picture will choose the transformation that provides her with the most significant information.

transformations are global and cannot be parameterized. They work on all the channels in the same way, although the Stretch HSV transformation operates on the HSV model rather than the RGB one. For comparison, Figure 7.36 shows the effect of using the Auto button in the Levels tool. That transformation operates separately on each channel, removing the lowest values in the histograms, so it takes away some

background noise but can also delete meaningful information.

Next, try some more complicated manipulations with the Curves tool. Work only on the Value channel (i.e., the grayscale values), although you could also work on the three color channels separately. In each case, first apply the curve modification shown in Figure 7.27 to remove the unrepresented extreme values.

In the sequence of figures from 7.37 to 7.44, you see the modification made to each curve, its effect (stated in each figure's caption), and the resulting image. The results are fairly diverse, and some of them are probably not very useful. In these last examples, the correlation among channels, and thus the general hue, was maintained in the images. Note that if you use the Auto button in the Levels tool, the correlation

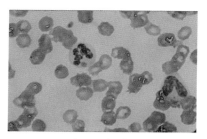

Figure 7.38 *The result of increasing pixel values*

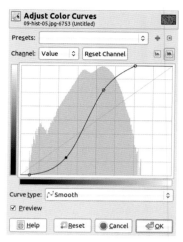

Figure 7.41 *Homogenizing gray pixel values*

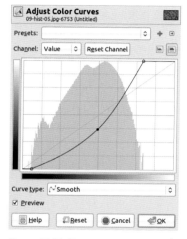

Figure 7.39 *Decreasing gray pixel values (lightening)*

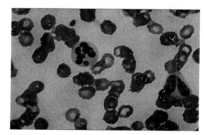

Figure 7.42 *The result of homogenizing pixel values*

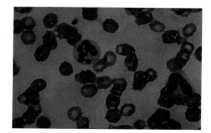

Figure 7.40 *The result of decreasing pixel values*

would not be maintained. For most users, this makes no difference.

A variety of manipulations are possible with the Curves tool. Changing the shape of the curves can lead to interesting results—but more often to weird and useless results. For example, Figure 7.45 shows a bizarre curve applied to the

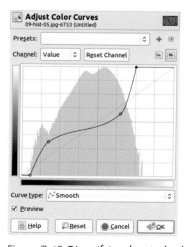

Figure 7.43 *Diversifying the pixel values*

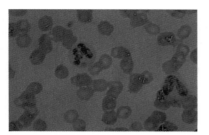

Figure 7.44 *The result of diversifying pixel values*

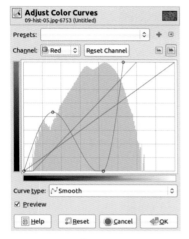

Figure 7.45 *A bizarre curve*

Red channel. A similar curve was applied to the two other channels to create Figure 7.46, which probably does not provide the biologist with any additional useful information.

7.3 Filtering

Filtering removes noise from an image. In this section, we'll introduce the concept behind filtering and show you some common techniques.

The Principles of Filtering

Noise occurs in images for several reasons:

- The photograph was taken in poor conditions; there was not enough light, as in

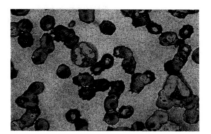

Figure 7.46 *The result of applying bizarre curves to all channels*

Figure 7.47 *Noise due to poor conditions*

Figure 7.48 *Noise because the photographer moved*

Figure 7.47, or the photographer moved, as in Figure 7.48.

- The camera was a very low-cost model with too few CCD sensors, which generated strong RGB noise, as shown in Figure 7.49.
- The sampling frequency was too low, as shown in Figure 7.50. This noise is typical in a photograph taken from a mobile phone.
- The printed photograph has been scratched or otherwise damaged, as in Figure 7.51.

Figure 7.49 *Noise caused by too few image sensors*

Figure 7.51 *Noise due to photograph scratching*

Figure 7.50 *Noise due to low sampling frequency*

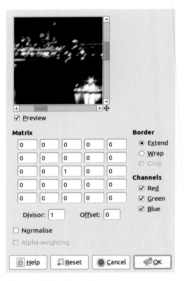

Figure 7.52 *The Convolution Matrix filter dialog*

The most common way to reduce the noise in an image is to use *filtering*. The idea is to reduce the amplitude of the perturbations in areas that should be consistent, such as a wall or the surface of an object, while preserving the transition areas, which are the borders between objects and their surroundings. If possible, these transition areas should actually be emphasized.

Characteristic Matrices

Filtering changes every pixel value, depending on the values of neighboring pixels. A filter is defined by the formula or mathematical mechanism that computes this new value.

We will consider only the simplest and most frequently used filters from among those available in GIMP. The noise reduction filters are found in various submenus of the **Image: Filters** menu. The most general one is **Image: Filters > Generic > Convolution Matrix**, which brings up the dialog shown in Figure 7.52.

The MATRIX is an array of numbers with five rows and five columns. Initially only the center point contains a value different from zero, in this

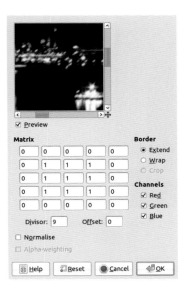

Figure 7.53 *A noise attenuation matrix*

Figure 7.54 *After applying an averaging filter to Figure 7.49*

0	0	0	0	0
0	1	2	1	0
0	2	4	2	0
0	1	2	1	0
0	0	0	0	0

Divisor: 16   Offset: 0

Figure 7.55 *A Gaussian filter matrix*

case 1. This means every pixel is replaced by itself (i.e., it is unchanged).

You can modify matrix entries to create various effects. If you change one entry, pressing the TAB key takes you to the next one, and its content is selected. If you then key in a new value, it replaces the previous one. In Figure 7.53, we set the eight entries that surround the center entry to 1, which means the new pixel is computed as the sum of itself and its eight immediate neighbors. To calculate the pixel value as the average of these nine values, set the DIVISOR to 9.

As the preview shows, this filter reduces the noise and smooths the image. Figure 7.54 shows the result on the image from Figure 7.49. The Convolution Matrix filter is easy to use, but be warned: The resulting image is blurred. Because its matrix has five rows and five columns, you could define a larger filter by adding the four points in the middle of the matrix sides. The DIVISOR would then be 13. The neighboring pixels used by the filter should be evenly spaced around the central target pixel.

You can use the same filter with different values in the matrix. For example, Figure 7.55 shows the values for a Gaussian blur, where the pixels closer to the central pixel are weighted more heavily. Of course, the DIVISOR must be adjusted appropriately. This filter blurs the image even more than the preceding one.

Comparing the Built-in Filters

Of the many filters in the **Image: Filters** menu, several are genuine preprocessing filters. For example, take the **Image: Filters > Blur** menu. The Blur entry is not very useful because you can't change the settings. Focus Blur and Motion Blur are used for specialized effects. The most useful entries for preprocessing are the two Gaussian filters. Figures 7.56 to 7.58 show various results of using these filters on the image in Figure 7.49. As you can see, the Selective Gaussian Blur filter worked best for this image.

Another useful filter is **Image: Filters > Enhance > Despeckle**. The Despeckle filter is called

Figure 7.56 *After applying an IIE Gaussian Blur filter with a radius of 5 to Figure 7.49*

Figure 7.58 *After applying the Selective Gaussian Blur filter with a radius of 8 to Figure 7.49*

Figure 7.57 *After applying an RLE Gaussian Blur filter with a radius of 8 to Figure 7.49*

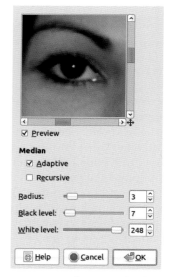

Figure 7.59 *The Despeckle filter dialog*

a *median filter*. It doesn't use the same method as the Convolution Matrix, although it relies on a matrix too. Figure 7.59 shows its dialog, and Figure 7.60 shows the result of applying the Despeckle filter to the image in Figure 7.51. You could hide the remaining scratches by adjusting the parameters. As a matter of fact, simply checking the RECURSIVE checkbox, which repeats the filter's last action, would work, but doing so would increase the blurring as well. Still, aesthetically, the result could be considered an improvement over the initial photograph.

The preprocessing filters that we've tried so far all have the same drawback: They blur the image to some degree. The blurring is because, by averaging the values of neighboring pixels, these filters decrease the image quality at strong transitions, which delimit the various regions of the image. Sharpening, on the other hand, strengthens the transitions.

Sharpening can be done by building a specific convolution matrix with a more complicated pattern than what you used before. You can also apply **Image: Filters > Enhance > NL Filter**, but

Figure 7.62 *After applying Unsharp Mask to Figure 7.48 twice*

Figure 7.60 *After using the Despeckle filter on Figure 7.51*

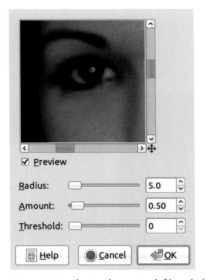

Figure 7.63 *The original photograph*

Figure 7.61 *The Unsharp Mask filter dialog*

7.4 Edge Detection

choosing the correct parameters is challenging. The best sharpening filter by far is the familiar filter with the paradoxical name: **Image: Filters > Enhance > Unsharp Mask**. Its dialog is shown in Figure 7.61.

RADIUS sets the thickness of the image edges. AMOUNT sets the effect intensity of the mask. Keeping the amount value low (0.25 to 0.5) is generally best. If necessary, repeat the action two or more times. This is what we did with Figure 7.48 to get the result shown in Figure 7.62.

In most cases, major variations in intensity in an image correspond to edges of objects. You can often extract objects in an image by detecting these variations through a process called *segmentation*. In GIMP, you can do this using the *edge detection* tools.

The Principles of Edge Detection

Technically, the edges in an image are any areas where the intensity presents a strong local

Figure 7.64 *After a strong Gaussian blur*

Figure 7.65 *The Edge-Detect menu*

variation. Edge detection is a fundamental part of extracting information from an image during preprocessing. Often, the discovered edges are then fed to a shape recognition system. Shape recognition has applications in robotics, medical image analysis, video surveillance, and other fields.

We won't go into the mathematical details of the various edge detection methods available. Instead, we'll demonstrate several of them on one image—the photograph in Figure 7.63. To make this image worthy of edge detection, we first apply a strong blur to it by applying **Image: Filters > Blur > Gaussian Blur**. The result is shown in Figure 7.64.

Edge Detection Methods

The edge detection filters in GIMP are all found in the **Image: Filters > Edge-Detect** menu (see

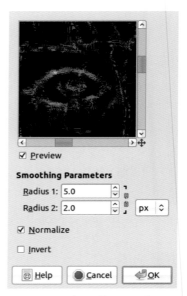

Figure 7.66 *The Difference of Gaussians dialog*

Figure 7.67 *After Difference of Gaussians edge detection*

Figure 7.65). Here, we explore the various entries on this menu.

Choosing **Image: Filters > Edge-Detect > Difference of Gaussians** brings up the dialog shown in Figure 7.66. Here, we adjusted the radius and suggest you do the same. We also unchecked the INVERT box. Figure 7.67 shows

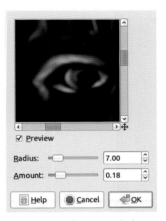

Figure 7.68 *The Neon dialog*

Figure 7.70 *After Laplace edge detection and applying Stretch Contrast*

Figure 7.69 *After Neon edge detection*

Figure 7.71 *The Edge dialog*

the result. Edge detection using the Difference of Gaussians filter worked rather poorly, at least for this image.

Image: Filters > Edge-Detect > Neon works better for this image. Figure 7.68 shows this filter's dialog with the settings we used. See the result in Figure 7.69. Note that the important features of the image are much more visible than with the previous filter.

The **Image: Filters > Edge-Detect > Laplace** filter is a bit disconcerting: When you apply it

to this image, no dialog pops up, and the result is completely black. But after applying **Image: Colors > Auto > Stretch Contrast** to this image, you get the result in Figure 7.70. Not great, but better than nothing.

Finally, the most handy tool is **Image: Filters > Edge-Detect > Edge**, which contains six different filters (algorithms). The dialog, shown in Figure 7.71, is simple. The only setting is the AMOUNT. A low amount value results in a black image with thin edges; a high amount value leads to thicker edges and multicolored dark regions.

Figure 7.72 *After Sobel edge detection*

Figure 7.74 *After Gradient edge detection*

Figure 7.73 *After Prewitt compass edge detection*

Figure 7.75 *After Differential edge detection and applying Stretch Contrast*

Figure 7.72 shows the result of applying Sobel edge detection with an AMOUNT of 6.5. Figure 7.73 shows the result of applying Prewitt compass edge detection with an AMOUNT of 10. Figure 7.74 shows the result of applying Gradient edge detection with the same AMOUNT.

Stretching the contrast of an image you've used edge detection on may be useful. For example, we got the image shown in Figure 7.75 by using Differential edge detection with an AMOUNT of 2.5 and then applying **Image: Colors > Auto > Stretch Contrast**.

You can use an edge detection filter to decompose the image into more readable objects. We show this in two different examples.

Figure 7.76 *Edge detection combined with the original image (Figure 7.63)*

To create Figure 7.76 from Figure 7.63, do the following:

1. Duplicate the layer.

2. Add an Alpha channel to the top layer (**Layers: right-click > Add Alpha Channel**).

3. Apply an edge detection filter to this layer (in this case, **Image: Filters > Edge-Detect > Edge > Sobel**).

4. Choose the Select by Color tool (SHIFT+O) and click a black area in the image.

5. Cut the selection (CTRL+X).

6. Hide the selection (CTRL+T).

Another possible use for edge detection is demonstrated in Figure 7.77. Begin with the image from Figure 7.22 on page 167. Duplicate the layer and apply the edge detection operator Sobel, as we did in the previous example. Finally, we experiment with the various merging modes in the Layers window to find the one that suits our needs. We choose Screen.

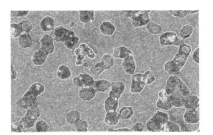

Figure 7.77 *Merging edge detection with the original image (Figure 7.22)*

7.5 Exercises

For these exercises, feel free to utilize the images on this book's website (*http://the-book-of-gimp.blogspot.com*).

Exercise 7.1. One simple tool we did not use in this chapter is **Image: Colors > Threshold**. Try using it on a poor-quality image. Experiment with the placement of the cursors. Try to remove noise and to emphasize the important parts of the image.

Exercise 7.2. Because the Threshold tool generates a black and white image, combine its result with the initial image in a different layer. Try various merging modes until you feel that you've increased the amount of information that a researcher could extract from your image.

Exercise 7.3. Try using the image generated by the Threshold tool to fill a layer mask added to the original image. Do this again, but this time invert the threshold image.

Exercise 7.4. Find an image that's difficult to interpret, either one that we've provided or one of your own. Try various methods for improving the edges and making the image's information more readable. Use a combination of edge detection tools, layer merging modes, and other tools that we demonstrated in this chapter.

8 Designing a Website

GIMP includes a number of tools that are handy for designing a website, including guides, grids, and layers. Guides and snaps to grid make the design process more accurate, and layers allow you to try various ideas and quickly toggle between them to see what works best.

8.1 Tutorial: Laying Out a Website

If you're planning to build a website or are designing one for someone else, you need to decide how the graphics will be laid out. Sometimes knowing what will look good until you actually see it is hard. In this tutorial, we create a prototype of a website about healthy food. This site will offer information about different foods and services to help people plan their meals, track their progress, and so on.

Planning

Before creating graphics or choosing colors, make a plan for the website. Start by writing down what the website should bring to its visitors.

Visitors can be divided into two main types: first-time and repeat. First-time visitors should be able to navigate the website easily and find what they're looking for quickly. Repeat visitors should find reasons to come back regularly. They should be able to check new content and use the website services effortlessly.

The next step is to lay out the blocks that will constitute the website. You should have a block for new content, displayed in a prominent place, which all visitors will see. New visitors, or returning visitors who are not yet registered members, will also see beginner blocks to help them decide what to read. Registered visitors will instead get member blocks that display their personal goals and progress.

Now arrange the blocks. You may want to draw a sketch on paper first to let your ideas take form, or you can fire up GIMP to sketch a draft digitally. In this tutorial, we use the 960 Grid System to help us calculate the dimensions of the blocks in a page that's 960 pixels wide. The 960 Grid System (*http://960.gs/*) offers a set of prototyping resources: templates in 12, 16, and 24 columns, including templates for GIMP with preset guides; sketch sheets like the one in Figure 8.1; CSS files; and example HTML files. You can also create a custom GIMP template if you prefer another page layout (**Image: File > Create Template**).

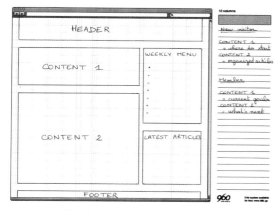

Figure 8.1 *Sketch on paper: laying out blocks*

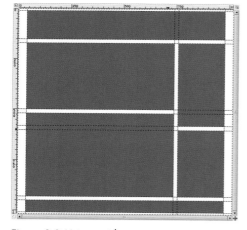

Figure 8.2 *Using guides*

Layout

If you decided to use the 960 Grid System to build this design, you can translate your sketch sheet into the provided GIMP template, as shown in Figure 8.2. If not, use your custom template with the guides placed where you prefer. You will have to define your own CSS files, however, without the help of 960 Grid System files.

Drag guides from the image rulers to mark the boundaries of the blocks. Choose 960 pixels as the total width of the page and delineate a right column that's 220 pixels wide; add 20-pixel margins around the design and 10-pixel margins between blocks. Verify that the **Image: View > Snap to Guides** option is checked so you can use the Rectangle Select tool to select a block and fill it. Use a middle-range gray (#808080) to fill the blocks. Figure 8.2 shows the result.

Being able to change the color of a block with one click makes color prototyping faster. To set this up, build a rectangular outline around each block:

- Create a new transparent layer, and place it at the top of the layers stack. It will contain all the block outlines.

- Select the Rectangle Select tool, and draw a rectangle using the guides.

- Select **Image: Edit > Stroke Selection**. In the dialog that opens, choose to stroke a line in a solid color with a width of 2 pixels. Choose a color that contrasts with your design.

- Repeat these steps for each of the six blocks.

Adding Color

To colorize a block, use the Bucket Fill tool in the transparent layer you created. From the Bucket Fill options, select FILL SIMILAR COLORS and uncheck SAMPLE MERGED. When you click inside a block, only that block is filled because the Bucket Fill tool fills only contiguous areas of the same color, and the outline surrounding the block is a different color. You can then build new layers with different colors and hide various layers to reveal the different options. If you click outside of any block, your color fills the margins of the layout, which is considered the background of the page you're building.

Always be aware of the margins, header and footer height, and column width. Changing any of these can drastically alter the feel of the design.

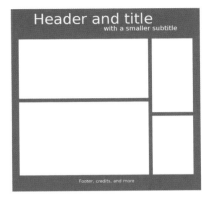

Figure 8.3 *Monochrome test*

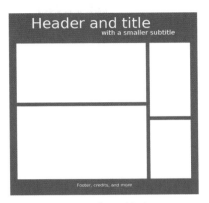

Figure 8.4 *One color added*

Choosing a Color Palette

Next, choose a color palette for the website. You can choose a palette in several ways: Pick colors using the Color chooser, use the eye dropper to pick colors from a photo or an illustration that will be included in the design, or browse through palette collections that other people have designed. With GNU/Linux, you can use the Agave color scheme generator.

For this website, we want a palette that includes red, orange, yellow, green, and brown. These colors seem bright and energetic, which is the feeling we want for our website. Choose at least one deep color and one soft color to add contrast to the design. Alternatively, start with a monochrome palette, and add different hues when the design looks good in black and white.

For our site, we first try a mid-dark background with bright blocks, as shown in Figure 8.3. The header and footer blend into the background, so we need bright text colors to make them readable. We add placeholder titles to see how text will look in this design. We start with a neutral font (Sans), with a size of 80 pixels for the main heading and 36 pixels for the subheading.

In the final website, header titles can either be text or an image. Text is nice because the reader (and search engines) can interact with it, but you need to choose a web-safe font, so your choices are limited. Note you'll need to make the titles

Figure 8.5 *Two colors added*

readable for vision-impaired viewers by adding the proper tags in the HTML file.

Now add colors: We add a deep green in the background to remind viewers of vegetables and nature (to convey the "healthy" feeling). See the result in Figure 8.4. Then, we fill the content blocks with a neutral pale yellow, which looks nice with the green but isn't too distracting. The result is shown in Figure 8.5. To make the side menus more colorful, we use orange, to complement the green and yellow, as shown in Figure 8.6.

The design has enough contrast, but it lacks energy. We need more bright colors. We can add color to the header, to the illustrations that will decorate the page, or to action buttons like "Buy now" or "Register". We decide to color the

Figure 8.6 *Three colors added*

Figure 8.7 *Four colors added*

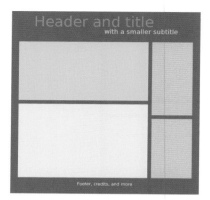

Figure 8.8 *Five colors added*

Figure 8.9 *Final palette for the website*

header a really bright orange, as you can see in Figure 8.7.

Next we add one more bright color. Bright yellow could fit, but bright lime green is even better as it looks nice with the dark green in the background. This website doesn't have any big action buttons, but we want new users to be drawn to the block that describes the website's strong points and its services. We color that block bright lime green so it stands out. Figure 8.8 shows the result, and our palette is shown in Figure 8.9.

This palette was built using the Color chooser: The first color (green) has an HSV value of (75, 100, 50); the second color (orange) is HSV (30, 100, 100); the third color (the darker yellow) is (44, 62, 100); the fourth color (the lighter yellow) is (60, 30, 100); the fifth color (a yellow-green) is (75, 50, 100). The H channel (the first number) determines the general hue; the S channel (the second number) determines whether the color is saturated or pastel; and the V channel (the last number) determines whether it's light or dark.

Save this palette in the Palettes dockable dialog (**Image: Windows > Dockable Dialogs**). Create a new palette by clicking the second button from left in the bottom row. In the Palette Editor, add colors to your palette from the current foreground or background color, edit a color, or delete it.

To use the new palette, click the color you want in the Palette Editor to set the foreground color or CTRL-click to set the background color.

We liven up the page by adding illustrations as new layers with transparent backgrounds. The result is shown in Figure 8.10.

Now we do some fine-tuning. We adjust the font to make the header more attractive and shrink the footer because it takes up too much space. Figure 8.11 shows the new layout.

The blocks look a little cramped, so we add white margins around them, as shown in

Figure 8.10 *Illustrations added*

Figure 8.12 *With white margins*

Figure 8.11 *With a new font and a smaller footer*

Figure 8.13 *Bigger margins*

Figure 8.12. To create the margins, add a layer below the blocks, create a rectangular selection around the blocks, increase it by 10 pixels (**Image: Select > Grow**), and fill it with white.

The margins around the blocks are barely visible, so we widen them from 10 pixels to 20 pixels, as shown in Figure 8.13. This time we want to shrink the blocks and move the guides 10 pixels toward the center of each block. We create a selection that's 10 pixels in from the current edges of the block by following the guides, invert the selection to select only the outer 10 pixels of the block, and then cut the selection to reveal more white border.

8.2 Fixed- and Variable-Width Designs

When creating a website, you can decide whether the size of the browser window affects the size of the page. A *fixed-width design* remains at a constant width (in pixels) regardless of the browser width. If the browser window is larger than the page width, borders appear. Fixed-width designs are generally centered, so a border appears to the left and to the right of the design. If the browser window is smaller than the page width, only part of the page is visible, and a horizontal scrollbar appears.

A *variable-width design* (also called *liquid design*) changes width with the browser width, and

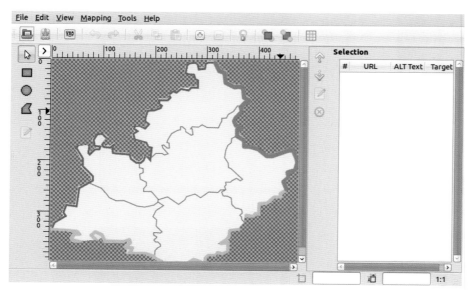

Figure 8.14 *The Image Map dialog*

at least one section of the design (usually, the main content block) is resized along with the browser window. Creating a design that will look good with any browser width is difficult, especially now that browsers can be very small (for handheld devices) or very large (for huge movie screens).

Variable-width designs can fill a variety of screens, unlike fixed-width designs that leave empty space or add a scrollbar. Fixed-width designs allow better readability, unlike variable-width designs whose content may be squeezed into a tiny column or expanded into long lines that are hard to read. On the other hand, fixed-width designs also give you more control over the layout, image placement, and column length.

To prototype a fixed-width design with GIMP, create a new image with the chosen width. Its height can be the minimum browser height, or it can be larger if users will need to scroll down to see the footer. If you're prototyping a variable-width web page, you can choose any width and height. If some of the elements on the page

will change size, while others remain fixed, you may want to create several prototypes of various widths to see how the elements look together as the page is resized.

8.3 Web Design Tools

Although GIMP wasn't designed for web development or design, it does include some useful tools for preparing images for the Web, including two found in the **Image: Filter > Web** menu, which let you delimit areas in an image so you can make something happen when a visitor clicks or hovers over those areas. This menu also contains a tool for handling GIF images.

Image Map

Image: Filters > Web > Image Map uses an image to build a clickable map that you can integrate into a web page. The map is divided into non-overlapping regions, and a link is attached to each region. When users click in one of the regions, they are taken to the corresponding link.

Figure 8.15 *The Area Settings dialog, Link tab*

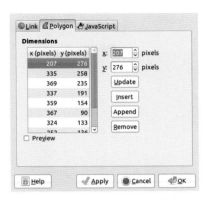

Figure 8.16 *The Area Settings dialog, Polygon tab*

Figure 8.17 *Access one Tools menu by right-clicking in the Image Map dialog.*

The Image Map dialog, shown in Figure 8.14, has two main regions: the source of the image map displayed on the left, and the URLs attached to regions of the image displayed on the right. The dialog also has a row of buttons at the top for editing the defined area and columns of buttons along both sides of the image preview. The left column contains buttons for selecting and defining areas and editing information linked to an area. The right column contains buttons for moving, editing, or deleting information linked to an area. To create the image map, click one of the three blue buttons defining a geometric shape, draw the shape on the image, and then attach a URL to it.

To draw a rectangle or a circle, click and drag to create the shape and then click once more to complete the shape. To draw a polygon, click at each vertex and double-click to place the final point and complete the shape. Once the shape is complete, a dialog similar to the one shown in Figure 8.15 appears. Choose the link type and then enter or paste in the link address. You can either use an absolute address beginning with `http://` or a relative address that is an internal link within your website. You can also enter ALT TEXT to display when the mouse hovers over the link and in the event the link doesn't work.

The second tab of the Area Settings dialog varies depending on the shape of the map. Here you can change some of the coordinates manually. Figure 8.16 shows the dialog for a polygon. The third tab, not shown, can be used to define JavaScript sequences and link them to specific events.

Image Map Tools

One TOOLS menu is accessed by clicking the triangle button at the top left of the another is accessed by right-clicking in the Image Map dialog while the pointer is active (Figure 8.17). Although these menus have the same name, they contain different entries. The first Tools menu is for handling the grid and the guides, whereas the second Tools menu contains the four tools also found in the left column of the Image Map dialog and in the MAPPING menu in the menu bar.

The Arrow tool, which appears as an arrow on the left side of the dialog, allows you to select an area that you've already defined and move or resize it. The Edit tool allows you to change

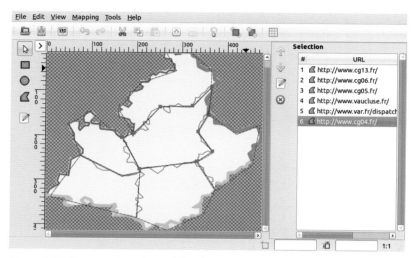

Figure 8.18 *Six areas have been defined.*

the parameters associated with the selected area. You can also select the link from the list on the right side of the dialog to select the corresponding area.

Figure 8.18 shows a map of Provence-Alpes-Côte-d'Azur, with six areas corresponding to French *départements* outlined and associated with appropriate URLs. If you click one of the shapes while the pointer tool is active, that shape is selected, and you can change the vertices. You can edit the information associated with a shape by double-clicking the URL in the right column or by clicking the Edit button in either of the two columns.

Useful Image Map Dialogs

Selecting **Edit > Preferences** opens the dialog shown in Figure 8.19, which has three tabs. Here, you can set various parameters that adjust the filter interface or the HTML page you are building. On the Menu tab, you can change the number of undo levels or the colors used in the tool dialog, for example.

The grid can be toggled on and off via **Tools > Grid**, and selecting **Tools > Grid Settings** opens the dialog shown in Figure 8.20, where you can set the grid's characteristics. The Image Map

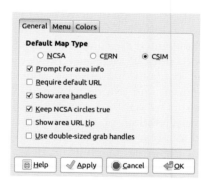

Figure 8.19 *Image Map preferences*

grid is similar to the grid used in the Image window, discussed in Chapter 10.

Selecting **Tools > Create Guides** opens the dialog shown in Figure 8.21. The guides delimit a predefined number of rectangles to which links can be associated. The guides help you to draw a simple map quickly. Note the default number of rectangles is zero, and if you don't change this number the tools will have no effect.

Selecting **Tools > Use GIMP Guides** produces a result similar to that produced by the Slice filter, discussed shortly.

When you save the image map (by selecting **File > Save**, pressing CTRL+S, or clicking the

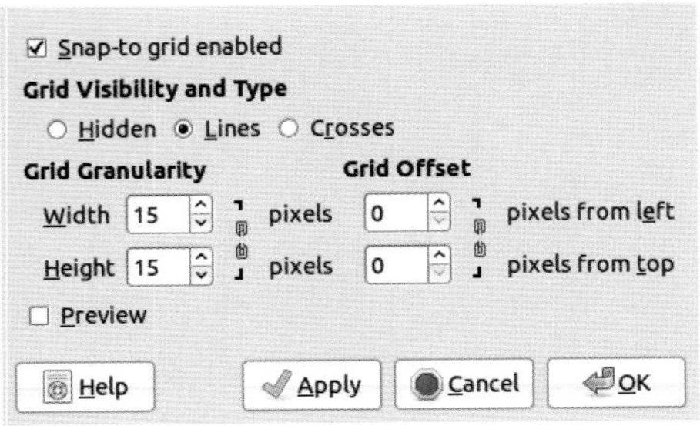

Figure 8.20 *The Grid Settings dialog*

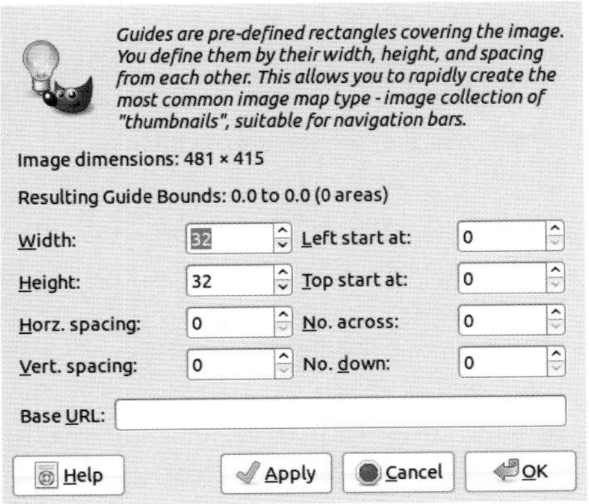

Figure 8.22 *Initial image*

Figure 8.21 *The Create Guides dialog*

Figure 8.23 *After semi-flattening*

SAVE button), the filter generates a file with a .map suffix. This HTML file contains the `<img>` tag for loading the image and the corresponding `<map>` tag with definitions of all the `<area>` tags. Note that the generated file does not necessarily contain the name of the image file to which it refers.

Semi-Flatten

Image: Filters > Web > Semi-Flatten has no dialog. It simulates antialiasing in a GIF image displayed on a web page.

Antialiasing smooths the edges of an object by making pixels along the boundary semi-transparent, as shown in Figure 8.22. Because GIF encoding can only represent 0% transparency or 100% transparency, you can't use anti-aliasing. You could use PNG instead of GIF, but some browsers don't handle PNG encoding properly. As a way to simulate semi-transparency, the Semi-Flatten filter creates pixels that contain a blend of the foreground color and the background color along the edge of the image. To use Semi-Flatten, set the background color to that of the web page background. Figure 8.23 shows the result when the background color is a deep pink.

Slice

Image: Filters > Web > Slice is another tool that lets you split an image into sections. Suppose you want to display a large rectangular image on a web page. The image will be cut into smaller rectangular fragments along a grid. Slice lets you choose to display only some of these fragments or to change their appearance when the mouse pointer hovers over them. Slice also lets you set fragments to trigger some specific action when clicked.

Figure 8.24 *The image to be cut into pieces*

Figure 8.25 *Guides for slicing*

For example, say we want to use the image shown in Figure 8.24 as a background for an HTML table. We define areas that correspond to the squares in the table, using a grid that covers the entire image.

Drag new guides from the image sides to the places where you want to make a slice. The result is shown in Figure 8.25.

Click **Image: Filters > Web > Slice** to finish the job. The image is sliced into several pieces, and a file with the .html suffix is created that

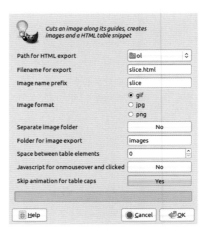

Figure 8.26 *Options for the files generated by Slice*

contains the code for the HTML table. You can add the contents of this file to the code of your web page. You'll also need to include the image fragments wherever you keep the web page's image files.

The options dialog that appears, shown in Figure 8.26, lets you choose the various parameters of the generated files and of the images built from the slices in the initial image. You can name the HTML file, choose where to store it, and enter a prefix and format for the separate cell files, as well as the location where they will be stored. If there are spaces between the images, the web page background will show through. A JavaScript snippet may be called when the mouse is on a cell, but you can choose to freeze the border cells so they can't be selected or changed.

8.4 Optimizing Images for the Web

The three formats best suited to the Web are JPEG, PNG, and GIF. These file formats can be handled by all the major browsers, with some restrictions in the case of Internet Explorer. These formats use compression algorithms to decrease the size of the file, which increases the page's download speed. Even though high-speed Internet access is common, users who still have a slow connection will appreciate any attempt to minimize the size of image files.

Here we summarize the most important aspects of these three formats, and in Chapter 20, we go into much more detail.

JPEG

The JPEG format is the best suited for photos due to its 24-bit color depth, which lets it render a large number of colors. JPEG is also good for rendering gradients, which are sometimes poorly rendered by the GIF format. The JPEG compression algorithm reduces the image size and results in a slight loss in detail and color. The loss is cumulative, so the more the image is compressed, the worse it looks.

When exporting a file to JPEG format, you can choose a quality level. The higher the quality, the larger the file. If you check SHOW PREVIEW IN IMAGE WINDOW, a preview of the image with that quality setting appears as a new layer. Under ADVANCED OPTIONS, OPTIMIZE lets you add additional compression. The expanded JPEG Export dialog is shown in Figure 8.27.

GIF

GIF is the oldest and the most limited file format. GIF can only represent up to 256 colors, so it's best suited for simple images with few colors. GIF is commonly used (and well suited) for small animations like the ones described in Chapter 18.

One way to optimize an image in GIF format is to reduce the number of colors in the palette. Begin with 8 colors and then double this number until you're happy with the result. If you get to 256 colors and are still not satisfied, try using a different format. Dithering, which can smooth the image, also increases its size.

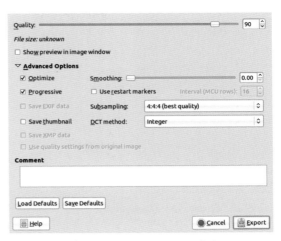

Figure 8.27 *The Export Image as JPEG dialog*

PNG

PNG is, in theory, a versatile format, with 24-bit mode for photographs and 8-bit mode for images with fewer colors. In practice, the 24-bit mode results in files that are too large for the Web, so JPEG is a better choice. The 8-bit mode gives better results than GIF in terms of file size, but PNG is not well supported by Internet Explorer.

You can optimize an 8-bit PNG file using the methods described for GIF: Limit the colors and avoid dithering.

Transparency

Transparency can be handy when you're building a website because it allows you to place graphics of any shape against the background easily. But no file format handles transparency perfectly. The GIF format represents transparency with only 1 bit, so a pixel is either completely opaque or completely transparent. The PNG format can represent transparency using 1 to 8 bits. Although all modern browsers support 8-bit transparency in PNG, many people still use obsolete versions of Internet Explorer, which don't support 8-bit transparency. The JPEG format can't represent transparency at all.

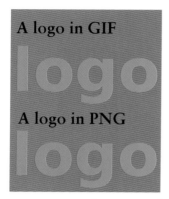

Figure 8.28 *Two logos on a web page*

Figure 8.29 *The PNG logo zoomed in*

If you want to use a round logo and you make the background transparent using 1 bit, the pixels along the edge of the circle will be either fully opaque or fully transparent, so the outline will look jagged and pixelated. If you fill the logo background with the web page's background color and then smooth the edges, the edges will be a mix of the logo color and the background color, which looks better but makes changing the background color of the web page more difficult. If you use 8-bit transparency, the edge is smooth, and you can easily change the background color.

Figure 8.28 shows two logos on a web page. With this zooming factor, the difference is not very visible. Figures 8.29 and 8.30 demonstrate the difference more clearly.

Figure 8.30 *The GIF logo zoomed in*

8.5 Exercises

Exercise 8.1. Download all the files from the 960 Grid System website (*http://960.gs/*). Unpack them in a folder. From the sketch_sheets subfolder, select and print the sketch sheet you prefer. Using this sheet, design the layout of a website to your taste, creating something different from what the tutorial suggests. Then open the proper template in GIMP, found in the templates/gimp subfolder, and fill it with blocks, using your sketch sheet as a model and the template guides to place the blocks correctly.

Exercise 8.2. On the book's website, in the files for this chapter, you'll find a file called tutorial.xcf. This file was used to build the example web page shown in Figures 8.3 to 8.13. Open the file in GIMP and experiment with different colors, images, and fonts to customize the design.

Exercise 8.3. Create a map from one of your own images. Link URLs to the various areas, and add text that visitors will see if they mouse over an area.

Exercise 8.4. Export one of your images as JPEG, GIF, and PNG using the optimization techniques described in Section 8.4. Each time, try to make the file as small as possible while maintaining an acceptable level of quality. Compare the results.

Part II
Reference

9 The GIMP Interface

In Chapter 1, we introduced the basics of the GIMP interface. In this chapter, we go into more detail. GIMP is a powerful, flexible application. A casual user can edit images without learning much about GIMP, but by digging a little deeper, you can better control your images and work more quickly and efficiently.

If you're new to image editing, this chapter teaches you how to work with your images more effectively. If you're switching from another image-editing application, this chapter teaches you the new language of GIMP. As of version 2.8, the GIMP interface has changed significantly, so even if you already know version 2.4 or 2.6, read this chapter carefully to learn about the differences in the new version.

9.1 The Main Windows

Once GIMP is installed on your computer, you can open it as you do other applications, via a shortcut or a menu. The first thing you see when you start GIMP is the splash window, followed by the main windows: the *Image window*, the *Toolbox window*, and the *multi-dialog window*.

The *splash window* is an image that's shown while GIMP loads. It changes with each version of GIMP and is a quick way to check

which version is currently installed on your computer. The splash also displays updates on the loading process. When the splash window disappears, GIMP's three main windows appear. By default, these windows appear as shown in Figure 9.1. If your screen is smaller than 1440×900 pixels, the two vertical windows will be shorter. If your screen is significantly larger, you'll see more space between the three windows. Because these are three separate windows, you'll also see your desktop in the background.

Multi-Window Mode

For some users, *multi-window mode* is a surprise. Most Windows and Mac OS applications, and even many GNU/Linux applications (like GNU Paint, Blender, Inkscape, or OpenOffice Draw), always use *single-window mode*. Multi-window mode doesn't work well in the Windows environment and has been a source of complaint about GIMP among Windows users. GIMP 2.8 also offers single-window mode, which we describe in "Single-Window Mode" on page 197. For now, let's focus on the classic multi-window mode. Most of the explanations that follow, however, also apply to single-window mode.

GIMP's screen layout is fully customizable—you can move the windows or change the height

Figure 9.1 *GIMP's initial windows displayed in multi-window mode*

and width of the two vertical windows, and when you quit GIMP, the changes are saved. Figure 9.2 shows a custom screen layout, where the two vertical windows are placed on the right side of the screen. The Toolbox - Tool Options window (also called the Toolbox dialog) is on the far right, and we've increased its width a little, so each row at the top contains six icons instead of five. To its left is the multi-dialog window, which contains several dialogs, organized into two sets of tabs.

Another GIMP window, Levels, is also shown here, along with the window of a text-editing program (which contains an early draft of Chapter 1 of this book) and a Terminal window. As you can see, multi-window mode lets you work with GIMP and other applications side by side.

The final window in Figure 9.2 is the Image window (shown in the top left). It appears once you open an image in GIMP and is labeled with the name of the image and other basic information about the image. This window also contains the menu bar (unless you're running Ubuntu's Unity interface or Mac OS X).

When GIMP opens, the Image window is empty, as shown in Figure 9.3. At the bottom left is the top of Wilber's head. Wilber is the GIMP mascot, so you'll see him all over GIMP. The top of Image window contains a menu bar with 11 or 12 entries, depending on whether you have the GAP plug-in installed. If you leave the mouse pointer in this window (or in the Wilber strip at the top of the Toolbox), you see a message that says "Drop image files here to open them."

You can access GIMP's features via the menus at the top of the Image window, but using keyboard shortcuts or the Toolbox icons is often more convenient. The Toolbox and the dockable dialogs also let you specify tool options and parameters.

If you're doing detailed work on more than one image at a time, you can quickly end up with over a dozen windows open at once. Although this can get confusing, the benefit is that GIMP allows you to do many things simultaneously, rather than forcing you to cancel one operation before trying another.

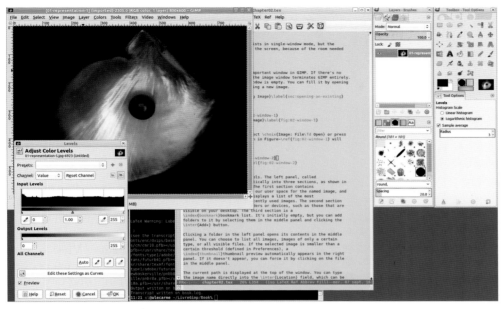

Figure 9.2 *A custom screen layout*

Figure 9.3 *An empty Image window*

Figure 9.4 *The Image: Windows menu*

You can hide all windows except the Image window by pressing TAB. Press TAB again to bring the windows back. By default, all the windows except the Image window are considered *utility windows*. You can change that using the Preferences dialog (see Chapter 22). Utility windows cannot be minimized or maximized, and they move above other open windows whenever you activate the Image window.

Single-Window Mode

As of version 2.8, you can choose between multi-window mode and single-window mode. As shown in Figure 9.4, the **Image: Windows** menu contains a checkbox for SINGLE-WINDOW MODE. If you check it, all the existing GIMP windows are collapsed into a single window that fills the screen. Figure 9.5 shows this window in its initial configuration, with the Toolbox on the left, reduced to the width of three tools, and the multi-dialog window on the right.

You can change this initial layout. In Figure 9.6, we widened the Toolbox and opened two images at the same time. The second image is only visible as a tab at the top of the current image, so we can't look at both images at the same time. We also opened a new dialog, Document History, which is on the bottom left, above the lower part of the Tool Options dialog. We

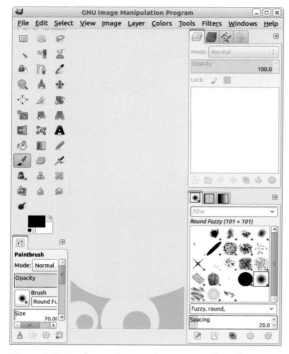

Figure 9.5 *Single-window mode in its initial configuration*

could move this dialog so it becomes a tab in an existing dock, as in multi-window mode, by clicking and dragging its title to the title bar of that dock. The only dialog that you can't move is the Toolbox, but you can temporarily switch to multi-window mode to do that.

As in multi-window mode, hide all docks by pressing TAB or checking the checkbox in the **Image: Windows** menu. Figure 9.7 shows the result. Press TAB again to restore the docks.

If you are working in single-window mode, you can reduce the single window so you can see other running programs, for instance, if you want to click and drag an image thumbnail from a browser or folder to GIMP. But in single-window mode, doing this is rather difficult unless you have a very large screen or a dual-screen configuration.

Sometimes when you open a new dockable dialog in single-window mode, it will be detached

(a separate window), which is counter to the idea of a single window.

If you select the ADD TAB entry in the configuration menu of a dockable dialog, the new dialog is added as a new tab in the current dock, so you'll still have just one window. If you select the **Image: Windows > Dockable Dialogs** menu, the new dialog is created detached.

You can drag a detached dialog to a dock, as explained in "Docking Windows and Dockable Dialogs" on page 198. You can detach a docked dialog using the DETACH TAB entry in its configuration menu (even in single-window mode).

The major limitation of single-window mode is that you cannot view multiple images at the same time, even if you use **Image: View > New View**. You can work on several images, but you must switch between them using tabs. You can click the tabs or press CTRL+PAGEUP or CTRL+PAGEDOWN to switch from image to image.

Many people claim that single-window mode is the most important feature that was missing from GIMP, but there are plenty of long-time GIMP users who still prefer multi-window mode. Try both and find out which works best for you. This will depend on the operating system you use, the size of your screen, and whether you frequently work on several images at the same time.

Docking Windows and Dockable Dialogs

The Toolbox window and the multi-dialog window are *docking windows*, or simply *docks*. They can contain several dialogs, and you can move a dialog from one window to another, hide it, place it outside of any dock, or dock it into another docking window.

By default, the Toolbox window contains a special dialog docked at the bottom, the Tool Options dialog, which changes automatically depending on the tool currently selected. In Figure 9.1, the current tool is the Paintbrush, and the bottom dialog contains the Paintbrush options. The multi-dialog window initially

Figure 9.6 *Single-window mode with two images open*

Figure 9.7 *Single-window mode without any docks*

Figure 9.8 *The Dockable Dialogs menu*

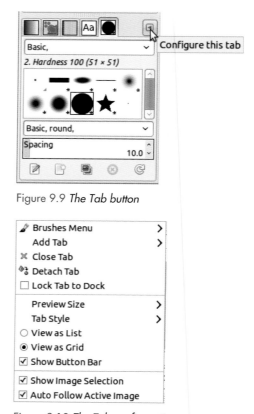

Figure 9.9 *The Tab button*

Figure 9.10 *The Tab configuration menu*

contains seven dialogs. Four of them are docked in the top part of the window, and you can switch among them using tabs, which are labeled with icons. The lower half of the window contains three more dialogs. These seven dialogs are the GIMP defaults because they're often the most useful, but you can remove any that you don't use or add any of the *dockable dialogs* shown in Figure 9.8.

Figure 9.9 shows the position of the Tab button at the top of a dockable dialog, next to the row of tabs. The button is marked with a small triangle, and if you click it, a Tab configuration menu opens, as shown in Figure 9.10. The menu is specific to each dialog, which, in this case, is the Brushes dialog.

If you close a dock, you can reopen it via **Image: Windows > Recently closed docks**. You can rebuild the Tool Options dialog in two ways: via **Image: Windows > Dockable Dialogs > Tool Options** or simply by double-clicking the current tool in the Toolbox. A new window is then created, as shown in Figure 9.11. This window is a new dock, so you can dock any dockable dialogs into it on any of its four sides.

To move a dockable dialog into a dock, grab it by its icon or title and drag it to one side of the dock, as shown in Figure 9.11. In this case, the two dialogs will be side-by-side. You could also dock a dialog on the left side or at the bottom. For example, in Figure 9.12, the Tool Options dialog is being docked at the bottom of the

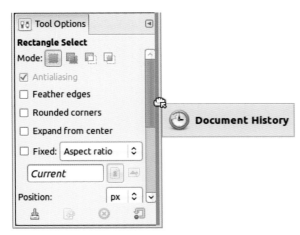

Figure 9.11 *Adding a dockable dialog to a dock*

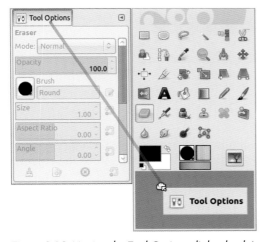

Figure 9.12 *Moving the Tool Options dialog back into the Toolbox window*

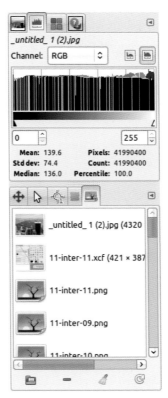

Figure 9.13 *A new dock with two parts and nine tabs*

Figure 9.14 *Selecting a tab to make active*

Toolbox. Note that as you drag the dialog close to the receiving dock, the place where it will dock is emphasized.

You can close dockable dialogs with the Tab configuration menu or open them with **Image: Windows > Dockable dialogs**. If you drag a dialog to the side of an existing dock, the dock enlarges on that side. If you drag a dialog to the top of the dock and drop it next to the existing tabs, the dialog is added as a new tab, without enlarging the dock. You can even make a tab into an independent dock by dragging its title or icon outside the dock.

You can also close all the docks, but it's probably a better idea to just temporarily hide them with $\boxed{\text{TAB}}$. You can create a dock with three levels of tabs, with all dockable dialogs as tabs in a

Menu button   Menu bar   Window resize
                                                                         button

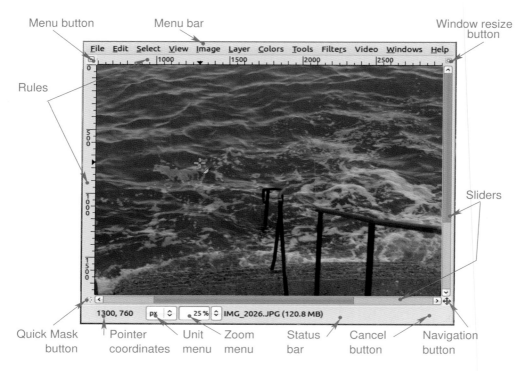

Rules

Sliders

Quick Mask   Pointer   Unit   Zoom   Status   Cancel   Navigation
  button   coordinates   menu   menu   bar   button   button

Figure 9.15 *The Image window and its components*

single dock, and so on. For example, Figure 9.13 shows a dock with two parts and nine tabs, none of which are opened by default.

Compared with many other graphic applications, the GIMP interface is amazingly customizable. GIMP gives you several ways to do the same thing, so you can choose the method you prefer. For example, instead of clicking and dragging, you can move dockable dialogs using the Tab configuration menu. In Figure 9.10, you see an entry for detaching the tab, as well as another menu entry for adding a tab in the same dock section as the current tab. The corresponding submenu lists all the dockable dialogs. You can even open the same dockable dialog in several different places.

In most dockable dialogs, right-clicking in the dialog opens a menu specific to that dialog, which is also the first entry of the Tab configuration menu. The LOCK TAB TO DOCK entry in the

Tab configuration menu, if checked, prevents you from dragging the dialog out of the current dock but not from closing it.

You can drag any tab to a new position in the tab list. To make a tab active, click it, or right-click somewhere in the tab list and choose its icon, as shown in Figure 9.14.

The Image Window

Because the Image window is at the heart of the GIMP interface, let's make sure we're familiar with all its features. Figure 1.15 on page 12 showed the Image window with its main components, and I've included a version here for reference (Figure 9.15).

When opened in GIMP, an image is placed on a *canvas*. The Image window displays a part of the canvas, and you use vertical and horizontal sliders to move the canvas within the window.

Figure 9.16 *Using the navigation button*

Figure 9.17 *The status bar and the cancel button*

If the canvas is smaller than the window, the unused area is filled with a neutral gray. You can also move the canvas in the window in three other ways:

- With the *navigation button* in the bottom-right corner of the window, as shown in Figure 9.16

- By pressing the SPACE key while moving the mouse (but not clicking)

- By using the mouse wheel to scroll up or down (pressing SHIFT while you scroll moves the canvas to the right or the left)

The status bar at the bottom of the window displays various information: the name and size (in memory) of the current layer, a message explaining how to use the current tool, or a progress bar and cancel button if GIMP is applying a filter (Figure 9.17). Note that since version 2.8, transformation tools display their status on the canvas rather than on the status bar.

The pointer coordinates, in the bottom left of the window, specify the exact position of the mouse pointer (if it's in the window). You can change the units for these coordinates using the

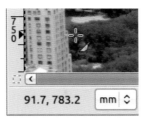

Figure 9.18 *Pointer coordinates in millimeters*

drop-down menu to the right. In Figure 9.18, the coordinates are displayed in millimeters. Note that the coordinates are relative to the image and have nothing to do with the screen coordinates. For more detail, see Chapter 10.

We consider the other components of the Image window later: the rules and the zoom menu in Chapter 10 and the Quick Mask button in Chapter 13.

9.2 Fundamental GIMP Commands

New GIMP users are sometimes put off by the presence of several separate windows and have complained for many years about that. Our advice is to try it first. Multi-window mode lets you view two images at once. It also allows for more control over the sizes of various windows and the placement of dialogs. If you still don't like working with multiple windows, then switch to single-window mode.

Closing Windows and Quitting GIMP

Many people are used to closing windows as soon as they don't need them, even if they plan to reopen them again soon. Users often also simply close a dialog window if they change their mind rather than press CANCEL or NO. This action is necessary in applications with a *blocking interface*. The GIMP interface is *nonblocking*: You can begin several things at the same time, change your mind, leave a question temporarily unanswered without canceling the dialog, and so on. The capability to do several things at once is particularly handy if you need some information before finalizing settings, for example.

What happens if you close one of the GIMP windows? It depends on the window itself. Closing the Image window has two different effects, depending on its contents. If the Image window is empty, closing it quits GIMP and is equivalent to selecting **Image: File > Quit** or pressing CTRL+Q.

Figure 9.19 shows the **Image: File** menu when the Image window is empty. Many entries are grayed out, which means they are irrelevant when there is no current image. The keyboard shortcut to quit GIMP (CTRL+Q) is also shown in the menu.

If the Image window contains an image, closing the window is equivalent to selecting **Image: File > Close** or pressing CTRL+W. If the image has been changed and not yet been saved, GIMP asks whether you want to save the image or discard the changes, as shown in Figure 9.20. Even if you've just exported the image, GIMP asks if you want to save it (as XCF). You can cancel if you decide not to close the image.

The Image window is the only window that closes GIMP when closed. The Toolbox window and the multi-dialog window are only auxiliary windows. You can open and close or hide and recall them (TAB).

In previous versions of GIMP, the Toolbox was the main window. It contained a menu bar different from the Image window menu bar, and closing the Toolbox quit GIMP.

In current versions of GIMP, you can work without the Toolbox because having it available is only a convenience. You can access all the tools it contains via the **Image: Tools** menu, and this menu actually contains more tools than the default Toolbox window. Other dialogs are more useful because you can't access the features they provide in other ways. These include the Tool Options dialog, the Layers dialog, and the Channels dialogs.

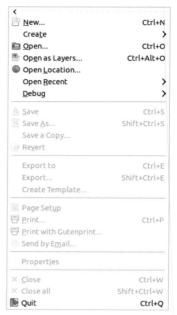

Figure 9.19 *The Image: File menu without an opened image*

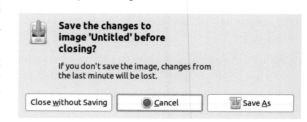

Figure 9.20 *Trying to close an altered image*

Working with Multiple Images

Up to now, we've referred to the Image window as if there was only one. But you can have several Image windows if you open multiple images at the same time. If you close one of them using CTRL+W, **Image: File > Close**, or the button at the top of the window, only that window is closed, and the others remain open. When you close the last open image, you'll see the empty Image window, which you first saw when GIMP started. You can also close all the open images without quitting GIMP by pressing $\boxed{\text{SHIFT+CTRL+W}}$ or selecting **Image: File > Close all**.

When you have several images open, you need to know which image is active. If you use a menu in an Image window, it operates on the image in that same window. If you are using a tool in the Toolbox, however, the active image is less obvious. In fact, clicking a tool icon in the Toolbox selects the tool but does not activate it. To activate it, you need to click in an Image window.

Although clicking generally works well, if your window manager allows for it, set up GIMP so that simply hovering the mouse pointer over a window makes it active without your needing to click. In the GNOME 2 desktop environment, check the first button in the window that opens via **System > Preferences > Windows**. In GNOME 3, install and call gconf-editor, then change **apps: metacity > general > focus-mode** to mouse. In Ubuntu Unity, this is the default behavior. In Windows, go to the control panel and find "Change how your mouse works." In Mac OS X, use TinkerTool.

This setup makes working in GIMP much easier. For example, suppose you choose the Rectangle Select tool, the first one in the Toolbox. Click the icon and move the mouse pointer to the Image window you want to work in, and you can immediately begin to draw the rectangular selection. If you need to click in the window to make it active first, you may accidentally make a tiny, virtually invisible selection if you're not careful. To use a keyboard shortcut ($\boxed{\text{R}}$ in this case), you must click the Image window before typing the shortcut—without accidentally editing the image with the current tool. Moving the mouse pointer above the image and typing the shortcut is much safer and easier.

The dialogs in the multi-dialog window also operate on only one of your Image windows. An image menu appears, by default, at the top of the multi-dialog window to show which image is currently active (Figure 9.14). When you press

Figure 9.21 *Options in the Tab button menu*

AUTO, the button is gray, and the current image changes automatically when you select an Image window (by clicking or by moving the mouse pointer, depending on your settings). If you don't press it, the button is white, and you must explicitly change the current image in the menu.

As Figure 9.21 shows, in the Tab button menu for an ordinary dockable dialog, you have two image selection options:

- SHOW IMAGE SELECTION specifies whether the image menu appears at the top of the dock.

- AUTO FOLLOW ACTIVE IMAGE specifies whether selecting another Image window changes the active image. This option is the same as AUTO at the top of the dockable dialog.

Although they appear in the Tab button menu of a specific dialog, these options apply to the whole dock.

Another way to see which image is active in the dockable dialogs is to add a thumbnail of it in the Toolbox, as shown in Figure 9.22. To add it (or any information thumbnail), select **Image: Edit > Preferences**. In the dialog that opens (covered in detail in Chapter 22), select TOOL-BOX and check the three buttons under the heading APPEARANCE, as shown in Figure 9.23.

Figure 9.22 *Information thumbnails in the Toolbox*

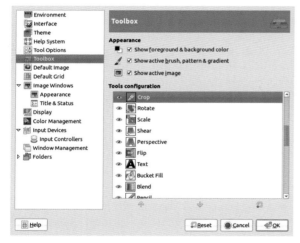

Figure 9.23 *The Preferences dialog, Toolbox entry*

Common Tab Menu Options

We already considered several of the entries on the Tab menu, which pops up when you click the small triangle button at the top right of a dockable dialog (Figure 9.21). Next we look at some of the other entries that appear in the middle of this menu. For some dialogs, some entries are grayed out or omitted.

PREVIEW SIZE opens the menu shown in Figure 9.24. Many dockable dialogs display thumbnails of an image or brushes, patterns, gradients, or fonts. You can display this thumbnail in eight

Figure 9.24 *The Preview Size submenu*

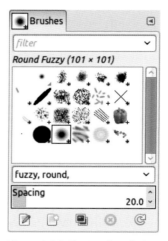

Figure 9.25 *The Brushes dialog with small thumbnails*

sizes. Figure 9.25 shows the Brushes dialog with small-sized thumbnails selected. The tiny size is useful if you have a very small screen, and the largest sizes are useful for users with impaired vision.

TAB STYLE opens the menu shown in Figure 9.26 and is used to change the appearance of the tabs. ICON uses only a descriptive icon. CURRENT STATUS displays a thumbnail of the currently selected brush, pattern, font, gradient, or so on. TEXT shows the dialog name. You can also choose to show both the name and the icon or the status. Figure 9.27 shows tabs with the icon and text. AUTOMATIC chooses the style depending on the available space in the dock: When only one tab is visible, the ICON & TEXT style is used; if several tabs are visible, the ICON or CURRENT STATUS styles are used.

Figure 9.26 *The Tab Style submenu*

Figure 9.27 *Changing tab styles*

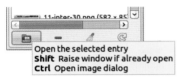

Figure 9.28 *The Dialog button tooltip*

VIEW AS LIST and VIEW AS GRID are radio buttons, so you can select only one at a time. VIEW AS LIST displays one item per line, while VIEW AS GRID displays as many items per line as possible.

SHOW BUTTON BAR specifies whether the button bar at the bottom of the dialog is displayed. The buttons in the bar vary by dialog. Some have up to eight buttons (such as the Paths dialog), whereas others have only three (such as the Patterns dialog). The button's function is shown in a tooltip message if you hover the mouse pointer over the button, as shown on Figure 9.28. Hide the button bar if the screen is crowded; the corresponding actions are still available in the right-click menu and in the first entry on the Tab menu.

9.3 Working with the GIMP Interface

In this section, we discuss the three main ways to interact with GIMP: opening a menu, using a keyboard command, and using the mouse to

click and drag a component from one dialog to another.

Menus

You can open a menu from the Image window in three ways:

- Click the menu name in the menu bar, as shown in Figure 9.29 (top).
- Use the Image menu button in the top-left corner of the Image window, as shown in Figure 9.29 (middle).
- Right-click the Image window, as shown in Figure 9.29 (bottom).

Menus that are opened from the Image menu button or from right-clicking the Image window display a dashed line at the top. If you click the dashed line, the menu becomes a separate window, as shown in Figure 9.30. This is handy if you need to use a menu multiple times. If you want to get rid of a detached menu, simply click the dashed line again. (You cannot detach a menu opened from the Image window menu bar.)

If you close the Image window from which the menu was detached, you should close the detached menu as well to avoid confusion.

Any image menu can be detached as long as it was opened by right-clicking or by pressing the menu button. Other menus, such as those opened from dockable dialogs, cannot be detached.

Keyboard Shortcuts

As you've certainly seen by now, GIMP gives you a number of ways to do the same task. Keyboard shortcuts are another way to access GIMP's features and tools. They provide an alternative way to access menu entries or to toggle settings. For example, if you press CTRL or SHIFT when scrolling with the mouse wheel in the Image window, you can zoom in or out or move the image horizontally on the canvas.

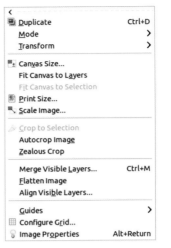

Figure 9.30 *A detached menu*

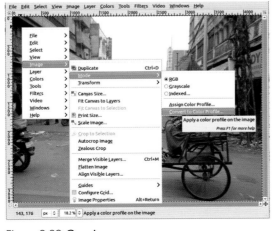

Figure 9.29 *Opening a menu*

As with many other applications, you can use the $\boxed{\text{ALT}}$ key instead of the mouse to open a menu. Provided that the Image window is active, you'll see that certain letters in the names of the entries in the Image window menu are underlined. Hold $\boxed{\text{ALT}}$ and press the corresponding key to open the corresponding menu. For example, in File, the letter F is underlined, as shown in Figure 9.31, so pressing $\boxed{\text{ALT+F}}$ opens the File menu. Underlined letters in this menu can then be used to access submenus, but you don't have to press the $\boxed{\text{ALT}}$ key. For example, the letter O in Open is underlined in the File menu. If you release $\boxed{\text{ALT}}$ and press $\boxed{\text{O}}$, the dialog for **Image: File > Open** appears. If the dialog that opens contains menu options with underlined letters, you need to press $\boxed{\text{ALT}}$ to select the corresponding entries. For example, if you type $\boxed{\text{ALT+C}}$ L $\boxed{\text{ALT+A}}$ $\boxed{\text{ALT+O}}$ the Levels tool opens, AUTO is selected, and then the tool is applied. The same technique works for the other Image window menus, but in some cases, no letters are underlined, which means that none of the menu's entries can be selected using the keyboard.

Figure 9.31 also shows the keyboard shortcuts for some menu entries displayed on the right. Many common GIMP commands are already

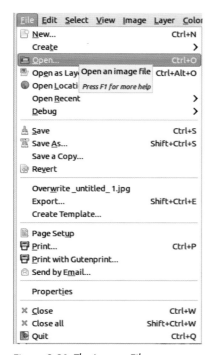

Figure 9.31 *The Image: File menu*

associated with a keyboard shortcut, and you can also define your own or change existing shortcuts, as we explain in Chapter 22.

Keyboard Tips

When you want to change a numerical value in an option field, like the size fields in the Create a new image dialog (see "Creating a New Image" on page 210), you can type an expression instead of a number. For example, if the field initially contains 640, type at its end *2 to get 1280, or +30 to get 670. You can also type 3000/7 to get 429. You can apply a percentage to the previous value or use different units in an expression, like 30in+40px or 4*5.4in. To check the result of the computation, use TAB. To apply the result, use ENTER.

As mentioned earlier, holding down the SPACE key and then clicking and dragging with the mouse is a handy way to move the image in its window.

You can toggle the options for several tools by pressing SHIFT, CTRL, or ALT. For example, the Dodge/Burn tool alternates between Dodge and Burn when you press CTRL.

Some keyboard shortcuts correspond to buttons rather than menu entries. For example, D restores the foreground and background colors to their default values, and X swaps them. CTRL+F searches in the entries shown list-style in a dockable dialog.

Some keyboard shortcuts are rather hidden but are useful to remember. CTRL+B opens and activates the Toolbox. CTRL+L does the same for the Layers dockable dialog. Pressing 1 zooms to 100%, 2 to 200%, 3 to 400%, 4 to 800%, and 5 to 1600%.

For the selection tools (Chapter 13), pressing SHIFT and/or CTRL *before* starting a selection toggles the available selection modes. For the Rectangle and Ellipse selection tools, if you press SHIFT *after* starting a selection, the selection will be centered on the starting point. Pressing CTRL or SHIFT+CTRL after starting a selection toggles different options.

When using a drawing tool, pressing < decreases the Opacity and > increases it. Pressing [decreases the Size of the current brush,] increases it, and \ resets the Size to its initial value.

Pressing ESC generally cancels a command and is equivalent to pressing the CANCEL button in the dialog. Pressing F1 opens the general GIMP Help, and SHIFT+F1 opens an interactive help mode. The cursor looks like a question mark, and you can click the menu or window that you want help with. F2 allows you to edit a name and is equivalent to double-clicking the name. Pressing F11 toggles between full-screen mode and normal mode.

Clicking and Dragging

Another way to work with GIMP is by clicking and dragging. We already saw this earlier in the chapter when we dragged and dropped dockable dialogs to add them to or remove them from docks. Here are some other clicking and dragging shortcuts.

Dragging an image thumbnail to the Toolbox or to an empty Image window opens the corresponding file as long as it's readable by GIMP. Dragging works with thumbnails of files stored on your computer or of images from a browser search, the Layers dialog, the Channels dialog, or even the Toolbox itself. Dragging an image thumbnail to an occupied Image window adds it as a new layer in the image.

Dragging the Toolbox image thumbnail to an XDS-compatible file manager saves the image as an XCF file.

Dragging a brush icon from the Brushes dialog to the Toolbox opens it in a new Image window, where you can edit it and then save it as a new brush. Again, if you drag the brush to an occupied Image window, the brush is applied as a new layer. You can do the same thing with a pattern, but if the pattern is dragged to an occupied Image window, it fills the current selection in the current layer.

You can click and drag layers up or down in the Layers dialog, and this also works for Channels and Paths.

In all dialogs with a delete icon at the bottom, dragging an item to this icon deletes it. Dragging to delete works in the Layers, Channels, and Paths dialogs; in a Palette Editor dialog; and in the Paint Dynamics, Patterns, and Gradients dialogs, as long as the dynamics, brush, palette, or gradient is user generated.

Dragging a color swatch to an occupied Image window fills the current selection with that color. Dragging works for the foreground and background colors in the Toolbox and for the components of a Palette Editor dialog. Dragging a color swatch to the Gradient Editor inserts this color into the gradient wherever it is dropped.

You can do many more things by simply clicking and dragging—actions that are generally quite intuitive.

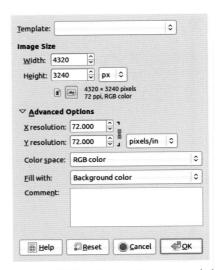

Figure 9.32 *The Create a New Image dialog*

9.4 Creating, Loading, Saving, and Exporting Files

An image loaded into GIMP is stored in the main memory of your computer, but when you save the image, it's stored as a file. In this section, we discuss how you can load images from a file and save or export your images to a file.

Creating a New Image

The first part of the **Image: File** menu (see Figure 9.31) deals with creating or opening an image. In this section, we look at the first two entries, which let you create a new image.

When you select **Image: File > New** or press CTRL+N, the dialog shown in Figure 9.32 appears. Click ADVANCED OPTIONS to expand the dialog as shown. The suggested IMAGE SIZE is either that of the current image, if there is one, or the last size used for creating a new image. The TEMPLATE drop-down menu, which offers several predefined sizes and resolutions, is shown in Figure 9.33. If you choose a template, the two buttons below HEIGHT let you swap the width and height.

Figure 9.33 *Predefined templates*

Figure 9.34 *The Image: File > Create menu*

Under ADVANCED OPTIONS, you can choose the X and Y resolution. The default value is 72, but change it to either the screen resolution or the intended printing resolution. You can also choose between RGB color or grayscale. Initially, the image must be filled with something, and you can choose the background color, fore-

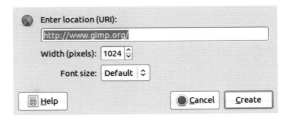

Figure 9.35 *The Create from Webpage dialog*

ground color, white, or transparency. Finally, you can add a comment if you want. When you click OK, the new image is created.

Image: File > Create opens the menu shown in Figure 9.34. The first entry is discussed in Chapter 13, and the next five entries are covered in Chapter 19, except the entry FROM WEBPAGE, described below. Some of these entries are only present if you have the XSane plug-in installed. The entries in the lower half of this menu open tools that automatically create new images designed to be buttons, logos, brushes, and so on. We cover these tools briefly in Chapter 21.

Loading a Web Page as an Image

Image: File > Create > From Webpage opens the dialog shown in Figure 9.35. Enter the URL of the page you want to download (the official GIMP site is entered by default). You can enter the width in pixels of the image to be built, such as the width of the browser window. For the FONT SIZE, you can choose between five predefined sizes, from TINY to HUGE, which will also change the size of the image.

When you press CREATE, the page is downloaded, rendered into an image, and opened in GIMP. If, for example, you leave all parameters to their default values, you'll get an image of the GIMP home page that's 1024 × 4066 pixels. Opening a web page as an image is a good way to control how it prints, since you can resize it in GIMP.

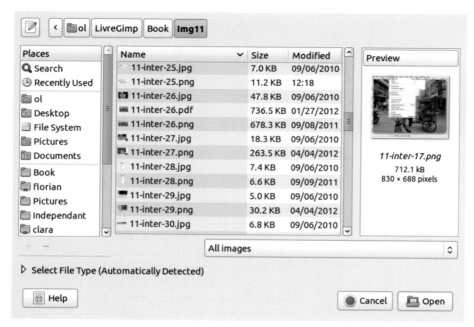

Figure 9.36 *The Open Image dialog*

Loading an Image from a File

The next four entries in the **Image: File** menu (see Figure 9.31) deal with opening an existing file. Selecting **Image: File > Open** or pressing CTRL+O opens the dialog shown in Figure 9.36. Because we already discussed this dialog in Chapter 1 and earlier in this chapter, here we present only what we didn't cover previously. The lower part of the PLACES pane contains *bookmarks*, which are saved paths. For example, you might bookmark the folder where you generally store photos. You can add or remove bookmarks with the ADD and REMOVE buttons. To add a bookmark, select the directory in the middle panel and then click ADD. To remove it, select it in the left panel and then click REMOVE. If you're on a GNU/Linux platform with the GNOME desktop environment, you can also manage your bookmarks outside of GIMP.

The button below the right panel opens the menu shown in Figure 9.37, which lists all the image formats, or file types, that GIMP can open.

You can choose to look for only certain types of images.

If you click SELECT FILE TYPE, you get a list of all the available file formats with the corresponding extensions. Let GIMP automatically detect the file type because GIMP knows how to do this reliably, using the file's internal characteristics. The extension is *not* what determines the file type.

Image: File > Open as Layers (CTRL+ALT +O) opens the same dialog, but the file you select is inserted into the current image as a new layer (or layers, if the image you're opening is a multilayer image).

Image: File > Open Location opens the dialog shown in Figure 9.38. You can paste a file path into the field, but clicking and dragging the image from the browser to the Toolbox (to open it as a new image) or to the current image (to open it as a new layer) is generally simpler.

Image: File > Open Recent opens a menu similar to Figure 9.39. The last 10 images you

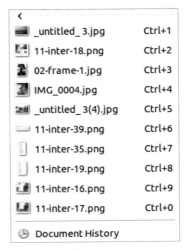

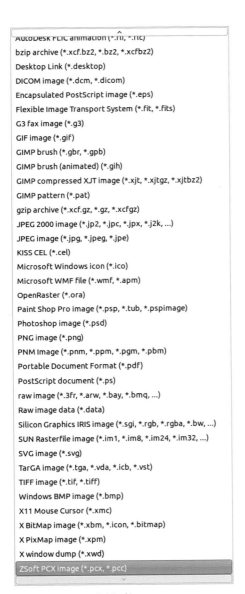

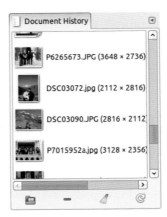

AutoDesk FLIC animation (*.fli, *.flc)
bzip archive (*.xcf.bz2, *.bz2, *.xcfbz2)
Desktop Link (*.desktop)
DICOM image (*.dcm, *.dicom)
Encapsulated PostScript image (*.eps)
Flexible Image Transport System (*.fit, *.fits)
G3 fax image (*.g3)
GIF image (*.gif)
GIMP brush (*.gbr, *.gpb)
GIMP brush (animated) (*.gih)
GIMP compressed XJT image (*.xjt, *.xjtgz, *.xjtbz2)
GIMP pattern (*.pat)
gzip archive (*.xcf.gz, *.gz, *.xcfgz)
JPEG 2000 image (*.jp2, *.jpc, *.jpx, *.j2k, ...)
JPEG image (*.jpg, *.jpeg, *.jpe)
KISS CEL (*.cel)
Microsoft Windows icon (*.ico)
Microsoft WMF file (*.wmf, *.apm)
OpenRaster (*.ora)
Paint Shop Pro image (*.psp, *.tub, *.pspimage)
Photoshop image (*.psd)
PNG image (*.png)
PNM Image (*.pnm, *.ppm, *.pgm, *.pbm)
Portable Document Format (*.pdf)
PostScript document (*.ps)
raw image (*.3fr, *.arw, *.bay, *.bmq, ...)
Raw image data (*.data)
Silicon Graphics IRIS image (*.sgi, *.rgb, *.rgba, *.bw, ...)
SUN Rasterfile image (*.im1, *.im8, *.im24, *.im32, ...)
SVG image (*.svg)
TarGA image (*.tga, *.vda, *.icb, *.vst)
TIFF image (*.tif, *.tiff)
Windows BMP image (*.bmp)
X11 Mouse Cursor (*.xmc)
X BitMap image (*.xbm, *.icon, *.bitmap)
X PixMap image (*.xpm)
X window dump (*.xwd)
ZSoft PCX image (*.pcx, *.pcc)

Figure 9.37 *Available file types*

Enter location (URI):
Help
Cancel
Open

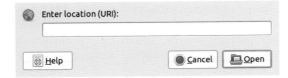

Figure 9.38 *The Open Location dialog*

_untitled_3.jpg Ctrl+1
11-inter-18.png Ctrl+2
02-frame-1.jpg Ctrl+3
IMG_0004.jpg Ctrl+4
_untitled_3(4).jpg Ctrl+5
11-inter-39.png Ctrl+6
11-inter-35.png Ctrl+7
11-inter-19.png Ctrl+8
11-inter-16.png Ctrl+9
11-inter-17.png Ctrl+0
Document History

Figure 9.39 *The Open Recent menu*

Document History
P6265673.JPG (3648 × 2736)
DSC03072.jpg (2112 × 2816)
DSC03090.JPG (2816 × 2112
P7015952a.jpg (3128 × 2356

Figure 9.40 *The Document History dialog*

opened are listed, which you can also open using CTRL+1, CTRL+2, and so on.

The last entry in the Open Recent menu opens the dockable dialog shown in Figure 9.40, which allows you to browse the list of the most recent images you opened. The list can contain hundreds of images, but no image occurs more than once in this history. If you open an image that was opened previously, its entry is moved to the top of the list.

You can search for an image in the list by name using CTRL+F. A small field opens at the

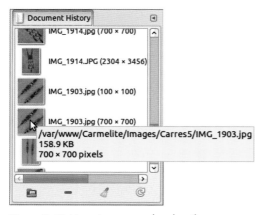

Figure 9.41 *Hovering over a thumbnail*

bottom of the list, and while you type, GIMP shows the first name beginning with the string you typed.

If you hover over a thumbnail, a message pops up with some general characteristics of the image (see Figure 9.41).

Right-clicking a thumbnail opens the menu shown in Figure 9.42, which lists some common actions. You can open the image as a new image, raise it if it's already open but hidden by other windows, open the File Open dialog with this file already selected, copy the image location to the clipboard, remove the thumbnail from the history, clear the full history, refresh this thumbnail, refresh all thumbnails, and clear the history of *dangling entries*, which are entries corresponding to files that no longer exist.

The four buttons in the bottom row of the Document History dialog let you do the following:

- Open the image (the leftmost button). If the image is already open, press SHIFT along with this button to bring it to the front. You can also press CTRL and this button to open the File Open dialog.

- Remove the selected entry (the button second from the left).

- Clear the entire document history (the button second from the right).

Figure 9.42 *The History menu*

- Refresh the thumbnails (the rightmost button). Press SHIFT and this button to refresh all thumbnails, or press CTRL and this button to remove the dangling entries.

If a thumbnail doesn't appear next to the image name, click to see one or double-click to open the corresponding image.

Saving an Image

The second part of the **Image: File** menu (see Figure 9.31 on page 209) lets you save images. If an image has been changed since you last saved it, an asterisk appears in front of its name in the title bar of the Image window. If you try to close an image without saving changes, the dialog we saw in Figure 9.20 on page 204 appears. You can choose to save the file before closing it, to cancel closing, or to discard the changes. If you discard the changes, you can't get them back.

In versions 2.6 and earlier, you could save an image in any of the output formats available. If the format was unable to represent all the information in the image, the information was discarded. If the image contained layers and the chosen format was unable to represent layers, a warning message was displayed, but after that, the image was saved without the layers. With version 2.8, you can save only in the XCF format, GIMP's native format, which can represent all the information contained in an image, including paths, layers, and layer groups. You can export an image in a variety of formats, but unless you save in XCF, some information will be lost,

Figure 9.43 *The Save Image dialog (short form)*

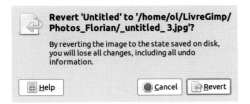

Figure 9.46 *Reverting an image*

GIMP Message

You can use this dialog to save to the GIMP XCF format. Use File→Export to export to other file formats.

OK

Figure 9.44 *Trying to save in a format other than XCF*

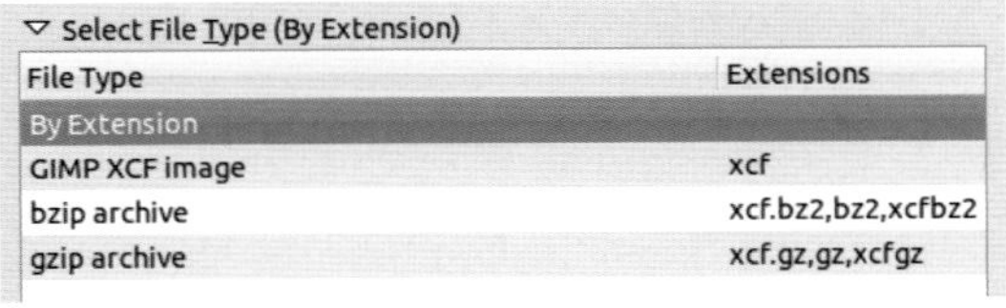

Figure 9.47 *The export options on the File menu, version one*

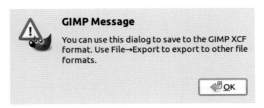

Figure 9.45 *Available file types for saving*

and GIMP warns you before closing the image. For example, if you add a legend to a photo, saving it as XCF saves the new text layer added for the legend. Thus you can later change the text of the legend or its presentation, which would be impossible in a JPEG image in which the text layer would be merged with the photo itself.

SAVE AS or SHIFT+CTRL+S opens the dialog shown in Figure 9.43. You can change the name of the file and change the path. You can select any folder or select from those you have bookmarked. The file type is automatically XCF because you're saving rather than exporting. If you try to change the file type, you'll get the message shown in Figure 9.44. If you expand SELECT FILE TYPE (BY EXTENSION), you get only the choices shown in Figure 9.45, which allow you to compress the file while saving it.

Clicking BROWSE FOR OTHER FOLDERS expands the Save Image dialog to let you browse for existing folders or create a new one. If you choose a filename that already exists, GIMP warns you so you can change it or replace the existing file.

SAVE A COPY works like SAVE, except that GIMP asks for a filename (and location) and the current image isn't changed or considered saved. If you plan to do anything that can't be undone easily, saving a copy is a good idea.

REVERT is a somewhat dangerous command because it cannot be undone. Basically, it discards all changes made to the image since you last saved. A warning message appears, as shown in Figure 9.46, reminding you that all the changes and undo information will be lost.

Exporting an Image

The next section of the **Image > File** menu covers the export options. When exporting any image, some information is lost. If no current image is available or the image is XCF, the first entry is grayed out. If the current image has already been exported, the first entry (EXPORT TO) is replaced by OVERWRITE (see Figures 9.47 and 9.48), and the word (exported) appears in its window title.

EXPORT (SHIFT+CTRL+E) is always available. This command opens a dialog similar to the Open Image dialog shown in Figure 9.36.

Figure 9.48 *The export options on the File menu, version two*

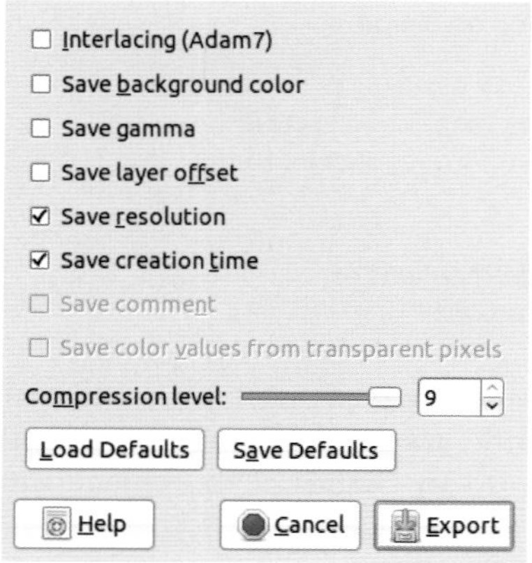

Figure 9.49 *Exporting as PNG*

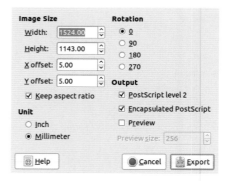

Figure 9.50 *Exporting to Encapsulated PostScript*

Figure 9.51 *Saving an image as a new template*

You can specify the file type by adding the appropriate extension to the filename or select a type via the SELECT FILE TYPE entry. All the major file types are available, and GIMP is even able to export to Photoshop. Although you cannot export to XCF from Photoshop, GIMP can read the PSD format. In addition to JPEG, GIF, and PNG, GIMP can export to PDF, Encapsulated PostScript (EPS), TIFF, and many other formats.

If the filename already exists, a warning message appears, and you can choose to cancel or overwrite the file. Depending on the output format, various dialogs appear. For example, Figure 9.49 shows the dialog for exporting to PNG, and Figure 9.50 shows the dialog for exporting to Encapsulated PostScript.

EXPORT TO (CTRL+E) uses the same name and file type as the last export, so no dialog pops up. This option is useful if you want to update an image that you're working on that's already been exported. If you're doing a lot of work on an image that won't be in XCF format, periodically save and export the image using CTRL+S

and CTRL+E, keyboard shortcuts that work silently (that is, without opening any dialogs) after you've saved and exported the image once.

OVERWRITE is available when the image has been imported from a format other than XCF. It exports to a file with the same name and file type as the imported file. If you like, you can also export the file as a different file type.

CREATE TEMPLATE opens the dialog shown in Figure 9.51, which lets you create a new template. Saved templates can be selected from the dialog shown in Figure 9.32 on page 210. The template is created from the dimensions, resolution, color space of the current image.

Manage the existing templates with the Templates dockable dialog, shown in Figure 9.52 (**Image: Windows > Dockable Dialogs > Templates**). The five buttons in the bottom row let you do the following:

- Create a new image from the selected template.

- Create a new template. Clicking this button opens the dialog shown in Figure 9.53

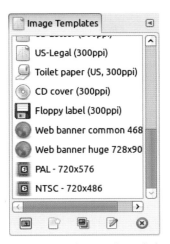

Figure 9.52 *The Templates dialog*

(with ADVANCED OPTIONS expanded). You can choose the name, size, resolution, color space, fill color, and even the icon for the new template. If you click the ICON button, you get a list of all the icons available in GIMP. Figure 9.54 shows a part of this list. The buttons in the bottom row zoom in or out and let you choose how the list is presented.

- Duplicate the selected template, which opens the dialog shown in Figure 9.53 with the same parameters as the selected template.

- Edit the selected template, which also opens the dialog shown in Figure 9.53, but this option allows you to change the parameters of an existing template.

- Delete the selected template.

You can also access these options by right-clicking in the list of templates.

9.5 Undoing

GIMP allows you to undo many steps, which makes undo a useful and powerful feature. This capability means that GIMP must store many successive states of the image you are working on, so the number of steps you can undo has

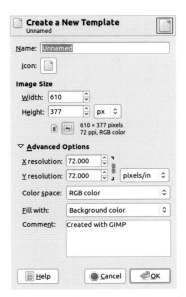

Figure 9.53 *The Create New Template dialog*

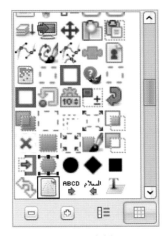

Figure 9.54 *Available icons*

a limit. We show how to adjust this limit in Chapter 22.

Figure 9.55 shows the entries in the **Image: Edit** menu that let you undo actions. We recently used IWarp and the Blend tool, but we chose to undo Blend. The menu, therefore, displays options for undoing the IWarp filter or redoing the Blend. If we did anything else before IWarp, we could then undo that, and if we undo

<
↰ Undo IWarp   Ctrl+Z
↱ Redo Blend   Ctrl+Y
↰ Fade IWarp...
🖌 Undo History

Figure 9.55 *The undo entries in the Edit menu*

anything after Blend, we can redo it after redoing Blend.

The text of the first two entries in the menu depends on what you've done to the image. CTRL+Z is the shortcut for undo, and CTRL+Y is the shortcut for redo. Even if a transformation or filter was processor intensive, undoing and redoing are not.

But computers have limited storage space, so GIMP has some limitations:

- If you undo something and then change the image, you cannot redo the operation. The undo history is like a path that forks every time you make a change to the image. If you turn around and go back (using undo) and then make a change, you are heading down a new fork, and the steps you took along the previous path are lost.

- Some operations cannot be undone, especially those dealing with saving and loading an image. If you save an image, close it, and then reload it, the undo history is lost. Reverting an image closes the image and then reloads it, so reverting cannot be undone.

- Some complicated selection tools, like the Scissors Select tool or the Free Select tool, don't allow you to undo while building a selection. You can undo the selection when you've completed it, but you cannot undo a step during its construction.

- Most filters and plug-ins have full undo capabilities, but some external plug-ins don't work properly and can even corrupt the undo history. Canceling a plug-in while it's running can also corrupt the undo history.

Figure 9.56 *The Fade dialog*

The FADE entry in the Edit menu is usually grayed out. Fade is only available after you've just used the Bucket Fill tool, the Blend tool, or a few of the filters. Its dialog is shown in Figure 9.56. Fade modifies the blending mode and the opacity of the last operation. For example, after applying the Bucket Fill tool in normal mode with full opacity, you can change the mode to Screen and reduce the opacity using Fade. Since fading is a modification, Fade doesn't add a step to the undo history. Unlike most things in GIMP, Fade is blocking: Once you begin, you must either fade or cancel. You can't do something else and then return to the Fade dialog.

As Figure 9.57 shows, all the layer-blending modes are available, plus BEHIND and COLOR ERASE, which are available only for painting tools, and REPLACE, ERASE, and ANTI ERASE. The effect of the mode and the opacity can be seen immediately, but the effects become permanent only when you click the FADE button.

The last entry in Figure 9.55 opens the Undo History dockable dialog, shown in Figure 9.58. This dialog initially appears in the multi-dialog window and shows all the actions that you can undo. The first state of the image is at the top of the list, and the last one that can be restored is at the bottom. If you click a state, it becomes the current one.

The three buttons in the bottom row, from left to right, let you undo, redo, or clear the undo history. Clearing the history isn't

Normal
Replace
Dissolve
Behind
Color erase
Erase
Anti erase
Lighten only
Screen
Dodge
Addition
Darken only
Multiply
Burn
Overlay
Soft light
Hard light
Difference
Subtract
Grain extract
Grain merge
Divide
Hue
Saturation
Color
Value

Figure 9.57 *Fading modes*

advisable unless you are in dire need of memory space.

9.6 The GIMP Help System

The GIMP Help system menu is shown in Figure 9.59. You can get help at any time by pressing F1. This command opens the Help system, displaying the table of contents of the full Help. The Help system launches in either the GIMP browser or your preferred browser, depending on the setting described in "Help System" on page 563.

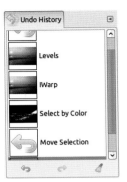

Figure 9.58 *The Undo History dialog*

Figure 9.59 *The Image: Help menu*

If you press SHIFT+F1 or use the corresponding entry in the **Image: Help** menu, a question mark appears under the mouse pointer, and you can click to get help with anything in the GIMP interface; for example, you could get help with the Toggle Quick Mask button or the Smudge tool.

An example of the Tip of the Day is shown in Figure 9.60. In previous versions of GIMP, this tip appeared by default when GIMP started. Now you have to open it explicitly. These tips are useful for neophytes, but they're rarely useful for veterans.

The About entry opens an informative window that specifies clearly the current version number, lists the members of the GIMP development team, and has buttons or links for visiting the GIMP site or reading the credits list and the license.

Figure 9.60 *The tip of the day*

Figure 9.61 *The GIMP Online menu*

Figure 9.62 *The User Manual menu*

The PLUG-IN BROWSER and PROCEDURE BROWSER entries are useful if you're writing plug-ins, which are discussed in Chapter 21.

The GIMP ONLINE entry opens the menu shown in Figure 9.61, which contains bookmarks to the four official GIMP websites. The websites open in the web browser specified in the Preferences dialog.

- The DEVELOPER WEB SITE is, as its name implies, mainly intended for GIMP developers.

- The MAIN WEB SITE is a must for any GIMP user. It announces new releases, contains download sections for most operating systems, and points to the following two sites, among others.

- The PLUG-IN REGISTRY gives you access to about 400 plug-ins written by many different people. This site offers various ways to search for plug-ins, as well as comments and forums.

- The USER MANUAL WEB SITE is the same content that you get by pressing F1 but displayed in your chosen browser rather than the GIMP browser. When you first launch this site, it opens a page where you can choose your preferred language.

The USER MANUAL entry opens the menu shown in Figure 9.62. This menu gives you yet another way to look at the user manual, listing its main chapters. It uses the Help browser specified in the Preferences dialog as well as the default language.

10 Display

In this chapter, we focus on ways to display images, delving more deeply into the properties of the Image window. Note that the tools presented in this chapter do not change the image itself, only the way it's displayed.

10.1 Rulers and Units

As soon as an image is opened in the Image window, two *rulers* appear, as shown in Figure 10.1. The horizontal ruler is just below the menu bar, and the vertical ruler is on the left side. In this figure, the mouse pointer is located at coordinates (1356, 1128), as the information on the left of the status bar shows. The coordinate units, displayed just to the right of these numbers, are pixels. Because the image zoom factor is 25%, as shown in the status bar, a pixel on the screen actually corresponds to a square of 4 × 4 pixels. Small black triangles on each of the rulers show the mouse pointer's current horizontal and vertical coordinates.

This is the default setup, and it works for most things in GIMP. The information provided allows you to place the mouse pointer with some precision, especially if you set the zoom factor to 100% or more, as you'll see later in this chapter.

Figure 10.1 *Rulers measuring in pixels*

Figure 10.2 looks a lot like Figure 10.1. But observant readers will notice the numbers on the rulers, and at the bottom left, have changed. We changed the units from pixels to millimeters. But what do these millimeters really represent? Because the zoom factor is 25%, these millimeters don't equate to millimeters in the image but rather to quarters of millimeters. If we change the zoom factor to 100% (for example, by using the menu in the middle of the status bar)

Figure 10.2 *Rulers measuring in millimeters*

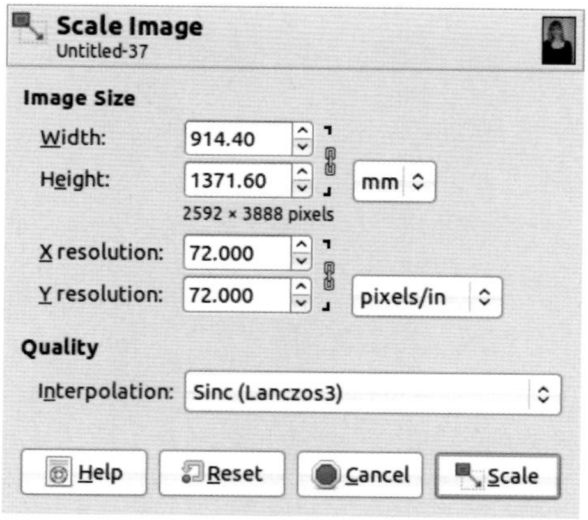

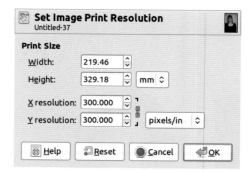

Figure 10.4 *The Set Image Print Resolution dialog*

Figure 10.3 *The Scale Image dialog*

and compare the ruler on the screen to a real ruler, we see they don't match.

The problem is that the image size is computed using its *resolution*. If we choose **Image: Image > Scale Image**, we get the dialog shown in Figure 10.3, which tells us the current resolution is 72 ppi in both directions. There's really no reason for this particular default resolution; most screens now use LCD technology and have a resolution close to 100 ppi. If we change the resolution of this image to 100 ppi, we see its dimensions changed in the Scale Image dialog

too. Now the image is 658.37×987.55 mm. When we apply the change, the size of the image on the screen doesn't change, but the numbers on the rulers do (unless the units are set to pixels).

Adjusting the resolution simply tells us the size at which this image would print given its chosen resolution. Since the resolution is really only important for printing purposes, we suggest making changes via **Image: Image > Print Size**. In Figure 10.4, we set the resolution to 300 ppi, the normal resolution for printing, and we see the printed image will be 219.46×329.18 mm, which is longer than a letter-size sheet and slightly larger than an A4 sheet. When we click OK in this dialog, the ruler graduations change once more, and now we can get the coordinates in the image with the exact values we'll get when the image prints.

But if you check against a real ruler once more, you'll see the rulers on the screen are still not displaying actual millimeters. We can fix this by making one final change. The **Image: View > Dot for Dot** box is still checked, which means that with a zoom factor of 100%, every pixel in the image corresponds exactly to one pixel on the screen. If we uncheck this box, set the image resolution to that of the screen, and set the zoom factor to 100%, the ruler displays actual millimeters.

Using actual millimeters may be handy if we want to build an image that must have specific

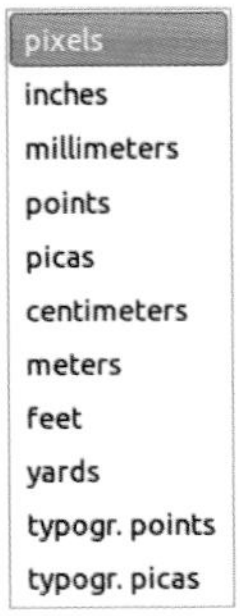

Figure 10.5 *Available units*

Figure 10.6 *Two guides set in an image*

Figure 10.7 *The Image: View menu*

dimensions when printed; for example, a business card or a label. Of course, the same manipulations may be done using inches.

The available units are shown in Figure 10.5. Pixels are the only exact measure, characteristic of the size of the image. All other measures are relative to the image resolution.

An inch is 25.4 mm. Centimeters, meters, feet, and yards are defined as multiples of millimeters or inches. Points and picas are typographic units, whose definition is not very clear, since the American pica is 4.2175 mm, the French pica is 4.512 mm, and the computer pica is 4.233 mm. It's probably best to avoid them if possible.

If the rulers bother you, hide them by unchecking the box (**Image: View > Show Rulers**) or pressing SHIFT+CTRL+R.

10.2 Guides

If we click and drag one of the rulers toward the center of the image, a movable dashed line appears in blue and black. This line is called a *guide*. In Figure 10.6, you see a vertical guide and a horizontal guide, which cross at coordinates (1000, 1000).

Guides have many useful options. Figure 10.7 shows the **Image: View** menu, which you use to access some of them. If the SNAP TO GUIDES box is checked, the mouse pointer "snaps up" to the nearest guide if it's closer than the set threshold (threshold adjustments are covered in Chapter 22). Figure 10.8 shows how the guides can be used to ensure the upper-left corner of a cropped area is located at (1000,1000) in the original image.

Figure 10.8 *Using the guides for precise cropping*

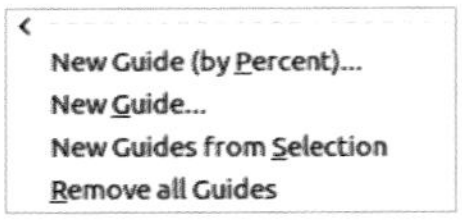

New Guide (by Percent)...
New Guide...
New Guides from Selection
Remove all Guides

Figure 10.9 *The Image: Image > Guides menu*

| Direction: | Horizontal |
| Position (in %): | 50 |

Help   Reset   Cancel   OK

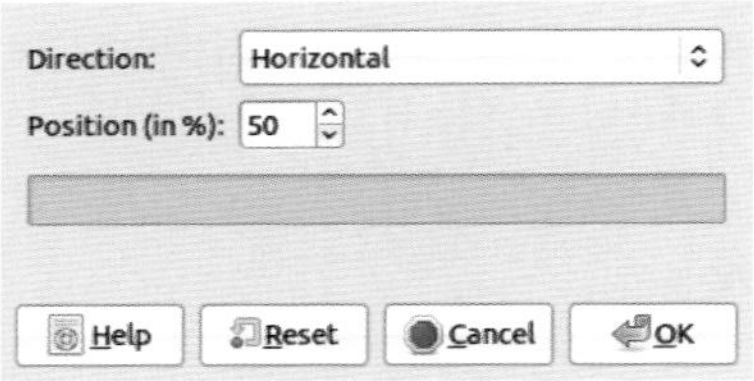

Figure 10.10 *Creating a new guide*

SHOW GUIDES is also available in the View menu. When this option is checked, the guides are shown; when it's unchecked, they are hidden. You can also toggle between these options using SHIFT+CTRL+T.

We can add any number of guides to an image. The **Image: Image > Guides** menu, shown in Figure 10.9, contains several entries; the first brings up the dialog shown in Figure 10.10. We can choose between a horizontal and a vertical guide and set its position as a percentage of the window (not the image). The second entry brings up a very similar dialog, but this time we

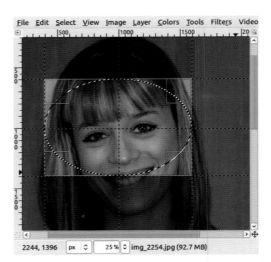

Figure 10.11 *Placing new guides from the current selection*

set the position of the guide in pixels.

The third entry allows us to place new guides around the current selection. For example, to make an elliptic selection centered on the intersection of existing guides, as shown in Figure 10.11, choose the Ellipse Select tool (E), click the intersection of the guides (with Snap to Guides enabled), press the CTRL key to expand the selection from the center, and move the mouse pointer to expand the selection. Then choose **Image: Image > Guides > New Guides from Selection** to get the result shown.

Two methods are available for removing a guide: We can click and drag it back to the corresponding ruler, or we can remove all guides at the same time using **Image: Image > Guides > Remove all Guides**.

As shown in Figure 10.7, the View menu contains three more buttons related to snapping:

- SNAP TO GRID is discussed in the next section.

- SNAP TO CANVAS EDGES, which uses the edges of the canvas as if they were guides. Moving the mouse pointer very close to an edge places it exactly on that edge.

- SNAP TO ACTIVE PATH, which does the same for the active path. See Section 13.3.

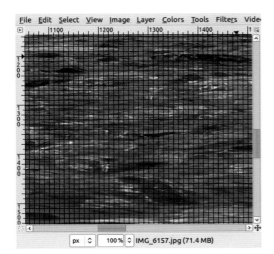

Figure 10.12 *Displaying the grid*

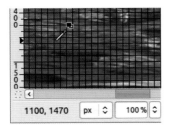

Figure 10.13 *Snapping the mouse pointer to the grid*

10.3 Grids

Guides can help us to position things within an image. A grid is another way to visualize placement. In fact, an image always has a grid, but it's hidden by default. You can permanently change this setting, as described in Chapter 22. You can make the grid visible by using **Image: View > Show Grid**. Figure 10.12 shows the result. Note that this image is displayed with a zoom factor of 100%.

This grid has a mesh size of 10 × 10 pixels. When **Image: View > Snap to Grid** is checked, the mouse pointer always snaps to the intersection of two lines, even if it appears to be somewhere inside the mesh, as shown in Figure 10.13. You can see that the coordinates displayed in the status bar are both multiples of 10.

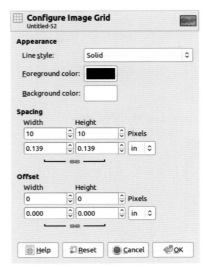

Figure 10.14 *The Configure Image Grid dialog*

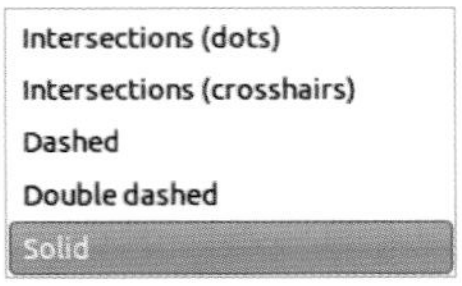

Intersections (dots)
Intersections (crosshairs)
Dashed
Double dashed
Solid

Figure 10.15 *Available grid line styles*

We can configure the grid by selecting **Image: Image > Configure Grid**. The dialog shown in Figure 10.14 pops up. We can change a number of parameters, which we'll consider in turn.

The grid's APPEARANCE is controlled by three parameters: LINE STYLE, FOREGROUND COLOR, and BACKGROUND COLOR. You have five choices for the LINE STYLE, as shown in Figure 10.15:

- INTERSECTIONS (DOTS) is shown in Figure 10.16. The dots are one pixel wide, regardless of the image's zoom factor. They can be hard to see.

- INTERSECTIONS (CROSSHAIRS) is shown in Figure 10.17. The crosses are more visible than the dots, but they can be distracting.

- DASHED is shown in Figure 10.18. We increased the zoom factor to make the details visible. This line style emphasizes the lines in the grid, rather than the intersections.

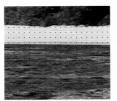

Figure 10.16 *The Intersections (dots) line style*

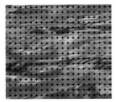

Figure 10.17 *The Intersections (crosshairs) line style*

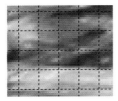

Figure 10.18 *The Dashed line style*

- DOUBLE DASHED is shown in Figure 10.19. Here again, we increased the zoom factor, so the lines are even more visible.

- SOLID is shown in Figure 10.20. SOLID is the default style, shown here at an intermediate zoom factor.

The FOREGROUND COLOR is the color of the dots, crosshairs, or lines. In Figure 10.20 we changed this to green.

The BACKGROUND COLOR is used only with DOUBLE DASHED, as shown in Figure 10.19, where the background color is cyan.

The SPACING of the grid determines the size of the grid mesh. Choose a size in pixels or in whatever units you prefer. The size depends on the image resolution, as discussed earlier in this chapter. To create a rectangular mesh, break the chain below the counters before inputting the new size.

Figure 10.19 *The Double dashed line style*

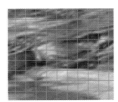

Figure 10.20 *The Solid line style*

The OFFSET of the grid specifies where the first coordinates are placed. Initially the first coordinates are (0, 0) (i.e., in the top-left corner of the canvas).

10.4　Zoom

You may want to change an image's zoom factor—either to view the complete image or to work on a specific detail. You can adjust the zoom in many ways; you access several methods directly from the Image window.

The zoom menu on the bottom bar of the Image window allows you to choose from among a few predefined zoom factors. You can also type in the desired factor directly.

Image: View > Zoom brings up another zoom menu, shown in Figure 10.21. Here you can choose among the same predefined zoom factors, plus two more. Note the keyboard shortcuts for common zoom factors. If you recently used a zoom factor that's not predefined, it appears at the end of the menu.

You can also step up or down this scale using the ZOOM IN or ZOOM OUT entries. Note that the keys ⊟ and ⊞ also do this. Go back to the preceding zoom factor by using REVERT ZOOM or the ` key (backtick).

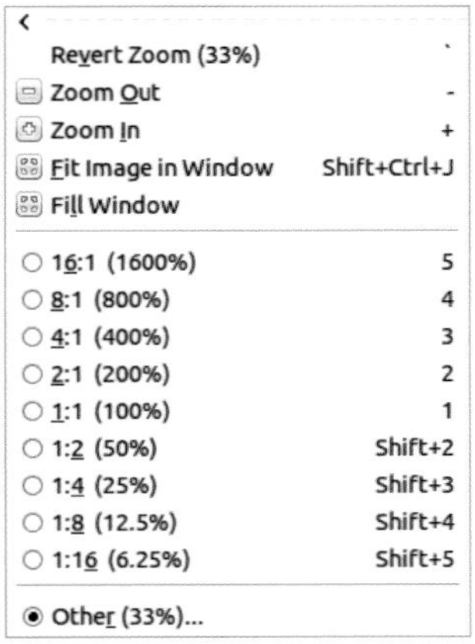

Figure 10.21 *The Image: View > Zoom menu*

Figure 10.22 *Starting with a 50% zoom factor*

Figure 10.23 *After Fill Window*

Figure 10.24 *After Fit Image in Window*

Figure 10.25 *The Zoom tool icon*

The two remaining entries are best explained using examples. Figure 10.22 shows a window with a zoom factor of 50%. If we choose **Image: View > Zoom > Fill Window**, we get Figure 10.23. The zoom factor has been changed so the image fills the window's dimensions. If we choose **Image: View > Zoom > Fit Image in Window** (or SHIFT+CTRL+J), we get Figure 10.24. In this case, the zoom factor chosen gives the closest possible zoom while still keeping the full image visible in the window.

Note that all these zoom changes do not change the size of the window. On the other hand, the command **Image: View > Shrink Wrap**, or CTRL+J, changes the window size without changing the image's zoom factor, in both single-window and multi-window mode.

When pressing the CTRL key, you can use the mouse wheel to zoom in or out using the standard zoom factors.

If the small window resize button in the top-right corner of the Image window is checked, then changing the window size changes the zoom factor. This can be useful or irritating, depending on the situation.

Figure 10.26 *Zooming in with the Zoom tool*

Figure 10.27 *After zooming in*

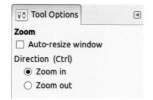

Figure 10.28 *The Zoom tool options*

Figure 10.29 *The Navigation dialog*

Yet another tool is available for adjusting the zoom factor: the aptly named Zoom tool, which can be accessed from the Toolbox (Figure 10.25) or by pressing Z. Figure 10.26 shows this tool in zoom-in mode (as indicated by the + sign beside the mouse pointer). To zoom in, click and drag a rectangle around the part of the image you want to fill the window. Figure 10.27 shows the result.

This tool can also be used to zoom out. The rectangle you draw shows the new scale of the image after it's zoomed out. Additionally, simply clicking the image with the Zoom tool zooms in or out along the zoom scale.

The Zoom tool has a few options, shown in Figure 10.28. You can zoom in or out or toggle this parameter by pressing the CTRL key. If you check the AUTO-RESIZE WINDOW checkbox, the window size changes so it contains the same part of the image as before.

If you still haven't found the perfect zoom tool, here's another one: **Image: View > Navigation window**. Choose this tool, and the small dockable dialog in Figure 10.29 pops up. The six buttons at the bottom provide the following functions:

- Zoom out.

- Zoom in.

- Zoom to 100%.

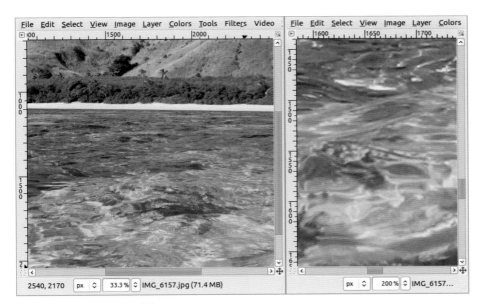

Figure 10.30 *Two views of the same image*

- Adjust the zoom ratio so the image becomes fully visible without changing the size of the Image window; this is equivalent to SHIFT+CTRL+J.

- Adjust the zoom ratio so the entire window is used; this is equivalent to **Image: View > Zoom > Fill Window**.

- Reduce the Image window to the size of the image display; this is equivalent to CTRL+J.

The slider allows us to choose any zoom factor from 0.39% to 25600%. Finally, the image preview displays a frame around the part of the image that is currently displayed in the Image window. You can move it with the mouse pointer.

10.5 Using Multiple Views

As you just saw, you can view an image at different sizes and zoom factors. But sometimes you may need several different views open at the same time. Suppose, for example, we are carefully retouching a photograph. We want a close-up view of the detail that we are retouching. At the same time, we want to see the effect of our work on the photograph at the size that it will be printed.

To open multiple views of an image, select **Image: View > New View**. The new Image window that opens is another view of the same image, not a new copy of it. For example, on the left side of Figure 10.30, you see a seaside landscape photo with a zoom factor of 33.3%, and on the right side, you see the ripple of a small wave from the foreground of the photo using a zoom factor of 200%. When we do something to the image on the right side, the effect is immediately visible in the left-side window as well. Note that this feature isn't as useful in single-window mode because in that mode you can't look at two different images at the same time, even if both of them are open in GIMP. You can only shift from one view to the other and then back.

Occasionally, you may want to enlarge the Image window to full screen. The best way to do this is not by using the button on the window bar but rather by applying **Image: View > Fullscreen** or by pressing F11, which is a toggle. The

Figure 10.31 *Enlarging the Image window to full screen*

result is shown in Figure 10.31. When setting
general parameters (see Chapter 22), you can
also choose to minimize what's displayed on
screen to give your image more room. You
can hide the rulers, the scroll bars, the status
bar, and even the menu bar, as shown in this
example. And you can recall them when needed
with the menu button at the top left of the Image window (if the rulers are displayed) or by
right-clicking the image.

11 Layers

Layers are so central to GIMP that without them, this powerful application would be almost useless. Instead, we would only be able to use GIMP for simple drawings or minor photo touch-ups. All of GIMP's more powerful and versatile features rely on layers.

When an image has multiple layers, the GIMP workspace acts as a stack of transparencies. Draw or paint on these transparencies, or arrange parts of an existing picture on separate layers. Set the layers' visibility, or adjust how transparent they are or how they blend with other layers. Move them around the canvas and control their order in the layer stack. Duplicate a layer before changing it so an intact copy remains in case you make a mistake or want to use the layer for other purposes. Layering makes possible so many things that this chapter covers only the basic concepts, while later chapters combine these concepts with the tools and features provided by GIMP. In this chapter, we examine the Layers dialog, the Layers menu, and the **Image: Layer** menu.

11.1 The Layers Dialog

Figure 11.1 shows an example of a Layers dialog for the painting created in Chapter 3. This dialog is probably the most important of all the GIMP dialogs, including the Toolbox, since the latter can be replaced with the **Image: Tools** menu (or keyboard shortcuts). The Layers dialog is a component of the multi-dialog window by default, and you will most likely want to keep it open. If you do close it, you can open it again by going to **Image: Windows > Dockable Dialogs > Layers** or pressing CTRL+L to bring it back. The keyboard shortcut brings up the dialog in the foreground, even if it was hidden by a TAB command.

Components of the Layers Dialog

Let's examine the components of the Layers dialog. The numbers below refer to Figure 11.1.

1. The image name is not really a component of the dialog but rather of the multi-dialog window. If you select a different tab (the Channels dialog, for example), the image name will remain visible. You can change whether the image name is visible in the Configuration menu (opened with the button labeled 4). To show the image name, check SHOW IMAGE SELECTION. Showing the image name is very useful when you're working with several images at the same time.

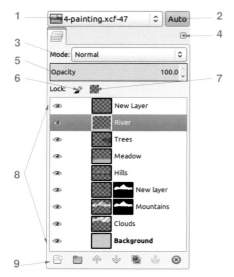

Figure 11.1 *The Layers dialog*

Figure 11.2 *The Configuration menu*

allows you to add, close, or detach tabs from the multi-dialog menu; change the preview size and the tab style; and show or hide elements in the dialog. The last entry allows you to navigate between multiple displays, if you're working with more than one monitor.

5. The Opacity slider allows you to set the opacity of the current layer. This is independent of the transparency, so a layer without an Alpha channel can be made semi-transparent with the Opacity slider. The layer opacity combines with the layer blending mode to determine the interaction between the pixels of the current layer and those of the underlying layers. For example, Dissolve mode is different from Normal mode only if the layer opacity is less than 100%.

6. The paintbrush icon is a toggle button. If pressed, the layer pixels are locked, which means they cannot be changed. This is useful if you want to protect a layer from accidental alterations. Painting on a layer with locked pixels is very similar to painting on it in Behind mode: When the pixels are locked, the painting tools will still work in transparent areas.

7. The square icon, another toggle button, locks a layer's Alpha channel, if there is one. If the Alpha channel is locked, painting tools don't work in transparent areas of the current layer, but they do work in opaque areas, as long as the pixels are unlocked. If both locks (pixels and Alpha channel) are checked, the layer cannot be changed at all. These buttons are useful, for example, when building logos, as shown in Chapter 4. If you want to blur the logo to add relief to it, the Alpha channel must be unlocked. If you want to paint the logo, the Alpha channel must be locked.

8. The main part of the Layers dialog contains as many entries as there are layers in the image. The current layer is noted by an emphasis on the corresponding entry (blue in Figure 11.1, where the current layer is named River).

2. This button toggles whether the multi-dialog window always reflects the current image.

3. The MODE drop-down menu sets the blending mode of the current layer. For a description of the 21 blending modes available, see Section 12.2.

4. This button brings up the Configuration menu, found in all dockable dialogs and shown in Figure 11.2. The first entry opens the Layers menu, which will be discussed later in this chapter. The Configuration menu also

Figure 11.3 *An example layer in the Layers dialog*

Always be aware of which layer is current, because anything you do to the image will be applied to that layer, which can be invisible or hidden by another layer. When the current layer is hidden, changes appear to have no effect, yet the current layer, hidden somewhere in the layer stack, is being affected by everything you do. Sometimes no layer is current, for example when a channel is active. In that case, when you apply changes to the image, the active channel is affected.

9. The bottom of the Layers dialog displays a row of seven buttons, which are shortcuts to entries in the Layers or **Image: Layer** menus. From left to right, these buttons allow you to do the following:

- Create a new layer. Hold down $\boxed{\text{SHIFT}}$ to use the previous parameters. Otherwise a dialog opens to set them.

- Create a new layer group.

- Raise the current layer in the layer stack. Press $\boxed{\text{SHIFT}}$ to move it to the top.

- Lower the current layer in the layer stack. Press $\boxed{\text{SHIFT}}$ to move it to the bottom.

- Duplicate the current layer.

- Anchor the floating layer.

- Delete the current layer.

A Layer Entry in the Layers Dialog

Figure 11.3 shows all the possible components of a layer displayed in the Layers dialog. From left to right, these are as follows:

- The eye icon denotes the fact that the layer is visible (if no upper layer hides it). Clicking it toggles visibility. An invisible layer does not contribute to the visible image, but this does not prevent it from being changed.

- The link icon denotes the fact that the layer is linked to something. This is meaningful only when it's activated for more than one object. We can link several layers together, or we can link channels and paths, using their respective dialogs. See Chapter 14 for information on channels, and see Section 13.3 for information on paths. When several objects are linked, the Move tool and the transformation tools (see Chapter 16) operate on the whole set of linked objects. However, each image is limited to only one set of linked objects. Clicking the chain turns the link on or off for that layer.

- The thumbnail provides a miniature view of the layer contents. If its frame is white, that layer is the current layer and any modification made will affect it. Otherwise, the frame is black. Clicking on the thumbnail makes the layer active. If you click and hold, a larger thumbnail pops out. Clicking and dragging the thumbnail to the Toolbox creates a new image from the layer. Dragging it into another image copies the layer as a new layer in that image.

- If the layer has a layer mask (see Section 14.2), its thumbnail appears to the right and has the same properties as the layer thumbnail. If the mask frame is white, the mask is active, and any modifications made will be applied to the mask. If the mask frame is red, the layer mask is inactive. When the layer mask is selected, the dashed outline in the Image window changes from yellow and black to green and black. $\boxed{\text{CTRL}}$-clicking the thumbnail toggles the layer mask activation, and $\boxed{\text{ALT}}$-clicking toggles the visibility of the layer mask.

  Drag the layer mask thumbnail into another image to add it as a layer or into the Toolbox to create a copy as a new image.

- The final item on the layer entry is the layer name. It is displayed in boldface if the layer does not have an Alpha channel. A name is assigned to the layer when the layer is created, but it can be changed. Double-click it, press F2, or select **Layers: right-click > Edit Layer Attributes** to change it.

If the layer is intended to be an animation frame (see Chapter 18), its name can be followed by text that alters the frame's behavior: the duration in milliseconds, as in (200ms), and the combination mode of the frame—either (combine) or (replace).

Keyboard Shortcuts in the Layers Dialog

Some handy keyboard shortcuts are available when the Layers dialog is active.

- The up arrow key selects the layer above the current layer as the new current layer. The down arrow key selects the layer below.
- The HOME key makes the top layer in the stack current, and the END key makes the bottom layer current.
- The horizontal arrow keys switch among the four (or five) components of the current layer: visibility, linking, layer thumbnail, layer mask thumbnail, and layer name.
- The SPACE and ENTER keys toggle the selected layer component (visibility, linking, activity of the layer or its layer mask, and the layer name), even if its layer is not active.
- Pressing CTRL along with the up or down arrow key moves from layer to layer without changing the current layer. You can use this in combination with the horizontal arrow keys or the SPACE or ENTER keys.
- The DELETE key erases the contents of the current layer (or the selection in this layer).

Uses of the Layers Dialog

In summary, the Layers dialog allows you to do the following:

- Open the configuration menu by clicking the top-right button. The first entry in this menu

opens the Layers menu (covered later in this chapter).

- Change the blending mode of the layer. See Section 12.2 for examples and a complete description of the blending modes.
- Set the layer opacity.
- Lock the pixels or the Alpha channel.
- Set the visibility of the layer by clicking the eye icon. Note that this is independent of the activity of the layer. An invisible layer can still be altered.
- Set the activity of the layer by clicking its thumbnail. Note that this does not change its visibility.
- Set the activity of the layer mask by clicking, CTRL-clicking, or ALT-clicking its thumbnail image.
- Change the name of the layer by double-clicking its name.
- Move the layer in the layer stack by clicking and dragging its thumbnail or name up or down the layer stack. This method can also be used to move a layer into, or out of, a layer group.
- Open the Layers menu by right-clicking anywhere in the layer's entry.
- Use the seven buttons in the bottom row to perform common layer-related tasks.

11.2   The Layers Menu

The Layers menu (Figure 11.4) is selected by right-clicking any of the layer entries in the Layers dialog or by selecting the first entry in the Configure menu of the Layers dialog. If the current layer is a text layer, this menu contains five additional entries, described in Section 15.8. In this section, we examine each of the entries in the Layers menu.

EDIT LAYER ATTRIBUTES opens the dialog shown in Figure 11.5. The only attribute that can be changed is the layer name.

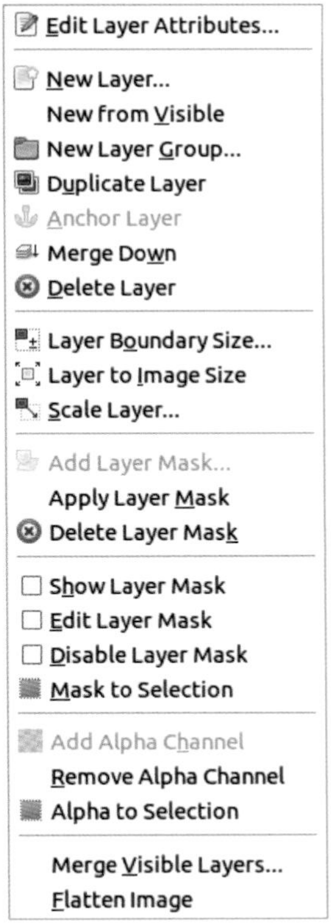

Edit Layer Attributes...

New Layer...
New from Visible
New Layer Group...
Duplicate Layer
Anchor Layer
Merge Down
Delete Layer

Layer Boundary Size...
Layer to Image Size
Scale Layer...

Add Layer Mask...
Apply Layer Mask
Delete Layer Mask

Show Layer Mask
Edit Layer Mask
Disable Layer Mask
Mask to Selection

Add Alpha Channel
Remove Alpha Channel
Alpha to Selection

Merge Visible Layers...
Flatten Image

Figure 11.4 *The Layers menu*

Figure 11.5 *The Edit Layer Attributes dialog*

Figure 11.6 *The Create a New Layer dialog*

NEW LAYER opens the dialog shown in Figure 11.6. A descriptive layer name can help you quickly identify the various components of an image. If you don't input one, a name is automatically generated, such as Layer #1. The width and height are initially the same as those of the canvas, but you can input different values. If the new layer is larger than the canvas, the areas of the layer that extend beyond the canvas won't be visible. The new layer's dimensions can be assigned as a percentage of the canvas dimensions, in pixels, or in a number of other units. Note that measurements in inches, millimeters, or other standard units of measurement are calculated with regard to the current resolution (see Section 10.1). Finally, the four radio buttons allow you to choose how the layer is initially filled. The layer can be filled with the foreground color, the background color, white, or transparency. Unless transparency is chosen, the new layer does not have an Alpha channel.

NEW FROM VISIBLE creates a new layer, initially called Visible, filled with the image as it currently appears. This new layer is placed in the stack just above the current layer. The layers contributing to this new layer are flattened before its creation such that only one new layer is created, even if several are visible.

NEW LAYER GROUP creates a new, empty layer group, initially called Layer Group. This concept is discussed in Section 11.3.

DUPLICATE LAYER makes a copy of the current layer (or layer group), places it into the layer stack just above the current layer, and names it the same name as that the current layer plus the word copy. The copy inherits all the characteristics of the original, including its blending mode, opacity, and locks.

ANCHOR LAYER is active only when there is a floating selection. See Section 13.4. The floating selection is anchored to the last current layer.

Figure 11.7 *The Layers Merge Options dialog*

MERGE DOWN merges the current layer with the layer below. If the current layer is invisible, it merges as if it were visible. However, if the layer below is invisible, and there is no visible layer below that, MERGE DOWN is inactive. MERGE DOWN is also inactive when the layers below the current layer form a layer group.

MERGE LAYER GROUP appears in the menu only if the current layer is a layer group. This group is replaced with a single layer, composed of all layers of the group.

DELETE LAYER deletes the active layer or layer group. Like the other Layers menu operations, this one can be undone.

The next four entry groups in the Layers menu are also found in the **Image: Layer** menu, and they are discussed in Section 11.4. Therefore we skip to the last two entries in the Layers menu.

MERGE VISIBLE LAYERS acts only on the layers with the eye icon checked, and it merges them according to their respective opacity and blending mode. The dialog is shown in Figure 11.7. The new layer can be sized to match the largest layer, the canvas, or the bottom layer. If the DIS-CARD INVISIBLE LAYERS box is checked, the invisible layers are deleted. Otherwise, they remain in the image. Note that this operation deletes the visible layers from the image, unlike NEW FROM VISIBLE, which is generally a better choice. If you do choose to use MERGE VISIBLE LAYERS, we strongly suggest that you save a copy of the image first with **Image: File > Save a Copy**.

FLATTEN IMAGE replaces all the layers with a single-layer representation of the image. This is a destructive operation and should be used only after you've saved a copy of the image with the layers intact.

11.3 Layer Groups

Layer groups are a new feature in GIMP 2.8, and the concept is still evolving.

To create a new layer group, click the corresponding button in the bottom of the Layers dialog or use **Image: Layer > New Layer Group** or **Layers: right-click > New Layer Group**.

The layer group appears just above the current layer and is initially empty. A good idea is to immediately give it a meaningful name. To add a layer to a group, click and drag it to the group in the layer stack. Do the same to move a layer out of its current group or to move an entire layer group around in the stack. You can also add a new layer to a layer group, using the corresponding button in the Layers dialog or the entry in the Layers menu. Click the small triangle to show (Figure 11.8) or hide (Figure 11.9) the contents of the group. A layer group can be placed within another layer group.

A layer group is a useful way to organize the layers in a complex image. The following operations can be done on a layer group:

- Locking the pixels
- Changing the group opacity
- Toggling visibility with the eye icon
- Toggling layer links with the chain icon
- Moving the group in the layer stack
- Moving the layers with the Move tool
- Applying a transformation to all layers (see Chapter 16)
- Duplicating the layer group and its contents
- Copying the layer group and its contents to another image by clicking and dragging it, or by copying and pasting it

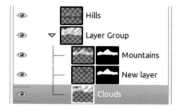

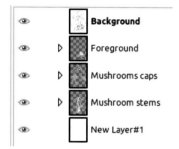

Figure 11.8 *This layer group has three layers*

Figure 11.9 *Three minimized layer groups*

Figure 11.10 *Moving the Mushroom caps layer group*

Figure 11.11 *Reducing the opacity of a layer group to 50%*

- Deleting the layer group and its contents

- Applying a layer blending mode to a layer group, which effects only the layers of the layer group

We'll use the result of the tutorial from Chapter 3 to demonstrate the properties of a layer group. This image has 20 layers, which we organized as we built the image. Each of the four mushroom caps is composed of two layers, one of which contains a layer mask. The mushroom stems are composed of six layers. The flower and stone in the foreground are composed of four layers. Finally, there is a white background for the whole image, and another layer on the top of the stack, named Background, which is in multiply blend mode and contains the original drawing. These layers can be organized intuitively into three layer groups: Mushroom stems, Mushroom caps, and Foreground. To do this without changing the layer order in the stack, click the New Layer Group button when the topmost layer of the future group is active, and then move layers into the group by clicking and dragging them to the upper layer or to an empty

layer group. Figure 11.9 shows the result when these three layer groups are minimized.

You can hide a layer group by clicking its eye icon, or you can move all of its layers simultaneously using the Move tool (see Figure 11.10). If a layer group is hidden, the layers it contains are invisible and their eye icons are stroked out. You can also change the opacity of an entire layer group (see Figure 11.11).

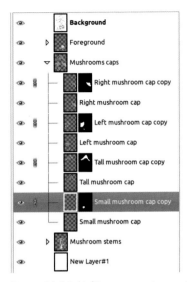

Figure 11.12 *Linking noncontiguous layers*

Figure 11.13 *Moving only the caps' spots*

All the layers in a layer group must be contiguous in the layer stack. This is not the case for linking layers. For example, let's chain together the second layer of all mushroom caps, the one containing a layer mask and used to draw the spots on the caps (see Figure 11.12). Now we can move the linked layers together, but separately from the group, as shown in Figure 11.13

Figure 11.14 *The Image: Layer menu*

(compare with Figure 11.10). The linked layers can even be in different layer groups.

Layer groups are saved in an XCF file, independently from the individual layers. In GIMP 2.8, it's possible to rotate or scale a layer group without rotating or scaling the individual layer components of the group. When the layer group is rotated or scaled, a floating selection is created with the result of the transformation, and the initial layer group is replaced with the merged, transformed components. The individual layers, however, are unchanged.

11.4   The Image: Layer Menu

The **Image: Layer** menu is shown in Figure 11.14. Some of the entries are also found in the **Layers: right-click > Layers** menu, but there are many new entries as well.

The first eight entries (or seven if there is no existing layer group) can also be found in the **Layers: right-click > Layers** menu, but in the **Image: Layer** menu three of these entries are accompanied by keyboard shortcuts:

- $\boxed{\text{SHIFT+CTRL+N}}$ opens the new layer dialog.
- $\boxed{\text{SHIFT+CTRL+D}}$ duplicates the current layer.
- $\boxed{\text{CTRL+H}}$ anchors the floating selection.

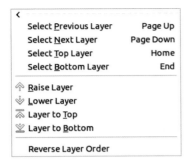

Figure 11.15 *The Stack menu*

This menu, and these shortcuts, allow us to make major changes to the layer stack without looking at it, which is generally not advisable. It's much easier to make a mistake when you can't see what you're doing. It's better to adjust layers in the Layers dialog whenever possible.

If the current layer is a text layer, the Layer menu will also contain four text-specific entries, described in Section 15.8. After that are the four menus discussed next.

The Stack Menu

The Stack menu is shown in Figure 11.15. Within it are four commands which are most useful when dealing with an image that has a lot of layers:

- SELECT PREVIOUS LAYER (PAGE UP) is equivalent to clicking in the previous layer in the Layers dialog, with one exception: If the current layer is within a layer group, this command does not extend to layers outside of the group.

- SELECT NEXT LAYER (PAGE DOWN) selects the next layer, with the same exception as above.

- SELECT TOP LAYER (HOME) selects the topmost layer in the stack or the topmost layer in the group.

- SELECT BOTTOM LAYER (END) selects the bottom layer in the stack or the bottom layer in the group.

Note that the arrow keys on the keyboard can be used to select the previous or next layer, but only when the Layers dialog is active. See "Keyboard Shortcuts in the Layers Dialog" on page 234 for other keyboard shortcuts available in this dialog.

The next four commands move the current layer in the layer stack:

- RAISE LAYER moves the layer up in the stack. It cannot raise a layer outside of its current group. To move a layer out of its group, click and drag it.

- LOWER LAYER moves the layer down in the stack.

- LAYER TO TOP moves the current layer to the top of the stack, or of its group if it belongs to a layer group.

- LAYER TO BOTTOM moves the layer to the bottom of the stack or group.

Finally, REVERSE LAYER ORDER can be called only from this menu. A layer group counts as a single layer, and there is no action to reverse the layer order within a layer group.

The Mask, Transparency, and Transform Menus

The Mask menu deals with layer masks and is discussed in Section 14.2. It offers slightly more options than are found in the **Layers: right-click > Layers** menu.

The Transparency menu is discussed in "Transparency and the Alpha Channel" on page 324. Only three of its entries also appear in the **Layers: right-click > Layers** menu.

Using the Transform menu is the easiest way to flip or rotate the current layer. You could also use the Flip tool (SHIFT+F) or Arbitrary Rotation, which is also accessed through the Rotate tool (SHIFT+R). See "Transforming a Layer" on page 375 for more information on the Transform menu.

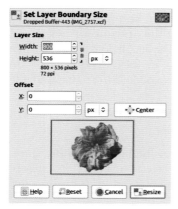

Figure 11.16 *The Set Layer Boundary Size dialog*

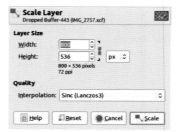

Figure 11.17 *The Scale Layer dialog*

Figure 11.18 *Autocropping a layer group*

The Final Five Entries

The remaining five entries in the Image: Layer menu provide the only access to their respective operations:

- LAYER BOUNDARY SIZE opens the dialog shown in Figure 11.16, which is very similar to the dialog of **Image: Image > Canvas Size**, described in "Resizing an Image" on page 371. You can choose the exact dimensions of the layer, and the position of its contents within the new dimensions. Adjust the position by setting the X and Y fields, by dragging the layer preview in its window, or by using the CENTER button. If you reduce the size of the layer, the clipped contents are deleted, but if you enlarge the layer beyond the border of the image, the contents outside of the image border are retained, though invisible. This tool also works with a layer group.

- LAYER TO IMAGE SIZE sets the layer to the image size, without a dialog and without moving the layer contents. Any part of the layer that's beyond the canvas limits is deleted. This tool also works with layer groups.

- SCALE LAYER opens the dialog shown in Figure 11.17, which is the same as the **Image: Image > Scale Image** dialog, described in Section 10.1 and in "Resizing an Image" on page 371. The only difference is that you

cannot change the layer resolution, which is fixed by the image resolution. This tool also works with layer groups.

- CROP TO SELECTION is active only if there is a current selection. The layer dimensions are set to the smallest rectangle that includes the selection.

- AUTOCROP LAYER crops the layer to the smallest rectangle that contains data of a color different from that of the layer border. It's similar to **Image: Image > Autocrop Image**, described in "Cropping an Image" on page 374. This tool also works with layer groups, as demonstrated in Figure 11.18, where the current layer is the entire Mushroom caps layer group.

12 Color

Representing and handling colors is one of the fundamental tasks of an image-manipulation program like GIMP. Thus, we cover the topic in several places in this book. In this chapter, we present the main concepts and tools. In Appendix A, we discuss the foundations of color perception, so refer to that appendix if you need to refresh your knowledge. The theories of color and vision form the foundation of color handling in GIMP, and a thorough understanding of that appendix will help you to understand this chapter fully.

Additionally, Chapter 19 contains information about 16-bit color depth and handling photographs from a digital camera in raw format. Chapter 20 describes all the image formats handled by GIMP, focusing on the definition and use of color palettes. And in Chapter 22, we explain how to set the parameters of color management.

12.1 Concepts

The concept of color is a very complex one, and many books have been written on the subject. Great thinkers like Aristotle, Huygens, Newton, Goethe, and many others developed theories of color. These theories dealt with physiology, philosophy, psychology, and even physics and high-level mathematics. The modern technology of computers, display screens, and printers now relies on a well-established theory that you can read about in any text on color theory.

In this section, we begin by briefly reviewing color models, which are presented in more detail in Section A.3. We'll then consider the three internal representations that GIMP uses to store image information while you work. External formats used to store images on hard disks or on the Web are considered in Chapter 20.

Color Models

GIMP handles raster images, which are composed of *pixels*. A pixel is the smallest image component and represents a single color (and any associated transparency). Each color is made up of a unique mixture of components, which depend on the chosen color model. Several color models exist, and GIMP uses three of them. In all the models, a given color is represented as coordinates in some number of dimensions, generally three. The size of the coordinate range indicates the number of possible colors. Due to file size constraints, the coordinates are generally integers, at least when stored on external media. A floating number needs 32 or even 64 bits, while all color representations on files use at most 8 bits per color.

The RGB model is additive, meaning that a color with a value of zero in each of its components is black, and a color with a maximum value in each of its components is white. The three fundamental colors are red, green, and blue, and the combination of two fundamental colors is a complementary color: red + green = yellow, red + blue = magenta, and green + blue = cyan. This model can be depicted as a cube, the contents of which define the gamut (or range) of colors that can be represented (see Figure A.37 on page 605).

The CMY model is a subtractive model, so a pixel with a value of zero in each of its components is white, and a pixel with a maximum value in each of its components is black. The three fundamental colors are cyan, magenta, and yellow. They are combined to create the complementary colors of the CMY model, which are the fundamental colors of the RGB model: cyan + magenta = blue, cyan + yellow = green, and magenta + yellow = red. The CMY cube (Figure A.40 on page 606) is the opposite of the RGB cube but defines the same gamut.

The HSV model is neither additive nor subtractive. The hue component represents an angle on a circle that goes from red to violet and purple, ending in red again. The saturation component is a percentage of color, from 0% for white (no color at all) to 100% for full saturation. The value component is also a percentage, from 0% for black (no light at all) to 100% for full intensity (maximum light). This model can be depicted as a cone or a cylinder.

Display devices generate color by combining the light of different colors and usually use the RGB model. This model also corresponds to the main internal representation in the computer, as you'll see later in this chapter. Printing devices, which generate color by superimposing inks, use the CMY model. To reduce the cost of ink, a fourth component, black, is often added, resulting in the CMYK model. With this model,

black can be represented in many ways. For example, 100% C, M, and Y with 0% K and 100% K with 0% C, M, and Y would both result in a black color, but the former would look muddier and require more ink and a longer time to dry. The CMY and CMYK models, therefore, have the same gamut, and the appropriate choice depends on the printer. The HSV model was designed to be intuitive for humans. It provides a visual interface. Rather than inputting a color as a combination of three numeric coordinates, you can choose a hue (H) component and then set the saturation (S) and value (V) components.

Stored Representations

In GIMP memory, a pixel is always represented in the RGB model. In GIMP 2.8, each RGB component is represented by 1 byte, which means that its range is [0 to 255]. The number of different colors is thus $256^3 = 16,777,216$. This seems like a lot of colors, but in some cases, it's not enough, as you'll see later. A pixel requires 3 bytes if there is no transparency. If there is an Alpha channel for transparency, this component is represented by one additional byte.

When an image is stored in the XCF format native to GIMP, just the three or four necessary bytes are stored. Storage and retrieval do not require any conversion, but an image file can still be quite large. A 10-megapixel image with an Alpha channel, for example, takes up 40MB.

The *mode* of an image, found in **Image: Image > Mode**, doesn't determine how an image is represented in memory. Rather, it determines how the image is handled. *RGB mode* is the most powerful because it corresponds to the stored representation of the image and allows for storage of a large number of different colors.

For a grayscale image, RGB representation is overkill. In *Grayscale mode*, only one component per pixel (assuming no Alpha channel) is present; this component represents the intensity of light, from 0 for black to the maximum value for white. In GIMP 2.8, a grayscale pixel uses

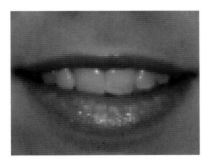

Figure 12.1 *The initial image*

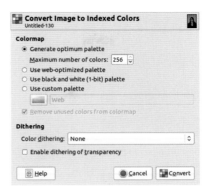

Figure 12.2 *The Indexed Color Conversion dialog*

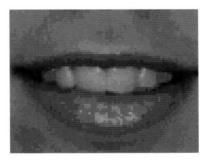

Figure 12.3 *Optimum palette with 256 colors*

1 byte, so the value range is [0 to 255]. This range is not very large, and a very large grayscale gradient—for example, in the sky of a landscape photograph—can appear striped. A grayscale image is best stored in that mode in GIMP, but keep in mind, any operation dealing with color won't work unless you change the image mode to RGB.

The third and last internal mode is the *Indexed mode*. In this mode, a pixel is not represented by the direct value of its color components but by an index in a table of predefined colors, called a *colormap*. This table can be of any size up to 256 entries, so an image in Indexed mode contains at most 256 different colors. This has several advantages and disadvantages:

- A pixel takes up only 1 byte or less if the colormap is smaller than 256 entries.

- By simply changing entries in the colormap, full image transformations can be done easily and efficiently.

- This mode is ideal if you're creating a tapestry or a mosaic because such designs contain only a limited number of colors.

- Many image manipulations are impossible to achieve because the necessary colors cannot be represented.

- The image quality that's achievable in this mode is acceptable only in very specific or simple cases, for example, when the image is small or is a sketch.

Now, let's consider Indexed mode in more detail.

Indexed Mode

Figure 12.1 shows a part of an image in RGB mode, zoomed to show the individual pixels. To convert it to Indexed mode, select **Image: Image > Mode > Indexed**, which opens the dialog shown in Figure 12.2. The following Colormap choices are available:

- GENERATE OPTIMUM PALETTE allows you to choose the maximum number of colors, and GIMP then attempts to generate the best palette for the image. Even with the maximum of 256 colors, Figure 12.3 shows that the conversion results in a clear decrease in image quality.

- USE WEB-OPTIMIZED PALETTE uses a specific palette that's supposed to have a consistent

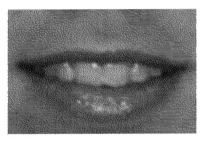

Figure 12.4 *An image dithered to black and white*

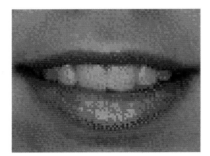

Figure 12.5 *Using Floyd-Steinberg (normal) dithering*

appearance on different screens. Unfortunately, the appearance is consistently bad, and this mode is now considered obsolete.

- USE BLACK AND WHITE (1-BIT) PALETTE converts the image to black and white in the same way as the **Image: Colors > Threshold** tool, unless color dithering is used. With color dithering, a usable black and white copy of an image can be created, as shown in Figure 12.4.

- USE CUSTOM PALETTE allows you to choose from the available palettes, which are usually not as good as the optimum palette that GIMP can generate.

The REMOVE UNUSED COLORS FROM COLORMAP checkbox is useful only when you select USE CUSTOM PALETTE.

As Figure 12.3 shows, indexing can lead to image degradation. A better result can be achieved with dithering, which uses a diffusion of pixels in available colors to approximate the colors that are not available. Four dithering algorithms are provided in the Index Color Conversion

| Normal |
| Dissolve |
| Lighten only |
| Screen |
| Dodge |
| Addition |
| Darken only |
| Multiply |
| Burn |
| Overlay |
| Soft light |
| Hard light |
| Difference |
| Subtract |
| Grain extract |
| Grain merge |
| Divide |
| Hue |
| Saturation |
| Color |
| Value |

Figure 12.6 *The available layer blending modes*

dialog, and Figure 12.5 shows the result of the first one. ENABLE DITHERING OF TRANSPARENCY can be used to help smooth boundaries in a GIF image that includes transparent areas.

12.2 Blending Modes

The blending modes apply an additional color plane to an image, either as a layer or as a design created with the painting tools. Figure 12.6 shows 21 of the 23 blending modes available for painting tools. In layers, the Behind and Color erase modes are not available.

The blending modes are arranged in the menu according to their effect. The first four modes (Normal, Dissolve, Behind, and Color erase, or just the first two for layers) leave the pixels intact and change only which pixels are displayed. The next four modes (Lighten only, Screen, Dodge, and Addition) lighten the

Figure 12.7 *The top layer*

Figure 12.9 *Normal mode, 50% opacity*

Figure 12.8 *The bottom layer*

image and are arranged by impact, from least to greatest. The next three modes (Darken only, Multiply, and Burn) darken the image, and they are also arranged by impact, from least to greatest. The next three modes (Overlay, Soft light, and Hard light) alter the image's luminosity. The next five modes (Difference, Subtract, Grain extract, Grain merge, and Divide) distort the image's hues rather than just its saturation and value. The last four modes (Hue, Saturation, Color, and Value) use the HSV model components as the basis for blending the layers.

To demonstrate the blending modes, we'll build an image with two layers. Figure 12.7 is the top layer, and Figure 12.8 is the bottom layer. We'll use specific examples for the two modes that exist only with the painting tools.

We also need a notation for explaining the mathematics underlying the blending modes. Recall that a pixel is made of three values—the channels R, G, and B—and so can be thought of as a vector. We'll use U to refer to the vector of a pixel in the upper layer, L to refer to the vector of a pixel in the lower layer, and R to refer to the vector of the resulting pixel.

Modes That Leave Pixels Intact

The four modes in this category have an important property in common: They all assign a value to R by taking the exact values either from U or from L.

In *Normal* mode, the upper pixel is always chosen (i.e., $R = U$). But if U isn't fully opaque, then the value of R is a combination of U and L. If the opacity of U is set to percentage x, then

$$R = \frac{Ux + L(100 - x)}{100}$$

Figure 12.9 shows the result when the top layer opacity is 50%. Opacity works in the same way for all of the blending modes.

In *Dissolve* mode, the choice between the upper and lower pixel is random but proportional to the opacity. Given a function $f(r)$ that yields a random result between 0 and 1, the formula is $R = [\text{if } 100 \times f(r) < x] \text{ then } U, \text{ else } L$. Figure 12.10 shows this result with 50% opacity,

Figure 12.10 *Dissolve mode, 50% opacity*

Figure 12.11 *Zooming in on a part of Figure 12.10*

Figure 12.12 *An image with transparency*

Figure 12.13 *Painting in Behind mode*

and Figure 12.11 magnifies a portion of this image.

To demonstrate *Behind* mode, we'll use Figure 12.12. We first removed the portrait's background, replacing it with transparency. An underlying white layer is visible beneath the portrait layer. If we paint on this image in Behind mode, only the transparent pixels are affected, as shown in Figure 12.13. If semi-transparency had been used rather than full transparency, we would see a combination of the green and semi-transparent background color.

Color erase mode removes the color that you're painting with from the image and replaces it with partial transparency. In Figure 12.14, we used a large round brush and selected the hue of the face as the foreground color by CTRL-clicking the girl's left cheek. The white background layer is visible through the semi-transparency.

Lightening Modes

When you use lightening modes, the image will be lighter than in Normal mode.

In *Lighten only* mode, the resulting pixel is the same as the lighter of the two pixels being blended. In Figure 12.15, the brightly lit seascape was taken from the upper layer, and the rest was taken from the lower layer. The formula is simply $R = \max(U, L)$.

Screen mode yields an even lighter result via a more complicated formula:

$$R = 255 - \frac{(255 - U) \times (255 - L)}{255}$$

The upper and lower pixels are inverted, which is done by subtracting their value from 255 (in 8-bit depth). The results are multiplied,

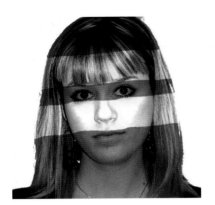

Figure 12.14 *Painting in Color erase mode*

Figure 12.16 *Screen mode*

Figure 12.15 *Lighten only mode*

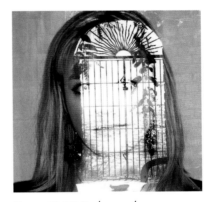

Figure 12.17 *Dodge mode*

and then the product is normalized to subrange [0 to 255] by dividing it by 255 and inverting it again. As you see in Figure 12.16, the dark areas of the upper layer disappear, the light areas look washed out, and the image seems to be more transparent.

Dodge mode exaggerates the lighting. The formula for this mode is:

$$R = \frac{L \times 256}{(255 - U) + 1}$$

The lower pixel value is multiplied by 256 and then divided by the inverse value of the upper pixel. To prevent division by 0, 1 is added to the divisor. Figure 12.17 shows the result. This mode works best when used with a painting

tool to simulate the dodging process used in the darkroom to decrease exposure in specific areas. This mode can be used to bring out details in the darkest areas of an image.

Addition mode exaggerates the lighting even further without any color inversion. Some areas may become completely white, as shown in Figure 12.18. To achieve this result, the pixel values are added, and then the result is truncated to 255 because greater values can't be represented in the RGB cube. The formula is $R = \min(U + L, 255)$.

Darkening Modes

With these modes, the resulting image is darker than the original.

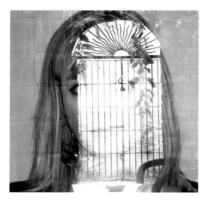

Figure 12.18 *Addition mode*

Figure 12.20 *Multiply mode*

Figure 12.19 *Darken only mode*

Figure 12.21 *Burn mode*

Darken only mode is the opposite of Lighten only mode: The resulting pixel is the darker of the two pixels being blended. As shown in Figure 12.19, the resulting image contains content from the upper layer where it's darker and the lower layer elsewhere. The formula is $R = \min(U, L)$.

In *Multiply* mode, the pixel values are multiplied, and the result is normalized by dividing by 255: $R = (U \times L)/255$. As Figure 12.20 shows, the result is much darker than the two layers.

Burn mode simulates a darkroom process, similar to Dodge mode, and also works best with painting tools. This mode decreases the exposure of the image and can lead to a loss of detail in dark areas. The formula for this mode is:

$$R = 255 - \frac{(255 - L) \times 256}{U + 1}$$

The lower pixel value is inverted and divided by the upper pixel value. That number is then normalized by multiplying by 256, and the result is inverted. Again, 1 is added to the divisor to prevent division by 0. In Figure 12.21, the only parts that are not completely burned out are those that were light in both layers.

Luminosity Modes

The three modes in this section are so similar that the first two currently have identical effects.

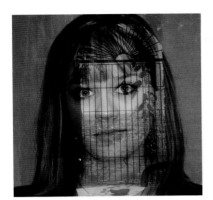

Figure 12.22 *Overlay or Soft light mode*

Figure 12.23 *Hard light mode*

These modes deal with the luminosity of the image rather than its colors.

Overlay mode combines Multiply and Screen modes, and it darkens the image a little less than Multiply. Its complicated equation is theoretically this:

$$R = \frac{L}{255} \times (L + \frac{2 \times U \times (255 - L)}{255})$$

But in GIMP 2.8, this mode actually uses the equation for Soft light mode. This bug has intentionally been left because correcting it would result in unexpected changes appearing in existing images that use Overlay mode. Developers are currently working on a strategy to correct the bug without altering existing images.

The equation for *Soft light* mode incorporates the result of the Screen mode calculation, here called R_S:

$$R = \frac{(255 - L) \times U \times L + L \times R_S}{255}$$

As Figure 12.22 shows, the resulting image is darker than the original image, having dim colors and softened edges.

Hard light mode uses the most complicated equation of all the modes. It handles darker colors differently than brighter colors. Hard light is yet another combination of Multiply and Screen, and it results in brighter colors and sharper edges (i.e., the exact opposite of

Figure 12.24 *Hard light mode with the layers reversed*

Soft light). The upper layer is treated differently than the lower layer, unlike most of the modes already considered. Figures 12.23 and 12.24 show two examples, with the layer order reversed in the second one. The equation is as follows:

If $U > 128$:

$$R = 255 - \frac{(255 - L) \times (255 - (2 \times (U - 128)))}{256}$$

If $U \leq 128$: $R = (2 \times U \times L)/256$

Color Distortion Modes

These modes distort colors in various ways.

In *Difference* mode, the resulting pixel is the absolute value of the difference between the

Figure 12.25 *Difference mode*

Figure 12.27 *Subtract mode with the layers reversed*

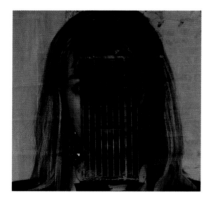

Figure 12.26 *Subtract mode*

Figure 12.28 *Grain extract mode*

upper and lower pixels: $R = |U - L|$. For example, if $U = 50$ and $L = 200$, then R will be the absolute value of -150, which is 150. When this occurs, the colors appear to be inverted, as shown in Figure 12.25.

Subtract mode is based on the same idea as Difference mode, but it doesn't take the absolute value after subtraction. This means the order of the layers affects the result, as illustrated by Figures 12.26 and 12.27. Subtract mode deals with negative values by setting them to 0, according to the following formula: $R = \max(U - L, 0)$. Any 0 values correspond to black areas.

According to its name, the *Grain extract* mode should extract the film grain from a layer, but whether it does this is debatable. Some people think it gives images an embossed appearance.

Figures 12.28 and 12.29 show the effect of Grain extract on our example images. The official formula is $R = L - U + 128$, but negative values or values greater than 255 are truncated. Negative values are replaced with 0, and values greater than 255 are replaced with 255.

Whereas Grain extract mode extracts the grain from the layer, *Grain merge* mode merges the grain layer into the current layer. This mode is symmetric, so the order of the layers doesn't matter. Our result is shown in Figure 12.30. The formula for this mode is $R = U + L - 128$, and again, values that are negative or greater than 255 are truncated.

Divide mode is yet another nonsymmetrical mode, wherein the value of the lower pixel is divided by that of the upper pixel (plus 1). The

Figure 12.29 *Grain extract mode with the layers reversed*

Figure 12.31 *Divide mode*

Figure 12.30 *Grain merge mode*

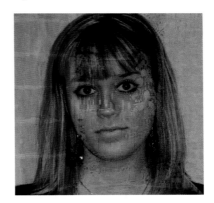

Figure 12.32 *Hue mode*

result is multiplied by 256 to normalize the value. The result, shown in Figure 12.31, is lighter than the original and completely white in some places. The equation is

$$R = \frac{256 \times L}{U + 1}$$

HSV Modes

The last four modes operate in the HSV space. They work by replacing one component (hue, saturation, or value) in the upper layer with the corresponding component from the lower layer.

In *Hue* mode, the resulting pixel has the hue of the upper pixel and the saturation and value of the lower pixel. But if the saturation of the upper pixel is 0, the hue is also taken

from the lower pixel. This explains why in Figure 12.32, the pixels corresponding to the black areas in the upper layer are completely replaced with the pixels from the lower layer.

In *Saturation* mode, the saturation is taken only from the upper layer. Because the saturation of the top layer was low throughout most of the image, the result, shown in Figure 12.33, is almost completely unsaturated.

In *Color* mode, the hue and saturation are taken from the upper layer, whereas the value is taken from the lower layer. As shown in Figure 12.34, the effect is that the lower layer is painted with the upper layer's colors.

In *Value* mode, the value is taken from the upper layer, and the saturation and hue are taken from the lower layer. As shown in Figure 12.35,

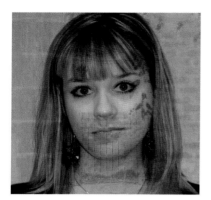

Figure 12.33 *Saturation mode*

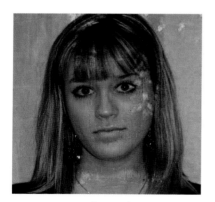

Figure 12.34 *Color mode*

the result of this mode is the reverse of Color mode: The upper layer is painted with the colors of the lower layer.

12.3 Color Management

Color perception is one of the most complicated aspects of image processing. We see images in the real world, capture them with a camera or maybe scan them, and then we look at them on a screen and perhaps print them. All these stages change the image, rendering the visible colors and the values differently. The purpose of color management is to control these changes so what others see on the screen or in print is the image as we intended them to see it.

Figure 12.35 *Value mode*

Color-Managed Workflow

The gamuts of devices (i.e., the sets of colors those devices are able to represent) are inevitably smaller than the gamut of normal human vision. (See "Digitalization" on page 598 for an in-depth discussion of image representation.) Furthermore, the digital camera or the scanner that digitalized the image, the monitor that displays it, and the printer that makes a copy all use different color spaces that are characterized by their gamuts and some adjustable parameters. Figure 12.36 shows a diagram of a computer using a device-independent *working color space*, usually RGB. A working color space includes the color spaces of the most commonly used devices. It should include the color spaces of a scanner and a camera and those of a standard screen and of most printers. The working color space should contain only colors that can be represented on the devices being used. When an image file is loaded from a scanner or a digital camera, it must first be converted from its initial color space to the working one, and a similar conversion must be done when displaying the image on a monitor or printing it.

This conversion process is automatic if we have the necessary information, which is stored as a *color profile*. A color profile provides the information needed to convert from one color space to another. One profile describes the camera color space and is attached to the image file

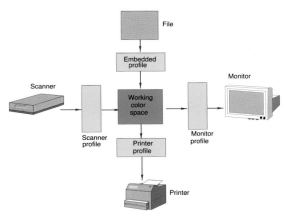

Figure 12.36 *A color-managed workflow*

Figure 12.37 *The Image: Image > Mode menu*

Figure 12.38 *Assigning a color profile*

of a digital photograph. Other profiles specify the color spaces of the scanner, printer, and monitor.

You can assign a color profile to an image if it doesn't have one or if you want to change the assigned one. The **Image: Image > Mode** menu (Figure 12.37) contains two entries that allow you to edit the color profile. Select the ASSIGN COLOR PROFILE entry to open the dialog shown in Figure 12.38. In the ASSIGN field, you can choose a previously used profile or search for a profile on the computer. On a GNU/Linux

Figure 12.39 *Converting to a color profile*

platform, the profiles are generally located in the /usr/share/color/icc/ folder.

Image: Image > Mode > Convert to Color Profile opens the dialog shown in Figure 12.39. In addition to the name of the profile, this dialog allows you to choose the rendering intent and black point compensation, which we'll discuss in "Using Color Management" on page 254.

Color management can also be used to simulate the result of converting an image to the color space of another device. The gamut of a printer is smaller than the gamut of a monitor. Printers are especially poor at rendering saturated colors, particularly shades of blue and green. A picture that we painstakingly crafted in GIMP may look terrible when printed if the conversion isn't managed. If you intend to print your image, displaying the image so it looks like the final printed result is best, rather than creating an image that exploits monitor capabilities that aren't shared by the printer. This technique is called *softproofing*.

Color profiles are generally known as *ICC profiles* because they are defined by the International Color Consortium. The two most frequently used profiles are shown in Figure 12.40. Although using the profile with the largest gamut (i.e., Adobe RGB) might seem best, this is generally not the case because color distortion can occur when converting the image to the more restricted printer gamut. Thus, the default color space is usually sRGB.

In fact, if we load an image into GIMP without any embedded color profile, GIMP assumes

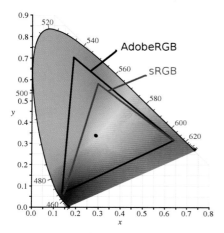

Figure 12.40 *Adobe RGB and sRGB gamuts*

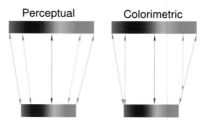

Figure 12.41 *Perceptual and colorimetric gamut mappings*

it's sRGB, although we can assign another profile. If an embedded profile exists, GIMP will ask whether you want to use it, and generally you should select yes.

Getting the color profile for a device is not always easy. This is especially true for monitors, which often require the purchase of a display calibration device. The retrieval of color profiles is beyond the scope of this book, but if you would like more information, we recommend the excellent website by Norman Koren (*http://www .normankoren.com/color_management.html*).

Using Color Management

You can set the color management parameters in two places in GIMP. One is the **Image: Edit > Preferences** dialog, described in "Color Management" on page 567. The other is the **Image: View > Display Filters** tool, described in "Display Filters" on page 573.

Apply *rendering intent* via the **Image: Edit > Preferences** dialog. Rendering intent can be used to generate the so-called softproof of an image that you want to print. It specifies how colors are converted from one gamut to another. If no conversion is carried out, the colors in the first gamut that cannot be represented in

the second one are simply clipped, leading to ugly distortions. By using a more sophisticated conversion technique, you can often achieve a much more satisfactory result. The two main techniques, perceptual and colorimetric, are shown in Figure 12.41.

With *perceptual intent*, the color spectrum is compressed, and so the differences among colors are maintained. This process affects fully saturated colors much more than those with low saturation. If it is done with a large enough color depth, this process is mostly reversible and so is a good choice if you will be converting the image between color spaces multiple times. This is also a good choice if the image contains saturated colors.

Colorimetric intent leaves the colors that belong to both gamuts completely unaltered and clips the others to the nearest color. This process is not reversible, and although it preserves the whites, it often yields poor results for images with saturated colors.

12.4   The Major Color Tools

In the rest of this chapter, we'll discuss the tools that you can use to adjust the colors in an image. Here we delve into the Color chooser, Levels, and Curves tools.

The Color Chooser

The Color chooser is the main tool for choosing a color for any painting tool. To open the Color chooser from the Toolbox, click one of the rect-

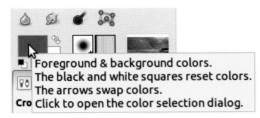

Figure 12.42 *Opening the Color chooser dialog*

angles that display the current foreground and background colors, as shown in (Figure 12.42).

The Color chooser appears as shown in Figure 12.43. This dialog is packed with features, so we'll break our discussion into several areas and look at them separately.

The top-right quadrant of the dialog contains six sliders corresponding to the channels in the HSV and RGB models. To the right of the sliders are counters that you can use to make precise changes. The radio buttons on the left are related to the first tab in the top-left quadrant, the one with Wilber's head displayed on it. If any of the other tabs are selected, these buttons are not active.

The sliders are correlated, so if we move one of them, several others are also affected. For example, moving the S slider also changes all the RGB sliders. Moving one of the RGB sliders changes the H slider and can also change the S and V sliders, depending on their initial values. The color spectrum for the sliders changes to display the effect based on the current selection. Only the H slider always displays the same rainbow of colors.

The bottom-right quadrant of the dialog contains a number of controls. The HTML NOTATION field contains the hexadecimal representation of the current color in HTML code. This code is composed of three groups of two hexadecimal digits, representing the values of the three RGB channels. If we choose a color elsewhere in the dialog, the code will change to match, but we can also type a number into the field and look at the result, or we can even type in a color name. If we type the beginning

of a name, all the available names that begin with those letters are displayed, as shown in Figure 12.44.

The small button to the right of the field is used to select a color from an image or from anywhere on the screen. If we click this button, the mouse pointer icon becomes an eyedropper. When we click somewhere on the screen (even outside of a GIMP window), the corresponding pixel color is selected for the Color chooser, and this color defines the value of the six sliders and the HTML notation field.

Below this field are 12 colored buttons that represent the *color history*. The button on the left with a > sign is used to add the current color to this history and remove the oldest color (the bottom-right one). If we click any of these buttons, its color becomes the current one.

The three buttons in the bottom-right corner of the dialog are mostly self-explanatory. RESET changes the current color to black but does not affect the history.

The bottom-left quadrant of the dialog contains only three controls. CURRENT and OLD represent, respectively, the current color as defined in the Color chooser dialog and the color defined before that. Click and drag the color from either of these two buttons to an image to fill the current selection. The HELP button does what you'd expect.

The top-left quadrant contains a rectangular display and five tabs, which give five different ways to finely tune the desired color. Figure 12.43 shows the Wilber tab, the only one that uses the six radio buttons to the left of the HSV and RGB sliders. Here, the selected radio button is H, which means the spectrum to the right of the large rectangular area shows the Hue scale. The pointer in this display indicates the current hue, whereas the rectangle on the left represents the possible variations of saturation and value when this hue is chosen. If we click this rectangle, we choose a specific value (in the horizontal scale) and a specific saturation (in the vertical scale). Two perpendicular lines

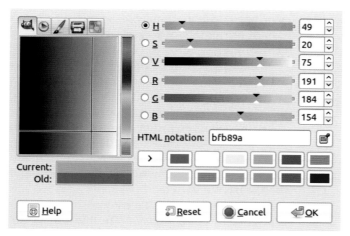

Figure 12.43 *The Color chooser*

Figure 12.44 *Typing a color name in the HTML notation field*

Figure 12.45 *The Wilber tab, Blue selection*

cross at the chosen point, and the sliders on the right side of the dialog change to reflect the new saturation and value.

Selecting a different radio button changes the rectangular display on the left. For example, Figure 12.45 shows the display when the B (blue) radio button has been selected. The thin vertical rectangle allows us to choose the quantity of blue, and the large rectangle allows us to adjust the quantities of red and green. Occasionally, the combination that's activated when you check the B radio button is more convenient, but usually the default (H) works best.

The Triangle tab has an icon showing a thumbnail of that tab's display (Figure 12.46). This tab offers another graphical way to choose

the color using the HSV model. Clicking the hue circle selects the H component. A click in the triangle then changes the values of the S and V components. At one of the triangle's points, S is 0; at another point, V is 0; at the final point, both are at the maximum (100). Some people find this tab more intuitive than the Wilber tab.

The tab with a paintbrush icon behaves like a simulation of watercolor painting (Figure 12.47). A click anywhere in the rectangle adds a small quantity of that color to the current one. The vertical slider sets the quantity of color being added, from 0 at the bottom to the maximum at the top. Because colors are added to the existing color, this tab uses the CMY model, and

Figure 12.46 *The Triangle tab*

Figure 12.47 *The Watercolor tab*

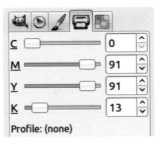

Figure 12.48 *The Print tab*

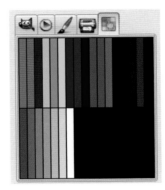

Figure 12.49 *The Palette tab*

the color obtained becomes stronger the more we click. If we click one of the rectangle's sides, the saturation increases. If we click in the center of the rectangle, the value decreases. This tab is especially useful for building a light color, like a pastel, beginning with a full white.

The tab marked with a printer icon contains options based on the CMYK color model (Figure 12.48). This tab is useful mainly for gathering information about how the colors will be mixed when printing rather than as a way to adjust a color, particularly because you can't automatically change the CMY channels when changing the K channel, which is a common printing adjustment.

The remaining tab has an icon showing a finger on a palette (Figure 12.49). The center square shows the contents of the current palette, a concept explained in Section 22.7. The only colors you can choose are from this palette, but you can change the palette in the Palettes dialog, which you open via **Image: Windows > Dockable Dialogs > Palettes**.

Access a simplified dockable dialog for choosing colors by selecting **Image: Windows > Dockable dialogs > Colors**, as shown in Figure 12.50. The Colors dialog is a modified version of the left portion of the Color chooser. The Wilber tab contains six buttons on the right, used to choose the color model and the master channel. The Triangle, Watercolor, Printer, and Palette tabs are identical to those on the Color chooser. The last tab is a slightly modified version of the right portion of the Color chooser dialog (Figure 12.51).

Figure 12.50 *The Colors dialog, Wilber tab*

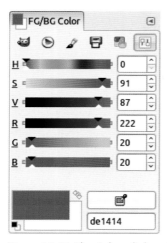

Figure 12.51 *The Colors dialog, Sliders tab*

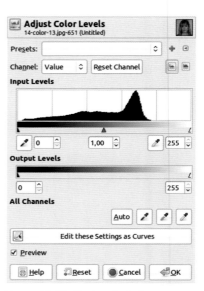

Figure 12.52 *The Levels dialog*

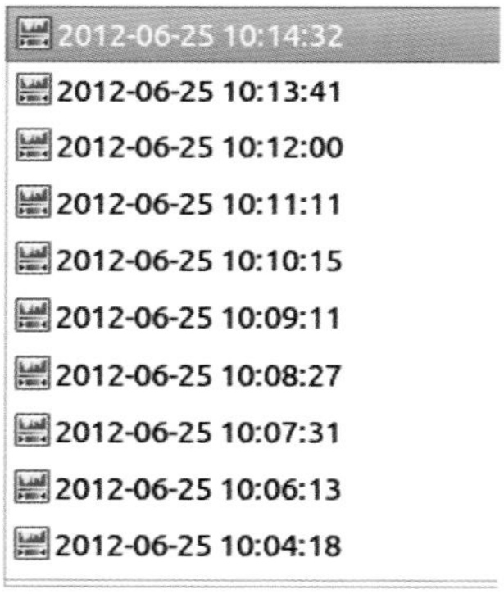

Figure 12.53 *Preset settings*

Levels

The Levels tool, opened by selecting **Image: Colors > Levels** or **Image: Tools > Color Tools > Levels**, is one of the most useful tools in GIMP

The bottom of the Colors dialog contains several useful buttons. On the left are the buttons for setting the foreground and background colors. On the right is the button for applying the eyedropper and the field containing the HTML notation for the current color.

for photo processing. In a nutshell, use the Levels tool (and the Curves tool, discussed in the next section) to adjust the relationship between initial pixel values (the input) and pixel values in the new, transformed image (the output). The Levels tool dialog is shown in Figure 12.52.

The PRESETS field at the top of the Levels dialog opens a menu of previously saved settings. The settings are identified in ISO format by the date and time they were saved (see Figure 12.53). The plus sign on the right saves the current settings. This is more convenient than

Figure 12.54 *The Levels dialog menu*

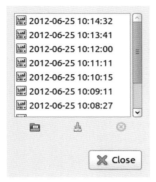

Figure 12.55 *Settings management*

Figure 12.56 *A logarithmic histogram*

remembering the ISO date and time when you used a specific setting. Named settings are listed at the end of the saved settings. The same capabilities are available in the other color tools. The small triangle on the far right opens the menu shown in Figure 12.54. Use the first two entries to import or export settings to or from a file. The last entry opens the dialog shown in Figure 12.55, which lists the saved settings and contains three buttons to import settings, export settings, and delete the selected settings.

The next line of the Levels dialog contains a menu to select the Channel that will be affected. The choices are Value, Red, Green, Blue, and Alpha (if an Alpha channel is available). When you select the Value channel, all three color channels change. The Value channel is the only channel available for a grayscale image. The RE-SET CHANNEL button resets the selected channel to its initial value without affecting any changes made elsewhere in the dialog.

The two buttons on the right set the characteristic of the histogram shown below. The histogram is a way to display the frequency of different values in the chosen channel. In 8-bit depth representation, there are 256 different values,

from 0 on the left to 255 on the right. The height of a bar in the graph is proportional to the number of pixels in the image with this value. If the leftmost button is pressed, the peak corresponds literally to the number of pixels, whereas in the logarithmic histogram, which you select with the rightmost button, the values are calculated using a logarithm. As Figure 12.56 shows, the logarithmic histogram better illustrates variations in the low values, whereas the linear histogram (shown in Figure 12.52) exaggerates the peaks.

The purpose of the Levels tool is to change the histogram by assigning new values to certain pixels. Generally, images look best when pixels are distributed across the full range. As you can see, the values greater than 200 are not represented at all in the example we've used.

Just under the histogram are three movable triangles. The black one on the left corresponds to the *black point*: All pixels with a value less than or equal to the position of this triangle are set to 0 (i.e., black for color channels or full transparency for the Alpha channel). When this point moves to the right, more pixels become black, which is generally only beneficial if the histogram is empty on the left. The white triangle on the right corresponds to the *white point*: All pixels with a value greater than or equal to the position of that triangle are set to 255 (i.e., the maximum). Our example image would benefit from this adjustment because values greater than 200 are not represented at all. If we move the white triangle to 200, the full range of available values is represented in the image, which improves the contrast. The result is shown in Figure 12.57, which you can compare to the original image, shown in Figure 12.8 on page 245.

Figure 12.57 *Figure 12.8 after moving the white triangle to 200*

Figure 12.58 *Figure 12.8 after restricting the output levels to [100 to 200]*

The middle, gray triangle corresponds to the *midpoint*. Moving it to the left makes the image lighter in the Value channel, more saturated in a color channel, or more opaque in the Alpha channel. Moving it to the right has the opposite effect. This slider changes the value of the *Gamma factor*, or Gamma correction, which specifies the shape of the *answering curve*. The answering curve represents the relationship between the input (initial pixel) and the output (new pixel) values. If Gamma = 1, the curve is a straight line. Increasing Gamma makes the curve convex, and decreasing it makes the curve concave.

Instead of moving one of the triangles by hand, we can also change the corresponding numeric field. Additionally, two eyedroppers, one for the black point and the other for the white point, are available. By clicking one of them and then clicking in the image on a pixel of the corresponding shade, we can adjust the triangles so they bracket the values that are represented in the image.

All the settings covered so far deal with the INPUT LEVELS, which enlarge the range of pixel values in the image to build a new image. Just below those controls are two triangles that alter the OUTPUT LEVELS. Moving the OUTPUT LEVELS triangles toward each other restricts the range of possible values. In the Value channel, for

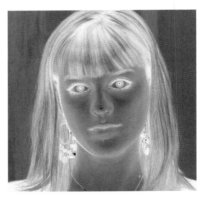

Figure 12.59 *Figure 12.8 after inverting the output levels*

example, this reduces the image contrast, making the image duller, as shown in Figure 12.58.

If we move the white triangle to the left side and the black triangle to the right side, then we invert the image, as illustrated in Figure 12.59. Doing this accomplishes the same thing as applying **Image: Colors > Invert**, except that when using the Levels tool, we can invert each of the RGB color channels separately.

So far we've discussed the manual settings, which alter only the selected channel. The Levels tool also includes some automatic settings, which act on all channels at the same time. The simplest and most useful of these is the AUTO button, which extends the input range of the three color channels as far as possible.

Figure 12.60 *Figure 12.8 after using the Auto button*

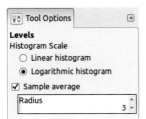

Figure 12.61 *The Levels tool options*

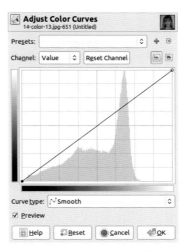

Figure 12.62 *The Curves dialog*

Figure 12.60 shows the result for our image. Generally this improves the image, but in this example, the change is too dramatic.

The three eyedroppers on the right, like the histogram eyedroppers, can be used to select the black and white points and also a midpoint in the image. But unlike the histogram eyedroppers, these eyedroppers change all the channels, which can lead to strange and unnatural effects. Note that the order in which these points are picked is significant, and picking them all is not necessary. Generally, the midpoint is the most difficult to pick accurately.

Although the Levels tool is, by default, not accessed from the Toolbox (change this in the **Image: Edit > Preferences** dialog, TOOLBOX entry), it does have Toolbox options, which appear when the tool is selected. These are shown in Figure 12.61. The HISTOGRAM SCALE radio buttons do the same thing as the buttons at the top right of the Levels dialog. The SAMPLE AVERAGE

option, if checked, sets the radius of the area used to pick a color in the image when using one of the eyedroppers. This square appears if you press the mouse button when clicking the image with the eyedropper selected.

Use the Curves tool to make the same adjustments as the Levels tool, but the Curves tool offers more control. Below the three eyedroppers in the Levels dialog is an EDIT THESE SETTINGS AS CURVES button, which retains any changes that were made in the Levels dialog and applies the Curves tool. The PREVIEW button allows you to see the effect of your changes and should always be checked. The four buttons at the bottom of the Levels dialog are self-explanatory.

Curves

The Curves tool is found via **Image: Colors > Curves** or **Image: Tools > Color Tools > Curves** and opens the dialog shown in Figure 12.62. The Curves tool's effect is similar to that of the Levels tool, but it offers fewer automatized options and more control.

The top and the bottom of the Curves dialog are the same as the Levels dialog. In the rectangle at the center of the Curves dialog, you'll see an image of the histogram. The diagonal of this

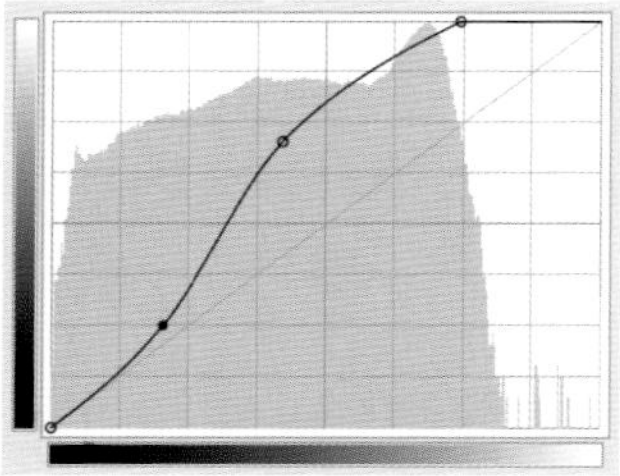

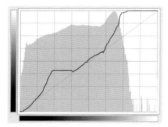

Figure 12.63 *A smooth curve*

Figure 12.65 *The result of the freehand curve*

Figure 12.64 *A freehand curve*

rectangle represents the answering curve. Input values vary horizontally, and output values vary vertically. Initially, the input and output values are equal. When the mouse pointer is in the rectangle, its coordinates are displayed in the top-left corner.

By clicking and dragging the answering curve, we can change its shape. If the CURVE TYPE button shows SMOOTH, as it does by default, the curve, which remains smooth, is adjusted to pass by the points added, as shown in Figure 12.63. These points, called *anchors*, are automatically added every time you click in the histogram. The current anchor is a black dot. Move it by clicking and dragging or by using the up and down arrow keys on the keyboard. Press SHIFT to move the arrow keys by 15 pixels at a time, rather than the default of 1 pixel. The left and right arrow keys select the next anchor in the corresponding direction. If you click near an existing anchor, you can drag it to another position, thus changing the curve. To remove an anchor, drag it into one of the other anchors.

While the tool is in use, the mouse pointer takes the form of an eyedropper when you hover over the image. If you click the image, a vertical line appears in the Curves dialog at the value of the clicked pixel. SHIFT-clicking creates an anchor in the selected channel, and CTRL-clicking creates an anchor in all the channels. The anchor is inserted only when the mouse button is released, so we can drag the point around the image to find a target value.

If the CURVE TYPE is set to FREEHAND, the curve is built by clicking and dragging in the rectangle and generally comes out jagged, as shown in Figure 12.64. The result is also more difficult to control, as illustrated in Figure 12.65. But if we then choose SMOOTH as the curve type, the curve is automatically smoothed, and the necessary anchors are added.

The options for the Curves tool are the same as for the Levels tool (see Figure 12.61).

The Curves tool does not have any automatic controls and can be more difficult to master than the Levels tool, but it allows for more precise color handling. If we keep the curve straight and move only its end anchors horizontally, the effect is the same as moving the end triangles under INPUT LEVELS in the Levels tool. Moving them vertically has the same effect as moving the triangles under OUTPUT LEVELS. Adding an anchor in the middle of the curve and moving it vertically does the same thing as moving the middle triangle in the Levels tool and is a more intuitive visualization of the Gamma value.

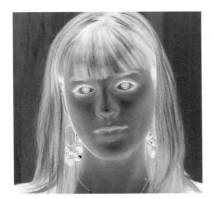

Figure 12.66 *Inverting the curve*

Inverting the curve by putting the left (lower) anchor in the top-left corner and the right (upper) anchor in the bottom-right corner results in a negative image, as shown in Figure 12.66. We can also do this in one channel only, with strange and colorful results. If we change the curves of individual color channels, they appear in their respective colors on the histogram, whereas the current curve is always black. These colored curves are not displayed when the Value channel is selected. Adjusting the shape of the curve can be tricky. Deforming the curve too much is easy and results in exaggerated, unnatural colors.

12.5 Additional Color Tools

The **Image: Colors** menu contains lots of entries (see Figure 12.67). The first section of the menu contains the more basic tools, including Levels and Curves, which we just discussed. Now, we'll demonstrate the other tools in this part of the menu using the photograph shown in Figure 12.68. (Tip: You can access these entries by placing them in the Toolbox or via **Image: Tools > Color Tools**.)

Color Balance

The adjustments you can make with the Color Balance tool can also be made with the Levels or Curves tool, but some people find the Color

Figure 12.67 *The Image: Colors menu*

Balance tool more intuitive. Its dialog is shown in Figure 12.69. The top of this dialog contains the same settings as the Levels and Curves tools, settings that are also shared by the next four tools in the menu: Hue-Saturation, Colorize, Brightness-Contrast, and Threshold.

Adjust the color balance using three sliders [−100 to +100], one for each combination of a fundamental color and complementary color in the RGB and CMY models. Recall that the pairings are the same in these two models, but the designation of fundamental versus complementary differs.

Balance tool to make adjustments in three different ranges: Shadows, Midtones, and Highlights. These ranges overlap, and precisely distinguishing them in an image is difficult. Because the sliders are very sensitive, achieving a natural-looking result is hard, as demonstrated in Figure 12.70. Each of the ranges can be reset

Figure 12.68 *A sample image*

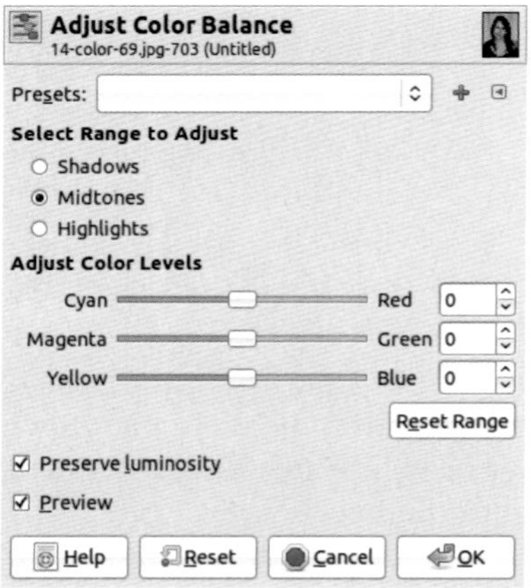

Figure 12.70 *After using the Color Balance tool*

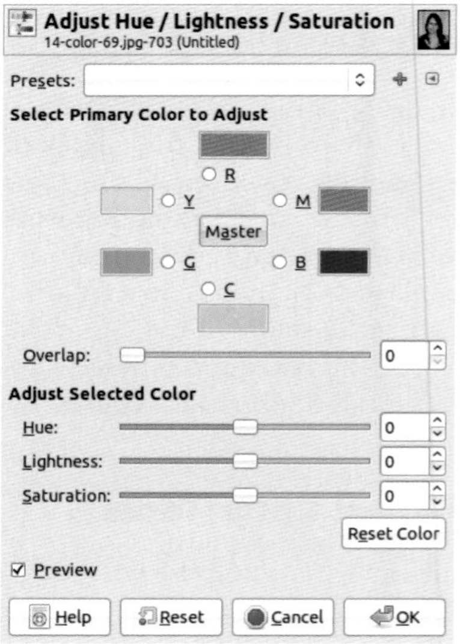

Figure 12.69 *The Color Balance dialog*

individually (by setting the value to 0), which makes adjusting an image by trial and error easier. Leave the two boxes at the bottom of the dialog checked to preview the effects of an adjustment.

Hue-Saturation

This tool offers yet another way to make adjustments that you could also make using the Curves tool. The advantage of Hue-Saturation is that the controls are based on the three color

Figure 12.71 *The Hue-Saturation dialog*

models: RGB, CMY, and HSV. Another important difference is that Hue-Saturation deals with color ranges rather than color channels. For example, how would you change the saturation of yellow pixels using the Curves tool? With Hue-Saturation, it's easy.

The Hue-Saturation dialog, shown in Figure 12.71, begins with the customary line for the PRESETS settings.

Figure 12.72 *After using the Hue-Saturation tool*

Figure 12.74 *Creating a sepia photo-graph with the Colorize tool*

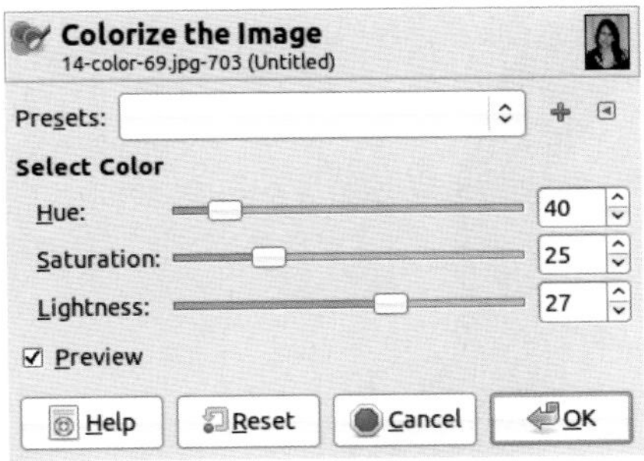

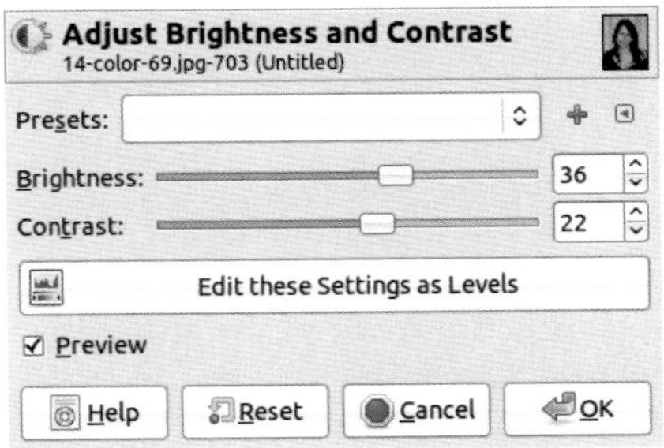

Figure 12.73 *The Colorize dialog*

Figure 12.75 *The Brightness-Contrast dialog*

The next part of the dialog lets us select what color range to change. The center button, called MASTER, allows us to change all the colors simultaneously. The six colored buttons specify color ranges, each representing a sixth of the hue circle. The OVERLAP slider [0 to 100] extends the chosen range into the two neighboring ranges.

The next three sliders are based on the HSV model. (Here, Value is called Lightness). The effect of adjusting any of the three sliders is visible not only in the image but also in the color buttons in the upper part of the dialog. Adjust the hue, saturation, or lightness of any of the six colors, or select the Master control. The many different possible combinations make this tool a difficult one to master. One possible result of the Hue-Saturation tool is shown in Figure 12.72.

Colorize

The Colorize tool first desaturates the image and then adds color to a grayscale version in RGB mode. Its dialog (Figure 12.73) begins with the standard color tool PRESETS option. Below that are sliders to specify the HSV components to apply to the image. The effect is similar to looking at a grayscale image through colored glass. The parameters shown in Figure 12.73 produce the sepia photograph in Figure 12.74.

Brightness-Contrast

The Brightness-Contrast tool is very simple, as you can see from its dialog (Figure 12.75). As the name implies, you can use it to adjust

Figure 12.76 *Adjusting brightness and contrast*

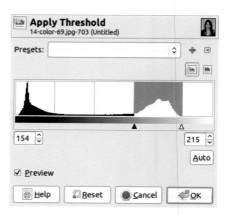

Figure 12.77 *The Threshold dialog*

two characteristics of an image: brightness and contrast.

Because this tool's abilities are rather limited, a button is included (EDIT THESE SETTINGS AS LEVELS) that opens the Levels tool, which you can use to edit brightness and contrast with much more flexibility. The sliders in the Brightness-Contrast tool work in the usual way, but when the tool is active, we can also click and drag in the image itself: Vertical strokes change the brightness, horizontal strokes change the contrast. Figure 12.76 shows the result of the settings shown in Figure 12.75.

Threshold

The Threshold tool transforms the current layer into a black and white image. Pixels that have a value within the set range are white, and those that have a value outside the range are black. Set the range by moving the two triangles below the histogram. Generally, you can achieve a better result by setting the threshold manually than by using the AUTO button. The settings shown in Figure 12.77 generate the result in Figure 12.78.

Use the Threshold tool to generate a *natural mask*, as described in "Building a Natural Mask" on page 323.

Figure 12.78 *After applying the Threshold tool*

Posterize

The Posterize tool reduces the number of colors in an image. The only slider, which has a range of [2 to 256], is used to set the number of colors in each RGB channel. Setting the level to 8 generates the result shown in Figure 12.79.

Desaturate

The Desaturate tool removes all color from the current layer, but the image remains in RGB mode, so you can add color later. The dialog includes three ways to compute the gray levels of the pixels.

Figure 12.79 *After posterization*

Figure 12.81 *After applying Invert*

Figure 12.80 *After desaturation*

Figure 12.82 *After applying Value Invert*

- LIGHTNESS is the average between the maximum and minimum of the three RGB values.

- LUMINOSITY is a weighted average among the three RGB values. The coefficients used correspond to *luminance* in colorimetry are: $0.21 \times R + 0.71 \times G + 0.07 \times B$.

- AVERAGE is the average of the three RGB values.

Figure 12.80 shows the result of applying LUMINOSITY.

Inversion

The two inversion tools operate instantly on the current layer. **Image: Colors > Invert** generates the result shown in Figure 12.81. The colors are inverted (i.e., they are replaced by their complementary color, as in a photographic negative). **Image: Colors > Value Invert** generates the result shown in Figure 12.82. When this tool is used, only the Value component in the HSV model is inverted via the formula $V = 100 - V$, where V is the pixel value. Rounding errors can lead to a strong color distortion.

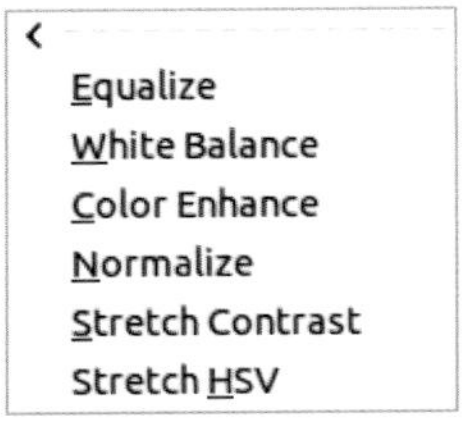

Equalize
White Balance
Color Enhance
Normalize
Stretch Contrast
Stretch HSV

Figure 12.83 *The Auto submenu*

Figure 12.84 *The initial image with its histogram*

12.6   The Color Submenus

The next part of the **Image: Colors** menu contains four submenus: Auto, Components, Map, and Info. We'll consider them each in turn.

The Auto Submenu

The Auto submenu is shown in Figure 12.83. It contains tools that have no corresponding dialogs. When selected, they adjust the image instantly, using automatic settings, as the name suggests. Because you can't customize the settings for these tools, their utility depends on the image being processed. To demonstrate their effects, we have included the Histogram dialog with each demonstration image and with the initial image, which is shown in Figure 12.84.

Figure 12.85 *After applying Equalize*

Equalize

The Equalize tool automatically adjusts the brightness of all colors, so that each possible brightness value occurs about the same number of times in the image. The histogram for the image in Figure 12.85 shows that the color values that occur most frequently, in this case [0 to 80], are stretched the most: See the flat part in the middle of the histogram. In this example, the result is bizarre and is not an improvement. In other cases, the result may look better.

White Balance

The White Balance tool operates separately on each of the RGB channels. It removes the least-used pixel values from both ends of the histogram and then stretches the remaining pixels to extend across the full range. In Figure 12.86, the brightest pixels disappeared, and the remaining pixels were stretched along the full range. The picture is much lighter, and this time the result could be considered an improvement.

Color Enhance

The Color Enhance tool makes adjustments using the HSV model: It increases the saturation

Figure 12.86 *After applying White Balance*

Figure 12.88 *Before applying Normalize*

Figure 12.87 *After applying Color Enhance*

Figure 12.89 *After applying Normalize*

without changing the hue or the value. The effect on this image, shown in Figure 12.87, is rather unpleasant. The Color Enhance tool flattened the histogram without extending the color range. The result is slightly better when we apply the White Balance tool first, but automatic tools such as this one clearly have limitations.

Normalize

The Normalize tool stretches the brightness of the image so the darkest point is black and the brightest point is as bright as possible in its current hue. To best demonstrate this, we'll use the image shown in Figure 12.88, which we modified with the Levels tool: We moved the right triangle under INPUT LEVELS to position 212 to remove the few pixels brighter than this value and the right triangle under OUTPUT LEVELS to the same

Figure 12.90 *After applying Stretch Contrast*

Figure 12.91 *After applying Stretch HSV*

position to retain the same overall brightness in the image. When applied to this modified image, the Normalize tool produces a visible effect (Figure 12.89), which it does only when there are no pixels on the far left or right of the histogram.

Stretch Contrast

The Stretch Contrast tool works the same way as the Normalize tool, but rather than stretching the Value channel, it stretches the RGB channels separately. These two tools result in visibly different effects only if the RGB channel ranges differ significantly, and when the Stretch Contrast tool does produce a unique result, it can generate color distortions. To create Figure 12.90, we began with the same modified example that we used for the Normalize tool, and the result is very similar.

Stretch HSV

The Stretch HSV tool works the same way as the Stretch Contrast tool, but it operates on the three channels of the HSV model instead of on the three RGB channels. This method can produce a better or worse result, depending on the image. Our result, shown in Figure 12.91, is almost identical to the initial image.

Figure 12.92 *The Components menu*

The Components Submenu

The Components menu is shown in Figure 12.92. Its four tools operate on the RGB channels.

Channel Mixer

This tool uses the values from all three of the RGB channels to compute new values for each one of them. Initially, each output channel receives only the corresponding input channel. Figure 12.93 shows the Red channel dialog.

At the top of the Channel Mixer dialog is a preview of the image, with zooming and panning enabled. Below that is the OUTPUT CHANNEL selection menu. The next three sliders, which have a range of [−200 to +200], allow you to set the percentage of the corresponding channel that will be assigned to the current output channel. If we change the output channel, we can define another set of percentages.

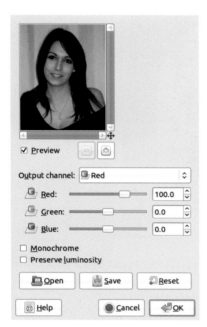

Figure 12.93 *The Channel Mixer dialog, Red channel*

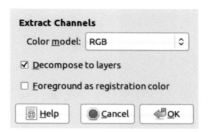

Figure 12.94 *The Decompose dialog*

Figure 12.95 *Color models*

If we check the MONOCHROME box, the image becomes grayscale, and we can use the sliders to set the proportion of each of the RGB channels that are used to build the monochrome image. For example, when we select **Image: Image > Mode > Grayscale**, a grayscale image is created using the values 21, 72, and 7 for the three RGB channels, from top to bottom.

The PRESERVE LUMINOSITY checkbox maintains the initial luminosity of each pixel, which prevents the resulting image from being overly bright.

The set of buttons at the bottom of the dialog allow us to save the current settings, reload previously saved settings, and reset everything to the initial values.

You can make very fine adjustments to the colors of an image with this tool, but mastering it is difficult.

Decompose

The Decompose tool separates the channels of the image into separate grayscale images or layers based on the chosen color model. Its dialog, shown in Figure 12.94, is fairly simple. At the top is the COLOR MODEL menu, and below that are two checkboxes. Checking the first box decomposes the image to layers; otherwise the decomposition results in separate images. The second box is included for CMYK printing purposes. When checked, every pixel that's part of the current foreground color will be black in the decomposed images or layers. This is commonly used to show crop marks on all channels as a way to aid in alignment.

The available color models, shown in Figure 12.95, are explained next.

- RGB: This decomposition allows us to work on the channels separately and then recompose the image. One of the channels can also be used as a mask.

Figure 12.96 *The Hue channel*

Figure 12.97 *The Saturation channel*

- RGBA: Similar to the RGB model, except with this model, an Alpha layer or image is also created for the image's Alpha channel.

- HSV: The layers or images represent the components of the HSV model. The Hue channel is rather compressed, and the result has no natural meaning, as shown in Figure 12.96. The Saturation channel is also not very meaningful (Figure 12.97). In contrast, the Value channel returns an accurate grayscale representation of the image.

- HSL: Similar to the HSV model, but the Value channel is replaced with Lightness, which is

Figure 12.98 *The Alpha channel*

similar conceptually but calculated a little differently. The calculations for the Saturation channel also differ slightly.

- CMY and CMYK: These models are generally used to decompose an image in order to pass it to printing software that requires decomposition.

- ALPHA: A new image is created from the Alpha channel of the image. For example, Figure 12.98 was generated from an Alpha channel built with **Image: Colors > Color to Alpha**, using white as the color.

- LAB: The Lab (or L*a*b*) color space includes several models that are intended to be more representative of human vision than the other color models. The L channel represents luminosity, and the A and B channels represent color in the form of *opponent color axes*. The Lab color space was designed based on the *opponent process theory*, which states that signals received by the rods and cones are processed antagonistically: red versus green signals (A channel), yellow versus blue signals (B channel), and black versus white signals (L channel).

- YCBCR: The last four color models are based on this color space, which has channels for Luminance, Blue, and Red. This color space

Figure 12.99 *The Compose dialog*

Figure 12.100 *Interpreting RGB channels as HSL channels*

Figure 12.101 *The Map submenu*

is used for digital video, and the various decompositions correspond to different recommendations by the International Telecommunication Union.

Generally, you'll use only the RGB, CMY, and HSV color models to make adjustments to an image. The other models are mainly for transferring the image information to an application.

Recompose

You can use the Recompose tool only on an image that has been decomposed with the Decompose tool. When this tool is applied, the original image is rebuilt using the component images or layers, allowing you to decompose the image, manipulate the layers or images separately, and then recompose the image.

Compose

The Compose tool is much more powerful than the Recompose tool because any grayscale image can be used to represent the channels. As Figure 12.99 shows, the dialog first asks us to choose the COLOR MODEL. The available choices are the same as for the Decompose tool.

Next, choose the CHANNEL REPRESENTATIONS. If the current image has multiple layers, use the successive layers as the channels. If the image is in grayscale with only one layer, then that layer is initially used for all the channels. For each channel, we can either choose one of the

available grayscale images or layers, or a mask value. If we choose a mask value, the slider on the right becomes operational, and we can choose a value in the range [0 to 255], which replaces the channel for all pixels. But at least one of the channels must be an image or a layer.

The Compose tool lets you exchange channels without changing the color model, use channels from one color model and interpret them with another model, add an Alpha channel taken from another image (if a model with an Alpha channel, such as RGBA, has been chosen), or replace a channel with a constant value. As you can see, this tool is powerful. Figure 12.100 was obtained by decomposing in the RGB model and then composing the layers in the HSL model.

Figure 12.102 *A sample image before colormapping*

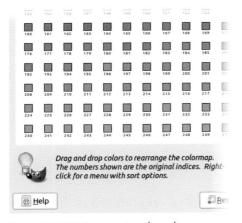

Figure 12.103 *Rearranging the colormap*

The Map Submenu

The Map submenu, shown in Figure 12.101, is separated into two sections. Tools in the first section apply only to images in Indexed mode. Tools in the second section apply only to images in RGB mode or, for some of the entries, Grayscale mode. We'll use the image in Figure 12.102 as an example and convert a copy of it to Indexed mode with an optimal palette of 256 colors and Floyd-Steinberg dithering to demonstrate the first two tools (see "Indexed Mode" on page 243 for more information about indexing).

Figure 12.104 *Choosing a colormap*

Rearrange Colormap

This tool does not change the image. It simply changes the numbering of the entries in the colormap. As shown in Figure 12.103 (only a quarter of the actual window is visible), we can move the entries by dragging and dropping. Right-click anywhere in the window to sort the colormap according to one of the HSV components or to reverse or reset the order.

Set Colormap

The Set Colormap tool opens a dialog in which we can only choose a new colormap from among those available (Figure 12.104). Some of the colormaps yield odd results, as you can see in Figure 12.105.

Alien Map

The Alien Map tool transforms the colors of an image in the RGB or the HSL model by applying trigonometric functions to the pixel values.

The dialog shown in Figure 12.106 begins with a preview. Then we choose the color model,

Figure 12.105 *After setting the colormap to Blues*

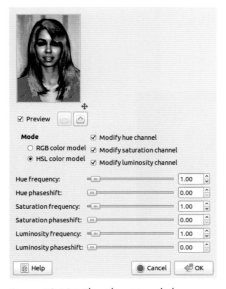

Figure 12.106 *The Alien Map dialog*

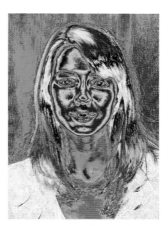

Figure 12.107 *After applying Alien Map*

and a phaseshift of 0.00 in the three HSV channels.

Color Exchange

As its name indicates, this tool replaces a color in the image with a different one.

The dialog, shown in Figure 12.108, contains a preview that you middle-click to define the FROM COLOR. This color can also be defined by clicking the corresponding button, which opens the Color chooser, or by setting the three sliders for the RGB channels. Each channel also has threshold sliders [0 to 1], which you adjust to set how much of the channel will be replaced.

The pixels in the image that are similar to the chosen FROM COLOR, within the threshold limits, are replaced with the TO COLOR, which you select using the button or the three sliders.

Gradient Map

The Gradient Map tool has no dialog. It uses the current gradient, which you can change in the Gradients dialog, usually a dockable dialog in the multi-dialog window below the layers tab. The mapping occurs between the color intensities in the image (represented as the Value channel in the Levels tool, for example) and the colors in the gradient. The left end of the gradient is mapped to the darkest pixel, and the

called *mode* in this dialog. The checkboxes on the right control which of the channels will be affected.

Each channel has two sliders: frequency [0 to 20] and phaseshift [0 to 360]. Frequencies that are less than 0.7 yield a result similar to the original. Higher values give an increasingly "alien" result. Figure 12.107 is the result of using a frequency of 6.00 in the three RGB channels

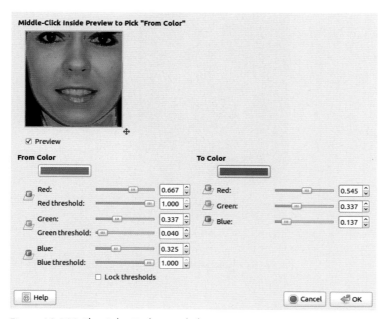

Figure 12.108 *The Color Exchange dialog*

Figure 12.109 *After applying Gradient Map*

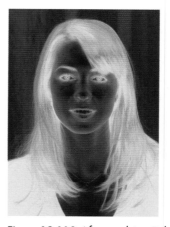

Figure 12.110 *After applying Palette Map*

right end to the lightest pixel. Figure 12.109 shows the result using the Greens gradient.

Palette Map

The Palette Map tool works like the Gradient Map tool, only it uses the current palette instead of the current gradient. Change the current palette via the Palettes dialog. This dialog can be opened by clicking the small button to the right of any dockable dialog or from the **Image: Windows > Dockable Dialogs** menu. Figure 12.110 shows the result using the Gold palette.

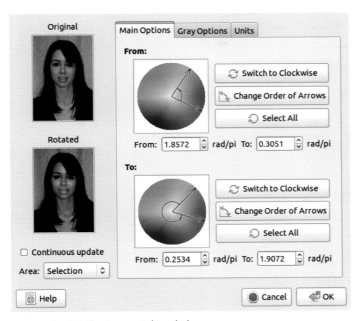

Figure 12.111 *The Rotate Colors dialog*

Figure 12.112 *After applying Rotate Colors*

Rotate Colors

The Rotate Colors tool uses the Hue color circle to alter the image colors. A hue subrange is defined on the FROM circle as a sector, and another sector is defined on the TO circle. The colors in the input range are mapped to the colors in the output range. The other colors are not affected.

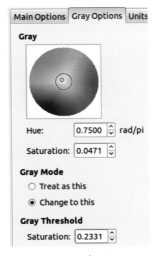

Figure 12.113 *The Gray Options tab*

This dialog is shown in Figure 12.111. You can adjust the two color ranges in various ways. The previews on the left show the original image and the current result. To get the dramatic change shown in Figure 12.112, we clicked the CHANGE ORDER OF ARROWS button.

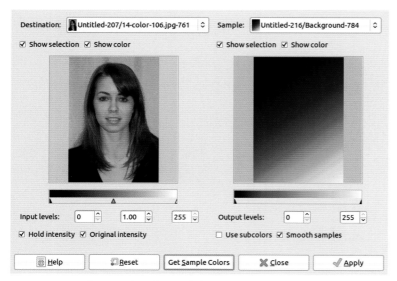

Figure 12.114 *The Sample Colorize dialog*

This dialog contains a second tab, shown in Figure 12.113. On this tab, we specify a color in the image to replace with gray, as long as the CHANGE TO THIS radio button is checked. The center circle is a visual representation of the GRAY THRESHOLD saturation: It extends when the threshold saturation is increased. The position of the small circle defines the hue and saturation of the color that will be converted to gray. If the TREAT AS THIS radio button is checked, the hue that will be converted to gray is defined by the rotation specified on the Main Options tab.

Sample Colorize

The Sample Colorize tool uses a sampling image to colorize a destination image.

The destination image must be in RGB mode but can be either grayscale or color. Its colors will be discarded; only the Value channel will be used in the resulting image. Figure 12.114 shows the dialog for this tool. We created a sample image by applying a linear gradient to a blank canvas, using the Blend tool and the Incandescent gradient. The drop-down menus at the top of the dialog contain all of the images currently open in GIMP; use them to select a sample or use the current gradient as the sample, either as is or reversed. We can use the triangles or the numbers below the sample image preview to restrict the output range. We can also change the prominence of dark, medium, and light tones, using the triangles or the numbers in the input range below the destination image preview.

Various checkboxes set the parameters. HOLD INTENSITY applies the average light intensity of the source image to the destination image. ORIGINAL INTENSITY inactivates the Input levels intensity settings. USE SUBCOLORS makes the colors of an output pixel a mixture of the source and destination image values; otherwise, only the dominant color (the color with the maximum value) is used. SMOOTH SAMPLES improves the transition between colors selected after clicking the GET SAMPLE COLORS button.

The Info Submenu

The Info submenu is shown in Figure 12.115. These entries don't change the image. Rather,

Figure 12.115 *The Info submenu*

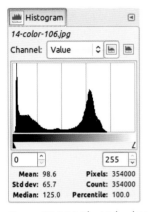

Figure 12.116 *The Value histogram*

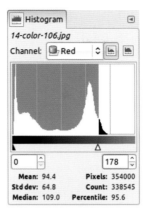

Figure 12.117 *The Red histogram with reduced range*

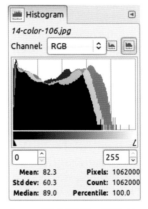

Figure 12.118 *The RGB histogram in Logarithmic mode*

they offer ways to gather information about the image properties, which allow you to make informed adjustments using the other tools.

Histogram

The Histogram tool opens a dockable dialog that can be selected via **Image: Windows > Dockable Dialogs > Histogram** and docked in one of the multi-dialog windows.

Keeping this dialog open on the screen is helpful, because it's automatically updated when the current image changes and it provides a way to track the effect of various adjustments. Adjust its size, either to reduce the histogram and save space on the screen or to extend the histogram and show more precise information. In Figure 12.116, only the Value channel is displayed in linear mode. Numeric data about the image pixels is displayed at the bottom of the dialog: the mean, standard deviation, and median of the values, and the number of pixels.

In Figure 12.117, we've displayed the Red channel and defined a subrange by moving the white triangle below the histogram. Because this is an informational dialog, the image doesn't change, but the data does: The pixel count is different from the total, and the percentile is less than 100.

In Figure 12.118, we've displayed the three RGB channels at the same time, and the histogram is logarithmic. In Logarithmic mode, the low values are more prominent, which is generally better since small differences in small values are much easier to see than small differences in high values.

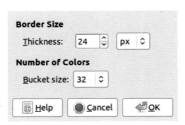

Figure 12.119 *The Border Average dialog*

Border Average

The Border Average tool is useful for finding an appropriate background color to go behind an image on a web page. It determines which color occurs most often along the border of the current layer and sets it as the foreground color. Because this does not change the image itself, this tool has no undo capability.

The Border Average dialog, shown in Figure 12.119, contains only two settings. The thickness of the BORDER SIZE specifies how much of the current layer is used in the calculation. The NUMBER OF COLORS is specified by the bucket size in the following way: Colors found in the border are placed in different buckets, depending on their similarity. The bucket containing the most colors is used to set the foreground color. A small bucket size leads to a large number of buckets and, often, an unexpected result. For example, when we applied the tool for the image in Figure 12.102 on page 274, a bucket size of 16 yielded black, because the model's black shirt spans much of the bottom border of the image and the tone is fairly consistent. A bucket size of 64 yielded a gray color, which is a mixture of the beige in the background of the photograph and the black of the woman's shirt.

Colorcube Analysis

This tool has been more or less obsolete since GIMP 2.4: Its dialog (Figure 12.120) only displays the RGB logarithmic histogram, the image dimensions, and the number of unique colors.

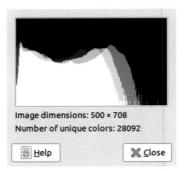

Image dimensions: 500 × 708
Number of unique colors: 28092

Figure 12.120 *The Colorcube Analysis dialog*

Figure 12.121 *The generated palette*

Figure 12.122 *The Smooth Palette dialog*

Smooth Palette

This tool uses the various colors in the current layer to generate a palette in the form of a series of color stripes, as shown in Figure 12.121. We use it mainly with the Flame filter (see "Flame" on page 454).

In the dialog shown in Figure 12.122, the first two parameters set the dimensions of the new image for the palette. SEARCH DEPTH [1 to 1024] generates more colors when you increase the value.

The Remaining Color Tools

The last part of the Colors menu contains six tools that aren't really related but are grouped here. We'll use the sample image shown in Figure 12.123 to demonstrate the effect of each of these tools.

Figure 12.123 *The sample image*

Figure 12.125 *After applying Color to Alpha*

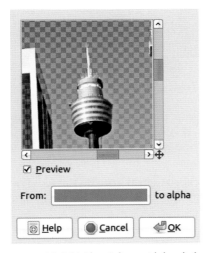

Figure 12.124 *The Color to Alpha dialog*

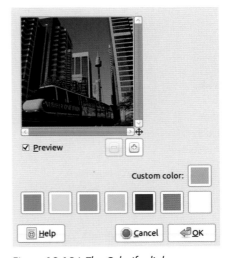

Figure 12.126 *The Colorify dialog*

Color to Alpha

The Color to Alpha tool replaces some chosen color with transparency. Its dialog, shown in Figure 12.124, contains a preview and a button for choosing the color, which opens a simplified version of the Color chooser. We chose a color from the picture using the eyedropper, and the result appears in Figure 12.125.

Colorify

The Colorify tool desaturates the image and then colorizes it, as if it were a grayscale image seen through colored glass. The Colorify tool actually does the same thing as the

Colorize tool but with a different user interface. Its dialog, shown in Figure 12.126, contains a preview; a small palette of fully saturated colors; and a button for defining a custom color, which opens a simplified version of the Color chooser. Choosing a light color is best because darker colors reduce the contrast in the image, as demonstrated in Figure 12.127.

Filter Pack

As its name suggests, this entry is actually a collection of tools, called *filters*, although they don't have any specific connection to the collection of tools found in the **Image: Filters** menu.

Figure 12.127 *After applying Colorify*

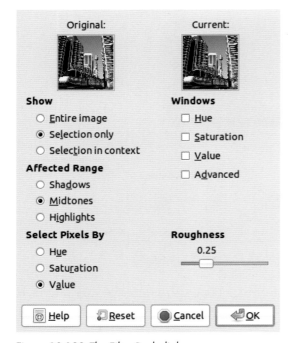

Figure 12.128 *The Filter Pack dialog*

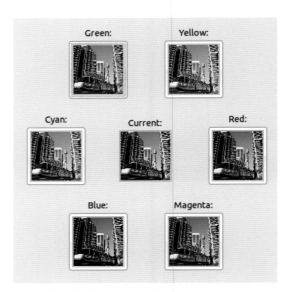

Figure 12.129 *The Hue variations*

- SHOW allows you to change what's shown in the preview. To use the trick just described, choose to show only the selection rather than the entire image.

- The four checkboxes in WINDOWS open corresponding windows, which are explained next.

- AFFECTED RANGE works in the same way as in the Color Balance tool (see "Color Balance" on page 263).

- SELECT PIXELS BY further determines which subrange will be affected by the changes.

- The ROUGHNESS slider [0 to 1] sets the strength of changes made when you click a window.

The windows, which open when the corresponding boxes in the Filter Pack dialog are checked, each contain a filter linked to the main dialog but offering a unique way to edit the image. The four windows are these:

- HUE: Its dialog, shown in Figure 12.129, contains seven previews. The center one displays the current state of the image. The others correspond to the three RGB colors and their complementary colors. Clicking one of the previews adds the corresponding color to the

Its dialog, shown in Figure 12.128, contains the following options:

- Two previews, before and after the filter. These previews are very small and you can't zoom in, so we often find it useful to first make a small selection in the image, work on that selection, invert it, and apply the tool again with the same parameters.

Figure 12.130 *The Saturation variations*

Figure 12.131 *The Value variations*

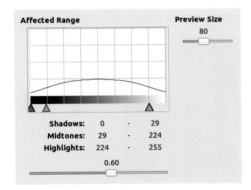

Figure 12.132 *The Advanced Filter Pack Options dialog*

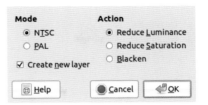

Figure 12.133 *The Hot dialog*

specifies the meaning of Shadows, Midtones, and Highlights. The blue triangle allows you to remove the darkest pixels from the affected subrange. You can use the two other triangles to define the limits of the three subranges. The shape of the curve depends on the range chosen in the main window, on the roughness, and on the position of the bottom slider [0 to 1]. This shape represents the intensity of the changes that will be made to the image.

Hot

The Hot tool selects pixels that could cause problems when displayed in NTSC or PAL video. In its dialog, shown in Figure 12.133, you can select the video mode as well as the process used to mitigate the potential problem. You can reduce luminance or saturation or blacken the pixels. By default, the changes made with this tool are done on an additional, transparent layer.

Maximum RGB

The Maximum RGB tool keeps only the RGB component with the maximum (or minimum) value. This explains why in its dialog, shown in Figure 12.134, the preview shows an image that's mainly red, except for the eyes, which are blue. If we choose the minimal channels, the result is mainly blue, except for the eyes, which are now red.

Retinex

Retinex algorithms are designed to mimic the dynamics of human vision, making images viewed on a screen appear more realistic. The

selected subrange (set in the Filter Pack dialog) with the current ROUGHNESS. Subtract a color by clicking its complementary color.

- SATURATION: Its dialog, shown in Figure 12.130, contains only three previews, allowing you to increase or decrease the saturation in the current subrange.
- VALUE: Its dialog, shown in Figure 12.131, also contains three previews, allowing you to increase or decrease the value in the image.
- ADVANCED: This checkbox opens the dialog shown in Figure 12.132. The PREVIEW SIZE slider [50 to 125] allows you to change the size of the preview slightly. The AFFECTED RANGE

Figure 12.134 *The Maximum RGB dialog*

Figure 12.135 *The Retinex dialog*

human eye distinguishes colors even in poor or colored lighting. The Retinex tool uses the MSRCR algorithm, which is used in digital photography or for processing astronomical and medical photographs.

The options in its Figure 12.135, assume that the user has some knowledge of the mathematics of the Retinex MSRCR algorithm. Those who don't possess the required knowledge can simply fiddle with the options and sliders until the result is appealing. An example is shown in Figure 12.136.

Figure 12.136 *After applying Retinex*

13 Selections

A selection allows you to apply changes to a specific part of the current image. You might copy and paste the selected area elsewhere, or adjust its color balance, or paint on it, or apply a transformation. In fact, the selection mechanism is central to many of GIMP's common uses.

13.1 What Is a Selection?

Without selections, GIMP would not be a very useful program. Because selections are so important, we begin by clarifying what they are.

A Selection as an Outline

The simplest definition of a selection is that it's an outline of a region within an image that will be selected. In fact, in GIMP terminology, the term *selection* is used for the outline itself and for the contents of this outline (i.e., what is selected). In this chapter we refer to the outline as the *selection* and the region of the image inside the outline as the *selected pixels*.

When you make a selection in GIMP, the selection's outline is indicated by *marching ants*. This is the name coined for the moving dotted line that surrounds the selected pixels. In Figure 13.1, we made a rectangular selection

Figure 13.1 *Marching ants delimit the selection.*

around the statue. All the pixels of the image inside the rectangle are selected; all the pixels outside are not.

If you make some adjustment to the image, only the selected pixels are affected. In Figure 13.2, you can see the result after we called the Levels tool and adjusted the gamma triangle in the three color channels.

You can also copy the selection and paste it elsewhere, as shown in Figure 13.3. To do this, follow these steps:

1. Copy the selection using **Image: Edit > Copy** or CTRL+C. The copy is placed in a buffer called the *clipboard*, which can hold only one image at a time.

Figure 13.2 *Using the Levels tool on the selected pixels*

Figure 13.3 *Copying and pasting the selection*

2. Paste the contents of the buffer into the same image, using **Image: Edit > Paste** or pressing CTRL+V.

3. Because this builds a *floating selection*, create a new layer to place the selection into. This can be done by choosing **Image: Layer > New Layer**, right-clicking in the Layers dialog and choosing **New Layer**, pressing CTRL+SHIFT+N, or clicking the first button in the Layers dialog bottom row. You could also *anchor* the copy to the current layer, which would replace the underlying pixels with the copied pixels. This is done by choosing **Image: Layer > Anchor Layer**, right-clicking in the Layers dialog, pressing CTRL+H, or pressing the second button from right in the Layers dialog bottom row.

4. Our new layer is pasted exactly in its original place, so to make sure we've been successful, select the Move tool (M) and move the new layer to the bottom of the image.

Figure 13.4 *Extending the selection made with the Fuzzy Select tool*

A Selection as a Grayscale Image

A selection made with the Rectangle Select tool is clearly defined by an outline. The delineation of a selection made with the Fuzzy Select tool (U) isn't as clear. When you click an image with the Fuzzy Select tool, all the pixels contiguous to the initial point, and those similar to it by some threshold defined in the tool options, are selected. Depending on the image and the threshold, calculating which pixels are selected and which are not is easy, but the outline is often complex and difficult to follow. If you drag the mouse pointer after clicking, you can adjust the threshold, thus increasing or decreasing the number of selected pixels. Figure 13.4 shows this process. The present selection outline appears as a thick, fuzzy line, and the new outline, which appears at the bottom of Figure 13.4, is still quite uneven.

By moving the mouse pointer as far as possible, you can select all the sky and a part of the misty woods in the background. Although the new selection appears, from a distance, to be a wavering line along the horizon and over the statue, some segments of the selection are much too complicated to be considered an outline. Figure 13.5 is an enlargement of the left part of this selection, which shows that pixels are selected in what appears to be a random fashion.

The selection is even more complicated than it looks. The pixels in the image are not simply selected or not selected; pixels can be partially

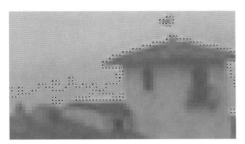

Figure 13.5 *Detail of the selection in Figure 13.4*

Figure 13.6 *Using the Toggle Quick Mask button*

Figure 13.7 *Applying a gradient fill to the selection*

selected along a continuous spectrum from 0% to 100%. Showing this is easy if you click the Toggle Quick Mask button in the bottom-left corner of the Image window (or press SHIFT+Q). Figure 13.6 shows Quick Mask with a similar selection that was also built with the Fuzzy Select tool.

As you can see, the selection is similar to a grayscale image that's been added as a layer of the current image, except the new layer appears in red (by default). Completely white pixels in this new layer are 100% selected in the current image. Completely red pixels aren't selected at all. Pink pixels (i.e., partially red ones) are selected to a degree that's inversely proportional to their redness—the lighter the pink of the mask, the greater the selection percentage in the image. In our example, the pixels in the middle of the sky are 100% selected, but in the upper part of the sky, they're only partially selected. Although we've described the selection based on the default color of red, you can change the setting to show the selection mask in any color you want by right-clicking the Quick Mask button.

In contrast, a selection built by the Rectangle Select tool appears as a purely red and white image when Quick Mask is activated. This is because pixels in the current image are either selected or they aren't.

The marching ants that surround a selection are simply a visual approximation of selections that contain partially selected pixels. The ants march along the average boundary of the selection. If you apply an action to a fuzzy selection, the effect on the pixels in the current image is proportional to their selection rate. Figure 13.7 shows this.

We look more closely at the mechanics of partial selections in Chapter 14.

13.2 The Seven Selection Tools

The first seven tools in the Toolbox (if they're in the default order) are the selection tools, shown in Figure 13.8.

Common Options

Like most tools initially present in the Toolbox, and like most other tools in general, selection tools have options, so keep the options dialog open and docked at the bottom of the Toolbox.

If you've accidentally closed it, just select **Image: Windows > Dockable dialogs > Tool Options**, double-click the tool icon, and drag the dialog that appears to the bottom of the Toolbox.

In the following section, we go through all the options for each of the selection tools. But some of these options are common to all tools, and

Figure 13.8 *The seven selection tools*

Figure 13.9 *Common selection tool options*

Figure 13.10 *A selection boundary with antialiasing*

Figure 13.11 *A selection boundary without antialiasing*

we describe those just once—right here at the beginning. Figure 13.9 shows common selection options when the Free Select tool is active.

The MODE option contains four ways to combine a new selection with an existing selection:

- Replace the existing selection with the new one. This is the default mode. The previous selection is discarded when a new selection is made.

- Add the new selection to the current one. Pressing and holding SHIFT before using the selection tool activates this mode even if you haven't checked it. Newly selected pixels are added to the pixels that were already selected. During construction of the selection, the mouse pointer is accompanied by a + sign.

- Subtract the new selection from the current one. Pressing CTRL before using a selection tool activates this mode. The newly selected pixels are removed from the current selection if they were part of it; otherwise, they are ignored. During construction of the selection, the mouse pointer is accompanied by a − sign.

- Select the intersection of the old and new selections. Pressing SHIFT and CTRL before using a selection tool activates this mode.

Only the pixels that were included in both the old selection and the new one are selected. During construction of the selection, the mouse pointer is accompanied by a ∩ sign.

Pressing and holding keys to change modes is often more convenient than clicking the mode icon; forgetting that a different mode is checked is particularly easy. Moreover, when changing the mode via the icons, the mode is changed for only that tool; if you change selection tools, the default, or previously selected mode, for that tool will be active.

The ANTIALIASING option, if checked, smooths the boundary of a selection. Figures 13.10 and 13.11 show the border of a selection with and without antialiasing, respectively. This option is clearly useful and should normally be checked.

The FEATHER EDGES option, when checked, blurs the boundary between the selected and unselected regions. The RADIUS specifies the width of the blurring boundary. Figure 13.12 shows the effect with a radius of 10 pixels.

Note that antialiasing and feathering both use the same technique, partial selection of pixels along the border of the selection.

Figure 13.12 *The effect of the Feather edges option*

Figure 13.13 *The Rectangle Select tool pointer*

Figure 13.14 *Moving the selection*

The bottom of the options dialog contains four buttons that are also present for all selection tools. The button on the far left saves the current settings. You can choose a name for the settings and can save an unlimited number of combinations. The next button allows you to restore previously saved settings. The third button allows you to delete settings that were saved previously. Finally, the fourth button allows you to reset all of the settings to their default values. If you press $\boxed{\text{SHIFT}}$ while clicking this button, all the tools will be reset to their default settings. Note that if you haven't saved any settings, only the first and fourth buttons are active.

The Rectangle Select Tool

The Rectangle Select tool can be accessed from the Toolbox (the leftmost icon in Figure 13.8), from the **Image: Tools > Selection Tools** menu, or by pressing $\boxed{\text{R}}$. When the Rectangle Select tool is active, the mouse pointer becomes a crosshair accompanied by a rectangular icon (Figure 13.13). When all options are set to the default values, you can use this tool to build a simple, rectangular selection by clicking in one corner of the intended rectangle, dragging the mouse pointer to the opposite corner, and then releasing the mouse button.

Simple, rectangular selections are not often useful in photo manipulation but can be useful for building textures or geometric shapes. In Section 13.4, we show you how to modify an existing selection, for example, to change its shape or rotate it, and these techniques will make the Rectangular Selection tool a great deal more versatile.

Although the selection is built the moment you release the mouse button, you can still move and change it. If the pointer is inside the selection, its icon is the crossed arrows that you see when the Move tool is active, as shown in Figure 13.14. You can move the selection itself (not the selected pixels) by clicking and dragging with the mouse, which is especially useful for making large changes to the position of the selection in the image. For minute adjustments, use the keyboard arrow keys, which move the selection by 1 pixel at a time. If you press and hold the $\boxed{\text{SHIFT}}$ key while using the arrow keys, the selection moves by 25 pixels at a time.

If you place the mouse pointer near the corners or edges of the selection rectangle, its icon changes, as shown in Figure 13.15. This icon signals that the tool will now move the edges or the corners of the selection, allowing you to change the dimensions of the rectangle. You can do this with the mouse pointer or with the arrow keys. While you are pressing the $\boxed{\text{SHIFT}}$ key, the arrow keys will again work in increments of 25 pixels. Otherwise, they move the border of the selection by one pixel, allowing you to

Figure 13.15 *Altering the selection*

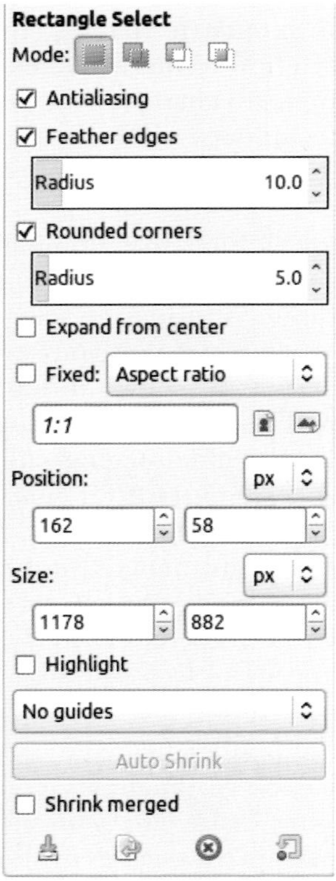

Rectangle Select

Mode:

☑ Antialiasing
☑ Feather edges

Radius   10.0

☑ Rounded corners

Radius   5.0

☐ Expand from center

☐ Fixed: Aspect ratio

1:1

Position: px

162   58

Size: px

1178   882

☐ Highlight

No guides

Auto Shrink

☐ Shrink merged

Figure 13.16 *The Rectangle Select tool options*

change the dimensions of the rectangle with a great deal of precision.

When not within the selection rectangle, the mouse pointer icon looks exactly like it did before you built a selection. If the mode is set to

Figure 13.17 *Highlighting the selection*

the default, when you click and drag outside the current selection, that selection is discarded and a new selection is built.

To finalize the selection, click in the rectangle, press the ENTER key, or choose a different tool.

The Rectangle Select tool has a number of options, as shown in Figure 13.16.

If checked, the ROUNDED CORNERS box displays options for the radius of the quarter circles that will replace the corners. See Figure 13.17 for an example.

If you check the EXPAND FROM CENTER box, the initial point where you click will be the center of the rectangular selection. Otherwise, it will be one corner of the rectangle. You can also activate this mode by pressing and holding the CTRL key *after* the initial click that begins the selection. Note that if you press CTRL *before* beginning the selection, it activates subtract mode, so the selected rectangle will be subtracted from the current selection. If the EXPAND FROM CENTER button is checked, pressing the CTRL key (while in the process of building a selection) toggles that option.

If the FIXED box in the tool options is checked, you can constrain the shape of the rectangle. The menu to the right contains the following choices:

- ASPECT RATIO: When this is selected, the box below specifies the ratio between width and height and is initially 1:1, which corresponds to a square. You can change it to 1:2 or 4:3, for example. The small icons to the right of this box allow you to invert the ratio.

Figure 13.18 *Using center lines*

Figure 13.19 *Using the rule of thirds*

Figure 13.20 *Using the rule of fifths*

- WIDTH: When this is selected, you can fix the width of the selection by typing a number in the box below. The drop-down menu to the right allows you to change the units or even use a percentage.

- HEIGHT works in the same way.

- SIZE: When this is selected, you can specify the exact dimensions of the rectangle in pixels. You can also enter a numeric expression like 257×7 or 85%.

Pressing and holding the $\boxed{\text{SHIFT}}$ key *after* you begin building the selection toggles the FIXED button.

The next four fields are used to adjust the position and size of the selection, either in pixels or in a variety of other units. The values shown change as you build or move the selection with the mouse pointer or the arrow keys. You can also set the size and position directly by typing in the boxes or clicking the arrows that appear to the right of each box.

If you check the HIGHLIGHT box, the selection is highlighted, as shown in Figure 13.17. This highlight disappears when the selection is finalized.

The next option allows you to display guides while building the selection. Guides can help you to apply common composition rules when cropping photographs, for example.

- NO GUIDES displays only the outer boundaries of the rectangle being built.

- CENTER LINES places two perpendicular lines in the middle of the rectangle, as shown in Figure 13.18.

- RULE OF THIRDS places two vertical and two horizontal lines in the rectangle, which divide it into nine identical parts. See Figure 13.19.

- RULE OF FIFTHS places four vertical and four horizontal lines in the rectangle, dividing it into 25 identical parts. See Figure 13.20.

- GOLDEN SECTIONS is similar to the RULE OF THIRDS, but the guides are aligned based on the golden ratio.

- DIAGONAL LINES draws a line from each corner at 45°, which bisects the selection only in the case of a square.

Note that if you change the guides while building a selection, the new guides appear immediately.

The next two entries deal with the AUTO SHRINK mechanism, which is occasionally useful. To illustrate this mechanism, we drew a simple black shape on a white background, shown in

Figure 13.21 *The original image*

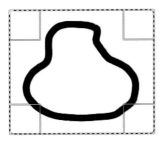

Figure 13.22 *The first selection*

Figure 13.23 *Shrinking the selection*

Figure 13.24 *The Ellipse Select tool pointer*

Figure 13.25 *Subtracting an elliptical selection*

Figure 13.26 *The resulting selection*

The Ellipse Select Tool

Access the Ellipse Select tool from the Toolbox (the second icon from the left in Figure 13.8 on page 288), from the **Image: Tools > Selection Tools** menu, or by pressing E. When this tool is active, the mouse pointer becomes a crosshair accompanied by a circular icon (Figure 13.24). It works in the same way as the Rectangle Select tool and has the same default options, except that the ANTIALIASING option is checked and enabled by default.

Figure 13.25 shows the process of subtracting an elliptical selection from a rectangular selection. Figure 13.26 shows the result after finalizing the selection.

Figure 13.21. We then made a rectangular selection roughly around the shape, as shown in Figure 13.22. When we click the AUTO SHRINK button, the selection shrinks to the smallest rectangle containing the object we drew, as shown in Figure 13.23.

Unfortunately, this option works only if the background is a solid color, so it's not very useful on a photograph or a complex illustration.

When the SHRINK MERGED box is checked, all the visible layers are considered rather than simply the current one.

Figure 13.27 *The Free Select tool pointer*

Figure 13.28 *Using the free drawing method*

The Free Select Tool

Access the Free Select tool from the Toolbox (the third icon from the left in Figure 13.8 on page 288), from the **Image: Tools > Selection Tools** menu, or by pressing F. When you select this tool, the mouse pointer appears as shown in Figure 13.27. The Free Select tool has only the options common to all selection tools. You can use this tool in two ways.

The first method is illustrated in Figure 13.28 and is best done with the stylus of a graphics tablet. To build a selection, click at the beginning of the outline of the intended selection and draw along it until you return to the initial point. When a white dot appears in place of the open circle, the outline is complete and will be closed once you release the mouse button. If you release the mouse button earlier, a hollow circle appears where the button was released. If you hover over the circle, it fills in, and the mouse pointer changes to the Move icon. If you move one of the endpoints of the selected curve, the orientation and size of the curve change, but the shape remains the same, as illustrated in Figure 13.29.

The Free Select tool can also be used to build a polygon by clicking on successive vertices, as

Figure 13.29 *Moving the curve*

Figure 13.30 *Using the polygon method*

illustrated in Figure 13.30. After each click, the point you just clicked is circled, and the pointer includes the Move icon, which indicates that you can move this last point. When the mouse pointer is close to the starting point, a closed circle appears on that point, and when you click, the path closes and the selection is finalized. As soon as this happens, the shape of the selection can't be changed, at least not with the Free Select tool itself.

You can also combine the two Free Select methods. As you build a selection, you can add points by clicking, or clicking and dragging, from a point to draw a curved segment. Pressing ENTER finalizes the selection no matter how far the last point is from the beginning, linking the first and last points with a straight segment.

This tool is handy for making a raw selection around a complex shape, which you can then refine using the Quick Mask, covered in depth in Chapter 14.

Figure 13.31 *The Fuzzy Select tool pointer*

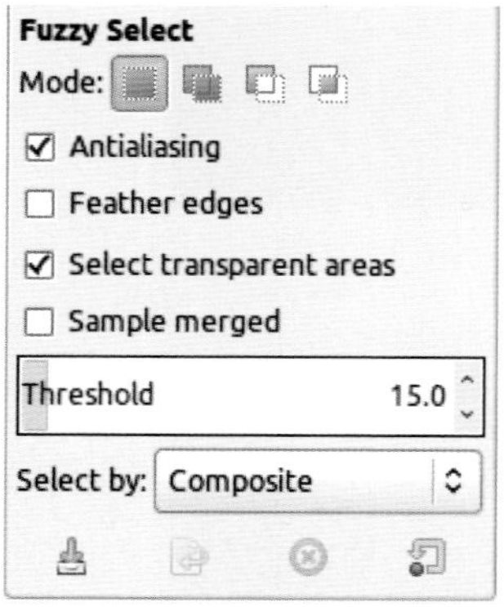

Figure 13.34 *The resulting selection*

Figure 13.32 *The Fuzzy Select tool options*

Figure 13.33 *Building the first selection*

The Fuzzy Select Tool

Access the Fuzzy Select tool from the Toolbox (the fourth icon from the left in Figure 13.8 on page 288), from the **Image: Tools > Selection Tools** menu, or by pressing $\boxed{U}$. When this tool is active, the mouse pointer is accompanied by the icon shown in Figure 13.31. The Fuzzy Select tool selects contiguous pixels with a similar color. Its options are shown in Figure 13.32.

When we click and hold the mouse button somewhere in the sky of the image in Figure 13.33, an outline of the selected area appears. When we release the mouse, we get the

selection shown in Figure 13.34, and the selection is indeed fuzzy. We've selected a portion of the sky using a very thick border, but our intention was to select the entire sky. You can extend the selected area in several ways:

- Add other areas to the first one by pressing the $\boxed{\text{SHIFT}}$ key while clicking in the nonselected areas. The best place to click in this case is within the fuzzy boundaries of the selection. $\boxed{\text{SHIFT}}$-click the grass to select the entire meadow. You can also, of course, remove areas that don't belong in the selection by pressing the $\boxed{\text{CTRL}}$ key while clicking those areas.

- Increase the THRESHOLD in the tool options with the slider. The default value is 15.0 but can be set to any value from 0 to 255. The number you select is the maximum difference between the values of the initial pixel and the pixels that are selected.

- Change the way the pixels are selected. The SELECT BY option brings up the menu shown in Figure 13.35. The default choice, COMPOSITE, uses all the components of an RGB pixel. But you can use only one of these components or one of the components of the HSV model. For example, in Figure 13.36, we used the Blue component, and one click was enough to select the whole sky—and only the sky.

- While building a selection, keep the mouse button pressed and move the pointer along

Figure 13.37 *An image with two layers*

Figure 13.35 *Methods to select pixels*

Figure 13.36 *Using only the Blue component*

Figure 13.38 *Zooming in to a part of Figure 13.37*

the diagonal from top left to bottom right. When you move the pointer up, the threshold decreases, and when you move it down, the threshold increases. The threshold change is reflected in the tool options dialog.

The Fuzzy Select tool has two more options that are handy if the image has transparency and multiple layers:

• SELECT TRANSPARENT AREAS, when checked, allows you to include transparent areas as part of the selection.

In Figure 13.37, we added a new sky, which we took from another photograph. To do this, we selected the sky with the Fuzzy Select tool by selecting only the Blue component. We added an Alpha channel to the layer and cut the selection with DELETE. Finally, we inserted the other photograph as a new layer, using **Image: Open as Layers** (CTRL+ALT+O also works), and placed this new layer below the first one.

Now our image has multiple layers and a transparent area where the old sky was, so the status of the SELECT TRANSPARENT AREAS checkbox matters. Figure 13.38 shows an enlargement of part of this image. The cloudy sky is in the bottom layer, and the corresponding part of the top layer is transparent. But a little bit of the old blue sky was left between the trees. If the SELECT TRANSPARENT AREAS button is unchecked, you cannot select any pixel in the new sky. If it is checked, you can select both the old and the new sky and thereby apply transformations to all the blue sky areas in the image simultaneously.

• SAMPLE MERGED allows you to make a selection that includes all visible parts of the image rather than just what's present in the current layer. If the relevant area is completely transparent or opaque, checking this box has no effect. If the area is semitransparent, such that you can see elements from

Figure 13.39 *The Select by Color tool pointer*

Figure 13.40 *Selecting in the Blue channel*

Figure 13.41 *A blue area selected far from the initial point*

Figure 13.42 *The Scissors Select tool pointer*

various layers, then the status of this option is important.

The Select by Color Tool

Access the Select by Color tool from the Toolbox (the third icon from the right in Figure 13.8 on page 288), from the **Image: Tools > Selection Tools** menu, or by pressing SHIFT+O. When this tool is selected, the mouse pointer appears as shown in Figure 13.39. Select by Color works in the same way as the Fuzzy Select tool (except the pixels selected need not be contiguous), and it has the same options. If we select in the Blue channel in the image shown in Figure 13.33, our selection now includes the blue areas beneath the trees, as shown in Figure 13.40.

Based on the example given, this tool may seem more useful than the Fuzzy Select tool. In reality, the best tool depends on the image and the goal. In this case, selecting the whole sky with the Select by Color tool was done with only one click. Unfortunately, however, the tool also selected blue areas in two other parts of the photograph. Figure 13.41 shows one of them, the shirt of a man walking on the path. To make this selection useful, you have to deselect these other blue areas before making adjustments to the sky.

The Scissors Select Tool

Access the Scissors Select tool from the Toolbox (the second icon from the right in Figure 13.8 on page 288), from the **Image: Tools > Selection Tools** menu, or by pressing I (because this tool is sometimes called *Intelligent scissors*). When the tool is active, the mouse pointer appears as shown in Figure 13.42. This tool is useful for selecting complicated forms, provided their outline contrasts with the background. To use this tool, place control points along the outline of the object you intend to select. If these control points are well chosen, the line between two consecutive points will trace the outline of the object. Figure 13.43 shows a work in progress. The + sign next to the mouse pointer indicates that when you click, another point is added.

If the points are placed too far from each other and the outline between them is not extremely clear, the tool may not trace the outline correctly. Unfortunately, this tool has no undo mechanism. But as long as the point you add is along the outline, you can salvage it by clicking the line to add another point and then

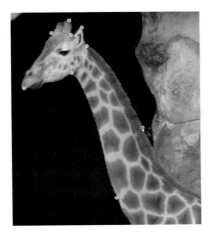

Figure 13.43 *Placing the first control points*

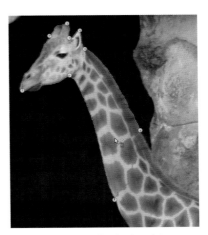

Figure 13.45 *The finished outline*

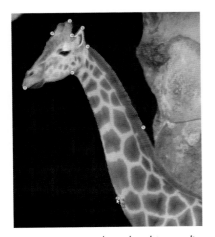

Figure 13.44 *Finishing the object outline*

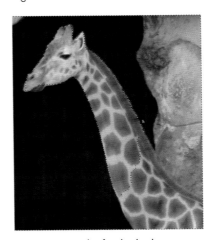

Figure 13.46 *The finished selection*

dragging the point into place while pressing the mouse button. If you accidentally add a point that's not along the object's border, add another point farther along the border and then click and drag the errant point into place. If a partial selection is unsalvageable, change to another tool, return to the Scissors tool, and start from the beginning.

When the mouse pointer is close to the start point, it changes, as shown in Figure 13.44. After you click, the mouse pointer changes again, as shown in Figure 13.45. If you click inside

the outline, it's transformed into a selection, as shown in Figure 13.46.

This figure illustrates the fact that the Scissors tool is not perfect. The lower jaw of the giraffe wasn't selected because its outline didn't contrast enough with the background. Errors such as this one are common. You will almost always need to refine a selection made with the Scissors tool by using another tool, such as Quick Mask, which is covered in Chapter 14.

The Scissors tool has only one option in addition to the standard selection options. INTERACTIVE BOUNDARY, when checked, shows

Figure 13.47 *Seeing the outline as it is built*

Figure 13.48 *Outlining the cat*

Figure 13.49 *After creating the outline*

Figure 13.50 *Marking the cat as the foreground object*

the outline between the previous control point and the one you're about to place. This outline appears as soon as you click on the new point and changes if you drag the mouse pointer without releasing it. This allows you to see how far you can move the new control point before the outline detection stops working properly, which helps you to outline an object accurately using fewer control points. Figure 13.47 shows an example where we managed to select the lower jaw correctly.

The Foreground Select Tool

Access the Foreground Select tool from the Toolbox (the rightmost icon in Figure 13.8 on page 288) or the **Image: Tools > Selection Tools** menu. It is a somewhat complex tool, best explained by demonstration.

This tool is designed to select a complicated object that's in the foreground of an image. When the tool is active, the pointer looks like the Free Select tool's pointer. The sentence "Roughly outline the object to extract" appears in the mode line of the Image window. Begin by outlining the object in the same way that you would when using the Free Select tool, as shown in Figure 13.48. A more precise outline will lead to a better result, so take care with this step.

When the mouse button is released, the outline is finalized, and the selection appears in blue (by default), as shown in Figure 13.49. The message "Mark foreground by painting on the object to extract" is now displayed in the mode bar of the Image window, and the mouse pointer is that of the Paintbrush tool. Next, paint roughly over the cat in one continuous stroke to select it, as shown in Figure 13.50. When you release the mouse pointer after your

Figure 13.51 *The new selection*

Figure 13.52 *The final selection*

first stroke, the message in the Image window will read "Add more strokes or press Enter to accept the selection." Our result, at this stage, is shown in Figure 13.51. If you haven't selected the cat completely, continue to paint over uns-elected areas. If you accidentally select some of the background, press the CTRL key to switch to deselect mode and paint over the areas that you accidentally selected. When you're satisfied, press ENTER to finalize the selection. Our final selection is shown in Figure 13.52.

Our final selection could still use a lot of work. The Foreground Select tool operates by selecting the colors that you paint over in the region that was outlined. If the colors of the object (the cat in this case) are similar to colors in the background, the selection won't be very accurate, particularly if the outline includes a lot of the background.

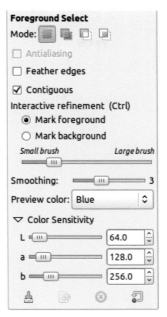

Figure 13.53 *The Foreground Select tool options*

The Foreground Select tool has many options, which are shown in Figure 13.53. When checked, CONTIGUOUS specifies that the selected area is a single, connected piece. Otherwise, the tool can select disjointed areas of similar color that fall within the outline drawn.

The following two radio buttons are equivalent to the CTRL key in that they allow you to toggle between selecting and deselecting colors with the paintbrush. The tool makes a new draft selection each time you release the mouse button. A slider lets you choose the size of the brush.

Use the SMOOTHING slider to adjust the precision of the selection. The smaller the value, the higher the precision, but small holes in the selection may also result.

The PREVIEW COLOR menu allows you to choose among Blue, Green, or Red, and the best choice is the color that contrasts most sharply with the image.

Finally, the COLOR SENSITIVITY option allows you to use the LAB color model to increase or

Figure 13.54 *The Paths tool icon*

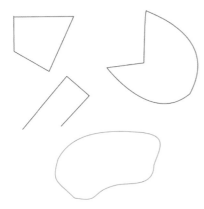

Figure 13.55 *Four example paths*

decrease the sensitivity of the tool to colors in the image by adjusting the three sliders. In this color model, L is the same as the Value channel in the HSV model, A is the difference between Red and Green, and B the difference between Blue and Yellow.

13.3   The Paths Tool

The Paths tool is not exactly a selection tool, but it does offer a powerful way to build complicated selections. You can access it from the Toolbox (see Figure 13.54), from **Image: Tools > Paths**, or by pressing B. The keyboard shortcut comes from *Bézier curves*, which is another name for paths.

A Bézier curve is a powerful mathematical tool for describing sophisticated curves. Although the mathematics are complicated, the curves, or paths, are fairly easy to create using a small set of *anchor points* and the corresponding *handles* of these points. Modifying the curve by moving, adding, or removing anchor points or by changing the orientation and length of the

Figure 13.56 *Building a path*

handles is easy. Figure 13.55 shows four different paths. As you can see, paths can be closed or open and may contain straight or curved segments, or both. When constructing a path, you can undo any action, which is not possible with most selection tools, including the Scissors Select tool and the Foreground Select tool. Every path you build is saved in the current image and can be retrieved in the Paths dialog, which is initially a part of the multi-dialog window. If it's no longer open, you can open the dialog from the **Image: Windows > Dockable Dialogs** menu. The Paths tab appears after the Layers and Channels tabs. When visible, the Paths dialog shows the paths that exist in the current image. By default, the paths are invisible, but clicking the left side of the line reveals the eye icon, which indicates that the path is now visible.

After creating a path, you can convert it to a selection or *stroke* it, which allows you to draw on the image. You can even convert the selection to the SVG format for vector graphics (see Chapter 20).

Building a Path

When you select the Paths tool, the mouse pointer is accompanied by the complicated icon shown in Figure 13.56. The tiny + sign means that clicking will add anchor points to the path. The points you have already placed appear as filled circles, except the most recent one, which appears as an empty circle. Straight lines link the points.

If you move the pointer close to an existing anchor point or a segment, the + sign changes to

Figure 13.57 *Moving an anchor point*

Figure 13.58 *Moving a segment in nonpolygonal mode*

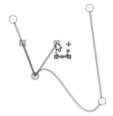

Figure 13.59 *Moving a handle*

Figure 13.60 *One example of moving a segment in polygonal mode*

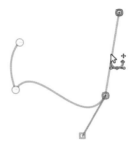

Figure 13.61 *A second example of moving a segment in polygonal mode*

the move sign (crossed arrows). In Figure 13.57, we clicked and dragged an existing anchor point, which then became the current point.

If you click and drag on a segment, the resulting effect depends on the status of the POLYGONAL checkbox in the tool options. If it is unchecked, the segment is deformed as shown in Figure 13.58. Handles extend from both ends of the resulting arc. If you move the handle, the arc is deformed, as shown in Figure 13.59.

If you click and drag a segment when the POLYGONAL box is checked, the segment is moved but not deformed. To make this possible without separating the segments, the adjacent segments must be deformed instead. In Figure 13.60, we moved the curved segment down, and both straight segments were lengthened. In Figure 13.61, we moved the straight segment on the right farther to the right, and the curved segment was deformed.

Modifying a Path

The Paths tool options are shown in Figure 13.62. We already discussed the POLYGONAL checkbox. The EDIT MODE option allows you to select among three choices. By default, the DESIGN button is checked; in this mode clicking outside the path adds a new point. When you add a new point, a segment is placed between the new

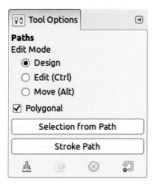

Figure 13.62 *The Paths tool options*

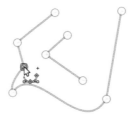

Figure 13.65 *Adding a new point in Edit mode*

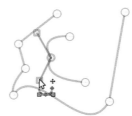

Figure 13.66 *Moving the handles of a point*

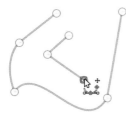

Figure 13.63 *Adding segments to an existing path*

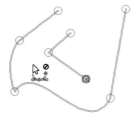

Figure 13.64 *The mouse pointer in Edit mode*

point and the previous one. If you switch to another tool and then back to the Paths tool, you can either continue the existing path or build a *disjointed path*, a single path that looks like two separate paths (Figure 13.63). To continue an existing path, click an existing anchor point and then add your new point. To build a disjointed path, click the existing path twice, activate Design mode, and begin adding points without first clicking an existing point.

If you click the EDIT radio button (or press the CTRL key), you can change the tool's

behavior. When outside of the anchor points or segments, the mouse pointer is not operational, as shown by the circle with a line through it in Figure 13.64.

If the pointer is close to a segment, the mouse pointer is accompanied by a tiny + sign, which means that you can add a new anchor point at this location, as shown in Figure 13.65.

If the pointer is close to an anchor point, the mouse pointer normally changes to the Move icon, which means you can move that point. But the effect of moving a point depends on the status of the POLYGONAL option. When this option is checked, the anchor moves; otherwise, a handle is moved, and the curve is deformed.

Depending on the direction of the move, a different handle appears; each handle corresponds to one of the curves attached to the anchor point. In Figure 13.66, both handles are visible.

Finally, if the current point (the one denoted with a hollow circle) is at the end of an open path and the mouse pointer is close to a different end point, the pointer changes to a link icon, as shown in Figure 13.67, and clicking

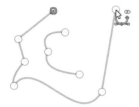

Figure 13.67 *Preparing to add a segment between existing points*

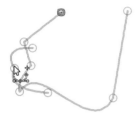

Figure 13.68 *Moving path components*

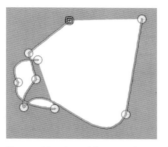

Figure 13.69 *Building a selection from a path*

Figure 13.70 *The Choose Stroke Style dialog*

draws a segment between the two endpoints. This closes the path.

If you click the MOVE radio button in the tool options (or press the ALT key), the mouse pointer is always accompanied by the move sign. If you click a segment or anchor point of a path component, you can move it, as shown in Figure 13.68. If you click and drag outside of the path, you move the whole active path.

You can also move a completed path without altering it with the Move tool. To do this, select the Move tool and click the rightmost button in its options dialog. You can also use the transformation tools on a path to apply perspective or rotation, for example.

Using a Path

Most often, a completed path is either converted to a selection or used to paint on the image. The path can be converted to a selection by clicking the SELECTION FROM PATH button in the options dialog.

Figure 13.69 shows the result when we do this for the path in Figure 13.68. The unse-lected parts appear pink because we've turned on Quick Mask (SHIFT+Q).

As expected, marching ants follow the path, and the outline of the selection is sharp.

Stroking the path is equivalent to painting on the image along the path. Clicking the STROKE PATH button opens the dialog shown in Figure 13.70. This dialog is where you specify the characteristics of the stroke that will be painted along the path. First, you must choose whether to stroke the line or to stroke with a paint tool.

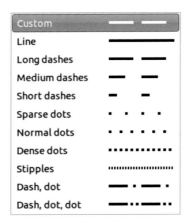

Figure 13.71 *The Dash preset menu*

If you choose to stroke the line, you can specify the width of the line, whether to use a SOLID COLOR (the foreground color) or a PATTERN, and which LINE STYLE to use. The LINE STYLE choices include the following:

- CAP STYLE affects the ends of the segments.

- JOIN STYLE affects the angle between two segments.

- MITER LIMIT also alters the appearance of joints. A level of zero results in a joint that ends abruptly where the two segments intersect, whereas a higher level results in a joint that tapers into a point.

- The DASH PATTERN is chosen from the DASH PRESET menu (shown in Figure 13.71), which contains a number of preset patterns, as well as an option for creating a custom dash pattern. Adjust the custom pattern by clicking and dragging the line that appears just above the Dash preset menu. The arrow buttons on the ends move the pattern back and forth along the line, changing where it begins and ends. Note that the third CAP STYLE can mask the intervals between dashes if they are too short. This effect will not be visible in the preview, but it will be apparent once you finalize the changes (see Figure 13.72). The path is still visible beneath the strokes, but it is not itself a part of the image. If you printed this

Figure 13.72 *Stroking a path*

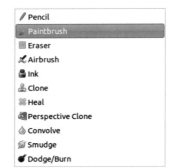

Figure 13.73 *The Paint tool menu*

Figure 13.74 *Stroking with the Paintbrush tool*

Figure 13.75 *Stroking with the Ink tool*

image, for example, the handles on the left would not appear.

- The ANTIALIASING option is best left checked, as usual.

If you select the STROKE WITH A PAINT TOOL option, you can choose from the paint tools shown in Figure 13.73. Figure 13.74 shows the result of stroking with the Paintbrush tool with a Hardness 075 brush scaled to size 20. For Figure 13.75, we used the Ink tool and checked

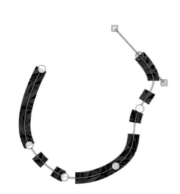

Figure 13.76 *Stroking with a pattern*

Figure 13.77 *The Paths dialog*

the EMULATE BRUSH DYNAMICS checkbox. See Chapter 15, and particularly "Paint Dynamics" on page 333, for more details about paint dynamics.

You can also stroke the path with a pattern by choosing STROKE LINE and then PATTERN. You must choose the pattern *after* opening the Choose Stroke Style dialog by selecting the pattern in the Patterns dialog, initially in the multi-dialog window. The path in Figure 13.76 was stroked using the Pine pattern.

The Paths Dialog

A path differs from a selection in the following ways:

- Although only one selection is available at a time, a given image can contain several paths. If you save the image in the XCF format, for example, the paths are saved with it and are available the next time you open it. Note that this is also true if you export the image in the TIFF format.

- When you are building a path, you can undo any action.

- Existing paths are available in the Paths dialog, which is a dockable dialog, normally open in the multi-dialog window.

Figure 13.77 shows a Paths dialog containing three paths. The top one, whose row is emphasized, is the current path. The other two are visible in the Image window, as the eye icon is visible. When a path is visible in the Image window, make it the current path by selecting the Paths tool and clicking it. Clicking its row in the Paths dialog has the same result. If the Lock is active, it prevents any change to the current path.

As in the Layers or Channels dialogs, each row in the Paths dialog has a position for a link. This is explained in more detail in Chapter 11. A path can be linked to one or more layers and channels and can then be deformed using any of the transformation tools—in the same way as the other linked components.

Right-clicking in the Paths dialog brings up the Paths menu, shown in Figure 13.78. This menu can also be accessed via the configure button at the top right of the dialog. The eight most useful entries in this menu also have corresponding buttons located at the bottom of the dialog.

EDIT PATH ATTRIBUTES only allows you to change the path name, which can also be done by double-clicking in the corresponding row.

NEW PATH creates a new empty path. Another way to create a new path is to click in the image with the Paths tool selected, without first clicking a visible path.

RAISE PATH and LOWER PATH move the paths up or down in the dialog, but this has no effect on the function of the paths, and you can also

Figure 13.78 *The Paths menu*

SELECTION TO PATH uses the marching ants of the existing selection to build a new path. Or you can apply **Image: Select > To Path** to do this.

STROKE PATH does the same thing as the corresponding button in the options dialog.

COPY PATH and PASTE PATH allow you to copy a path from one image to another. You can also do this by clicking and dragging a path from the Paths dialog to the Image window.

EXPORT PATH converts the path to the SVG format. In the dialog that opens, you can choose whether to export only the current path or all the paths in the image.

IMPORT PATH converts an existing SVG file into a path. This can be handy for creating extremely complicated paths, which would be beyond the capabilities of the Paths tool. Note that GIMP can also load an SVG file as an image.

Paths can also be used in conjunction with the Text tool. Text can be converted to a path, or it can be typed along a path. Refer to Section 15.8 for more details.

rearrange them by clicking and dragging their rows in the dialog.

DUPLICATE PATH and DELETE PATH have obvious meanings. Clicking and dragging a row to the delete icon also deletes that path.

MERGE VISIBLE PATHS is a way to build one path from several, but all the paths being merged must be visible. Make them visible (by clicking the eye icon) before using this menu entry.

The next four menu entries are equivalent to the SELECTION FROM PATH button in the options dialog. The difference is that in the options dialog, you must make additional selections to control how the new selection is combined with the existing one, whereas in the Paths menu, four distinct entries correspond to the different combination methods. Note that the default method (replacing the existing selection) can also be accomplished by applying **Image: Select > From Path** or by pressing SHIFT+V.

13.4 Using Selections

Once you've built a selection, you can use it for a number of purposes. Here, we discuss how you may use a selection that you've just built. If you'd like to save the selection for later use, we will discuss masks in depth in the next chapter.

When a selection is active, it's outlined by marching ants. You can hide this outline, if it's distracting, by pressing CTRL+T or selecting **Image: View > Show Selection**. But use this toggle wisely. One of the main pitfalls a new GIMP user encounters is a forgotten hidden selection. When a hidden selection exists, transformations to the image seem to work strangely, or not at all. If a transformation doesn't work as expected, always toggle the visibility of marching ants to check whether a hidden selection is to blame.

Changes to an image, whether via drawing or painting, color correction tools, or filters, are

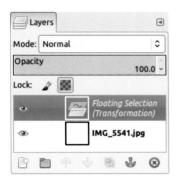

Figure 13.79 *A floating selection*

applied to the current selection only. This allows you to delimit precisely which part of the image the action affects. We've included many examples of this throughout the book.

Suppose you select some building in a photograph and want to correct its perspective with the corresponding transformation tool (see Chapter 16). As soon as you apply the transformation tool, a new layer, called a *floating selection*, appears in the image. Figure 13.79 shows a floating selection in the Layers dialog.

This new layer is temporary, but while it exists, you cannot change anything elsewhere in the image, nor can you change the active layer. GIMP gives us three ways to get rid of this temporary anomaly and regain control of the other image layers:

- Delete the floating selection if you don't really need it for anything.

- Create a new layer to contain the floating selection.

- *Anchor* the floating selection to the current layer. That is, add it to that layer, in effect replacing all the pixels that will be hidden by the selection.

Any of these actions can be applied by right-clicking the Layers dialog or from the **Image: Layer** menu. Press CTRL+H to anchor the floating selection to a layer. Note that this shortcut doesn't always operate on a layer, however. It

Figure 13.80 *The Select menu*

can also operate on a layer mask or on a channel, depending on previous actions.

When transformations are applied to a selection, the initial content of the selection will be replaced. For instance, if you rotate a selection, the part of the image that was selected will not be at the same place and position as before. If the layer doesn't have an Alpha channel, the area that the selection occupied, but has moved out of, is filled with the current background color. If an Alpha channel does exist, the empty area becomes transparent. If you want to retain a copy of the selection in its original form, you must duplicate the layer prior to transforming the selection.

The Select Menu

The **Image: Select** menu appears in Figure 13.80. Its entries affect the selection rather than the image as a whole. We will discuss each of the entries in turn.

ALL or CTRL+A creates a selection that covers the entire canvas. If you'd like to manipulate the entire canvas, it is not always necessary to press

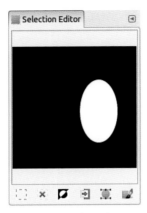

Figure 13.81 *The Selection Editor dialog*

Figure 13.82 *After clicking in the display window*

Figure 13.83 *Feathering a selection*

CTRL+A. For example, if there is no selection and you choose **Image: Edit > Copy**, the whole canvas is copied. However, if you wish to move the canvas, you must select it first.

NONE or SHIFT+CTRL+A dismisses any current selection, leaving nothing selected.

INVERT or CTRL+I inverts the selection, so all the pixels that were fully selected are not selected, and vice versa. Partially selected pixels remain selected, but the amount of selection is inverted. For example, if a pixel is 80% selected, after inversion, the other 20% is selected. If you think about the selection as a grayscale image, inverting the selection means that a black pixel becomes white, a white pixel becomes black, and a pixel that is gray at 60% becomes gray at 40%.

FLOAT or SHIFT+CTRL+L makes the selected pixels a floating selection. This option is rarely useful, especially because it cuts pixels from the initial layer. This command is generally thought of as an obsolete feature.

BY COLOR is simply another way to access the Select by Color tool (see "The Select by Color Tool" on page 296).

FROM PATH or SHIFT+V builds a new selection from the current path if one exists. The previous selection is discarded.

SELECTION EDITOR opens the dockable dialog shown in Figure 13.81. This dialog allows easy access to some of the most common selection-related tasks via the six buttons along the bottom of the dialog. The current selection is displayed in the window.

If you click the display window of the dialog, the Select by Color tool's method is used to build a selection automatically, as shown in Figure 13.82. Press the SHIFT, CTRL, and ALT keys to change the selection mode as usual.

FEATHER opens the dialog shown in Figure 13.83. This option is useful if you forget to check the FEATHER EDGES checkbox when using a selection tool, choose too small a value, or build a selection using a tool that doesn't include this option.

SHARPEN removes all feathering from the selection, and the result is dramatic only if the fuzzy outline of the selection was the result of feathering. If you use it on a selection made with the Fuzzy Select tool, for example, the effect is barely noticeable, and the border of the selection remains convoluted, as shown in Figure 13.84.

SHRINK opens the dialog shown in Figure 13.85. The size of the selected area is reduced

Figure 13.84 *Sharpening a fuzzy selection*

Figure 13.85 *The Shrink dialog*

Figure 13.86 *The Border dialog*

Figure 13.87 *Bordering a selection*

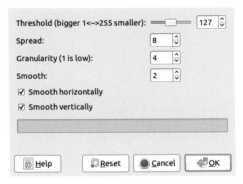

Figure 13.88 *The Distort dialog*

Figure 13.89 *Distorting with the default parameters*

by a specified number of pixels. This means that fewer pixels are selected than before, regardless of the shape of the selection. The SHRINK FROM IMAGE BORDER checkbox is meaningful only if the selection is larger than the canvas. If that is the case, and if this option is checked, the initial selection is treated as if it extends only to the canvas edges.

GROW has the opposite effect and brings up a similar dialog.

BORDER opens the dialog shown in Figure 13.86. Border can be used to build a new selection that extends along the outline of the current selection. Figure 13.87 shows the result when the initial selection was an ellipse. You can choose the width of the border, which is applied symmetrically along the selection. A checkbox allows you to feather the border, but you cannot control the width of the feathering. The other checkbox, LOCK SELECTION TO IMAGE EDGES, constrains the new selection to within the canvas limits.

DISTORT opens the dialog shown in Figure 13.88. This tool is used to distort the selection outline randomly. By playing with the parameters, you can get different effects, but the outcome is difficult to predict. From an initial simple ellipse, using the default parameters, we get Figure 13.89. If we double the three parameters—SPREAD, GRANULARITY, and

Figure 13.90 *Distorting with doubled parameters*

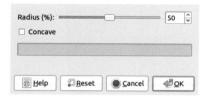

Figure 13.91 *The Rounded Rectangle dialog*

Figure 13.92 *A rectangle with concave corners*

SMOOTH—we get Figure 13.90.

ROUNDED RECTANGLE opens the !dialog in Figure 13.91. This tool builds a rectangular selection with rounded corners with the specified radius around the current selection. If you check the CONCAVE option, the selection will be shaped like the one in Figure 13.92.

The next two entries on the Select menu, TOGGLE QUICK MASK and SAVE TO CHANNEL, will be considered in the next chapter. The last entry, TO PATH, uses the marching ants of the existing selection to build a path.

The Edit Menu

The Edit menu is shown in Figure 13.93. In this section, we cover only the entries that apply to selections.

CUT or CTRL+X deletes the selected pixels in the current layer and copies them to the clipboard. The contents of the clipboard can be retrieved via the Paste command, but they're also

Figure 13.93 *The Edit menu*

available as the first entry in both the Brushes dialog and the Patterns dialog. This provides an easy way to build an interesting temporary brush or pattern.

If the current layer has no transparency (no Alpha channel), then any deleted pixels are replaced with the current background color. If the layer has an Alpha channel, the deleted pixels become transparent. If there is no current selection, all the pixels of the current layer are deleted.

COPY or CTRL+C works like the Cut command, but it doesn't delete anything. Note that every time you put something on the clipboard, the previous contents are discarded.

COPY VISIBLE or SHIFT+CTRL+C works like Copy, but it copies all the selected visible pixels regardless of whether they belong to the current layer. It acts as if the image was flattened.

PASTE or CTRL+V places the current contents of the clipboard into the current image as a floating selection, discussed at the beginning of this section. Note that if you select a part of

Figure 13.94 *A fuzzy selection*

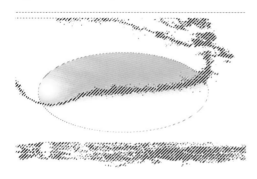

Figure 13.95 *Pasting one selection into another on a white canvas*

Figure 13.96 *The Paste as menu*

Figure 13.97 *The Buffer menu*

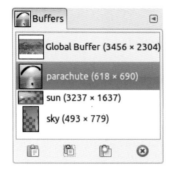

Figure 13.98 *The Buffers dialog*

the canvas that is larger than the contents of the clipboard, the floating selection will be centered within that selection once you press CTRL+V.

PASTE INTO works like Paste, except that the contents of the clipboard are only pasted within the current selection in the target image. Figure 13.94 shows a selection made with the Fuzzy Select tool. Figure 13.95 shows the result of pasting this selection into an elliptic selection on a white canvas.

PASTE AS opens the menu shown in Figure 13.96. The contents of the clipboard can be used to create a new image (also SHIFT+CTRL +V), a new layer in the current image (equivalent to simply pasting and then creating a new layer for the floating selection), a new brush, or a new pattern. The last two entries make more permanent the temporary brush or pattern derived from the clipboard contents.

BUFFER opens the menu shown in Figure 13.97. These four commands operate on *named buffers*. You can have any number of such buffers, and you can name them anything you like. You can see any existing buffers in the Buffers dockable dialog, which can be opened via **Image: Windows > Dockable Dialogs > Buffers** if it's not already open. Figure 13.98 shows this dialog after we created two buffers. The contents of the clipboard appear on top (named Global Buffer). The first three buttons along the bottom of the dialog allow you to paste the selected buffer into a selection or as a new image.

CLEAR (or the DELETE key) deletes the contents of the selection without affecting the clipboard.

The next three commands in the **Image: Edit** menu offer a convenient means for filling the selection with the foreground color, the background color, or the current pattern without changing from the current tool. Their keyboard abbreviations—CTRL+,, CTRL+., and CTRL+;—are handy, and we suggest committing them to memory.

STROKE SELECTION works in exactly the same way as STROKE PATH (which appears next in the menu). This option is equivalent to changing the selection to a path and then stroking the path.

Modifying the Selection Border

Once a selection is built using any of the techniques discussed in this chapter, you can modify the border of the selection to include or exclude pixels from the selected area. We've already introduced many of the tools to do this, here and in previous chapters, but now we provide a brief summary for quick reference:

- If the selection was built with the Rectangle Select or the Ellipse Select tool, you can change its size or move it whenever the tool is active.

- All the transformation tools discussed in Chapter 16 can be applied to selections. When using them, simply select the second choice in the TRANSFORM option in their options dialog. This modifies the selection, not the image contents (i.e., the selection changes, but the image is left unchanged). Note that these tools can also transform the current path, if you select the third choice.

- The Move tool works the same way: It can move the current selection (or a path).

- When building a new selection, combine it with an existing one by pressing SHIFT or by changing the mode in the tool options.

- As we discussed in "The Select Menu" on page 307, use the entries in the middle section of the **Image: Select** menu to change the boundaries of the selection.

- The Quick Mask tool, which we discuss in Chapter 14, is an excellent tool for refining a complicated selection. It's intuitive and simple, yet it allows you to make extremely precise adjusts to a selection.

- The Selection Editor is a convenient tool for making various changes to the current selection, such as inverting it, saving it, and creating a path from it. See "The Select Menu" on page 307 for more details.

- With channels, which we cover in Chapter 14, you can manipulate a selection as if it were a grayscale image, using any of the GIMP tools. You can also create selections in this grayscale image, which allow you to make selections within a selection. The possibilities are endless.

14

Masks

A *mask* is a grayscale image that is used to represent either a selection within an image (called a *selection mask*) or the transparency of a layer (called a *layer mask*).

You use a selection mask to save a particular selection. This way you can maintain a collection of selections that you've built, ready to use when you need them. In a selection mask, pixels that are completely selected in the image are represented as white, pixels that are not selected at all are represented as black, and pixels that are partially selected are represented as intermediate shades.

Although a selection mask is an independent object, a layer mask is part of a specific layer used to specify the transparency of the layer's pixels. The pixels themselves don't change—in other words, their RGB components remain intact. With layer masks, you can manipulate a layer's transparency independent of its colors.

You can use all GIMP tools on a mask: drawing tools, transformation tools, and even selection tools. This makes doing very precise work on a mask possible—and creating a selection much more complex than what you saw in Chapter 13.

14.1 Selection Masks

Figure 14.1 shows a photograph where we made a selection with the Select by Color tool (SHIFT+O). In the tool options, we increased the Threshold value to 20.0 to select the entire sky. Then we applied **Image: Select > Save to Channel**.

The Channels Dialog

Figure 14.2 shows the Channels dialog, which is a dockable dialog initially located in the multi-dialog window. The first three rows correspond to the image's Red, Green, and Blue channels. These channels are grayscale images; each of their pixel values corresponds to the value of that color component in the image itself. That's why the thumbnail appears as a grayscale image.

Figure 14.1 *A selection made with the Select by Color tool*

Figure 14.2 *The Channels dialog*

Figure 14.3 *Looking at the thumbnail*

Click and hold the thumbnail to see a somewhat larger, color thumbnail (see Figure 14.3).

Click and drag the Red channel thumbnail to the Toolbox to create a new grayscale image, as shown in Figure 14.4. Or drag the thumbnail to the Image window to add the channel as a new layer of the image.

Clicking a channel toggles it on and off. If a channel is deactivated, none of the changes made to the image affects that particular channel. Use this to your advantage, for example, by selecting only the Red channel when removing red eye in a photograph. If no channels are active, you won't be able to change the image at all, leading to confusion and frustration. We recommend always keeping the Channels dialog open and checking it if the adjustments you make don't yield the results you expect.

Clicking the eye next to a channel toggles that channel's visibility. For example, Figure 14.5

Figure 14.4 *Extracting the Red channel*

Figure 14.5 *Hiding the Green channel*

shows the result of hiding the Green channel. Note that visibility and activating a channel are two different things: You can blindly alter a channel that's not visible and vainly attempt to edit a channel that's visible but inactive.

As soon as you add an Alpha channel or a second layer to an image, the global Alpha channel, which represents the transparency of the whole image, appears in the Channels dialog.

Below the rows for the three or four actual channels, a horizontal strip separates the dialog into two parts. You find the layer pixels lock icon (which you saw in Chapter 11) in this strip. Activating the lock prevents changes to the mask. The lower part of the dialog holds the selection masks. Figure 14.2 has only one, and its name was chosen by GIMP. Change this name the same way you do with layers: by double-clicking the name itself, selecting **Channels: right-click > Edit Channel Attributes**, or clicking the leftmost icon at the bottom of the Channels dialog, which brings up the dialog shown in Figure 14.6. Here, change the channel name and adjust its

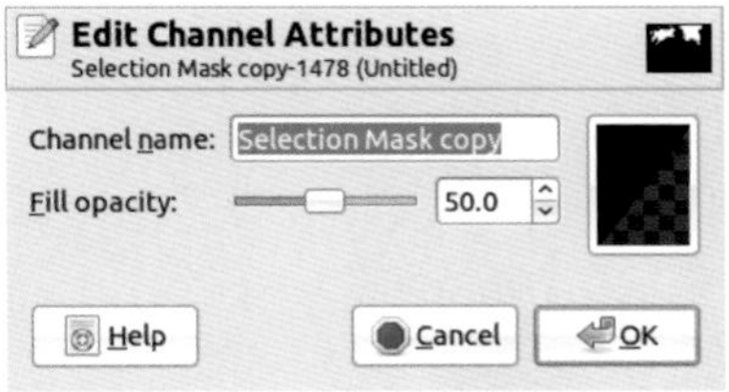

Figure 14.6 *Editing the channel attributes*

Figure 14.7 *Making the mask visible*

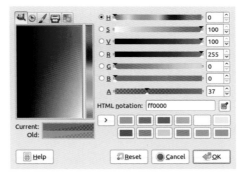

Figure 14.9 *Editing the channel color*

Figure 14.9, you can change the Alpha value by using the bottom slider.

Between each channel's eye icon and thumbnail, notice room available for an additional icon: the chain. The chain links selection masks together. If you have several selection channels and link some of them together by selecting the chain icons, any changes applied to one of them also affect the others.

To access the Channels menu, either click the configuration button in the top-right corner of the Channels dialog or right-click one of the rows. This menu has the same options as the seven buttons in the dialog's bottom row (see Figure 14.2). These buttons allow you to do the following:

- Edit the channel attributes.

- Create a new channel. This option brings up the dialog shown in Figure 14.10, which is identical to the one shown in Figure 14.6 except for the additional INITIALIZE FROM SELECTION checkbox. Checking this box saves the current selection to a channel. Press SHIFT while clicking CREATE A NEW CHANNEL to use the last parameter values.

- Move the current channel up or down. This option has no effect on the image itself.

- Duplicate the current channel.

- Create a selection with the current channel. The CTRL and SHIFT keys work the same way as they do when using the selection tools.

Figure 14.8 *After changing the channel attributes*

opacity and color to make it temporarily visible in the image.

These last two attributes are used when you click the eye icon for the Red, Green, or Blue channel. If you use the settings shown in Figure 14.6, you get the result shown in Figure 14.7: The mask is 50% opaque and is shown in black. In Figure 14.8, you see the result when the opacity is set to 37% and the color is set to a bright green. Note that the Color chooser dialog, which pops up when you click the box on the right of the Edit Channel Attributes dialog, has more components than usual. As shown in

Figure 14.10 *Creating a new channel*

In the Channels dialog menu are four entries that create a selection from the channel, each corresponding to the different selection modes.

- Delete the current channel.

All of these menu options, except New Channel, are available only when a selection mask is active.

Only one selection mask can be active at a given time, and when a mask is active, GIMP's various drawing and transformation tools work on the mask, not on the image itself. In fact, if you switch to the Layers dialog, you can see there is no active layer. Conversely, if you activate a layer in the Layers dialog, the selection mask deactivates. If you're trying to change the current image and nothing is happening, make sure a layer is actually selected in the Layers dialog. You could be inadvertently changing a mask!

Creating a Selection Mask

You can create a selection mask using one of two methods, each with several possible pitfalls. The first method is to use the selection tools (covered in Chapter 13) and then to save the selection to a channel. After doing this, no layer is active, the image mask is active but might not be visible in the image, and the selection used for creating the mask is still active.

As a result, if you try to paint on the image, you're actually painting on the mask. When you create the mask, the Channels dialog appears, even if it was previously hidden. This should

Figure 14.11 *Another photograph*

Figure 14.12 *A mask that needs to be cleaned up*

alert you that the mask is active. But the selection also remains active—even if it's hidden—so if you try to paint on the mask, you're only able to alter areas that fall within the selection.

The second method for creating a selection mask is to use the Channels dialog directly. Create a new channel by clicking the appropriate button, and it immediately appears in the image. Then use the drawing tools to edit it. Painting white on the mask selects pixels, and painting black deselects pixels. Use the Blend tool and paint with various shades of gray to partially select pixels. You can also use colors other than gray, although only the color's value component is used.

For example, we took the photograph shown in Figure 14.11 and made a selection with the Select by Color tool. But we set the THRESHOLD cursor to 15.0, which is too low for a clean selection. Figure 14.12 shows a part of the image after saving the selection to a channel and making this channel visible.

Figure 14.13 *Resetting the foreground and background colors*

Figure 14.14 *The Quick Mask button*

The mask needs to be cleaned up, which you can do with the Paintbrush tool. First set the foreground and background colors to their default values of black and white. The simplest way to do this is to click the small buttons in the lower-left corner of the Toolbox (see Figure 14.13) or to press D̲. Then select the Paintbrush tool (P̲) and an appropriate brush. Paint the parts that shouldn't be selected black and the parts that should be selected white. Switch between the foreground and background color by pressing X̲.

You want either full selection or no selection at all, so if you're using a tablet pen, set the Paint Dynamics so that pressure changes the brush size, rather than the opacity. This dynamic allows you to press down to fill large areas quickly or zoom in and press gently to touch up the mask's finer details.

The Quick Mask Tool

If you want to create a complicated selection, but don't need to save it for later, use the Quick Mask tool. Toggle it via **Image: Select > Toggle Quick Mask**, by clicking the button in the bottom-left corner of the Image window (see Figure 14.14), or by pressing S̲H̲I̲F̲T̲+̲Q̲.

When the Quick Mask is active, it appears in the Channels dialog as an active and visible red selection mask. Figure 14.15 shows a part of our photograph after making a selection with the

Figure 14.15 *A part of a Quick Mask*

Figure 14.16 *The Quick Mask menu*

Select by Color tool, using a THRESHOLD of 20.0. To edit the selection, paint the mask with black or white. When satisfied, toggle the Quick Mask again, which has the following effects:

- The mask is converted to a selection.
- The selection mask is removed from the Channels dialog.
- The current layer is reactivated.

This is a very simple and convenient way to make changes to a selection without formally creating a selection mask. Also note that using a Quick Mask doesn't prevent saving the final selection to a channel.

Right-clicking the Quick Mask button brings up the menu shown in Figure 14.16. This menu allows us to toggle the mask, change its color and opacity, and invert the coloration, as shown in Figure 14.17. The color inversion reveals that quite a bit of blue sky in the top-left portion of the photograph remains unselected. Painting in black still adds red pixels to the mask, but now the red pixels are selected. If you toggle Quick Mask off, you see the selection wasn't inverted. The sky is still selected.

Figure 14.17 *Inverting the mask coloration*

Figure 14.18 *The initial image*

14.2   Layer Masks

A layer mask is a grayscale image attached to a specific layer; it is the same size as that layer. The mask's pixels set the transparency of the corresponding pixels in the layer. A white pixel in the mask specifies that the corresponding pixel in the image is completely opaque, and a black pixel specifies full transparency. A gray pixel specifies partial opacity. The pixel's color components are unchanged, so a pixel can be strongly colored and completely transparent at the same time. This means that in a layer with a layer mask, every pixel requires 4 bytes.

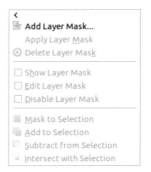

Figure 14.19 *The Mask menu*

Figure 14.20 *Adding a mask to the layer*

Building a Layer Mask

Start with the image shown in Figure 14.18. Select **Image: Layer > Mask**, and the menu shown in Figure 14.19 appears. The same menu, minus the last three entries, can also be selected via **Layers: right-click**.

Select Add Layer Mask, and the dialog shown in Figure 14.20 appears. Several options are available for the layer mask's initial contents:

- WHITE (FULL OPACITY): The mask appears as a white thumbnail in the Layers dialog just beside the layer thumbnail. Because all its pixels are white, the layer is completely opaque, and the image looks no different. Note that this does not prevent us from manipulating the OPACITY slider in the Layers dialog, which

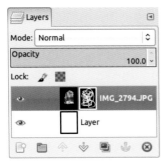

Figure 14.21 *Two layers and a layer mask*

Figure 14.22 *Painting in white on the layer mask*

is independent of the mask. This slider operates in combination with the layer's MODE to specify how its pixels are combined with the underlying layers. This opacity is a characteristic of the layer, not of the individual pixels.

- BLACK (FULL TRANSPARENCY): The mask appears as a black thumbnail, and the layer becomes fully transparent. Now wherever you paint on the mask with white, areas of the layer reappear. Figure 14.21 shows the Layers dialog of an image we created to demonstrate this. We loaded a photograph, added a new white layer, moved it down in the layer stack, and added a black layer mask to the top layer.

Then we painted in white on the mask with the Paintbrush tool, using the Hardness 075 brush in a large size. In the resulting image, shown in Figure 14.22, the transparent areas of the top layer appear white because of the white background layer, whereas the areas where we painted on the layer mask are filled with the contents of the top layer.

- LAYER'S ALPHA CHANNEL: If the layer already has an Alpha channel, its contents are copied to the layer mask. Note that the Alpha channel remains intact.

- TRANSFER LAYER'S ALPHA CHANNEL: This does the same thing as the previous entry, but the Alpha channel is reset to full opacity.

- SELECTION: As stated previously, a selection is a grayscale image. This image is copied to the layer mask. The selected pixels are opaque; the unselected pixels are transparent.

- GRAYSCALE COPY OF LAYER: The current contents of the layer are converted to a grayscale image and used for initializing the layer mask. Most of the pixels in the image are partially selected, and the level of selection is proportional to the pixel's value. White pixels are fully selected, and darker pixels are selected to a lesser degree.

- CHANNEL: If at least one channel exists, use it to initialize the layer mask. Select a channel from the menu that appears.

INVERT MASK inverts the mask. The transparent parts become opaque, and vice versa.

Manipulating a Layer Mask

When the layer mask is created, the Layers dialog changes, as shown in Figure 14.23. A thumbnail of the mask appears to the right of the layer thumbnail. It's enclosed in a white frame to show that it's active, whereas the layer thumbnail is enclosed in a black frame.

Here, choose a grayscale copy of the layer as a mask and invert it. The result, shown in Figure 14.24, is that the parts of the image that

Figure 14.23 *A layer mask has been added.*

Figure 14.24 *The result of using the layer mask*

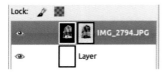

Figure 14.25 *Activating the layer itself*

Figure 14.26 *An inactive layer mask*

Figure 14.27 *The Layers dialog when only the layer mask is visible*

Figure 14.28 *The Image window when only the layer mask is visible*

were very dark are now much more visible because they are highly selected and thus opaque. But the sea landscape is now pale and dull because the layer's light pixels are now almost transparent and reveal the white layer underneath.

When the layer mask is active, all tools operate only on it, not on the layer itself. To toggle between the mask and the layer, click the corresponding thumbnail in the Layers dialog. The white frame always shows whether the layer or the mask is active. In Figure 14.25, the layer is active.

To hide the effect of the layer mask without deleting it, CTRL-click the mask thumbnail. Its frame is now red, as shown in Figure 14.26, and the mask effect is temporarily canceled. If you CTRL-click again, the mask is activated.

To see the mask itself, ALT-click the mask thumbnail. Its frame is now green, as shown in Figure 14.27, and the Image window displays the mask as a grayscale image, as shown in Figure 14.28. Notice the green dotted line framing

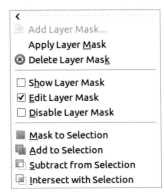

Figure 14.29 *The Mask menu after the layer mask is created*

the image; this tells you a layer mask is active. If you ALT-click again, the layer reappears.

You can also create, edit, or activate a layer mask via the **Image: Layer > Mask** menu, as shown in Figure 14.29. The checkboxes give you simple tools to display and manipulate a layer mask, and the remaining entries in this menu (and in the **Layers: right-click** menu) relate to the ways you can use a layer mask:

- APPLY LAYER MASK: Save the effect of the layer mask in the layer's Alpha channel, and delete the layer mask. This change should be the last one you make to a layer. Prior to applying the mask, the layer itself is unchanged—regardless of what you do to the layer mask.

- DELETE LAYER MASK: Discard the layer mask; this has no effect on the layer itself.

- MASK TO SELECTION: Convert the layer mask to the current selection. Where the mask's pixels are white, the associated layer's pixels are selected; where they are black, the layer's pixels are deselected. But mask pixels with intermediate values lead to partially selected pixels in the associated layer. A selection is thus initiated, but the layer and the mask remain unchanged.

- ADD TO SELECTION, SUBTRACT FROM SELECTION, and INTERSECT WITH SELECTION also convert the mask to a selection. Whereas

Figure 14.30 *The final image*

Mask to Selection replaces the current selection, these three entries allow you to combine the new selection with the previous selection in various ways. These entries do not appear on the **Layers: right-click** menu.

Using a Layer Mask

The following example uses two layers with layer masks and two ordinary layers to create the composite image shown in Figure 14.30. Take the following steps to transform the image:

1. Open the photograph shown in Figure 14.18, and choose the Select by Color tool. Click the sky and then the sea and foam while pressing the SHIFT key to select all of the landscape behind the window—except the rocks in the lower right. To select them as well, use Quick Mask, and this time use the Pencil tool to paint the rocks white. The Pencil tool works like the Paintbrush but without feathering or antialiasing.

2. When the selection is complete, add a layer mask to the background layer and initialize it with the inverted selection. Now the full window opening is transparent (Figure 14.31).

Figure 14.31 *Making the opening transparent*

Figure 14.33 *Removing the background*

Figure 14.32 *A portrait to add to the image*

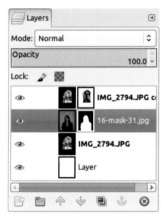

Figure 14.34 *The Layers dialog when the image is finished*

3. Add a new layer to the image using the photograph shown in Figure 14.32. Because this image is much larger than the previous one, scale this new layer to the canvas size with **Image: Layer > Scale Layer**.

4. Using the Fuzzy Select tool, click several times while pressing SHIFT to select the portrait's

background. Then add a layer mask to this layer, and initialize it with the selection (not inverted). The result is shown in Figure 14.33.

5. Duplicate the layer containing the window, and delete its layer mask. You can see the scenery behind the subject has been retained. Reorder the layers as shown in Figure 14.34, and discard the white background layer.

Figure 14.35 *The initial photograph*

Figure 14.36 *The new channel*

14.3 Using Masks and Channels

In this section, we show you two specific uses for masks and channels that cannot be accomplished by other means.

Building a Natural Mask

The *natural mask* of an image is a quick way to generate a mask that selects the subject of an image. This particular mask is not always accurate, but, in many cases, it yields good results. This concept is the brainchild of Carey Bunks,

Figure 14.37 *The Channels dialog*

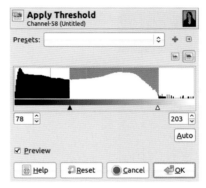

Figure 14.38 *The Threshold tool dialog*

author of an excellent, early book about GIMP, *Grokking the GIMP* (New Riders, 2000).

Start with the photograph shown in Figure 14.35. You want to select only the girl. First, select the whole image ([CTRL+A]) and copy it ([CTRL+C]). Then go to the Channels dialog and create a new channel by clicking the proper button (the second icon from the left at the bottom of the Channels dialog).

Paste the copied data ([CTRL+V]), and anchor the floating layer to the new channel ([CTRL+H]). If you leave the visibility on in the new channel and turn it off in the layer, you see a grayscale image of the photograph, as shown in Figure 14.36. The Channels dialog for this image is shown in Figure 14.37.

The values of the pixels in this image are used to build the selection. To do this, choose the **Image: Colors > Threshold** tool. The dialog shown in Figure 14.38 appears, and the image changes

Figure 14.39 *The selection mask transformed by the Threshold tool*

Figure 14.40 *Making the mask more visible*

Figure 14.41 *Improving the mask*

button, and choose yellow and 50% opacity. The result is shown in Figure 14.40.

Touch up the mask under the chin, in the corners of the mouth, on the nostrils, and on the eyes. You can do this easily by painting directly on the mask. Choose the Paintbrush tool and a large brush, and paint the selected facial features with white. Figure 14.41 shows the improved mask. Then convert the mask to a selection, and remove the mask's visibility. The result is the selection shown in Figure 14.42.

Transparency and the Alpha Channel

The Alpha channel is necessary when an image contains transparency. When an image has more than one layer, it always has a global Alpha channel. Individual layers may or may not have Alpha channels, but when they don't, you can see the pixels in the underlying layers unless you use certain blend modes or set the layer opacity to a value less than 100%. But if a given layer does not have an Alpha channel, its name appears in boldface in the Layers dialog.

A single layer image can also use transparency. Images displayed on a website, for example, often have transparent backgrounds,

to black and white. The positions of the small triangles in the Threshold dialog determine which pixels are white and which are black.

Adjust the triangles as shown in Figure 14.38, and you get the image shown in Figure 14.39. This mask selects only the lightest parts of the image.

To see what the mask actually selected, click the eye icon for the image layer, but be careful not to activate the layer. As you can see, the mask is black and doesn't contrast well with the image. Change its color using the Edit channel

Figure 14.42 *The resulting selection*

Figure 14.43 *The Transparency menu without an Alpha channel*

Figure 14.44 *The Transparency menu with an Alpha channel*

Figure 14.45 *The Color to Alpha dialog*

which allow them to blend naturally with other design elements on the page.

Figure 14.43 shows the **Image: Layer > Transparency** menu when the corresponding layer has no Alpha channel, and Figure 14.44 shows the same menu when there is an Alpha channel. A few of these entries also appear in the **Layers: right-click** menu.

Let's discuss what these menu entries do.

The first two entries, ADD ALPHA CHANNEL and REMOVE ALPHA CHANNEL, add and remove Alpha channels, respectively.

COLOR TO ALPHA also appears in the **Image: Colors** menu. Select it to make the dialog shown in Figure 14.45 appear. Check PREVIEW, and select the color that will be made transparent. Initially this color is white, as the figure shows.

Clicking the FROM: button brings up a simplified version of the Color chooser, shown in Figure 14.46. If you click the small button to the right of the HTML NOTATION field, you can choose the exact color from the image that you want to make transparent and see the resulting effect in the Preview window.

Figure 14.47 shows a photographic portrait. To get the image shown in Figure 14.49, choose **Image: Layer > Transparency > Color to Alpha** and select a flesh-tone pixel near the woman's necklace. Because all similar pixels become transparent, add a white layer under the image layer. Note that because the chosen color appears in the woman's hair, parts of her hair will also be altered. You could avoid this if you first selected the face and then used Color to Alpha.

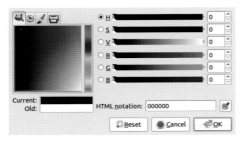

Figure 14.46 *The Color to Alpha Color chooser*

Figure 14.48 *Altering the skin color*

Figure 14.47 *The initial image*

If you paint the underlying layer in the color you made transparent, the image looks exactly like the original portrait. This makes changing a specific color in the active layer easy. For example, Figure 14.48 shows the result when we slightly alter the underlying layer color by decreasing the hue and increasing the value in the HSV color model.

SEMI-FLATTEN is also found in the **Image: Filters > Web** menu. We discuss it in depth in Chapter 17, but in brief, it replaces partial transparency with the current background color. If you apply it to the image layer shown in Figure 14.49 and choose the skin tone as the background color, you get the result shown in Figure 14.48.

Figure 14.49 *Making the skin tone transparent*

THRESHOLD ALPHA applies a threshold filter to the Alpha channel. Clicking this entry brings up the dialog shown in Figure 14.50. If you choose the value shown for the threshold, apply it, and add another layer filled with the initial skin color under the original layer, you get the result shown in Figure 14.51.

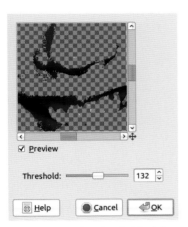

Figure 14.50 *The Threshold Alpha dialog*

Figure 14.51 *After thresholding the Alpha channel*

ALPHA TO SELECTION transforms the Alpha channel of the layer into a selection. Because both are represented as grayscale images, this transformation is very simple, and the new selection replaces any existing one.

The final three entries in the Transparency menu allow you to choose a different selection mode when creating a selection from the Alpha channel. You can then transform the selection into a channel, but you can't transform an Alpha channel into a channel directly.

Converting Masks, Selections, and Channels

As you've seen, selections, channels, masks, and layer transparencies are strongly related. Let's review how to convert back and forth among these.

To convert a selection to

- a selection mask (channel): **Image: Select > Save to Channel**.
- a layer mask: **Layers: right-click > Add Layer Mask** and choose SELECTION.
- an CTRL+X. As a side effect, the contents of the selection are placed on the clipboard.

To convert a selection mask to

- a selection: **Channels: right-click > Channel to Selection**.
- a layer mask: **Layers: right-click > Add Layer Mask** and choose CHANNEL.
- an Alpha channel: **Channels: right-click > Channel to Selection** and then press CTRL-X. As a side effect, the contents of the selection are placed on the clipboard.

To convert a layer mask to

- a selection: **Layers: right-click > Mask to Selection**.
- a selection mask: **Layers: right-click > Mask to Selection** and then **Image: Select > Save to Channel**.
- an Alpha channel: **Layers: right-click > Apply Layer Mask**.

To convert an Alpha channel to

- a selection: **Layers: right-click > Alpha to Selection**.
- a selection mask: **Layers: right-click > Alpha to Selection** and then **Image: Select > Save to Channel**.
- a layer mask: **Layers: right-click > Add Layer Mask** and choose LAYER'S ALPHA CHANNEL.

15 Drawing Tools

Drawing is an art, and as such, many people think they have to be born with the talent to draw well. Although drawing comes more easily to some people, with practice, anyone can learn to draw and can develop a unique style.

15.1 Digital Art

You may think digital art is easier than traditional art because the computer draws for you, but in fact digital art requires practice, just as traditional art does. If you already practice sketching and painting, you'll pick up digital art more easily than if you have never touched a pencil.

Digital art does allow for some tricks and shortcuts that would be impossible with traditional media. Undo is one of the most powerful tools digital art brings to the scene. If you're painting and make a mistake, you can try to hide the mistake, or you can try to take advantage of it, which can lead to unexpected results. If the painting is digital, however, you can simply undo the mistake and try again, which is convenient but takes away the challenge and the possibility of working with mistakes.

Another valuable tool that's inherent to digital art is superimposed layers. You can store each element of a painting as a new layer, and you can, in a click, hide layers or lock them.

One major benefit of digital art tools is they can speed up tedious processes like filling an area with a color, pattern, or gradient. But imperfections (e.g., seeing the paper grain through watercolor or visible brush strokes in an oil painting) can enhance the beauty of a work of art. In fact, many digital tools are designed to simulate these traditional imperfections.

To see examples of what digital art can be used to create, check out *http://www.cgsociety.org/* and *http://mattepainting.org/*.

The more you practice, the better you'll be at drawing, and the more you use GIMP, the better you'll be at using its tools. Even if you're only interested in making digital art, consider carrying around a small sketch pad and pencil so you can practice drawing when you have a free moment during the day. And don't be deterred if your initial sketches are crude—if you keep practicing, your sketches (and your digital art) will improve.

15.2 An Overview of the Drawing Tools

Drawing tools are used to modify the colors in an image—throughout the entire image, within

Figure 15.1 *The drawing tools in the Toolbox*

a selection, or brush stroke by brush stroke. By default, the drawing tools are at the bottom of the Toolbox, as shown in Figure 15.1.

While *brush tools* change the pixels along the brush stroke, *filling tools* affect a whole image or selection:

- *Bucket fill* fills an area with a solid color or a pattern.
- *Blend* fills an area with a gradient.

The other drawing tools are brush tools. They modify the image via manual brush strokes using the current brush or along a selection or path, as explained in "The Paths Dialog" on page 305.

The brush tools are divided into three categories: painting tools, cloning tools, and modifying tools. We'll discuss these categories in detail after discussing the properties common to all drawing tools.

Painting tools add (or remove) strokes of color:

- *Pencil* creates a hard-edged stroke.
- *Paintbrush* creates a soft-edged stroke.
- *Eraser* removes colors along the stroke.
- *Airbrush* creates a soft stroke.
- *Ink* creates a solid but antialiased stroke.

Cloning tools copy something and render it in brush strokes:

- *Clone* copies from an image or a pattern.
- *Heal* copies from an image and mixes with the surroundings.
- *Perspective clone* copies from an image and renders along perspective lines.

Modifying tools transform pixels along brush strokes:

- *Convolve* blurs or sharpens pixels.

- *Smudge* smears pixels.
- *Dodge/Burn* lightens or darkens pixels.

We will also cover the Text tool, Color Picker tool, and Measure tool in this chapter. Even though they are not strictly drawing tools, they are very useful for creating original art.

15.3 Shared Features

In this section, we describe the features and characteristics that are common to all or most of the drawing tools.

Drawing Tool Options

All drawing tools have options, which are normally shown in a dockable dialog attached to the Toolbox. If you close the options dialog by mistake, you can re-open it by selecting **Image: Windows > Dockable dialogs > Tool Options** or by double-clicking the tool icon in the Toolbox. No two drawing tools have exactly the same set of options, but most of the options are shared by a number of tools. In this section, we cover all the options that are common to at least two drawing tools.

Figure 15.2 shows all the options for the Paintbrush tool, which has the largest set of options.

Click the small triangle icon in the top right of the dialog to open the menu shown in Figure 15.3. This menu is similar for all the dockable dialogs, but some have additional entries. The figure also shows the selections available in the Tool Options Menu. We describe them in detail in Section 15.10.

Below the triangle icon is the name of the tool (Paintbrush in this case), and below that are the following options:

- MODE is a selection of the 23 blending modes explained in Section 12.2.
- OPACITY changes the transparency. The opacity percentage combines with the blending mode to determine the tool's exact effect. Opacity is also affected by paint dynamics.

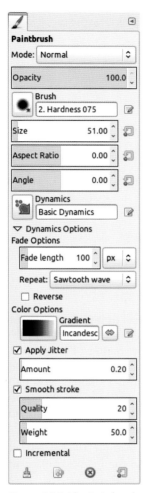

Figure 15.2 *The Paintbrush tool options*

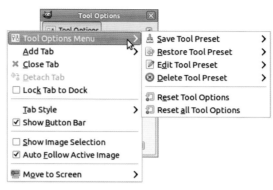

Figure 15.3 *The menus for an options dialog*

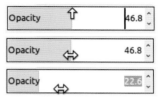

Figure 15.4 *Using the Opacity slider*

in Figure 15.4 (middle). Click and drag horizontally to change the opacity factor with better precision.

You can use the mouse wheel to change the factor in increments of one percentage point, or you can use the small arrows on the right to do the same thing.

You can also type a value directly into the numeric field on the right. Clicking the top half of the slider places the cursor just in front of the numeric field. You can erase the value by pressing the DELETE key or add digits in front of value. Clicking the bottom half of the slider selects the whole numeric field, as shown in Figure 15.4 (bottom), and then you can type in a new value.

Two handy keyboard shortcuts exist: < decreases the opacity, and > increases it. The step is always 1, but you can keep the key pressed to decrease or increase more. Thus you can change the opacity with one hand and paint with the other.

The sliders were updated with some interesting new capabilities in version 2.8. If the mouse pointer is located in the top half of the slider, its icon takes the form of a vertical arrow, as shown in Figure 15.4 (top). Click any part of the slider to get a rough approximation of the opacity factor.

If the mouse pointer is located in the bottom half of the slider, its icon takes the form of a double horizontal arrow, as shown

• BRUSH changes the type of brush. This option, as well as the next six, is present only for the brush tools. Click the brush icon to see a grid of all the available brushes. You can also type the brush name in the field on the right. As soon as you start typing, brushes matching what you've typed appear below.

Each physical device has its own independent settings, so if you choose a brush for the stylus, it won't affect which brush is used with the mouse or the eraser. On the contrary, if you attach a specific brush to the stylus, it stays the same whether the stylus is using the Paintbrush tool, Smudge tool, or any other brush tool. You may also associate a different brush with each of these tools by changing the settings in the **Image: Edit > Preferences** dialog (see Chapter 22).

• SIZE changes the brush size, and although the range appears to be [1 to 1000], if you move the cursor far to the right of the slider, you can choose any size. This option is also affected by the current Paint Dynamics. The curved arrow on the right resets the size to the default for the current brush. The mouse wheel changes it by increments of one hundredth.

Two keyboard shortcuts are handy for changing the size of the brush: [decreases it, and] increases it. As with the opacity changes, the step is always 1, and you can keep the key pressed.

• ASPECT RATIO changes the proportions of the brush in the range [−20 to +20]. This option is new in GIMP 2.8. If the value is positive, the brush is stretched vertically, and if it's negative, the brush is stretched horizontally. Paint Dynamics can control this option.

• ANGLE rotates the brush, so it has no effect if the brush is perfectly round. Again, Paint Dynamics can control this option.

• DYNAMICS is where you can change the current paint dynamics (explained in "Paint Dynamic" on page 333). Clicking the button

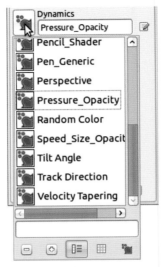

Figure 15.5 *The Paint Dynamics menu in a tool options dialog*

opens the menu shown in Figure 15.5 for choosing a specific dynamic. The bottom buttons allow you to get smaller or larger previews, to display them as a list or as grid, and to open the Paint Dynamics dialog. You can also begin typing in the field to the right, and GIMP completes the name. The button on the right opens the Paint Dynamics Editor.

• If you click the small triangle to the left of DYNAMICS OPTIONS, the menu expands, and you'll see the following options:

– FADE LENGTH affects how the parameters change over the length of a stroke. Any parameter can be set to fade, and the brush fades in or out along the fade length. When REPEAT is set to NONE, the stroke stops changing after reaching the fade length. When it's set to SAWTOOTH WAVE or TRIANGULAR WAVE, the effect repeats in various patterns. If REVERSE is checked, the way the brush changes as you paint is reversed. This option can also be assigned to pointer movement via paint dynamics.

– COLOR OPTIONS does not use the foreground color to paint; it gets its colors from the specified gradient. This is true even in the case of a color brush. But this option is subject to the current paint dynamics, so the effect depends on at least one box being checked in the Color row of the Mapping matrix for the current paint dynamics.

- APPLY JITTER jitters the brush stroke from side to side within the range [0 to 50]. If no box is checked in the Jitter line of the current paint dynamics, the jitter is inversely proportional to pressure. If at least one box is checked in the Jitter line of the current paint dynamics, the behavior just described is suppressed.

- SMOOTH STROKE makes the stroke more homogeneous using two settings. QUALITY [1 to 100] specifies the stroke's uniformity. WEIGHT [3 to 1000] limits the stroke's minimum diameter.

Note that the last two options apply to all drawing tools.

Another behavior that all brush tools share is the effect of pressing and holding SHIFT and CTRL:

- If you press SHIFT while using a brush tool, you can draw a straight line.

- If you press CTRL while using the Pencil, Paintbrush, Eraser, or Airbrush tools, the pointer becomes an eyedropper, and the next color you click becomes the foreground color (or background for the Eraser).

- If you press SHIFT and then CTRL, the straight line is constrained to the nearest 15°, which is helpful if you're drawing parallel or perpendicular lines.

Paint Dynamics

Every brush tool uses a general feature called *paint dynamics*, which is especially useful if you have a graphics tablet. With paint dynamics, you can change the parameters of the brush tool based on how you move the mouse or

tablet stylus. This is part of GIMP that has been largely improved in version 2.8. Seven pointer-movement characteristics can be detected, although some of these work only with a tablet and a specialized stylus:

- PRESSURE is the amount of force applied when painting a stroke and can be controlled only with a stylus and tablet.

- VELOCITY is the relative speed with which you move the pointer.

- DIRECTION is the direction of the movement.

- TILT is the angle of the stylus. You can use this dynamic only with a tablet, and even some tablets cannot detect tilt.

- WHEEL controls wheel rotation if you're using a tablet stylus with a wheel, like the Airbrush Pen from Wacom. When used with the Intuos Art Pen, this dynamic controls the effect of the pen rotation.

- RANDOM varies a parameter randomly as you draw (within the limits you set).

- FADE determines how a stroke changes as you draw. After reaching the fade length, the parameter stops changing. It returns to the initial value and changes along the fade length repeatedly (like a sawtooth wave), or it can change in the opposite way (like a triangular wave). For example, if the brush size increases, it could decrease again after the fade length was reached.

These 7 movement characteristics have 11 possible tool options:

- OPACITY alters the transparency of the stroke according to the tool's OPACITY settings.

- SIZE makes the brush smaller or larger based on the brush size and the tool's SIZE settings.

- ANGLE rotates the brush starting from the initial angle set in the tool's ANGLE option.

- COLOR changes the brush color along the gradient specified in Color of the DYNAMICS OPTIONS section of the tool's options dialog.

COLOR works with the Pencil, Paintbrush, and Airbrush tools.

- HARDNESS alters the stroke's edges within the limits set by the brush type.

- FORCE works with all brush tools except the Pencil. Its effect is specific to each tool and is designed to mimic the tool's physical equivalent. For example, when force is correlated with pressure, the Paintbrush paints a thicker, darker stroke when you press hard, whereas Airbrush adds more paint.

- ASPECT RATIO changes the height and width of the brush within the limits set by the brush type and the tool's ASPECT RATIO option.

- SPACING makes the brush spacing smaller or larger within the limits set by the Spacing slider in the Brushes dialog.

- RATE varies the speed of the Airbrush, Convolve, or Smudge tools within the limits fixed by the tool's RATE option.

- FLOW changes the flow of the paint within the limits fixed by the tool's FLOW option. It affects only the Airbrush tool.

- JITTER makes the brush spacing more or less uniform within the limits set by the Amount tool option when you check the tool's APPLY JITTER option.

These movement characteristics are assigned to tool options based on the current *paint dynamics*, which are found in the Dynamics Options section of the painting tool options or in the Paint Dynamics dockable dialog, shown in Figure 15.6. Like all the resource dockable dialogs, this dialog contains a tags field, as well as five buttons along the bottom that you can click to edit, create, or delete Paint Dynamics. You'll also find a button for refreshing the list.

GIMP comes with 17 predefined paint dynamics. Dynamics Off, the default, turns off all links between pointer movement and tool options. The other paint dynamics will be considered in Section 15.10.

Figure 15.6 *The Paint Dynamics dockable dialog*

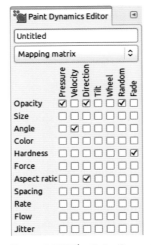

Figure 15.7 *The Paint Dynamics Editor, Mapping matrix tab*

You can't change predefined paint dynamics. If you double-click one of them in the paint dynamics dialog or click the EDIT DYNAMICS button, the Paint Dynamics Editor, shown in Figure 15.7, opens. Even though you can't change the predefined dynamics, you can see which boxes are checked. If you create a new dynamic, you can check the boxes to link the corresponding row and column. Type a name in the box at the top of this dialog.

Figure 15.8 *The Paint Dynamics Editor, drop-down menu*

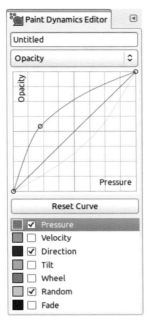

Figure 15.9 *The Paint Dynamics Editor, Opacity tab*

Under the name field is a drop-down menu (Figure 15.8) that lists the tool characteristics tabs. Each of these options opens a tab similar to the Curves tool dialog, showing the answer curve of the corresponding characteristic. The bottom part of the tab (Figure 15.9) contains a list corresponding to the columns of the mapping matrix. When you select one (indicated by the highlight), you can change its curve.

You can change any of the 7 answer curves for each of the 11 tool characteristics. This means GIMP has 77 different adjustable curves, but note that only the curves that are actually linked to an action (via the checkboxes in the matrix map) have an effect.

Using Dockable Dialogs with Drawing Tools

A number of dockable dialogs are useful with all of the drawing tools. These dialogs are global, which means their settings affect any drawing tool unless the PAINT OPTIONS SHARED BETWEEN TOOLS option is unchecked in the **Image: Edit > Preferences > Tool Options** dialog. One example is the Paint Dynamics dialog. The others are Brushes, Patterns, Gradients, and Palettes.

The Dialog Menu

All dockable dialogs have a *dialog menu*, as shown in Figure 15.10. To open this menu,

Figure 15.10 *A dockable dialog menu*

click the small triangular button at the top right of the dialog. In this section, we cover some of the entries that are especially helpful with the drawing tools. We cover some of the more general entries in "Docking Windows and Dockable Dialogs" on page 198.

Dockable dialogs can display lists of options (such as available brushes or gradients) as either a list or a grid, and you can switch between views using the dialog menu. Grid view is more compact, but the list view shows the name and some information about each visible entry. When in grid view, you can see the same information at the top of the dialog by clicking an entry.

You can change the size of the icons using the PREVIEW SIZE option in the dialog menu. Eight sizes, from TINY to GIGANTIC, are available. The large sizes are useful for certain dockable dialogs, like the Images dialog.

The first entry in the dialog menu is specific to the dialog and can also be selected by right-clicking the dialog body.

Using Tags

Another new feature introduced in version 2.8 is *tags*. As shown in Figure 15.6 on page 334, most dockable dialogs now have a filter field near the top of the dialog and a tag assignment field near the bottom. Type a tag and press ENTER, and GIMP saves the tag even if you quit and restart the program. Tags are especially useful if you have a lot of choices (as with brushes, patterns, or gradients). For example, if you download a set of several hundred brushes, scrolling through the Brushes dialog in search of a brush that paints stars becomes cumbersome, but if all such brushes are tagged *stars*, then you can simply search in the filter field.

Tags can be simple or compound words, separated by commas. If you highlight a tag and press BACKSPACE, the tag is deleted.

The Brushes, Paint Dynamics, and Tool Presets already have some tags. They are stored in subfolders of the corresponding system folders (see Chapter 22), and they automatically bear the name of their subfolder as a tag. For example, the Brushes system folder contains subfolders called Basic, Legacy, Media, Sketch, Splatters, and Texture, and these tags are attributed to the corresponding brushes.

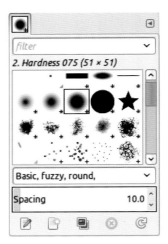

Figure 15.11 *Using tags (the Brushes dialog)*

Figure 15.11 shows that the Hardness 075 brush is in the Basic subfolder and has been tagged round and fuzzy by the user.

If you set the dialog to VIEW AS LIST, then you can CTRL-click to select (or unselect) more than one object (handy for tagging multiple entries). Or if you click an entry and SHIFT-click another entry, then you select everything between the two entries.

Clicking the down arrow at the right of the field brings up a menu of the existing tags. Click one or more tags and press any key on the keyboard to enter the tag into the filter or tag field. While in the tags field, you can delete a tag from the current object by simply clicking it. If you SHIFT-click the tags field and tap the left or right arrow, the tags are selected from right to left. BACKSPACE deletes all the selected tags. If you haven't selected a tag in the tag list, BACKSPACE selects the tag on the left, and DELETE does the same on the right. If a tag is no longer used for any object, it disappears from the drop-down menu.

When one tag is in the filter field, only the objects with that tag are displayed. When two or more tags are listed, only the objects with all of the tags are shown. To go back to the full list, delete all tags in the filter field.

Six Useful Dockable Dialogs

In this section, we cover six dockable dialogs that are especially useful for digital drawing and painting.

The Brushes Dialog

The Brushes dialog is shown in Figure 15.11. Because user-defined brushes appear in this dialog, it might look different on your screen.

Brushes are divided into four major categories:

- An *ordinary* brush is a grayscale image painted on a white background. It paints with the foreground color (or a color from a gradient if the color paint dynamics is enabled), except for the Erase tool, which paints with the background color.

- A *color* brush is an RGB image with an Alpha channel and a mask that's a grayscale image of the brush. A color brush uses its own color rather than the foreground color, as long as a box is not checked in the Color row of the current Paint Dynamic. If one is checked, only the mask of the color brush—with colors from the current gradient—is used.

- An *animated* brushcan be an ordinary brush or a color brush. It is actually a sequence of brushes, so the brush changes depending on the current paint dynamics.

- A *parametric* brush is a resizable brush created with the Brush editor, as explained in Section 22.4. Parametric brushes are grayscale and use the foreground color, much as ordinary brushes do.

When the brush image is larger than its icon, you'll see a small + sign in the bottom-right corner of the icon. Click and hold the icon to see the actual size.

Animated brushes have a small red triangle in the bottom-right corner, and if you click and hold their icons, you can view the animation.

A brush paints by repeatedly stamping the brush at regular intervals, and the SPACING

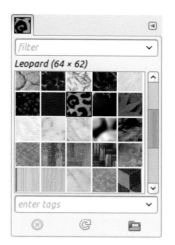

Figure 15.12 *The Patterns dialog*

slider specifies the distance between two successive stamps. Its initial value is specified in each brush's file. If you download or create a brush, you can delete it; the delete button at the bottom of the dialog will be active.

The Patterns Dialog

The Patterns dialog is shown in Figure 15.12. GIMP's set of patterns is rather small, but you can build your own, as explained in Section 22.5. A Google search for "GIMP patterns" also yields tons of patterns, which you can add to GIMP by saving them in the `patterns` folder. The three buttons at the bottom of the dialog allow you to delete the current pattern, refresh the list, and open the current pattern as an image.

The Gradients Dialog

Unlike the Patterns and Brushes dialogs, the Gradients dialog is viewed as a list by default, as shown in Figure 15.13. GIMP's set of gradients is quite large. Some of these gradients are designed for use with specific filters; for instance, the gradients that start with `Flare` are designed for the Gradient Flare filter, described in "Gradient Flare" on page 415.

The only unique feature of the Gradients menu is the option to save a gradient in POV-Ray

Figure 15.13 *The Gradients dialog*

Figure 15.14 *The Palettes dialog*

format, used with ray-tracing software. Again, you can download more gradients, or you can build them, as explained in Section 22.6.

The Palettes Dialog

The Palettes dialog is also displayed as a list by default, as shown in Figure 15.14. GIMP comes with a large set of predefined palettes.

From the Palettes menu, you can import a palette from a gradient or an image. You can also build a new palette, as discussed in

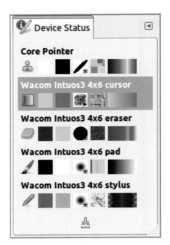

Figure 15.15 *The Device Status dialog*

Section 22.7, or you can download palettes from the Web.

The Device Status Dialog

The Device Status dockable dialog (**Image: Windows > Device status**) is shown in Figure 15.15. This dialog displays information about input devices. In this figure, you see five current devices: the normal mouse (core pointer), the tablet mouse (called cursor), the tablet eraser, the tablet pad, and the tablet stylus. Assign tools and options to devices simply by selecting the tool with the device. The tool and its current settings are then set for that device. In the figure, the tablet mouse is using the Blend tool, and the tablet stylus is using the Pencil tool with a dark red foreground color and green background color. Note that you can't change settings directly in the dialog—this dialog is strictly informative. But you can save the current device status, using the button at the bottom of the dialog.

The Tool Presets Dialog

The Tool Presets dialog (**Image: Windows > Tool presets**) is shown in Figure 15.16. A *tool preset* is a group of saved settings for a specific tool, similar to those in the Device Status dialog,

Figure 15.16 *The Tool Presets dialog*

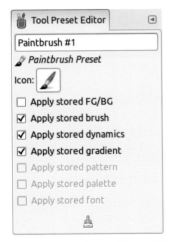

Figure 15.17 *The Tool Preset Editor*

but tool presets contain additional settings—the current paint dynamics and the font. They are different from the preset settings used by color tools like Levels or Curves (see Chapter 12).

You can create a new tool preset by selecting **Tool Presets: right-click > New Tool Preset** or by clicking the second button from the left at the bottom of the Tool Presets dialog to open the

Figure 15.18 *The Bucket Fill tool icon and pointer*

dialog shown in Figure 15.17. Note that you can choose to save certain settings and to leave the others unchanged when you use the preset.

Tool presets are powerful, and they will be explained in detail in Section 15.10.

15.4 The Fill Tools

GIMP has tools that fill an entire layer, selection, or image. The only options they share with other painting tools are MODE and OPACITY.

The Bucket Fill Tool

The Bucket Fill tool ($\boxed{\text{SHIFT+B}}$) can fill a layer, a selection, or all pixels of a similar color in the layer or selection. Its icon and pointer are shown in Figure 15.18, and its options are shown in Figure 15.19. To use it, click once in the area that you want to fill.

Here are the options specific to this tool:

- FILL TYPE determines whether the area is filled with the foreground color, background color, or a pattern. The $\boxed{\text{CTRL}}$ key toggles between the foreground and background colors.

  If you choose to fill using a pattern, the current pattern is used, but you can change the pattern in the dialog. You can also change the current pattern in the Toolbox or the Patterns dialog.

- AFFECTED AREA lets you choose whether to fill the whole selection (or the layer when there is no selection) or just an area of similar color. Pressing the $\boxed{\text{SHIFT}}$ key toggles between these choices.

- FINDING SIMILAR COLORS is active when FILL SIMILAR COLORS is selected. This option lets you select how similar colors are determined.

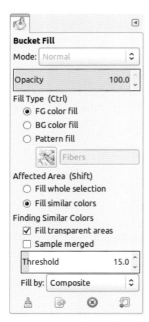

Figure 15.19 *The Bucket Fill tool options*

Figure 15.20 *The Fill by drop-down menu*

Figure 15.21 *Original image*

- Fill transparent areas allows transparent pixels to be filled, unless the Lock alpha channel button in the Layers dialog is checked.

- Sample merged decides whether GIMP uses the pixels of other layers. When this option is checked, all visible layers participate to the area definition.

- The Threshold option [0 to 255] determines how similar the pixel color must be to be included in the fill. A threshold value of 0 means only pixels of exactly the same color are filled. The area filled must be contiguous.

- Fill by changes how the pixel data is used when calculating what to fill based on the threshold. The choices are shown in Figure 15.20. Composite means that all the pixel's components are taken into account. The other entries use only one component in the RGB or HSV model. For example, say we want to add a pattern fill of stone bricks to the image shown in Figure 15.21.

We fill similar colors throughout the layer, first using Composite (Figure 15.22) and then using only the pixel's Blue value (Figure 15.23). In this case, filling by the Blue value means more area is filled, but the effect is different for every image.

The Bucket Fill tool has some useful keyboard shortcuts:

- CTRL+, fills the entire selection or layer with the current foreground color.

- CTRL+. fills with the current background color.

- CTRL+; fills with the current pattern.

The Blend Tool

The Blend tool (L) fills a layer or a selection with a gradient. Its icon and pointer are shown in

Figure 15.22 *Filling by Composite*

Figure 15.23 *Filling by Blue*

Figure 15.24, and its options are shown in Figure 15.25.

To use it, click and drag to draw a segment. The gradient will span this segment, but the entire selection or image will be filled regardless of the segment length.

Here are the options specific to this tool:

- GRADIENT is used to select the gradient. You can also change the gradient in the Toolbox or in the Gradients dialog.

- The small button to the right reverses the gradient direction.

- SHAPE is a drop-down list for selecting a gradient shape. We explain it in detail shortly.

Figure 15.24 *The Blend tool icon and pointer*

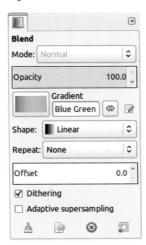

Figure 15.25 *The Blend tool options*

- REPEAT has three choices: no repetition (none), sawtooth wave, or triangular wave. However, these choices are active only for the first four shapes. To demonstrate the effect of repeats, we filled a blank image with the Abstract 3 gradient and a linear SHAPE. The red arrow shows where the stroke was made. With no repetition, the end color extends from the stroke to the edge of the layer or selection on both sides (Figure 15.26). With sawtooth-wave repetition, the gradient simply repeats (Figure 15.27). With triangular-wave repetition, the direction of the gradient reverses for every other repeat (Figure 15.28).

- The OFFSET slider [0 to 100] effectively shortens the gradient segment by moving the starting point. Again, it works only with the first four shapes.

- DITHERING is designed to smooth the transition between different colors in the gradient.

- ADAPTIVE SUPERSAMPLING smooths the gradient's edges, which you may find useful with a spiral shape.

Figure 15.26 *A linear gradient shape with no repetition*

Figure 15.27 *A linear gradient shape with sawtooth wave repetition*

Figure 15.28 *A linear gradient shape with triangular wave repetition*

Figure 15.29 *A bi-linear gradient shape*

Figure 15.30 *A radial gradient shape*

Now we describe the SHAPE options in detail. These are the available gradient shapes:

- LINEAR puts the gradient in the segment you draw and fills the outer areas with either the first and last colors or the same gradient (sawtooth- or triangular-wave repeats).

- BI-LINEAR mirrors the gradient at the starting point, as shown in Figure 15.29. We used a short gradient segment for this figure. (We use the same segment for Figures 15.30 to 15.38.)

Figure 15.31 *A square gradient shape*

Figure 15.32 *A conical gradient shape, symmetrical*

Figure 15.33 *A conical gradient shape, asymmetrical*

- RADIAL creates a circle centered on the starting point with a radius that is the length of the segment drawn, as shown in Figure 15.30.

- SQUARE creates a square centered on the starting point. The square is twice as wide as the segment you draw (Figure 15.31).

- CONICAL makes a cone with a tip on the starting point. The effects of the symmetrical and asymmetrical shapes are shown in Figures 15.32 and 15.33, respectively.

- SHAPED follows the image or selection borders. The segment that you would normally draw to add a gradient has no effect. Instead, three different algorithms are used to apply the gradient within the shape, as shown in Figures 15.34, 15.35, and 15.36. Here, we applied the gradient to a flower-shaped selection.

Figure 15.34 *A gradient along a shape, angular algorithm*

Figure 15.35 *A gradient along a shape, spherical algorithm*

Figure 15.36 *A gradient along a shape, dimpled algorithm*

- SPIRAL draws a spiral centered on the starting point, going clockwise or counterclockwise. The segment length sets the distance between two whorls. A clockwise spiral is shown in Figure 15.37. Figure 15.38 shows the interesting effect of using a very short segment.

Figure 15.37 *A spiral gradient shape, clockwise*

Figure 15.38 *A spiral gradient shape, very short segment*

15.5 The Painting Tools

Painting tools are intuitive because they behave like traditional drawing media.

We already discussed the features shared by the painting tools ("Drawing Tool Options" on page 330). In this section, we discuss each tool individually, focusing on options and features unique to that tool.

The Pencil Tool

The Pencil tool ($\boxed{\text{N}}$) paints hard-edged strokes. Its icon and pointer are shown in Figure 15.39. The characteristic that makes the Pencil tool unique is that the stroke edges are not anti-aliased. See "The Pencil Tool" on page 69.

The Pencil tool options are shown in Figure 15.40. The FADE OPTIONS settings work only if the Paint Dynamics Mapping matrix contains a check in the Fade column, and the COLOR OPTIONS settings work only if there is a check in the Color row.

Figure 15.41 (top) shows the result of painting with Basic Dynamics. Because no check appears in the Color row in the Mapping matrix, the tool uses the foreground color. Size and Velocity are correlated, however, so the stroke is

Figure 15.39 *The Pencil tool icon and pointer*

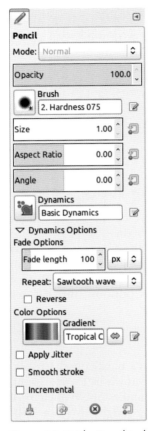

Figure 15.40 *The Pencil tool options*

Figure 15.41 *Some examples of different dynamics options*

Figure 15.42 *The Paintbrush tool icon and pointer*

In the third stroke in Figure 15.41, Color is correlated with Random, so the colors are taken at random from the gradient, and Size is correlated with Fade, so it decreases along a path of 100 pixels and then starts again.

In the last example in Figure 15.41, Color is correlated with Direction, so the colors vary along the gradient based on the direction of movement, and Opacity is correlated with Fade. Note that we changed the REPEAT option to TRIANGULAR WAVE for this example, so the opacity decreases and then increases again.

The Paintbrush Tool

The Paintbrush tool ([P]) paints soft-edged strokes but otherwise is similar to the Pencil tool. Its icon and pointer are shown in Figure 15.42.

The Paintbrush is the most general-use tool for creating digital illustrations in GIMP. The Paintbrush options are the same as the Pencil options, so we won't show the dialog again. Instead we'll demonstrate a couple of options that we haven't explored yet, with no checked box in the Fade column or the Color row of the current paint dynamics. In Figure 15.43, we make the top stroke with APPLY JITTER checked and a value of 0.20, and we make the bottom stroke without jitter.

narrower when the movement is faster. Opacity is correlated with Pressure and Fade, so the stroke is less opaque when the pressure is lower. Because the SAWTOOTH WAVE repeat is selected, the opacity fades and then starts again after a distance of 100 pixels (the fade length).

For the second stroke in Figure 15.41, we defined a new paint dynamics that links only Color and Fade. The colors follow the current gradient, which is used along a path of 100 pixels and then starts again.

Figure 15.43 *Drawing with and without jitter*

Figure 15.44 *Incremental painting with an acrylic brush*

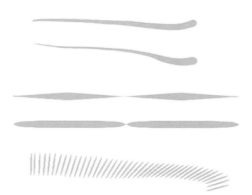

Figure 15.45 *Variations in size and angle*

Figure 15.46 *The Eraser tool icon and pointer*

In Figure 15.44, we set the OPACITY to 43% and scribble with the dynamic `Acrylic 02` brush. We make the scribble on the left with the INCREMENTAL option turned off and the scribble on the right with INCREMENTAL turned on.

In Figure 15.45 (top), we draw a stroke with the tablet stylus, increasing the pressure along the stroke. The paint dynamics correlates Size with Pressure. We draw the top stroke with the default, straight answer curve. For the bottom stroke, we make the curve strongly concave by moving its center toward the bottom-right corner, so the brush size is constant at the beginning of the stroke and then increases at the end of the stroke.

In Figure 15.45 (middle), we draw the horizontal strokes with paint dynamics that correlate Size with Fade. For the top stroke, the answer curve is flat. For the bottom stroke, the answer curve is strongly convex, the middle point having been moved toward the top-left corner.

To demonstrate the Wheel parameter, we use the Art Pen, which has a rectangular tip. If the tip is flat on the tablet, the greatest surface area touches the tablet, and if the pen is rotated by 180°, the smallest area touches the tablet. The best way to translate this to paint dynamics is to invert the answer curve that correlates Wheel with Size. This way of using the Art Pen becomes very natural. But in Figure 15.45 (bottom), we correlate Wheel with Orientation and use the

Hardness `100` brush with ASPECT RATIO set to −10. Rotating the pen then rotates the brush.

The Eraser Tool

The Eraser tool ([E]) removes color from the current layer by painting with transparency if the layer has an Alpha channel or with the background color if it does not. Its icon and pointer appear in Figure 15.46.

As Figure 15.47 shows, the Eraser tool has fewer options than the Pencil and Paintbrush tools because it has no mode or color option. Two new options appear, however, that are unique to the Eraser: HARD EDGE and ANTI ERASE.

To illustrate this tool, we create a simple image filled with green. We add a second transparent layer (which, therefore, has an Alpha channel) and paint a purple blob with the Paintbrush tool and the Hardness `050` brush at size 40. In Figure 15.48, we use the Eraser tool with the same brush. We make the two left strokes with HARD EDGE unchecked. Because we use the Hardness `050` brush, the edges are fuzzy. On the right, the HARD EDGE option is checked so the full

Figure 15.47 *The Eraser tool options*

Figure 15.48 *Erasing with or without Hard edge*

Figure 15.49 *Anti-erasing*

diameter of the brush erases pixels, making the stroke appear wider.

When ANTI ERASE is checked, the color that was erased appears again, as shown in Figure 15.49. This feature works only on layers with an Alpha channel. When pixels are made transparent, the color information is retained. Antierasing toggles the transparency, revealing the color that was invisible. Pressing ALT temporarily toggles this option.

Figure 15.50 *The Airbrush tool icon and pointer*

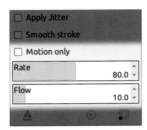

Figure 15.51 *Airbrush-specific options*

Many tablets come with a double-ended stylus, the ends of which look like a drawing tip and an eraser. GIMP can remember which tool is attached to each end, so you can associate the drawing tip with the Paintbrush, for example, and then flip the stylus over to use the Eraser tool. To create the association, click the Eraser tool icon with the proper end, and as long as you don't use it to click another tool icon, it remains associated with the Eraser.

The Airbrush Tool

The icon and pointer associated with the Airbrush tool ([A]) appear in Figure 15.50. The Airbrush tool is similar to the Paintbrush tool, but the amount of paint deposited on the canvas is more variable. If you paint more than once over the same spot, Airbrush adds more paint, and if you paint a stroke faster, it adds less paint. If you click and hold the mouse over one spot (or press the stylus on one spot), it keeps adding more paint unless you check MOTION ONLY (this can also be affected by the current paint dynamics).

The Airbrush tool options are the same as those of the Paintbrush tool, except that INCREMENTAL is always active with this tool.

Three options are specific to the Airbrush tool, however, as shown in Figure 15.51. When MOTION ONLY is checked, no paint is added

Figure 15.52 *The Ink tool icon and pointer*

unless the brush is moving. The RATE slider [0 to 150] changes how quickly the paint comes out of the airbrush. The FLOW slider [0 to 100] sets the strength of the paint stream, so it also affects how much paint ends up on the canvas. If you correlate Rate with Pressure in paint dynamics, set the Rate to the maximum because at lower settings the result is too subtle.

The Ink Tool

The Ink tool (K) simulates a calligraphy pen with a changeable nib. Its icon and pointer are shown in Figure 15.52. The Ink tool draws an antialiased stroke using the nib settings rather than the current brush, and it has its own settings for paint dynamics, so the current brush and paint dynamics don't affect this tool.

As Figure 15.53 shows, the Ink tool's Mode and Opacity options are like the other painting tools. But its other options are unique. Let's take a look at these options. We'll start at the bottom, with the SHAPE of the pen nib. You can choose among a round, square, or diamond-shaped nib. If you click and drag the small white square in the SHAPE window, you can customize the shape of the nib. You can then simulate a felt-tip pen, a quill pen, a brush, or any other pen type.

The SENSITIVITY options control the effect of the stylus movements (like paint dynamics). SIZE sets the maximum size of the nib, depending on how hard you press with the stylus. Because the minimum size is set in the ADJUSTMENT field, the greater the value, the more the size can vary. TILT uses the tilt of the stylus to change the nib shape. SPEED controls the size of the nib: The faster you draw, the narrower the stroke. You

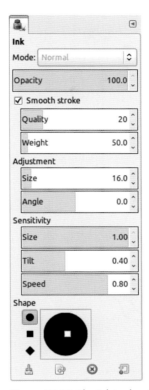

Figure 15.53 *The Ink tool options*

need a low speed value to get a wide stroke. These three options are in [0 to 1]. Of course, the effect of all of these depends on your tablet's capabilities.

ADJUSTMENT sets the initial stroke parameters. SIZE [0 to 200] is the size of the nib, and ANGLE [−90 to +90] is its angle relative to the horizontal.

Figures 15.54 to 15.56 show three examples of a signature for Wilber, the GIMP mascot. We drew the first signature slowly using all the default settings, except we used a narrow diamond-shaped nib. In the second signature, we applied pressure to change the stroke width and set TILT to 1.0. In the third signature, we reduced the adjustment size to 2.9 and signed more quickly.

Figure 15.54 *The first Wilber signature*

Figure 15.55 *The second Wilber signature*

Figure 15.56 *The third Wilber signature*

15.6 The Cloning Tools

The three cloning tools (Clone, Heal, and Perspective Clone) let you paint cloned content from an image onto another image or another area of the same image. Like other brush tools, these tools use the current paint dynamics. Here are the features shared by all three tools:

- The CTRL key is used to set the starting point in the image to clone. CTRL-click the area that you want to clone. Then, use the current brush to "paint" the pixels from the place that you clicked onto the target.

- The SHIFT key is used to clone in a straight line.

- MODE, OPACITY, BRUSH, SCALE, ASPECT RATIO, ANGLE, FADE OUT, and APPLY JITTER work the same way that they do for all other brush tools.

Figure 15.57 *The Clone tool icon and pointer*

Figure 15.58 *Options specific to the Clone tool*

- HARD EDGE works like it does with the Eraser tool: When it's checked, the fuzziness of the brush is ignored.

- The ALIGNMENT option is described later.

The Clone Tool

The Clone tool (C) is the simplest and most broadly useful cloning tool. Its icon and pointer are shown in Figure 15.57. First select the source to clone by CTRL-clicking and then paint the target area. A thin cross marks the position that is cloned from the source layer.

The options specific to the Clone tool are shown in Figure 15.58. These are SOURCE and ALIGNMENT.

SOURCE has two radio buttons:

- IMAGE clones from a layer in an image that's open in GIMP. The source can be in a different image or a different layer in the same image or even the same layer. CTRL-click selects the initial position of the source. SAMPLE MERGED, if checked, makes all the visible pixels the source. When SAMPLE MERGED isn't checked, only the active layer is used as the source, and transparent pixels are painted as transparent (and, therefore, have no effect).

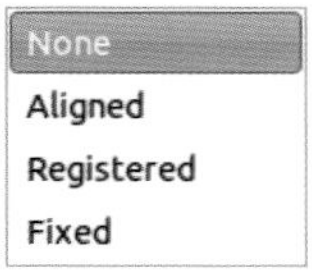

None
Aligned
Registered
Fixed

Figure 15.59 *The Alignment drop-down menu*

Figure 15.60 *Source image*

- PATTERN clones from a pattern rather than an image, so it paints with that pattern. You can change the pattern by clicking in the corresponding field or in the Patterns dialog. No initial CTRL-click is necessary.

ALIGNMENT determines how the source is painted on as you move the brush. You have four choices, shown in Figure 15.59. To demonstrate, we'll use a portrait (Figure 15.60) as the source and a plain white canvas as the target. We'll apply the tool options shown in Figure 15.58. First, we CTRL-click the left eye and paint on the left side of the target image, and then we paint another eye shape on the right side of the image without changing the source.

In Figure 15.61, ALIGNMENT is set to NONE, so every time we move the pointer to a different place in the target image, we start copying at the place that we last CTRL-clicked in the source image. In this case that meant we copied the left eye twice.

Figure 15.61 *Alignment set to None*

Figure 15.62 *Alignment set to Aligned*

Figure 15.63 *Alignment set to Registered*

Figure 15.64 *Alignment set to Fixed*

In Figure 15.62, ALIGNMENT is set to ALIGNED. With this option, when we move the pointer, the area being copied in the source image moves in the same way. This time when we paint on the right side, we copy the right eye rather than making a second copy of the left one.

In Figure 15.63, ALIGNMENT is set to REGISTERED. With this setting, the CTRL-click is irrelevant. The cloned pixels are in the same position in the source image as the pointer is in the target image, so even though we click the left eye again, we end up cloning the top of her head.

In Figure 15.64, ALIGNMENT is set to FIXED, so the source area is fixed by the CTRL-click. Since

Figure 15.65 *The Heal tool icon and pointer*

Figure 15.67 *The Perspective Clone tool icon and pointer*

Figure 15.66 *Using the Heal tool*

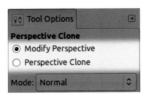

Figure 15.68 *Options specific to the Perspective Clone tool*

tern. An example is shown in Figure 15.66. We chose a source point where the skin is smooth. Then we painted over blemishes to blend them away. We left the blemishes on the right side of the portrait for comparison. This tool requires a fair amount of processor power, so it may lag depending on your computer's capabilities.

The Perspective Clone Tool

The Perspective Clone tool has no keyboard shortcut assigned to it. Its icon and pointer are shown in Figure 15.67. This tool basically combines the Clone tool and the Perspective tool (see Chapter 16). It has the same options as the Clone tool, except for a couple of additional radio buttons (Figure 15.68):

- MODIFY PERSPECTIVE establishes the perspective: Click the image and then move the corners of the rectangle to set the perspective.

- PERSPECTIVE CLONE actually clones objects in perspective after you've used MODIFY PERSPECTIVE mode.

Figure 15.69 shows a house in Grasse, France. We want to replace the rightmost, closed window with the open window on the left. We set up the perspective as shown in the figure and CTRL-click the leftmost window. Next, we switch to PERSPECTIVE CLONE mode, and paint on the rightmost window, as shown in Figure 15.70.

we click the eye, it's copied over and over again as if it were a brush.

If the source is a pattern, ALIGNED and REGISTERED both fill the painted area with the pattern. FIXED alignment uses the pattern as if it were a color brush. NONE (or no alignment) works like ALIGNED or REGISTERED alignment, except if you move the pointer, the pattern starts over, whereas in the other two modes, it continues seamlessly.

The Heal Tool

The Heal tool (H) is like the Clone tool, but instead of replacing the pixels, it combines them. This tool is designed to smooth over blemishes in an image. Its icon and pointer are shown in Figure 15.65.

The Heal tool options are the same as those of the Clone tool, but you can't heal with a pat-

Figure 15.69 *Setting up the perspective*

Figure 15.70 *After cloning the window*

This tool gives the best results if you clone simple geometric shapes and create a subtle perspective.

15.7 The Modifying Tools

The three modifying tools, which are often used in photo retouching, are brush tools that transform an image rather than adding or removing color. They have all the shared options of the brush tools except for MODE, and they are af-

Figure 15.71 *The Convolve tool icon and pointer*

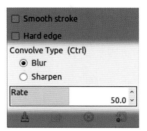

Figure 15.72 *Options specific to the Convolve tool*

fected by the current paint dynamics. They differ from the other brushes in that they use the CTRL key in a unique way and have a couple of additional options.

Convolve and Smudge are *timed tools*, which means their effect is cumulative if the same area is covered more than once. You control this effect with the RATE slider and the Rate characteristic in the current paint dynamics.

The Convolve Tool

The Convolve tool (SHIFT+U), also called the Blur/Sharpen tool, blurs or sharpens the image. Its icon and pointer are shown in Figure 15.71.

Convolve's unique options are shown in Figure 15.72. Depending on the CONVOLVE TYPE, this tool can blur or sharpen using the current brush, opacity, rate value, and paint dynamics. The CTRL key toggles the CONVOLVE TYPE.

The RATE slider [0 to 100] sets the speed of the transformation. This tool is cumulative, so painting over the same area twice intensifies the blurring or sharpening. Although it can be used with a large brush and a high rate, this tool is not designed to transform large areas. It's best for touch-ups and details. For large areas, we recommend using a filter.

Figure 15.73 shows how the Convolve tool, set to BLUR mode with the Hardness 075 brush,

Figure 15.73 *Using the Convolve tool*

Figure 15.74 *The Smudge tool icon and pointer*

helps flowers stand out against a bright, leafy background. The left half is unchanged, and the right half shows the result.

The Smudge Tool

The Smudge tool (S) does just what you'd expect: It smudges. Figure 15.74 shows its icon and pointer. This tool can be used to blend shading in a drawing; to subtly manipulate a photo; or even to draw hair, fur, or grass in a digital illustration, as shown in Section 3.5.

We'll demonstrate two uses of the Smudge tool on the photo shown in Figure 15.75. To create bangs, we choose a Hardness 050 brush set to a large size (about half as large as the woman's head) and smudge from left to right along the her head. Then we reduce the size of the brush to about half as large as an eye and extend the edges of her mouth. The result is shown in Figure 15.76.

If you make changes on a copy of the layer, then if you make a mistake, you can use the Clone tool to restore the image by copying from the original layer.

Figure 15.75 *Initial image before smudging*

Figure 15.76 *Smudging with two different brush sizes*

The Dodge/Burn Tool

The Dodge/Burn tool (SHIFT+D) simulates two traditional photography techniques. Its icon and pointer are shown in Figure 15.77. The Dodge effect lightens colors, whereas the Burn effect darkens them. Because this is a brush tool, it's great for adding light or shadow to specific parts of an image or object.

This tool's unique options are shown in Figure 15.78. The TYPE radio buttons switch between Dodge and Burn, and the CTRL key

Figure 15.77 *The Dodge/Burn tool icon and pointer*

Figure 15.78 *Options specific to the Dodge/Burn tool*

Figure 15.79 *Dodging the face and burning the hair*

toggles those options. The RANGE radio buttons change which parts of the image are affected, depending on the lighting.

We'll demonstrate the tool on the image shown in Figure 15.75. We dodge the face in the MIDTONES and burn the hair in the MIDTONES and HIGHLIGHTS. The result is shown in Figure 15.79. This tool cannot change the hues, so

Figure 15.80 *The Text tool icon and pointer*

even though the shadows are enhanced, the hair is still blond.

If you're a traditional photographer, note that the dynamic range of photo paper is much higher than in digital photography, so you won't be able to extract as many details by dodging as you would in a darkroom.

15.8   The Text Tool

The Text tool (⊤) is used, unsurprisingly, to set text. Its icon and pointer are shown in Figure 15.80. To use it, click the image where you want to place the top-left corner of the text and then enter your text. Each time you click and add text, a new layer is created.

The Text Tool Options

The Text tool options are shown in Figure 15.81. Here they are from top to bottom:

- FONT determines how the text will look. The Aa button opens a drop-down menu of the available fonts (Figure 15.82). The buttons at the bottom of this menu, from left to right, do the following:

  - Reduce the size of the font previews
  - Enlarge the font previews
  - Show the font previews as a list (currently selected)
  - Show the font previews as a grid
  - Open the Fonts dialog (Figure 15.83)

  You can scroll through the fonts using the mouse wheel. When you begin typing a name in the field at the top of the dialog, a drop-down menu of the matching fonts appears.

Figure 15.81 *The Text tool options*

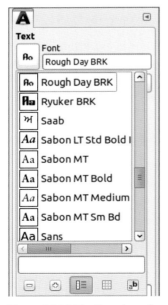

Figure 15.82 *The Font drop-down menu*

Figure 15.83 *The Fonts dialog*

- SIZE is the font size in pixels, by default, but you can switch to resolution-dependent units like millimeters or inches.

- USE EDITOR switches to using the Text editor rather than editing the text directly in the image, as explained in "Using the Text Tool" on page 356.

- ANTIALIASING smooths the edges of the fonts, but it doesn't work on an image in Indexed mode.

- HINTING sets the level of *hinting instructions*, which improve rendering at small sizes. Clicking the button opens a drop-down menu with four choices—from NONE to FULL.

- COLOR opens the Color chooser, described in "The Color Chooser" on page 254.

- JUSTIFY sets the alignment of the text using four small icons that act like radio buttons. The justification can be left, right, center, or justified. These options are only available if the BOX option value is FIXED.

  The next three options use the same units as SIZE and can be set to negative values:

  - Indent the first line

  - Line spacing

  - Letter spacing

Figure 15.84 *The Text options: Language > right-click menu*

Figure 15.85 *The Fonts dialog, grid view*

- BOX changes how the text box works. You can choose either FIXED or DYNAMIC. With fixed text, you can change the dimensions of the box and the text, and the justify, indentation, and spacing parameters automatically operate. With dynamic text, the box extends while you are typing, and you must press ENTER to start a new line.

- LANGUAGE changes the language, which can affect the way the text is rendered. If you type in this field, a drop-down list of the available languages appears. Right-click to open the menu shown in Figure 15.84. The last two entries open a menu of input methods and a menu for inserting a Unicode control character, respectively.

Figure 15.86 *The Fonts menu*

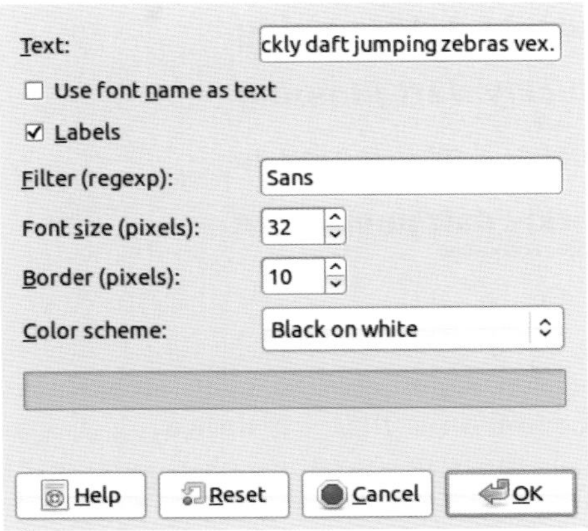

Figure 15.87 *The Render Font Map dialog*

Choosing a Font

As you just learned, you can change fonts in the Text tool options dialog. You can also use the Fonts dockable dialog. Figure 15.83 shows its default appearance, and Figure 15.85 shows the fonts in a grid; you can select the display format in the dialog menu. To change fonts, just click the one you want. If you change the font in the Text tool options, the change is reflected in the Fonts dialog. If you click and hold the Aa button in the Fonts dialog, a temporary window appears, showing a sentence that uses all 26 letters of the alphabet.

The Fonts menu, which opens if you right-click the Fonts dialog, contains the two entries shown in Figure 15.86. RESCAN FONT LIST refreshes the list; you'll find it useful after you install new fonts. RENDER FONT MAP opens a dialog (Figure 15.87) where you can search for a suitable font. It displays example text in the available fonts. The default TEXT contains all 26 letters, but you can change this. You can also choose to show the font name as the text. When checked, LABELS shows the name of the

How quickly daft jumping zebrc
Comic Sans MS

How quickly daft jumping zebr
Comic Sans MS Bold

How quickly daft jumping zek
DejaVu Sans

How quickly daft jumping
DejaVu Sans Bold

How quickly daft jumping
DejaVu Sans Bold Oblique

How quickly daft jumping ze
DejaVu Sans Bold Oblique Semi-Condensed

How quickly daft jumping ze
DejaVu Sans Bold Semi-Condensed

Figure 15.88 *Rendered fonts*

font under the example text. FILTER reduces the number of fonts that are shown. You can also choose the size and the color scheme of the example text. Part of our result appears in Figure 15.88. Although this tool is useful, keep in mind it doesn't show all of the available fonts.

On Windows and GNU/Linux machines, GIMP uses a general tool called Fontconfig to manage fonts. To add a font, simply place it in the appropriate directory, and Fontconfig does the rest. Mac OS X, as explained on the GIMP website (*http://docs.gimp.org/en/gimp-using-fonts.html*), is slightly different.

Using the Text Tool

To use the Text tool, click the image, and if the box is dynamic, the embedding box automatically adjusts around the text you enter. You can also click and drag the box corners and sides to adjust it to the dimensions you want, but when you do, the box becomes fixed. When the box is fixed, line breaks are automatic.

Above the text box is an option box (Figure 15.89) with several fields and buttons that you can use to edit a selection within your text. The top-left field is used to change the font. The top-right field is the font size in pixels.

The bottom-left button (broom icon) clears all the style settings in the text box. The next four

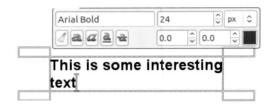

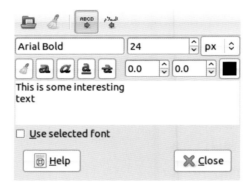

Figure 15.89 *Typing the text*

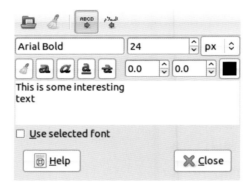

Figure 15.90 *The Text Editor*

buttons toggle boldface, italics, underline, and strike through, respectively. The next two fields move the selected text vertically and change the character spacing, respectively.

If you check the USE EDITOR option in the Text tool options dialog, the Text editor, shown in Figure 15.90, opens. The top buttons let you load text from a file, delete the text, and align the text on the left or on the right. The next two rows are the same settings as shown in the options for the text box. When you check the USE SELECTED FONT box at the bottom, the text above should be displayed in your chosen font.

You can add or edit text in either the Text editor or in the image, but if you're working with text directly in the image, the function of several keyboard shortcuts temporarily changes. For example, CTRL+A selects all text instead of the entire layer, and P just adds the letter p to the text rather than opening the Paintbrush tool. Any single-letter shortcut behaves the same way.

Figure 15.91 *The Text layer: right-click menu*

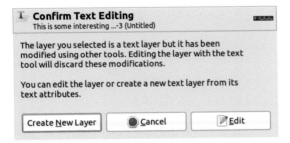

Figure 15.92 *A warning dialog*

The text is created as a new layer that's the size of the text box. This layer has the special properties of a text layer and is named using the beginning of the text itself.

If you right-click the text box, the menu shown in Figure 15.91 opens. Some of these options are also found in the Text editor, and others are standard editing commands (Copy, Cut, etc.). You'll see a submenu of INPUT METHODS at the bottom, which you can also access from the LANGUAGE field in the Text tool options. The two commands, PATH FROM TEXT and TEXT ALONG PATH, are discussed in the next section.

You can edit your text as long as it's in a text layer. Simply select the Text tool and click somewhere in the text. If the layer properties have changed—after you edit it with a transformation tool, for example—the warning dialog shown in Figure 15.92 opens. If you choose to edit

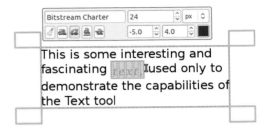

Figure 15.93 *Changing some text characteristics*

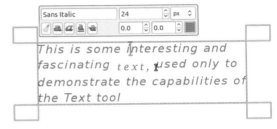

Figure 15.94 *Changing global characteristics*

the text, the transformations you made are removed. Alternatively, you can choose to create a new text layer above the transformed one.

Editing Your Text

The Text tool is not a word processor, so its capabilities are limited. This tool is useful for creating text effects (see Chapter 4) or for adding a little text to a larger image.

As mentioned earlier, you can edit the look of a selection within your text. In Figure 15.93, we selected the word text (hence the yellow box) and changed its font to Bitstream Charter and italics, set its size to 24 pixels, moved it down 5 pixels, and increased the character spacing by 4 pixels.

If you change the parameters in the tool options, all the text in the layer is affected. In Figure 15.94, we changed the font, text color, line spacing, and character spacing.

Some of the ways to work with text are hidden around the GIMP interface. As you saw previously, you can open menus by right-clicking the text layer, its option box, or the LANGUAGE field

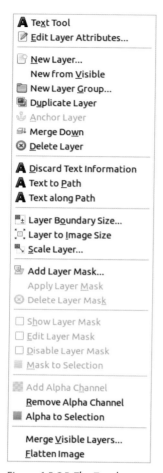

Figure 15.95 *The Text layer menu*

Figure 15.96 *A path built from text*

Figure 15.97 *Modifying and filling the path of the first character*

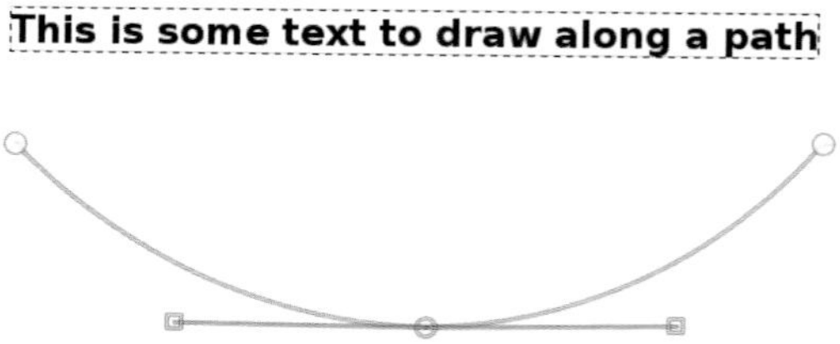

Figure 15.98 *Building a new path*

of the tool options. Right-clicking the text line in the Layers dialog opens the menu shown in Figure 15.95. This menu can also be accessed via the triangle button in the top-right corner of the Layers dialog.

This menu has three new entries:

- DISCARD TEXT INFORMATION: This entry transforms the text layer to an ordinary layer. The characters are represented with pixels, so you won't be able to edit them as text.

- TEXT TO PATH: This entry is called PATH FROM TEXT in the menu accessed when you right-click the text box. Use it to change the shape of characters. For example, Figure 15.96 shows the path built from some text, and Figure 15.97 shows the result of moving some of the anchors, converting the path to a selection, and filling the selection.

- TEXT ALONG PATH: For this transformation to work, a path must already be active in the Paths dialog. After making a path (Figure 15.98), select the text layer and then choose TEXT ALONG PATH.

GIMP builds a new path out of the text that curves along the path (Figure 15.99). As before, we converted the path to a selection and filled it with black (Figure 15.100). The original, horizontal text remains as well.

15.9 The Color Picker Tool and the Measure Tool

Two more tools that are useful in digital art and drawing are the Color Picker tool and the Measure tool.

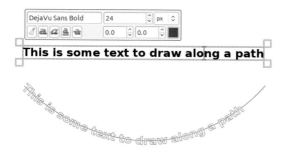

This is some text to draw along a path

Figure 15.99 *Converting the text to a path*

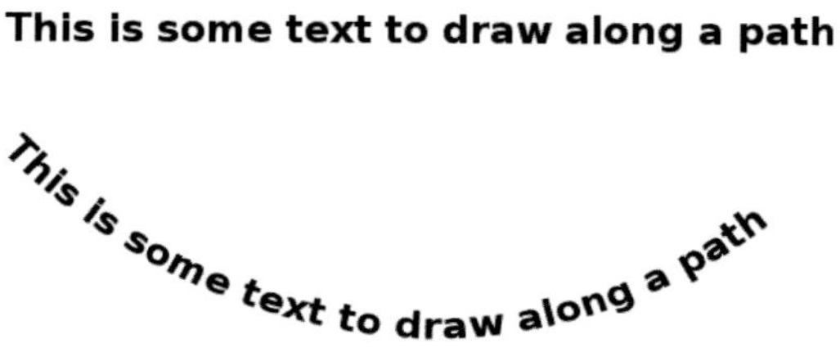

This is some text to draw along a path

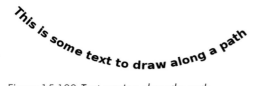

Figure 15.100 *Text curving along the path*

The Color Picker Tool

The Color Picker tool ([O]) is used to choose a color from an image open in GIMP. Its icon and pointer are shown in Figure 15.101. After selecting the tool, click a color in an open image, and it becomes the foreground or background color. When you press the [CTRL] key while using a painting tool, the pointer temporarily acts as a color picker, but you can pick only one pixel in the current layer and set only the foreground color. When you release [CTRL], the painting tool is restored. Figure 15.102 shows the tool options.

- SAMPLE AVERAGE, when checked, takes the average pixels in a square centered on the clicked pixel. Use the slider to set the radius of this square, which is outlined when you click in the image. Otherwise, only the clicked pixel is used.

- SAMPLE MERGED, when checked, uses all the visible layers in an image; otherwise, only the current layer is used.

Figure 15.101 *The Color Picker tool icon and pointer*

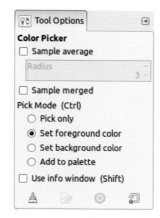

Figure 15.102 *The Color Picker tool options*

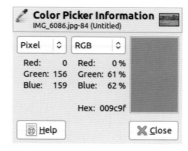

Figure 15.103 *The Color Picker Information dialog*

- PICK MODE has four choices:

  - PICK ONLY shows information about the pixel you click in the Information dialog (Figure 15.103), but it does not change the foreground or background color.

  - SET FOREGROUND COLOR and SET BACKGROUND COLOR let you choose which color to set, and you can toggle between these options with [CTRL].

  - ADD TO PALETTE sends the picked color to the active palette, using the Palette editor described in Section 22.7.

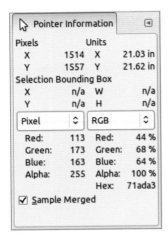

Figure 15.104 *The Pointer dialog*

Figure 15.105 *The Measure tool icon and pointer*

Figure 15.106 *Using the Measure tool*

- USE INFO WINDOW, when checked, opens the Color Picker Information dialog (Figure 15.103), which you can also open with SHIFT. This dialog contains the following information:

  - A large rectangle containing the selected color.

  - The hexadecimal value of this color.

  - Two sets of more detailed information. By default, the information shown uses the RGB channel values as percentages. You can change the models to HSV, CMY, or CMYK.

  You can also get pixel information from the Pointer dockable dialog. Figure 15.104 shows an example. This dialog displays detailed information about the pointer's current position. No option is available for sample averaging, and the SAMPLE MERGED option is checked by default. This dialog also displays the dimensions of the current layer and selection.

The Measure Tool

The Measure tool (SHIFT+M) is used to measure a distance and angle in an image. Its icon and

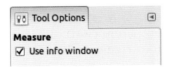

Figure 15.107 *The Measure tool option*

pointer are shown in Figure 15.105. Click an initial point to measure from and then drag to the final point.

The results are displayed in the status bar at the bottom of the Image window, as shown in Figure 15.106. You can see the distance in pixels between the two points, the angle of the line with regard to the horizontal, and the dimensions in pixels of the rectangle drawn using the line's end points. You can move the points into new positions, and the results reflect the new values.

This tool has only one option, shown in Figure 15.107. If it's checked, the tool opens a dialog, shown in Figure 15.108, which displays the same information that appears in the status bar of the Image window but with labels.

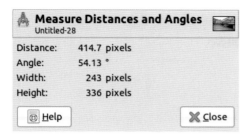

Figure 15.108 *The Measure dialog*

15.10 Combining Tool Presets, Brushes, and Paint Dynamics

We briefly discussed tool presets earlier in the chapter, but let's take a closer look at them now. Tool presets are a new feature of version 2.8, and they are especially powerful when combined with brushes and paint dynamics.

Getting to Know the Dialogs Involved

Figure 15.109 (inspired by Ramón Miranda) shows how tool presets, brushes, and paint dynamics interact. In the Paintbrush's tool options dialog (1), click the DYNAMICS button (2) to open a temporary menu of the available paint dynamics. From this menu, you can select the dynamic you want or click the button in the bottom-right corner to open the Paint Dynamics dialog (3). In this dialog, you can use the tag field only to select the dynamics of some category, here FX. You cannot edit the settings of a predefined dynamic like Confetti, but you can edit a copy of it by pressing the button labeled (4) in the Paintbrush tool options dialog. This opens the Paint Dynamics Editor (5).

In Figure 15.109, the Paint Dynamics Editor dialog appears twice. The top copy (5) shows the Mapping matrix (6) for the chosen dynamic. In this example, you see a checked box at the intersection of the SIZE row and the RANDOM column. When you display the SIZE parameters in the Paint Dynamics Editor (7), you see that the corresponding answer curve is not linear at all.

If you're satisfied with your current settings for the Paintbrush tool and want to save them, click the bottom-left button in the Paintbrush tool options dialog to open the Tool Preset Editor (8). Here, you can choose the name of the new tool preset and its icon. If you click the suggested icon, you get a list of the many icons available, the same as in Figure 9.54 on page 217. More important, you can choose what settings to save. In this example, the current foreground and background colors are not saved because the colors are selected at random in the chosen gradient. The current brush, dynamics, and gradient are saved because they are fundamental to this FX Confetti preset. Finally, the current pattern, palette, and font are irrelevant with the Paintbrush tool.

The Tool Presets dialog (9) is opened by selecting **Image: Windows > Dockable Dialogs > Tool Presets**. You can also open the Tool Preset Editor by clicking the first button in the bottom row of the Tool Presets dialog.

Predefined Paint Dynamics

As you've seen, GIMP comes with 17 predefined paint dynamics. The Basic category contains seven dynamics:

- Basic Simple links Opacity to Pressure and Angle to Random in the Mapping matrix of the Paint Dynamics Editor, which means that for a round brush, only opacity varies. The Angle-Random answer curve begins in the middle of the square, so the angle changes even if random is null.

- Dynamics Random links Size to Random.

- Negative Size Pressure has the same settings as Basic Simple, plus a link from Size to Pressure, with an inverted linear answer curve, which makes the drawing more transparent when you press more on the stylus.

- Pencil Generic is a complex dynamic that links Opacity to Pressure and Velocity (steep

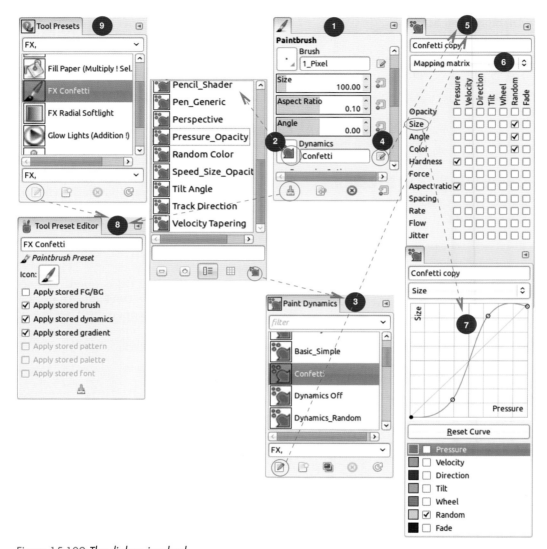

Figure 15.109 *The dialogs involved*

answer curve), Size to Pressure (concave answer curve), Angle to Direction, Force to Pressure, and Jitter to Pressure and Velocity (concave answer curve).

- `Pencil Shader` has the same settings as `Basic Simple`. Only the answer curves are different: Opacity-Pressure is steeper in the middle, and Angle-Random is simply linear.

- `Pen Generic` links Opacity to Pressure, Velocity, and Fade; Size to Pressure and Velocity; and Angle to Random. The Size-Pressure answer curve is almost linear up to the middle and then decreases to zero for the maximum pressure. The Size-Velocity curve is concave.

- `Pressure Opacity` links Opacity to Pressure, first with a concave and then a convex answer curve.

The FX category contains three Paint Dynamics:

- Confetti is a complex dynamic, with Size, Angle, and Color linked to Random, and Hardness and Aspect ratio linked to Pressure. The Angle-Random answer curve is linear and begins in the middle.

- Perspective links Opacity and Aspect ratio to Pressure and links Angle to Direction. All the curves are linear.

- Speed Size Opacity links Opacity to Pressure, Size to Pressure and Velocity, and Angle to Direction.

Finally, seven dynamics have no category. Their answer curves are linear unless otherwise noted:

- Basic Dynamics links Opacity to Pressure and Fade, Size to Velocity, and Angle to Tilt. This dynamic is the most natural for simple painting.

- Dynamics Off has an empty mapping matrix. Select this dynamic when you want no effect at all.

- Fade Tapering links Opacity and Size to Fade.

- Random Color links Color to Random.

- Tilt Angle links Angle to Tilt and is useful only with a tablet that records the pen tilt.

- Track Direction links Angle to Direction.

- Velocity Tapering links Opacity and Size to Velocity.

You can extend this set of paint dynamics as needed. Use the predefined dynamics as models. Avoid defining a dynamic with too many checked boxes in its mapping matrix because its behavior will be difficult to predict.

Several of the predefined paint dynamics are especially handy when combined with some predefined tool presets, as you'll see in "Predefined Tool Presets" on page 364.

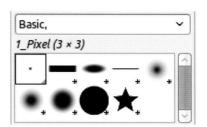

Figure 15.110 *Basic brushes*

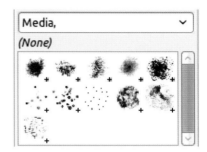

Figure 15.111 *Media brushes*

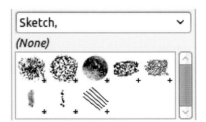

Figure 15.112 *Sketch brushes*

Predefined Brushes

As already mentioned, GIMP's 54 predefined brushes are divided according to their tags: Basic, Media, Sketch, Splatters, Texture, and Legacy (Figures 15.110 to 15.115).

You can define your own brushes, as detailed in Section 22.4. Any brushes you've created are listed first in the Brushes dialog, followed by the predefined brushes, which are listed in alphabetical order. A brush's appearance in the list depends on its tag filter at the top of the dialog. Remember that when no tag is specified, the first brush in the dialog is the contents of the clipboard cropped to a maximum size of 512×512.

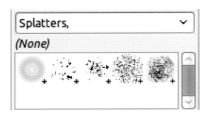

Figure 15.113 *Splatters brushes*

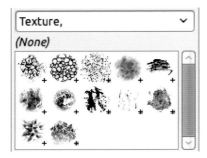

Figure 15.114 *Texture brushes*

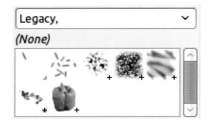

Figure 15.115 *Legacy brushes*

A wide variety of brushes is available on the Web at, for example, *http://www.noupe.com/how-tos/1000-free-high-resolution-gimp-brushes.html* and *http://www.pgd-design.com/gimp/br.php*. The Gimp Paint Studio (*http://code.google.com/p/gps-gimp-paint-studio/*) offers a large collection of brushes specifically designed for GIMP.

Brushes designed for Photoshop can also be used in GIMP. Simply place the downloaded brushes into you GIMP's brushes folder, and refresh the Brushes dialog by pressing the button at the bottom.

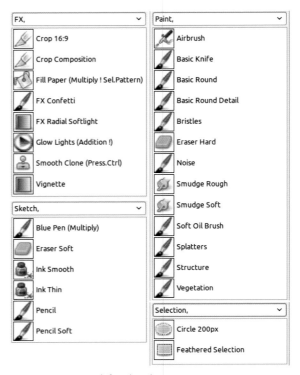

Figure 15.116 *Predefined tool presets*

Predefined Tool Presets

GIMP now contains 29 predefined tool presets, divided into 4 categories.

FX contains eight presets (top left of Figure 15.116):

- `Crop 16:9` crops in a 16:9 ratio.
- `Crop Composition` applies the Crop tool without any setting other than HIGHLIGHT and RULE OF THIRDS.
- `Fill Paper (Multiply! Sel. Pattern)` opens the Bucket Fill tool in Multiply mode, selecting the `Paper` pattern (Figure 15.117) with an opacity of 50%.
- `FX Confetti` opens the Paintbrush tool with the `1.Pixel` brush, the `Confetti` paint dynamics, the `Tropical Colors` gradient, and a significant jitter (Figure 15.118).

Figure 15.117 *Using the Fill Paper tool preset*

Figure 15.119 *Original photo*

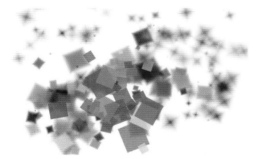

Figure 15.118 *Using the FX Confetti tool preset*

- FX Radial Softlight applies the Blend tool with the FG to Transparent gradient in SOFT LIGHT mode and a RADIAL shape. You can choose the foreground color. From Figure 15.119, we achieved Figure 15.120 by choosing a bright green for the foreground color and placing the center of the gradient on the sun.

- Glow Lights (Addition!) opens the Paintbrush tool at 40% opacity and in ADDITION mode, using the Hardness 050 brush and the Pressure Opacity paint dynamics. The brush size is set to 400, and the INCREMENTAL box is checked. For example, if we take Figure 15.121, we can get Figure 15.122 by choosing a bright green color and drawing across the image with increasing pressure.

- Smooth Clone (Press Ctrl) opens the Clone tool with all default options, except SIZE set to

Figure 15.120 *Using the FX Radial Softlight tool preset*

150, the Dynamics Off paint dynamics, and the SAMPLE MERGED box checked. Choose your brush, preferably Hardness 075 or Hardness 050, and begin cloning.

- Vignette opens the Blend tool in MULTIPLY mode at 75% opacity, using the FG to BG (RGB) gradient, a RADIAL shape with an OFFSET of 25, and the DITHERING box checked. It simulates the so-called vignette effect produced by old-time, low-value cameras.

Figure 15.121 *Original photo*

Figure 15.122 *Using the Glow Lights tool preset*

Paint contains 13 presets. All these presets but the last two use the Pressure Opacity paint dynamics. These tool presets differ in terms of the tool and brush they apply and the various tool options settings mentioned next. They constitute a set of daily tools with carefully chosen characteristics ideal for painters.

- Airbrush uses the Hardness 050 brush with a Size of 500 and sets Rate to 30 and Flow to 10.

- Basic Knife applies the Paintbrush tool (as do the next three presets) with the Block 03 brush and a Size of 180.
- Basic Round uses the Hardness 100 brush with a Size of 80.
- Basic Round Detail uses the Hardness 075 brush with a Size of 20.
- Bristles uses the Bristles 01 brush with a Size of 60. This tool simulates drawing as if with an old toothbrush.
- Eraser Hard uses the Block 01 brush with a size of 80 to erase with a strong square eraser.
- Noise uses the Paintbrush tool with the Sponge 01 brush with a size of 450 and an Angle of 90, which is meaningful only if you change the Aspect Ratio.
- Smudge Rough uses the Acrylic 01 brush with an Opacity of 50 and a Size of 100, with the Rate set to 60.
- Smudge Soft is the same as Smudge Rough, except it uses the Hardness 050 brush.
- Soft Oil Brush and the next three presets use the Paintbrush tool. Soft Oil Brush applies the Oils 02 brush with a Size of 80. It simulates painting with oil paint.
- Splatters applies the Splats 01 dynamic brush with a Size of 200. It simulates the result of shaking your brush above your canvas.
- Perspective applies the Structure brush with a Size of 283.55, using the Perspective Paint Dynamics. Use this preset to draw strokes that follow the shapes of forms on the canvas.
- Vegetation applies the Vegetation 02 dynamic brush with a Size of 250 and the Pressure Opacity paint dynamics (Figure 15.123).

Selection contains two presets, handy for two common situations. Use these presets to generate your own ideas for defining presets:

- Circle 200px creates a circular selection with a diameter of 200 pixels. The Antialiasing box is checked.

Figure 15.123 *Using the Vegetation tool preset*

Figure 15.124 *Using the Blue Pen tool preset*

Figure 15.125 *Fragment from a black and white portrait*

- Feathered Selection opens the Rectangle Select tool with the ANTIALIASING, FEATHER EDGES (RADIUS set to 25), and ROUNDED CORNERS (RADIUS set to 50) boxes checked. The guides are set to CENTER LINES.

Sketch contains six presets, similar to the Paint presets:

- Blue Pen (Multiply) applies the Paintbrush tool in MULTIPLY mode with OPACITY set to 75%, the Hardness 075 brush at SIZE 15, and the Pen Generic paint dynamics. The foreground color is set to (26, 47, 152) RGB, that is, a dark blue. The result simulates a sketch made with a blue ballpoint pen (Figure 15.124).

- Eraser Soft is the same as Eraser Hard, but it uses the Hardness 050 brush.

- Ink Smooth applies the Ink tool with SMOOTH STROKE checked, QUALITY set to 75, WEIGHT to 300, ADJUSTMENT SIZE to 10, TILT to 0, and

SPEED to 0.9. The tip is a round size, deformed as a narrow oval tilted to the right. These settings are good for calligraphy.

- Ink Thin applies the Ink tool with ANGLE set to 0.5 and SPEED to 1. The tip shape is a simple round size. This preset is good for simulating handwriting.

- Pencil opens the Paintbrush tool with OPACITY set to 50%, the Pencil 01 brush set to a SIZE of 50, and the Pencil Generic paint dynamics. APPLY JITTER (AMOUNT set to 0.2) and INCREMENTAL are checked. This preset simulates using a soft pencil on drawing paper.

- Pencil Soft has the same settings, except the Charcoal 02 brush is set at a SIZE of 200. It simulates using a charcoal pencil.

By experimenting with this set of predefined tool presets, you'll get ideas for defining your own tool presets. Don't forget to tag them, too, so you can retrieve them easily. You can use existing tags, but you can also invent new ones, and you can apply several tags to the same object. Defining a new tool preset is much easier than defining a new brush. And, of course, if you miss a specific paint dynamics, you can easily define it as a tool preset. Figures 15.125 to 15.127 show a few examples of work that combines custom

Credit: Ramón Miranda

Figure 15.126 *Fragment from a color portrait*

Credit: Ramón Miranda

Figure 15.127 *Fragment from a color painting*

predefined brushes, paint dynamics, and tool presets, courtesy of Ramón Miranda, the main author of the GIMP Paint Studio (see *http://code. google.com/p/gps-gimp-paint-studio/*). GIMP Paint Studio offers a huge collection of brushes and presets designed to speed up repetitive tasks by minimizing the need to reset tool options manually when changing tools. Its main goal is to support painting tasks, as its name implies.

16 Transformation Tools

Transformation tools change the position or geometry of an image or part of an image. These tools do not alter the colors or the transparency of pixels, although, in some cases, regions of the image are left vacant and new pixel values must be determined. For example, if a section of an image is rotated, empty areas are created, which are automatically filled with the current background color. Also, when pixels are rearranged, they are usually not in exactly the same relative positions, so some pixels are lost and others must be computed.

16.1 Global Transformations

Global transformations are transformations that act on an entire image or layer, rather than on an object or region, and act by rearranging pixels, rather than by calculating new values. Perhaps counterintuitively, global transformations require relatively little computing power because they change the position of pixels but don't create empty spaces within the image or require interpolation. (To interpolate pixels is to compute new pixels by using the values of neighboring pixels.) For example, when using the Rotate tool to rotate an image, all the pixels in the image layer must be interpolated.

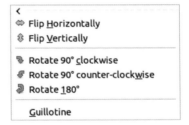

Figure 16.1 *The Image: Image > Transform menu*

Rotation is not a global transformation. The Flip tool, which does perform a global transformation, simply changes the position of the pixels, which requires no interpolation.

Transforming an Image

Figure 16.1 shows the **Image: Image > Transform** menu. All the entries on this menu act on the image as a whole, which means the transformation is applied to all layers in the image. We demonstrate these transformations on the image shown in Figure 16.2 by applying each transformation in the **Image: Image > Transform** menu to the original image.

- FLIP HORIZONTALLY produces the result shown in Figure 16.3. After the transformation, the flowers are a mirror image of the original.

Figure 16.2 *The original image*

Figure 16.3 *Flipped horizontally*

Figure 16.4 *Flipped vertically*

Figure 16.5 *Rotated 90° clockwise*

Figure 16.6 *Rotated 90° counterclockwise*

This transformation exchanges pixels symmetrically around the central vertical axis.

- FLIP VERTICALLY exchanges pixels symmetrically around the central horizontal axis. The result appears in Figure 16.4.

- ROTATE 90° CLOCKWISE does *not* involve symmetry around the main diagonal. The resulting image is not mirrored but is simply rotated 90°. See Figure 16.5.

- ROTATE 90° COUNTER-CLOCKWISE is *not* a horizontal flip of the preceding rotation; the flowers are rotated from the original position in a counterclockwise direction. See Figure 16.6.

- ROTATE 180° does not produce the same result as FLIP VERTICALLY; the flowers are not changed, simply rotated. See Figure 16.7.

- GUILLOTINE is, in fact, named after the obsolete French execution device. The GIMP feature is quite handy—and much less dangerous.

Before using GUILLOTINE, place guides to delimit regions of the image, as shown in Figure 16.8.

When GUILLOTINE is selected, GIMP creates a separate Image window for each distinct rectangle delimited by the guides. In this example, nine windows are created, as

Figure 16.7 *Rotated 180°*

Figure 16.8 *The original image with guides*

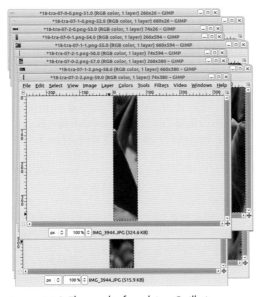

Figure 16.9 *The result of applying Guillotine*

Figure 16.10 *The central rectangle*

shown in Figure 16.9. Figure 16.10 shows the central rectangle containing the flowers. This tool is sometimes used in web development to cut a large image into many components that are each associated with a different link. See also "Slice" on page 189.

Resizing an Image

The *canvas* of an image is the full visible area, which may extend beyond the area visible in the Image window, especially if the zoom factor is high. Conversely, the window may display areas outside the canvas, generally represented as a neutral color. Layers are often, but not necessarily, the same size as the canvas; layers can be smaller than the canvas, or regions of a layer can extend beyond the canvas. When a layer is larger than the canvas, the regions that extend beyond the canvas aren't visible, but they still exist and can be moved into view.

Selecting **Image: Image > Canvas Size** brings up the dialog shown in Figure 16.11. We broke the chain that links the WIDTH and HEIGHT fields and reduced both values, so the new canvas is smaller than the original and has different proportions. In the preview, we moved the image so the flowers dominate. The new canvas boundaries are clearly shown in the preview. You could also increase the canvas size and press the CENTER button to place the image in the center of the new canvas.

If an image contains several layers, you can specify how the layers are handled via the RESIZE LAYERS drop-down menu at the bottom of

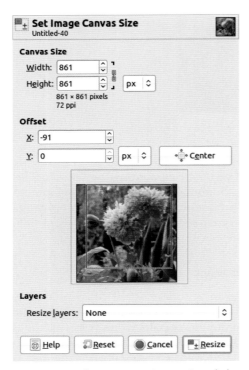

Figure 16.11 *The Set Image Canvas Size dialog*

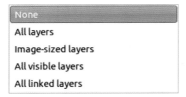

Figure 16.12 *Resizing layers*

the SET IMAGE CANVAS SIZE dialog, shown in Figure 16.12. The options are these:

- NONE: Leaves the layers unchanged.

- ALL LAYERS: Resizes all layers to the canvas size.

- IMAGE-SIZED LAYERS: Resizes only the layers that are the same size as the original canvas.

- ALL VISIBLE LAYERS: Resizes only the layers whose visibility eye is checked.

- ALL LINKED LAYERS: Resizes only the layers whose link icon is checked.

Figure 16.13 *The canvas size was increased.*

If you increase the size of the canvas, but do not resize any of the layers, then one or more areas will be created that contain no data. These areas are displayed as transparent, as shown in Figure 16.13. The empty area cannot be edited with any of the GIMP tools because no layer is present there. To make the empty space usable, enlarge at least one layer to the size of the canvas or select something other than NONE in the RESIZE LAYERS menu.

Select **Image: Image > Fit Canvas to Layers** to fit the canvas around all the existing layers. The edges are determined by whichever layer extends the farthest in a given direction. The canvas size can also be reduced if all layers are smaller than it is.

Image: Image > Fit Canvas to Selection is demonstrated in Figure 16.14, where we made a loose selection around some of the buildings, and in Figure 16.15, which shows the result.

Selecting **Image: Image > Print Size** brings up the dialog shown in Figure 16.16. This command doesn't alter the image or compute any new pixel values. PRINT SIZE affects only how the image is printed; it only works with some printer software; and even when it does work, its parameters are overridden by those of the printer software. This command is useful as a means to compute the print size but not to specify it.

In the Set Image Print Resolution dialog, sets of values are linked together: If WIDTH is changed, the X RESOLUTION changes in

Figure 16.14 *Defining a selection*

Figure 16.15 *Fitting the canvas to the selection*

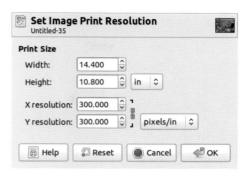

Figure 16.16 *The Set Image Print Resolution dialog*

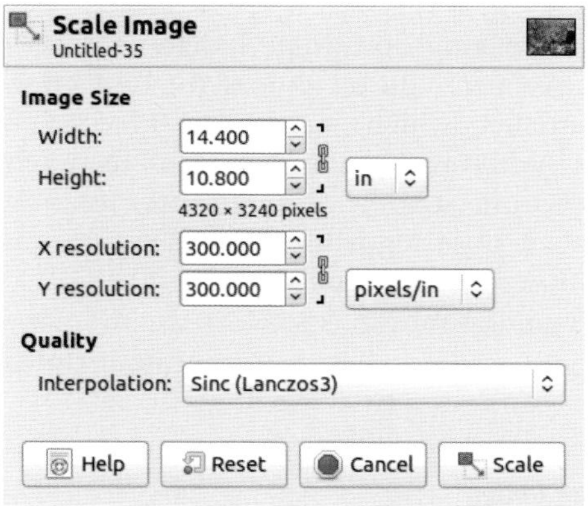

Figure 16.17 *The Scale Image dialog*

proportion, and vice versa. Likewise, if HEIGHT is changed, the Y RESOLUTION changes. Moreover, if the chain beside the resolutions is not broken, all the values change when one value changes. Several different units are available for size (inches, millimeters, points, and picas, or even feet, yards, centimeters, and meters) and for resolution (pixels per inch, millimeter, point, pica, and others).

Selecting **Image: Image > Scale Image**, on the other hand, changes the entire image, sometimes dramatically. Its dialog, shown in Figure 16.17, is almost identical to the previous one. But a chain now appears beside the WIDTH and HEIGHT fields, which allows you to change the image proportions (see Figure 16.18). Note also that dimensions can be expressed as a percentage of the original size. The actual size in pixels is always displayed just below. And

Figure 16.18 *A scaled-down image with altered proportions*

Figure 16.19 *Adding a frame to the image*

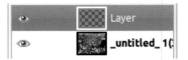

Figure 16.20 *The Layers dialog for Figure 16.19*

Figure 16.21 *An autocropped image*

a new field, QUALITY, has a few options. Unless you're working on a huge image or have a very old computer, always choose the best interpolation quality, which is the SINC (LANCZOS3) algorithm. When resizing an image, all its pixels must be computed anew using an interpolation algorithm. A poor algorithm causes significant deterioration in image quality.

A good rule of thumb is to work on an image at the largest size possible and to scale it down only when you're ready to use it.

Cropping an Image

When an image is resized, all its contents are retained, although a loss of quality can occur. When an image is cropped, on the other hand, some of the content is removed.

Image: Image > Crop to Selection appears to do exactly the same thing as FIT CANVAS TO SELECTION. Actually, however, FIT CANVAS TO SELECTION doesn't remove any information from the image; it just hides certain areas, which you can reveal by moving the layer and thus changing which areas are hidden. On the other hand, CROP TO SELECTION removes part of the image, as the layers are cropped to the new canvas size. After using CROP TO SELECTION, the image size is reduced. You can see the current image size in the Image window's status bar.

To demonstrate **Image: Image > Autocrop Image**, we added a frame to the example

Figure 16.22 *Preparing an image for Zealous Crop*

photograph, as shown in Figure 16.19. To do this, we added a transparent layer, built a rectangular selection around the photo, inverted the selection, and filled it with bright blue. Figure 16.20 shows the Layers dialog. AUTOCROP IMAGE crops all the layers of an image based on a frame in the current layer. The frame must be a homogeneous color. The result of our example appears in Figure 16.21.

Image: Image > Zealous Crop works like AUTOCROP IMAGE, but it can remove central regions of an image in addition to an outer frame. Figure 16.22 shows an image prepared for a ZEALOUS CROP, and Figure 16.23 shows the result.

Figure 16.23 *After Zealous Cropping*

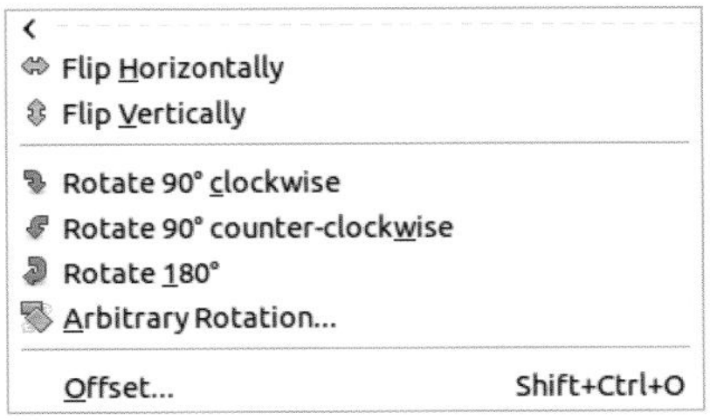

<
⇔ Flip <u>H</u>orizontally
⑧ Flip <u>V</u>ertically
⬛ Rotate 90° <u>c</u>lockwise
⬛ Rotate 90° counter-clock<u>w</u>ise
⬛ Rotate <u>1</u>80°
⬛ <u>A</u>rbitrary Rotation...
<u>O</u>ffset...　　　　　　Shift+Ctrl+O

Figure 16.24 *The Image: Layer > Transform menu*

Figure 16.25 *The initial image with two layers*

Transforming a Layer

Figure 16.24 shows the **Image: Layer > Transform** menu. We demonstrate each of the tools in this menu on the image shown in Figure 16.25. The upper layer of this image contains only the rose, and the lower layer contains the city background.

Figure 16.26 *Flipped horizontally*

Figure 16.27 *Flipped vertically*

The first five entries on the **Image: Layer > Transform** menu are identical to those of the **Image: Image > Transform** menu, but they act on the current layer rather than on the entire image. The entries are demonstrated in Figures 16.26 to 16.30.

The ARBITRARY ROTATION entry applies the Rotate tool, described in "The Rotate Tool" on page 385.

Figure 16.28 *Rotated 90° clockwise*

Figure 16.30 *Rotated 180°*

Figure 16.29 *Rotated 90° counterclockwise*

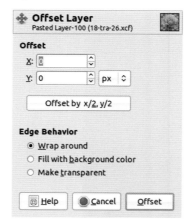

Figure 16.31 *The Offset Layer dialog*

The OFFSET entry (which is also available via SHIFT +CTRL+O) brings up the dialog shown in Figure 16.31. This command moves the contents within a layer without moving the layer relative to other layers in the image. The X and Y offset are set individually, in pixels or a variety of other units, including percentage. The OFFSET BY X/2, Y/2 button automatically sets these two fields to half the width and height of the layer, but you can adjust these values manually after pressing the button. EDGE BEHAVIOR is a set of radio buttons with the following three options:

- WRAP AROUND: All pixels moved out of the layer from one side reenter it again from the other side. Figure 16.32 shows the result after pressing the OFFSET BY X/2, Y/2 button with this option selected.

- FILL WITH BACKGROUND COLOR: The vacated areas of the layer are filled with the current background color. This option doesn't work well on a layer with a transparent background and so is not shown.

Figure 16.32 *Offset by x/2, y/2 with Wrap around*

Figure 16.33 *Offset by y/2 with Make transparent*

- MAKE TRANSPARENT: The vacated parts of the layer are filled with transparency. Figure 16.33 shows the result with a vertical offset of y/2 and no horizontal offset.

16.2 Local Transformations

The Toolbox contains nine local transformation tools, as shown in Figure 16.34. You can also find them in the **Image: Tools > Transform**

Figure 16.34 *The transformation tools in the Toolbox*

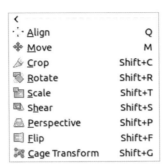

Figure 16.35 *The Image: Tools > Transform Tools menu*

Tools menu, which is shown in Figure 16.35. *Local transformations* act only on an object or region of an image or layer. Keyboard shortcuts also exist for these tools—and for almost all the other tools in the Toolbox. As we present each tool, we show the Toolbox icon, the keyboard shortcut, and the tool pointer.

Shared Properties

All the tools in the **Image: Tools > Transform Tools** menu (except Align and Crop) operate on the current layer, the current selection, or the current path but not on multiple layers simultaneously. Figure 16.36 shows the options for the Move tool. The top row of buttons allows you to decide whether the tool acts on the current layer, the current selection (rather than the selected layer content), or the current path. These buttons are, in fact, the only way to switch among the layer, selection, and path when using a tool from the **Image: Tools > Transform Tools** menu. You make this choice in the individual options for each tool, and your choice does not propagate to the other transformation

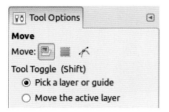

Figure 16.36 *The Move tool options*

Figure 16.37 *Moving the selection*

tools. But changes to the parameters do remain in place for a specific tool until you restart GIMP, so if you use GIMP for a long period of time and change the settings for one of the transformation tools, check the settings before using the tool again. Figure 16.37 shows the result of moving the current selection (which was built with **Image: Layer > Transparency > Alpha to Selection**). The selection, rather than its contents, is moved.

The Rotate, Scale, Shear, and Perspective tools share the same set of options. Although the options shown in Figure 16.38 are for the Rotate tool, the only difference is the dialog's name, which appears in bold at the top, and, in some cases, the presence of a checkbox at the bottom of the dialog, which is discussed later. In this section, we examine all these options in turn.

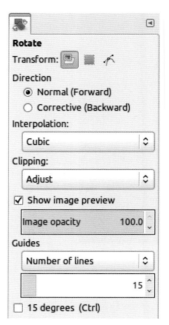

Figure 16.38 *The Rotate tool options*

The DIRECTION can be NORMAL (FORWARD), in which case the image moves with regard to the canvas, or CORRECTIVE (BACKWARD), which causes the grid to move with regard to the image. The CORRECTIVE (BACKWARD) option works well for correcting object deformities within an image, such as warped perspective. When using this option, align a grid with the warped object, like we did in "The Perspective Tool" on page 387.

The INTERPOLATION menu contains four possible algorithms to compute new pixels from old ones. Although NONE is the fastest, the result is very poor, as shown in Figure 16.39. The other three methods do a reasonably good job, but the most processor intensive, SINC (LANCZOS3), yields the best result. Unless your computer is extremely slow or the image being processed is huge, choose SINC (LANCZOS3).

The CLIPPING menu (Figure 16.40) specifies what happens if the layer is larger after a transformation.

Figure 16.39 *Using None as the interpolation algorithm*

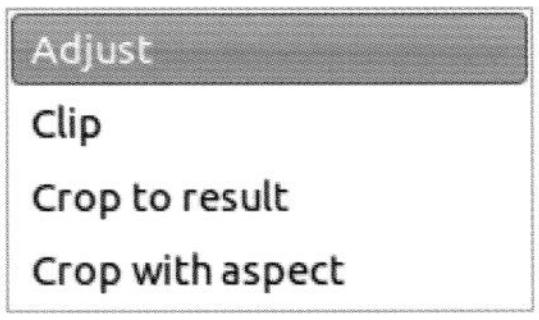

| Adjust |
| Clip |
| Crop to result |
| Crop with aspect |

Figure 16.40 *The Clipping menu*

Figure 16.42 *Clipping with Clip*

Figure 16.43 *Clipping with Crop to result*

Figure 16.41 *Clipping with Adjust*

- ADJUST enlarges the layer to the size of its new contents, as shown in Figure 16.41. If the layer no longer fits in the canvas, use **Image: Image > Fit Canvas to Layers** to enlarge the canvas.

- CLIP clips the layer's contents to the layer's boundaries, as shown in Figure 16.42.

- The other two choices, CROP TO RESULT and CROP WITH ASPECT, work like CLIP and ADJUST, respectively, but they remove any border with no content, a situation that may occur after the transformation. Figure 16.43 shows the case of CROP TO RESULT.

Figure 16.44 *Previewing with an outline*

Figure 16.46 *The Guides menu*

Figure 16.47 *Previewing with the image and with diagonal lines*

Figure 16.45 *Previewing with the image itself*

If the SHOW IMAGE PREVIEW button is unchecked, when you click and drag the image to operate the transformation, the transformed part of the image is not shown, and you see only an outline or some guides. In Figure 16.44, the button is unchecked and there are no guides.

If the SHOW IMAGE PREVIEW button is checked, you can choose the opacity of the image preview, which can help when you want a very precise

transformation. For example, in Figure 16.45, the opacity of the preview was set to 50%.

The GUIDES menu (Figure 16.46) offers a number of choices:

- When NO GUIDES is selected, only an outline of the layer appears while the transformation is in progress. The image appears unchanged until you accept the transformation. See Figures 16.44 and 16.45.

- The next five choices are the same as for the Rectangle Select tool, and they are described in "The Rectangle Select Tool" on page 289. For example, Figure 16.47 shows the case of Diagonal lines, with an image preview.

Figure 16.48 *Previewing with a grid but without the image*

Figure 16.49 *Previewing with the image and a grid*

- When LINE SPACING is selected, a grid is displayed over the layer, as shown in Figure 16.48. You can change the spacing of grid lines by using the field at the bottom of the options dialog, as shown in Figure 16.38.

You can combine the guides and a visible image preview, as shown in Figure 16.49.

Figure 16.50 *The Move tool's icon and pointer*

Figure 16.51 *The Alignment tool's icon and pointer*

The Move Tool

The Move tool is the simplest transformation tool. Select it by pressing $\boxed{\text{M}}$ or clicking its icon in the Toolbox. Its icon and pointer are shown in Figure 16.50. Once you select the Move tool, click and drag a layer, selection, or path to move it. In the tool options (see Figure 16.36), you can choose whether to move the active layer, selection, or path, or you can select the object to be moved by clicking it. In the present example, we wanted to move the rose, so we were careful to click a nontransparent pixel so as not to accidentally move the underlying layer instead. If the image has a guide, you can move it if you click close enough to it (the guide turns red). Toggle between the two options by pressing the $\boxed{\text{SHIFT}}$ key.

If a selection exists, but LAYER MOVE mode is active, temporarily shift to SELECTION MOVE mode by pressing $\boxed{\text{CTRL+ALT}}$ before making a move.

Use the arrow keys on the keyboard to move the active layer or path. Each key press moves the layer or path by 1 pixel in the corresponding direction. If you press and hold $\boxed{\text{SHIFT}}$, each key press moves the layer or path by 50 pixels.

The Align Tool

Select the Align tool by pressing $\boxed{\text{Q}}$ or clicking its icon in the Toolbox. Its icon and pointer are

Figure 16.52 *The Align tool options*

Figure 16.53 *An image with three layers and a selection*

Figure 16.54 *The Layers dialog for Figure 16.53*

Figure 16.55 *The Relative to menu*

shown in Figure 16.51, and its options dialog is shown in Figure 16.52. In this case, the buttons in the options dialog are actually used to operate the tool.

We used the image in Figure 16.53 to demonstrate the Align tool. The Layers dialog for this image is shown in Figure 16.54. The outline of the middle layer, which contains the rose, is visible in Figure 16.53. We selected the portrait in the top layer with the Scissors Select tool

and then cut and pasted it into the image as a new layer with a transparent background. A selection, built around the rose and then moved down in the image, is also present.

When you select the Align tool, the mouse pointer changes to a hand. Click in the image to select the object (i.e., a layer) that you will move, called the *source*. To select several objects, either SHIFT-click all the objects after the first one or click and drag to build a rectangle around all the objects. The selected objects are indicated by small squares in the corners of the enclosing rectangle.

When you select at least one object, the buttons in the options dialog become active. Choose the alignment *target*, which is the object that the selected objects will be aligned to. Six choices are located in the RELATIVE TO menu, which is shown in Figure 16.55:

- FIRST ITEM: The target is the first selected object. If only one object is selected, or if the selection is a rectangle, this choice behaves the same as IMAGE.

- IMAGE: The target is the image itself. In Figure 16.56, we selected the portrait layer and clicked the middle button in the lower row.

- SELECTION: The target is an invisible rectangle around your selection whose height

Figure 16.56 *Aligning the source to the middle of the image*

Figure 16.58 *Aligning the source to the middle and center of the active layer*

Figure 16.57 *Aligning the source to the middle and center of the selection*

Figure 16.59 *Aligning two layers along the left and top edges of the image*

and width match that of the selection exactly. For example, in Figure 16.57, we clicked the middle button in both button rows to center the portrait in the middle of our selection, the outline of the rose, which is visible in Figure 16.53.

- ACTIVE LAYER: The idea is simple, as demonstrated in Figure 16.58. Again, we clicked the two middle buttons to position the portrait in the center of the rose.

- ACTIVE CHANNEL: This option allows you to align to a selection made previously that's saved in a channel.

- ACTIVE PATH: This option allows you to align to a path.

The second set of buttons, labeled DISTRIBUTE, act based on the OFFSET field setting. In Figure 16.59, we selected the two upper layers as the source and aligned them along the left and

Figure 16.60 *Using the same options as in Figure 16.59 but with an offset of 100 pixels*

Figure 16.61 *The Crop tool's icon and pointer*

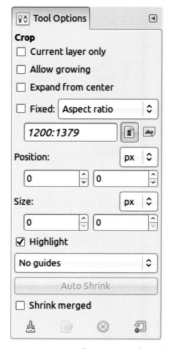

Figure 16.62 *The Crop tool options*

top edges of the image. In Figure 16.60, we did the same thing but used the DISTRIBUTE buttons and an offset of 100 pixels.

The Crop Tool

To select the Crop tool, press SHIFT+C or click its icon in the Toolbox. Its icon and pointer are shown in Figure 16.61, and its options are shown in Figure 16.62. This tool removes any parts of the image that are outside a selected rectangle. Build the rectangle the same way you would build a selection with the Rectangle Select tool. Normally the selected area is highlighted, as shown in Figure 16.63. When you're satisfied with the selection, click inside it or press ENTER to crop the image.

The Crop tool has several options.

- The CURRENT LAYER ONLY checkbox allows you to crop just the current layer, rather than the whole image. The selection automatically stops at the layer's boundary, as shown in Figure 16.64.

- The ALLOW GROWING checkbox allows the selection to cross the boundaries of the image or the layer. For example, in Figure 16.65 both the ALLOW GROWING and the

CURRENT LAYER ONLY checkboxes are checked. Figure 16.66 shows the result. Notice that the boundaries of the flower layer are extended based on the selection.

- The EXPAND FROM CENTER checkbox works as it does with the selection tools: The first click will be the center of the selection, rather than a corner. Note, however, that you can't toggle this option with the CTRL key, as you can with the selection tools.

- All the remaining fields—FIXED, POSITION, SIZE, HIGHLIGHT, AUTO SHRINK, SHRINK MERGED, as well as the use of guides—work in the same way as they do with the Rectangle Select tool, described in "The Rectangle Select Tool" on page 289.

Figure 16.63 *Selecting the cropping rectangle*

Figure 16.65 *Cropping the current layer with Allow growing active*

Figure 16.64 *Cropping the current layer only*

Figure 16.66 *The result of Figure 16.65*

The Rotate Tool

To select the Rotate tool, press $\boxed{\text{SHIFT+R}}$ or click its icon in the Toolbox. Its icon and pointer appear in Figure 16.67. Note that you can also access the Rotate tool via **Image: Layer > Transform > Arbitrary Rotation**. Almost all of its options have been discussed previously (see Figure 16.38 on page 378). Only one option is specific to this tool: the 15 DEGREES checkbox, which you can toggle by pressing $\boxed{\text{CTRL}}$. When

active, this option forces the rotation angle to be a multiple of $15°$.

After selecting the tool, click the image. The dialog shown in Figure 16.68 pops up. The rotation center is initially the center of the object being rotated, but you can change it by clicking and dragging. You can change the angle in three ways: Drag the object in the Image window; move the slider in the dialog; or adjust the number displayed in the ANGLE field by typing,

Figure 16.67 *The Rotate tool's icon and pointer*

Figure 16.68 *The Rotate dialog*

Figure 16.69 *Rotation in progress*

using the mouse wheel, or clicking the small arrows. Click the ROTATE button to finalize the rotation.

If a selection is active, only its content is affected by the transformation tools. Figure 16.69 shows a rotation in progress: Only the region of the portrait layer within the selection is being rotated. The result is shown in Figure 16.70. The selected pixels from the portrait layer are now a floating selection.

Figure 16.70 *The result of rotation*

Figure 16.71 *The Scale tool icon and pointer*

The Scale Tool

Select the Scale tool by pressing SHIFT+T or clicking its icon in the Toolbox. Its icon and pointer are shown in Figure 16.71. Although the Scale tool appears to do the same thing as **Image: Layer > Scale Layer**, it's actually rather different. **Image: Layer > Scale Layer** acts on the entire image, not on a selection or path, and it doesn't offer a preview or the corrective mode option.

Figure 16.72 shows the scaling process with this tool. The current layer is the portrait layer, which has an active selection. The preview is the image, with the opacity of the region being scaled set to 60%. The center of the scaled area is marked with a circle and a cross, and you move it by clicking and dragging. Press ENTER to scale the selection, which then becomes a floating selection.

Figure 16.72 *Scaling a selection*

Figure 16.74 *Shearing a layer*

Figure 16.73 *The Shear tool icon and pointer*

Figure 16.75 *The Perspective tool's icon and pointer*

The Scale tool is surprisingly versatile. Try the following:

- Click and drag the circle at the center of the area being scaled to move it around in the image, just as the Move tool does.

- Click and drag any other part of the selection or layer to adjust the scaling amount.

- Keep the current aspect ratio by clicking the checkbox in the tool options and the chain in the tool's dialog or by pressing the CTRL key. If you drag the handles on the sides, only one dimension is changed, and the aspect ratio is maintained.

The Shear Tool

Select the Shear tool by pressing SHIFT+S or clicking its icon in the Toolbox. Its icon and pointer are shown in Figure 16.73. Its options are the same as those shown in Figure 16.38

on page 378. It's impossible to shear both vertically and horizontally at the same time. The tool sets the direction of a shearing based on the direction that you drag the mouse after the first click. To shear, click and drag the selection. Figure 16.74 shows the transformation in progress. The preview is opaque, but in the figure, the opacity of the layer being sheared was reduced to 50%. The selection that's acted on by this tool becomes the current selection, and any previous selection is dismissed.

The Perspective Tool

To select the Perspective tool, press SHIFT+P or click its icon in the Toolbox. Its icon and pointer are shown in Figure 16.75. Its options are the same as those presented in Figure 16.38 on page 378.

Figure 16.76 shows the Perspective tool being used on an image with a perspective that's

Figure 16.76 *Applying perspective to an image*

Figure 16.77 *The result of the transformation shown in Figure 16.76*

slightly skewed. For this type of adjustment, Corrective direction mode works best because you can align the grid's vertical and horizontal lines to those of the building.

The result appears in Figure 16.77. Although the adjustment helped, the image is no longer rectangular, and the lens distortion of the camera is visible.

The Flip Tool

You can select the Flip tool by pressing SHIFT+F or clicking its icon in the Toolbox. Its icon and pointer are shown in Figure 16.78. You can choose whether to flip horizontally or vertically (CTRL toggles between these) and whether to flip the current layer, selection, or path. As with previous tools, if a selection exists in the current layer, flipping the layer flips only the part that's

Figure 16.78 *The Flip tool's icon and pointer*

Figure 16.79 *Flipping a selected portion of a layer horizontally*

within the selection. Figure 16.79 shows the image after a selected part of the rose layer was flipped horizontally. As with the other transformation tools, a floating selection is built to contain the flipped pixels.

The only difference between the Flip tool and those tools found in **Image: Layer > Transform** is that this tool allows you to flip a selection or a path instead of just the layer or a portion of the layer.

The Cage Transform Tool

The Cage Transform tool was added to GIMP in version 2.8. Its icon and pointer are shown in Figure 16.80, and its options are shown in Figure 16.81.

Use the Cage Transform tool to distort an object. A *cage* is a polygon built around a target portion of the image. Move the corners of the cage to distort the object within. Our example figure has two layers, one containing the city and one

Figure 16.80 *The Cage Transform tool's icon and pointer*

Cage Transform
- ◉ Create or adjust the cage
- ○ Deform the cage to deform the image
- ☐ Fill the original position of the cage with a plain color

Figure 16.81 *The Cage Transform tool options*

Figure 16.82 *Building the cage*

Figure 16.83 *Deforming the cage*

containing the rose. Select the rose layer and enlarge it to the same size as the image, using **Image: Layer > Layer to Image size**.

Select the Cage Transform tool and make sure the first option, CREATE OR ADJUST THE CAGE, is checked. Build the cage by clicking around the rose. You can move each point after placing it, but you can't delete points, and you can move only the most recently placed point. But once the cage is closed and GIMP has worked for a moment, you can go back and add points or move existing points. This tool has no undo capability, so if you make a mistake, you'll have to start over by temporarily switching to another tool. When you're satisfied, finalize the cage by clicking the first point. Figure 16.82 shows the cage being built.

Once the cage is finalized, two successive on-canvas messages appear briefly, indicating that GIMP is processing. Then the options dialog changes, and DEFORM THE CAGE TO DEFORM THE IMAGE is selected by default. However, you can change it back to CREATE OR ADJUST THE CAGE. This allows you to add a point by clicking and dragging in a segment or to delete a point by clicking it and pressing BACKSPACE. After that, you can click DEFORM THE CAGE TO DEFORM THE IMAGE to go to the next step.

Now you can move the points of the cage to deform the rose. But the computations involved take a while, and you have to wait for the transformation to finish before moving another point. Figure 16.83 shows the result after moving the bottom points of the cage. To finish the transformation, press ENTER. To cancel the transformation, change to another tool.

When used properly, this tool can generate smooth, natural transformations. It works best on multilayer images, particularly on layers that contain objects and transparent background pixels, as with the rose we just transformed. But this

Figure 16.84 *Poor use of the Cage Transform tool (left); filling from the first point (right)*

tool does a poor job on objects that are part of an image because the limits of the cage are sharp and visible, and the cage transformation is only defined on the interior of the cage. Figure 16.84 (left) shows the result of building a rectangular cage in the middle of an image and then enlarging it. Shrinking the cage results in empty geometric spaces. If you check the FILL THE ORIGINAL POSITION OF THE CAGE WITH A PLAIN COLOR option, these spaces are filled with the color of the first point, as shown in Figure 16.84 (right). If the option is unchecked, these spaces show the original contents of the corresponding areas of the image.

17

Filters

Filter is a name used in GIMP to describe a variety of tools: More than 120 filters ship with GIMP. Some filters apply a simple transformation to the current layer, while others do processor-intensive alterations to the entire image and sometimes even build a new image. Note that the word *filter* was used in a more specific way in Chapter 7. Some of the filters described in this chapter conform to that meaning; for example, Unsharp Mask and Convolution Matrix. Others are called filters simply because they are accessed from the **Image: Filters** menu.

In this chapter, we walk through almost all of the entries found in the **Image: Filters** menu. They have little in common besides being in the same menu. After trying in vain to find a logical way to organize this chapter, we decided to just follow the order of the menu. The GIMP developers devised this order using their own logic, and the order they came up with is as good as any we could think of. However, we will omit the following entries:

- WEB is presented in Chapter 8.
- ANIMATION is presented in Chapter 18, along with the other filters that are added by the GAP plug-in set.
- PYTHON-FU and SCRIPT-FU deal with scripts and are presented in Chapter 21.

- ALPHA TO LOGO contains a subset of the logo creation tools that appear in the **Image: File > Create > Logos** menu. They use the Alpha channel of the current image as the source of the logo, while the tools in the LOGOS submenu act on text. As explained in Chapter 4, we won't cover them in this book since they're self-explanatory.

We will also omit the following 10 filters, which we consider no longer useful to anybody: Erase Every Other Row, Video, Xach-Effect, Blinds, Predator, Slide, Filmstrip, Stencil Carve, Stencil Chrome, and Fog. In case you really need one of them, you'll find its description on this book's companion website.

17.1 Common Properties

In this section, we introduce the common properties of all the filters to avoid repetition in the individual descriptions.

The Filters menu begins with four generic entries. The first two entries allow you to quickly repeat or reshow the last filter used.

The first entry ($\boxed{\text{CTRL+F}}$) repeats the previous filter with exactly the same parameters. This is very convenient if you're doing something repetitive that requires multiple applications of the

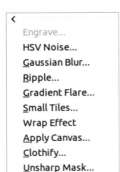

Figure 17.1 *The Image: Filters > Recently Used menu*

same filter. However, it's important to note that this command also repeats the last plug-in used, which may or may not be from the Filters menu. For example, pressing CTRL+F will repeat **Image: Colors > Colorify** but not **Image: Colors > Desaturate**. Colorify is a plug-in; Desaturate is built in to GIMP.

The second entry in the **Image: Filters** menu (SHIFT+CTRL+F) allows you to reshow the dialog of the previous filter and repeat the filter with different parameters. To see the effect of using the same filter with different parameters, apply the filter, then press CTRL+Z to undo the change, followed by SHIFT+CTRL+F to choose new parameters.

The third entry, RECENTLY USED, is a convenient way to access any of the last 10 filters used. As Figure 17.1 shows, some of the filters may be grayed out if they cannot be applied to the current image.

The fourth entry, RESET ALL FILTERS, allows you to set all the filters to their initial state. Most filters have at least one, and often several, parameters, which each have default (initial) values. If you change any of these parameters, the change will be maintained until you quit GIMP or change the parameter again. This is generally convenient, but in some cases you may want to restore the default parameter values for all the filters. Restarting GIMP also restores the parameters to their default values.

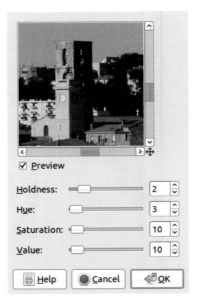

Figure 17.2 *An example of a filter dialog*

Figure 17.2 shows the dialog of the HSV Noise filter, which contains three buttons that are present in all filter dialogs:

- HELP brings up the GIMP help documentation for the filter, as explained in Section 9.6.

- CANCEL closes the filter dialog without applying any changes, but the first three entries in the Filters menu will still refer to that filter, even though it was canceled.

- OK applies the filter with the current parameter values. Some filters act quickly, while others apply many complex changes that take a long time to process. Pressing CTRL+Z undoes any filter.

Many filter dialogs also contain a preview, which is generally rather small by default. Some dialogs allow zooming in, but even at the maximum zoom, the preview is small. Fortunately, when you enlarge the dialog window, the preview is enlarged as well. The preview is either square or in the same proportions as the image, and the proportions of the preview are always maintained when the window size changes. To enlarge the preview, click and drag a corner of the dialog. If you extend one of the sides of the dialog, the proportions of the dialog change, but the preview will stay the same.

Most of the filter descriptions that follow are accompanied by at least one example. Most examples were created using the settings shown in an associated dialog figure, so often we simply show the example without mentioning the settings, to prevent this lengthy chapter from becoming a separate book.

Figure 17.3 *The initial image*

17.2   The Blur Filters

The Blur menu has six entries. All but the first one end with an ellipsis, which indicates that those filters bring up a dialog to set their parameters before acting on the image.

Blur

The Blur filter has no parameters and operates instantly. It works by computing the average of each pixel and its immediate neighbors. On a large image, its effect is imperceptible. Figure 17.3 shows only a small part of a photograph, which is zoomed in to make the effect visible. Figure 17.4 shows the same image after three applications of the Blur filter. This a rather clunky way to adjust the amount of blur on an image, but it is very fast.

Figure 17.4 *After using Blur three times*

Gaussian Blur

Gaussian Blur is the most useful blur filter. Like many filter dialogs, its dialog (see Figure 17.5) contains a preview and a button to toggle the preview on and off, which is checked by default. The preview is smaller than the image itself, but you can scroll around or enlarge it.

Adjusting the BLUR RADIUS determines the intensity of the effect. The blur radius is the radius of the circle containing the pixels that are averaged to compute new pixel values (see

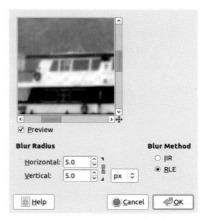

Figure 17.5 *The Gaussian Blur dialog*

Figure 17.6 *Figure 17.3 after Gaussian Blur*

Figure 17.7 *The initial image*

Chapter 7). You can change the units (pixels or an actual distance), but the result depends on the size of the image, so consult the preview when choosing the blur radius. A radius of 10 leads to a visible blur on a 600×400 image but has no perceptible effect on a 3000×4000 image.

You can break the chain between the horizontal and vertical radii and choose different values. The effect is that of a motion blur, as shown in Figure 17.6, where we chose a horizontal radius of 30 pixels and a vertical radius of 0 pixels.

Two blur methods are available, selectable via radio buttons on the right side of the dialog:

- IIR (Infinite Impulse Response) is best suited to photographs and large radius values.
- RLE (Run Length Encoding) is best suited to computer-generated images or images with large areas of the same intensity.

Usually, the difference between these is minor, and you can safely choose either one.

Motion Blur

The Motion Blur filter is actually three different filters, with different properties. We demonstrate on the photograph shown in Figure 17.7. The Motion Blur filter dialog (see Figure 17.8) contains the following:

- A preview similar to the one in the Gaussian Blur filter dialog.

Figure 17.8 *The Motion Blur dialog*

- Three blur types: LINEAR, RADIAL, and ZOOM.
- Parameters that may be available, depending on the blur type: For linear type, LENGTH and ANGLE are available; for radial type, BLUR CENTER and ANGLE; for zoom type, BLUR CENTER and LENGTH.

The BLUR CENTER is set numerically, which is not very intuitive. The default value is the center of the image. The easiest way to choose a specific location as the new center is to hover the mouse

Figure 17.9 *A linear motion blur*

Figure 17.11 *A zoom motion blur*

Figure 17.10 *A radial motion blur*

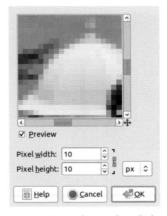

Figure 17.12 *The Pixelize dialog*

over the new center and note the pointer coordinates, which appear in the bottom bar of the Image window. You can then input the relevant coordinates into the field in the dialog.

Linear motion blur appears to move the pixels in a direction determined by the angle and by the distance determined by the length parameter. This simulates the effect of movement in a photograph (see Figure 17.9).

Radial motion blur simulates a spinning motion around the given center and by the given angle (see Figure 17.10). This effect is processor intensive and so takes a long time to run.

When a zoom motion blur is applied, the subject appears to be moving toward the camera (if BLUR OUTWARD is checked) or away from the camera (if BLUR OUTWARD is unchecked).

The blur center determines where the image is sharp, and the length determines the intensity of the simulated movement. This blur type also takes a long time, but not as long as the radial motion blur (see Figure 17.11).

Pixelize

The Pixelize filter creates the effect often used for blurring out the face of a person captured on film or video who has not given the photographer permission to use his likeness. The filter divides the image into equal rectangles, and each one is filled with the average of all the pixels it replaces. In the dialog, shown in Figure 17.12, you can choose the size of the rectangles. They're

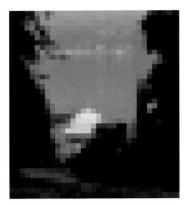

Figure 17.13 *After applying Pixelize*

Figure 17.14 *The initial picture*

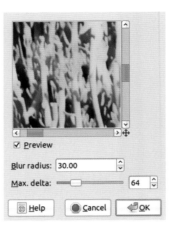

Figure 17.15 *The Selective Gaussian Blur dialog*

Figure 17.16 *After applying Selective Gaussian Blur*

square by default, but you can break the chain to make them rectangular. Figure 17.13 shows the result of this filter with 30×30 pixel squares.

Selective Gaussian Blur

Selective Gaussian Blur applies a Gaussian blur selectively (as you may have guessed). Rather than applying the blur to all the pixels, Selective Gaussian Blur acts on pixels only if the value difference between the pixel and its neighbors is less than the MAX. DELTA value.

We demonstrate on the photograph shown in Figure 17.14, which we also used in Chapter 2. The Selective Gaussian Blur filter is designed to blur the background more than the foreground. We chose the parameter values shown in Figure 17.15 to exaggerate the effect so that it's easy to see. In the result, shown in Figure 17.16,

the cat is too blurry, but it does stand out from the background.

Tileable Blur

Tileable Blur is useful for building a tilable design from a single image, using **Image: Filters > Map > Small Tiles**. This filter blurs the image so that the left side fades into the right side, and the top fades into the bottom.

In the Tileable Blur dialog, shown in Figure 17.17, you can choose the radius of the blur and the algorithm. We chose a large radius to exaggerate the effect. The result, shown in Figure 17.18, is somewhat tilable, as shown in Figure 17.19.

Tileable Blur affects the entire image. To avoid this, you could copy a central rectangle from the image and place it in a new, upper

Figure 17.17 *The Tileable Blur dialog*

Figure 17.18 *After applying Tileable Blur*

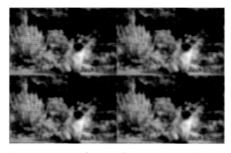

Figure 17.19 *After applying Image: Filters > Map > Small Tiles*

Figure 17.20 *After adding a copy of an unblurred rectangle of the original image*

Figure 17.21 *The initial image, and after applying Antialias*

layer, then apply the Tileable Blur filter to the background layer. Merge the layers and apply the Small Tiles filter. The result is shown in Figure 17.20. The blurred border would look more natural if we feathered the outer edge of the crisp top layer.

17.3 The Enhance Filters

There are eight entries in the Enhance menu. As in the Blur menu, the first entry lacks a dialog.

Antialias

The Antialias filter can be used to add antialiasing to borders within an image.

Figure 17.21 (left) shows a line drawn with the Pencil tool, zoomed to 800%. Figure 17.21 (right) shows the same line after antialiasing. The filter operates instantly, without any dialog.

Deinterlace

A video camera simulates motion by capturing a large set of images, usually 25 or 30 frames per second. More accurately, the video camera captures 50 or 60 half-frames per second. These half-frames, called *fields*, are composed of horizontal lines separated by a distance equal to their height. A frame is built by *interlacing* two fields from top to bottom. A line is taken from the first field, then a line is taken from the second field, and so on.

The two fields that are interlaced in a frame are not captured at precisely the same moment,

Figure 17.22 *The initial image*

Figure 17.23 *The Deinterlace dialog*

Figure 17.24 *Deinterlace, using only the odd field*

Figure 17.25 *Deinterlace, using only the even field*

Figure 17.26 *The initial image*

which can result in a strange effect if the subject is moving quickly. This effect is shown in Figure 17.22.

The Deinterlace filter removes half of the scan lines, either the odd ones or the even ones, and replaces each of them with an interpolation between the neighboring lines. Its dialog (see Figure 17.23) contains only a choice between the odd and even fields.

If you compare Figures 17.24 and 17.25, you can clearly see the movement of the cat's head.

Despeckle

Despeckle removes dots or scratches from images and can correct the speckled appearance of a scanned magazine page. However, it works automatically and can accidentally remove details from an image, so it should be used with care.

The photograph shown in Figure 17.26 is marred by tiny black dots due to its age. The

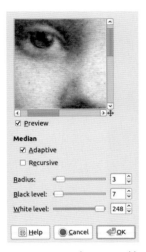

Figure 17.27 *The Despeckle dialog*

Despeckle filter dialog (see Figure 17.27) contains a preview and the following parameters:

- ADAPTIVE mode computes the radius based on the histogram. If unchecked, the radius is set manually using the corresponding slider (see RADIUS, below).

- RECURSIVE mode causes the filter to act repeatedly on the image, which intensifies the effect.

- RADIUS is relevant only in non-adaptive mode. It specifies the size of the area around each pixel, from 1, which corresponds to 3×3, to 20, which corresponds to 41×41. A larger radius blends surrounding colors and increases the filter's processing time.

- BLACK LEVEL sets the threshold value below which dark pixels are removed.

- WHITE LEVEL sets the threshold value above which light pixels are removed.

Figure 17.28 shows the result of applying Despeckle in adaptive mode on Figure 17.26. Figures 17.29 and 17.30 show non-adaptive mode results, with a radius of 2 for the first image and 7 for the second.

Figure 17.28 *After applying Despeckle in adaptive mode*

Figure 17.29 *After applying Despeckle without adaptive mode*

Figure 17.30 *After applying Despeckle with a large radius*

Figure 17.31 *The initial image*

Figure 17.33 *After applying Destripe*

Figure 17.32 *The Destripe dialog*

Destripe

Destripe is used to remove vertical stripes generated by a poor-quality scanner. This filter creates a pattern of vertical stripes that cancel out the striping produced by the scanner. While this filter can be effective, selecting optimal settings can be challenging.

Figure 17.31 shows an initial, striped image, Figure 17.32 shows the filter dialog, and Figure 17.33 shows the effect of the filter. The only setting is WIDTH, which specifies the strength of the filter. High values are generally not advisable, since they often have no effect or, worse, they actually generate more stripes. Checking CREATE HISTOGRAM replaces the image with the pattern that would be used to destripe the image, which can be used to create interesting textures.

NL Filter

NL (Non Linear) Filter does a variety of things. It requires a layer without an Alpha channel, and it uses a hexagonal block of pixels surrounding the target pixel instead of the square blocks used by most other filters. Depending on the mode setting, NL Filter can apply three transformations (see Figure 17.34):

- ALPHA TRIMMED MEAN smooths the image when the ALPHA value is low, and it removes noise when ALPHA is at its maximum. RADIUS specifies the effect's intensity.

- OPTIMAL ESTIMATION uses an adaptive method to smooth the image, which is good for removing noise due to dithering in color images. ALPHA specifies the noise threshold, above which the filter has no effect, and RADIUS specifies the effect's intensity.

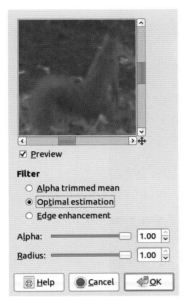

Figure 17.34 *The NL Filter dialog*

- EDGE ENHANCEMENT sharpens the image, and ALPHA sets the intensity of the effect, while RADIUS controls the width of the edges.

Red Eye Removal

Red Eye Removal is an automated tool for correcting the effect of flash photography on a person's pupils. Depending on the image, this filter can work well or quite poorly.

First, try this filter on the photograph shown in Figure 2.77 on page 47. The red color in the girl's eyes isn't very saturated or bright. When the filter is selected, the dialog shown in Figure 17.35 appears. The preview shows that if the default parameters are used, the lips and the left cheek will be discolored. The dialog informs us that "Manually selecting the eyes may improve the results."

Select the eyes by drawing a rough outline around them with the Free Select Tool, and choose the filter again. This time, after an adjustment with the THRESHOLD slider, the result

Figure 17.35 *First attempt with the Red Eye Removal filter*

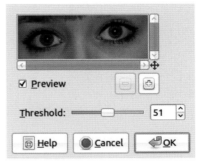

Figure 17.36 *Second attempt with Red Eye Removal*

Figure 17.37 *After applying Red Eye Removal*

Figure 17.38 *Another example of red eye*

Figure 17.39 *A rather poor result*

Figure 17.40 *The initial image*

Figure 17.41 *After applying Sharpen*

looks good. The dialog is shown in Figure 17.36, and the result is shown in Figure 17.37.

In the second example (see Figure 17.38), the red color is very bright but not very saturated. In the HSV model, the S value is 48 and the V value is 100. The filter doesn't work very well under these conditions, as shown in Figure 17.39. In the final image, the eyes look dull, and the bridge of the nose has a red cast.

For more tips on removing red eye, see "More Correction Methods for Red Eye" on page 47.

Sharpen

Sharpen is a simplified version of Unsharp Mask, which is the next filter in the menu. Sharpen works well for simple tasks, like enhancing a photograph that's blurry because of the interpolation that occurs in a digital camera or a scanner or due to an image's being scaled up or down. Edges are almost always slightly blurred in a digital photograph, and the simple Sharpen filter in GIMP works much better than the built-in correction features of current digital cameras. The filter's dialog has only one parameter: SHARPNESS.

Figure 17.40 is a good example of a photograph that would benefit from sharpening. Color and size adjustments led to interpolation, which left the image very blurry. Figure 17.41 shows the result of using the Sharpen filter with a sharpness of 77.

Unsharp Mask

Despite its paradoxical name, the Unsharp Mask filter is an excellent sharpening tool, offering much more control than the Sharpen filter.

Figure 17.42 *A very strong application of Unsharp Mask*

Figure 17.43 *The Value layer after decomposition*

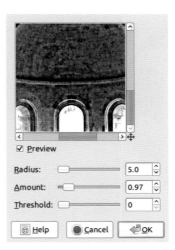

Figure 17.44 *The Unsharp Mask dialog*

Figure 17.45 *The Value layer after sharpening*

Figure 17.46 *After applying Unsharp Mask with decomposition*

The parameters allow you to adjust the amount of sharpening. Note that color distortions may occur if the amount is really high. A dramatic example is shown in Figure 17.42. To sharpen a picture dramatically without color distortion, first decompose the initial image to HSV layers. Select **Image: Colors > Components > Decompose**, and choose the HSV model and DECOMPOSE TO LAYERS.

Hide the Hue and Saturation layers, and from the Value layer (Figure 17.43), select the Unsharp Mask filter and set the parameters as shown in Figure 17.44.

After sharpening the Value layer, as shown in Figure 17.45, select **Image: Colors > Components > Recompose**. The result is shown in Figure 17.46. By carefully adjusting the parameters, it's possible to get a much better result than

Figure 17.47 *After applying Apply Lens*

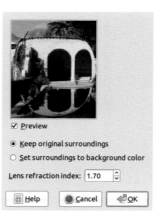

Figure 17.48 *The Apply Lens dialog*

with the Sharpen filter. Note that it's always best to sharpen an image after it's been scaled to its final size and resolution.

The three parameters of Unsharp Mask are as follows:

- RADIUS specifies the width of the mask and, as a result, the visibility of the sharpening effect. The optimal value depends on the resolution of the image and the size of the details within it.

- AMOUNT specifies how much edge contrast will be created. A large value exaggerates the edge by adding a rim to it (see Figure 17.42).

- THRESHOLD specifies the minimum difference between pixel values that indicates an edge. In effect, it separates signal from noise. A high value prevents false detection of edges but also reduces the effect of the filter.

17.4 The Distorts Filters

The Distorts menu includes 18 loosely related filters. All 18 filters have a dialog, but the Engrave filter requires an Alpha channel and will be grayed out if none exists. We omit three filters because they are seldom useful: Blinds, Erase Every Other Row, and Video.

Apply Lens

Apply Lens simulates a distorted view of the image through a spherical lens, as shown in Figure 17.47.

The dialog, shown in Figure 17.48, contains settings for the refraction index of the lens [1 to 100] and the handling of the image surroundings, which can be retained, made transparent (an Alpha channel is required), or filled with the background color.

Curve Bend

Curve Bend deforms the contents of an image based on a curve that you can manipulate in the filter dialog.

When the filter is selected (in this case to work on the image in Figure 17.49), it brings up the dialog shown in Figure 17.50. The AUTOMATIC PREVIEW button is unchecked by default, because it's processor intensive, and generally it's best to use PREVIEW ONCE instead. On the right are the curves. You can choose to deform the UPPER or LOWER curve. If the Curve Type is SMOOTH, add points to the curve and move the points to deform it further. If the Curve Type is FREE, build the curve by drawing in the grid with the mouse.

You can COPY the upper curve to the lower one, and vice versa, or MIRROR them or SWAP them. You can also RESET the current curve. The

Figure 17.49 *The initial picture*

Figure 17.51 *After applying Curve Bend*

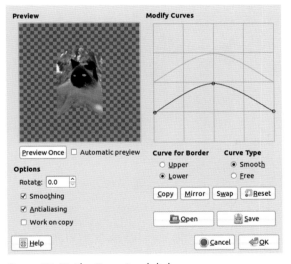

Figure 17.50 *The Curve Bend dialog*

settings of the curves can be saved to a file and loaded later.

The SMOOTHING and ANTIALIASING buttons on the left should usually be left checked. When WORK ON COPY is checked, the transformation is done to a new layer, and the original layer isn't changed. Finally, you can use the ROTATE field to rotate the curves on the layer. If the rotation angle is 90°, the curves will align vertically, with the upper curve on the left side.

Figure 17.51 shows our result. The current background color fills empty areas in the image.

Emboss

Emboss is available only for RGB images. It uses the values of the image's pixels to create relief. Bright areas are raised, and dark ones lowered.

The dialog, shown in Figure 17.52, has three parameters:

- AZIMUTH is the direction of the light source. When this is set to 0°, the light appears to be coming from the right. When this is set to 90°, the light appears to come from above.

- ELEVATION is the angle of the light source above the horizon.

- DEPTH specifies the intensity of the relief. With a very low value, the embossed relief is almost flat. With a high value, the image is dark and shadowy.

The result, shown in Figure 17.53, is a grayscale image in RGB mode. If BUMPMAP is checked, the result is in color, and the relief is smoother (see Figure 17.54).

Engrave

Engrave requires an Alpha channel. It simulates the engraving found in old books, in which horizontal stripes of variable width give an impression of relief.

In the Engrave dialog, HEIGHT is the width of the lines, and small values correspond to thinner

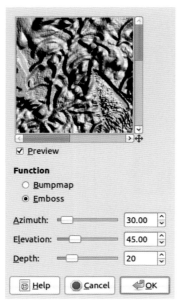

Figure 17.52 *The Emboss dialog*

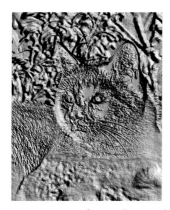

Figure 17.53 *After applying Emboss*

lines. LIMIT LINE WIDTH, if checked, ensures that the parallel lines don't touch.

The result of this filter is a black and white image in RGB mode (Figure 17.55).

IWarp

Because it can be used in animation, this filter is covered in detail in Chapter 18. It can be

Figure 17.54 *After applying Emboss with Bumpmap mode*

Figure 17.55 *After applying Engrave*

used to create a silly caricature or to make subtle changes to a photograph.

We demonstrate on a picture of one of the authors of this book, who will surely not sue us for what we're doing to him (see Figure 17.56). With a deform radius of 20, we moved the nose down, enlarged both eyes, swirled the mouth in both directions, and shrank the chin. With a radius of 72, we moved the hair down on the forehead. The disturbing result appears in Figure 17.57.

Lens Distortion

Lens Distortion simulates the various distortions that can occur due to camera lens imperfections. Since a distortion in the reverse direction can

Figure 17.56 *The initial image*

Figure 17.57 *After applying IWarp*

Figure 17.58 *The Lens Distortion dialog*

Figure 17.59 *The initial image*

cancel an existing one, this filter may also be used to correct real camera distortions.

Figure 17.58 shows the filter dialog when applied to the photograph shown in Figure 17.59. The preview has two zoom buttons, and there are six setting sliders, which all have a range of [−100 to +100]:

- MAIN is the strength of the spherical distortion. If it's positive, the effect is convex, and if it's negative, the effect is concave.

- EDGE works like MAIN, above, but it acts on the edges of the image.

- ZOOM enlarges or reduces the image.

- BRIGHTEN sets the so-called *vignetting* effect: if positive, the edges of the image are darker, and if negative, they're brighter.

- X SHIFT specifies a horizontal image shift caused by poor lens alignment.

- Y SHIFT does the same but vertically.

If the values of MAIN and EDGE are both low, the effect of changing the other sliders may not be perceptible.

The result is shown in Figure 17.60. To find the proper settings to correct the results of a digital camera, you could take a picture of a large rectangular sheet with straight lines on it. Since the pattern is simple and bold, you can adjust the

Figure 17.60 *After applying Lens Distortion*

parameters until you have corrected any distortion and then note the parameter values.

Mosaic

Mosaic simulates a mosaic by breaking the image up into small tiles. Its dialog, shown in Figure 17.61, has many settings:

- TILING PRIMITIVES allows you to pick the shape of the tiles.
- TILE SIZE [5 to 100] is the size of the largest side of the tiles.
- TILE HEIGHT [1 to 50] controls the amount of relief. If this value is large relative to tile size, the tiles become spherical.
- TILE SPACING [1 to 50] is the width of the black channels between tiles.
- TILE NEATNESS ranges from 0 (totally random tile shapes) to 1 (totally regular tile shapes).
- LIGHT DIRECTION determines how the tiles are lit. It is generally best left at the default value of 135° (lit from the upper left).
- COLOR VARIATION ranges from 0 (homogeneous blocks of tiles) to 1 (strong color variations between neighboring tiles).
- ANTIALIASING smooths the tile contours.
- COLOR AVERAGING makes each tile a single color, which is the average of the pixels it contains.

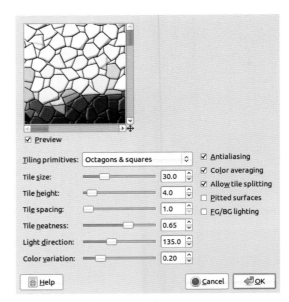

Figure 17.61 *The Mosaic dialog*

- ALLOW TILE SPLITTING allows very small tiles such that the tile pattern follows the object borders in the image.
- PITTED SURFACES gives the tiles a rough surface texture.
- FG/BG LIGHTING uses the foreground color for light areas and the background color for shadowy areas.

The result is shown in Figure 17.62.

Newsprint

Newsprint simulates the dithering used to convert an image for offset printing, for a newspaper for example.

The dialog is shown in Figure 17.63. (We have omitted the preview to save space.) The parameters are divided into three groups:

- RESOLUTION specifies the size of the colored spots that will make up the image.

  - INPUT SPI is the input resolution in samples per inch. It's automatically set to the image resolution.

Figure 17.62 *After applying Mosaic*

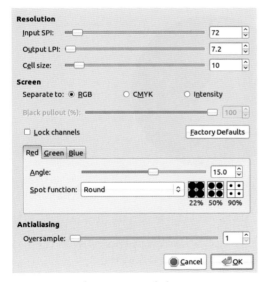

Figure 17.63 *The Newsprint dialog*

Figure 17.64 *After applying Newsprint*

CMYK, the image is internally converted, then dithered, and then converted back to RGB. In INTENSITY, the image is internally converted to grayscale, and the final result is used as an Alpha channel for the image.

- BLACK PULLOUT determines the percentage of black used when converting RGB to CMYK.

- LOCK CHANNELS copies the settings below it from one channel to the others.

- FACTORY DEFAULTS resets the channel parameters to their default values.

- For each channel, the ANGLE of the cell grid and the SPOT FUNCTION can be set.

- ANTIALIASING is useless when printing but useful if this filter is being used for special effects.

Figure 17.64 displays the result.

Pagecurl

Pagecurl simulates the curling of paper. The dialog (Figure 17.65) has the following parameters:

- CURL LOCATION: The four radio buttons allow you to choose the corner that will curl, and

- OUTPUT LPI is the desired output resolution in lines per inch.

- CELL SIZE changes the size of the spots. It's correlated to the Output LPI.

- SCREEN controls the dithering parameters.

  - SEPARATE TO has three radio buttons that determine the color space for decomposition. In RGB, there is no conversion. In

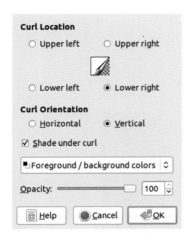

Figure 17.65 *The Pagecurl dialog*

Figure 17.66 *After applying Pagecurl*

an icon in the middle illustrates the current selection.

- CURL ORIENTATION: The fold can be horizontal or vertical, and the icon in the dialog also reflects this selection.

- SHADE UNDER CURL: Checking this box adds a shadow to the image, beneath the curl.

- The colors used for the underside of the page are the current foreground and background colors, the current gradient, or the current gradient reversed.

- The fold is created as a new layer, and its opacity can be set in the dialog of the filter, as well as in the Layers dialog.

Figure 17.66 shows the result of the Pagecurl filter.

Polar Coordinates

Polar Coordinates transforms a rectangular image into a circular one by wrapping and stretching the image.

In the dialog of Polar Coordinates, CIRCLE DEPTH IN PERCENT determines how circular the result will be. At 100%, the result is a perfect circle, and if it is 0%, it is a square. Intermediate values yield a square with rounded sides. OFFSET ANGLE rotates the image by the specified angle.

Figure 17.67 *After applying Polar Coordinates*

The three checkboxes do the following:

- MAP BACKWARDS maps the pixels from right to left, instead of from left to right.

- MAP FROM TOP maps the top of the image to the center of the circle. By default, the bottom is mapped to the center.

- TO POLAR maps the image to a circle, cuts along the top and vertical radius, and then extends the image to create a rectangle.

The result of Polar Coordinates is shown in Figure 17.67. The background color is white, and the MAP FROM TOP button is checked.

Using the photo shown in Figure 17.68, and unchecking the MAP FROM TOP button, we get in

Figure 17.68 *The initial image*

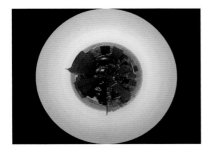

Figure 17.69 *A new, weird planet created with Polar Coordinates*

Figure 17.69 a new planet in the black sky provided by the background color.

Ripple

Ripple simulates the reflection of the image on a rippled water surface.

Its dialog, shown in Figure 17.70, offers the following parameter settings:

- ANTIALIASING softens the borders in the image and is best left checked.

- RETAIN TILABILITY should be checked if you're building a tilable pattern.

- ORIENTATION allows you to select horizontal or vertical ripples.

- EDGES specifies what should be done with empty spaces along the image's edges:

  - WRAP: Pixels that shift off the canvas on one side re-enter on the other side.

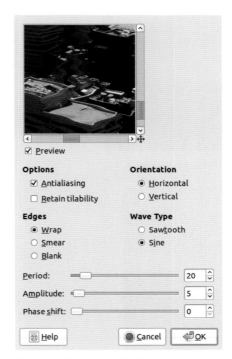

Figure 17.70 *The Ripple dialog*

  - SMEAR: Neighboring pixels are extended to fill the holes.

  - BLACK: Black pixels fill the holes.

- WAVE TYPE may be SINE for smooth ripples or SAWTOOTH for spiky ones.

- PERIOD [1 to 200] specifies the distance between two consecutive ripples.

- AMPLITUDE [0 to 200] specifies the height of the ripples.

- PHASE SHIFT [0 to 360] changes the distance between the beginning of the first ripple and the edge of the image.

Figure 17.71 shows the result of Ripple.

Shift

Shift displaces all pixels in the image, vertically or horizontally, by a random amount within set limits.

Figure 17.71 *After applying Ripple*

Figure 17.72 *After applying Shift*

The dialog contains only a few settings:

- Direction of the shift, either vertical or horizontal
- Maximum amount of the shift, in pixels or alternative units

Figure 17.72 shows the result of Shift on our garden photo.

Value Propagate

Value Propagate spreads pixels at the color borders of the image.

We demonstrate on the image shown in Figure 17.73. Since there are many adjustable parameters, we show a couple of interesting alternative results.

Figure 17.73 *The initial image*

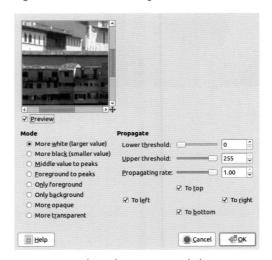

Figure 17.74 *The Value Propagate dialog*

The many parameters are shown in Figure 17.74. First, take a look at the PROPAGATE section. At the bottom, there are four checkboxes for the four directions; most of the time it's best to check all four. The three sliders specify the intensity of the transformation. A pixel will not be propagated if its value difference from its neighbor is lower than the LOWER THRESHOLD or greater than the UPPER THRESHOLD. The amount of propagation is specified by the PROPAGATING RATE.

Figure 17.75 *Value Propagate in More white mode*

Figure 17.77 *Value Propagate in Middle value to peaks mode*

Figure 17.76 *Value Propagate in More black mode*

Figure 17.78 *Value Propagate in Foreground to peaks mode*

The mode determines which pixels will propagate. The available modes are these:

- MORE WHITE propagates the bright pixels to the dark ones. Figure 17.75 shows the result after three applications.

- MORE BLACK propagates the dark pixels to the bright ones. Figure 17.76 shows the result after three applications.

- MIDDLE VALUE TO PEAKS adds a thin border to the edges, computing its color as the average of the neighboring pixels. Figure 17.77 shows an enlargement of its effect.

- FOREGROUND TO PEAKS fills the propagated pixels with the foreground color. In

Figure 17.78, the foreground color was bright green.

- ONLY FOREGROUND/BACKGROUND propagates only the pixels that are the foreground or background color.

- MORE OPAQUE/TRANSPARENT propagates the pixels that are opaque or transparent.

If the current layer has an Alpha channel, two more checkboxes appear in the dialog. If PROPAGATING ALPHA CHANNEL is unchecked, the propagated pixels use the Alpha of neighboring pixels instead of their own Alpha. If PROPAGATING VALUE CHANNEL is unchecked, the filter operates only on the Alpha channel.

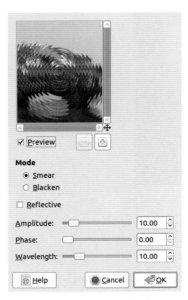

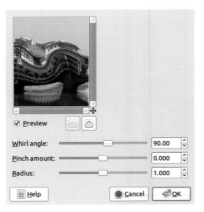

Figure 17.81 *The Whirl and Pinch dialog*

Whirl and Pinch

Whirl and Pinch applies two different distortions to the image. Whirl swirls the image in a pattern similar to water going down the drain, and Pinch distorts the image as if it were a sheet of rubber.

The dialog shown in Figure 17.81 contains only three sliders:

- WHIRL ANGLE [−720° to +720°] is the angle of rotation of the whirl distortion.

- PINCH AMOUNT [−1 to +1] is the intensity and direction of the pinch. A negative value expands from the center, while a positive value squeezes the image inward.

- RADIUS specifies how much of the image is distorted, from 0 (none) to 2 (the entire image).

See Figure 17.82 for the result.

Figure 17.79 *The Waves dialog*

Figure 17.80 *After applying Waves*

Waves

The Waves filter simulates the concentric waves that occur when a stone is dropped into water.

In the dialog, shown in Figure 17.79, the parameters are very similar to those of the Ripple filter. The only new parameter is REFLECTIVE: If this is checked, the waves bounce off the image edges and interfere with one another.

Figure 17.80 shows the result of Waves.

Wind

The Wind filter adds thin horizontal lines to the image in order to create the illusion of strong wind.

The dialog shown in Figure 17.83 offers the following parameters:

- STYLE is WIND (very thin lines) or BLAST (thicker lines).

- DIRECTION is from LEFT or RIGHT.

Figure 17.82 *After applying Whirl and Pinch*

- EDGE AFFECTED is the leading one, the trailing one, or both.

- THRESHOLD [0 to 50] is used to detect borders.

- STRENGTH [1 to 100] is the strength of the effect.

Figure 17.84 shows the result.

17.5 The Light and Shadow Filters

This is yet another menu with a series of disjointed entries. The first five are related to light, the next three to shadows, and the last two are glass effects. We omit the Xach-Effect filter, which we consider not very useful.

Gradient Flare

Gradient Flare simulates the effect that a strong light source can have on a camera lens. The flare is made up of three parts: the Glow, which is the central circle of light; the Rays, which are the streaks of light that extend from the Glow; and the Second Flares, which are the smaller circles of light that sometimes appear in a line, extending out from the Glow.

We demonstrate on the image shown in Figure 17.85. The dialog of Gradient Flare has two

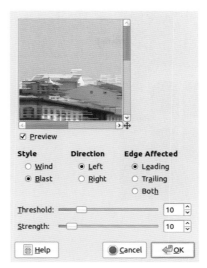

Figure 17.83 *The Wind dialog*

Figure 17.84 *After applying Wind*

tabs, as shown in Figure 17.86. From the Settings tab, you can set the position of the main flare by typing in coordinates, or you can click the preview to specify the position. The other parameters are these:

- RADIUS [0 to 248] specifies the radius of the glare. The slider stops at a rather low value, but you can type a much larger value into the field on the right.

- ROTATION [−180 to +180] changes the rotation of the Glow.

Figure 17.85 *The initial image*

Figure 17.86 *The Gradient Flare dialog, Settings tab*

- HUE ROTATION [−180 to +180] changes the color of the flare.
- VECTOR ANGLE [0 to 359] changes the orientation of the Second Flares.
- VECTOR LENGTH [1 to 1000] changes the length of the Second Flares.
- ADAPTIVE SUPERSAMPLING contains parameters for antialiasing.

The Selector tab of the Gradient Flare filter, shown in Figure 17.87, offers seven predefined flares, which you can select by clicking them. See Figure 17.88 for the result of choosing DIS-TANT_SUN.

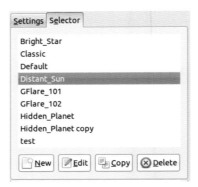

Figure 17.87 *The Gradient Flare dialog, Selector tab*

Figure 17.88 *After applying Gradient Flare*

In the Selector tab (Figure 17.87), four buttons at the bottom allow you to copy an existing flare, edit it, or delete it, or create a new one. The EDIT button brings up the dialog shown in Figure 17.89, with four tabs. The General tab lets you set OPACITY and PAINT MODE. PAINT MODE contains four options: NORMAL, ADDITION, OVERLAY, and SCREEN.

In the Glow tab of the Gradient Flare editor (Figure 17.90), you can choose gradients for the three elements that define the Glow component. Any of the predefined gradients called Flare ... will generally create a nice effect. RADIAL GRA-DIENT determines the main color scheme of the Glow. ANGULAR GRADIENT determines the wrapping pattern of the Glow gradient. The angular gradient begins at the rotation angle

Figure 17.89 *The Gradient Flare editor, General tab*

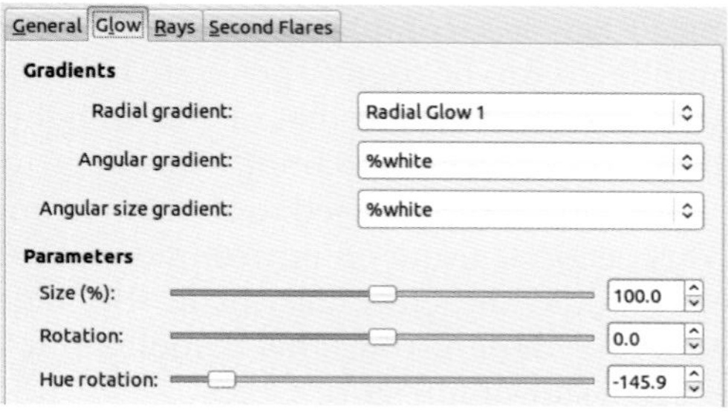

Figure 17.90 *The Gradient Flare editor, Glow tab*

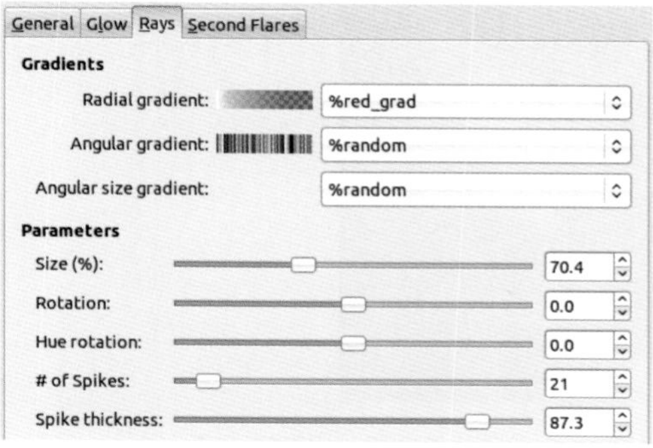

Figure 17.91 *The Gradient Flare editor, Rays tab*

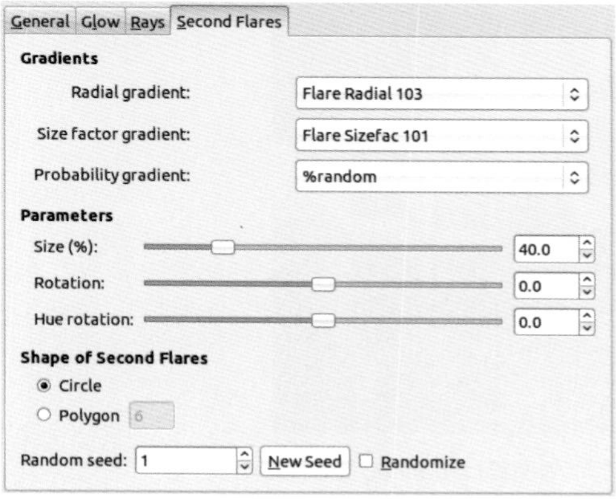

Figure 17.92 *The Gradient Flare editor, Second Flares tab*

specified below and then wraps the radial gradient into a circle or spiral. The colors of the angular gradient are combined with the radial gradient in Multiply blending mode. The third gradient, ANGULAR SIZE GRADIENT, is used to change the radius of the Glow. The brightness of the gradient is used to change the shape of the flare. White enlarges the flare to the full radius, and black shrinks the flare to the central point. A progressive gradient from black to white, for example, results in a spiral glow.

The last three parameters in this tab specify the size of the glow, the rotation angle of the angular gradient, and the color of the glow according to the hue circle.

The number and pattern of the rays can be adjusted using the Rays tab (Figure 17.91). As in the Glow tab, the radial, angular, and angular size gradients determine the color, wrapping pattern, and radius of the Rays, respectively. The parameters below also have the same

effect as those in the Glow tab. The number and thickness of the spikes can also be changed. Experiment with the number of spikes: A large number will lead to an interesting moiré effect.

The parameters of the secondary flares can be specified using the Second Flares tab (Figure 17.92). The three gradients and the three parameters below have the same meaning as they do in the Glow tab and the Rays tab, except that PROBABILITY GRADIENT specifies the position of the second flares, rather than the radius. The shape of the Second Flares can be a circle or a polygon with three or more sides, or it can be a straight line, if the number of sides is set to 1. The RANDOMIZE button uses a random number to randomize everything. However, if you input a random seed, the effects are reproducible (the

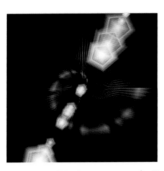

Figure 17.93 *A custom-made Gradient Flare*

Figure 17.94 *After applying Lens Flare*

same seed always produces the same effect). The NEW SEED button generates a new seed.

Figure 17.93 shows an example of a custom-made Gradient Flare.

Lens Flare

Lens Flare simulates the effect of the sun striking the objective lens of a camera.

In the dialog, only one parameter can be changed: the position of the flare effect. The position can be set by clicking the preview or by changing the coordinates. You can also hide the cross that shows the position if you like, although this has no effect on the result. There is currently no way to change the size, shape, or hue of the lens flare.

Figure 17.94 shows the result of the Lens Flare filter.

Figure 17.95 *The Lighting Effects dialog, Options tab*

Lighting Effects

Lighting Effects is a complicated filter. As the name implies, it can be used to generate lighting effects in an image, such as that of a lamp light. In addition, it can be used to bump the image to create relief, and it can be used to simulate complicated reflections using an environment map. This filter would therefore also fit in the Map submenu. We demonstrate this complex filter on the image shown in Figure 17.85.

The Lighting Effects filter dialog has five tabs. Figure 17.95 shows the first one: the Options tab. If the INTERACTIVE button is checked, the light position can be changed by dragging the blue dot in the preview on the left. The DISTANCE slider sets the height of the light above the image relative to the image center. The position and the distance both contribute to the light effect, as you can see if you adjust each in turn. The dialog also contains a checkbox that allows you to create a new image with the effect, rather than altering the original image. An example of Lighting Effects, for which we adjusted parameters only in the Options tab, is shown in Figure 17.96.

The Light tab (Figure 17.97) contains parameters for six different light sources. These parameter settings can be saved in a file for later use. Each source has the following options:

- TYPE can be set to POINT, DIRECTIONAL, or NONE. NONE turns the selected source off, reducing the number of light sources. There

Figure 17.96 *After applying Lighting Effects, no mapping*

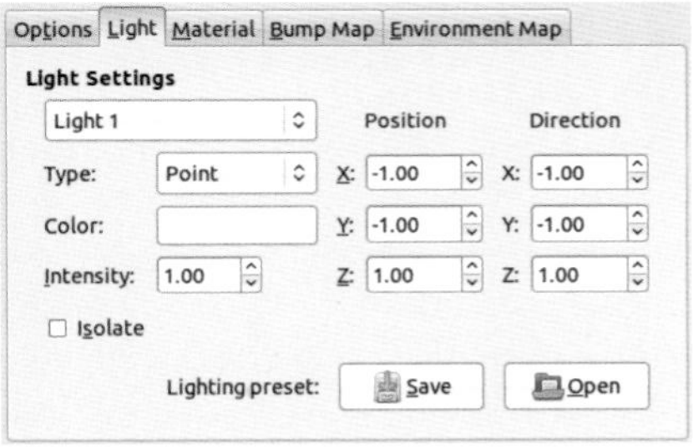

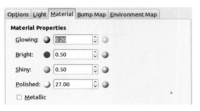

Figure 17.97 *The Lighting Effects dialog, Light tab*

can be anywhere from zero to six active light sources at the same time.

- COLOR is set with the standard Color chooser.

- INTENSITY changes the brightness of the light source and can be set to a number from [0 to 100].

- POSITION is set relative to the center of the image and can be adjusted in the X, Y, and Z directions to any number from [−2 to +2]. POSITION is only active when the POINT type is selected.

- DIRECTION is the same as POSITION, but it affects the direction of the light source and is only active when the DIRECTIONAL type is selected.

Figure 17.98 *The Lighting Effects dialog, Material tab*

Figure 17.99 *The Lighting Effects dialog, Bump Map tab*

- ISOLATE, if checked, alters the preview so that only the light source being set is shown.

The Material tab (Figure 17.98) contains settings for five characteristics of the image surface. Each of them can be set to any positive value, or to zero, but usually values less than 1 work best for the first three:

- GLOWING sets the intensity of areas that are not directly lighted.

- BRIGHT sets the intensity of areas that are directly lighted.

- SHINY sets the highlight intensity.

- POLISHED sets the highlight focus: For low values, the highlight is wide; for high values, it's more focused.

- METALLIC, if checked, simulates the effect of a metallic surface.

The Bump Map tab (Figure 17.99) can be used to add a bump map based on a different picture. The other image must be the same size as the image being transformed, and it must be open in GIMP when the filter is called. Only its Value channel is used to create the bump map, so it doesn't matter whether it's a grayscale or a color image. If the ENABLE BUMP MAPPING box is checked, a bump map image can be chosen. The response curve can be LINEAR, LOGARITHMIC, SINUSOIDAL, or SPHERICAL, and the relief

Figure 17.100 *After applying Lighting Effects, bump mapping*

Figure 17.101 *The Lighting Effects dialog, Environment Map tab*

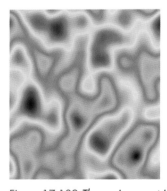

Figure 17.102 *The environment image*

Figure 17.103 *After applying Lighting Effects, environment mapping*

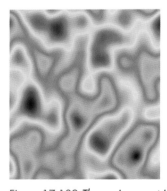

Figure 17.104 *The Sparkle dialog*

can be controlled by adjusting the MAXIMUM HEIGHT field.

Figure 17.100 shows the result of the Lighting Effects filter with bump mapping enabled and the parameters shown in Figure 17.99. The bump map image is the portrait from Figure 5.44 on page 133.

In the Environment Map tab (Figure 17.101) you can choose the Environment image, which must be an RGB image already open in GIMP.

There are no other parameters. In our example, we used Figure 17.102. Figure 17.103 shows the result.

Sparkle

Sparkle adds star-like sparkles to the lightest points in the image, based on a set threshold.

The dialog is shown in Figure 17.104. There are several parameter sliders:

- LUMINOSITY THRESHOLD [0 to 0.1]: Small values lead to fewer sparkles, while large values lead to more sparkles.
- FLARE INTENSITY [0 to 1] specifies the width of the central spots.
- SPIKE LENGTH [1 to 100] alters the length of the sparkles' spikes.
- SPIKE POINTS [0 to 16] determines the number of spikes on each sparkle.
- SPIKE ANGLE [−1 to 360] specifies how the angle of the first large spike is generated with regard to the horizontal axis. If the value is −1, the angle is random.
- SPIKE DENSITY [0 to 1] is the percentage of visible sparkles. A set number are generated by the filter's algorithm, but only a subset will actually appear on the image, based on the density setting.
- TRANSPARENCY [0 to 1] determines the opacity of the sparkles.
- RANDOM HUE [0 to 1] changes the hue, unless the color is set to NATURAL (the color in the image where the sparkle was placed).
- RANDOM SATURATION [0 to 1] operates in the same way as RANDOM HUE, except that it alters the saturation.

There are also three checkboxes:

- PRESERVE LUMINOSITY applies the luminosity of the brightest pixels in the image to the center of the sparkle, which makes the sparkles almost invisible except in the lightest areas of the image.
- INVERSE generates dark sparkles in the darkest parts of the image.
- ADD BORDER generates an image border of sparkles. Try creating an image border with the Spike angle set to −1.

Finally there is a set of three radio buttons to choose the color of the sparkles: foreground, background, or natural (i.e., the color of the brightest—or darkest, if INVERSE is selected—point where the sparkle is drawn).

Figure 17.105 shows the result.

Figure 17.105 *After applying Sparkle*

Supernova

Supernova adds a large spiky star that is vaguely similar to a supernova. In the dialog, shown in Figure 17.106, you can move the center of the supernova by setting the coordinates or by clicking the preview. If the SHOW POSITION box is checked, crosshairs are also shown. Here are the other parameters:

- COLOR is the base color, and clicking the box brings up the Color chooser.
- RADIUS [1 to 100] specifies the size of the supernova's central circle.
- SPOKES [1 to 1024] is the number of 1-pixel-wide spikes extending from the supernova's center.
- RANDOM HUE [0 to 360] randomizes the spike colors.

The result of Supernova is shown in Figure 17.107.

Drop Shadow

Drop Shadow adds a drop shadow to an image or a selection without altering the contents of the image or generating a background layer. You can choose to add a background layer if Drop Shadow is applied to the full image.

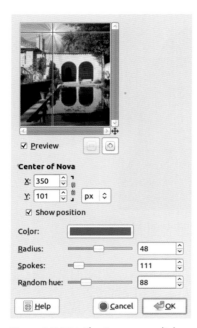

Figure 17.106 *The Supernova dialog*

Figure 17.107 *After applying Supernova*

Figure 17.108 *The initial image and selection*

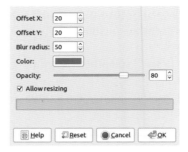

Figure 17.109 *The Drop Shadow dialog*

Figure 17.110 *After applying Drop Shadow*

We built a simple green ellipse, shown in Figure 17.108, to demonstrate this filter.

The dialog is shown in Figure 17.109. The first three parameters set the position and width (called BLUR RADIUS) of the drop shadow. Below that is COLOR, which brings up the Color chooser, and then OPACITY, which sets the opacity of the new layer built by the filter. If the ALLOW RESIZING box is checked, the filter can enlarge the image if necessary once the shadow has been added.

Figure 17.110 shows the result.

Perspective

Perspective applies a shadow with perspective to an image or selection.

In the dialog, shown in Figure 17.111, you can set the ANGLE [0 to 180] between the light source and the target. If it's less than 90°, the shadow is on the right; otherwise it's on the left. The RELATIVE DISTANCE OF HORIZON [0.1 to 24.1] changes the distance of the horizon line relative to the height of the selection. The RELATIVE LENGTH OF SHADOW works the same way, but the shadow

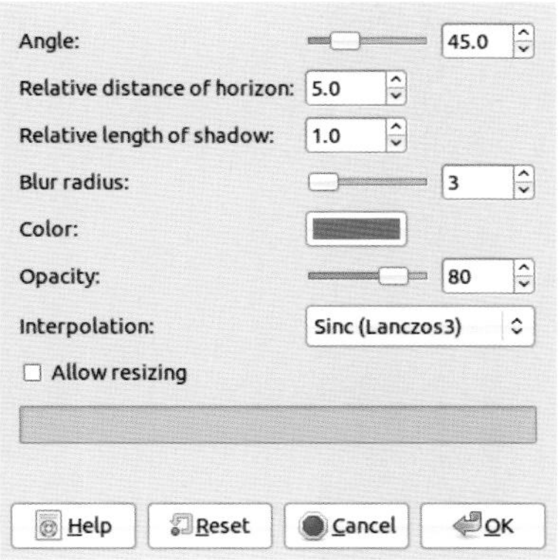

Figure 17.111 *The Perspective dialog*

Figure 17.113 *The HSV Noise dialog*

Figure 17.112 *After applying Perspective*

cannot extend beyond the horizon. The BLUR RADIUS [0 to 1024] is applied to the edges of the shadow. The OPACITY is that of the new layer that's created. Finally, you can set the INTERPO-LATION algorithm and allow or disallow image resizing.

The result is shown in Figure 17.112.

17.6 The Noise Filters

The six Noise filters add noise to an image and therefore do the opposite of the Enhance filters.

HSV Noise

HSV Noise adds noise using the HSV model, so you can adjust the dynamics of the H, S, and V components.

In the dialog, shown in Figure 17.113, you can adjust the strength of the random variation in the three HSV components. HUE varies from [0

Figure 17.114 *The initial image*

to 180], SATURATION and VALUE from [0 to 255]. HOLDNESS [1 to 8] is inversely proportional to the hue variation: 2 results in a stronger variation than 8.

The initial image is shown in Figure 17.114 and the result in Figure 17.115.

Hurl

Hurl applies randomization to all channels of every pixel, including the Alpha channel (if one exists), so the image will be semitransparent.

Figure 17.115 *After applying HSV Noise*

Figure 17.117 *After applying Hurl*

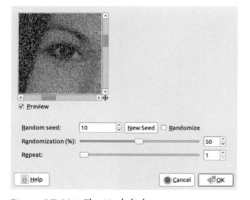

Figure 17.116 *The Hurl dialog*

Figure 17.118 *After applying Pick*

Pick

Pick replaces every pixel with one randomly chosen from the 3 × 3 square of pixels around it.

The dialog is very similar to that of the Hurl filter. However, because of the way the filter works, repeating it results in a very mild effect.

The result is shown in Figure 17.118.

RGB Noise

RGB Noise works like the HSV Noise filter, but its randomization is normalized, which means that dramatic changes are much less probable than minor ones. Additionally, RGB Noise allows you to make changes to the Alpha channel.

The dialog, shown in Figure 17.116, contains the following parameters:

- In the first line, you can set the randomization process by inputting a seed value, clicking NEW SEED, or selecting full randomization.

- RANDOMIZATION is the percentage of pixels that are changed. If it is set to 100%, the image will be unrecognizable.

- REPEAT [1 to 100] sets the number of times the filter is applied; this compounds the effect.

The effect of Hurl is shown in Figure 17.117.

Figure 17.119 *The RGB Noise dialog*

Figure 17.120 *After applying RGB Noise*

In the dialog, shown in Figure 17.119, the RED, GREEN, and BLUE sliders have a range of [0 to 1]. If INDEPENDENT RGB is unchecked, all three have the same value, resulting in gray noise. The CORRELATED NOISE box, if checked, enables multiplicative noise; otherwise the noise is additive. In correlated mode, the noise is correlated to the channel values in the pixel and so

Figure 17.121 *After applying Slur*

is exaggerated for bright pixels and subdued for dark ones.

The result is shown in Figure 17.120.

Slur

Slur simulates melting, as if the pixels were dripping down. A random percentage of the pixels are selected to be slurred, and there is an 80% chance that those selected will be replaced with the pixel above; otherwise the remaining 20% are replaced with the pixel on the right or left.

The dialog is very similar to those of the Hurl and Pick filters. RANDOMIZATION sets the proportion of pixels that are changed. This filter works best if REPEAT is set to a high value. On the other hand, a very high randomization percentage can reduce the effect.

The result is shown in Figure 17.121.

Spread

Spread exchanges randomly matched pixels within a given distance, and it has no effect in areas that are a single, flat color.

The dialog is minimal, containing only two fields used to set the maximum distance between swapped pixels. You can break the chain to input uncorrelated values and select alternative units.

The result is shown in Figure 17.122.

Figure 17.122 *After applying Spread*

Figure 17.123 *The initial image*

17.7   The Edge-Detect Filters

The five filters in the Edge-Detect menu all detect the edges in the image and emphasize them. They find places where there is a strong change of color intensity, which often indicates the edge of an object. The result is generally an outline of the image, with the colors diminished or removed, set on a black or white background. Often, a better result can be obtained by first adding a blur to the image to smooth small irregularities and avoid false edges. We added a mild blur to the image shown in Figure 17.123, which will be used to demonstrate the Edge-Detect filters.

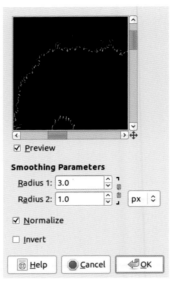

Figure 17.124 *The Difference of Gaussians dialog*

Difference of Gaussians

Difference of Gaussians works by applying two separate Gaussian blurs of different radii to the image and then blending the resulting images using the subtract method.

In the dialog, shown in Figure 17.124, the most important parameters are the two radii. They must be different, and usually RADIUS 1 is greater than RADIUS 2. The ideal settings depend on the image being processed. The NORMALIZE checkbox stretches the contrast of the result when checked, and the INVERT checkbox inverts the result, yielding dark lines on a white background.

The result, with the INVERT box checked, is shown in Figure 17.125.

Edge

Edge is in fact six different edge-detect filters, each of which applies a unique algorithm.

In the dialog, ALGORITHM contains the six different algorithms. AMOUNT [1 to 10] sets the threshold used to determine what is an edge. Low values yield thin lines on a black

Figure 17.125 *After applying Difference of Gaussians*

Figure 17.127 *After applying Edge, Gradient algorithm*

Figure 17.126 *After applying Edge, Sobel algorithm*

Figure 17.128 *After applying Edge, Differential algorithm*

background; high values yield thick lines on a colored background. The three radio buttons determine where the algorithm finds the missing pixels along the threshold, but the effect is very subtle.

The results of some of the six algorithms are shown in Figures 17.126 to 17.129. In all these cases, the color of the result was inverted (**Image: Colors > Invert**), and the AUTO button of the Levels tool was used to make the result easier to see.

Laplace

The Laplace filter is the same Laplace found within the Edge filter, but without any parameters. Since it produces very thin edges, create a more visible result by stretching the contrast (**Image: Colors > Auto > Stretch Contrast**) and

Figure 17.129 *After applying Edge, Laplace algorithm*

inverting the color (**Image: Colors > Invert**). Our result is shown in Figure 17.130, which differs from Figure 17.129 because of the Laplace filter's implicit parameters.

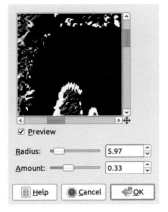

Figure 17.130 *After applying Laplace*

Figure 17.132 *After applying Neon*

Figure 17.131 *The Neon dialog*

Figure 17.133 *The Sobel dialog*

Neon

Neon adds bright colors to the edges, as if they were fluorescent.

In the dialog, shown in Figure 17.131, RADIUS sets the thickness of the edges, and AMOUNT changes the intensity of the filter's effect. See the result in Figure 17.132.

Sobel

Sobel detects horizontal edges and vertical edges separately. The dialog, shown in Figure 17.133, contains no numeric parameters. The checkboxes allow you to render the horizontal or vertical edges, or both. If only one direction is active, the KEEP SIGN OF RESULT checkbox will

Figure 17.134 *After applying Sobel*

build a relief surface with the discovered edges when checked. An example of this is shown in Figure 17.134, which was improved by using the AUTO button in the Levels tool.

17.8 The Generic Filters

There are only three filters in the Generic menu, and only the first one has a dialog. The filters in this section are only vaguely related; all of them use a matrix to calculate new pixel values, which is a common property of filters. The truth is, the three filters in this menu are here because they didn't fit anywhere else.

Convolution Matrix

Convolution Matrix can rightly be called a generic filter, since it's used to generate custom filters for blurring, sharpening, embossing, inverting, and much more.

The main part of the dialog, shown in Figure 17.135, is the MATRIX, a 5 × 5 array of numbers. The middle box corresponds to the current pixel. The other boxes correspond to the neighboring pixels. The filter works by multiplying every pixel near the current pixel, and the current pixel itself, by the corresponding factor in the matrix, then adding those numbers together, and dividing the total by the divisor. The process is similar to taking an average. If an offset is included, that number will be added to the calculated value. The result will be the new value for the current pixel.

The calculation is done separately for each of the three RGB channels and for the Alpha channel if there is one. Checkboxes on the right side of the dialog allow you to choose which channels are filtered. If the NORMALIZE box is checked, the divisor will be automatically set to the sum of the values in the boxes of the matrix, or 1 with an offset of 128 if the sum is zero. If the sum is negative, an offset of 255 is used.

When the current pixel is near the edge of the image, the missing pixels can be added in one of two ways: EXTEND duplicates the pixels on the border to fill the empty boxes; or WRAP takes pixel values from the opposite border, as if the image were wrapped around a cylinder.

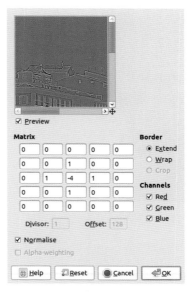

Figure 17.135 *The Convolution Matrix dialog*

Figure 17.136 *After applying Convolution Matrix*

The ALPHA-WEIGHTING box, if checked, includes the Alpha channel of the current pixel when calculating new pixel values.

Since this is such a flexible filter, an entire chapter (at least) would be needed to show all the possible interesting uses. For the sake of space, we picked one example: an edge-detect type of filter, shown in Figure 17.136. We also used the Levels tool to improve the result.

Figure 17.137 *After applying Dilate*

Figure 17.138 *After applying Erode*

Dilate

Dilate uses a simple, preset 3×3 matrix. The value of the central pixel is changed to the highest value of the eight neighboring pixels. Figure 17.137 shows the result after three applications of the filter.

Erode

Erode works the same as Dilate, but it takes the lowest value of the neighboring pixels as the new pixel value. Figure 17.138 shows the result after three applications of the filter.

Figure 17.139 *The first image*

Figure 17.140 *The second image*

17.9   The Combine Filters

The filters in the Combine menu are used to combine two or more images. We omit Filmstrip, since film is rarely used nowadays.

Depth Merge

Depth Merge merges two images using two image maps as guides. It requires four images in total, and they must all be the same size. An image map must be grayscale. The dark areas correspond to areas that will be visible in the associated image, and light areas of the map will be transparent areas in the associated image. In other words, the map acts as a mask.

The images shown in Figures 17.139 and 17.140 were used to demonstrate the filter. First they were cut and scaled until they were the same

Figure 17.141 *The map of the first image*

Figure 17.142 *The map of the second image*

size. To build the maps shown in Figures 17.141 and 17.142, we did the following:

1. Chose the Select by Color tool.

2. Clicked a light area of the image, pressed and held SHIFT, and then clicked other light areas until all of the light areas in the image were selected.

3. Created a new white layer.

4. Inverted the selection and filled it with black.

5. Dragged the new layer to the Toolbox to create a new image with it.

6. Deleted the mask layer from the image.

When the Depth Merge filter is selected, the dialog shown in Figure 17.143 pops up. The menus on the right are used to set the source and depth image maps. The remaining parameters are as follows:

- OVERLAP [0 to 2] smooths the transition between images using semitransparency.

- OFFSET [−1 to +1] adjusts the respective visibility of the Source images in the resulting image.

- SCALE [−1 to +1] does the same thing as OFFSET, but separately for each image, by darkening its map when the value of Scale is lowered.

See the result in Figure 17.144.

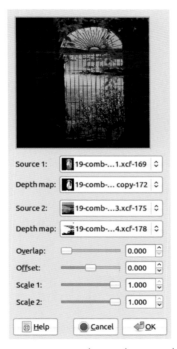

Figure 17.143 *The Depth Merge dialog*

17.10 The Artistic Filters

The Artistic menu is long and contains many complex filters. The filters in this menu create artistic effects, from simulating canvas to imitating cubist or impressionist paintings. We omit Predator, which refers to the science-fiction film from 1987.

Figure 17.144 *After applying Depth Merge*

Figure 17.146 *After applying Apply Canvas*

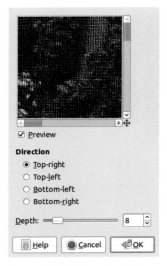

Figure 17.145 *The Apply Canvas dialog*

Apply Canvas

Apply Canvas simulates a canvas texture. The coarseness of the canvas cannot be changed, and the filter has few options.

The dialog, shown in Figure 17.145, contains controls for adjusting the direction of the light and the relief of the canvas. The effect of this filter is shown in Figure 17.146.

Cartoon

Cartoon simulates a drawing that was done in black ink and then colorized. The filter works by

Figure 17.147 *The initial image*

blackening the darkest areas in the image. The Cartoon filter is demonstrated on the photograph shown in Figure 17.147. The filter dialog is shown in Figure 17.148. There are only two parameters:

- MASK RADIUS [1 to 50] controls the coarseness of the cartoon drawing, and the optimal value depends on the image size. As a starting point, try a radius that is $1/100$ of the length (in pixels) of a side of the image.

- PERCENT BLACK [0 to 1] controls the intensity of the effect by changing the amount of black added to the image.

See the result in Figure 17.149.

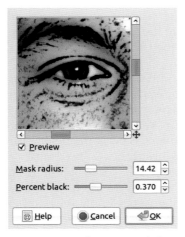

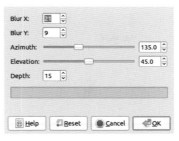

Figure 17.150 *The Clothify dialog*

☑ Preview

Mask radius: ▭ 14.42

Percent black: ▭ 0.370

Help Cancel OK

Figure 17.148 *The Cartoon dialog*

Figure 17.151 *After applying Clothify*

Cubism

Cubism simulates the cubist painting style. It builds small squares of semitransparent colors taken from the image and randomly scatters the squares, placing them near the source of the color.

The dialog, shown in Figure 17.152, contains the following parameters:

- TILE SIZE [0 to 100] sets the size of the squares.

- TILE SATURATION [0 to 10] sets the opacity of the squares, but it also affects their size. With low values, the image is dark and partially transparent, with a few small squares, and is generated very quickly. With high values, the image is colored with large squares and takes a long time to process.

- USE BACKGROUND COLOR, when checked, substitutes the background color in place of black below the semitransparent tiles.

Our result is shown in Figure 17.153.

Figure 17.149 *After applying Cartoon*

Clothify

Clothify has an effect similar to that of Apply Canvas, but the cloth is more textured and doesn't look as much like stretched canvas.

The dialog, shown in Figure 17.150, contains two sets of parameters. The two BLUR parameters control the appearance of the cloth texture, and the last three parameters control the lighting effects: direction and height of the light and depth of the relief.

The result is shown in Figure 17.151.

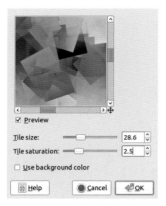

Figure 17.152 *The Cubism dialog*

Figure 17.153 *After applying Cubism*

GIMPressionist

GIMPressionist is the most complex and powerful of all the artistic filters in GIMP, and it is sometimes called the king of the artistic filters. The general idea is that the image is displayed on simulated paper with specific properties, painted with a brush with its own properties. There are many other parameters that can be adjusted as well.

Its dialog appears in Figure 17.154. There are eight tabs, and each one contains a lot of parameter settings, which leads to a gigantic number of possible combinations. Since the filter's process is very complex, the preview must be updated manually by clicking the UPDATE button. Moreover, the RESET button changes the preview back to the initial image.

The filter comes with a lot of predefined combinations of parameters, and new ones can be added to the list. To create a preset, adjust the parameter values in the various tabs, type the name of the new combination in the field at the top of the Presets tab, and click SAVE CURRENT.

After selecting a preset combination from the list, you must click APPLY before you can change the parameter values in the other seven tabs. The DELETE button is active only if the selected preset is not a predefined one. Finally, the REFRESH button will load any new preset combination that was added to GIMPressionist outside of GIMP.

The preview is only an indication of the possible result, not a preview of the actual outcome of the filter. The real effect depends on the size of the image, which affects how large the brush strokes appear, as it would in reality. The preview would be accurate if the image was the same size as the preview.

The Paper tab (Figure 17.155) can be used to adjust the texture of the paper that the image will appear to be painted on. There are nine textures to choose from. The preview in the tab is only an approximation, since the image size will impact the effect, and only a generic preview of the texture is shown. The SCALE slider [3 to 150] changes the size of the texture relative to that of the image, and the RELIEF [0 to 100] slider changes the depth of the pattern embossing. The INVERT box, when checked, inverts the texture, which is represented as a grayscale image in GIMP. The OVERLAY box, when checked, creates the texture as a new layer, whose opacity is set by the RELIEF percentage.

The Brush tab (Figure 17.156) works in a similar way. There is a long list of existing brushes, which are small grayscale images. If other images or layers were open in GIMP before the filter was selected, they will appear in the SELECT

Figure 17.154 *The GIMPressionist dialog, Presets tab*

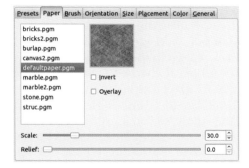

Figure 17.155 *The GIMPressionist dialog, Paper tab*

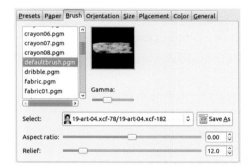

Figure 17.156 *The GIMPressionist dialog, Brush tab*

menu and can be saved as brushes. The GAMMA slider sets the luminosity of the brush. ASPECT RATIO [−1 to +1] changes the brush proportions: A negative value reduces the height, and a positive value reduces the width. The brush size can be changed in the Size tab. RELIEF [0 to 100] specifies the amount of virtual paint used for each stroke.

The Orientation tab (Figure 17.157) sets the orientation of the brush strokes. The DIRECTIONS slider specifies the number of pixels [1 to 30] in a stroke (i.e., the width of the stroke). The START ANGLE [0 to 360] sets the direction of the first stroke, and ANGLE SPAN [0 to 360] sets the possible range of strokes that follow the first one. There are eight aspects of the image that can direct the ORIENTATION of the strokes:

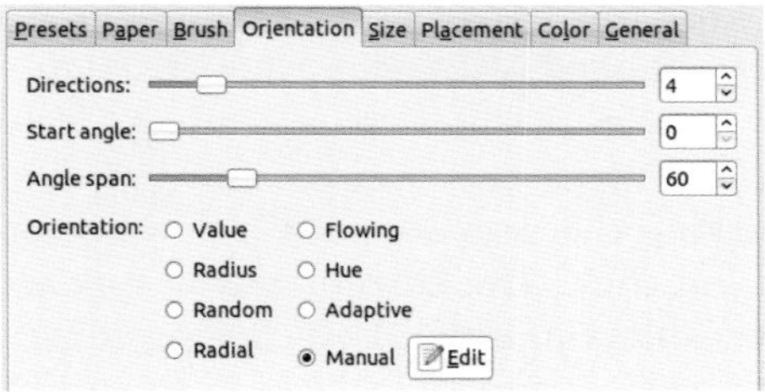

Figure 17.157 *The GIMPressionist dialog, Orientation tab*

- VALUE: Luminosity determines the direction of the stroke.

- RADIUS: The stroke direction is based on the distance from the center of the image.

- RANDOM: The stroke direction is random.

- RADIAL: The stroke direction is a based on the direction to the center of the image.

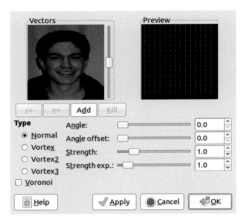

Figure 17.158 *The Orientation Map Editor*

- FLOWING: A flowing pattern is generated, independent of image properties.

- HUE: The hue determines the direction of the stroke.

- ADAPTIVE: The direction follows the contours of the original image.

- MANUAL: The EDIT button opens the Orientation Map editor.

The Orientation Map editor window (Figure 17.158) can be used to define the orientation of successive strokes based on vectors, shown in the image preview on the left (called VECTORS). A vertical slider changes the preview brightness to make the vectors more visible. Middle-clicking the preview adds a new vector wherever you click. The current vector appears in red, the others in gray. Left-clicking moves the current vector, and right-clicking rotates it. Two arrow buttons below the preview change which vector is current, and the ADD button adds a new vector in the center of the preview. The KILL button deletes the current vector. The preview on the right, called PREVIEW, shows the effect of the vectors on brush stroke orientation.

The first and third sliders below the previews modify parameters of the current vector: ANGLE does the same thing as right-clicking, and STRENGTH [0.1 to 5] changes the vector length,

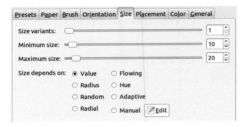

Figure 17.159 *The GIMPressionist dialog, Size tab*

which represents the breadth of the effect of each vector. The two other sliders affect all of the vectors: ANGLE OFFSET changes all of the vector angles, and STRENGTH EXP changes the length of all vectors. *Exp* stands for exponent and is likely related to the mathematical algorithm used to calculate the result.

On the left side, TYPE sets the arrangement of brush strokes, shown in the right-hand preview. The VORONOI box, if checked, causes only the closest vector to affect a given point.

There is no way to save the orientation map built with the editor, so you must re-create maps that you want to use again. However, the APPLY button allows you to see the effect of the orientation map in the GIMPressionist preview window. Note that you'll have to update the preview after applying the effect.

The Size tab (Figure 17.159) sets the size of the strokes and works a lot like the Orientation tab. You can set the amount of variation, the minimum and maximum size, and which of eight possible image characteristics influence the brush stroke size. When the manual method is selected, the EDIT button brings up the Size Map editor.

The Size Map editor window (Figure 17.160) is similar to that of the Orientation Map editor, except there are no choices for types and the angle settings are replaced with size settings.

The Placement tab (Figure 17.161) is used to specify how the strokes are distributed in the image: randomly or evenly, focused around the center if CENTERED is checked, and with a STROKE DENSITY in the range [1 to 50].

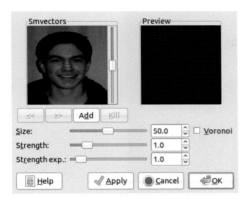

Figure 17.160 *The Size Map Editor*

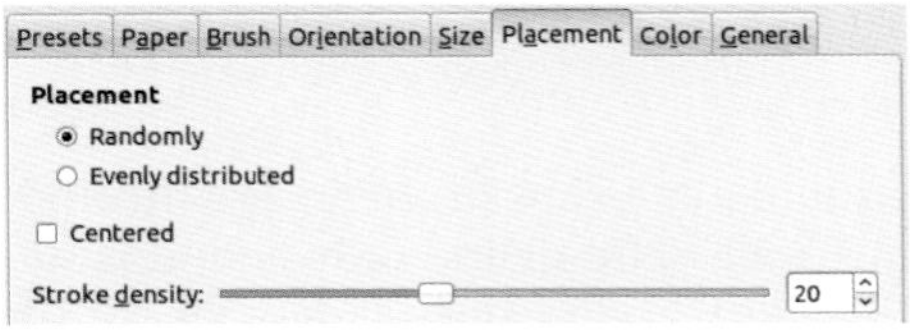

Figure 17.161 *The GIMPressionist dialog, Placement tab*

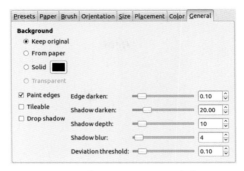

Figure 17.163 *The GIMPressionist dialog, General tab*

Figure 17.164 *One example of GIMPressionist*

Figure 17.162 *The GIMPressionist dialog, Color tab*

The Color tab (Figure 17.162) is used to specify what color will be used for each brush stroke. A stroke can be an average of the pixels it covers or the same color as the center pixel. COLOR NOISE [0 to 100] (random color variation) can also be added.

The General tab (Figure 17.163) sets the background color and the relief of the brush strokes. The background color (the color between brush strokes) can be taken from the initial image or from the chosen paper, or it can be a solid color, selected with the color chooser. If the image has an Alpha channel, the background can also be transparent.

The three checkboxes do the following:

- PAINT EDGES creates a thin border around all brush strokes.

- TILEABLE makes the image tilable.

- DROP SHADOW adds a slight shadow beneath each brush stroke.

The five sliders on the right add relief to the brush strokes:

- EDGE DARKEN [0 to 1] sets the depth of the relief.

- SHADOW DARKEN [0 to 99] sets the darkness of the shadows.

- SHADOW DEPTH [0 to 99] sets the distance between the brush stroke and the shadow.

- SHADOW BLUR [0 to 99] blurs the shadow.

- DEVIATION THRESHOLD [0 to 1] is rather mysterious and can be left at the default value.

Figure 17.167 *After applying Glass Tile*

Figure 17.165 *A second possible result of GIMPressionist*

Glass Tile

Glass Tile simulates a view of the image through a glass brick wall. The dialog only contains settings for the width and height of tiles. The result is shown in Figure 17.167.

Oilify

Oilify is designed to simulate an oil painting with large brush strokes. It's possible to get the same effect with the GIMPressionist filter, but this filter makes the process fast and easy.

Figure 17.166 *A third example of GIMPressionist*

GIMPressionist has a wide variety of parameter settings, and as a result, there are a vast number of possible results. Be warned that some of the settings can lead to a prohibitively long computation time. The GIMPressionist filter is so diverse that it can actually replicate a number of other artistic filters, such as Apply Canvas or Cubism. Figures 17.164 to 17.166 are varied examples of GIMPressionist on the image shown in Figure 17.147.

The dialog, shown in Figure 17.168, contains parameter settings similar to those of the Depth Merge filter. MASK SIZE [3 to 50] specifies the size of the brush strokes. The mask-size map option requires that another image the same size as the image being edited, preferably in grayscale, also be open in GIMP. The brightness of the image map determines the size of the strokes in the target image. EXPONENT [1 to 20] sets the variation between strokes, and this can also be specified using an image map. Finally, the USE INTENSITY ALGORITHM box, if checked, preserves the details and colors of the initial image. This filter often processes for a long time before producing a result. Figure 17.169 shows a possible result of Oilify.

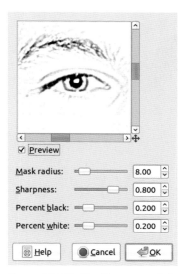

Figure 17.170 *The Photocopy dialog*

Figure 17.168 *The Oilify dialog*

Figure 17.169 *After applying Oilify*

Photocopy

Photocopy creates a simulation of a black and white photocopy. The result is similar to a grayscale edge-detect image.

The Photocopy filter darkens areas of the image that are darker than the average of the neighboring pixels, and it lightens the other areas. In addition to making simulated photocopies, you can use this filter to sharpen an image: Apply it to a layer copy that's above the original in the layer stack and then put it in Multiply mode.

The dialog, shown in Figure 17.170, has the following parameters:

- MASK RADIUS [3 to 50] sets the size of the neighboring area that will be averaged and thus alters the coarseness of the effect.

- SHARPNESS [0 to 1] sets the sharpness of the result.

- PERCENT BLACK [0 to 1] controls the amount of solid black added to the image. The effect is generally quite subtle.

- PERCENT WHITE [0 to 1] sets the proportion of white pixels in the image. If PERCENT WHITE is set to zero, the filter effect is very similar to desaturation.

Figure 17.171 shows the result.

Figure 17.171 *After applying Photocopy*

Figure 17.173 *After applying Softglow*

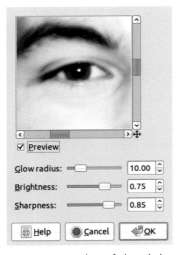

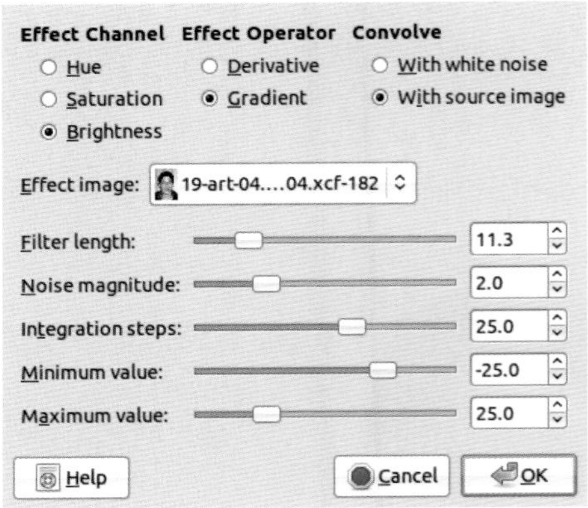

Figure 17.172 *The Softglow dialog*

Softglow

Softglow makes the image glow by further brightening the areas of the image that are already the brightest.

The settings in the dialog, shown in Figure 17.172, are simple. GLOW RADIUS [1 to 50] affects the sharpness of the resulting image. BRIGHTNESS [0 to 1] sets the intensity of the effect. SHARPNESS [0 to 1] determines how harsh the lighting is. See Figure 17.173.

Figure 17.174 *The Van Gogh (LIC) dialog*

Van Gogh

The Van Gogh filter is officially called Van Gogh (LIC), where LIC stands for Line Integral Convolution. This filter adds a blur to an image in one of two ways: based on the gradients in an image map or based on white noise. The dialog, shown in Figure 17.174, does not include a preview. There are three sets of radio buttons:

- EFFECT CHANNEL specifies which HSV channel is used.

- EFFECT OPERATOR allows you to select among the gradients in the image or the derivative (the reverse) of the gradient.

Figure 17.175 *The effect image*

Figure 17.176 *After applying Van Gogh with the target image as the effect image*

- CONVOLVE changes what is convoluted (combined) with the target image: either white noise (noise with the same amplitude in all frequencies), an effect image, or the target image itself.

The effect image must be the same size as the image processed, and only its gradients will be used by the filter. It must be open in GIMP when the filter is called. We used the image shown in Figure 17.175, created with the Blend tool.

The sliders are difficult to explain, and you'll probably learn best by just trying them. FILTER LENGTH [0.1 to 64] is the only one that's really useful when dealing with the source image. It controls the amount of blur, or the coarseness of the texture.

Figure 17.177 *After applying Van Gogh with white noise*

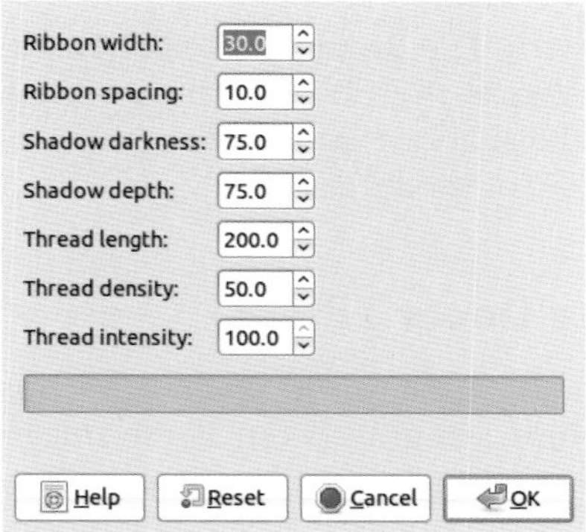

Ribbon width:	30.0
Ribbon spacing:	10.0
Shadow darkness:	75.0
Shadow depth:	75.0
Thread length:	200.0
Thread density:	50.0
Thread intensity:	100.0

| Help | Reset | Cancel | OK |

Figure 17.178 *The Weave dialog*

Figure 17.176 shows the effect when the target image is also the effect image and CONVOLVE is set to WITH SOURCE IMAGE. Figure 17.177 shows the result when white noise was chosen.

Weave

Weave simulates painting the image on a weave of ribbon or perhaps straw. The ribbons are striped so that they appear to be made out of some fibrous material. These stripes are referred to as *threads*.

The dialog, shown in Figure 17.178, does not include a preview. The filter builds an additional layer that contains the weave pattern and combines it in Multiply mode. This pattern is shown

Figure 17.179 *After applying Weave*

Figure 17.180 *The initial image*

in Figure 17.179. The parameters specify the width and spacing of the ribbons; the darkness and depth of the shadow; and the length, density, and intensity of the threads.

17.11   The Decor Filters

The Decor menu contains nine entries, but the first and third are grayed out if the image is in grayscale mode, and the last two entries are grayed out if the image is in a color mode. These filters are referred to as decor filters because they add some embellishment to the image, such as a border. We omit the last three filters (Slide, Stencil Carve, and Stencil Chrome) because they are not very useful.

Figure 17.181 *After applying Add Bevel*

Figure 17.182 *After applying Add Border*

Add Bevel

Add Bevel adds a slight bevel to a selection in the image by creating a new layer from the selection. The dialog contains one parameter, which allows you to set the thickness of the bevel [0 to 30]. The filter can generate a new image instead of changing the source, and the bump layer used for the bevel can be saved as an underlying layer.

We applied the Add Bevel filter to the image shown in Figure 17.180, with the central square selected. The result is shown in Figure 17.181.

Add Border

Add Border adds a border (with relief) around the image. The dialog is simple. It allows you to set the border size in X and Y; the color via the Color chooser; and the delta value [0 to 255], which specifies the difference in brightness between the top, bottom, left, and right borders. The delta value is added to the HSV value of the top border and subtracted from that of the bottom border, and half its value is added to the left border and subtracted from the right one. See Figure 17.182.

Figure 17.183 *The initial image*

Figure 17.184 *After applying Coffee Stain*

Coffee Stain

Coffee Stain simulates coffee stains.

The dialog has only two parameters: the number of stains [1 to 10] and a box to allow you to create the stain layers in Darken only mode. By default the layers are in Normal mode. Each stain is created in its own layer, each of which can be moved or removed afterwards.

The initial image is shown in Figure 17.183 and the result in Figure 17.184.

Fuzzy Border

Fuzzy Border adds another type of border, one that seems to crumble into pieces at the transition between the image and the border.

The dialog shown in Figure 17.185 contains options for the color and size of the border. The first checkbox can be used to blur the border edge with the image. Granularity, set with a slider [1 to 16], changes the size of the pieces of border that are crumbling. A low value leads to smaller pieces. The next checkbox adds a shadow, and the Shadow weight slider [1 to 100] sets the shadow's opacity. Two checkboxes

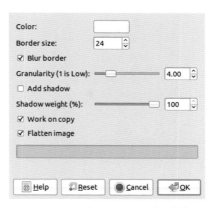

Figure 17.185 *The Fuzzy Border dialog*

Figure 17.186 *After applying Fuzzy Border*

at the bottom of the dialog can be used to create a new image (instead of altering the original) or flatten the result (rather than creating the border as a new layer).

The result of Fuzzy Border is shown in Figure 17.186.

Old Photo

Old Photo applies several transformations to an image in order to make it look like an old photograph.

In the dialog, shown in Figure 17.187, you can choose whether to defocus the photograph, add a blurred border of a specified size, convert the colors to a sepia hue, or add some imperfections. Once the settings have been chosen, either generate a copy of the image or work directly on the original.

The result is shown in Figure 17.188.

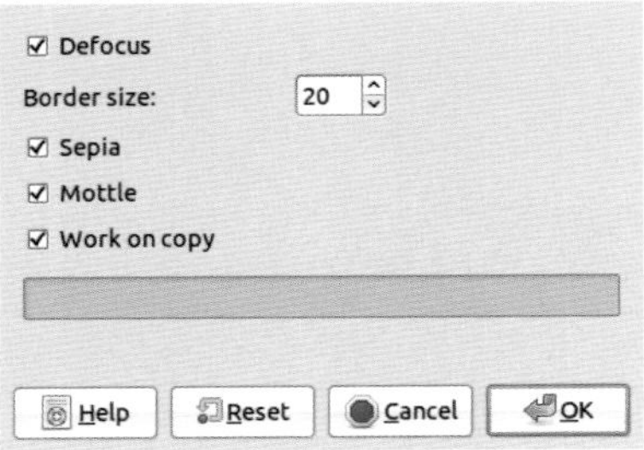

Figure 17.187 *The Old Photo dialog*

Figure 17.190 *After applying Round Corners*

and Y as well as the radius of the shadow blur. At the bottom of the dialog are checkboxes to add a background (in the current background color) and to generate a new image.

The result of Round Corners is shown in Figure 17.190.

17.12   The Map Filters

All 10 filters in the Map menu map an image onto an object in order to deform the image; for example, by adding relief to it, curving it, or making it seamless. The map filters often produce very dramatic effects.

Bump Map

Bump Map embosses an image using another image as a map. If the map is smaller than the image, some areas of the image will be left unaltered.

In the dialog, shown in Figure 17.191, the BUMP MAP menu lists all of the images open in GIMP and the images previously open in the same session. MAP TYPE can be set to one of three modes, which determine how the bump height is related to the map image luminosity: linear, spherical, or sinusoidal.

It's generally advisable to leave the COMPENSATE FOR DARKENING box checked to avoid overly dark results. By default, bright pixels generate bumps, and dark pixels generate hollows; if the INVERT BUMPMAP box is checked, bright pixels will be hollows, and dark pixels will be bumps. When TILE BUMPMAP is checked, the resulting

Figure 17.188 *After applying Old Photo*

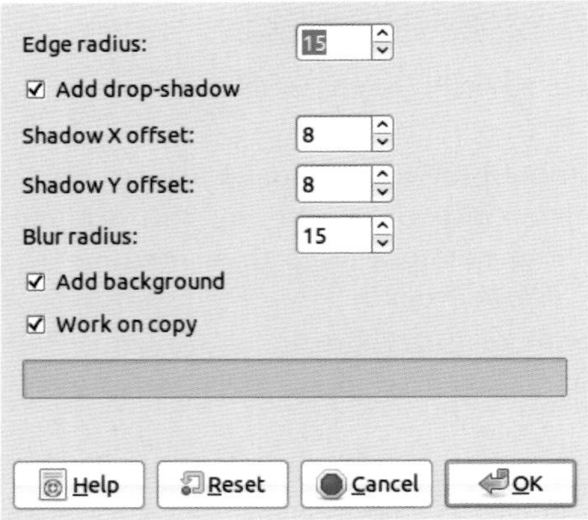

Figure 17.189 *The Round Corners dialog*

Round Corners

Round Corners simulates a photograph with round corners placed on some background with a drop shadow behind it.

At the top of the dialog (Figure 17.189) is a field that sets the radius of the round corners. Below that is a checkbox that turns the drop shadow on or off and fields to set its offset in X

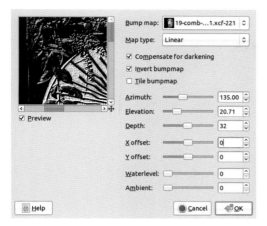

Figure 17.191 *The Bump Map dialog*

Figure 17.192 *One example of Bump Map*

Figure 17.193 *Another example of Bump Map*

is increased, these hollows progressively disappear. AMBIENT [0 to 255] is the level of ambient light, which reduces the effect of the relief when it's very high.

Our result is shown in Figure 17.192. The image itself was used as a map. Figure 17.193 shows the application of the filter to the same image, using the portrait from Figure 5.44 on page 133 as a map and with slightly increased DEPTH and ELEVATION.

Displace

Displace uses two images as *displace maps*, one for X and the other for Y. These two images must be the same size as the original image, which is being altered. All three images must be open in GIMP when the filter is selected. Only the value component of the map images is used, so it makes no difference whether they're color or grayscale images.

Most of the options in the dialog, shown in Figure 17.194, deal with displacement. When the DISPLACEMENT MODE is CARTESIAN, the displacement in the target image is calculated by multiplying the chosen displacement value (X or Y) by the value component of the pixel in the map. It's possible to uncheck one of the dimensions and displace the target image in only one

image will be a tilable relief, which can be used as a background for a web page, for example.

AZIMUTH [0 to 360] sets the direction of the light. ELEVATION [0.5 to 90] sets the position of the light above the horizon (90 means vertical). DEPTH [1 to 65] sets the difference in height between hollows and bumps. X OFFSET [−1000 to +1000] displaces the map horizontally with regard to the image, and Y OFFSET displaces it vertically. WATERLEVEL [0 to 255] has an effect only if the image contains transparency: Transparent areas are treated as darker and become hollows (if the bump map is not inverted). If Waterlevel

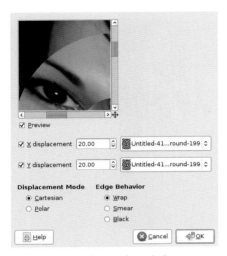

Figure 17.194 *The Displace dialog*

Figure 17.196 *After applying Displace in Cartesian mode*

Figure 17.195 *Our displace map*

Figure 17.197 *After applying Displace in Polar mode*

direction. When the displacement mode is PO-LAR, X is the radial distance (called Pinch) and Y the tangential one (called Whirl). The EDGE BEHAVIOR specifies how the image edges are handled: If the mode is WRAP, the missing pixels are taken from the opposite side; if it is SMEAR, neighboring pixels are duplicated in areas that are missing pixels; if BLACK is chosen, missing pixels are filled with black.

Computing the actual displacement is rather complicated. In the X and Y dimensions, a pixel value in the displace map that's less than 127 results in a displacement to the left, and a value

greater than 127 results in a displacement to the right. In polar displacement, pixels with a value greater than 127 are displaced outward, and pixels with a value less than 127 are moved toward the center of the image.

To demonstrate Displace, we built the map shown in Figure 17.195 by creating a new image the same size as the image to be filtered and filling it with a spiral gradient. The result of Displace in CARTESIAN mode is shown in Figure 17.196. Figure 17.197 shows the result of the same filter and parameters, in POLAR mode.

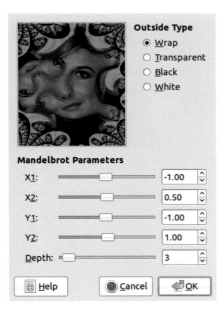

Figure 17.199 *After applying Fractal Trace*

Figure 17.198 *The Fractal Trace dialog*

Fractal Trace

Fractal Trace maps the image to a Mandelbrot fractal.

The dialog of Fractal Trace is shown in Figure 17.198. The OUTSIDE TYPE option determines what appears in the area around the original image. Only WRAP produces a fractal-like pattern of smaller copies of the image. The other three options, TRANSPARENT, BLACK, and WHITE, replace the background with transparency, black, or white. The MANDELBROT PARAMETERS sliders are sensitive and should be set with care, especially the DEPTH: At high values (the maximum is 50), the initial image is unrecognizable.

The result of Fractal Trace is shown in Figure 17.199.

Illusion

Illusion doesn't use a second image as a map. Instead, it uses multiple copies of the image itself, at various sizes, orientations, and levels of bright-

Figure 17.200 *After applying Illusion*

ness, to build something like a kaleidoscope image.

There are only two adjustable parameters in the dialog: the number of copies of the image [−32 to +64] (a negative value inverts the rotation direction) and the mode.

The result is shown in Figure 17.200.

Make Seamless

Make Seamless has no dialog and no options. It transforms the image to make it tilable. To

Figure 17.201 *After applying Make Seamless*

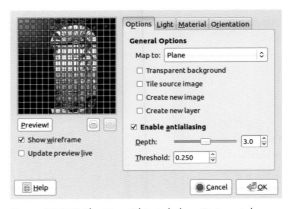

Figure 17.202 *The Map Object dialog, Options tab*

achieve this, it cuts a copy of the image into quarters, puts each quarter in the corner opposite to its original position, and creates a smooth transition with the original image.

Our result is shown in Figure 17.201.

Map Object

Map Object maps one or more images onto a plane, a sphere, a box, or a cylinder. The light source, the material properties, and the orientation of the object can be adjusted.

The dialog of the filter contains four or five different tabs, depending on the objects chosen. The Options tab appears in Figure 17.202, along with the preview. There are zoom buttons, as well as a PREVIEW! button, which is useless in the Options tab but is useful in the other tabs. The SHOW WIREFRAME checkbox, if checked, adds a wireframe of the object to the preview.

The MAP TO option in the orientation tab allows you to choose among the four different objects. There are also checkboxes to replace the background with transparency and to create a new image. Another works only for a plane: TILE SOURCE IMAGE fills the area of the image that is left empty with the content that was pushed off the opposite side.

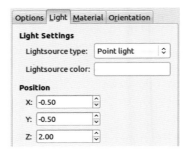

Figure 17.203 *The Map Object dialog, Light tab*

ENABLE ANTIALIASING should generally be left checked, and the corresponding slider and counter can also be left as they are.

In the Light tab (Figure 17.203), the LIGHTSOURCE TYPE can be set as a point, as directional lighting, or as no light at all. The three coordinates determine the POSITION of the point of light or the DIRECTION VECTOR for directional light. LIGHTSOURCE COLOR brings up the Color chooser.

In the Material tab (Figure 17.204), the INTENSITY LEVELS change the properties of the indirect (AMBIENT) or the direct (DIFFUSE) light. On the default setting, areas that aren't directly lighted are very dark. The REFLECTIVITY of the object is specified by three parameters: DIFFUSE sets the brightness of reflecting parts, SPECULAR the intensity of the highlights, and HIGHLIGHT changes the precision of the highlights. These

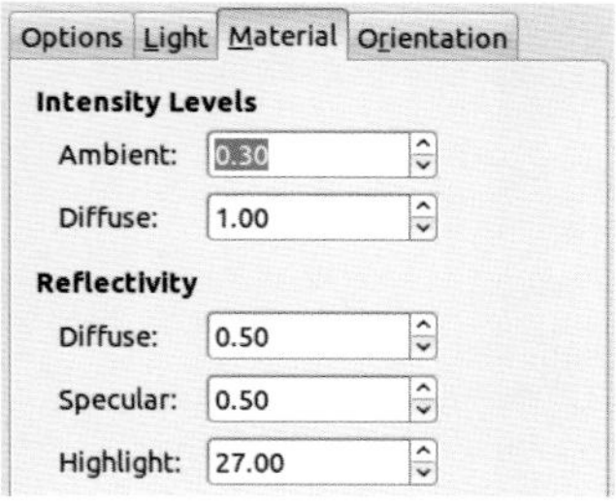

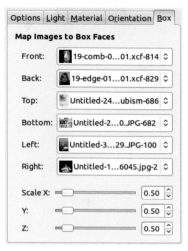

Figure 17.204 *The Map Object dialog, Material tab*

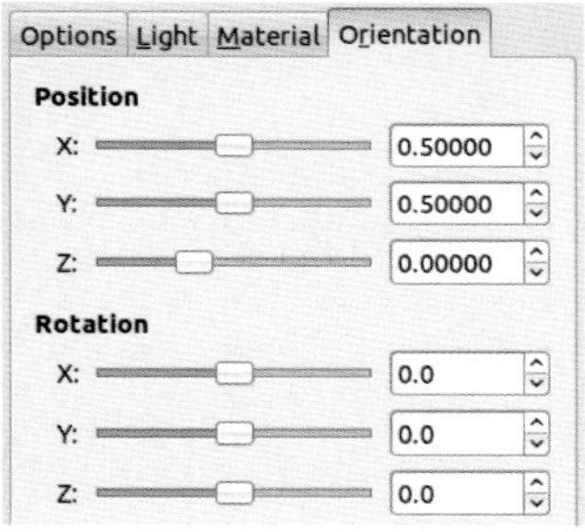

Figure 17.205 *The Map Object dialog, Orientation tab*

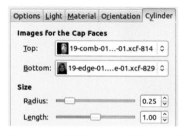

Figure 17.206 *The Map Object dialog, Box tab*

Figure 17.207 *The Map Object dialog, Cylinder tab*

parameters can be difficult to set properly, and the PREVIEW! button really comes in handy.

The Orientation tab (Figure 17.205) contains a couple of three-dimensional coordinate sliders, which set the position and rotation of the object. The origin (0,0) is always the top-left corner of the object. The position coordinates have the range [−1 to +2], and the rotation coordinates have the range [−180 to +180]. The PREVIEW! button should be used regularly to check the new object position, since it is very difficult to accurately predict the effect of these sliders.

The Box tab (Figure 17.206) is present only if the object is a box. The tab is mainly used to choose images that will be mapped to the six faces of the box. The images must be open in GIMP when the filter is selected, and they're automatically scaled to fit on the box. The three sliders [0 to 5] change the size of the box edges.

The Cylinder tab (Figure 17.207) is present only if the object is a cylinder. It allows you to choose the images that will be mapped to the

cap faces of the cylinder. The image on the curved face of the cylinder is always the current image. The two size sliders [0 to 2] can be used to change the dimensions of the cylinder.

Figures 17.208 through 17.211 show examples of the Map Object filter mapping some of our sample images to a box, a cylinder, a sphere, and a plane, respectively.

Paper Tile

Paper Tile cuts the image into many squares of the same size and moves them around randomly, leaving small spaces between some and overlapping others.

In the dialog, shown in Figure 17.212, you can set the size of the squares and the number of squares in the horizontal and vertical

Figure 17.208 *Mapping to a box*

Figure 17.211 *Mapping to a plane*

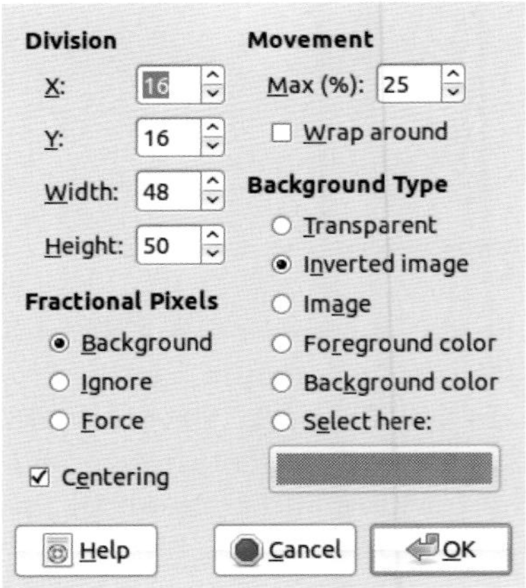

Figure 17.209 *Mapping to a cylinder*

Figure 17.210 *Mapping to a sphere*

Division

X: 16

Y: 16

Width: 48

Height: 50

Fractional Pixels

- Background
- Ignore
- Force

☑ Centering

Movement

Max (%): 25

☐ Wrap around

Background Type

- Transparent
- Inverted image
- Image
- Foreground color
- Background color
- Select here:

Help | Cancel | OK

Figure 17.212 *The Paper Tile dialog*

directions. These parameters are linked: Setting the X and Y parameters automatically changes the WIDTH and HEIGHT, and vice versa. MOVEMENT is randomly computed within a percentage limit of the size. If pixels are shifted out of the image, they can be simply cut, or they can be wrapped around the image so that they'll appear on the other side. FRACTIONAL PIXELS are pixels not covered by any paper squares. They can be filled based on the selected background type (BACKGROUND), left as they are (IGNORE), or cut out (FORCE). BACKGROUND TYPE specifies what is done to the spaces between the paper tiles after they are moved. The space can be

Figure 17.213 *After applying Paper Tile*

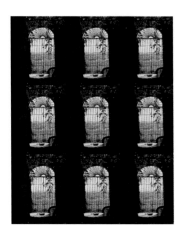

Figure 17.215 *After applying Small Tiles*

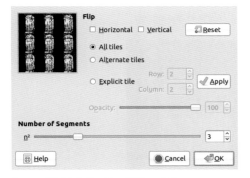

Figure 17.214 *The Small Tiles dialog*

Figure 17.216 *The Tile dialog*

transparent; it can contain the original image, as is or inverted; or it can contain the foreground or background color or a different color selected with the Color chooser. The CENTERING box, if checked, gathers the tiles toward the center of the image.

Our result is shown in Figure 17.213.

Small Tiles

Small Tiles creates smaller duplicates of the image, displayed in a grid.

In the dialog, shown in Figure 17.214, the most important setting is the NUMBER OF SEGMENTS (i.e., the number of rows and columns of small images in the resulting image). For example, a value of 3 results in a total of 9 copies.

Copies can be flipped, horizontally or vertically or both. The flip can be applied to all tiles, to every other tile, or to an EXPLICIT TILE, which you can specify by its column and row. Finally, if the image layer has an Alpha channel, the OPACITY of the result can be set to less than 100%.

See Figure 17.215 for the result.

Tile

Tile builds an image that contains as many copies of the original image as needed to fit the new size.

The dialog, shown in Figure 17.216, is very simple. The new size of the image can be set using the linked fields, and the change can be applied to the current image or to a new image. If the new size is smaller than the current image, the image will be cropped in the result. If the new size is larger, there will be several copies of the original image tiled in the new image.

Figure 17.217 *After applying Tile*

Our result is shown in Figure 17.217. The initial image size was 768 × 1024.

Warp

Warp is a complicated filter, and the result is difficult to predict, since there is no preview. The trial-and-error approach is often impractical, as the filter's processing time is rather long. Warp displaces the pixels of the image according to the gradient slopes of a grayscale displacement map.

The dialog is shown in Figure 17.218. To demonstrate the filter, we built a displacement map by creating a new image, the same size as the original one (Figure 17.139), filled with solid noise (**Image: Filters > Render > Clouds > Solid Noise**). This displacement map contains gradients in random directions. The STEP SIZE is set to 10 by default, which would result in image pixels being displaced by only 1 pixel. We increased the step size to 100 in this example. The filter effect is repeated the number of ITERATIONS times. The ON EDGES radio buttons do not need explanations. Figure 17.219 shows the result.

The second part of the dialog, ADVANCED OPTIONS, includes the following options:

- DITHER SIZE can be used to create a dithered effect, as shown in Figure 17.220. The step

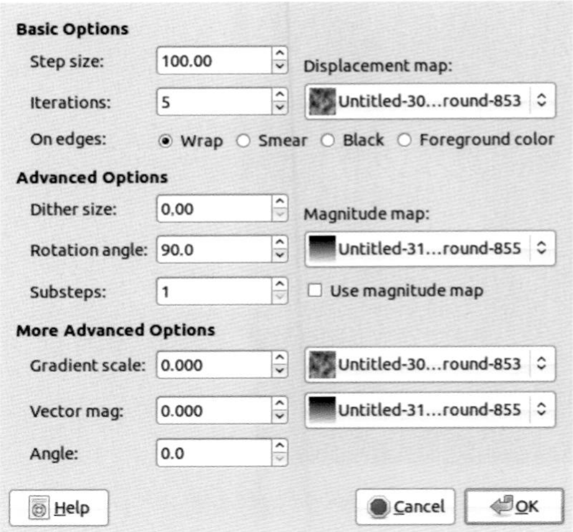

Figure 17.218 *The Warp dialog*

Figure 17.219 *After applying Warp with a displacement map*

size was set to zero, so there was a dithering effect but no displacement.

- A MAGNITUDE MAP alters the target image based on the map's brightness rather than its gradients, and it is used in conjunction with the displacement map to create the final effect. Black regions of the magnitude map cancel the filter effect, while white regions result in the strongest effect. In Figure 17.221, the magnitude map used was a simple vertical

Figure 17.220 *After applying Warp with dithering but no displacement*

Figure 17.221 *After applying Warp with a magnitude map*

gradient from black at the top to white at the bottom, so the effect of the displacement map was strongest at the bottom of the image. The changes are applied some number of times specified by SUBSTEPS.

- ROTATION ANGLE is the angle between the displacement and the gradient. In Figure 17.221 it was set to 90.

The third part of the dialog, MORE ADVANCED OPTIONS, allows you to use two additional maps.

Figure 17.222 *The initial image*

These maps will have an effect only if the corresponding coefficient is greater than zero.

17.13 The Render Filters

The Render menu contains three submenus and seven normal entries. All the filters in the Render menu replace the current layer or selection with a pattern, and they are generally used on an empty image or an empty layer.

Clouds Filters

The Clouds submenu contains four filters for generating cloud-like effects, but the first filter is almost exactly the same as the fourth one. We omit Fog, which does not seem very useful.

Difference Clouds

Difference Clouds first generates Solid Noise, which will be discussed below. This filter acts on a new layer, then puts this new layer in Difference mode and merges it with the original layer. We used this filter on the image shown in Figure 17.222 and got the result shown in Figure 17.223.

Plasma

Plasma generates a colorful, opaque cloud that fills the current layer or the selection. It can be used to generate textures or to add wild colors to a desaturated layer.

The dialog, shown in Figure 17.224, contains randomization parameters that are similar to

Figure 17.223 *After applying Difference Clouds*

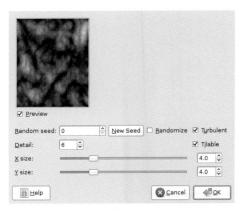

Figure 17.225 *The Solid Noise dialog*

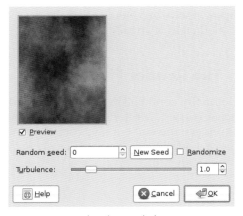

Figure 17.224 *The Plasma dialog*

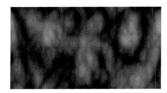

Figure 17.226 *After applying Solid Noise*

Y SIZE [0.1 to 16] set the level of detail in each dimension.

An example is shown in Figure 17.226.

those of a number of other filters. The NEW SEED button allows you to generate random patterns until you find an interesting one. TURBULENCE [0.1 to 7] controls the smoothness and complexity of the pattern.

Solid Noise

Solid Noise is very similar to Plasma, but it generates a grayscale image and has more settings. It is often used as a way to generate displacement maps or embossing maps.

The dialog, shown in Figure 17.225, begins with randomization settings. The rest of the parameters can be used to modify the generated pattern. TURBULENT makes it rougher. TILABLE makes it tilable. DETAIL [1 to 15] changes the pattern from cloud-like to gravel-like. X SIZE and

Nature Filters

The Nature submenu contains only two entries, but they correspond to powerful and complicated filters.

Flame

Flame can be used to generate an infinite array of patterns, including some extraordinary fractals. Almost every attempt leads to compelling computer-generated art, but it is extremely difficult to predict the result, which can be frustrating. Flame paints on the current layer, which means that it can be used several times to generate combinations of successive patterns. If the layer has an Alpha channel, the filter makes the layer transparent before applying the flame

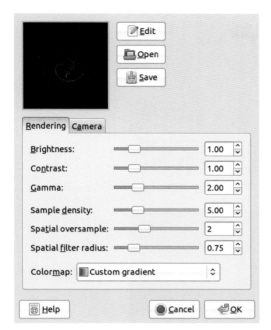

Figure 17.227 *The Flame dialog, Rendering tab*

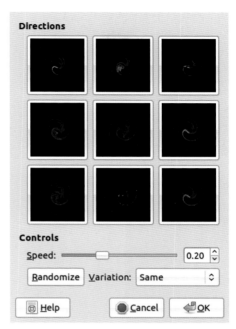

Figure 17.228 *The Edit Flame window*

pattern so that the current layer disappears and the flames appear on the layer beneath.

The dialog, shown in Figure 17.227, contains two tabs and a preview window. Next to the preview window are three important buttons. SAVE and OPEN allow you to save and restore a set of parameters that previously generated an interesting pattern.

EDIT brings up a new window (Figure 17.228) in which nine variants of the current pattern are displayed. The current one is in the center. Clicking any of the patterns makes that pattern current and generates a new set of patterns around it. SPEED changes the pattern in a way that only the author of the filter fully understands. VARIATION offers 32 fractal themes. RANDOMIZE generates a new set of patterns with the same parameters.

Now switch back to the Rendering tab. The first three settings have an effect that's apparent in the preview and alter the general color properties of the pattern. The COLORMAP menu

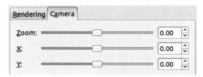

Figure 17.229 *The Flame dialog, Camera tab*

changes the color scheme of the pattern. There are six predefined colormaps to choose from. The current gradient is selected by default and is called CUSTOM GRADIENT. The other choices are based on all of the images previously open in this session of GIMP. The other three settings do not have a visible effect in the preview, and to use them with intention you need to understand the mathematics behind the filter (see *http://flam3.com/*).

The Camera tab (Figure 17.229) contains only three settings, and these settings change only the preview. The most useful is ZOOM [−4 to +4], which lets you look at the pattern from different distances. The X and Y settings [−2 to +2] move the pattern in the workspace.

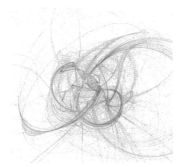

Figure 17.230 *One example of the Flame filter*

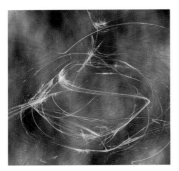

Figure 17.231 *A second example of the Flame filter*

Figure 17.232 *A third example of the Flame filter*

Figures 17.230 to 17.234 show five different examples of results that can be achieved with the Flame filter. The second and third examples (Figures 17.231 and 17.232) show the Flame layered over images from earlier in this chapter, while the fourth and fifth examples (Figures 17.233 and 17.234) resulted from multiple applications of the filter.

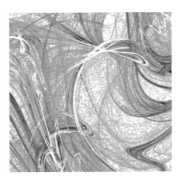

Figure 17.233 *A fourth example of the Flame filter*

Figure 17.234 *A fifth example of the Flame filter*

IFS Fractal

IFS Fractal (IFS means Iterated Function System) is even more complicated and difficult to master than the Flame filter. However, with some practice, it is possible to use the filter with some goal in mind and to produce a result that's reasonably similar to the intended result.

The dialog of the filter (Figure 17.235) contains two sections on top and two tabs on the bottom. The upper-left window shows the geometric figures used to generate the fractal, and the upper-right window shows the result. Initially there are three triangles in the left window, arranged into a larger triangle, and the right window displays what is called a Sierpinsky triangle. On the left, the geometric object (a triangle to start) that is selected is emphasized in boldface. Clicking an object selects it.

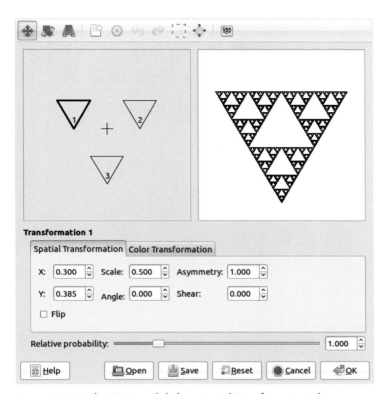

Figure 17.235 *The IFS Fractal dialog, Spatial Transformation tab*

The 10 buttons in the top row of the dialog have the following functions:

- Move the selected object. The other objects will also move and be deformed when any one object is moved, and the fractal pattern on the right will change as well.

- Rotate and scale. Unlike Move, this operates only on the selected object. To rotate an object, select it and move the mouse in a circle centered on that object. To change the size of an object, move the mouse perpendicular to the object's center. A larger object has more influence on the fractal pattern.

- Extend and deform. The effect of this operation can be difficult to control, especially if the mouse pointer is too close to the object center. It's best to click near the edges of the object. While the object can take on many shapes, its perimeter is constant during this operation.

- Create a new object. This operation adds a new object in the center of the left window. As soon as this has been moved, all of the objects, including the one in the preview on the right, will gain a side. If they're triangles, they become deformed rectangles. Thus if there are five objects, they will all be irregular pentagons. Note that if you add an object immediately after adding the previous one, only this last object will add sides to all the objects when moved. Thus, you could have five irregular rectangles, for example.

- Delete the selected object.

- Undo the last operation.

- Redo the last operation.

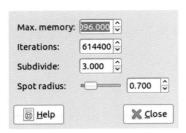

Figure 17.236 *The IFS Fractal dialog, Render options*

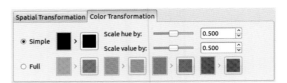

Figure 17.237 *The IFS Fractal dialog, Color Transformation tab*

- Select all the objects. This may be used before any transformation, such as moving or rotating, to allow you to move or rotate all of the objects at once.

- Recompute center.

The last button of the top row brings up the IFS Fractal Render options dialog (Figure 17.236), which contains four options. MAX. MEMORY can speed up rendering time, which is especially important if you're using a large spot radius or a lot of iterations. A high value for MAX. MEMORY can make the computation faster. The number of iterations is the number of times the fractal will repeat. SUBDIVIDE also affects the level of detail, and a high value can lead to a longer computation time. SPOT RADIUS is like a brush size: A large one corresponds to a large brush, while a small one leads to a fractal pattern that is a cloud of small points.

The Spatial Transformation tab displays the parameters of the current object (a triangle at first) as numbers, which can be adjusted directly or by pressing the up or down buttons to the right of each one.

The RELATIVE PROBABILITY slider in the bottom of the dialog sets the degree of influence that the selected object has on the whole pattern.

The Color Transformation tab (Figure 17.237) can be used to add color to the fractal pattern. By default, the pattern is generated using the current foreground color. The changes made in the Color Transformation tab are applied to the selected object. SIMPLE changes the object's color to a chosen color, with settable scales for its hue and value components. FULL allows you

Figure 17.238 *An example of two superimposed IFS fractals*

to choose a specific color for each of the three RGB components and for the Alpha channel, which is displayed in black.

The best way to learn to use the IFS Fractal filter is to experiment with moving and deforming the three initial objects. Mouse movements should be very precise, since a small movement has a large effect. A tablet and stylus is preferable. Once you've found a pattern that you like, you can add a new object to make the pattern richer. Generally, it's not a good idea to add too many objects, but it's hard to say exactly how many is too many. Add the color once the pattern is complete. Figure 17.238 is a simple example of an IFS fractal pattern. The filter was used twice on the same layer.

Pattern Filters

The Pattern submenu contains eight entries for building patterns, some completely predefined, others generated from a large combination of parameters and randomization.

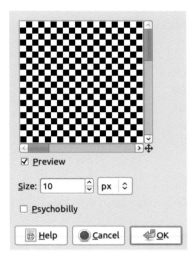

☑ Preview

Size: 10 ⌄ px ⌄

☐ Psychobilly

[🖶 Help] [⬤ Cancel] [⬅ OK]

Figure 17.239 *The Checkerboard dialog*

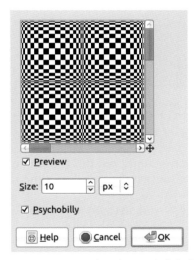

☑ Preview

Size: 10 ⌄ px ⌄

☑ Psychobilly

[🖶 Help] [⬤ Cancel] [⬅ OK]

Figure 17.240 *When the Psychobilly box is checked*

Checkerboard

Checkerboard is a very simple filter. It fills the current layer with a regular checkerboard or a distorted one, depending on the settings.

Figure 17.239 shows the dialog of the filter. The SIZE of the squares can be set in a number of different units. Figure 17.240 shows the distorted result of Checkerboard when the PSYCHOBILLY box is checked.

Figure 17.241 *The CML Explorer dialog*

CML Explorer

CML (Coupled-Map Lattice) Explorer, the king of all pattern filters, is a very complex tool, difficult to understand and master. It relies on a mathematical model called a cellular automaton.

In the top left of the dialog (Figure 17.241) is a long, rectangular preview of the filter result, which does not reflect the shape of the current layer. Below are buttons for altering the randomization: requesting a new seed and switching between a fixed seed or a random one. Below that are buttons for saving the current configuration of parameters and opening a previously saved configuration. The filter dialog also contains six tabs, summarized briefly next.

The filter works in the HSV space, and the Hue, Saturation, and Value tabs contain the same set of parameters, but changes are applied only to the specified component. Next we'll walk through the components that are common to all three tabs.

FUNCTION TYPE includes the list of options and functions shown in Figure 17.242. The

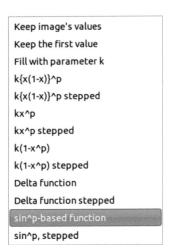

Figure 17.242 *The Function type menu*

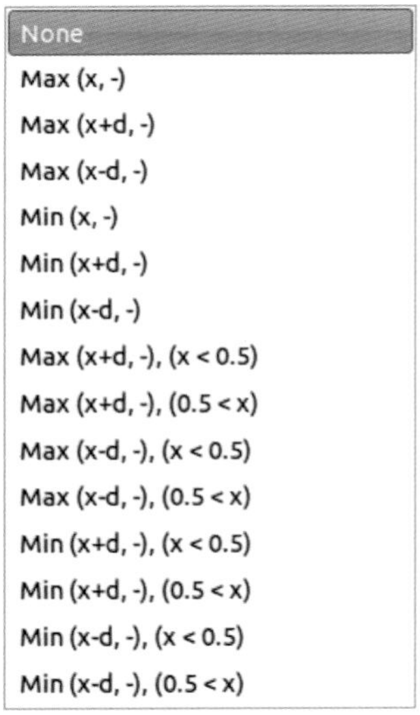

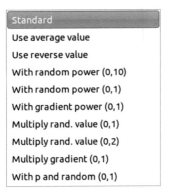

Figure 17.244 *The Misc arrange menu*

Figure 17.245 *A graph of the settings*

Figure 17.243 *The Composition menu*

corresponding parameter (Value, Saturation, or Hue) can be taken from the image; be standard cyan; or be computed using one of the functions, which may use a parameter k, specified below in the dialog, or a power factor p, also specified below.

The COMPOSITION function can be chosen from the list shown in Figure 17.243. An entire book could be written about the theory behind

and effect of these functions, but this is not that book, so we simply suggest that you experiment with the various functions.

MISC ARRANGE also contains a list of functions, shown in Figure 17.244. As with COMPOSITION, the effect of these functions is difficult to explain. Below MISC ARRANGE, the tab contains a checkbox and a lot of sliders. The best way to understand their purpose is to try them out.

The PLOT A GRAPH OF THE SETTINGS button displays the graph shown in Figure 17.245. This graph provides a visual display of the settings and may help you to better understand the influence of the different functions.

The Advanced tab is shown in Figure 17.246. It contains three sliders for each component of the HSV model. The MUTATION RATE affects the changes to a pixel relative to its neighbors.

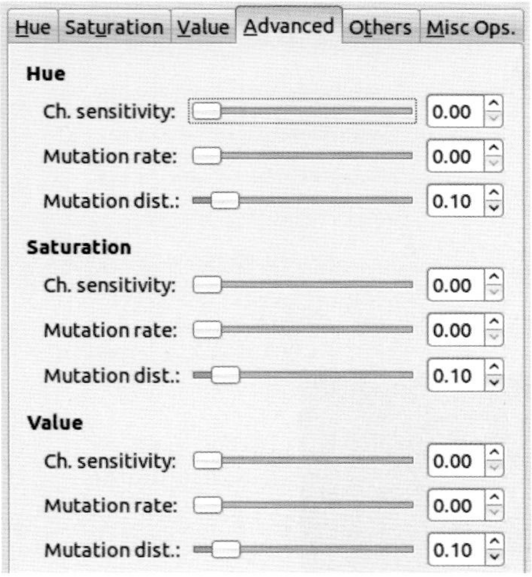

Figure 17.246 *The CML Explorer dialog, Advanced tab*

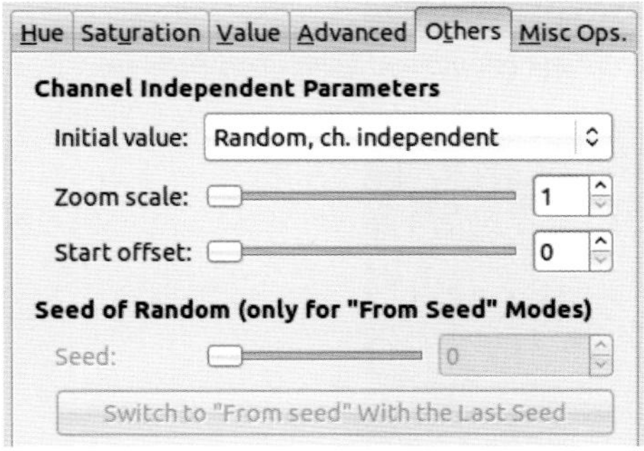

Figure 17.247 *The CML Explorer dialog, Others tab*

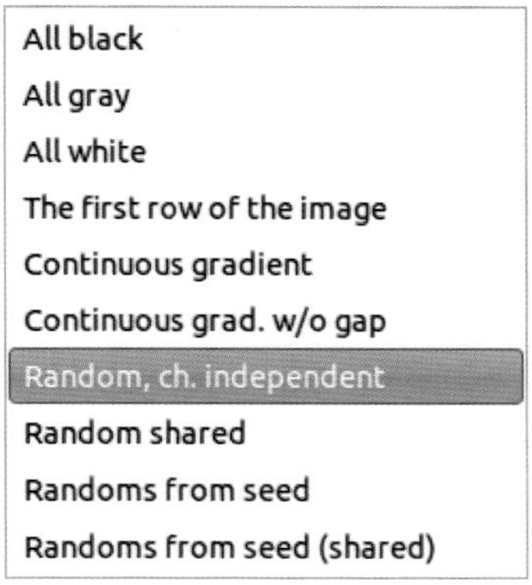

Figure 17.248 *The Initial value menu*

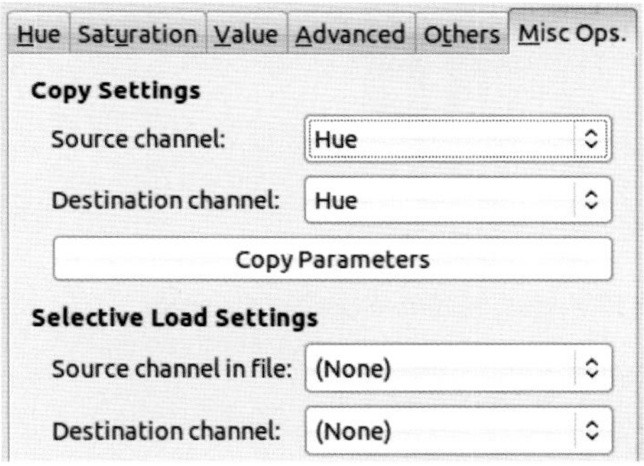

Figure 17.249 *The CML Explorer dialog, Misc Ops. tab*

Experimentation is again the best way to understand what effect changes will have.

The Others tab is shown in Figure 17.247. The INITIAL VALUE field contains the menu shown in Figure 17.248, which allows you to choose the initial value and includes several methods of selecting random sources in addition to fixed values such as black or white. The random seed can be changed with the lower slider. The ZOOM SCALE slider lets you look more closely at the pattern, but zooming in too far can lead to a strong pixelation effect.

The Misc Ops. tab (Figure 17.249) lets you copy the parameters from one of the HSV channels to another. The two parameters at the bottom change the effect of the OPEN button, on the left of the dialog. They allow you to load only one channel from the source file and to put the parameter values from one channel into a different channel.

The number of possible combinations of the different functions in the CML Explorer is huge, and with the addition of the parameters, the number of possible results is incredibly vast. The name of the filter, CML *Explorer*, reflects the fact that the best way to use this tool is to explore the innumerable capabilities of the CML algorithm. Figures 17.250 to 17.253 show just a few random examples of the results it can produce. Readers are strongly encouraged to explore the filter for themselves.

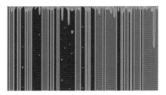

Figure 17.250 *One example of CML Explorer*

Figure 17.251 *A second example of CML Explorer*

Figure 17.252 *A third example of CML Explorer*

Figure 17.253 *A fourth example of CML Explorer*

Diffraction Patterns

Diffraction Patterns creates wave interference patterns from an image. The authors of the filter never wrote an explanation for the function of the parameters, so the only way to learn what they do is to experiment. The preview is rather small and doesn't update automatically. To update it, click the PREVIEW! button.

The dialog, shown in Figure 17.254, contains four tabs. However, the first three are identical. Each contains three sliders [0 to 20] for the three components of the RGB model. The tabs alter the frequencies, contours, and sharp edges. The last tab contains options for

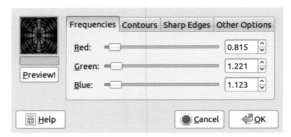

Figure 17.254 *The Diffraction Patterns dialog*

Figure 17.255 *One example of Diffraction Patterns*

Figure 17.256 *A second example of Diffraction Patterns*

BRIGHTNESS [0 to 1], SCATTERING [0 to 100], and POLARIZATION [−1 to 1].

Diffraction Patterns inevitably yields an interesting result, but it is very difficult to predict what the result of changes to any one parameter will be. Figures 17.255 to 17.257 show three examples.

Grid

Grid simply draws a grid on the current layer. The dialog, shown in Figure 17.258, allows you to set the parameters separately for the horizontal lines, the vertical lines, and the intersections.

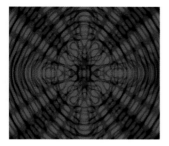

Figure 17.257 *A third example of Diffraction Patterns*

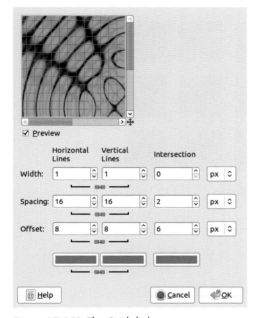

Figure 17.258 *The Grid dialog*

It's possible to generate intersections that are thinner or thicker than the lines themselves. These intersections look like plus signs. You can set the following parameters:

- The width of the lines, including the arms of the intersection plus signs.

- The spacing of the lines. For intersections, this clears the space between the line crossing and the plus sign arms. If this is confusing, try it out and see the effect for yourself.

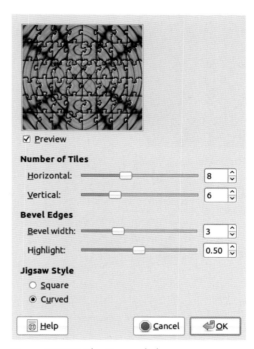

Figure 17.259 *The Jigsaw dialog*

- The offset of the lines with regard to the upper-left corner. For the intersections, this is the length of the plus sign arms.

- The color of the lines or intersections.

Jigsaw

Jigsaw draws the pieces of a very uniform jigsaw puzzle on the current layer.

The dialog, shown in Figure 17.259, allows you to specify the number of tiles in the horizontal and vertical directions. The relief effect can be adjusted by changing the BEVEL WIDTH [0 to 10] and the HIGHLIGHT [0 to 1]. Finally, the tiles can either have sharp edges or be slightly curved. The result is shown in Figure 17.260.

Maze

The Maze filter creates a maze that fills the current layer. The walls are black, and the paths are white.

Figure 17.260 *After applying Jigsaw*

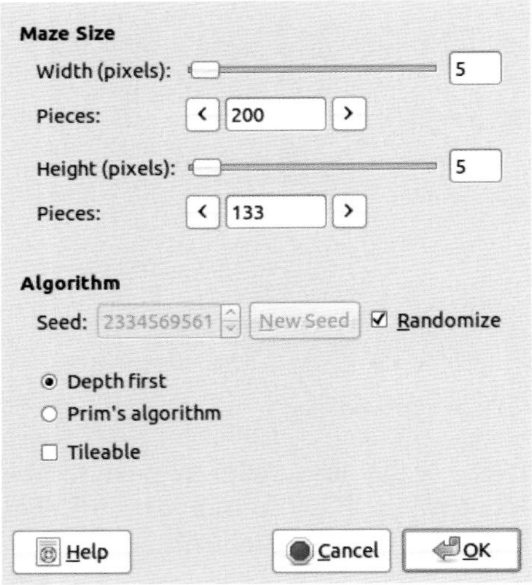

Figure 17.262 *After applying Maze*

Maze Size

Width (pixels): [====O————————] 5

Pieces: [<][200][>]

Height (pixels): [==O—————————] 5

Pieces: [<][133][>]

Algorithm

Seed: [2334569561 ⇕] [New Seed] ☑ Randomize

⦿ Depth first
◯ Prim's algorithm
☐ Tileable

[⊕ Help]   [● Cancel] [⏎ OK]

Figure 17.261 *The Maze dialog*

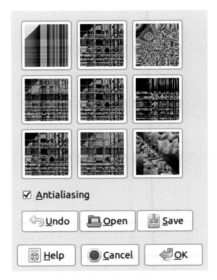

☑ Antialiasing

[↩ Undo] [🖵 Open] [🖫 Save]

[⊕ Help] [● Cancel] [⏎ OK]

Figure 17.263 *The Qbist dialog*

The dialog, shown in Figure 17.261, allows you to choose the width of the paths and the number of paths, horizontally and vertically. The maze generally looks best when the width and height are equal. The number of paths (called number of pieces) is linked to the width and height. The maze can be completely randomized, or you can set a seed or generate one with the corresponding button. There are two algorithms that can be used to generate the maze, and the result can be made tilable, in which case the maze extends to the boundaries of the layer. Otherwise, there is a white frame around it.

Our result is shown in Figure 17.262.

Qbist

Qbist is a random texture generator.

The dialog shown in Figure 17.263 is simple. Nine patterns are generated at the same time. The center one is the current selection, and the eight surrounding patterns are random variations on that selected pattern. If you click any of the nine patterns, that pattern becomes the new center pattern, and eight new derivative patterns are generated. Clicking the center pattern does not change it, but new derivative patterns are generated. There is no way to control the generation, since the patterns that appear are a matter of random chance. Although you can't intentionally generate a pattern again, you can

Figure 17.264 *One example of Qbist*

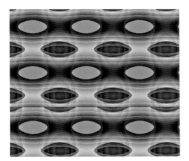

Figure 17.265 *Another example of Qbist*

Figure 17.266 *A third example of Qbist*

save an interesting pattern and reload it later. It is also possible to undo the generation process and return to a previous set of patterns.

Figures 17.264 to 17.266 show three random examples of Qbist-generated patterns.

Sinus

Sinus is yet another texture generator. It uses two colors to create wave-like patterns using the

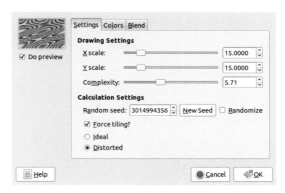

Figure 17.267 *The Sinus dialog, Settings tab*

Figure 17.268 *The Sinus dialog, Colors tab*

mathematical function sine. The texture fills the current layer.

The dialog, shown in Figure 17.267, contains three tabs. In the Settings tab, X SCALE and Y SCALE [0.0001 to 100] set the number of curves in the X and Y directions. The higher the value, the more compressed the curve is. COMPLEXITY controls how the two colors are combined. The randomization is similar to that of other filters. The FORCE TILING? checkbox allows you to make the texture tilable. Finally, an IDEAL texture is more symmetrical than a DISTORTED texture.

The Colors tab (Figure 17.268) allows you to choose the two colors, which can be set to black and white or the current foreground and background colors, or they can be chosen using the Color chooser. Two sliders can be used to make these colors semitransparent if the layer has an Alpha channel.

The Blend tab (Figure 17.269) contains a selection of three function types that determine

Figure 17.269 *The Sinus dialog, Blend tab*

Figure 17.270 *One example of Sinus*

Figure 17.271 *Another example of Sinus*

the shape of the waves. The SMALL EXPONENT slider sets the respective weight of the two colors.

Two examples of patterns generated with Sinus are shown in Figures 17.270 and 17.271.

Circuit

Circuit builds a maze that looks like a jumble of curved roads or a plate of spaghetti. It also vaguely resembles a diagram of circuitry, hence its name.

The dialog does not contain many parameters. The filter generates a maze and then oilifies it. The settings include the mask size for the Oilify filter and a randomization seed,

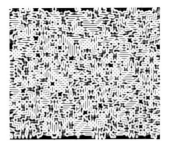

Figure 17.272 *After applying Circuit*

which allows the filter to generate a unique maze each time it's used. The width of the paths and the number of walls cannot be set. When the SEPARATE LAYER checkbox is checked, the circuit will be created on a new layer. If there is a selection, the circuit is generated within the selection, and a checkbox allows you to keep the selection active after the filter operates. Finally, if the NO BACKGROUND box is checked, the intervals between the paths are transparent, and the remaining selection excludes these transparent parts.

The result of Circuit is shown in Figure 17.272.

Fractal Explorer

Fractal Explorer is a fractal generator that's much simpler than the IFS Fractal filter. Its most interesting feature is the long list of available predefined fractals.

The dialog is unusually wide, so only the left side, which is common to all tabs, is shown in Figure 17.273, while the first of the three tabs, Parameters, is shown in Figure 17.274.

The left side of the dialog contains a large preview, a checkbox that turns the automatic update on or off, and a button that can be used to manually update the preview. Below that are buttons to zoom in or out and buttons to undo or redo changes in the zoom. ZOOM IN and ZOOM OUT zoom by a predefined amount. You can click and drag in the preview window to create a new viewing rectangle, which will zoom in on a specific part of the fractal.

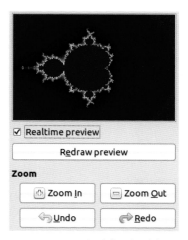

Figure 17.273 *The left side of the Fractal Explorer dialog*

| Parameters | Colors | Fractals |

Fractal Parameters

Left: -2.00000
Right: 2.00000
Top: -1.50000
Bottom: 1.50000
Iterations: 50
CX: -0.75000
CY: -0.20000

Open   Reset   Save

Fractal Type

- Mandelbrot
- Julia
- Barnsley 1
- Barnsley 2
- Barnsley 3
- Spider
- Man'o'war
- Lambda
- Sierpinski

Figure 17.274 *The Fractal Explorer dialog, Parameters tab*

| Parameters | Colors | Fractals |

Number of Colors

Number of colors: 256
☐ Use loglog smoothing

Color Density

Red: 1.00
Green: 1.00
Blue: 1.00

Color Function

Red	Green	Blue
○ Sine	○ Sine	● Sine
● Cosine	● Cosine	○ Cosine
○ None	○ None	○ None
☐ Inversion	☐ Inversion	☐ Inversion

Color Mode

- ● As specified above
- ○ Apply active gradient to final image

Figure 17.275 *The Fractal Explorer dialog, Colors tab*

a very large number of iterations can enhance the MANDELBROT fractal, which then has a great depth of detail that you can zoom in on.

The other parameters change the aspect and form of the fractals. The CX and CY sliders have a dramatic effect on the aspect, except with MANDELBROT and SIERPINSKI. The four direction parameters simulate rotating a plane on which the fractal is drawn.

The SAVE and OPEN buttons allow you to save an interesting combination of parameters for use later.

The Colors tab (Figure 17.275) allows you to adjust the appearance of a fractal. A gradient at the bottom of the tab shows the available colors, which change as the NUMBER OF COLORS slider is changed. The COLOR DENSITY sliders do not change what colors are available but how colors are used in the fractal. The COLOR FUNCTION radio buttons, along with the INVERSION checkboxes, also change how the available colors are applied. The color gradient (which changes the available colors) can be replaced using the

In the Parameters tab, skip down to the bottom and begin by choosing a FRACTAL TYPE. (If you've used this filter before, click the RESET button first.) The appearance of a fractal strongly depends on the number of ITERATIONS [1 to 1000], set using the corresponding slider. The BARNSLEY 1 fractal is invisible unless you zoom out. The BARNSLEY 2, SPIDER, MAN'O'WAR, and SIERPINSKI become invisible if the number of iterations is greater than 50. On the other hand,

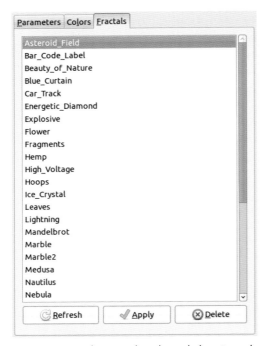

Figure 17.276 *The Fractal Explorer dialog, Fractals tab*

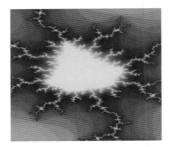

Figure 17.277 *One example of Fractal Explorer*

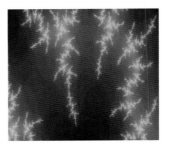

Figure 17.278 *A second example of Fractal Explorer*

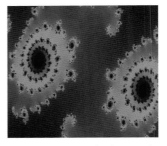

Figure 17.279 *A third example of Fractal Explorer*

COLOR MODE radio buttons along with the large gradient selection button.

The Fractals tab (Figure 17.276) is simply a list of 33 predefined fractals. When you choose one of them and click the APPLY button, the two other tabs change to reflect the corresponding parameters. You can subsequently change some of the parameters to personalize the fractal.

As is the case with other render filters, this filter is the source of endless experiments. Three example fractals are shown in Figures 17.277 through 17.279.

Gfig

Gfig is something special within the framework of GIMP. It is not really a filter but rather a tool to create geometric figures. Although GIMP is intended to create raster or pixelized images, Gfig works like a vector graphics tool, but the graphics it creates are pixelized. They are created in a new layer, on top of the source image.

The dialog, shown in Figure 17.280, shows the initial image. We chose a dark blue as the stroke color and a vivid yellow as the fill color, and we drew a regular star heptagon using the Star tool, selected from the bar at the top of the dialog.

The preview shows the entire initial image, zoomed out to fit the dialog size. The preview size cannot be changed. The top bar contains buttons for 21 tools, of which only the first 14 are shown here. The remaining 7 can be accessed using the drop-down menu on the far right. Most of the tools have no options. However,

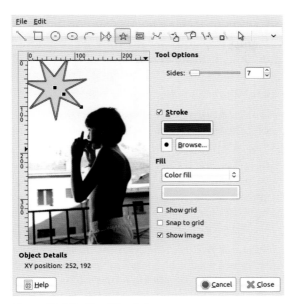

Figure 17.280 *The Gfig dialog*

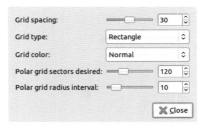

Figure 17.281 *The Grid function dialog*

the Star tool does have a slider for adjusting the number of sides that the polygon will have.

The geometric figures created using the first nine tools in the bar (from left to right) can be stroked and filled. Stroking is done using the selected color and brush, which can be changed by clicking the relevant buttons. Filling can be done with a color, pattern, shape gradient, vertical gradient, or horizontal gradient. The color, the pattern, or the gradient can be changed using a button that appears just below the field.

Note that there is no way to change the scale of the brush, so to adjust the brush, you must have a collection of brushes of different sizes. There is one in the brush folder, in a subfolder called `gimp-obsolete-files`. Since this subfolder is not visible from the Brushes dialog, you must copy all the brushes it contains to your own brush folder. Place them in a subfolder called `Obsolete`, so they all automatically bear the corresponding tag. See Chapter 22 for more details about the location of the brush folder.

Three checkboxes can be used to do the following:

- Show a regular grid.
- Snap to this grid.
- Show the image (i.e., preview the result of the filter).

This filter has its own menus, which replace the general GIMP image menus, making this filter very different from any other. The File menu contains three entries:

- OPEN ($\boxed{\text{CTRL+O}}$) reloads a previously saved geometric drawing.
- SAVE ($\boxed{\text{CTRL+S}}$) saves the current geometric drawing in a file.
- CLOSE ($\boxed{\text{CTRL+C}}$), which is equivalent to the CLOSE button in the bottom right of the dialog, applies changes and closes the dialog.

The Edit menu contains four entries:

- UNDO ($\boxed{\text{CTRL+Z}}$) undoes the last action. However, there is no redo provision.
- CLEAR deletes the current drawing. This can be undone.
- GRID ($\boxed{\text{CTRL+G}}$) opens the dialog shown in Figure 17.281, where you can set the characteristics of the grid:
  - Spacing [10 to 50]
  - Type: rectangle, polar, or isometric
  - Color: normal, black, white, gray, darker, lighter, or very dark

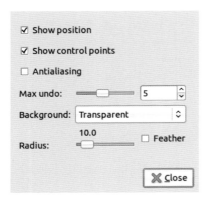

Figure 17.282 *The Preferences function dialog*

– In the case of a polar grid, the number of grid sectors [5 to 360] and the grid radius interval [5 to 50]

• PREFERENCES (CTRL+P) opens the dialog shown in Figure 17.282. There are three checkboxes that show the mouse position (in OBJECT DETAILS), show control points in the image, and turn on antialiasing. You can also set the maximum number of undo [1 to 10], and you can choose whether the background is transparent, the foreground or background color, white, or a copy of the image. A checkbox can be used to feather the drawing, with a radius set by the slider [0 to 100].

You can create several geometric shapes in the drawing, but when you add a new form, build it first and then change its stroke and fill parameters, or the changes will affect the previous shape.

The object-creating tools, corresponding to buttons in the top bar, are as follows:

• Line: Click the origin and drag to the end. This creates a straight line.

• Rectangle: Click one corner and drag to the opposite corner.

• Circle: Click the center and drag to the radius.

• Ellipse: Click the center and drag to the corner of the embedding rectangle.

• Arc: Click the three points defining the arc.

• Regular polygon: Set the number of sides [3 to 200], click the center, and drag to one of the vertices.

• Star: Works like the Regular polygon tool.

• Spiral: Set the number of turns [1 to 20], the orientation (right or left), and then click and drag as with the Circle tool.

• Bézier curve: Click the successive control points and SHIFT-click the final one. The options allow you to close the curve and to show the *line frame*, which is composed of the tangents from the last control point.

The next five buttons can be used to make adjustments to the shapes you've drawn. First select the shape by clicking one of its control points. Then, depending on which button you've selected, you can move the entire shape, move one of the control points, copy the shape, or delete it.

The shapes are superimposed in the order they were built. The additional tools available on the right of the top bar raise or lower the selected shape by one position, put it at the top or the bottom of the stack, display only one object, or show all objects.

Gfig offers a set of operations that allow you to create complicated geometric objects. One example is shown in Figure 17.283, where very precise shapes could be drawn thanks to the large image size (2304 × 3456).

Lava

The Lava filter simulates lava as seen in a volcano crater.

The dialog, shown in Figure 17.284, has no preview. You can set the randomization seed, the size of the waves [0 to 100], and the wave roughness [3 to 50]. The gradient determines the colors used in the waves, which can be a nice lava red or something completely unrealistic. If there is a selection in the current layer, you can choose whether to keep it. You can create the

Figure 17.283 *After applying Gfig*

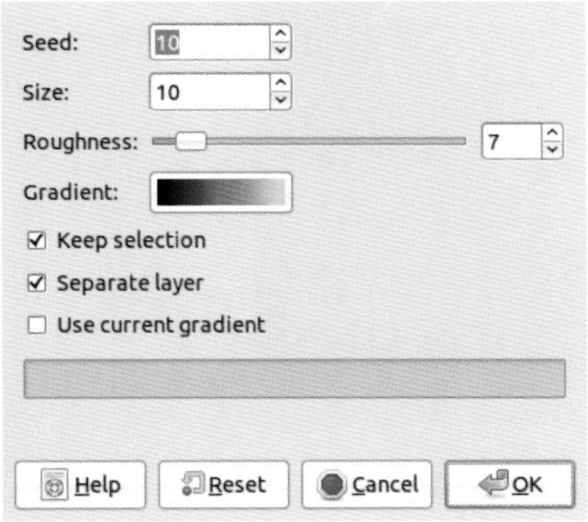

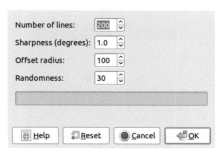

Figure 17.286 *The Line Nova dialog*

Figure 17.287 *After applying Line Nova*

Line Nova

Line Nova draws a multispiked star on the current layer, in the foreground color.

In the dialog, shown in Figure 17.286, only four parameters can be set: the number of spikes (at least 40), their sharpness [0 to 10], the offset radius (the radius of the central circle), and the randomness of the spike lengths.

A star created with Line Nova is shown in Figure 17.287.

Sphere Designer

Sphere Designer creates a 3D sphere on the current layer, which covers up most of the layer contents.

The dialog, shown in Figure 17.288, contains a preview that is automatically updated. The sphere image is built with several texture layers (which are merged when the sphere is generated). These layers are listed on the top right in the dialog. The dialog also has buttons to create a new layer, duplicate the current one,

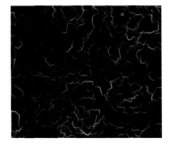

Figure 17.284 *The Lava dialog*

Figure 17.285 *After applying Lava*

lava on a new layer, and you can choose to use the current gradient to color the lava.

An example made with the Lava filter is shown in Figure 17.285.

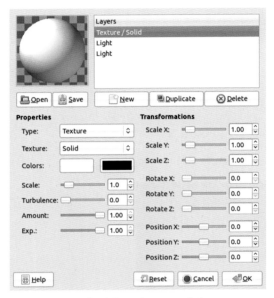

Figure 17.288 *The Sphere Designer dialog*

Figure 17.289 *Possible textures for the sphere*

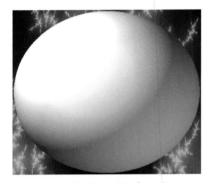

Figure 17.290 *Example of a sphere*

or delete it. The OPEN and SAVE buttons allow you to save the current settings into a file or to restore a previously saved set.

When a layer is selected, its PROPERTIES can be set. The layer's TYPE can be TEXTURE, BUMP, or LIGHT, and its TEXTURE can be chosen from the list shown in Figure 17.289. Two color buttons can be used to select colors for TEXTURE type layers. LIGHT type layers only use the first color, while BUMP type layers are colorless.

Four sliders set the characteristic of the texture. SCALE and TURBULENCE [1 to 10] are general settings with effects that depend on the layer type. AMOUNT [0 to 1] sets the influence of the layer on the sphere. EXP [0 to 1] sets the strength of the pattern and affects only the texture types MARBLE, LIZARD, NOISE, and SPIRAL.

The TRANSFORMATIONS section of the dialog contains three groups of sliders, and each group has a slider for the X, Y, and Z coordinates. SCALE [0 to 10] stretches or compresses the pattern in the corresponding direction. ROTATE [0 to 360] rotates the pattern, but not the sphere itself. POSITION [−20 to +20] sets the position of

the texture on the sphere, or the position of the light if the layer type is LIGHT.

See Figure 17.290 for an example of a sphere generated with Sphere Designer.

Spyrogimp

Spyrogimp simulates a spirograph (a geometric drawing toy) on the current layer. Although the concept is fairly simple, there is a wide range of possible results, so this filter can be yet another source of endless experimentation.

In the dialog, shown in Figure 17.291, the first option is the curve type. Figures 17.292 to 17.294 illustrate the three available types.

The parameters mimic the properties of a spirograph, which creates designs using gears with various numbers of teeth [1 to 120] and various shapes (see Figure 17.295). Each design

Type:	Spyrograph	⌄
Shape:	Circle	⌄
Outer teeth:	[slider]	86 ⌄
Inner teeth:	[slider]	70 ⌄
Margin (pixels):	0 ⌄	
Hole ratio:	[slider]	0.40 ⌄
Start angle:	[slider]	0 ⌄
Tool:	Pencil	⌄
Brush:	· Browse...	
Color method:	Solid Color	⌄
Color:	[black bar]	
Gradient:	[gradient bar]	

[⊕ Help] [⟳ Reset] [● Cancel] [⏎ OK]

Figure 17.291 *The Spyrogimp dialog*

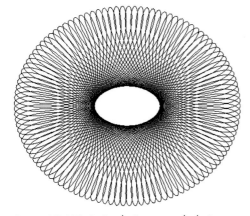

Figure 17.292 *A simple Spyrograph design*

is done using two gears, and the complexity of the design depends on the value of the greatest common multiple of the numbers of teeth. The combination of 120 and 60 leads to a very simple curve, while 120 and 61 yield an extremely complex curve, with a moiré effect. The most complicated design in the given range occurs when the gears with 120 and 119 teeth are used. More complicated designs take longer to render.

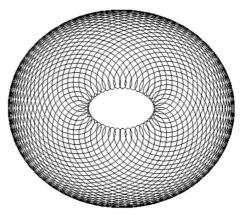

Figure 17.293 *A simple Epitrochoid design*

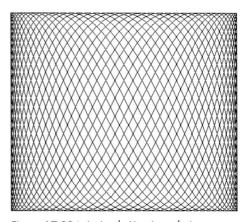

Figure 17.294 *A simple Lissajous design*

Circle
Frame
Triangle
Square
Pentagon
Hexagon
Polygon: 7 sides
Polygon: 8 sides
Polygon: 9 sides
Polygon: 10 sides

Figure 17.295 *Shapes available for Spyrogimp*

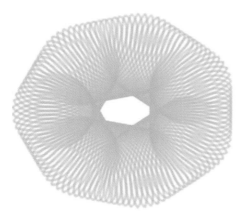

Figure 17.296 *One example of Spyrogimp*

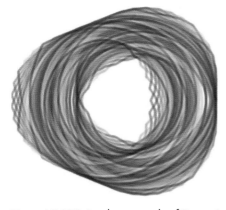

Figure 17.297 *Another example of Spyrogimp*

MARGIN sets the width of the border of the image, where the design is not drawn. It can be negative, which causes the design to extend beyond the edges of the image. HOLE RATIO sets the diameter of the center hole. START ANGLE sets the angle of the first line that's drawn, which is not very important since the design is circular and closed. Changing the START ANGLE just rotates the design.

The TOOL option can be used to select among Pencil, Brush, or Airbrush. The Brush works best when a very small diameter is used. See "Gfig" on page 468 for more information on adjusting the brush size. The COLOR METHOD can be a solid color or a gradient with a repeated sawtooth or triangle pattern. The color or gradient can be changed using the buttons below the COLOR METHOD menu.

See Figures 17.296 and 17.297 for examples of designs made with Spyrogimp.

18 Animation Tools

Many powerful tools are designed specifically for digital animation. Blender, for example, is free software for creating professional 3D animation (see *http://www.blender.org/*). Compared to Blender, GIMP offers limited animation tools. But if you just want to make a simple animation, GIMP can get the job done. As you saw in Chapter 6, you can use GIMP to make animated GIFs for a web page, and as you'll see in this chapter, you can also use GIMP to edit a short digital video.

We begin this chapter with the principles of animation, and then we discuss the file formats specific to animations. We also cover GIMP's various tools for building animations, including GAP (GIMP Animation Plug-in; installed separately from GIMP).

18.1 Principles of Animation

To use the animation building tools available in GIMP and the GAP plug-in effectively, you must first understand the underlying principles of animation. First, we present the physiology of viewing animations and their internal and external digital representations, and then we discuss how these principles work in GIMP.

Frame Frequency and Vision

Animations are made with a sequence of images, called *frames*. Images persist on the eye's retina, especially when there is a strong contrast between light and dark (as in a movie theater), so when images are displayed in quick succession, they appear to be a continuous animation.

Currently, the standard frame frequency is 24 frames per second. Hand-drawn cartoons were usually filmed at 12 frames per second, and each frame was photographed twice. But in the earliest movies, the frequency was only 20 frames per second, which is why actors appear to move too fast in very old films.

Television is different from movies projected in a theater. Because the contrast between the screen and the surroundings is generally less than in a movie theater, the image persistence is shorter, so frames must be shown at a higher frequency. Usually only every other line is drawn on each screen refresh, so at a rate of 60 refreshes per second, the full image is redrawn only 30 times per second.

The refresh frequency may be even higher for digital animation viewed on a monitor, thanks to the capabilities of the screen and the computer itself. Because people use computers in bright offices and even outside, the contrast with the environment is often weak, so a (in animation) minimum of 60 frames per second is necessary.

If you were to view the frames independently, you would see motion blur on fast-moving objects, but when you watch the video, everything looks sharp because the visual centers in the brain process the blurry frames into a moving object. The ability to create a sharp image from blurred frames depends on the image's persistence. If persistence is too short due to low contrast between the room and the screen, then the motion blur can become visible. Because of this, computer games with very quick movement often need a frame frequency greater than 60 frames per second.

Frames and Layers

Depending on the tool used, frames in GIMP can either be layers in one image or separate image files. When stored as layers, frames cannot include multiple layers, but when stored as multiple images, they can.

To use layers as frames, you have to give each layer a *duration* and *replacement mode*. You do this by editing the layer name itself, by double-clicking it in the Layers dialog, by selecting **Layers: right-click > Edit Layer Attributes**, or by pressing F2 when the mouse pointer is in the Layers dialog. The frame duration is specified in milliseconds and within parentheses, as in (200ms), and the replacement mode is also designated in parentheses, as in (replace). The order in which the layers appear on the screen is *from bottom to top*.

When frames are independent images, they're all stored in one folder and named in order. The names are something like *name_*00001.xcf, *name_*00002.xcf, and so on (where *name* is whatever you designate). The frames' duration cannot be changed, so to slow down part of the animation, you must duplicate the frames, and to speed it up, you delete frames. Because frames are images and not layers, no

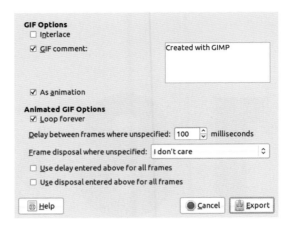

Figure 18.1 *The GIF Export File dialog*

replacement mode is available. Every new frame replaces the preceding one.

Output Formats

Simple animations are represented in GIF encoding, and the GIF Export File dialog (shown in Figure 18.1) can be set to save the frames as an animation instead of being set to flatten the image. When you choose to export as an animated GIF, you can also choose

- whether the animation runs only once or forever

- the duration of frames

- the replacement mode (called *frame disposal*)

- whether to use the specified duration for all frames

- whether to use the specified replacement mode for all frames

The default delay of 100 milliseconds per frame results in only 10 frames per second. This delay is fine for a slow animation, but the frame frequency should be much higher if the animation has fast movements or else it will look jerky. To increase the frame frequency, reduce the frame duration, for example, to 40 milliseconds to obtain a frequency of 25 frames per second.

Using GIF for animation has all the drawbacks of this encoding, the biggest of which is the indexed representation, explained more thoroughly in Chapter 20. Basically, GIF can represent at most only 256 different colors, which is fine for a cartoon or logo but not for a home movie.

GIF animations can be viewed on any graphical web browser, so they're popular on web pages. You can use the <img> HTML tag to display an image inside a page. It has to be loaded in full before the animation begins, so keep animations to a few hundred KB maximum, and avoid using more than one animation on a page.

JPEG encoding can't be used for animations, but the corresponding MPEG encoding can. According to the official MPEG website (*http://mpeg.chiariglione.org/*), MPEG-1 was established in 1988 and is the standard on which Video CD and MP3 are based. DVDs are based on MPEG-2, and MPEG-4 is the multimedia standard. Other versions, like MPEG-7 and MPEG-21, also have modern applications.

An MPEG is a video made of JPEG frames. When the difference between successive frames is small (as when only a person's mouth is moving), you don't need to represent the entire frame again, reducing the video file size and increasing the feasible frame frequency and definition.

So an MPEG video comprises several frame types: complete JPEG images, frames of the differences between the current and the previous frame, and frames of the differences between the current and the next frame. The video recorder must save three different frames at the same time, including full JPEG frames at regular intervals.

The MPEG format also encodes the audio, as most video formats do. The GAP plug-in set generates MPEG-1 and MPEG-2 formats.

Similar to JPEG, PNG has a corresponding encoding for animations, called MNG. Unfortunately, this format is not supported by some web browsers, so it's not a viable replacement for animated GIFs. For this reason, we won't cover it, but GIMP can work with MNG animation.

Although they can use indexed representation, PNG and MNG generally use RGB, whereas GIF always uses indexed representation. Converting to indexed representation inevitably results in a loss in quality, and the loss is even worse when working with animation. If the MNG format were supported by more browsers, it would be much better than GIF for web animations.

Some proprietary formats are also supported by GIMP with GAP, but we won't cover those either, except to say that GAP can generate the Apple QuickTime format and read other proprietary formats like Microsoft AVI.

Because animations can be represented as layers or images, using several different formats, you'll find conversion tools handy. GAP provides tools to

- convert a multilayer image to a multi-image animation, and vice versa

- convert an MPEG or AVI animation to a multi-image animation, and vice versa

Optimizing Animations

An animation is generally a huge file. For example, if one JPEG is 33KB and you build an animation with a total of 21 frames (about 2 seconds!), the resulting animation will be 1.8MB. You can easily extrapolate that a one-minute animation using similar photos will be more than 54MB, which is far too large for a web page.

Fortunately, animation size can be reduced via optimization. For example, GIMP has a tool for optimizing animated GIFs. If only a small area in the animation is changing (a hand moves, a person smiles), then the parts of the image that don't change from frame to frame are represented only once in the background layer. Subsequent layers are transparent except when things change, leading to a much smaller file size.

When we applied this tool to the 1.8MB animation, we reduced its size to 337KB (one-fifth the original size). This reduction is significant, but the 54MB one-minute animation would still be too large for a web page because it would reduce only to about 10MB, and a nonstreaming video on a web page should probably be 2MB maximum. The MPEG format can reduce the size of a video more than GIF optimization can; therefore, it is the standard for video on the Web.

18.2 Tools for Building Multilayer Animations

In this section, we cover tools for building animations that will be stored as a single image, with each layer acting as a frame. Some of these tools were used in Chapter 6, where we demonstrated simple animation techniques.

Animating by Hand

Suppose you want to move an object on a fixed background, as cartoon animators did 50 years ago. For example, how might you animate an old biplane landing in a field? You might try the method shown in Section 6.1, placing the plane in its successive positions in separate layers. But you have a problem: Each plane you position is added to the image instead of replacing the previous one, so the final animation is full of planes. And if you choose the replace mode in the layers, the background disappears as soon as the plane appears.

To make this animation work, you can do the following:

1. Duplicate the background for each plane layer.

2. Place the background layers below each plane layer.

3. Merge each plane layer with the underlying background layer.

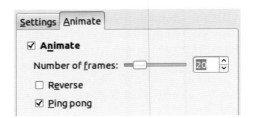

Figure 18.2 *The IWarp dialog, Animate tab*

Now the animation works, but making even a short animation by hand takes a long time. Wouldn't it be great to have tools that automate parts of the animation-building process? With GIMP, we do.

The IWarp Tool

The IWarp tool, accessed via **Image: Filters > Distorts > IWarp**, is demonstrated in "Interactive Deformation" on page 151, and its dialog is shown in Figure 6.32 on page 152.

To use IWarp for animation, warp the image as you would warp a still photo, and then click the ANIMATE tab and choose to generate an animation. In Figure 18.2, we chose to create 20 frames between the first and last image, and we selected PING PONG, which repeats the animation in reverse. These settings result in 40 layers (20 forward and another 20 in reverse order), numbered from 0 to 39. Because the number of frames determines the animation's smoothness, don't reduce the number of frames unless the final file size is critical. If you plan to export the animation as a GIF file, you can optimize it to reduce file size later.

The Morph Tool

The Morph tool is part of GAP. It generates multilayer animations by progressively transforming one image into another. Use it to morph between images of people, as demonstrated in Chapter 6. You can also use it to morph one word into another, as we'll demonstrate now.

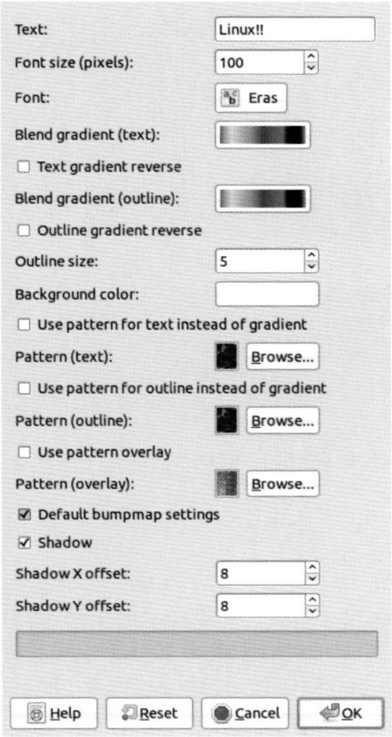

Text:	Linux!!
Font size (pixels):	100
Font:	Eras
Blend gradient (text):	
☐ Text gradient reverse	
Blend gradient (outline):	
☐ Outline gradient reverse	
Outline size:	5
Background color:	
☐ Use pattern for text instead of gradient	
Pattern (text):	Browse...
☐ Use pattern for outline instead of gradient	
Pattern (outline):	Browse...
☐ Use pattern overlay	
Pattern (overlay):	Browse...
☑ Default bumpmap settings	
☑ Shadow	
Shadow X offset:	8
Shadow Y offset:	8

 Help   Reset   Cancel   OK

Figure 18.3 *Building one of the logos*

Morphing Text

In this example, the word "Windows" will be progressively morphed to the word "Linux!!" with just a few clicks.

First, build the logos using **Image: File > Create > Logos > Glossy**, with the default parameters, as shown in Figure 18.3. Enter *Windows* in the text field to create the first logo (Figure 18.4), and then enter *Linux!!* to create the second logo (Figure 18.5). Flatten both logos (**Layers: right-click > Flatten Image**) so they each contain only one layer. Copy the Linux layer to the Windows image as a new layer by dragging the layer thumbnail to the image.

Because the Linux layer is narrower than the Windows layer, you must increase its size to match via **Image: Layer > Layer to Image Size**. Also add an Alpha channel to both layers.

Now apply the Morph tool by selecting **Image: Video > Morphing > Morph**, which opens the dialog in Figure 18.6.

Figure 18.4 *The initial logo*

Figure 18.5 *The final logo*

How you place the *shape points* determines how a point in the first image is morphed into a point in the second image. For a more complicated project, you should choose points carefully, but in this case, just click the SHAPE button, and the tool automatically creates and places points on the sides of both images.

The number of STEPS is the number of frames in the animation. Choose 20, click OK, and that's it! The animation plays on a loop, but you can pause it between iterations by increasing the duration of the top layer. Optimize the animation and save it as a GIF.

The Morph Tool Dialog

Let's explore this dialog section by section. In the top-left section, the SOURCE menu allows you to choose the source layer from the images open in GIMP. The X and Y boxes display the coordinates of the current shape point in the source layer. You can set these points by clicking the layer image, and you can adjust the coordinates using the vertical arrows at the right. Click FIT ZOOM to reset the zoom to show the entire source layer.

The top-right section is similar to the top-left section, except that it deals with the destination instead of the source layer. This section also includes POINT, which shows the current shape point. You can choose any shape point and then change or check its position with the X and Y boxes.

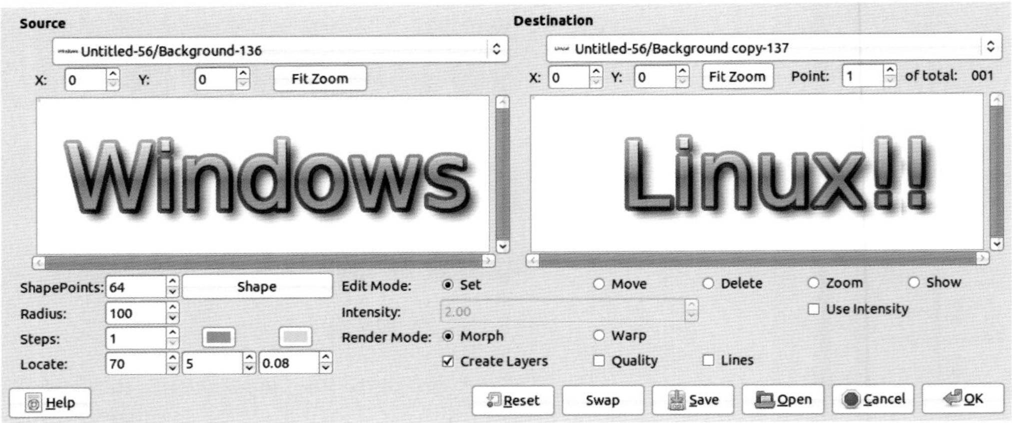

Figure 18.6 *The Morph tool dialog*

The bottom-left section of the dialog includes these options:

- SHAPEPOINTS and SHAPE are used to set the number of shapepoints that are automatically placed and to place them. The more shape points you use, the more precise the morphing. But when you use more shape points, you also use more computing power. As a rule, place shape points where things change: You don't need two points close to each other if no important variation occurs in the image between them.

  The automatic shape points are placed along the outline of the source layer. Transparent pixels are not included in the outline.

  If you SHIFT-click the SHAPE button, the number of points specified is *added* to the existing number of points. Otherwise the specified points replace the existing ones.

- RADIUS sets the size of the area influenced by every shape point.

- STEPS sets the number of layers to be added or modified between the source layer (at the bottom) and the target layer (at the top). Any preexisting middle layers are modified.

- The two color buttons to the right of the STEPS box set the colors of source and destination shape points.

- LOCATE is useful for automatically locating features in the source and destination layers, but it can be time consuming because of the computations involved. It is triggered when you CTRL-click a shape point. The source shape point is automatically placed on the closest feature and the destination point on the feature that best matches the source. The first field in the dialog sets the radius in the source layer, the second field sets the radius of the area to be searched in the destination layer, and the last field is the edge-detection threshold for detecting a feature. You can play with these parameters, but their default values are already well chosen.

Finally, the bottom-right portion of the Morph tool dialog covers these settings:

- EDIT MODE has five options. SET is the most versatile. It lets you add a new shape point by clicking in the source layer. SHIFT-click to create a new point that's near an existing one. Right-click to delete an existing point. This mode also lets you drag existing points to a new position. MOVE mode is similar to SET, but clicking doesn't create a new point.

  DELETE mode is used only to delete a point. The ZOOM mode allows you to zoom in on a specific point. CTRL-clicking zooms out. SHOW mode should simply show the coordinates of the point you clicked, but as this book goes to press, this mode is unusable.

- INTENSITY is active if you select USE INTENSITY. When this box is checked, the shape point's influence decreases geometrically with increasing distance from the point to the deformation radius. When the USE INTENSITY box is unchecked, the influence decreases linearly.

- RENDER MODE can be set to Morph or Warp. MORPH is the normal mode. In this mode, the source layer transforms progressively into the destination layer by *forward warps* (warping the source layer into the destination layer), *backward warps* (warping the destination layer into the source layer), and *cross fades*. WARP makes the transition using only forward warps, but every time we've tried it, the results were strange and not very useful.

- When checked (which it is by default), CREATE LAYERS creates the number of new layers indicated in the STEPS box. When unchecked, the existing layers are modified, but no new layers are created.

- When checked, QUALITY uses a better transformation algorithm, but this algorithm is much more processor intensive and may crash the tool.

- When checked, the LINES box displays small vectors that show how a specific shape point will be moved.

- The RESET button removes all existing shape points.

- The SWAP button exchanges the source and destination, but it does not move the layers in the image.

- The SAVE and OPEN buttons do what you'd expect: SAVE saves all the shape point coordinates in a file, and OPEN loads previously saved coordinates. Open allows you to use the same shape points for different images or to save a partially completed project so you can return to it later, for example, to try different values for options.

Filtering All Layers

This tool, accessed via **Image: Filters > Filter all Layers** is also part of GAP but operates on multilayer animations. The concept is simple:

1. Build a bunch of layers, for example, by duplicating a layer over and over.

2. Apply a transformation to all the layers using one of the many GIMP filters.

You can apply this filter using the same parameters for all layers, or you can change the parameter values progressively from layer to layer.

Figure 18.7 shows the Filter all Layers dialog. The menu on the left lists the many available filters, called `plug-in-filter-name`. The names are in alphabetical order. You can search for a specific filter using the buttons at the bottom right of the dialog:

- SEARCH BY NAME compares the characters typed in the SEARCH box to the names of the available filters.

- SEARCH BY BLURB searches in the filter's description, located just above PARAMETERS in the top-right area of the dialog.

- SEARCH BY MENU PATH searches in the menu path, located above the description.

In the first two cases, the string entered in the SEARCH box is treated as a *regular expression*. Searching using expressions is a complex concept, so we'll provide just the basic explanation that you need to search efficiently. In short, a normal character, like a letter or a number, matches itself. A dot can stand in for any character, so `c.l.r` matches `color` and `celar`. An asterisk can match any number of occurrences of the preceding character, including none, so `sear*ching` matches `seaching`, `searching`, and `searrrching`. The dot and asterisk notations can also be combined, so `color.*hance` matches `color-enhance`, `colorhance`, and `colorabcdhance`.

When you select a filter in the left menu, its description appears on the right in the dialog. Most descriptions are written for GIMP developers rather than typical users, but you can still

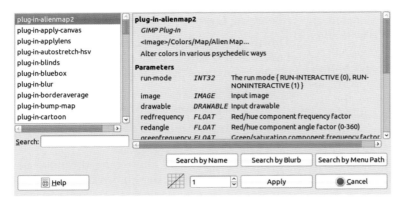

Figure 18.7 *The Filter all Layers dialog*

learn from them. The description gives you a general sense of what the filter does, and the parameter description gives you an idea of what you can change in the filter dialog.

Once you've chosen a plug-in, the first two options at the bottom of the dialog may be active. They are inactive if the chosen plug-in does not have any parameters, as is the case for plug-in-blur. If these options are active, they let you choose *acceleration characteristics*:

- 0 means that the filter will be applied with the same parameter values for all layers. In this case, the box on the left is empty.

- 1 means that the parameters will vary, from the first value given to the last one, with constant speed. The box on the left displays an ascending diagonal line.

- A negative value means the speed of variation will decrease (deceleration). The box on the left displays a convex curve.

- A positive value (other than 1) means the speed of variation will increase (acceleration). The box on the left displays a concave curve.

- You can set the acceleration value numerically or by using the small arrows on the right or by dragging the curve.

After making your selections, click APPLY. If the filter has parameters, its dialog opens, with a preview and the variable parameters displayed.

If the acceleration is 0, this dialog appears only once because the parameters are the same for all the layers. If the acceleration is not 0, the filter dialog appears twice, first for the bottom layer and then for the top layer. Remember, animations are played from bottom to top. A tiny warning dialog precedes the second filter dialog. In this second filter dialog, you choose the final values of the filter parameters. A new dialog appears and asks for the name of a backup file to be used for building the intermediate layers. This file is about the same size as the final animation, but you don't need to save it, so the name isn't important and the file can be stored in a temporary folder.

Click CONTINUE, and the filter is applied to all the layers, with parameters interpolated between the first and last values according to the acceleration factor.

You'll also see a button for skipping a frame. It displays the number of the frame to skip, and if you click it, the dialog appears again, asking for the filename. You can choose to continue or to skip the next frame also. You can't skip the first frame, however. One way to use the skip feature is to set the initial parameters so the filter does nothing and then begin applying the filter after skipping several frames. Doing this is the same as setting the acceleration to a high positive number.

Blend...
Burn-In...
Rippling...
Selection to AnimImage...
Spinning Globe...
Waves...

Optimize (Difference)
Optimize (for GIF)
▷ Playback...
Unoptimize

Figure 18.8 *The Animation menu*

Intermediate frames: 8
Max. blur radius: 0
☑ Looped

Help   Reset   Cancel   OK

Figure 18.9 *The Blend dialog*

Filter all Layers has no undo capability, but you can use the normal undo (CTRL+Z) over and over, or you can open the UNDO HISTORY dialog. Of course, if you have many layers, undoing one layer at a time will be tedious, so save the original image before filtering all the layers.

18.3   The Animation Menu

We've already covered most of the tools for creating multilayer animations, but we need to discuss a few minor tools in the **Image: Filters > Animation** menu, shown in Figure 18.8.

Blend

The Blend tool requires at least two layers plus a background layer.

You choose the number n of intermediate frames in the tool dialog (Figure 18.9). The intermediate frames are a composite of the previous frame and the next one. A new image is built, with the number of layers equal to $(n + 1) \times f$, where f is the total number of layers in the original image (not including the background layer). If you only have two layers,

Glow color:
☐ Fadeout
Fadeout width: 100
Corona width: 7
After glow: 50
☑ Add glowing
☐ Prepare for GIF
Speed (pixels/frame):   50

Help   Reset   Cancel   OK

Figure 18.10 *The Burn-In dialog*

the new image has $2(n + 1)$ layers. The first layer fades out, then the next layer appears, and then the first one fades in again. If you have more layers, the layers fade in and out from the bottom layer to the top layer and then again from the top to the bottom layer.

The animation created by this tool is very specific, so the applications are pretty limited.

Burn-In

The Burn-In tool generates an animation in which one image fades into another. This tool requires a starting image with two layers. The top layer *must* have an Alpha channel, and this layer must be selected or the tool is grayed out in the menu. Figure 18.10 shows the tool dialog. The upper part of the dialog specifies how the transition between layers is done.

When FADEOUT is checked, the upper layer progressively fades out from left to right, revealing the layer beneath. Figure 18.11 shows an intermediate layer of the animation, with the FADE-OUT WIDTH set to 200 pixels.

If ADD GLOWING is checked, a "glow" effect is added to the transition in the color specified in the GLOW COLOR box. Figure 18.12 shows an intermediate layer of the animation, with the width of the Fadeout set to 250 pixels to take into account the width of the glow (50 pixels).

When FADEOUT is unchecked, the upper layer completely disappears. Figure 18.13 shows an

Figure 18.11 *Fading out, without glowing*

Figure 18.12 *Fading out, with glowing*

Figure 18.13 *With glowing, but without fading out*

Figure 18.14 *The Rippling dialog*

Figure 18.15 *One layer of the rippled animation*

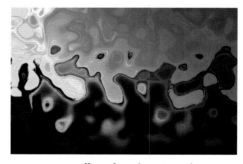

Figure 18.16 *Effect of rippling strength*

intermediate layer of the animation when the glow effect is used. The animation speed is specified as the number of pixels in the upper layer that becomes transparent in every frame. The number of frames is automatically computed from this number.

Rippling

This tool takes an image with one layer and builds an animation that simulates the reflection of the image on water with ripples created as if by wind. Figure 18.14 shows the Rippling tool dialog, and Figure 18.15 shows one layer of a rippled animation. RIPPLING STRENGTH sets the force of the wind. NUMBER OF FRAMES is the number of layers that are created.

EDGE BEHAVIOR specifies how the layer edges are handled. BLACK keeps image borders straight, and the two other modes (WRAP and SMEAR) deform the border in different ways.

The edge behavior effect is only apparent when the rippling strength is greater than the default value of 3.0. A high rippling strength leads to dramatic image distortion, as shown in Figure 18.16, where the strength is set to 80.

Figure 18.17 *A portrait with the face selected*

Figure 18.18 *The Selection to Animimage dialog*

Selection to Animimage

The Selection to Animimage tool is very similar to the Filter all Layers tool, discussed in "Filtering All Layers" on page 481. In this section, we focus on the differences between them.

Figure 18.17 shows an image with a single layer and a selection that has been made using the Free Select tool and corrected with the Quick Mask.

The Selection to Animimage tool dialog, accessed via **Image: Filters > Animation > Selection to Animimage**, is shown in Figure 18.18. You can choose the number of layers to be generated. This plug-in automatically creates the layers, unlike the Filter all Layers tool. You can also choose the color used to fill the new image outside of the selection and whether to apply the

filter to all new layers. If the filter is not applied to all new layers, the tool generates the layers without applying a filter.... So it just duplicates the layer!

When you apply the filter, two new windows replace the dialog:

- A new image containing a copy of the selection made in the initial image, with the number of copies of the background layer specified in the preceding dialog
- A dialog identical to Figure 18.18 that lets you select a filter

You can choose the Cartoon filter, for example, and select APPLY VARYING to open the Cartoon filter dialog (see Figure 17.148 on page 433) for the first layer. Set the PERCENT BLACK to 0, and click OK. In the next dialog, set PERCENT BLACK to 1.000 for the final layer.

The result is an animation that progressively transforms the portrait into a cartoon.

Spinning Globe

The Spinning Globe tool automatically maps an image to a globe and then makes it spin. Simply select an image, open the tool, set the two parameters, and decide whether the three checkboxes should be checked, and the computer does the work.

The image you use determines the shape of the globe. If the image is a true square, the globe is a sphere. Otherwise, it is an ellipsoid.

To demonstrate, we used the same portrait as before. When we select the Spinning Globe tool (**Image: Filters > Animation > Spinning Globe**), the dialog shown in Figure 18.19 appears. Here, we choose the number of frames. For a photograph, 10 is too few and would make the animation jerky. For a simple graphic, however, 10 frames might be enough. You can also choose the rotation direction, which is right to left by default, and whether the background of the animation is transparent (you can add a background later) or uses the background color. The animation can use indexing with a given number of

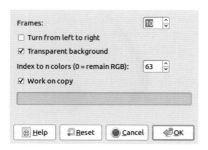

Figure 18.19 *The Spinning Globe dialog*

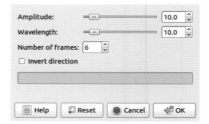

Figure 18.21 *The Waves dialog*

Figure 18.20 *Final animation*

looks like the waves created when a stone is thrown into a still lake.

When you select the Waves tool, the dialog shown in Figure 18.21 appears. The rock always falls in the center of the image, and the proportions of the concentric waves are determined by the image itself. But you can choose the following:

- The number of frames. Six frames is normally enough.
- The amplitude and wavelength of the waves. The default values are usually fine.
- The direction of the movement. If you click INVERT DIRECTION, the waves move toward the center of the animation and disappear, which is a weird effect since it runs contrary to known physics.

Click OK to generate the frames. Figure 18.22 shows the initial image and the animation's effect.

Optimizing and Playing an Animation

The Animation menu has four additional entries, which let you optimize and play back your animations:

- OPTIMIZE (FOR GIF) is probably the option you'll use most frequently. It saves a multilayer image as a GIF animation. This tool has no dialog and generates a new image with the same layers as the original image but at a (hopefully) reduced size.
- PLAYBACK tests an animation generated as a multilayer image. In this tool's dialog, the

colors, which is wise if you plan to export the animation to GIF. Finally, you can choose to work on a copy of the image.

Here, we change FRAMES to 30 and uncheck TRANSPARENT BACKGROUND. Figure 18.20 shows the animation stopped on frame 2.

Waves

The Waves tool is even easier to use than Spinning Globe, and the result isn't too bad either. The Waves tool generates an animation that

Figure 18.22 *The Waves animation, before (left) and after (right)*

image appears in its original size without any zoom, which can be problematic if the image is larger than the screen because the toolbar may appear off-screen. If that happens, just use CTRL+W to close the dialog.

The toolbar buttons should be self-explanatory with the exception of DE-TACH, which removes the image animation from its frame and allows you to move the frame. If you then want to use CTRL+W to close the frame, make sure the frame window (and not the full animation) is selected first.

- OPTIMIZE (DIFFERENCE) has almost the same effect as OPTIMIZE (FOR GIF). The main difference is that OPTIMIZE (DIFFERENCE) keeps all layers the same size as the image, whereas OPTIMIZE (FOR GIF) tries to make every layer as small as possible. The size of the generated file can vary slightly, but predicting which filter will produce the smallest file is difficult.

- UNOPTIMIZE is useful if you're editing an animation that's already optimized. If you want to add or remove frames, you need to undo the optimization first, then make the changes, and finally reoptimize the animation.

18.4 The Move Path Tool

The rest of this chapter focuses on multi-image animations. As explained in "Method Three: Moving Along a Path" on page 142, multi-image animations are usually stored in a specific folder

with each frame as a separate file named systematically (*name*-0001.xcf, for example). The number of digits determines the maximum number of frames, which would be 9999 in this example. The number changes, but the *name* is the same for all frames. The file could be any type handled by GIMP, but XCF is the best choice because it is the only one that handles layers and selections.

In this section, we explore GAP's primary tool, accessed via **Image: Video > Move Path**.

This tool copies layers from a source image to a target animation. During the copy process, the layers can be transformed in various ways. The source image can be a single- or multilayer image or a multiframe animation. The target animation must be multiframe because the Move Path tool does not generate frames.

Before using the Move Path tool, open the first frame of the target animation and the source image or animation in GIMP. The source and target images must be of the same type: RGB, indexed, or grayscale, but they cannot be the same file. If you want to duplicate something in an animation using this tool, you must copy the animation first, so the source and target are different files.

To demonstrate the Move Path tool, we chose a multilayer animation as the source and the multiframe animation in Figure 6.43 on page 155 as the target. The tool's large and complex dialog is shown in Figure 18.23. To make

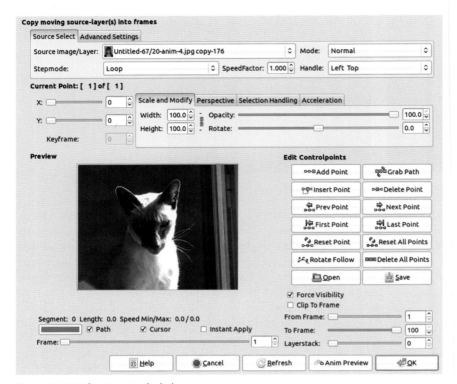

Figure 18.23 *The Move Path dialog*

things clearer, we'll highlight certain parts of the dialog in subsequent figures.

Choosing the Source Layers

Because the tool's purpose is to copy layers to frames, you need to decide which layers to copy to which frames. One copy of the selected layer from the source image is added to each frame of the target.

You choose the source layer in the top-left part of the dialog (Figure 18.23). The menu SOURCE IMAGE/LAYER shows all the layers of the source image or all the frames of the source animation. If the source is a multiframe animation and the individual frames have more than one layer, the layers are flattened before being copied. We chose 1 layer from a 41-layer image as the source.

The STEPMODE menu lets you choose how to select a layer when the source image is multi-layer or a frame when it is multiframe. When the source image is a single layer, choose NONE. When the source is a multilayer image, as in our example, you can choose from five different step modes:

- LOOP selects the layers in sequence, one for each successive target frame (depending on SPEEDFACTOR, discussed in a bit). When the last layer is the source, the loop starts with this layer, followed by the first layer and then the rest of the layers in order.

- LOOP REVERSE is the same as LOOP, except the source layers are selected in reverse order.

- ONCE is the same as LOOP, except that copying stops after the last layer instead of looping back to the first layer.

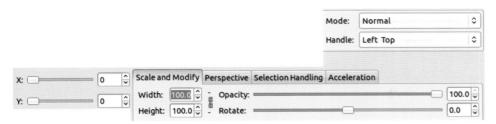

Figure 18.24 *Choosing transformation parameters for the selected layer*

- ONCE REVERSE is the same as ONCE, except that source layers are selected in reverse order.

- PING PONG selects the layers in sequence first and, once the last layer has been selected, reverses the sequence.

When the source animation is multiframe, STEPMODE offers six equivalent modes whose names all begin with FRAME. When a frame has several layers, the layer selected in one frame is irrelevant because all visible layers in the frame are flattened and the step mode selects among the frames, not the layers.

The last parameter dealing with layer selection is SPEEDFACTOR, which changes how fast the source layers are stepped through. When its value is 1.0, the source and target step are synchronized. When its value is 0.5, the source steps to half speed, so each layer is copied into two successive frames before stepping to the next one. When its value is 2.0, the source steps to double speed, so every other layer is copied. The speed factor is irrelevant if STEPMODE is NONE or FRAME NONE.

Choosing the Destination Frames

You choose the target animation in the bottom-right part of the dialog (Figure 18.23). The FROM FRAME and TO FRAME cursors delimit the range of target frames. They are set to the full range of the target by default, so the changes are applied to the entire animation, but you can choose to target only a part of the animation.

FORCE VISIBILITY makes all source layers visible even if they are not visible in the source. CLIP TO FRAME clips the copied layers to the image boundaries of the target frames. LAYERSTACK specifies where the copied layers should be inserted in the layer stack of target frames. The default value, 0, is the top of the stack because existing layers are numbered from top to bottom, starting at 0.

Applying Transformations

Figure 18.24 shows the sections of the Move Path dialog where you can choose to apply transformations. You can decide where the transformation will be applied using the X and Y coordinates. The HANDLE menu specifies where in the selected layer the origin of these coordinates is located. The possibilities are LEFT TOP, LEFT BOTTOM, RIGHT TOP, RIGHT BOTTOM, and CENTER. CENTER is generally the best choice, especially if rotation or scaling is applied to the layer.

A blending mode can be applied to the layer in the target frame using the MODE menu.

You can scale the source later by setting WIDTH and HEIGHT. These values are percentages. If the chain to the right of the counters is broken, the values can be changed independently.

OPACITY is specified as a percentage. ROTATE is specified in degrees, and a negative value results in a counterclockwise rotation. The rotation center is the image's handle.

Two more tabs deal with layer transformation. Figure 18.25 shows the PERSPECTIVE tab for

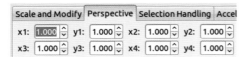

Figure 18.25 *The Perspective tab for transforming the perspective*

Figure 18.28 *Acceleration handling*

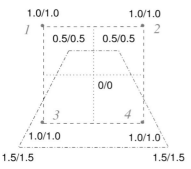

Figure 18.26 *Perspective deformation*

Figure 18.27 *The Selection Handling tab*

transforming perspective. The eight counters specify the factors for the x- and y-coordinates of the four corners of the layer. If the values for all factors are 1.0, no transformation occurs. Scaling with factor 0 moves the point toward the middle. Scaling with factor 2.0 moves the point outward by half the layer's original dimension. Figure 18.26 shows the layer's four corners numbered in red. The black numbers show factors, and the dotted outlines show the resulting positions of pixels.

If the source image has a selection, you can control how it's handled on the SELECTION HANDLING tab shown in Figure 18.27. The menu at the top of the tab has three options:

- IGNORE SELECTION (IN ALL SOURCE IMAGES) ignores the selection.

- USE SELECTION (FROM INITIAL SOURCE IMAGE) applies the selection found in the first frame

to all copied layers. The unselected pixels are transparent.

- USE SELECTIONS (FROM ALL SOURCE IMAGES) is the same as the previous choice if the source image is a multilayer animation. If the source is multiframe, then the selection within each frame is used, and if a frame has no selection, that frame is copied in its entirety.

When selection handling is used, you can adjust feathering with the SELECTION FEATHER RADIUS cursor, which changes the number of pixels that are applied in the feathering boundary.

All the preceding parameters (movement, scale, perspective, opacity, rotation, and feathering) are controlled on the ACCELERATION tab (Figure 18.28). Each of those six parameters is associated with a numeric field $[-100$ to $100]$ and a small square. If the field value is zero, the movement has a constant speed (i.e., there is no acceleration). If the field value is positive, the movement accelerates, and the small square displays a curve showing the steepness of the acceleration. If the field value is negative, the movement decelerates. You can change the field by typing a value, clicking the small up and down arrows, or dragging in the small square.

Control Points

A *control point* is the set of transformation parameters that are applied to a layer. You can define a single control point for all frames being handled by the Move Path tool, or you can define a sequence of control points, which together constitute a *control path*.

When you have a single control point, the transformation parameters are applied with the same values to all layer copies to the target frames. If you have several control points, they

Figure 18.29 *Specifying the control points*

are distributed among target frames. The first and last control points always correspond to the first and last frames. Other control points are usually distributed evenly among rest of the target frames.

Figure 18.29 shows the section of the dialog that is focused on control points. The number of the current control point is displayed at the top of the dialog, just above the X and Y cursors. Any changes to transformation parameters apply only to the current control point. Note that in the following discussion, when we refer to transformation parameters, we are not referring to the x- and y-coordinates. This dialog has 14 buttons associated with control points.

- ADD POINT adds a control point after the last one, with the same transformation parameters as that last point.

- GRAB PATH deletes all control points and replaces them with the path's anchor points (see Section 13.3) in the image from which the Move Path tool was opened. All of these points are initialized with transformation values identical to the current settings.

  If you press SHIFT and click GRAB PATH, control points are created for all target frames, with intermediate points defined by the Bézier curve that follows the anchor points.

- INSERT POINT duplicates the current control point, and the new copy becomes the current point.

- DELETE POINT removes the current control point. Note that undo is not available.

- PREV POINT makes the previous control point the current one. When you define key frames (discussed in "Key Frames" on page 492) and press SHIFT, the control point from the previous key frame becomes the current control point.

- NEXT POINT does the same for the next control point or key frame.

- FIRST POINT does the same for the first control point (or key frame when pressing SHIFT).

- LAST POINT does the same for the last control point or key frame.

- RESET POINT resets the transformation parameters of the current control point to the default values of 100.0 for width, height, and opacity; 0.0 for rotation; and 1.0 for all perspective coordinates.

- RESET ALL POINTS resets all control points to the default values. If you press SHIFT, this button resets all control points to the values of the first point. If you press CTRL, it sets all control point parameters to values interpolated from the first and last control points.

- ROTATE FOLLOW computes rotation values for all the control points based on the path defined by the x- and y-coordinates. If an object moves horizontally from left to right, its rotation is set to 0°. When moving from right to left, its rotation is set to 180°; and when moving vertically, from top to bottom, it's set to 90°. When you press SHIFT, a rotation offset is taken from the rotation of the first point and added to the rotation of all other points, which allows you to move an object from right to left without turning it upside down.

- DELETE ALL POINTS removes all control points except the first one, which is reset to the default value.

- OPEN loads control point parameters from a file.

- SAVE saves the control point parameters to a file.

Key Frames

You will always have fewer control points than target frames, and, by default, the control points are distributed equally among the frames. You can use *key frames* to change this.

The KEYFRAME counter is at the top of the dialog, just below the X and Y coordinates. If its value is zero, the current control point is not attached to any key frame. Otherwise, the current control point is attached to the target frame specified by that number, which means the control points don't have to be assigned to frames evenly. So you can apply transformations that accelerate or slow down as the animation plays.

The Preview Window

The preview window in the center of the dialog initially shows only the first target frame. Several buttons and a cursor help you control this preview (Figure 18.30).

The FRAME cursor determines which frame is displayed when you click REFRESH. When INSTANT APPLY is checked, changes are applied as soon as you change the counter value, which can be processor intensive if you're working with large target animations.

When CURSOR is checked, crossed lines are displayed in the preview window, showing the position of the *x*- and *y*-coordinates. When PATH is checked, the path between the coordinates of the successive control points is also displayed in the preview window.

The small box to the left of the PATH button lets you change the path color via the Color chooser.

Testing the Move Path Tool

When you click OK at the bottom right of the Move Path dialog, the transformation specified

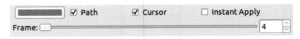

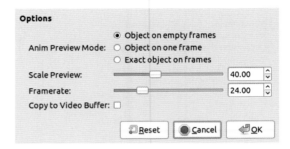

Figure 18.30 *Controlling the preview*

Figure 18.31 *The Anim Preview dialog*

by the control points is performed. Not every transformation can be undone, so always click ANIM PREVIEW first to make sure all the control points and parameters are set up properly.

When you click either OK or ANIM PREVIEW, the Move Path tool first checks whether the number of control points is greater than the number of target frames and whether the key frames are in ascending or descending order (if key frames are used).

If the tool finds more control points than target frames, or if the key frames are not all ordered in the same way, you'll see an error message, and no transformation is performed.

If you don't get an error message, ANIM PREVIEW opens the dialog shown in Figure 18.31. The animation preview is a scaled-down, multilayer file, and the Playback tool (usually selected via **Image: Filters > Animation > Playback**) opens automatically.

ANIM PREVIEW MODE can have one of three values:

- OBJECT ON EMPTY FRAMES shows the copied layers on blank frames (rather than the target frames) filled with the background color.

- OBJECT ON ONE FRAME shows the copied layers on the frame displayed in the preview window of the tool dialog.

Figure 18.32 *The Advanced Settings tab*

- EXACT OBJECT ON FRAMES shows a scaled-down version of the final animation.

The third option takes much longer to generate, but the preview more closely approximates the final result.

SCALE PREVIEW changes how much the preview is scaled down. If the setting is 100.0, the preview isn't scaled down and takes a long time to process. Usually a value between 20 to 40 is ideal. FRAMERATE sets the animation speed in frames per second. COPY TO VIDEO BUFFER, when checked, may produce a smoother animation.

The preview is generated as a new, multilayer animation, which you can delete once you've watched it.

Advanced Settings

The Move Path dialog has an Advanced Settings tab, shown in Figure 18.32.

When checked, BLUEBOX applies the Bluebox filter to the selected layer, as explained in "Bluebox" on page 503. KEYCOLOR is used with the Bluebox filter and opens the Bluebox dialog.

The TRACELAYER box, when checked, creates an additional layer in all target frames. This layer shows all positions of the moving layer from the beginning of the animation to the previous frame. TRACEOPACITY1 specifies the opacity of this additional layer. TRACEOPACITY2 specifies how much this opacity fades out.

TWEENSTEPS specifies the number of virtual frames, called *tweens*, that are computed between two consecutive frames and included in a *tween layer* in the target frame below the stack position of the inserted layer. This tween layer shows the positions of the moving object in all virtual frames. The opacity of this layer is spec-

ified by the TWEENOPACITY1 counter and fades out at the older positions, depending on the value of the TWEENOPACITY2 counter.

When you have both a trace layer and a tween layer, the tween layer is invisible so the opacity of the moving object does not increase. These additional layers can be useful for simulating the motion blur of fast-moving objects.

18.5 The Video Menu

We've already covered two tools in the **Image: Video** menu—the Morph tool and the Move Path tool. In this section, we'll discuss the remaining tools. This menu is organized alphabetically, but we'll discuss the tools in a logical order instead.

Manipulating Frames

Many entries in the Video menu deal with frame manipulations, but quite a few also perform very simple actions.

The **Image: Video > Go To** menu contains five entries that change the current frame in a multiframe animation. The function of the FIRST FRAME, LAST FRAME, NEXT FRAME, and PREVIOUS FRAME entries are obvious. ANY FRAME opens a dialog where you can select a frame by number.

DELETE FRAMES lets you delete a subrange of frames, beginning at the current frame and ending at the chosen number.

DUPLICATE FRAMES opens the dialog in Figure 18.33. You can choose the starting and ending frame numbers and the number of times to duplicate that range.

EXCHANGE FRAME opens a dialog where you can select the number of the frame to be exchanged with the current one.

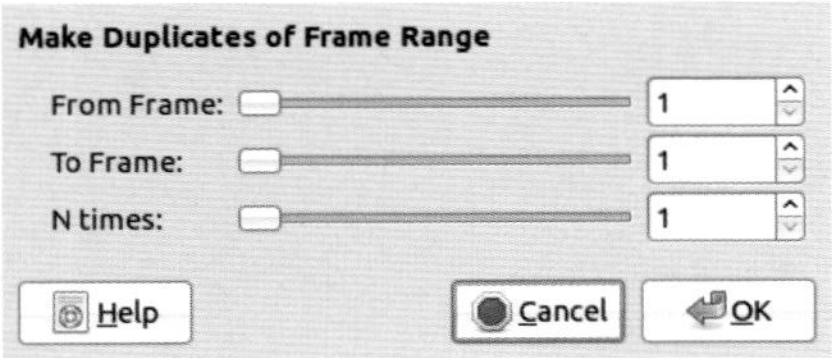

Make Duplicates of Frame Range

From Frame: 1

To Frame: 1

N times: 1

Help   Cancel   OK

Figure 18.33 *The Duplicate Frames dialog*

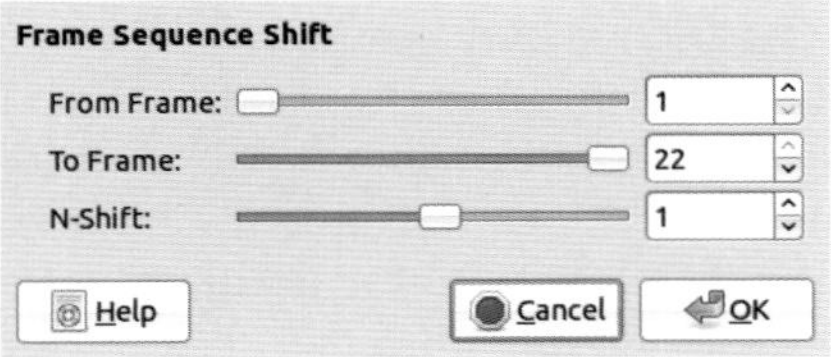

Frame Sequence Shift

From Frame: 1

To Frame: 22

N-Shift: 1

Help   Cancel   OK

Figure 18.34 *The Frame Sequence Shift dialog*

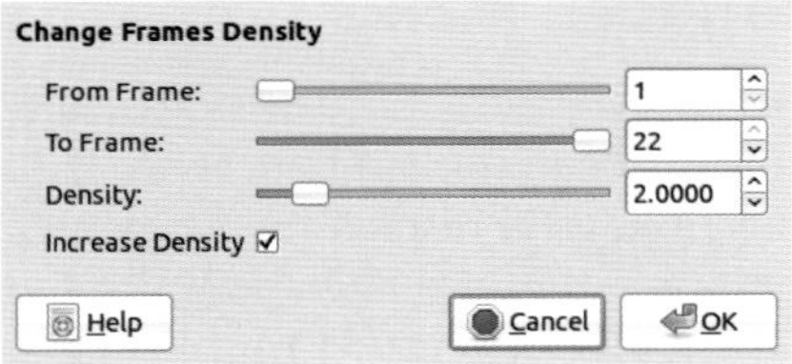

Change Frames Density

From Frame: 1

To Frame: 22

Density: 2.0000

Increase Density ☑

Help   Cancel   OK

Figure 18.35 *The Frames Density dialog*

FRAME SEQUENCE REVERSE opens a dialog with two sliders, one for the numbers of the FROM FRAME and the other for the TO FRAME. This tool reverses the sequence, so 3-4-5-6-7 becomes 7-6-5-4-3.

FRAME SEQUENCE SHIFT opens the dialog shown in Figure 18.34. The first two sliders define a frame subrange, and the last cursor, N-SHIFT, specifies the amount of circular shift that will be applied to the subrange. The first frame of the sequence is renumbered N places farther along in the range, and so on, until the last frame, which is $N-1$ places farther than the first frame.

FRAMES RENUMBER opens a dialog with two sliders. The first specifies the new number of the first frame, and the second specifies the number of digits of the frame numbers. All the frames are renumbered.

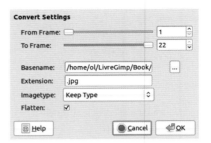

Figure 18.36 *The Frames Convert dialog*

Selecting FRAMES DENSITY opens the dialog shown in Figure 18.35. This dialog allows you to duplicate frames if the density is increased and delete frames if the density is decreased.

The first two cursors are used to select a subrange of the animation. DENSITY can range from 1.0 to 100.0. When INCREASE DENSITY is checked, the density is multiplied by this factor. Otherwise it's divided by this factor.

Use the Frames Density tool to combine two animations with different frame rates without changing playback speed. For example, you could convert an animation with a frame rate of 8 frames per second to 24 frames per second by choosing a density of 3.0, which will add two copies of every frame to the original animation. If your animation is jerky after you increase the density, try creating *onionskin* layers (see "Onionskin" on page 504).

Because the Frames Density tool has no undo, work with a copy of your animation so you can return to the original if you make a mistake.

Converting Between File Formats

FRAMES CONVERT converts a subrange of the multiframe animation to a different format. The Frames Convert dialog is shown in Figure 18.36. FROM FRAME and TO FRAME set the subrange. The BASENAME specifies where the new frames are stored. The small box at the right opens the file manager dialog that you can use to select the location.

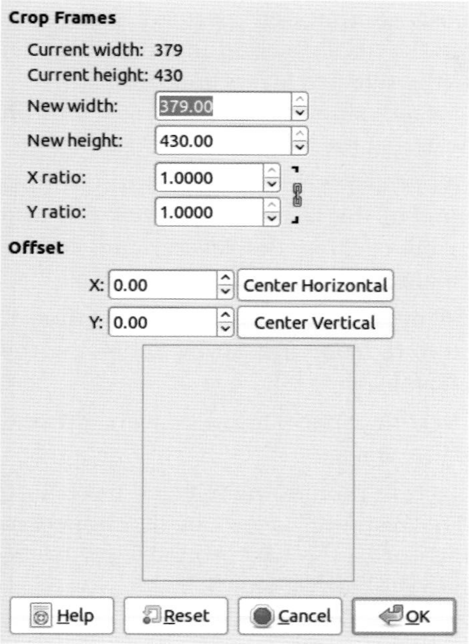

Crop Frames

Current width: 379
Current height: 430

New width: | 379.00
New height: | 430.00
X ratio: | 1.0000
Y ratio: | 1.0000

Offset

X: | 0.00 | Center Horizontal
Y: | 0.00 | Center Vertical

Help Reset Cancel OK

Figure 18.37 *The Frames Crop dialog*

Use the EXTENSION field to select the format that you want to convert the animation to. The IMAGETYPE menu allows you convert the animation to RGB, indexed, or grayscale. Be sure to convert to indexed if you choose GIF as the output format.

When checked, FLATTEN flattens the layers in the output files, which is necessary for most output formats. This tool can be used to convert numerous files at the same time, using many possible input and output formats, as long as the files share a systematic naming scheme.

FRAMES CROP is used to crop *all* frames of a multiframe animation to a new width and height. Its dialog is shown in Figure 18.37. This tool acts on the animation (not a copy), and the regions of the frames outside the cropped area are discarded.

You can change the width and height of the crop with the NEW WIDTH and NEW HEIGHT fields. The X RATIO and Y RATIO fields also modify the cropping. If the chain to the right of these

Scale Frames

Current width: 379
Current height: 430

New width: | 379.00
New height: | 430.00
X ratio: | 1.0000
Y ratio: | 1.0000

Help Reset Cancel OK

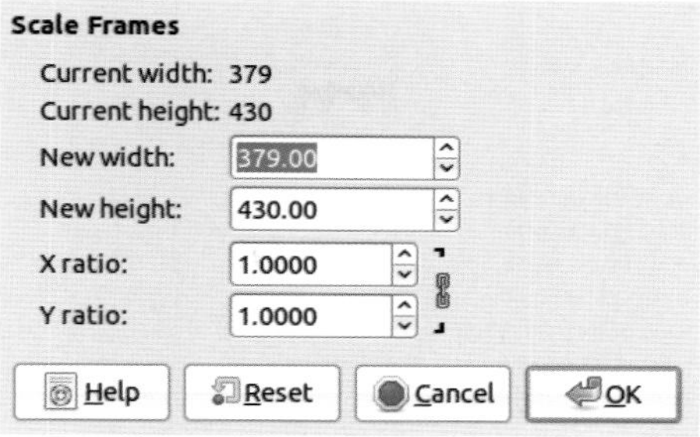

Figure 18.38 *The Frames Scale dialog*

fields is broken, the X and Y dimensions can be changed independently.

Once you've changed the dimensions, you can define what part of the source image remains after cropping using the X and Y fields or using the CENTER HORIZONTAL and CENTER VERTICAL buttons. You can also click and drag in the small rectangular area at the bottom of the dialog.

Use FRAMES RESIZE to change the canvas size of all frames of a multiframe animation. It opens the same dialog as the Frames Crop tool. If the new canvas is smaller than the original, the result is the same as cropping.

FRAMES SCALE changes the scale of all frames in a multiframe animation. Its dialog, shown in Figure 18.38, contains the same fields as the top half of the Frames Crop and Frames Resize dialogs. The algorithm used to scale the frames can be changed in the GIMP Preferences (**Image: Edit > Preferences**, TOOL OPTIONS entry, DEFAULT INTERPOLATION field).

Modifying Frames

FRAMES MODIFY is a very powerful tool that you can use to modify selected layers in a subrange of the current multiframe animation. Its dialog is shown in Figure 18.39. The layers are selected based on their name or their number in the layer stack (0 at the top). Under the heading LAYER SELECTION are seven radio buttons, the first six of which use the LAYER PATTERN field just below. Most of the radio buttons are self-explanatory.

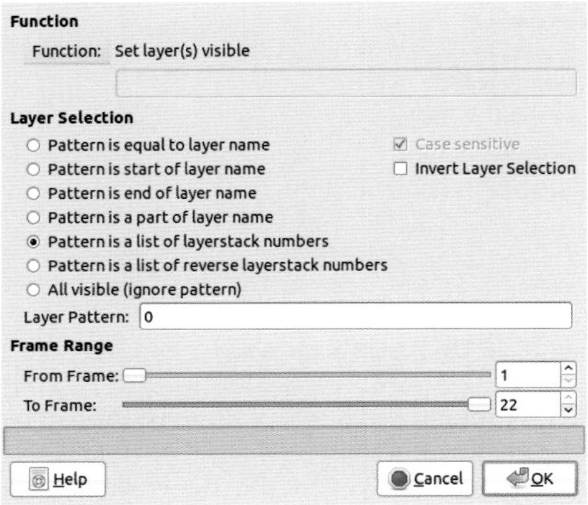

Function

Function:　Set layer(s) visible

Layer Selection

○ Pattern is equal to layer name　☑ Case sensitive
○ Pattern is start of layer name　☐ Invert Layer Selection
○ Pattern is end of layer name
○ Pattern is a part of layer name
◉ Pattern is a list of layerstack numbers
○ Pattern is a list of reverse layerstack numbers
○ All visible (ignore pattern)

Layer Pattern:　0

Frame Range

From Frame:　1
To Frame:　22

Help　　Cancel　OK

Figure 18.39 *The Frames Modify dialog*

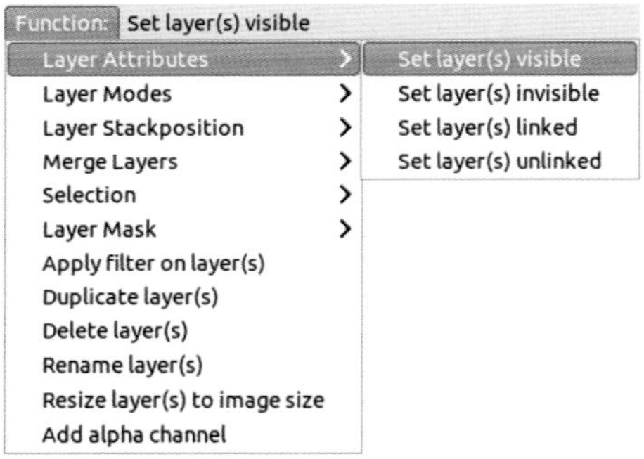

Function:　Set layer(s) visible

Layer Attributes ＞	Set layer(s) visible
Layer Modes ＞	Set layer(s) invisible
Layer Stackposition ＞	Set layer(s) linked
Merge Layers ＞	Set layer(s) unlinked
Selection ＞	
Layer Mask ＞	
Apply filter on layer(s)	
Duplicate layer(s)	
Delete layer(s)	
Rename layer(s)	
Resize layer(s) to image size	
Add alpha channel	

Figure 18.40 *Choosing a function*

The first four buttons match a string pattern to the exact name of the layer or to a part of its name. The next two choices use a list of layer stack numbers as the pattern. For example, the list "0, 4–6, 8" selects layers 0, 4, 5, 6, and 8. The last choice selects all visible layers.

When you use a string pattern, the CASE SENSITIVE box allows you to distinguish Background from background. In all cases, checking the INVERT LAYER SELECTION box selects all layers that don't match your criteria.

As usual, select the frame subrange with the FROM FRAME and TO FRAME sliders.

The most complicated part of using the Frames Modify tool is choosing the function to apply to the selected layers and frames.

Figure 18.40 shows the FUNCTION button menus, located at the top of the dialog.

- LAYER ATTRIBUTES lets you perform simple operations in the layers, which you can also do by right-clicking the layer name in the Layers dialog.

- LAYER MODES contains the 22 blending modes, also selected from the MODE menu in the Layers dialog.

- LAYER STACKPOSITION moves layers up and down in the stack.

- MERGE LAYERS merges the selected layers into one. The resulting layer can be clipped to the canvas or to the background layer or expanded to the canvas.

- SELECTION has several functions. The first four functions (REPLACE, ADD, SUBTRACT, and INTERSECT) take the selection from the frame that was used to open the tool and combine it with existing selections in all frames of the subrange. The remaining functions alter selections in the same ways as the entries in the **Image: Select** menu.

- LAYER MASK includes several functions. The first seven functions are found by selecting the **Image: Layer > Mask > Add Layer Mask** dialog or by right-clicking the layer name in the Layers dialog. The next three functions are also found in the **Image: Layer > Mask** menu. The remaining two copy a layer mask from the layer above or below and then apply that mask to all selected layers. The meaning of the other entries in this menu should be clear from their names alone.

Note that some functions require you to enter a name in the field just below the name of the function in the tool dialog.

The function APPLY FILTER ON LAYER(S) opens a dialog when you click OK. This dialog is the same as the one shown in Figure 18.18, and it works the same way. But this tool operates on several layers at the same time, within a subrange of frames.

The function APPLY FILTER ON LAYER MASK (in the LAYER MASK submenu) applies the selected filter to the layer mask instead of the layer itself. If the first selected layer in the first frame in the subrange does not have a layer mask, you'll get an error. If the selected filter is applied with varying values, the first selected layer in the last frame in the subrange must have a layer mask too. If intermediate layers in intermediate frames have no layer mask, they are skipped while GIMP processes the frame subrange.

To use this powerful tool properly, you should use the same layer stack structure in all frames. We also recommend using meaningful names for the layers—and to do so systematically for all frames.

Altering Layers

Several tools in the Video menu, such as FRAMES MODIFY (discussed in the previous section), deal with the layers of the animation frames. In this section, we discuss other tools in the Video menu that alter layers.

FILENAME TO LAYER creates a new layer in all frames of the subrange that contains the filename. Its dialog is shown in Figure 18.41. In the MODE menu, you can choose to use only the number from the filename, the full name, or a combination of the path and the name. Specify the font in the FONTNAME field with the FONT BROWSER button.

You can also choose the font size and the co-ordinates of the upper-left corner of the name. Leave the ANTIALIAS box checked. If the CREATE LAYER box is unchecked, the name is written on the active layer.

To use the tool to number all of the frames in a subrange of an animation, you must select the Filename to Layers tool from the **Image: Video > Frames Modify** menu, using

Figure 18.41 *The Filename to Layer dialog*

the APPLY FILTER ON LAYER(S) function (called `plug_in_gap_renumber`).

FRAMES FLATTEN flattens all frames (merges all layers) in the specified subrange. It has a dialog with two sliders, similar to the top part of Figure 18.33 on page 494.

FRAMES LAYER DELETE deletes one specific layer in all frames of the subrange. It opens a dialog with three sliders, similar to Figure 18.33 on page 494.

The **Image: Video > Layer** menu has several entries that can be accessed directly but are much more useful when accessed from the **Image: Filters > Filter all Layers** tool or the **Image: Video > Frames Modify** tool.

Converting Between Multilayer and Multiframe

Two tools can be used to convert a multilayer animation to a multiframe one, and vice versa.

SPLIT IMAGE TO FRAMES must be opened from a multilayer image. Its dialog appears in Figure 18.42. You can't choose names for the new frames or their position in the folder hierarchy. To save the new frames in a particular folder, place the source image in that folder before splitting it into frames.

The EXTENSION is XCF, by default, and it is the safest extension to use, but you can enter any format supported by GIMP. The dialog has four checkboxes that, when checked, do the following:

- INVERSE ORDER starts with the first frame (the top layer) instead of the bottom frame.

Split Settings

Make a frame (diskfile) from each layer.
Frames are named in the style:
<basename><framenumber>.<extension>
The first frame for the current case gets the name

/home/ol/LivreGimp/Book/Img20/Animation/Broglie_000001_000001.xcf

Extension:	xcf
Inverse Order:	☐
Flatten:	☐
Only Visible:	☐
Copy properties:	☐
Digits:	6

Reset Cancel OK

Figure 18.42 *The Split Image to Frames dialog*

- FLATTEN flattens the new frames, and any transparent areas are filled with the background color .

- ONLY VISIBLE ignores invisible layers. When unchecked, all layers generate a frame, regardless of their visibility.

- COPY PROPERTIES copies the channels, paths, and guides existing in the image to all the frames. When unchecked, these properties are ignored.

Finally, the DIGITS counter specifies the number of digits contained in the numeric part of the frame names.

FRAMES TO IMAGE creates a multilayer image from frames, so it must be opened from a multiframe animation. Its dialog is shown in Figure 18.43.

The first two sliders specify the subrange of the frames that will be used to build the multilayer image. The LAYER BASENAME field lets you name the layers. By default, all layer names begin with frame_, but you can change that to any string. The number signs in the square brackets will be replaced by the frame number, but you can change the number of digits. The duration of each layer is 24 images per second, by default, but you can change that as well.

The new layers are created by merging the layers in the source frames (unless FLATTENED

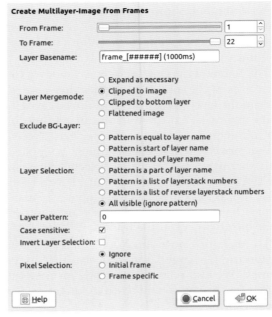

Create Multilayer-Image from Frames

From Frame:		1
To Frame:		22
Layer Basename:	frame_[######] (1000ms)	

Layer Mergemode:
- ○ Expand as necessary
- ● Clipped to image
- ○ Clipped to bottom layer
- ○ Flattened image

Exclude BG-Layer: ☐

Layer Selection:
- ○ Pattern is equal to layer name
- ○ Pattern is start of layer name
- ○ Pattern is end of layer name
- ○ Pattern is a part of layer name
- ○ Pattern is a list of layerstack numbers
- ○ Pattern is a list of reverse layerstack numbers
- ● All visible (ignore pattern)

Layer Pattern: 0

Case sensitive: ☑

Invert Layer Selection: ☐

Pixel Selection:
- ● Ignore
- ○ Initial frame
- ○ Frame specific

Help Cancel OK

Figure 18.43 *The Frames to Image dialog*

IMAGE is selected). LAYER MERGEMODE lets you choose how the image size is determined.

- EXPAND AS NECESSARY expands the image size to fit around all layers.

- CLIPPED TO IMAGE clips the layers to the image size.

- CLIPPED TO BOTTOM LAYER clips the image to the size of the bottom layer of the source.

- FLATTENED IMAGE creates the new layer by flattening rather than merging the source layers, so the resulting layer, which is the same size as the image, has no transparent part.

When checked, EXCLUDE BG-LAYER excludes the background layer from all source frames. When unchecked, this layer is handled like any other.

LAYER SELECTION determines how the source layers are selected. For the first four options, the LAYER PATTERN field is a character string, which should match at least part of the name of the layers you want to select. The next two options

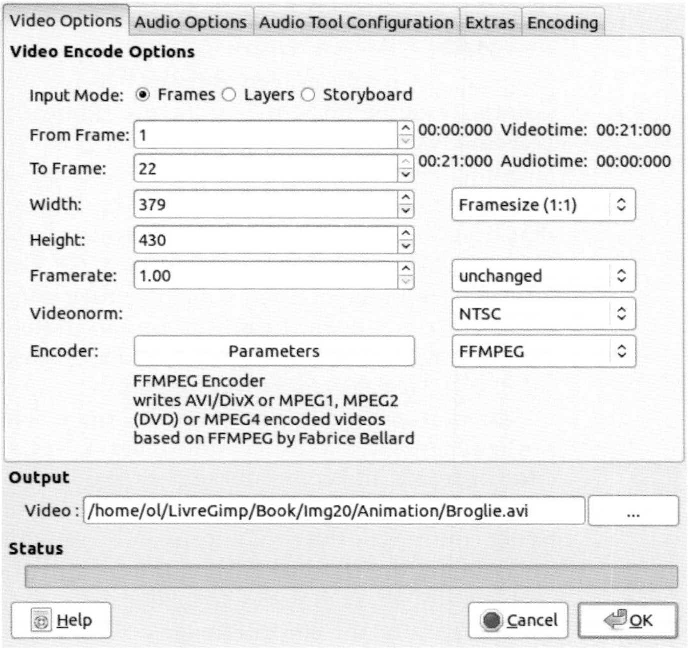

Video Options	Audio Options	Audio Tool Configuration	Extras	Encoding

Video Encode Options

Input Mode: ● Frames ○ Layers ○ Storyboard

From Frame: `1` 00:00:000 Videotime: 00:21:000

To Frame: `22` 00:21:000 Audiotime: 00:00:000

Width: `379` Framesize (1:1)

Height: `430`

Framerate: `1.00` unchanged

Videonorm: NTSC

Encoder: Parameters FFMPEG

FFMPEG Encoder
writes AVI/DivX or MPEG1, MPEG2
(DVD) or MPEG4 encoded videos
based on FFMPEG by Fabrice Bellard

Output

Video : `/home/ol/LivreGimp/Book/Img20/Animation/Broglie.avi` ...

Status

Help   ● Cancel   OK

Figure 18.44 *The first tab of the Master Videoencoder dialog*

require a list of layer numbers ("1, 3–5, 9" for example). Layers are numbered from zero, beginning at the top layer (or at the bottom layer if the third option is chosen). The final option selects all visible layers. If CASE SENSITIVE is checked, the case of the string must match for the layer to be selected. All of these options can be inverted by checking INVERT LAYER SELECTION.

PIXEL SELECTION specifies how an existing selection is handled. IGNORE ignores all selections in the source frames. INITIAL FRAME uses the selection from the first frame of the subrange and applies it to all frames. The unselected areas are transparent, and the layer shape is determined by the selection. FRAME SPECIFIC uses the selection in each selected frame.

Encoding

MASTER VIDEOENCODER converts multiframe or multilayer animations into a specific video file encoding. Its dialog is shown in Figure 18.44.

You can also use a storyboard with this option, as explained in "Storyboard" on page 505.

OUTPUT allows you to name the output file. The extension is added by GIMP, depending on the chosen encoder. The button to the right opens the local file manager. The STATUS field shows the conversion progress.

The first tab in this dialog is VIDEO ENCODE OPTIONS. You can select the INPUT MODE; however, the tool automatically chooses one based on the source file. The next two fields define the subrange of frames or layers to be used as the source.

WIDTH and HEIGHT specify the size, in pixels, of the resulting video frames. The menu to the right lists a set of standard sizes.

FRAMERATE specifies the number of frames per second. The menu to the right has a set of standard rates.

The VIDEONORM menu contains the usual norms (NTSC, PAL, SECAM), which generally depend on the country in which the video will

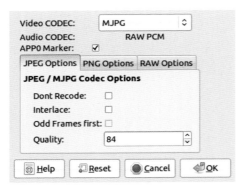

Figure 18.45 *The parameter dialog of the AVI1 encoder*

be broadcast.

ENCODER is operational only after you choose an encoder plug-in in the box to the right. For example, Figure 18.45 shows the parameters of the AVI1 encoder.

The remaining tabs in the Master Videoencoder dialog deal with audio options and the audio tool configuration, which is beyond the scope of this book.

Playback and Navigator

Use PLAYBACK to preview a multiframe animation (but not a multilayer one). It cannot play MPEG or AVI files. You can open Playback via **Image: Video > Playback**, but you may also open it from the VCR Navigator (discussed next) or from the Storyboard dialog (see "Storyboard" on page 505).

The lower part of the Playback dialog (Figure 18.46) contains the standard play forward, pause, and play backward buttons. SHIFT-clicking one of the two play buttons creates a "snapshot" image, which is a small multilayer animation containing all the frames that have been played up to this point. When an animation is playing, you can jump to the first, middle, or last frame by clicking the pause button with the left, middle, or right mouse buttons, respectively.

The top of the Playback dialog contains a set of 50 rectangles, which are the *GO array*, an array of the 50 current frames. Move the pointer over the array to display the frames in real time. You can stop at a particular point in an animation or play the animation at a different speed. Clicking one of the rectangles displays that frame in the source animation window. If the animation is larger than 50 frames, the GO array is a subrange of frames, and by moving the pointer to one side or the other, you can change the subrange contained in the array. The mouse scroll wheel can also move the animation frames.

The buttons and counters at the right side of the dialog let you display information on the current frame and set a subrange of the animation to play. Two counters below the current frame counter, or the two buttons at the right of the counter, are used to select a range. SHIFT-click one of these buttons to make the corresponding frame the current image.

You can also set the frame rate and the size (in pixels) of the preview window, which also changes when you resize the dialog.

The five boxes at the bottom right of the dialog control playback and are mostly self-explanatory. Check THUMBNAILS once you've seen the animation because that lets you reuse the small images generated. Use EXACT TIMING to skip frames and save time in an animation's playback.

VCR NAVIGATOR lets you perform simple edits on an animation or play it back. The VCR Navigator dialog is shown in Figure 18.47. In the middle is a scrollable list of frame thumbnails. You can see the frame numbers, as well as the time elapsed from the beginning of the animation. FRAMERATE and TIMEZOOM let you control the frequency and timing of the frames, and the result is immediately visible in the thumbnail area.

Figure 18.46 *The Playback dialog*

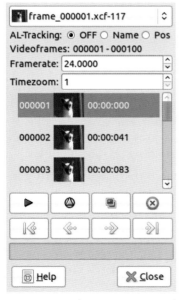

Figure 18.47 *The VCR Navigator dialog*

At the top of the VCR Navigator is the animation selector. Next is AL-TRACKING (Active Layer Tracking). Active Layer Tracking finds a layer in the newly loaded frame that matches the active layer of the previous frame and sets that layer as the active one. Three options are available:

- OFF disables Active Layer Tracking.

- NAME compares the layer names from left to right and chooses the layer that best matches.

- POS uses the layer's stack position; onionskin layers are not counted.

In the thumbnail area, you can select frames: A single click selects one frame; CTRL-click adds (or removes) the frame to the selected frames; and SHIFT-click selects all layers between the previous and the current layer. Right-click to open a simple editing menu (copy, cut, paste, and so on).

Below the thumbnails are two rows of buttons. The playback button opens the Playback tool. $\boxed{\text{SHIFT}}$-click it to use the selected frames to build a temporary multilayer animation and then open the Playback tool.

The next button (a triangle in a circle) updates only those thumbnails that are out of date; press $\boxed{\text{SHIFT}}$ to update all thumbnails. The next button duplicates the selected frames, and the last one deletes them. The lower row of buttons lets you navigate through the frames of an animation.

Split Video into Frames

The menu **Image: Video > Split video into frames** contains two entries.

MPLAYER-BASED EXTRACTION is the best tool for converting a video file to a multiframe animation, but it works only if you have MPlayer installed. MPlayer is free software, available for all platforms. See *http://www.mplayerhq.hu/* for more information.

The MPlayer-based extraction tool, shown in Figure 18.48, supports many input formats. The most useful fields are as follows:

- INPUT VIDEO is where you can enter the name of the input video or click the button on the right to browse for the file.

- START TIME is the place in the video where you want to begin extracting, entered in *hours:minutes:seconds*.

- FRAMES sets the number of frames to extract.

- VIDEOTRACK and AUDIOTRACK are useful if the input video file is multitrack, but that isn't very common. Enter 0 to ignore the audio or video track.

- FRAMENAMES sets the base name of the new frames. To use the file navigator, click the button on the right.

- FORMAT lets you choose JPEG, PNG, or XCF (generally the best choice). Below that you can adjust the compression or optimization, depending on the output format.

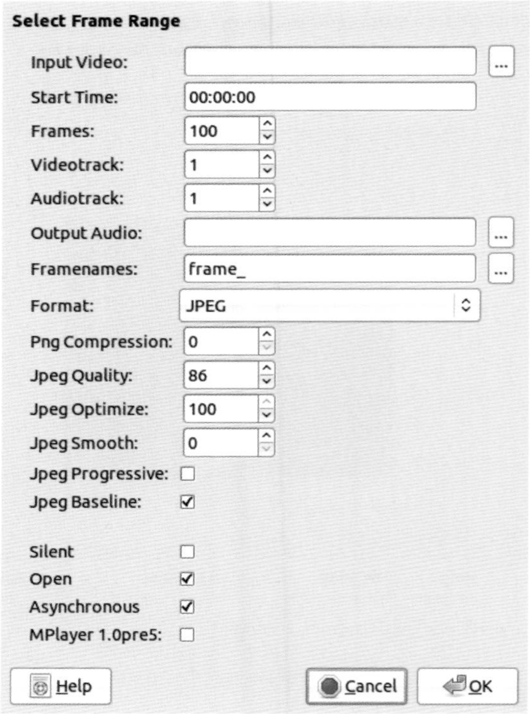

Figure 18.48 *The MPlayer-based extraction dialog*

- SILENT, if checked, ignores any audio track.

- OPEN opens the first frame once the extraction is finished.

- ASYNCHRONOUS, when checked, sets MPlayer to run asynchronously, so it doesn't block other processes running on the computer.

The frames of the input video are first converted to PNG and then to the chosen output format, which is normally XCF. Because the frames are processed twice, and a one-minute video sequence contains 1440 frames, these conversions can take half an hour or more.

The other entry in the **Image: Video > Split video into frames** menu is EXTRACT VIDEORANGE. When no additional video software is installed, this tool can only process an MPEG input file. Its dialog is shown in Figure 18.49. At the top of the dialog, choose the input file and then the range, either using

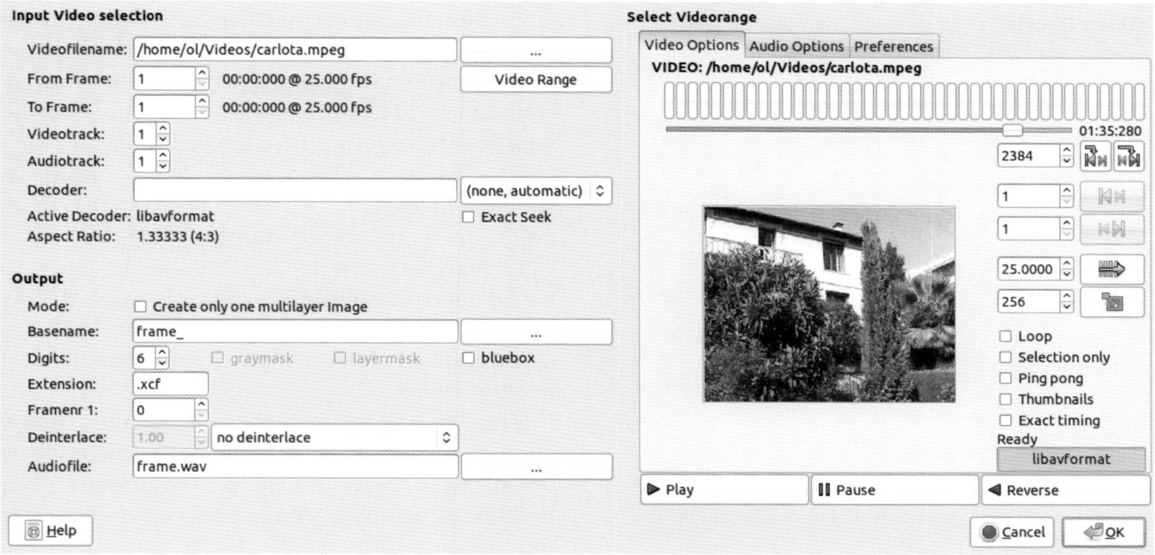

Figure 18.49 *The Extract Videorange dialog, extended*

the counters FROM FRAME and TO FRAME or the extended dialog that opens if you click VIDEO RANGE, as shown on the right of Figure 18.49.

You can generally leave the remaining fields in the input portion of the Extract Videorange dialog set at the defaults. In the OUTPUT section, you can choose whether to generate a multilayer or multiframe animation. You can also choose the base name of the frames, the number of digits, the extension (and format), and the number of the first frame. The audio track is extracted into a WAV file.

Bluebox

Bluebox uses a technique often called *blue screen* in cinematography. It's also called *chroma key*, *color keying*, or *color-separation overlay*. Basically, a scene is filmed with the actor(s) in front of a blue (or green) screen. The blue (or green) part of the video frame is then replaced with a different background. This technique can also be used to make an actor appear more than once in the same scene.

The Bluebox dialog is shown in Figure 18.50. Bluebox is actually a filter and works best when opened through the Move Path tool because it operates on a single layer. You can also open it through the Frames Modify tool from the Apply filter on layer(s) function.

KEYCOLOR chooses the color of the background to removed. You can choose any color via the Color chooser. Pixels similar to this chosen color are made transparent according to the threshold setting.

The THRESHOLD MODE can be RGB (three values), HSV (three values), VALUE (one value), or ALL (HSV and RGB combined, six values). These thresholds range from 0.0 to 1.0, where 0.0 only targets the exact color and 1.0 makes the widest range of colors transparent. The ALPHA TOLERANCE also changes how much of the background becomes transparent.

SOURCE ALPHA sets a maximum Alpha value to prevent transparent pixels from becoming part of the selection. TARGET ALPHA specifies the transparency of the selected pixels after the

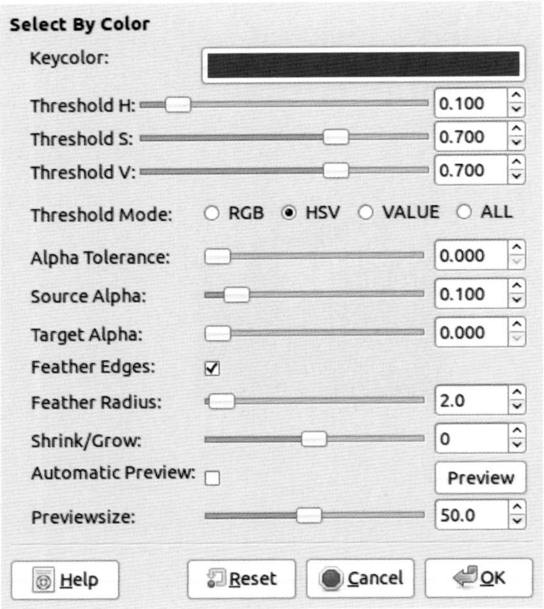

Select By Color

Keycolor:	
Threshold H:	0.100
Threshold S:	0.700
Threshold V:	0.700
Threshold Mode:	○ RGB ⦿ HSV ○ VALUE ○ ALL
Alpha Tolerance:	0.000
Source Alpha:	0.100
Target Alpha:	0.000
Feather Edges:	☑
Feather Radius:	2.0
Shrink/Grow:	0
Automatic Preview:	☐ Preview
Previewsize:	50.0

⊙ Help   ♫ Reset   ● Cancel   ⬅ OK

Figure 18.50 *The Bluebox dialog*

transformation. You can feather (smooth) the edges of the selection and shrink or grow it.

You can also adjust the size of the preview window, which is useful because this filter has no undo capability.

Onionskin

An onionskin layer is used to show the previous (or next) frame of an animation in the current frame. This is useful when painting moving characters, for example. The onionskin is automatically deleted when you move on to the next frame.

Onionskin layers can also be used for smoothing very fast movement to simulate motion blur, as we discussed in "Manipulating Frames" on page 493. Onionskin layers behave like normal layers for the most part, but special tools are available for doing some things like toggling visibility.

By default, onionskin layers are built by merging the visible layers of the previous frame without the background or any other onionskin layers. They are usually placed above the background layer in the current frame.

The **Image: Video** menu has a submenu called ONIONSKIN. CONFIGURATION, the main entry, opens the dialog shown in Figure 18.51.

LAYER SELECTION lets you choose the layers to be selected and is similar to the Frames Modify tool (see "Modifying Frames" on page 495). An additional field lets you ignore a number of background layers.

The large field displaying the name of the current multiframe animation is actually a button used to set the video's parameters. The two boxes below it are used to create or delete onionskins automatically when you select the tool from the VCR Navigator tool or when you move to the next frame using **File: Video > Go To > Next Frame**. When both boxes are checked, onionskins are automatically added when you load a frame and deleted when you save the frame.

The top of the dialog, ONIONSKIN SETTINGS, specifies how the layers from the previous frames are copied. FRAME REFERENCE refers to the source frame number from which the onionskin layer is copied. If the frame reference is −1, it means that the first onionskin layer will be copied from the previous frame, the second from the frame before that, and so on. A positive frame reference means that the onionskin is made up of frames that come after the current frame.

REFERENCE MODE specifies the way neighboring frames are used. In Normal mode, the delta provided by FRAME REFERENCE is used in one direction only. This delta value determines which onionskin layers are built and copied in the current frame. In Bidirectional (single) mode, this delta is used alternately in both directions, but a given offset is used only once, as in the

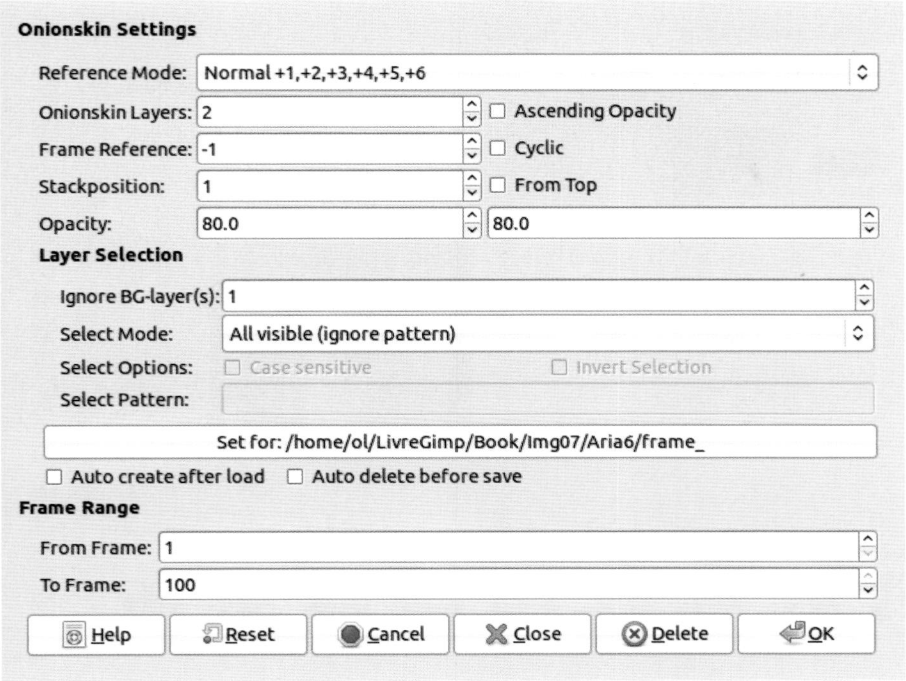

Onionskin Settings

Reference Mode:	Normal +1,+2,+3,+4,+5,+6
Onionskin Layers:	2 ☐ Ascending Opacity
Frame Reference:	-1 ☐ Cyclic
Stackposition:	1 ☐ From Top
Opacity:	80.0 80.0

Layer Selection

Ignore BG-layer(s):	1
Select Mode:	All visible (ignore pattern)
Select Options:	☐ Case sensitive ☐ Invert Selection
Select Pattern:	

Set for: /home/ol/LivreGimp/Book/Img07/Aria6/frame_

☐ Auto create after load   ☐ Auto delete before save

Frame Range

From Frame:	1
To Frame:	100

[ⓘ Help]   [Reset]   [● Cancel]   [✕ Close]   [⊗ Delete]   [OK]

Figure 18.51 *The Onionskin Configuration dialog*

sequence $-1, +2, -3, +4, \ldots$. In Bidirectional (double) mode, each delta is used twice, as in the sequence $-1, +1, -2, +2, -3, +3, \ldots$

You can also specify the number of onionskin layers to generate, their stack position, and their opacity.

Clicking OK adds the onionskin layers, whereas clicking DELETE removes them. CLOSE uses the parameters to define the settings throughout the current animation without generating an onionskin layer.

Once the settings are defined, the remaining entries in the **Image: Video > Onionskin** menu let you make global changes to the selected frames. You can create the onionskin layers or replace layers that you created previously. You can also delete specified onionskin layers or toggle their visibility.

The Onionskin tools are designed to work with the VCR Navigator or the **Image: Video > Go To** operations. When you move between frames, the actions specified by the AUTO boxes (if checked) are performed automatically. When both AUTO boxes are checked, the frame is saved after deleting the onionskin, and a new onionskin is created in the next frame according to the parameters saved in the **Image: Video > Onionskin > Configuration** dialog.

Storyboard

A *storyboard* is a text file that describes how to assemble video clips, images, and audio files to build a single output video file. Storyboards are useful for creating and cutting long video sequences. In fact, the Storyboard Editor,

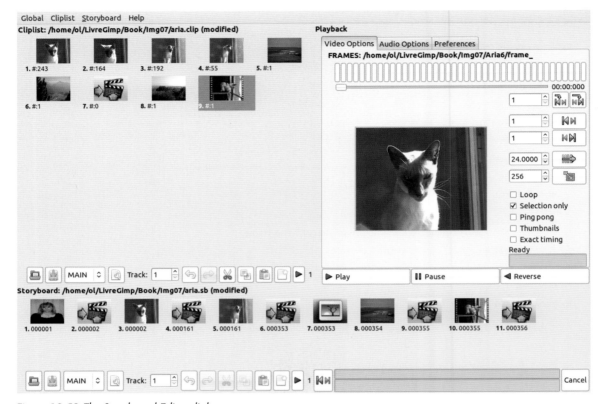

Figure 18.52 *The Storyboard Editor dialog*

together with its accompanying tools, provides a means for editing a video sequence by assembling video clips, multiframe animations, and single images. It does not provide as many features and capabilities as more specialized video-editing tools (such as Kdenlive at *http://www.kdenlive.org/* or Cinelerra at *http://cinelerra.org/*), but it does allow you to use GIMP's image-editing capabilities to work on individual frames.

Selecting **Image: Video > Storyboard** opens the dialog in Figure 18.52. The right side of this dialog is similar to the Playback dialog and is fairly intuitive. The left side is divided into the Cliplist and the Storyboard itself. The menu bar

at the top of the window contains two identical menus (CLIPLIST and STORYBOARD) for the two sections. In the GLOBAL menu, check the VIDEOTHUMBNAILS button to view thumbnails of the Cliplist and Storyboard. The PROPERTIES entry opens a dialog where you can choose the layout of the Cliplist and Storyboard sections, including the size of the thumbnails.

To use the Cliplist or Storyboard, you first must choose a video or animation file. To begin a new project, select **Storyboard > New**. In the dialog that appears, select the characteristics of the video animation you plan to build and enter the name of the storyboard file. Also select **Cliplist > New**. Its dialog is the same, but

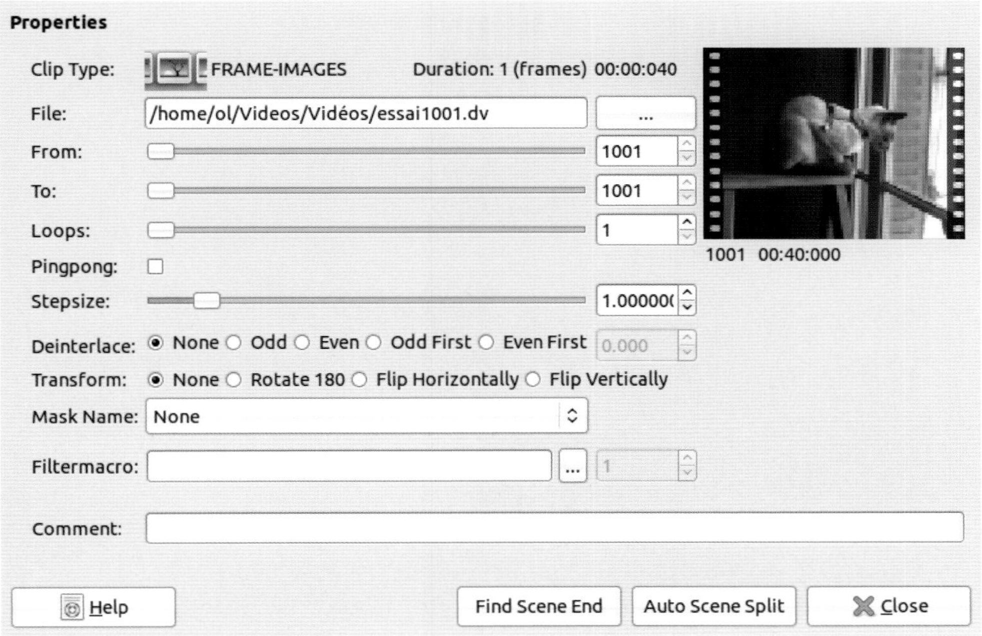

Properties

Clip Type:	[Y] FRAME-IMAGES Duration: 1 (frames) 00:00:040
File:	/home/ol/Videos/Vidéos/essai1001.dv [...]
From:	[slider] 1001
To:	[slider] 1001
Loops:	[slider] 1
Pingpong:	☐
Stepsize:	[slider] 1.00000(
Deinterlace:	◉ None ○ Odd ○ Even ○ Odd First ○ Even First 0.000
Transform:	◉ None ○ Rotate 180 ○ Flip Horizontally ○ Flip Vertically
Mask Name:	None
Filtermacro:	[ ] [...] 1
Comment:	[ ]

1001 00:40:000

[⊙ Help]   [Find Scene End] [Auto Scene Split] [✗ Close]

Figure 18.53 *Clip properties*

you must choose a different name for the file. Both menus contain additional entries that are fairly self-explanatory.

To add a clip, select **Cliplist > Create Clip**, which opens the dialog shown in Figure 18.53. You can load frames or layers from another animation and set several parameters for this new clip. Note that if the new clip is significantly different from the video that it's added to, the frames may be deformed.

A single image can also be used as a new clip. You can even drag and drop an image from a file manager.

After a clip is selected, it's displayed as a thumbnail in the PLAYBACK section of the Storyboard Editor dialog. You then choose the frame range to be used as a clip and add it to the Cliplist by clicking the first button on the right. The second button adds the inverse range.

Once you have clips in the Cliplist, add them to the Storyboard by

- CTRL-clicking and SHIFT-clicking to select the clips
- using the CUT, COPY, and PASTE buttons at the bottom of the Cliplist to arrange the clips in sequence
- using the CUT, COPY, and PASTE buttons in the Storyboard to copy and arrange clips
- clicking the play button at the bottom right of the Cliplist to play the sequence of clips or only the selected clips
- double-clicking a clip thumbnail to play it
- right-clicking a clip thumbnail to change its properties (Figure 18.53)

Playing a clip or clip sequence is useful when selecting a subrange of frames and defining a new clip. Pasted clips are added after the last selected clip or at the end of the sequence.

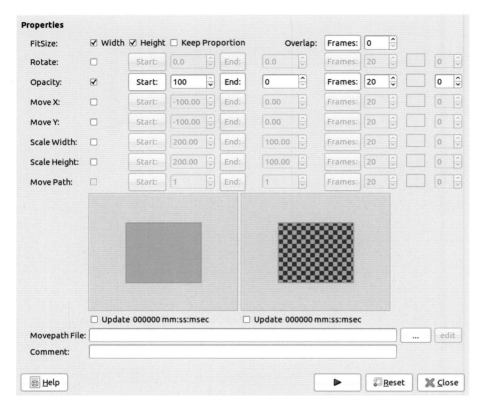

Figure 18.54 *Transition attributes*

The **Cliplist** and **Storyboard** menus also allow you to create a transition. This menu entry
opens the dialog shown in Figure 18.54. Create
transitions by changing the opacity of frames,
scrolling frames, or zooming. You can also combine these effects.

Once you've finished building a storyboard,
you can save it as a text file. These files use a well-
defined syntax, and you can modify them with a
text editor if you know the syntax.

19 Obtaining and Printing Images

You can get an image into GIMP using several methods, but there's basically only one way to output an image onto paper (in other words, to print it). You obtain or print images via the **Image: File** menu. We begin this chapter by exploring the **Image: File > Create** submenu, shown in Figure 19.1.

19.1 Capturing Screenshots

Figure 19.2 shows the dialog that opens when you select **Image: File > Create > Screenshot**. You can create screenshots in three ways:

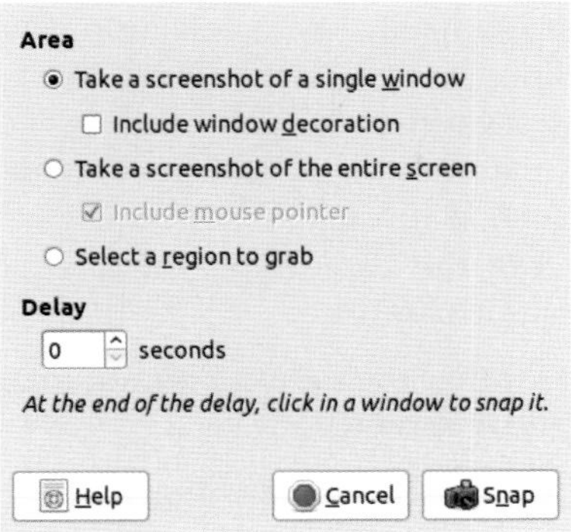

- TAKE A SCREENSHOT OF A SINGLE WINDOW: In this case, a checkbox toggles the visibility of the window decoration, which is added by the window manager, not by GIMP. Most illustrations in this book do not include the window decoration to save space and avoid distractions. Once you've made your selections in the dialog, press the SNAP button. The mouse pointer changes to a cross, and you can click the window that you want to take a screenshot of.

  But this makes taking a screenshot of a temporary window, such as one that appears when you right-click, difficult. You

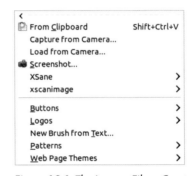

Figure 19.1 *The Image: File > Create submenu*

Figure 19.2 *The Screenshot dialog*

can get around this by setting a delay and then right-clicking to open the desired window. If that doesn't work (for example, for a GIMP menu), try right-clicking to open the menu and then clicking the dotted line at the top of the dialog, which opens the dialog as a window. This method results in screenshots of detached menus, as you've seen in this book.

- TAKE A SCREENSHOT OF THE ENTIRE SCREEN: With this option, check or uncheck the checkbox to include the mouse pointer in the screenshot; a visible pointer can be useful if you want to demonstrate an application. Generally setting a delay is best so you can prepare the screen before taking the screenshot (for example, by opening or closing menus or dialogs). A beep sounds at the beginning and end of the capture. The mouse pointer appears in a separate layer of the resulting image, so you can move it around.

- SELECT A REGION TO GRAB: After the optional delay, the mouse pointer changes to a cross, and you can click and drag to outline the region you want to capture. Select a region larger than you need, and crop it afterward.

Taking a screenshot is not the same as saving the current state of an image. A screenshot uses the screen definition and is preferable only when you want to include features that do not appear in the image itself, like a selection outline, a layer outline, guides, or the Quick Mask. Saving the image saves the real definition of the photograph but cannot store the features outside the image, such as those just mentioned.

Choosing among the three types of screenshots is fairly straightforward:

- If you want to capture the mouse pointer, take a shot of the entire screen.

- If you want to press a mouse button while taking the screenshot—to show a right-click menu, for example—take a shot of the entire screen.

- If you just want to capture the menu, take a single-window shot.

- Selecting a region is useful if you need only a part of a larger window (for instance, the Toolbox but not the options dialog, or any part of the window in single-window mode) or if you need to capture several windows but not the entire screen.

- Taking a clean, well-framed screenshot of a single window is optimal, so choose that option when possible.

Most operating systems have the capability to capture a fullscreen copy or a copy of a single window. For instance, the GNOME desktop environment under GNU/Linux includes the tool GNOME-screenshot, which offers the same screen capture capabilities as GIMP, except it has no option to select a region. The PRINT SCREEN key usually takes a screenshot of the entire screen, which you can save wherever you choose.

Under Windows, the PRINT SCREEN key places the screen copy on the clipboard without providing any feedback, so although it seems as though nothing happened, you can open the screenshot in GIMP with **Image: Edit > Paste as > New Image** or SHIFT+CTRL+V.

Generally, if you plan to edit an image in GIMP, it's more convenient to use GIMP's Screenshot tool, which is has as many options, or more, than the operating system screen-capture tools.

19.2 Scanning

Scanning is the conversion of an image to a digital representation using a specific device called a *scanner*. The process is also called *digitizing* or *digitization*.

Scanners and Drivers

An image scanner is an independent device that connects to the computer by a USB or an IEEE 1394 (Firewire) connection. In this book, we cover only the flatbed type, where the document is placed on glass and the charged coupled device (CCD) sensors move across the glass while the document is lit. The same manufacturers that make printers (such as Canon and Epson) generally also make scanners. The prices are in the same range, and multifunction devices in which a scanner and printer are combined are more and more common, including in low-cost models.

Most people buy a scanner to digitize photographs or sketches, so, for most people, an automatic feeder is unnecessary and a letter-size (or A4) glass size is sufficient. If you need to scan a large quantity of documents, you may consider buying a scanner with an automatic feeder, and if you're an artist who works in large format, you may need a larger glass size. Many people want to scan photographic negatives or slides, which requires a specific device lit from behind; look for this capability in the scanner's specifications.

Scanning speed is generally not very important, as long as scanning a normal-sized photograph does not take more than a minute. Scanning resolution is more important, but be warned that, as always with numeric information, resolution is used as a marketing point—a larger number is not necessarily better. A scanner has an intrinsic maximum resolution, depending on the number of CCD cells that compose the sensor array. Larger resolutions can be obtained by interpolation, which means they are a digital simulation of a higher resolution, which can also be done in GIMP. The physical, true resolution of a scanner is called the *optical resolution*, and only the optical resolution should be considered when comparing different models.

Actually, a large resolution is often not needed. If you intend to print the scanned image in the same size, 300 ppi (pixels per inch) is enough. If you intend to enlarge the image a lot—for example, the original is a 35 mm slide and you want to print it in letter-size format—1200 ppi is probably enough. So resolutions of 4800 or 9600 ppi, frequently advertised for scanners, are not only artificially inflated but also useless for most people.

The most important factors to take into account when buying a scanner are its precision and fidelity in rendering the values and colors of the image's pixels. Look at websites that compare the capabilities, performance, and prices of various scanner models.

If you are a GNU/Linux user, we recommend looking at the Scanner Access Now Easy, or SANE, website (*http://www.sane-project.org/*) to make sure a scanner model will be recognized on your platform. Don't worry if you cannot buy the most recent scanner with all the bells and whistles: The bells and whistles are often useless, and the standard model, when correctly handled by SANE, will meet all your needs.

What exactly is SANE all about? All too frequently, scanner manufacturers build their devices without any thought to free and open source software. They provide drivers and applications only for Windows and Mac operating systems. The goal of the SANE project is to provide a free software version of the drivers for as many scanner models as possible. It constitutes a front-end for the scanner, which also requires a back-end to handle the digitized image. Several back-ends are available for GNU/Linux and Mac OS but not for Windows. Windows users can use the application shipped with the scanner, or they can use a client back-end, which gets its information from a GNU/Linux server running SANE, or from a SANE to TWAIN converter application.

Scanners are generally sold with accompanying software on CDs. Some come with trial or feature-limited versions of commercial image-processing applications, but since we're using GIMP, we don't need them. The scanner comes with its own specific application as well, which allows you to use its unique front panel buttons. You can use the scanner without these buttons without any real problem; they're designed to make the scanner faster or easier to use but are

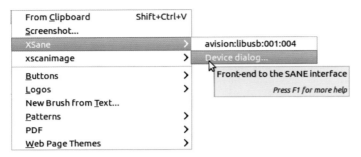

Figure 19.3 *Opening XSane*

not the only way to interface with it. For the purposes of this book, we want to digitize a picture so it's as unchanged as possible, and then we want to process it in GIMP.

XSane and GIMP

If GIMP is installed without any additional plug-ins, it can't communicate with a scanner. Several scanner plug-ins are available for GIMP, but XSane is the best-developed and maintained tool. The XSane package is available for most GNU/Linux distributions, and installing it also installs the XSane plug-in for GIMP. We'll be using the XSane plug-in for scanning in this chapter. If you're using different software, the interface will be different, but similar options should be available.

Once you've installed the plug-in and restarted GIMP, you'll find XSane in the **Image: File > Create** menu, as shown in Figure 19.3. The first entry is the only one most users will need, but if you have two scanners, or a scanner and a webcam, you'll see additional entries that let you choose which device will be the image source. A temporary window appears first, telling the tool is scanning for devices. If no scanner is available, an error window appears. Note that XSane can also use a webcam as input, but we'll not consider this capability.

When you select XSane from the **Image: File > Create** menu, you'll normally see two different dialogs. Figure 19.4 shows the main dialog, which has most of the controls and

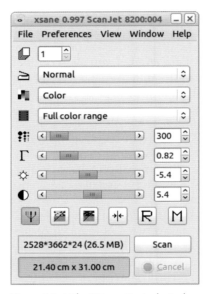

Figure 19.4 *The XSane Control window*

parameters. For that reason, we call it the Control window. Figure 19.5 shows the preview window, which is especially useful for selecting a subsection of the image to scan.

Other SANE back-ends have similar dialogs and controls.

Selecting an Area to Scan

First, place a photograph or drawing on the scanner glass. If the picture is on thin paper, place a black sheet on top of it, especially if there is anything on the reverse side of the paper.

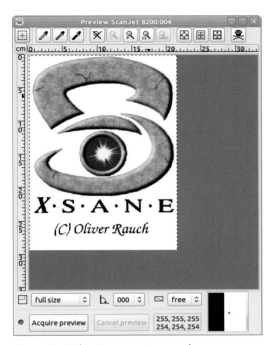

Figure 19.5 *The XSane preview window*

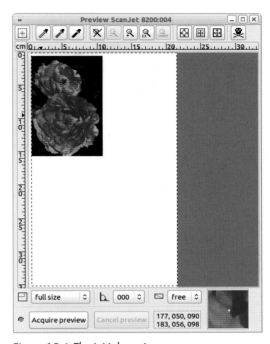

Figure 19.6 *The initial preview*

Adjust the controls in the XSane control window if you'd like to and then acquire a preview by clicking the corresponding button in the preview window.

Figure 19.6 shows our initial image preview. The preview window is square to accommodate any orientation that you choose for the scan. Change the orientation using the middle button in the second row of buttons from the bottom. The large dashed rectangle is what the scanner thinks the image size is. Fortunately, we can change it by clicking and dragging the sides or corners of this rectangle. It is best to delimit a rectangle that's slightly larger than the image because the scanner doesn't always capture precisely what's in the rectangle. Figure 19.7 shows a much better preview. To get this preview, we dragged the rectangle so it outlined the photograph and then clicked ZOOM INTO THE SELECTED AREA (the button with a magnifying glass and a plus sign).

Let's take a look at the other buttons at the top of the preview window. The button with the plus sign at the far left is used for batch processing. The three eyedropper buttons are used to adjust the levels, as in GIMP. The next five buttons control the zoom. From left to right, they are: use the full scan area (no zoom), zoom 20% out, click at the position to zoom to, zoom into the selected area, and undo the last zoom. The three rectangular buttons that follow are, from left to right, autoselect the scan area, autoraise the scan area, and select the visible area. The intriguing button on the far right, the one that looks like a skull and crossbones, deletes everything that's stored in the preview cache. Press it each time you start a new scan to be sure that all the previews of images that you scanned in the past have been cleared.

Below the preview are two rows of buttons. The upper-row buttons control the area to be scanned. Each opens a menu:

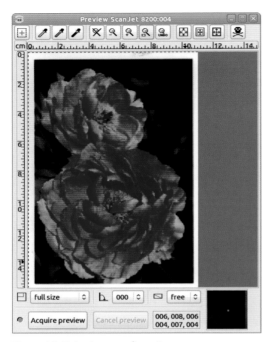

Figure 19.7 *An improved preview*

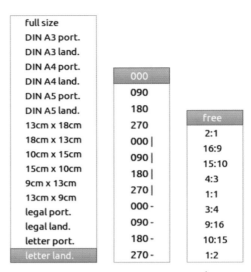

Figure 19.8 *Scanning area, rotation angle, and aspect ratio settings*

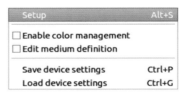

Figure 19.9 *The Preferences menu*

- The preset areas are shown in Figure 19.8 (left). These presets allow you to select some standard dimensions automatically.

- The rotation angles are shown in Figure 19.8 (center). They are all multiples of 90° with three variants. The minus signs indicate the image will be mirrored horizontally, and the pipes indicate it will be mirrored vertically.

- The aspect ratios are shown in Figure 19.8 (right). Use the aspect ratios to set the relationship of width to height and thus control the shape of the region you select to scan.

Although you can use XSane to adjust the image, we recommend scanning the image as is and then making any necessary adjustments in GIMP.

Setting the Scanning Parameters

The Control window, shown in Figure 19.4 on page 512, changes depending on the status of

the two checkboxes shown in Figure 19.9 and can also be affected by some of the buttons at the bottom of the dialog. The PREFERENCES entry in the menu bar brings up the menu shown in Figure 19.9. The SETUP option, which is highlighted, opens a large dialog with nine tabs. Many of those tabs are useful only when XSane is opened independently of GIMP and are used for things like storing, copying, faxing, emailing, or simply displaying files.

If we check ENABLE COLOR MANAGEMENT in the Preferences menu, the Control window changes to the one shown in Figure 19.10. The fields in this dialog, from top to bottom, are these:

- Number of pages to scan: If the scanner has an automatic feed, you can set the number of pages to scan, but if you want to scan in

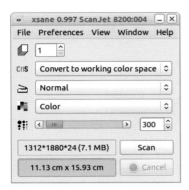

Figure 19.10 *The XSane Control window with color management enabled*

Figure 19.11 *Scan modes*

bulk, use XSane as an independent program, rather than in GIMP. Once all the images have been digitized, you can open them in GIMP as you're ready to edit them.

- Color management function: This allows you to choose how colors are managed in the acquired file. If the choices don't make sense to you, please refer to Section 12.3.

- Scanning method: Choose NORMAL when manually placing the images on the glass, but choose ADF FRONT if you're using an automatic feeder. When using GIMP, you should always choose NORMAL.

- Scan mode: The available scan modes are shown in Figure 19.11 and discussed in the following section.

- Scanning resolution: Set this manually or from the menu if you've checked the SHOW RESOLUTION LIST box on the VIEW menu. For more information on how to choose the best scanning resolution for your needs, see "Scanning Resolutions" on page 517.

Figure 19.12 *Source medium types*

- Size of the scanned image in pixels and MB.

- Size of the scanned image in a variety of measurement units (centimeters is shown).

If color management is not enabled in the Preferences menu, the Control window will contain all the entries shown in Figure 19.4 on page 512. The entry below the scan mode allows you to choose the source medium type. The choices are shown in Figure 19.12. As you can see, specific settings are listed for many types of negatives. FULL COLOR RANGE is the only choice for positives.

The rest of the Control window, between the source medium type and the image size, is covered in "Color Handling" on page 518.

Scan Modes

As shown in Figure 19.11, six scan modes are available in the XSane Control window. The last four are the most useful for GIMP users. You can choose between a color or grayscale image and between depths of 8 or 16 bits. The scan mode selected affects the size of the resulting file, and it affects what you can do to the file in GIMP.

With an 8-bit depth, you have 256 possible gray values or 256^3 colors. XSane has the capability to scan in 16-bit depth, which results in 65,536 gray values or $65,536^3$ colors. Presently GIMP cannot handle 16-bit depth, but plans are to change that in version 2.10 or 3.0. For most

Figure 19.13 *The initial gradient*

Figure 19.14 *After reducing the output range*

Figure 19.15 *After enlarging the input range*

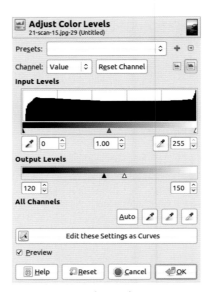

Figure 19.17 *Reducing the output range*

Figure 19.16 *The original image*

Figure 19.18 *The result of reducing the output range*

users, 8-bit depth is plenty. The human eye is unable to distinguish 65,536 shades of gray, and most monitors and printers are only able to handle up to 8-bit depth images.

That's not to say that 16-bit depth is completely pointless. If you happen to reduce the output levels range of a gradient (Figure 19.13) dramatically with the Levels tool, you get an almost uniform gray (Figure 19.14). If you then enlarge the resulting narrow histogram to the full range, with an 8-bit depth image, you see stripes (Figure 19.15), whereas with a 16-bit image, you once again have a smooth gradient.

Reducing the output range severely restricts the number of different values. We show the

effect on the image in Figure 19.16. First, open the Levels dialog. As shown in Figure 19.17, reduce the output range to the 31 values between 120 and 150. The result appears in Figure 19.18.

Then open the Levels dialog again, and this time enlarge the input range by using only the values between 120 and 150 (Figure 19.19). The 31 values that remain in the image are spread

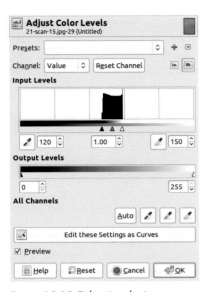

Figure 19.19 *Enlarging the input range*

Figure 19.20 *The result of enlarging the input range*

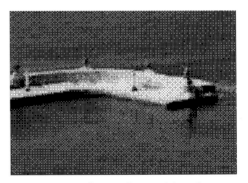

Figure 19.21 *Enlarging from a dithered scan*

across the 256 possible values, as shown in Figure 19.20. The result is rather ugly because the image has too few values. The effect is especially apparent in the sky. If this image had a 16-bit value range, the effect wouldn't be noticeable.

You may be wondering why you would ever want to reduce and then enlarge an image's value range. In reality, you probably won't ever do that, but it does demonstrate that 16-bit depth can make a difference. The impact is important for high-level photograph handling, and that category of users is waiting impatiently for GIMP to include 16-bit depth.

The LINEART scan mode applies an effect that GIMP can also do and can probably do better. The image is scanned in grayscale, and then a threshold is applied for generating the line art. In GIMP, you can do this with the **Image: Colors > Threshold** tool, presented in Chapter 12.

The DITHERED scan mode results in a dithered grayscale image, which was, many years ago, the required format for newspaper printing (see Figure 19.21).

Scanning Resolutions

Which scanning resolution you choose depends on the size of the image being scanned, the capabilities of your computer, and what you intend to use the resulting image for.

The available resolutions depend on your scanner and may differ from those shown in Figure 19.22. The lowest ones are available for every scanner, but the highest resolution may be 2400 pixels per inch or less for a low-cost scanner model (like those found on all-in-one printers). For more discussion of scanning resolutions and hardware, see "Scanners and Drivers" on page 510.

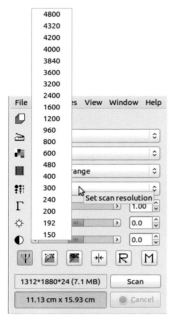

Figure 19.22 *Choosing a resolution from the list*

Olivier's scanner bed is legal sized (8.5 inches × 14 inches). If the definition is set to 300 ppi, the resulting image is 2552×4205 pixels, or 31.4MB if the color depth is 8 bits. If the resolution is 4800 ppi and the color depth is 16 bits, the resulting image is $40,818 \times 67,276$ pixels, or 16,090MB, or 16GB. Obviously, 16GB is far too large for today's personal computers, and that resolution is overkill for the vast majority of users anyway.

Let's consider image resolution in another way. If you want to put an image on a web page, the final resolution should be 96 ppi. If you want to print it, the resolution should be 300 ppi for normal-quality printing or 1200 ppi or greater for high-quality photo printing. Since the final resolution depends on what the image will be used for, you should have a goal in mind when choosing the scanning resolution. Choose a resolution that's a little higher than you need. You can scale it down at the very end of the process.

For example, let's say we have a 4×6 inch photograph that we want to publish on a website, with a maximum size of 1024×768 pixels. In the XSane Control window, the image's pixel size is updated when the scanning resolution is changed. Using trial and error, we determine that 192 ppi would be enough. But if we round up to 300 ppi, we have some wiggle room. If the photograph was printed recently, it was probably printed at 300 ppi, so that's the highest resolution we can actually get. If the photo was printed in the traditional way (in a darkroom), a better resolution is possible. But for this example, 300 ppi is plenty.

Here's a second example: Let's imagine we have a 24×36 mm film negative and we want to make a high-quality print of the photograph—1200 ppi in 4×6 inch format. The scanned image will need to be about 4700×7000 pixels. In the Control window, we see that the best resolution possible with our scanner, 4800 ppi, is not quite enough.

If this happens, don't worry. You can get good results by using interpolation to enlarge an image, as long as you don't overdo it.

Color Handling

In the next section of the Control window, below the settings for scanning resolution, you find a series of parameters for color handling. By default, the dialog has three sliders: one for the gamma value, one for brightness, and one for contrast.

Basically, the *gamma value* measures the brightness of the median values of the image. If the gamma value is set to 1, the image remains in its original state. If gamma is greater than 1, the image is lighter. If gamma is less than 1, the image is darker. This is also the case when we move the gamma triangle in the Levels tool dialog (see "Levels" on page 258).

Brightness measures the intensity of light in each pixel. Intuitively, increasing the brightness

Figure 19.23 *The expanded XSane Control window*

makes an image lighter, and decreasing brightness makes it darker.

Contrast may be loosely defined as a ratio of the brightness of the lightest pixels to the brightness of the darkest pixels in an image. When contrast increases, the lightest parts of the image grow lighter and more saturated, while the darkest parts grow darker and blacker. Although you can adjust brightness and contrast in XSane when scanning, you have more control in GIMP with the **Image: Colors > Brightness-Contrast** tool (see Chapter 12) or, better yet, with the Levels tool.

If you click the leftmost button in the bottom row of buttons in the XSane Control window (Figure 19.4 on page 512), the window expands, as shown in Figure 19.23. The expanded window contains settings for gamma, brightness, and contrast in each of the four

channels: Value, Red, Green, and Blue. Making adjustments with these controls can be difficult and tedious, so we recommend ignoring them and using the equivalent tools found in GIMP instead. Also, all changes to brightness and contrast that you make in the Control window are done automatically for all scans until you change the parameters again. Additionally, if you make adjustments in XSane, you won't see the raw result created by the scanner. You'll see the scan only after it's been adjusted.

To summarize, we recommend using XSane simply as a means to scan images. Transformations, such as changes in brightness or contrast, can and should be done in GIMP rather than in XSane. Note that after you acquire the preview, the Control window automatically sets the autoadjust parameters. If you want to use only GIMP for these adjustments, choose SET DEFAULT ENHANCEMENT VALUES by clicking the fourth button in the row of six at the bottom of the Control window.

The following buttons are also found in the bottom row (from left to right):

- RGB DEFAULT (CTRL+B): Toggles the size of the Control window, which you can use to adjust gamma, brightness, and contrast values in the Value, Red, Green, and Blue channels.

- NEGATIVE (CTRL+N): Inverts all the color values.

- AUTO ADJUST (CTRL+A): Automatically adjusts the gamma, brightness, and contrast values.

- SET DEFAULT ENHANCEMENT VALUES (CTRL+0): Sets gamma to 1.0 and brightness and contrast to 0.

- RESTORE (CTRL+R): Restores the enhancement values as set in the preferences.

- STORE (CTRL++): Stores the current enhancement values in the preferences.

19.3 Digital Cameras

Almost everybody has a digital camera now and can take countless photographs without worrying about the cost of film or developing. Digital photographs are probably the most common type of images edited in GIMP. A wide range of digital cameras are on the market today, with prices ranging from less than ten dollars to tens of thousands of dollars. The CCD sensors generate from 1 megapixel to more than 50 megapixels for the most expensive models. The optics of a reflex camera account for a huge proportion of the total cost, with the many possible features and gadgets available contributing less to the cost.

Many, many models are on the market, and there are at least as many unique user needs, so we won't offer any camera-shopping advice. If you need help choosing a camera, you can find detailed reviews online. From this point on, we assume you already have a camera in hand.

Importing Photographs into GIMP

As you saw in the **Image: File > Create** menu, shown in Figure 19.1 on page 509, two entries involve a camera, assuming the gtkam-gimp plug-in is installed. (If it is not, simply install the gtkam-gimp package as described in Appendix E.) CAPTURE FROM CAMERA allows you to take photographs from inside GIMP by controlling the camera. LOAD FROM CAMERA allows you to access the photographs stored on a camera's memory card.

You don't need to use GIMP to retrieve photographs from a camera, as several applications will do this. However, if you plan to edit your photographs in GIMP, retrieving them in GIMP can be simpler than using a complicated application for managing photo albums.

Note that you don't have to connect the camera to the computer if you have a card reader. When the camera's card is inserted into a reader, the computer treats it like a new storage disk.

Figure 19.24 *The initial dialog for Load from Camera*

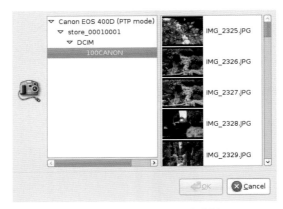

Figure 19.25 *Opening the photograph folder*

You should see a hierarchy of folders with all the photographs as files in one or several folders. The files are named using a pattern specific to the camera. You can open one of these files in GIMP in the same way that you would open any saved file.

LOAD FROM CAMERA is useful when you want to load just one photograph from the camera, not a lot of photographs at once. When you select LOAD FROM CAMERA, you get the dialog shown in Figure 19.24. The name of the camera obviously depends on what model you have.

After choosing your camera and navigating through its folder hierarchy in the left frame of the dialog, you'll arrive at the window shown in Figure 19.25, where thumbnails of the available photographs appear in the right frame. Now you can select one thumbnail and click OK to load the corresponding photograph into GIMP. The dialog then closes, and you'll have to select it again if you want to load another photograph.

Choosing a Format

The simplest cameras store photographs in JPEG format only, due to the compression capabilities of this format. For example, if the camera's CCD sensors generate 10 megapixels, then, assuming 3 bytes per pixel, a full photograph would take up 30MB. Even with a memory card of considerable size, this severely limits the number of pictures that you can store. Moreover, saving large image files onto the card takes time, so you wouldn't be able to take several pictures in quick succession.

A high-quality camera should offer a choice among several definitions and several compression factors. Usually image files can range from 30KB for the lowest definition and highest compression factor to 4MB for the highest definition and lowest compression. Of course, the number of images the memory card can store is inversely related to the picture file size. Unless you want to take a lot of pictures in a short time, choose the best photograph quality: The result that you can get when editing a picture in GIMP is limited by the quality of the initial image. Although JPEG is standard, some people prefer TIFF because they say it uses a lossless compression algorithm. TIFF doesn't actually use any compression algorithm, but a TIFF image may specify an algorithm, which can be lossless. It can also use a JPEG compression algorithm, which is lossy. A TIFF file is always much larger than the equivalent JPEG file and can't be read by as many software applications. The TIFF format is actually a container for several formats, so there's no guarantee that all the features specified in an image will be properly handled by an application. JPEG is a better choice for most users, and if a lossless format is absolutely needed, PNG is a better choice than TIFF.

The compression algorithm used by JPEG sometimes generates artifacts. If the quality factor is large enough, these artifacts won't be visible, even when the image is zoomed in substantially. But you should avoid repeatedly exporting an image in the JPEG format because

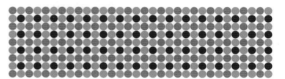

Figure 19.26 *The Bayer pattern*

the compression deterioration is cumulative. Also, note that setting the quality factor higher than when the image was loaded is pointless. Doing so only increases the file size without actually increasing the quality.

Most quality cameras also allow you to save photographs in *raw format*, which is not a specific format. As many different raw formats exist as camera manufacturers, and the same manufacturer often defines different raw formats for different camera models. Moreover, all these raw formats are incompatible with each other, so the proprietary software used for decoding one is incompatible with the software released with a new camera model from the same manufacturer.

The main drawback of any raw format is that you have no guarantee you'll be able to open files in a specific raw format in a few years. Raw format is, therefore, not a good choice for storing photographs. Choose an internationally standardized format; for photographs, JPEG with a high quality rate (85 or greater) is the best solution.

Raw format is often called the *digital negative*, but this term is misleading because raw format is a mathematical approximation of the image, whereas a true negative is the actual image projected on the back of the camera. The definition of a negative depends on the size of the crystals that compose it, but it's always many times better than the definition of the best CCD matrix.

The reason the raw format is called a digital negative is that it represents the data emitted by the CCD sensors. These data are generally sampled to create 4096 different values, which equate to 12 bits per sensor. The sensors are arranged in a *Bayer pattern*, shown in Figure 19.26. Note that there are twice as many green cells as

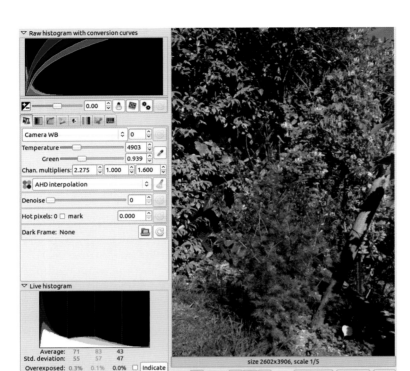

Figure 19.27 *The UFRaw plug-in dialog*

there are red and blue ones. This is because the human eye is much more sensitive to the green wavelengths.

Color pixels are interpolated from the information generated by the cells via *Bayer interpolation*, which is the first transformation done to the data. After that, the camera executes several successive processes: White balance, contrast, and saturation are adjusted, and the sharpness is enhanced, among other things.

Finally, the data generated are compressed to 8 bit and then compressed to JPEG format. The compression from 12 to 8 bit doesn't cause much loss because the compression is logarithmic, which preserves information with precision where it is most needed: in the low values. But in the high values, only a few different brightness levels are retained. The information lost

during the compression to JPEG can vary from nominal (with a high quality setting) to severe.

The one advantage of raw format is that it is the only format that allows you to do all the transformations to your images manually. People often promote the use of raw format because it allows for correcting extreme exposure errors. This assumption is partly true because less data are present after the automatic transformations. But if you know how to use your camera correctly, you probably won't make mistakes that are too extreme for the camera to handle.

If you don't mind complicated software applications and fiddling with numerous parameters, and you want full control over what happens after the sensors measure the light arriving on them, raw format might be for you. Also, if you absolutely need 16-bit depth and if you have a lot of time to spend on every photograph, then raw format is a fine choice. But as long as a high quality setting is used, JPEG isn't inferior to raw format, although some people who present themselves as professionals might argue otherwise. Even if raw format is ideal for you, we recommend generating both raw and JPEG images, as long as you don't need to take a lot of photographs very quickly. And you should always choose a different format (such as JPEG or XCF) for long-term storage.

Handling Raw Photographs

If you do choose to work with raw images, you can use the generic, free software tool called UFRaw (see *http://ufraw.sourceforge.net/*), which reads most raw formats, is regularly updated, costs nothing, and is available on all GNU/Linux distributions, as well as on Mac OS X and various versions of Windows. You can use it as a separate application or as a GIMP plug-in.

Darktable (see *http://www.darktable.org/*) is a more powerful tool, also generic and free software. But it is not available for any version of Windows, and it's not interfaced with GIMP. Thus, in this section we suppose that you installed UFRaw and the corresponding GIMP plug-in.

When you open a raw image in GIMP, it automatically calls the UFRaw plug-in, which displays the dialog shown in Figure 19.27. On the right is a preview of the image, with buttons for zooming in or out. On the left, you'll see a number of information windows, tabs, buttons, sliders, and other controls. These controls show the transformation process that UFRaw applies to the image in place of the transformations normally done by the camera.

The top histogram shows the raw data coming from the sensor cells and the curves that represent how the data will be converted. The histogram is bunched up on the left, which means that most of the pixels have a low luminosity. By right-clicking the histogram, you can switch between a logarithmic view, as shown in

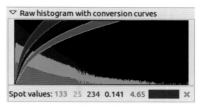

Figure 19.28 *The logarithmic histogram and spot values*

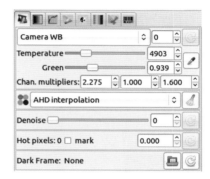

Figure 19.29 *The White balance tab*

Figure 19.28, and a linear view. In the same figure, we see the RGB values for whatever point we've clicked in the image, as well as the luminosity and the Adams zone.[1]

The row just below the raw histogram contains a slider for adjusting the exposure, two buttons for restoring highlights and controlling how corrections are applied, and a button for automatically adjusting the exposure.

Next are eight tabs, which you can use to set successive transformations that will be applied to the data:

- White balance (Figure 19.29, top): The initial value is chosen on the camera but not applied to the raw data. The TEMPERATURE slider changes the relative amounts of warm and cool colors. The slider below is for adjusting the Green channel, which is not affected

---

1. Ansel Adams is a celebrated photographer who defined the *zone system* to mitigate the exposure issues caused by the fact that light meters assume that the average of all scenes is middle gray. See *http://www.normankoren.com/zonesystem .html* for a more thorough explanation.

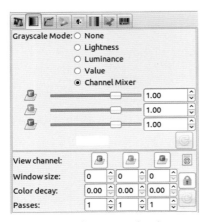

Figure 19.30 *The Grayscale tab*

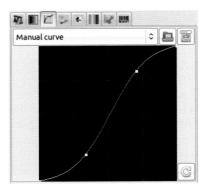

Figure 19.31 *The Base curve tab*

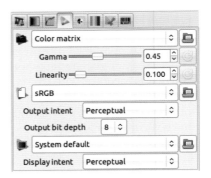

Figure 19.32 *The Color management tab*

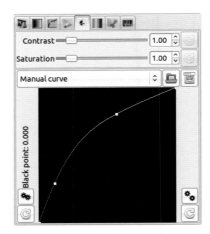

Figure 19.33 *The Saturation tab*

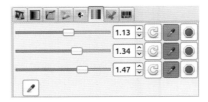

Figure 19.34 *The Lightness adjustments tab*

by the color temperature. Several preset white balance settings are available.

- Interpolation (Figure 19.29, middle): This allows you to choose among several different algorithms for Bayer interpolation.

- Grayscale (Figure 19.30): This tab contains a number of methods for generating a grayscale image from a color one.

- Base curve (Figure 19.31): This tab works like the **Image: Colors > Curves** tool, but it operates only on the Value channel.

- Color management (Figure 19.32): This tab contains settings for the various color parameters and for ICC profiles.

- Saturation (Figure 19.33): This tab has a correction curve that works like the one for the Value channel.

- Lightness adjustments (Figure 19.34): This tab lets you select up to three colors from the image and then to adjust its lightness from [0 to 2].

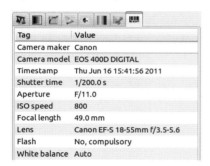

Figure 19.35 *The Crop and rotate tab*

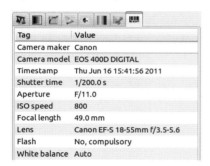

Tag	Value
Camera maker	Canon
Camera model	EOS 400D DIGITAL
Timestamp	Thu Jun 16 15:41:56 2011
Shutter time	1/200.0 s
Aperture	F/11.0
ISO speed	800
Focal length	49.0 mm
Lens	Canon EF-S 18-55mm f/3.5-5.6
Flash	No, compulsory
White balance	Auto

Figure 19.36 *The EXIF data tab*

- Lightness adjustments (Figure 19.34): This tab lets you select up to three colors from the image and then adjust its lightness in [0 to 2].

- Crop and rotate (Figure 19.35): This tab contains some simple controls for cropping and rotating the image, but GIMP offers more powerful and convenient tools.

- EXIF data (Figure 19.36): This tab lists information generated by the camera and describes how the picture was taken. This information cannot be changed.

The final histogram (Figure 19.37) displays the properties the image will have when all the selected transformations are applied. You can select different display options by right-clicking. Various checkboxes and buttons reveal any of the overexposed or underexposed areas.

When you click OK, the transformations are applied to the image, and it's loaded into GIMP.

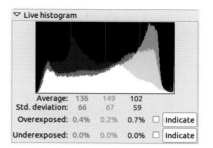

Figure 19.37 *The final histogram*

19.4 Printing

Printing an image is easy as long as you have a printer and the proper drivers, but printing a faithful representation of what you see on the screen can be challenging.

The Principles of Printing

Purchasing a printer is the first step in printing your images. There are many printer manufacturers and brands and an overwhelming number of different models. The price range is also huge, from less than $50 for the smallest and slowest ones to $15,000 and more for professional models that can print on three-foot-wide paper. There are also several printing techniques and a myriad of additional capabilities to choose from. Because this book is intended for general users, we consider only the printers intended for nonprofessional use.

The most common printing techniques are inkjet and laser. The least expensive color laser printers cost three to five times as much as the least expensive inkjet printers, but they're much faster. On the other hand, low-cost inkjet printers generally produce much nicer images than laser printers in the same price range. You can also use glossier and heavier papers with an inkjet printer.

If you print mainly text or simple illustrations, and if you print a lot (say, several pages every day on the average), then a laser printer is probably the best choice. If you want to print mainly photographs and want a better quality output, then you should buy an inkjet printer.

The major cost in printing is not the printer or the papers but the inks. A replacement set of all the inks used by a printer can cost as much as the printer itself, or even more. This cost model is the result of a rather underhanded business model. Printer manufacturers sell printers below their fabrication cost, but they sell ink cartridges well above their real cost. In fact, the inks they use are very cheap to manufacture, and a one-liter bottle in some countries costs the same as a 5 ml cartridge in other countries. Moreover, manufacturers have devised imaginative devices and tricks to prevent customers from using generic ink cartridges that would be 5 to 10 times cheaper.

Note, however, that laser ink cartridges generally print many more pages than inkjet cartridges. The business model used here is more respectable.

Printers generally use the CMYK color model, which is explained in Chapter 12. Because the colors are layered on a white paper, using a subtractive model makes sense. The CMY model isn't enough because generating a good black color by mixing the three basic colors is almost impossible. A standard laser or inkjet printer, therefore, uses at least four different color cartridges: Cyan, Magenta, Yellow, and Black.

Inkjet printers designed for high-quality photo printing generally have more than four different inks. In addition to CMYK, they usually have a light Cyan and a light Magenta. More expensive printers may add a matte Black and a light Gray in order to replicate the qualities of the blacks and grays present in analog black and white photography.

The quality of the output paper is also important. You will get a much better result on glossy photo paper (which is unrelated to the analog photography process), but printing on glossy paper requires more ink and takes much longer. If you make several test prints in a rather large format, you can quickly empty the ink cartridges.

Figure 19.38 *Printing entries in the Image: File menu*

When planning to buy a printer, ask yourself the following questions:

- What do I intend to print?
- How many pages will I print per week?
- What print quality do I need?
- What monthly or annual budget can I devote to printing?

When you consider all the factors, the cheapest printer is probably not the best buy. Although the initial investment is low, cheap models usually break more quickly, produce a lower-quality result, and use ink cartridges that may cost more than the printer itself. Also consider how boring it will be to watch a low-cost printer slowly exude a photograph over the course of several minutes.

To create high-quality photo prints, you should look for an inkjet printer with, at the very least, six different ink colors. Printers with separate cartridges for the various inks are preferable because they allow you to change only the cartridge that's empty, which can save you money. Also, some printer cartridges contain the print head, whereas for other printers, the print head is a part of the printer itself. We prefer the former, despite its slightly higher cost, for two reasons:

- If the print head is damaged, replacing it is extremely simple.
- If you don't print anything for several weeks, the ink generally dries in the print head and can clog the micro-holes. If the head is fixed to the printer, the only solution is to run the cleaning program, which consumes a lot of ink and does not always work.

Some printers have replaceable print heads, separate from the cartridges, which is also a better choice than fixed print heads.

Figure 19.39 *The Print dialog*

If you are a GNU/Linux user, check the Open Printing page of the Linux Foundation (*http://www.linuxfoundation.org/collaborate/workgroups/openprinting*) before buying a printer to be sure drivers are available.

Printing with the GTK Interface

Figure 19.38 shows the section of the **Image: File** menu that contains entries related to printing or digitally outputting the image via email.

The last entry, **Image: File > Send by Email**, allows you to send a digital copy of a file directly from GIMP. Note that this tool works only if a Mail Transfer Agent is installed on the computer, which is uncommon on personal computers, so you may get an error message when you try to send the image. If so, simply save the image and attach it to an email message as you normally would.

The first entry shown in Figure 19.38 is always present, but the second one is available only if Gutenprint is installed. The print command uses printing mechanisms specific to the operating system. We're using the GTK interface, which is available in a GNU/Linux environment. If you're using a different operating system, the interface will be slightly different, but the concepts and features should be similar.

Image: File > Print opens the dialog shown in Figure 19.39. On the GENERAL tab, you'll see a list of local printers. PRINT TO FILE allows you to convert the image to PDF or PostScript and save it to a chosen folder. This is the simplest way to convert an image to either of those formats. The RANGE and COPIES entries are relevant only if you're printing more than one image at a time. The PRINT PREVIEW button converts the image to PDF and displays it using the default PDF reader. This option may be useful if you're preparing to print a large image and want to check the parameters.

The PAGE SETUP tab is shown in Figure 19.40. In previous versions of GIMP, these options appeared in their own dialog, accessed via **Image: File > Page Setup**. Now everything is located in the same dialog. As is the case throughout most of the Print dialog tabs, the contents of this tab change depending on the capabilities of the printer selected on the GENERAL tab. PAPER SIZE offers a predefined selection of formats, shown in Figure 19.41. You can also add new formats with MANAGE CUSTOM SIZES, which opens the dialog shown in Figure 19.42. Here you can

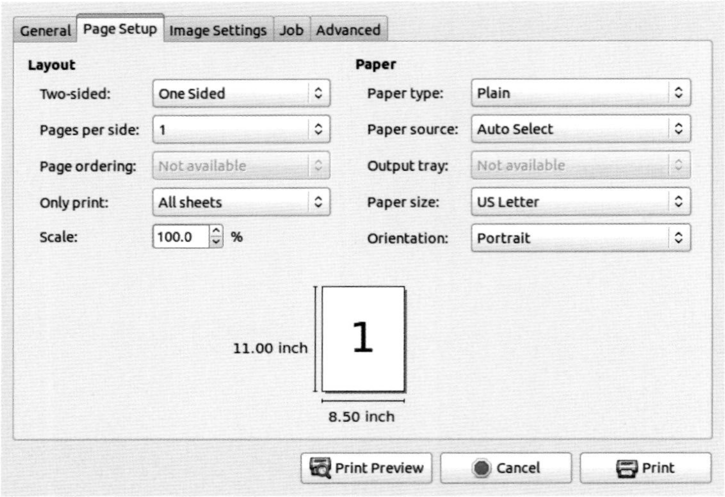

Figure 19.40 *The Print dialog, Page Setup tab*

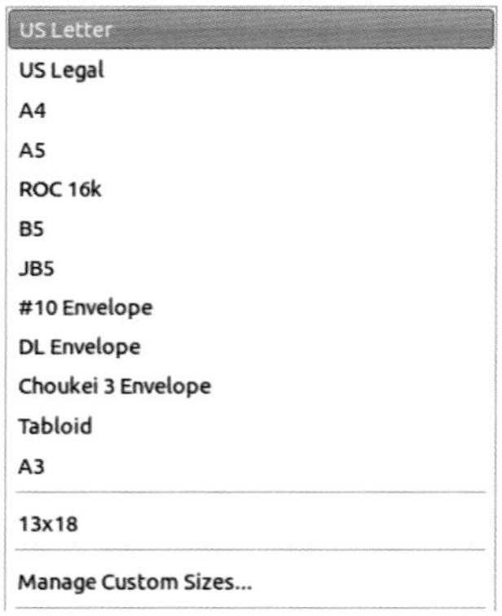

Figure 19.41 *Available paper sizes*

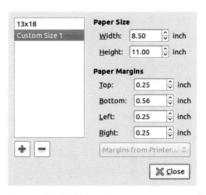

Figure 19.42 *Managing custom paper sizes*

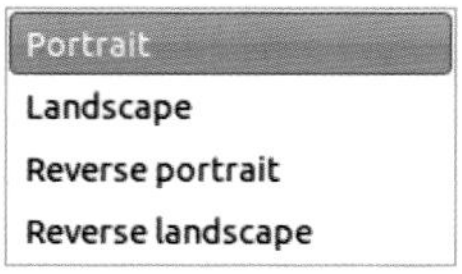

Figure 19.43 *Available orientations*

create, name, and specify a new size or change or delete an existing one. ORIENTATION offers the four possibilities shown in Figure 19.43.

The IMAGE SETTINGS tab (Figure 19.44) can be used to change the size of the printed image via adjustments to the margins and the resolution. Note that the paper size was set in the PAGE SETUP tab. You can also add crop marks, which are useful if you plan to crop the printed picture physically.

The other tabs are not always present, depending on the active printer. Figure 19.45

shows the ADVANCED tab, in the case of a laser printer. The settings deal with printing quality, color control, and fine-tuning. For an inkjet printer, the ADVANCED tab provides more controls, and two additional tabs may precede the ADVANCED tab (IMAGE QUALITY and COLOR).

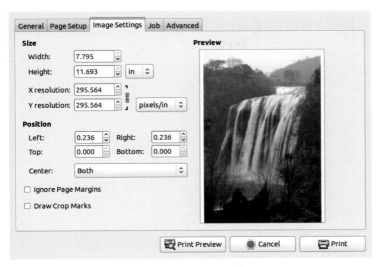

Figure 19.44 *The Print dialog, Image Settings tab*

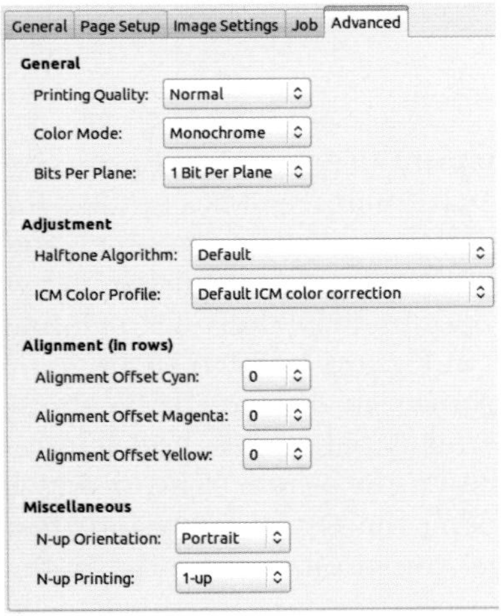

Figure 19.45 *The Print dialog, Advanced tab*

In the case of a monochrome printer, there are no extra tabs.

Printing with Gutenprint

Gutenprint is not a component of GIMP, although it was initially developed for it to provide more options than the GTK interface. You can easily install it on any GNU/Linux distribution as well as on Mac OS X, but installing it on Windows is more difficult. To run it in GIMP, you must also install the plug-in (see Chapter 21 for more about installing plug-ins). **Image: File > Print with Gutenprint** should then appear and, when selected, open the dialog shown in Figure 19.46.

A preview of the current image appears on the left. If you hover the pointer over this preview, a detailed tooltip explains how to position the image. These instructions are especially important if the image is much smaller than the sheet of paper. The IMAGE POSITION and IMAGE SIZE frames at the bottom of the dialog display the numeric equivalents of what you see in the preview. The SIZE UNITS tab offers a choice among inches, points, picas, centimeters, and millimeters.

The two frames on the top right vary depending on the printer. In particular, the possible paper sizes in the PAPER SIZE frame are different for a traditional laser printer versus a multipurpose inkjet printer. Similarly, the rectangle above SET PRINTER OPTION DEFAULTS in the PRINTER SETTINGS tab shown in Figure 19.46 may contain buttons or sliders depending on the selected printer.

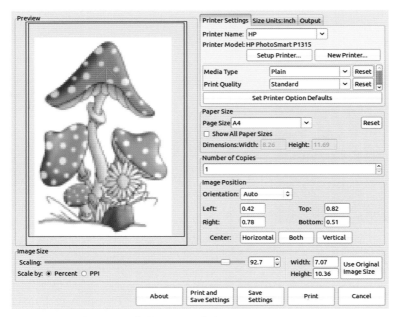

Figure 19.46 *The Print with Gutenprint dialog*

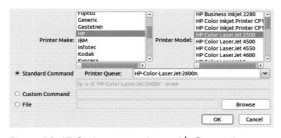

Figure 19.47 *Setting up a printer with Gutenprint*

The PRINTER SETTINGS tab allows you to select a predefined printer, add a new one, or set up the current printer. The SETUP PRINTER button opens the dialog shown in Figure 19.47. You can choose the PRINTER MAKE and then the PRINTER MODEL. The number of possible printer models is huge and always increasing; although the Gutenprint developers work hard to be up-to-date, a new model may not yet be compatible.

Figure 19.46 shows the Print with Gutenprint dialog with an HP PhotoSmart P1315 printer selected. There are only a few settings available. For comparison, Figure 19.48 shows the

Print with Gutenprint dialog for an Epson Stylus Photo P50. As you can see, it has options for various print qualities, media types, sources, and more. The Print with Gutenprint dialog always contains more options than the GTK printing interface, shown in Figures 19.39 to 19.44.

The dialog shown in Figure 19.49 shows just a few of the many parameters and settings available with the Epson printer. This dialog is accessed by clicking the OUTPUT tab and then clicking the large ADJUST OUTPUT button in the center. These parameters are intended to be adjusted specifically for each image. Many of the sliders are inactive by default but can be activated if you check the box to the left.

Because many parameters are available, you will likely want to save settings that work well. You can do this by using the buttons at the bottom of the main window (see Figure 19.46) to either save the settings and continue fiddling with them or save them and print immediately.

If you want to use Gutenprint with a printer that is not (yet) supported, you can choose to

Printer Settings	Size Units:Inch	Output

Printer Name: Epson ⌄
Printer Model: Epson Stylus Photo P50

Setup Printer...	New Printer...

Print Quality	Photo ⌄		Reset
Media Type	Ultra Glossy Photo Pap ⌄		Reset
Media Source	Rear Tray ⌄		Reset
Double-Sided Printing	Off ⌄		Reset
Ink Set	EPSON Standard Inks ⌄		Reset
	Borderless		Reset
Resolution	Default ⌄		Reset
Printing Direction	Automatic ⌄		Reset
Interleave Method	Standard ⌄		Reset
Ink Type	Standard ⌄		Reset
☐ Quality Enhancement		0	Reset
☐ Print Method		0	Reset
☐ Platen Gap		0	Reset

Set Printer Option Defaults

Figure 19.48 *The options that appear on the Printer Settings tab depend on your printer.*

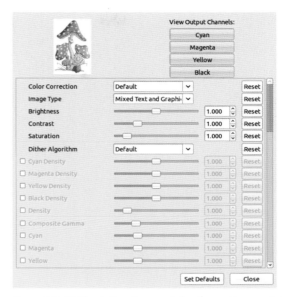

View Output Channels:

Cyan
Magenta
Yellow
Black

Color Correction	Default ⌄		Reset
Image Type	Mixed Text and Graphi ⌄		Reset
Brightness		1.000	Reset
Contrast		1.000	Reset
Saturation		1.000	Reset
Dither Algorithm	Default ⌄		Reset
☐ Cyan Density		1.000	Reset
☐ Magenta Density		1.000	Reset
☐ Yellow Density		1.000	Reset
☐ Black Density		1.000	Reset
☐ Density		1.000	Reset
☐ Composite Gamma		1.000	Reset
☐ Cyan		1.000	Reset
☐ Magenta		1.000	Reset
☐ Yellow		1.000	Reset

Set Defaults	Close

Figure 19.49 *The Adjust Output dialog for an Epson printer*

generate a PostScript or PDF file by selecting Adobe as the printer, and then print this file using the system tool. But doing so greatly reduces the flexibility and power of Gutenprint. If you intend to use Gutenprint and are shopping for a printer, check whether the printer you're considering is one of the more than 1400 printers supported.

19.5 Scanning and Printing with Windows

Gutenprint is supposed to have been ported to Windows, but installing it and getting it up and running properly is not easy. XSane is even more complicated because SANE itself doesn't currently run smoothly under Windows. Windows users can access SANE through a SANE GNU/Linux server, but doing so requires at least two computers on a local network, and one of them must be a GNU/Linux server running SANE. If you have a Linux server running

SANE, you might as well bypass the Windows machine and print from the server.

If you're using a Windows machine, generally you must use the scanning software provided with your device. The features are similar to those of the XSane dialogs—just organized in a different way. Proprietary scanning software can be unintuitive and make scanning several images in sequence unduly complicated. For example, the scanning resolution may be hidden in a menu and not immediately visible in the main menu.

As Gutenprint is not readily available in Windows, GIMP's default printing capabilities are slightly different on Windows machines. When you select **Image: File > Print**, a dialog with only two tabs opens. In the first tab, you select the printer in a way similar to GNU/Linux. The second tab is the IMAGE SETTINGS tab, identical to Figure 19.44.

In order to finely tune the printing parameters, click PREFERENCES in the first tab. You get a dialog with several tabs, specific to your printer. This dialog is intended for text documents and does not have many image-specific capabilities.

20

Image Formats

GIMP can manage more than 40 file formats for representing images. It can read 35 input formats and generate 39 output formats. Moreover, it accepts these formats in a compressed form, using either the Gzip or Bzip2 compression techniques.

If we covered all these formats in detail, this chapter would be enormous. Instead, we cover only the formats that are popular with, or at least useful to, many GIMP users. We also discuss the general principles that govern the various image formats.

20.1 An Overview of File Formats

An image on a computer screen is comprised of a matrix of pixels. This holds true on all current displays: cathode-ray tube, plasma, liquid crystals, and others. This is also true for laser and inkjet printers. Even the eye breaks down images into an array of rods and cones, as described in Appendix A.

The *file format* is how a file is stored in memory and is independent of how an image was captured and how it will eventually be viewed. So the representation of an image as a file, whether stored on disk or downloaded online, is not necessarily a representation of the final matrix of pixels. And because pixel density varies widely among mobile phone displays, computer monitors, cheap inkjet printers, and professional laser printers, any representation needs to be converted from the internal representation to the external one. Images that you produce must also be converted—be it from a phone's camera, a scanner, or a professional digital camera.

Raster and Vector Formats

Image formats can be divided into two main families: raster and vector.

- In the *raster formats*, an image is stored as a representation of the pixels it contains. A *bitmap* image, which can represent black and white only (no gray levels), contains 1 bit per pixel, whereas a *pixmap* image, which can represent gray levels and colors, contains several bits per pixel.

- In the *vector formats*, an image is stored as a geometric description of its contents.

Each format has its advantages and drawbacks. An image file in vector format is generally much smaller than a file in raster format,

Figure 20.1 *An icon*

Figure 20.2 *The icon enlarged as a vector image*

Figure 20.3 *The icon enlarged as a raster image*

and a vector image will be displayed at any size with the same sharpness because the pixels are computed each time the zoom factor changes. Figure 20.1 shows a 48×48 icon generated as a vector graphic image. The file is 63KB in the SVG format (which is a textual format in the XML convention). It is 1.3KB in JPEG because the image is very small.

Figure 20.2 shows the same icon enlarged to 480×480 as a vector graphic image at 300 dpi. The SVG file is the same size as before, but the JPEG file is now 30KB. Figure 20.3 shows the same icon enlarged as a raster graphic image. The JPEG file is 19KB, but the image is badly pixelated.

Figure 20.4 *A typical vector graphic image*

Although vector graphics clearly have advantages, their main drawback is they cannot represent complicated images like photographs accurately. For example, describing the relief and shading of a human face with mathematical formulas is not feasible. Figure 20.4 is a typical example of a portrait done in vector graphics. Although tools are available for converting an image from a raster format to a vector image, the results tend to be poor.

GIMP works on the raster representation of images, so it works well for photographs and illustrations. A pixmap cannot be zoomed in indefinitely, however, so when working with a raster image, work with as large a definition as possible. You can always reduce the size before sending the file to somebody or posting it online.

Lossless and Lossy Compression

Raster images are generally large, and they keep getting larger as digital cameras improve. The data size of a single pixel also increases when the number of colors that can be represented increases. And the number of pixels increases with the size and resolution of the image. A digital camera can now create images as large as 10 (or even 12) million pixels, which generally means at least 30MB if the number of colors in each channel is 256.

A 30MB file is rather large, even for current hard disks, especially if you store a lot of photos. This file size is also large for most memory

Figure 20.5 *A photo of a rose with decreasing image quality*

cards and would be difficult to send via email or to post online. One solution is to compress the file to decrease its size. A number of algorithms are available for compressing files, especially image files. These algorithms can be either lossless or lossy.

- A *lossless* compression algorithm rebuilds the original data without losing any information. The image quality remains stable, but sometimes the original image is transformed in a lossy way. If the image isn't transformed first, then applying lossless compression won't reduce the file size by very much.

- A *lossy* compression algorithm results in some loss of information, but the differences may be invisible to the human eye. Generally, lossy compression reduces the file size considerably, but you cannot rebuild the original image exactly as it was, and if you apply lossy compression more than once, the deterioration is cumulative. Eventually, you can see the difference.

If you want maximum image quality and don't care about size, use only lossless compression. If you can accept some loss in image quality in exchange for significant size reduction, choose a lossy algorithm.

	Column 1		Column 2		Column 3	
	Factor	Size (KB)	Factor	Size (KB)	Factor	Size (KB)
Row 1	100	233	80	47	60	33
Row 2	40	26	30	23	20	19
Row 3	10	14	8	13	5	11.7

Figure 20.6 *Sizes and quality factors of the images shown in Figure 20.5*

Figure 20.7 *The initial photo of the rose (left); the same image after saving and reloading several times (right)*

Figure 20.5 shows the same image nine times. Each time the image's quality factor and size decrease, as shown in Figure 20.6.

You cannot see any obvious loss of quality down to factor 60. When the factor is 10 or less, however, the loss is very apparent.

Another problem with lossy compression is that defects accumulate if you save the image several times. Figure 20.7 (left) shows an enlarged section of the rose photo, and Figure 20.7 (right) shows the same photo after we saved and reloaded it several times with a low quality factor (less than 60). The compression artifacts are clearly visible on the edge of the middle petal.

Layout Engines and Browsers

These days many people view images through browsers like Firefox or Internet Explorer. Unfortunately, not all image formats are supported by all browsers. In fact, the three common formats discussed in the next section are the only ones that are displayed by all existing browsers,

and sometimes even those formats don't work perfectly.

Many different browsers exist, and some browsers vary depending on your operating system. Browsers use *layout engines* to display images on the screen. Fewer than 10 layout engines are available, and only a handful are widely used. Different browsers using the same layout engine handle images in the same way. The following table lists popular layout engines and the browsers that use them:

Layout Engine	Browsers
Gecko	all Mozilla software: Firefox, Galeon, Seamonkey, etc.
KHTML	Konqueror
Presto	Opera
Trident	Internet Explorer 4 to 9
Webkit	Safari, Epiphany, Google Chrome

Because many people still use Internet Explorer, many people use Trident. No layout engine is perfect, but unfortunately Trident is one of the worst. Its main problem, with regard to image display, is that it does not handle PNG format very well. Other free software browsers handle PNG images much better.

20.2 JPEG, GIF, and PNG

In this section, we discuss the common formats that all layout engines handle (though not always well) and which are generally the most useful.

JPEG

Surprisingly, JPEG is not the name of the format, which is called JFIF, but of the working group that defined it—the Joint Photographic Experts Group. This committee defined what became an ISO standard in 1994. The format they designed is the usual output format of most, if not all, digital cameras. JFIF stands for *JPEG File Interchange Format*.

JPEG uses a lossy compression algorithm, which means that some information is lost, but the file size is decreased substantially while maintaining a fairly high image quality. JPEG is the format of choice for photographs and digital illustrations because it can present complex images as files that are small enough to send by email or to post on the Web.

As shown in Figure 20.7, exporting a JPEG over and over is not a good idea because the quality loss accumulates. Each time you load a picture you start with the last state, which suffered some loss of quality when you last exported it. Always work on the image as an XCF in GIMP, and export it from the XCF to store it as a JPEG. This issue is one of the reasons why, since version 2.8, GIMP only exports an image as JPEG and doesn't consider the image to be saved until you have saved it as an XCF file.

The JPEG format is not well suited to images containing line drawings, text, or a sharp contrast between adjacent pixels. A lossless

Figure 20.8 *Sharp contrast with a lossy compression algorithm*

Figure 20.9 *Sharp contrast with a lossless compression algorithm*

compression algorithm is needed in such a case, because it means that only some pixels from the initial image are saved and the missing pixels are interpolated when the image is loaded. If pixels along a sharp border in a line drawing are not saved, the interpolation assigns them an average value based on the surrounding pixels, which smooths the border and can make the image look blurry.

Figures 20.8 and 20.9 show the difference between a lossy and lossless compression algorithm used on an image with high contrast. In the first figure, the character contours are blurred by the lossy compression algorithm, whereas in the second figure, they remain sharp, thanks to the lossless compression algorithm.

Another weakness of the JPEG format is that it cannot handle transparency. Although generally fine for photos, if you want to display a non-rectangular graphic on a web page, for example, and it's a JPEG, you have to fill the background with a color or pattern.

A JPEG file can contain an ICC color profile, which defines the color space used (see Chapter 12). If this is the case, when you load the file, GIMP asks whether you want to use the embedded profile. Generally, you should answer yes. Many simpler image applications simply ignore the profile.

Exporting to JPEG

When you export an image to JPEG (`.jpeg` or `.jpg`), GIMP opens a dialog, which in its simplest form only allows you to set the compression quality [0 to 100].

The QUALITY slider determines how much the image quality will be degraded to decrease the file size. Images at values greater than 85 generally look the same, and the loss in quality is practically indiscernible at such values. The degradation usually becomes apparent only if the value is less than 50. Check SHOW PREVIEW IN IMAGE WINDOW to see the effect of the current setting before exporting the image.

If you click ADVANCED OPTIONS, you'll see the extended dialog shown in Figure 20.10. Here are the most useful ADVANCED OPTIONS:

- PROGRESSIVE: The file loads progressively in a web page. First, a crude version appears, and then the image becomes more and more refined. This setting is useful for large files that inevitably take time to load, but it increases the file size slightly.

- SAVE EXIF DATA: The EXIF data, which is generally added to the file by digital cameras, contains information about a photo, including the date and time the photo was taken, the camera brand and model, and the camera settings used.

- SAVE THUMBNAIL: This option saves a thumbnail of the image in the file.

- USE QUALITY SETTINGS FROM ORIGINAL IMAGE: These settings determine how the compression algorithm works. The original image may have an unusual set of values; in this case, checking this box guarantees that if you make minor changes to the image, the result will have the same quality as the original.

- SMOOTHING: This slider smooths imperfections created by a high level of compression. Smoothing also blurs the image.

The other ADVANCED OPTIONS are useful only under very specific circumstances, so just ignore them unless you know that you need to change them. Note that the COMMENT field, which adds text to the file, will not be visible in the image itself, but you can see it in GIMP with **Image: Image > Image Properties**, on the third tab. The COMMENT field can be handy for adding a copyright notice, for example.

In addition to transparency, JPEG cannot save multiple layers. Although it has some popular applications, JPEG can't store nearly as much information as XCF, which is another reason why it's always better to save files as XCF and export them as JPEG rather than storing them only as JPEG.

GIF

The Graphics Interchange Format (GIF) has a long and tumultuous history. Although this format has many major drawbacks, it remains popular partly because it's the simplest format for building small animations (Chapter 18) and because people are familiar with it.

This format was defined in 1987 by CompuServe, now a subsidiary of AOL. At that time, the compression of images was considered much more important than the number of colors, which was limited by most existing display

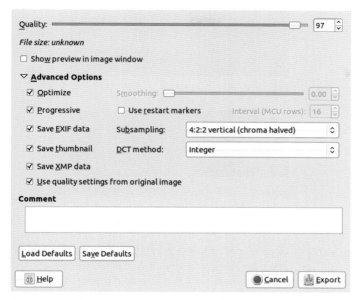

Figure 20.10 *The Export Image as JPEG dialog*

screens. For this reason, the GIF format, with its efficient compression algorithm and limited palette, was widely used in the first browsers and graphic tools.

The compression algorithm used by GIF is known as LZW. It was designed in the late 1970s by Jacob Ziv and Abraham Lempel and improved in 1983 by Terry Welch. Welch immediately filed an application for a US patent on his algorithm and extended this patent later to various other countries.

When the GIF format was published, the authors were not aware of the patent, and it was only in 1993 that the current patent owner, Unisys, tried to exercise rights to the algorithm. They tried to get royalties when the format was used, at least in commercial products. This triggered much indignation in the Internet world and was one of the main reasons for the development of the PNG format (see "PNG" on page 541). The patent expired in 2003 in the US and one year later in other countries, so you can now use the format freely, but its reputation hasn't fully recovered.

The GIF format was actually pretty good when it was developed, but today PNG is superior in all respects but one: animation. Internet Explorer's poor support of PNG remains a major obstacle to the full adoption of this format, however.

GIF's main characteristic is that the image must be in *indexed mode*. An indexed image is encoded using a color table, as we explained in Chapter 12. The pixels are represented as indexes in the table, and the size of each pixel depends on the size of the table: A table with 4 colors requires 2 bits, a table with 64 colors requires 6 bits, and a table with 256 colors requires 8 bits (1 byte), the maximum for GIF.

Indexed mode saves space because a pixel needs at most 1 byte instead of 3 (with 8-bit depth RGB encoding). But even more space is saved by the increased probability that neighboring pixels are the same. Instead of storing the value of every pixel separately, a compression algorithm can store the shape and size of a contiguous area with identical pixels and the pixel value for the area.

Figure 20.11 *The rose in Figure 20.7 indexed with 32 colors*

Figure 20.12 *A color gradient*

Figure 20.13 *The color gradient indexed and dithered*

The LZW compression algorithm doesn't quite work that way, but the compression rate is still better if neighboring pixels have the same value. LZW doesn't work if there are more possible values for pixels than pixels in the image, which is often the case with RGB encoding. With 8-bit RGB, you have 2^{24} possible pixel values (more than 16 million), but a 4000 × 4000 pixel image is unusually large. GIF also doesn't work well for photos, as the probability that neighboring pixels have the same value is low.

The LZW algorithm works best when the image contains large areas of the same color, which means the GIF format is best suited for simple graphics, line drawings, and cartoons. A smooth change in hue or value is not easy to represent because the palette does not have enough colors. A technique known as *dithering* can smooth transitions to a degree. When dithering is applied, two different colors are used in neighboring pixels, and because the pixels are so small, the eye blends the two colors together. Dithering can lead to a loss of detail, and the result doesn't always look very good. Another consequence is that neighboring pixels are no longer identical, so the LZW algorithm can't compress the image as effectively.

Figure 20.11 shows the effect of indexing on the rose from Figure 20.7. The image was indexed with 32 colors, and the colors look blocky.

Figure 20.12 shows a simple image built with the Blend tool and the `Full saturation spectrum CW` gradient. Figure 20.13 shows the same image after we indexed it using 256 different colors. Even though we used the maximum number of colors, the image didn't look right, so we added dithering to smooth the transitions. But it still doesn't look right.

Among the 256 different colors available in GIF, one can be used for transparency. When the image is displayed on the Web, a transparent pixel lets the background show through. Although transparency isn't possible with a JPEG, GIF doesn't allow for progressive transparency.

Exporting to GIF

When you export an image to the GIF format (`.gif`), GIMP opens the dialog shown in Figure 20.14.

If you're saving a still image, this dialog allows you only to add a comment and check the INTERLACE box. Interlace builds an image that displays progressively, which may be useful for a large image coming over a slow Internet connection.

If the image has more than one layer, the option to save it as an animation is available. Checking AS ANIMATION expands the dialog, and you can set the animation parameters explained in "Output Formats" on page 476.

If the image is in RGB mode when you export it as a GIF, it is automatically converted to indexed mode using a default colormap.

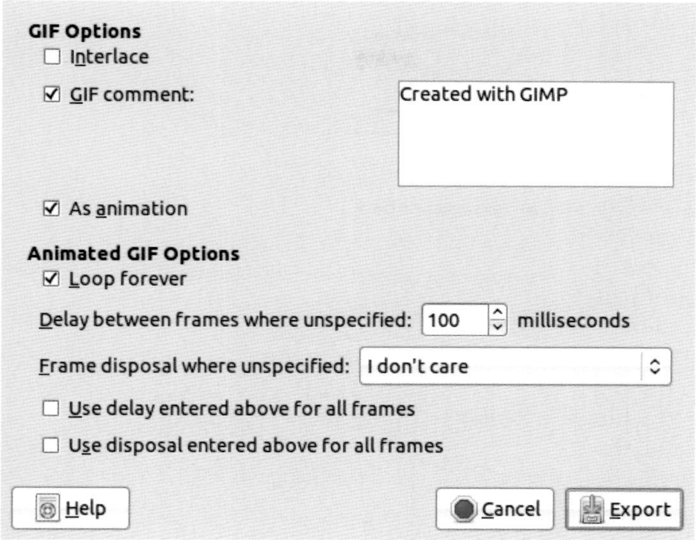

GIF Options
☐ Interlace

☑ GIF comment: | Created with GIMP

☑ As animation

Animated GIF Options
☑ Loop forever

Delay between frames where unspecified: 100 ⌄ milliseconds

Frame disposal where unspecified: | I don't care ⌄

☐ Use delay entered above for all frames

☐ Use disposal entered above for all frames

[⊚ Help]   [● Cancel] [▤ Export]

Figure 20.14 *The Export Image as GIF dialog*

Converting it to indexed mode (**Image: Image > Mode > Indexed**) first is safer; this way you can choose the colormap and whether to use dithering.

PNG

The Portable Network Graphics (PNG) format was first defined as a free replacement for GIF at the peak of the battle over the patented LZW compression algorithm used with GIF. PNG uses a lossless, patent-free compression algorithm and is also designed to avoid most of GIF's drawbacks, including the restriction to indexed representation.

The PNG format became an ISO standard in 2003 and was revised a year later. Although PNG is clearly superior to GIF, it hasn't completely replaced it for two reasons: its lack of support for animation and Microsoft's unwillingness to implement it correctly in Internet Explorer. Later versions of Internet Explorer (7 and above) handle PNG better, however, and IE 9 seems faultless, so we have hope.

PNG supports RGB, grayscale, and indexed images, but it doesn't support other color spaces

Figure 20.15 *Some text in a PNG image*

Figure 20.16 *The same text in a JPEG image*

like CMYK. It also supports progressive transparency as an additional channel when the image is in RGB or grayscale mode or by adding Alpha values to palette entries in indexed mode.

Because PNG uses lossless compression, it produces larger files than JPEG, but the format is clearly superior to JPEG in the case of a photograph on which text is printed. The lossy algorithm used for JPEG blurs the outline of the characters, as Figures 20.15 and 20.16 show. The lossy compression used by JPEG does result in smaller files, however, and image quality is just as good for a photo as long as you select a quality factor greater than 50.

Compared to GIF, PNG actually generates smaller files if the conditions are the same (that is, if the image is in indexed mode). If you export an RGB image as a PNG, it stays in RGB mode and, therefore, takes up more space because it contains more colors. If you first convert the image to indexed mode and then export it to both GIF and PNG, the PNG file is about half the size of the GIF file.

The PNG format works well for all kinds of images—except animations. (But for photos without text, JPEG is preferable because the file size is smaller.) When storing simple illustrations like cartoons that have only a few colors, do not forget to convert the image to indexed mode before exporting it. Because the compression algorithm is lossless, you can repeatedly export an image as PNG without the cumulative deterioration seen with JPEG.

Exporting to PNG

When you export an image as a PNG (.png), the dialog in Figure 20.17 opens. Here are the most useful entries in the dialog:

- INTERLACING: This option creates an image that loads progressively.

- SAVE BACKGROUND COLOR : This option is for obsolete browsers that can't handle progressive transparency. Using this option, you can choose the color that is displayed in place of the transparent pixels. Unfortunately, Internet Explorer does not recognize these settings.

- SAVE RESOLUTION: This option is useful only if the program that opens the image can read the saved resolution.

- SAVE CREATION TIME: This option stores the time and date when the image was last saved.

- SAVE COMMENT: Any comments added via **Image: Image > Image Properties** on the COMMENT tab are saved.

Figure 20.17 *The Export Image as PNG dialog*

- SAVE COLOR VALUES FROM TRANSPARENT PIXELS: Fully transparent pixels may still have a color value, which will appear if the transparency is decreased or removed later.

20.3   GIMP's Native Formats

In GIMP, a work in progress often includes multiple layers, transparency, and an active selection. It might also have layer masks, channels containing saved selections, and paths. It probably also includes undo history. Anything you can do in GIMP can be represented by the *native format*, XCF. A native format is a file structure designed specifically for a piece of software.

GIMP also has tools for defining new brushes, patterns, palettes, and gradients. Each of those also has a native format in GIMP. You can download custom brushes, patterns, palettes, and gradients from the Web or even create your own and post them for other users to download. We show you how in Chapter 22.

XCF

XCF is GIMP's most important native format. When you save an image in XCF, you're saving all its components, layers, layer groups, masks, channels, paths, guides, and so on. The only thing that isn't saved is the undo history, which would increase the file size significantly.

XCF is the only format that is guaranteed to store all the information in an image that you're working on in GIMP, and it's the best format for a work in progress. If you want to store a file in another format, but you want to make additional changes at some point, always save a copy of your work as XCF.

Because XCF stores so much information, an XCF file can be rather large, but GIMP allows you to compress it using one of two lossless external compression algorithms: the one used by Gzip and the one used by Bzip2. Bzip2 yields better results than Gzip but only by 30% or 40% at most. Bzip2 is also much slower. GIMP can load and save files compressed using these algorithms without first having to unpack the files. The compression is indicated by a second extension, which is either .gz or .bz2. On a GNU/Linux operating system, the suffix does not determinate the file format, which is specified by the file's first few bytes, but it can be helpful for users.

Although XCF can be read by several other applications, including ImageMagick, Krita, and Inkscape, it's not intended as a universal format.

When you save an image with **Image: File > Save As** or SHIFT+CTRL+S, GIMP automatically assumes the file format is XCF and adds the corresponding extension to the filename. For all other output formats, you must export the image with **Image: File > Export As** or SHIFT+CTRL+E. The export commands cannot generate XCF. If an image is modified and then exported, GIMP does not consider the image saved and opens a warning window if you try to close it.

Other Native Formats

In addition to images, whose natural format is XCF, four other objects have their own native formats in GIMP. These are brushes, patterns,

gradients, and palettes. Each of these objects has a specialized dockable dialog: The Brushes dialog, the Patterns dialog, and the Gradients dialog are present, by default, in the multi-dialog window; and the Palettes dialog can be opened via **Image: Windows > Dockable dialogs** or from the dialog menu, which you open by clicking the small triangle found at the top of all dockable dialogs.

These objects are stored on the computer in special folders, which you can define using **Image: Edit > Preferences** in the Folders entry. Each category has a systemwide folder, where objects are stored when installing or updating GIMP, and a personal folder, where you can store objects you create.

You can create, edit, or delete a brush, pattern, and palette by using the buttons at the bottom of the corresponding dialog. These let you do the following:

- Edit the current object. Editing works only if the object is in the personal folder. Otherwise, you can only look at the characteristics of the object.

- Create a new object.

- Duplicate the current object.

- Delete the current object (if it's in your personal folder).

- Refresh the object list in the dialog.

You can also access these options via the dialog menu or by right-clicking a brush, palette, or pattern. Patterns are not built using a specific tool, so the Patterns dialog only contains buttons for deleting, refreshing, and opening the current pattern as an image.

Building and saving new brushes, patterns, dialogs, and palettes is described in Chapter 22.

20.4   Other Useful Formats

In this section, we cover the image formats that, although useful to know when using GIMP, are less frequently used.

PostScript and PDF

PostScript is not exactly an image format; rather it is a programming language, designed in 1982 for document page description. Early laser printers, and even many current ones, use PostScript to describe pages being printed. These printers contain an interpreter for the language, and executing this interpreter tells the printer where to put dots on the page.

PostScript is a proprietary language that belongs to Adobe, but its description is public. The Ghostscript interpreter is free software under GPL that lets you print PostScript files on printers that don't use PostScript (for instance, on most inkjet printers).

PostScript is a vector graphics language. It rasterizes the image at the last moment when the printer definition is received from the printer. The character fonts can be defined in vector geometry and zoomed in or out without pixelation.

When you export an image as PostScript (.ps), GIMP opens the dialog shown in Figure 20.18. The dimensions of the image are predefined in millimeters or inches. You can change them, but if you do, you freeze the printer definition attached to the image. Leaving the conversion from image to PostScript to whatever application you use to add it to a document is best.

Encapsulated PostScript (EPS) is PostScript with additional information on the box that encapsulates the image. This information tells the application importing the file the image's exact dimensions and generally works more smoothly than regular PostScript when inserting an image into a document.

GIMP can also import a PostScript file using the dialog in Figure 20.19. The resolution you choose is very important. The image is immediately rasterized when you import it, and the vector information in the input file is lost.

The Portable Document Format, generally known as PDF, is a simplified version of

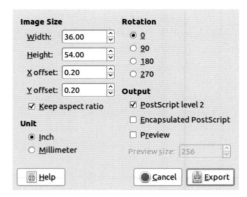

Figure 20.18 *The Export Image as PostScript dialog*

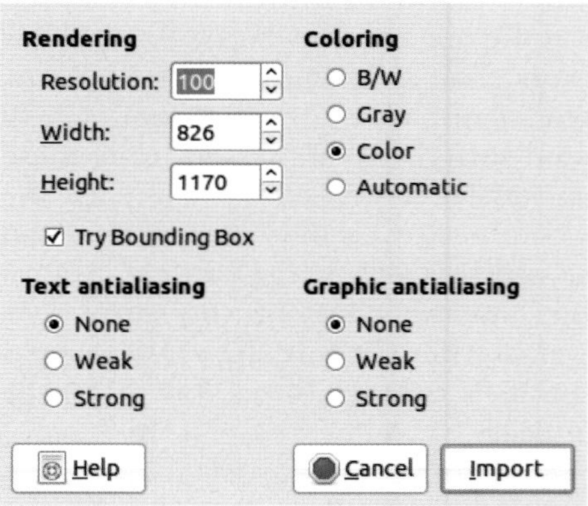

Figure 20.19 *The Import from PostScript dialog*

PostScript. PDF also belongs to Adobe but was accepted as an ISO standard in 2008. PDF is slowly replacing PostScript and offers several advantages. GIMP is able to import and export PDF files.

When you import a PDF file into GIMP, it opens the dialog shown in Figure 20.20. You can select the input file's resolution, the pages to import, and whether to import them as layers of a single image or as multiple images.

When you export an image to PDF, GIMP opens the dialog shown in Figure 20.21. You can choose options for decreasing the size of the generated PDF file.

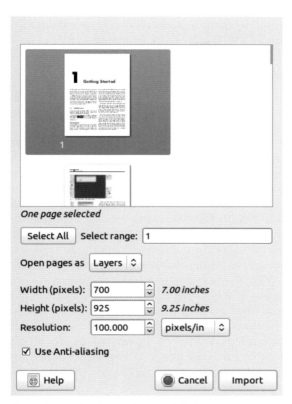

One page selected

Select All Select range: 1

Open pages as Layers ↕

Width (pixels): 700 | 7.00 inches
Height (pixels): 925 | 9.25 inches
Resolution: 100.000 | pixels/in ↕

☑ Use Anti-aliasing

Help | ● Cancel | Import

Figure 20.20 *The Import from PDF dialog*

TIFF

The Tagged Image File Format, also known as TIFF, is not an international standard. It also belongs to Adobe, was defined in the mid-1980s, and has not been updated since 1992.

TIFF is a complicated and flexible format that can use several different compression algorithms—lossy or lossless. It can also use different numbers of bits per color, different color spaces, and more. But most applications can't handle all the TIFF features, which means you may lose information when transferring images from one application to another.

The TIFF format is the format of choice in scientific imaging and is widely accepted in the printing business, however.

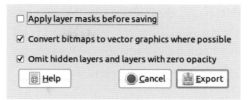

☐ Apply layer masks before saving
☑ Convert bitmaps to vector graphics where possible
☑ Omit hidden layers and layers with zero opacity

Help | ● Cancel | Export

Figure 20.21 *The Export Image as PDF dialog*

Compression
◉ None
○ LZW
○ Pack Bits
○ Deflate
○ JPEG
○ CCITT Group 3 fax
○ CCITT Group 4 fax

☐ Save color values from transparent pixels

Comment:

Help | ● Cancel | Export

Figure 20.22 *The Export Image as TIFF dialog*

When you export an image in TIFF format (.tiff), GIMP opens the dialog shown in Figure 20.22. The radio buttons let you choose the compression algorithm. LZW, Pack Bits, and Deflate are lossless; JPEG is lossy. The two CCITT compression algorithms work only with black and white images (without gray levels). If the image contains paths, they are saved too.

Netpbm Formats

Netpbm is a public domain, portable collection of programs for converting from one graphic format to another. These programs handle a large set of graphic formats and define four new ones that are supported by GIMP:

- Portable Bit Map (PBM) is for bitmaps (black and white images).

- Portable Gray Map (PGM) is for grayscale images.

- Portable Pixmap (PPM) is for color pixmaps.

- PNM refers to these three formats together.

Netpbm offers an additional format called PAM, but GIMP doesn't support it. All these formats use a textual representation, which results in very large files. For example, the rose in Figure 20.5 on page 535 has the following sizes (the TIFF was saved with Deflate compression):

Format	Size (KB)
GIF	109
JPEG	26
TIFF	300
PPM	3600

Despite their size, these formats are handy because you can convert them to or from almost any existing image format.

SVG

Scalable Vector Graphics (SVG) is the format of choice for vector graphics. It is an open standard defined by the World Wide Web Consortium that relies on the textual nature of XML. More and more application programs accept this format in their input files, including GIMP.

SVG is the native format for some vector graphics programs like Inkscape (free software). Others, like Adobe Illustrator, CorelDRAW, Blender, or Xara Xtreme (the last two are free software), can import and export SVG files. Note that Adobe Photoshop does not offer SVG support.

Most browsers can display SVG images. The only exception is Internet Explorer, but plug-ins are available that allow Internet Explorer to display SVG.

GIMP can import SVG images like the one shown in Figure 20.2 on page 534, but exporting a raster image to SVG is not possible, and the result probably wouldn't look very good anyway. But a GIMP path can be exported to SVG.

Additional Formats Supported by GIMP

GIMP can import Photoshop image files, which is useful for people who want to abandon proprietary software in favor of free software.

The BMP format is a very simple Microsoft format that lacks compression. The image in Figure 20.5 on page 535 takes up 1100KB when saved in BMP. This format is notably used for icons in the Microsoft Windows system as well as in OS/2. GIMP can import and export BMP files. When exporting, you can choose the number of bits of the color space and the representation of the Alpha channel, if one exists.

The X window system (the windowing system on all Unix-like operating systems) uses the XPM and XBM graphic formats for icons and such. The first one is for pixmaps and the second one for bitmaps. Both are fully textual, so they aren't suitable for large images. The image shown in Figure 20.5 on page 535 occupies 2400KB when exported to XPM.

An image format popular among professional photographers is *raw format*. We discuss this format in more detail in "Choosing a Format" on page 521 and "Handling Raw Photographs" on page 523.

21

Scripts and Plug-ins

GIMP is not a monolithic program. Much of it is made up of plug-ins, components that are not part of the core of the system. In fact, most of the tools found in the **Image: Filters** menu are plug-ins, as are many of the tools in the **Image: Colors** menu. Besides these built-in plug-ins, many third-party plug-ins are available; some of these are quite large, like the GIMP Animation Package (GAP; discussed in Chapter 18). Other, much smaller ones, are used for simple tasks.

Scripts and plug-ins are very similar. One difference is that they are stored in different places. When you open the FOLDER entry in the **Image: Edit > Preferences** dialog, you'll see the Plug-Ins and Scripts folders.

21.1   About Scripts and Plug-ins

In this chapter, we explain the concepts underlying GIMP scripts and plug-ins and show you how to find and install new ones. Then we briefly describe some important plug-ins that are worth installing. Finally, we show examples of plug-ins written in Python and C, as well as a script written in Scheme.

Another difference between a script and a plug-in is the programming language in which the components are written. Scripts are written in Scheme (called Script-Fu in GIMP) and stored in the Scripts folder. Plug-ins are written in Python or C and stored in the Plug-Ins folder.

Scheme, Python, and C

Scheme is a very simple and rather old language, directly interpreted without any translation needed. GIMP includes an interpreter for a subset of Scheme, so Scheme scripts are always operational. In fact, many of the predefined plug-ins you've used so far (for example in Chapter 12 or in Chapter 17) are in fact scripts programmed in Scheme. Scheme is a functional language that uses only parentheses and whitespace for syntactic punctuation.

Python, also directly interpreted, is more powerful than Scheme. It has become popular in the last few years and is probably progressively replacing another scripting language, Perl, because of its much more pleasant syntax and its wider range of capabilities. Python's interpreter is not part of GIMP and needs to be installed separately on Windows. (It comes packaged with Linux and Mac operating systems.)

C is the language in which the core of GIMP is programmed, as well as most of the GNU/Linux

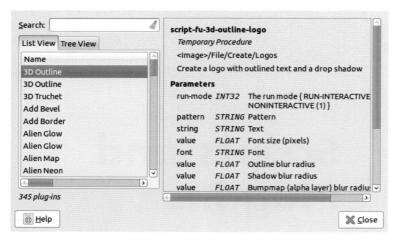

Figure 21.1 *The Plug-in Browser, List view*

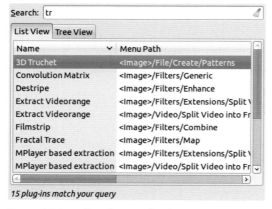

Figure 21.2 *Looking for specific plug-ins*

operating system. An old language, C is extremely well supported because it allows programs to use all the capabilities of the computer efficiently. Programs written in C cannot be directly executed but must first be translated into machine language and then loaded. You do this with a *compiler*. In order to write a C plug-in, you must have a C compiler and development environment on your computer. A compiler is easy to set up on GNU/Linux and Mac OS but a bit trickier on Windows.

GIMP plug-ins can be written in other programming languages, especially if the language is compiled. Perl used to be the language of choice for writing GIMP plug-ins but is used less frequently today. For this reason, we consider only Scheme, Python, and C. To write your own plug-in, you need some knowledge of at least one of these languages; a complete introduction to programming in each language is beyond the scope of this book.

Installed Plug-ins

To find out which plug-ins are already a part of your GIMP installation, use the Plug-in Browser (**Image: Help > Plug-in Browser**), as shown in Figure 21.1. As you can see, this installation has 345 plug-ins. The first tab on the left lists them alphabetically.

When you begin typing in the SEARCH field at the top left of the Plug-in Browser, the plug-ins list is automatically filtered to the names that contain this substring, as shown in Figure 21.2. Click the broom at the top right to clear the filter.

The second tab offers a tree view of all plug-ins, which can be useful for searching plug-ins by category. In Figure 21.3, we've enlarged this view by clicking and dragging its right boundary. As you can see, this view shows the image types accepted by each plug-in, as well as the

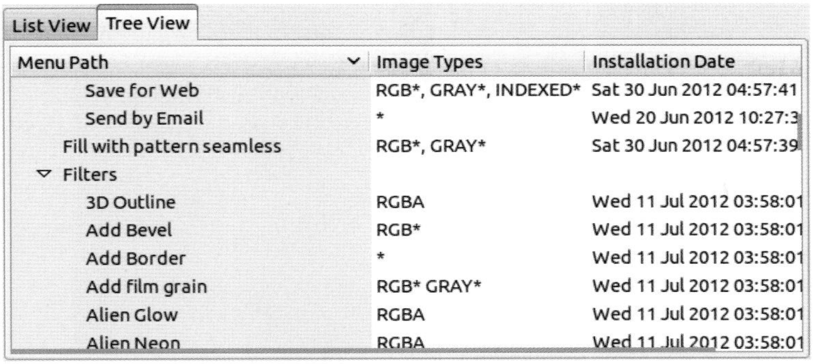

Figure 21.3 *The Plug-in Browser, Tree view*

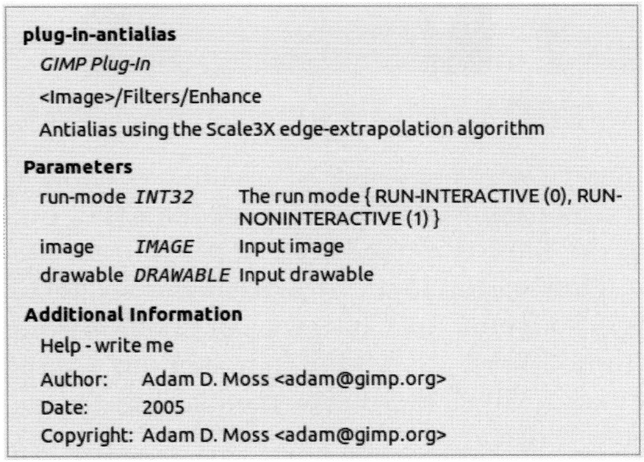

Figure 21.4 *The Plug-in Browser, plug-in description*

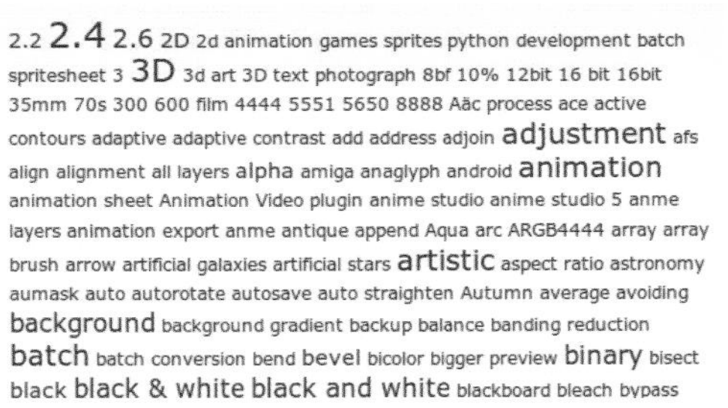

Figure 21.5 *The beginning of the tag cloud*

installation date. In the image types, the letter *A* means that there is an Alpha channel, and the star is a wildcard. For example, *RGB** means that the Alpha channel may or may not be present.

The right part of the dialog describes the plug-in selected at the left. For example, in Figure 21.4, you see the description of the Antialias tool, which is found in **Image: Filters > Enhance**.

Finding New Plug-ins

The main source of existing GIMP plug-ins is the GIMP Plugin Registry at *http://registry.gimp.org/*. Here you'll find plug-in descriptions, links to the plug-in itself or to its home page, and tags that

help in searching. Click a tag for a list of all matching plug-ins.

One convenient way to browse the registry is the *Content by tags view* (also called *tag cloud view*), which shows a list of all the tags with a font size proportional to their frequency, as shown in Figure 21.5. The tags are clickable, so browsing all the plug-ins related to a given tag is easy.

Most plug-ins have a very detailed and complete home page, explaining how they work and how to install them.

21.2 Noteworthy Plug-ins

The following sections describe some interesting plug-ins available on the GIMP Plugin Registry. This selection is obviously subjective, and we've excluded a couple of plug-ins that we've already discussed, like GAP, presented in Chapter 18,

Figure 21.6 *The initial image (left); after applying the Wrap Effect tool (middle); after applying the ev_crayon_full preset*

and UFRaw, presented in "Handling Raw Photographs" on page 523.

Photo Effects

Photo Effects is a set of plug-ins that you can use to add artistic effects to photos. You can find it by searching for photo effects at *http://registry.gimp.org/*. Once it's installed, you'll see a menu called PHOTO EFFECTS in the **Image: Filters > Decor** menu. Let's use Figure 21.6 (left) as an example. When we apply the Wrap Effect tool, found in **Image: Filters > Decor > Photo effects > Artist**, we get the result shown in Figure 21.6 (middle).

Photo Effects also comes with 22 predefined presets for the GIMPressionist filter (see "GIMPressionist" on page 434). Figure 21.6 (right) shows the result of applying the ev_crayon_full preset.

G'MIC

G'MIC (*http://gmic.sourceforge.net/gimp.shtml*) is a huge collection of filters (229 as this book goes to press) and effects. It operates as a single entry in the **Image: Filters** menu, which opens the dialog shown in Figure 21.7.

The G'MIC's preview is updated as soon as you select a filter. When you click the APPLY button, the filter is immediately applied to the image, allowing you to transform it using several filters in sequence. Because we can't demonstrate all these filters, we've chosen a random sample here and will demonstrate them using the default settings.

Figure 21.8 (left) shows the result of applying the Local normalization filter found in the Colors submenu to our sample image. Figure 21.8 (middle) shows the result of applying the B & W pencil filter found in the Artistic submenu. Figure 21.8 (right) shows the same photograph after applying the Anisotropic smoothing filter, which is found in the Enhancement submenu.

G'MIC is a complex plug-in, and these examples give only a taste of its capabilities.

Liquid Rescale

Liquid Rescale (*http://liquidrescale.wikidot.com/*) is a powerful tool that allows you to stretch or squeeze an image without changing the shape of objects. You'll find the tool in the **Image: Layer** menu. In Figure 21.9, a 2000 × 1333 photograph is shown in the preview window. We'll make it more panoramic by stretching it horizontally.

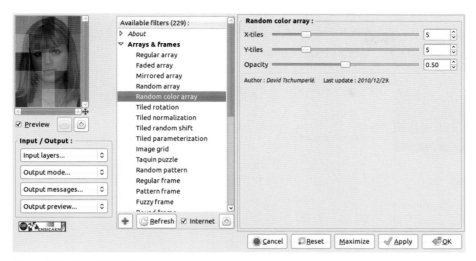

Figure 21.7 *The G'MIC dialog*

Figure 21.8 *After applying the Local normalization filter (left), the B & W pencil filter (middle), and the Anisotropic smoothing filter (right)*

If we simply change the canvas width to 3000 pixels using Liquid Rescale, the result (shown in Figure 21.10) is unsatisfactory because the person's head is misshapen. To fix this, check the NEW button at the right of the tool dialog, in the FEATURE PRESERVATION MASK section, to activate the PRESERVE FEATURES button. Doing so creates a new layer with 50% opacity and temporarily changes the foreground color to a vivid green.

Now we can paint the man and, as you can see in Figure 21.11, we don't need to be very precise.

After painting the subject, return the width to 3000 pixels to get the result shown in Figure 21.12. Admittedly, the ship is a bit too stretched, but we could have preserved its aspect ratio if we'd painted it as well.

You can also use Liquid Rescale to discard certain features in an image. For example,

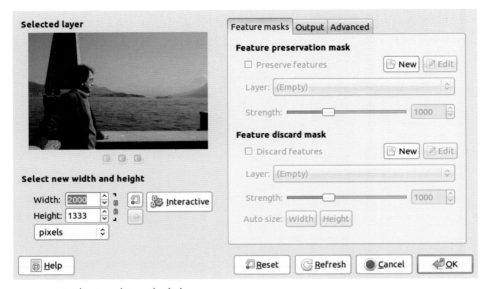

Figure 21.9 *The Liquid Rescale dialog*

Figure 21.10 *The result of resizing without preservation*

Figure 21.11 *Defining the preservation mask*

suppose that in Figure 21.13 we want to discard the potted plants on both sides of the peacock. To do this, we click the NEW button in the FEA-TURE DISCARD MASK tool dialog. The DISCARD FEATURES button is automatically checked, a new layer is created, and the foreground color changes to a vivid red.

Next, we paint the mask shown in Figure 21.14, which is a bit more challenging than before because the peacock tail is very close to the left pot. Then, we click the WIDTH button to the right of AUTO SIZE to get a width of 1103 pixels. The final result, shown in Figure 21.15, needs some retouching, but you should get the idea.

As described on its home page, the Liquid Rescale tool offers many other possibilities,

Figure 21.12 *The result of resizing with preservation*

including an interactive mode, the ability to output a seam map (which shows how the image was resized), and so on. For example, Figure 21.16 shows the seam maps when we make a portrait narrower (80% original width) and Figure 21.17

Figure 21.13 *Initial image*

Figure 21.14 *Defining the discard mask*

Figure 21.15 *Resizing with the Discard feature*

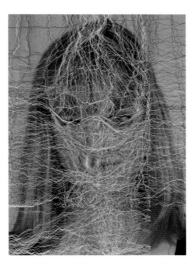

Figure 21.16 *The seam maps when shrinking a portrait*

Figure 21.17 *The seam maps when enlarging a portrait*

Elsamuko Scripts

shows the seam maps when we make it wider (120% original width). On the Output tab, we checked OUTPUT ON A NEW LAYER, OUTPUT THE SEAMS, and SCALE BACK TO THE ORIGINAL SIZE. In both cases, the rescaling left the eyes and most of the mouth intact but changed the rest of the face in an unnatural and unpleasant way.

The Elsamuko collection of scripts offers a wide variety of ways to transform or improve pictures. The collection can be found at *http://sites.google.com/site/elsamuko/gimp/* and is part of the `gimp-plugin-registry` Debian package (usable on Debian and Ubuntu). This site also contains many other plug-ins and scripts.

Figure 21.18 *After applying the National Geographic filter (left), the Obama Hope filter (middle), and the Lomo filter (right)*

We'll demonstrate only three of the Elsamuko scripts, using the same photograph as before. These scripts generally require lots of computing power, and most build an image with numerous layers and layer masks.

Figure 21.18 (left) shows the result of applying the **Image: Filters > Generic > National Geographic** filter, designed to generate high-quality portraits like those found in the celebrated magazine.

Figure 21.18 (middle) shows the result of applying the **Image: Filters > Artistic > Obama Hope** filter, inspired by the famous Obama "HOPE" poster.

Figure 21.18 (right) shows the result of applying the **Image: Filters > Light and Shadow > Lomo** filter, designed to simulate the results of using a Lomo camera, an inexpensive Russian model from the early 1990s.

21.3 Writing Plug-ins

Using predefined plug-ins is convenient, but you won't always find exactly what you need, and if you have a little programming experience, writing your own plug-ins can be more fun anyway.

After you have written the first three or four, you'll find writing them easy. In this section, we present plug-ins written in the three main programming languages: Scheme, Python, and C.

Scheme

Scripts written in Scheme are called Script-Fu. Take, for example, the script for **Image: Colors > Map > Colormap**. This script includes the function `script-fu-makecmap-array`, which returns an array containing the colors for a specified palette. This function can be used in other scripts that need color palette information.

The function is written in Scheme, and the code is shown in Figure 21.19. Scheme is written as a sequence of embedded expressions in parentheses. Briefly, a Scheme function definition takes the form of `(define (name parameters) (expr) (expr) ...)`. This snippet of code defines the function `name` whose value is that of the last expression. An expression calls a function, whose name or symbol appears as the first element in the expression, along with any arguments that follow the function. An argument itself can be an expression that calls functions.

```
1   ; Set Colormap v1.1  September 29, 2004
2   ; by Kevin Cozens <kcozens@interlog.com>
3   ;
4   ; Change the colourmap of an image to the colours in a specified palette.
5   ; Included is script-fu-make-cmap-array (available for use in scripts) which
6   ; returns an INT8ARRAY containing the colours from a specified palette.
7   ; This array can be used as the cmap argument for gimp-image-set-cmap.
8   (define (script-fu-make-cmap-array palette)
9     (let* (
10          (num-colours (car (gimp-palette-get-info palette)))
11          (cmap (cons-array (* num-colours 3) 'byte))
12          (colour 0)
13          (i 0)
14          )
15
16     (while (< i num-colours)
17       (set! colour (car (gimp-palette-entry-get-color palette i)))
18       (aset cmap (* i 3) (car colour))
19       (aset cmap (+ (* i 3) 1) (cadr colour))
20       (aset cmap (+ (* i 3) 2) (caddr colour))
21       (set! i (+ i 1))
22     )
23
24     cmap
25     )
26  )
27  (define (script-fu-set-cmap img drawable palette)
28    (gimp-image-set-colormap img
29                             (* (car (gimp-palette-get-info palette)) 3)
30                             (script-fu-make-cmap-array palette))
31    (gimp-displays-flush)
32  )
33
34  (script-fu-register "script-fu-set-cmap"
35     _"Se_t Colormap..."
36     _"Change the colormap of an image to the colors in a specified palette."
37     "Kevin Cozens <kcozens@interlog.com>"
38     "Kevin Cozens"
39     "September 29, 2004"
40     "INDEXED*"
41     SF-IMAGE      "Image"      0
42     SF-DRAWABLE   "Drawable"   0
43     SF-PALETTE    _"Palette"   "Default"
44  )
45  (script-fu-menu-register "script-fu-set-cmap" "<Image>/Colors/Map/Colormap")
```

Figure 21.19 *A Script-Fu example: the cmap array function from the Set Colormap script*

For example, on line 29 in Figure 21.19, the function * (multiplication) is called with two arguments. The first argument is an expression that calls the function car, and the second argument is the number 3. The call to function * is actually the second argument to the call to gimp-image-set-colormap that appears on the previous line. The first argument is the first function parameter, and the third argument is the result of the script-fu-make-cmap-array function with the third function parameter as an argument.

Select **Image: Help > Procedure Browser** to learn about a function's arguments and their purpose. For example, in Figure 21.20, we enter colormap in the Search field and then select a function from the list. At the right of the dialog, we see the type and meaning of the parameters for the chosen function, as well as a detailed comment.

Lines 9 to 14 of Figure 21.19 contain the declaration and initialization of the local variables of function script-fu-make-cmap-array. We can use these variables in the function body.

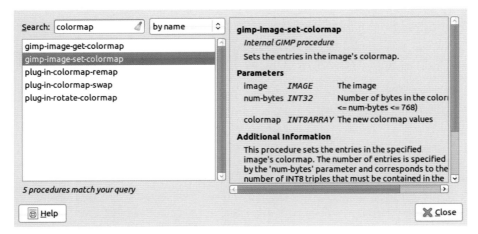

Figure 21.20 *The Procedure Browser dialog*

One of the most important parts of any Script-Fu is the script registration, as shown in lines 34 to 44 of Figure 21.19. The script registration gives GIMP all the information it needs to integrate the script into GIMP. The various parameters of `script-fu-register` provide this information in the following order.

- Entry in the menu, with an underscore (_) before the character used as an abbreviation
- Contents of the tool tip
- Author name
- Copyright notice
- Copyright date
- Type of image to be handled
- Description of the type, name, and initial value parameters

Finally, calling `script-fu-menu-register` places the Script-Fu in the GIMP menus.

Testing Script-Fu is easy, thanks to **Image: Filters > Script-Fu > Console**, which opens the dialog shown in Figure 21.21. All you need to do is enter the Scheme expressions in the bottom field and press ENTER. The expressions are evaluated immediately, with the result shown in the main dialog window.

The BROWSE button opens the Procedure Browser dialog. When you choose a specific

Figure 21.21 *The Script-Fu console*

procedure and click APPLY, a call to this procedure is inserted in the Script-Fu console field, and then you simply need to enter your parameters.

You'll find many Script-Fus on the Web. Some are well advertised on the GIMP Plug-in Registry, whereas others are available on independent websites and blogs. See, for example, *http://gimpfx-foundry.sourceforge.net/* or *http://gimpscripts.com/*.

Python

Like the name *Script-Fu* coined for Scheme scripts, *Python-Fu* is what Python plug-ins are called. Figure 21.22 shows a sample Python

```
1    #!/usr/bin/env python
2    #   Gimp-Python - allows the writing of Gimp plugins in Python.
3    #   Copyright (C) 1997  James Henstridge <james@daa.com.au>
4    from gimpfu import *
5    import time
6    gettext.install("gimp20-python", gimp.locale_directory, unicode=True)
7
8    def foggify(img, layer, name, colour, turbulence, opacity):
9
10       gimp.context_push()
11       img.undo_group_start()
12
13       if img.base_type is RGB:
14           type = RGBA_IMAGE
15       else:
16           type = GRAYA_IMAGE
17       fog = gimp.Layer(img, name,
18                        layer.width, layer.height, type, opacity, NORMAL_MODE)
19       fog.fill(TRANSPARENT_FILL)
20       img.add_layer(fog, 0)
21
22       gimp.set_background(colour)
23       pdb.gimp_edit_fill(fog, BACKGROUND_FILL)
24
25       # create a layer mask for the new layer
26       mask = fog.create_mask(0)
27       fog.add_mask(mask)
28
29       # add some clouds to the layer
30       pdb.plug_in_plasma(img, mask, int(time.time()), turbulence)
31
32       # apply the clouds to the layer
33       fog.remove_mask(MASK_APPLY)
34
35       img.undo_group_end()
36       gimp.context_pop()
37
38   register(
39       "python-fu-foggify",
40       N_("Add a layer of fog"),
41       "Adds a layer of fog to the image.",
42       "James Henstridge",
43       "James Henstridge",
44       "1999,2007",
45       N_("_Fog..."),
46       "RGB*, GRAY*",
47       [
48           (PF_IMAGE,    "image",      "Input image", None),
49           (PF_DRAWABLE, "drawable",  "Input drawable", None),
50           (PF_STRING,   "name",       _("_Layer name"), _("Clouds")),
51           (PF_COLOUR,   "colour",     _("_Fog color"), (240, 180, 70)),
52           (PF_SLIDER,   "turbulence", _("_Turbulence"), 1.0, (0, 10, 0.1)),
53           (PF_SLIDER,   "opacity",    _("Op_acity"),   100, (0, 100, 1)),
54       ],
55       [],
56       foggify,
57       menu="<Image>/Filters/Render/Clouds",
58       domain=("gimp20-python", gimp.locale_directory)
59       )
60
61   main()
```

Figure 21.22 *A Python-Fu example: a fog-rendering filter*

program, the **Image: Filters > Render > Clouds > Fog** filter. In lines 4 to 6, the contents of the gimpfu module are imported, the time module is imported, and the gettext function is used to internationalize all the text in the program.

The Python-Fu body of the Render Clouds plug-in, shown from lines 8 to 36, is a good example of a Python program. Statements end when the line ends, except when they are within parentheses, as in line 17. Embedding is denoted by indentation, as shown in lines 13 through 17. Some Python syntax is inspired by the C language, with = used for assignment and == for comparison. The workings of this particular function are easy to follow once you know the meaning of GIMP's predefined functions.

Python-Fu is registered in GIMP in the same way as Script-Fu (lines 38 to 59), except for some slight differences in the arguments of the register function, especially in the description of the Python-Fu arguments.

Selecting **Image: Filters > Python-Fu > Console** opens a dialog similar to the Script-Fu Console. You can use this dialog to enter Python statements directly and test their effect. The Procedure Browser is used in a similar way, allowing you to insert typed code into the proper function call.

C

By nature, a C program is longer than its equivalent in Scheme or in Python because it is programmed in a lower-level language. You'll find a good three-part tutorial about building a C plug-in for GIMP at *http://developer.gimp.org/plug-ins .html*.

The shortest C plug-in is the Semi-Flatten plug-in, found in the **Image: Filters > Web** menu. We removed as many blank lines as possible but still had to cut it into two parts (Figures 21.23a and 21.23b) to display the full program. The file's heading is shown in lines 1 to 20, along with its declaration of three visible functions, some static variables, and one constant.

This C plug-in contains four function definitions. Because none of these functions returns a result, their type is always static void. The query function (lines 23 to 48) has no parameter and is called the first time the plug-in is used. It calls gimp_install_procedure to register the plug-in (in a similar way to a Python plug-in). Note that the semiflatten plug-in is installed both in the **Image: Filters > Web** and in the **Image: Layer > Transparency** menus.

The semiflatten_func function (lines 50 to 60) is a simple auxiliary function called indirectly by semiflatten (lines 61 to 69), itself an auxiliary function. The run function (lines 71 to 111) is called when we call the plug-in and makes the actual changes. Note that Semi-Flatten does not open a dialog.

The most crucial point in the plug-in definition is the GimpPlugInInfo PLUG_IN_INFO structure, declared in the heading. This definition declares the query and run functions. The call to MAIN() shown on line 21 is a C macro that initializes the arguments and calls PLUG_IN_INFO. These sorts of definitions are required for all C plug-ins.

Although a casual programmer with a good knowledge of GIMP should be able to program a short Script-Fu or Python-Fu plug-in, using the Procedure Browser to search in the GIMP procedural database, most likely only a serious C programmer will be able to build even a simple C plug-in.

Moreover, installing a C plug-in is nontrivial and requires a C compiling environment. The libgimp headers must be installed on the computer to provide all needed declarations, and a tool called gimptool is also needed to compile and install the plug-in (see *http://developer.gimp .org/plug-ins.html* for more information).

```
1   /*
2    *  Semi-Flatten plug-in v1.0 by Adam D. Moss, adam@foxbox.org.  1998/01/27
3    */
4   /* Declare local functions.
5    */
6   static void   query      (void);
7   static void   run        (const gchar    *name,
8                             gint           nparams,
9                             const GimpParam *param,
10                            gint           *nreturn_vals,
11                            GimpParam      **return_vals);
12  static void   semiflatten (GimpDrawable   *drawable);
13  static guchar bgred, bggreen, bgblue;
14  const GimpPlugInInfo PLUG_IN_INFO =
15  {
16    NULL,  /* init_proc  */
17    NULL,  /* quit_proc  */
18    query, /* query_proc */
19    run,   /* run_proc   */
20  };
21  MAIN ()
22
23  static void
24  query (void)
25  {
26    static const GimpParamDef args[] =
27    {
28      { GIMP_PDB_INT32,    "run-mode", "The run mode { RUN-INTERACTIVE (0), RUN-NONINTERACTIVE (1) }" },
29      { GIMP_PDB_IMAGE,    "image",    "Input image (unused)"       },
30      { GIMP_PDB_DRAWABLE, "drawable", "Input drawable"             }
31    };
32    gimp_install_procedure (PLUG_IN_PROC,
33                            N_("Replace partial transparency with the current background color"),
34                            "This plugin flattens pixels in an RGBA image that "
35                            "aren't completely transparent against the current "
36                            "GIMP background color",
37                            "Adam D. Moss (adam@foxbox.org)",
38                            "Adam D. Moss (adam@foxbox.org)",
39                            "27th January 1998",
40                            N_("_Semi-Flatten"),
41                            "RGBA",
42                            GIMP_PLUGIN,
43                            G_N_ELEMENTS (args), 0,
44                            args, NULL);
45
46    gimp_plugin_menu_register (PLUG_IN_PROC, "<Image>/Filters/Web");
47    gimp_plugin_menu_register (PLUG_IN_PROC, "<Image>/Layer/Transparency/Modify");
48  }
49
50  static void
51  semiflatten_func (const guchar *src,
52                    guchar       *dest,
53                    gint         bpp,
54                    gpointer     data)
55  {
56    dest[0] = (src[0] * src[3]) / 255 + (bgred * (255 - src[3])) / 255;
57    dest[1] = (src[1] * src[3]) / 255 + (bggreen * (255 - src[3])) / 255;
58    dest[2] = (src[2] * src[3]) / 255 + (bgblue * (255 - src[3])) / 255;
59    dest[3] = (src[3] == 0) ? 0 : 255;
60  }
```

Figure 21.23a *A C plug-in example: Semi-Flatten (part 1)*

```
61   static void
62   semiflatten (GimpDrawable *drawable)
63   {
64     GimpRGB background;
65     gimp_context_get_background (&background);
66     gimp_rgb_get_uchar (&background, &bgred, &bggreen, &bgblue);
67
68     gimp_rgn_iterate2 (drawable, 0 /* unused */, semiflatten_func, NULL);
69   }
70
71   static void
72   run (const gchar      *name,
73        gint               nparams,
74        const GimpParam  *param,
75        gint              *nreturn_vals,
76        GimpParam        **return_vals)
77   {
78     static GimpParam    values[1];
79     GimpDrawable        *drawable;
80     gint32              image_ID;
81     GimpPDBStatusType   status = GIMP_PDB_SUCCESS;
82     GimpRunMode         run_mode;
83     run_mode = param[0].data.d_int32;
84     *nreturn_vals = 1;
85     *return_vals = values;
86     values[0].type          = GIMP_PDB_STATUS;
87     values[0].data.d_status = status;
88     INIT_I18N();
89     /*  Get the specified drawable  */
90     drawable = gimp_drawable_get (param[2].data.d_drawable);
91     image_ID = param[1].data.d_image;
92     if (status == GIMP_PDB_SUCCESS)
93       {
94         /*  Make sure that the drawable is indexed or RGB color  */
95         if (gimp_drawable_is_rgb (drawable->drawable_id))
96           {
97             gimp_progress_init (_("Semi-Flattening"));
98             gimp_tile_cache_ntiles (2 * (drawable->width / gimp_tile_width ()
99                                          + 1));
100
101   semiflatten (drawable);
102             gimp_displays_flush ();
103           }
104         else
105           {
106             status = GIMP_PDB_EXECUTION_ERROR;
107           }
108       }
109     values[0].data.d_status = status;
110     gimp_drawable_detach (drawable);
111   }
```

Figure 21.23b *A C plug-in example: Semi-Flatten (part 2)*

22

Customizing GIMP

In the tradition of free software, GIMP is highly configurable, and many of its characteristics can be changed. Although GIMP has only one specific Preferences dialog, you'll find other tools for changing parameters scattered in various places. In this chapter, we'll show you how to customize GIMP so it works best for you.

22.1   The Preferences Dialog

Open the Preferences dialog via the **Image: Edit** menu. It is a large and complex dialog, as shown in Figure 22.1 (left). The menu on the left in the dialog displays the list of preference tabs; we'll consider each in turn. Anytime you change parameters in GIMP, your work is saved to a file called gimprc and stored on your machine, typically in the main GIMP directory. The changes usually take effect immediately, unless the program says otherwise.

Environment

The first tab of the Preferences dialog deals with the ENVIRONMENT. You can set the following parameters, as shown in Figure 22.1 (left).

- RESOURCE CONSUMPTION determines how GIMP uses system resources.

- MINIMAL NUMBER OF UNDO LEVELS sets the number of levels of undo history for each image. Because undo requires a certain amount of memory, you are limited in the amount of history that GIMP can keep, but this parameter guarantees that at least a set number of levels are always available.

- MAXIMUM UNDO MEMORY tells GIMP to delete the oldest saves when this amount of undo memory is exceeded. If you have a lot of memory on your machine, increase the default value.

- TILE CACHE SIZE can affect both GIMP's and your computer's performance. If you intend to use GIMP seriously and to work with large images, set this parameter to something like half the size of your installed RAM. Experiment with different values. Sizes that are too small will cause GIMP to swap frequently to disk, which slows things down. On the other hand, values that are too large may prevent other applications from starting or may cause processes to fail.

- MAXIMUM NEW IMAGE SIZE sets a maximum allowed size for new images. If a new image is larger than this maximum, GIMP asks

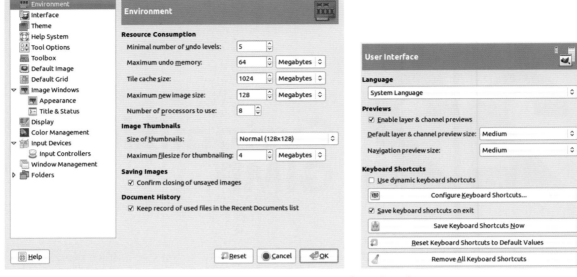

Figure 22.1 *The Preferences dialog, Environment tab (left) and User Interface tab (right)*

for confirmation but does not prevent its creation.

- NUMBER OF PROCESSORS TO USE is set automatically, due to the prevalence of multi-core processors, to the number of cores on your machine. Reduce this value if you need to use additional processors for other applications.

- IMAGE THUMBNAILS appear in the Open Image, Save Image, and Export Image dialogs. You can choose between two sizes or none. If the file size is larger than the maximum specified, GIMP does not automatically generate the thumbnail, but you can click the filename to generate the thumbnail.

- SAVING IMAGES should be left checked, or you will not be warned when you try to close an unsaved image.

- DOCUMENT HISTORY keeps a record of all open files in the Document History dialog (generally a good idea). Access the Document History dialog from the **Image: File > Open Recent** submenu or via **Image: Windows > Dockable Dialogs > Document History**.

User Interface

Figure 22.1 (right) shows the User Interface settings that deal with the system language, the small thumbnails that appear in the Layers and Channels dialogs, and the keyboard shortcuts.

- LANGUAGE allows you to set the language. Like most free software, GIMP is fully internationalized. The default is to use the base language of the host operating system, but you can choose from 71 different languages, although some of the translations are incomplete. Changes are applied after GIMP restarts.

- PREVIEWS are the layer or channel thumbnails, which are enabled by default. You can choose from nine predefined sizes, from TINY to GIGANTIC. The former is useful only on a very small screen, the latter only if you have severe vision problems.

- KEYBOARD SHORTCUTS can help you use GIMP more efficiently. GIMP has a rather small set of predefined keyboard shortcuts, mentioned throughout this book, but you can add more or change them to suit your needs. This dialog allows you to change, add, or remove keyboard shortcuts using several checkboxes and buttons:

- USE DYNAMIC KEYBOARD SHORTCUTS is unchecked by default because it is somewhat dangerous. When checked, you can define a new keyboard command simply by pressing a key combination while a menu entry is highlighted. This feature is handy for defining new commands but makes it much too easy to redefine existing shortcuts accidentally.

- CONFIGURE KEYBOARD SHORTCUTS is explained in "Keyboard Shortcuts" on page 571.

- SAVE KEYBOARD SHORTCUTS NOW is useful only when automatic saving is not specified.

- RESET KEYBOARD SHORTCUTS TO DEFAULT VALUES is useful if you want to reset GIMP to its defaults.

- REMOVE ALL KEYBOARD SHORTCUTS is for people who do not want any shortcuts.

Theme

As Figure 22.2 shows, the Theme tab is simple. You can choose between two themes, Default and Small (shown in Figure 22.3). Other themes are available on sites like *http://art.gnome.org/*.

Help System

GIMP has numerous help features, as discussed in Section 9.6. The dialog shown in Figure 22.4 allows you to set certain parameters that control the sort of help that you receive while using GIMP:

- SHOW TOOLTIPS is normally checked.

- SHOW HELP BUTTONS is also normally checked, and when it's checked, a HELP button is added

Figure 22.2 *The Preferences dialog, Theme tab*

Figure 22.3 *Using the Small theme*

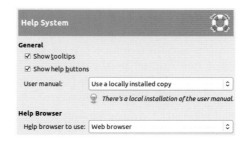

Figure 22.4 *The Preferences dialog, Help System tab*

to most dialogs. When clicked, this button takes you to the help documentation.

- USER MANUAL lets you choose between the locally installed or the online user manual.

- HELP BROWSER lets you use your default browser or the GIMP help browser. The GIMP help browser is faster and always opens in the current desktop in a multidesktop environment.

Tool Options

The Tool Options tab is shown in Figure 22.5. The first checkbox and first two buttons let you save or restore tool options settings. The other options are described as follows.

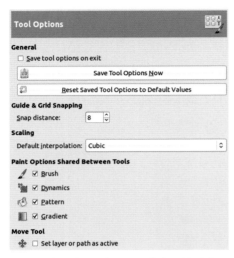

Figure 22.5 *The Preferences dialog, Tool Options tab*

Figure 22.6 *The Preferences dialog, Toolbox tab*

- GUIDE & GRID SNAPPING sets the minimum distance needed for "snapping" the pointer to the closest guide or grid in the Image window. This parameter sets the distance, but the snapping itself is determined by the corresponding parameters in the **Image: View** menu (see "Padding Colors and Snapping" on page 576).

- SCALING allows you to choose among the various interpolation algorithms, from NONE to SINC (LANCZOS3). The choice you make here will be the default for all the tools that use scaling, though you are still able to change the particular scaling method for each tool in its options dialog.

- PAINT OPTIONS SHARED BETWEEN TOOLS has four checkboxes that allow you to specify certain options to be shared by the painting tools (Pencil, Paintbrush, Eraser, Airbrush, and so on). By default, all the checkboxes are selected. So changing the brush used by the Paintbrush, for example, also changes the brush used by the Smudge tool or the Clone tool. But if BRUSH is unchecked, then each tool remembers its own brush.

- MOVE TOOL sets the active layer or path. If this is checked, moving a layer or a path with the Move tool makes it active.

Toolbox

In the tab shown in Figure 22.6, you can choose to display three different objects at the bottom of the Toolbox:

- The foreground and background colors, plus the small buttons for switching them or resetting them

- The active brush, pattern, and gradient

- The active image

The TOOLS CONFIGURATION list allows you to choose which tool icons appear in the Toolbox. The first 32 are present by default, but you can add 10 more or remove existing ones by clicking the visibility eye. When a tool is selected, you can change its position in the Toolbox with the arrows at the bottom of the dialog.

Default New Image

The Default New Image tab in Figure 22.7 specifies the default characteristics of the image created when you select **Image: File > New** or CTRL+N. This dialog is almost identical to the one shown in Figure 9.32 on page 210 and is described in detail in Section 9.4. But it also contains a button for changing the default Quick Mask color.

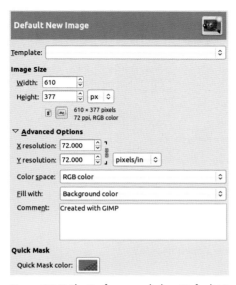

Figure 22.7 *The Preferences dialog, Default New Image tab*

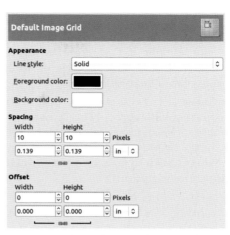

Figure 22.8 *The Preferences dialog, Default Image Grid tab*

Default Image Grid

The tab shown in Figure 22.8 is where you customize the initial characteristics of the grid that appears when you select **Image: View > Show Grid**. This tab is the same as **Image: Image > Configure Image Grid**. See Section 10.3 for more information.

Image Windows

You set the Image window parameters on three tabs. On the first tab, shown in Figure 22.9, you specify the following:

- USE "DOT FOR DOT" BY DEFAULT: This box is normally checked, in which case, if the zoom factor is 100 percent, the displayed image pixels are the same size as the screen pixels. When unchecked, the size of the displayed image is determined by its internal resolution. (See Section 10.1 for more details.)

- MARCHING ANTS SPEED: Set the time in milliseconds between movements of the dotted line around a selection.

- RESIZE WINDOW ON ZOOM: When this is checked, GIMP tries to resize the Image

Figure 22.9 *The Preferences dialog, Image Windows tab*

window as the zoom factor changes. Selecting this option is basically the opposite of checking the resize button at the top-right corner of the Image window, which, if you recall, allows you to enlarge the window to zoom in and shrink the window to zoom out.

- RESIZE WINDOW ON IMAGE SIZE CHANGE: When this is checked, the Image window is resized as the size of the image changes when you crop or resize it (**Image: Image > Scale image**).

- INITIAL ZOOM RATIO: You have two choices: Fit to window or 1:1. The second choice is probably not suitable if you intend to open images that are larger than the size of your screen at this zoom factor.

- WHILE SPACE BAR IS PRESSED: One option in this list is particularly useful: The "pan view" allows you to move an image within the Image window simply by moving the pointer. Alternatively, you can set it to no action or to switch to the Move tool temporarily.

- SHOW BRUSH OUTLINE: Normally checked, but if you are using a very large brush or your computer is slow, consider unchecking this option.

- SHOW POINTER FOR PAINT TOOLS: When this is checked (the default), a small icon of the painting tool being used accompanies the mouse pointer. When this box and the previous one are both unchecked, no pointer or outline follows the mouse, meaning you are painting without seeing where you are painting.

- POINTER MODE: This option offers three ways to show the pointer: as the tool icon with a pointed arrow if the preceding box is checked, as a crosshair pointer instead of the arrow, or as a crosshair alone.

- POINTER RENDERING: This option specifies whether to display the pointer in black and white or as a grayscale image (FANCY). Choose FANCY unless you encounter serious performance problems.

The tab shown in Figure 22.10 specifies the parts of the Image window that are shown initially and includes the initial status of the various checkboxes that appear in the **Image: View** menu. You can specify different components for the Image window's normal mode and for fullscreen mode (**Image: View > Fullscreen** or F11).

You can also set parameters for the color of the canvas padding, the part of the Image window that is not part of the canvas. Some of the

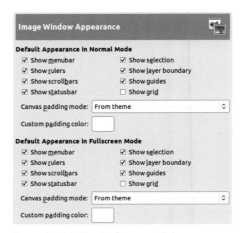

Figure 22.10 *The Preferences dialog, Image Window Appearance tab*

padding is shown if the image is smaller than the window in at least one dimension. Choose from these options:

- FROM THEME: Assuming you've loaded additional themes, a collection of themes can define a custom color.

- LIGHT CHECK COLOR: This option refers to the light color in the checkerboard pattern that represents transparency. This pattern is specified in the Display tab, discussed in the next section.

- DARK CHECK COLOR: This sets the darker color in the checkerboard pattern for transparency.

- CUSTOM COLOR: Choose a custom color using the Color chooser.

The tab shown in Figure 22.11 allows you to specify the text that appears in the Image window's title and status bar . (Note that the title bar is controlled by the operating system's window manager, so it may not appear exactly as GIMP specifies.) Predefined formats are available for both title and status bars. You can also define a new format by editing the proper field, which contains a format string that should be familiar to programmers.

A format string contains ordinary characters and variables that begin with a % sign. GIMP

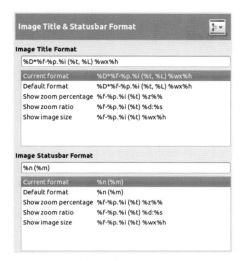

Figure 22.11 *The Preferences dialog, Image Title & Statusbar Format tab*

offers more than 20 variables; only the most important ones are described here:

- D*: Image not saved since the last time it was changed (displays an asterisk)
- f: Image filename
- p: Unique image identification number
- i: View number (useful if the image is viewed several times)
- t: Image type
- L: Number of layers
- w: Image width in pixels
- h: Image height in pixels
- m: Memory amount used by the image
- n: Name of the current layer

These string options let you choose what to display in the title or status bar. Depending on your own preferences and needs, you may choose to display or hide different types of information about the image.

Display

The tab of options shown in Figure 22.12 allows you to specify the representation of

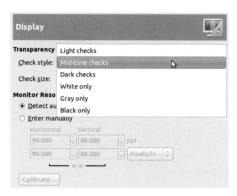

Figure 22.12 *The Preferences dialog, Display tab*

transparency. As you can see in this figure, you can choose from six different representations. The first three use a checkerboard pattern, whereas the other three use a continuous color. If you use a checkerboard pattern, you can choose one of three square sizes.

This tab also lets you specify your monitor's resolution manually. Monitor resolution is detected automatically, but to enter it manually, check the corresponding radio button to define your monitor's horizontal and vertical resolutions and choose among the different measurements. If you do not know the exact value that corresponds to your screen, click the CALIBRATE button to open a window with measurements in your chosen units. Measure the vertical and horizontal rulers displayed on the screen carefully, and input your measurements into the corresponding fields in the window. Then GIMP computes the actual resolution.

Color Management

Color management is described in Section 12.3. The tab of options in Figure 22.13 shows the various parameters that you can set.

- MODE OF OPERATION: Choose from three modes:
  - NO COLOR MANAGEMENT: GIMP's color management capabilities are bypassed, which is probably a bad idea.

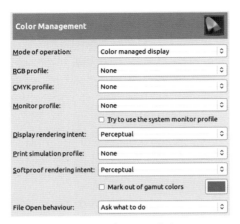

Figure 22.13 *The Preferences dialog, Color Management tab*

- COLOR MANAGED DISPLAY: Use the display color profile to display colors as accurately as possible.

- PRINT SIMULATION: When this is selected, GIMP uses the printer profile you provide so you can preview the color results you'll achieve with this profile. Note that this option does not deal with actual printing, as discussed in Section 19.4.

The next three options require an ICC profile: a file whose name ends with .icc. The location of these files depends on your operating system. On GNU/Linux, look in */usr/share/color/icc/*; on Mac OS X, look in */Library/ColorSync/Profiles/*; and in Windows, check *\Windows\system32\spool\drivers\color*. You can also find profiles on sites like the European Color Initiative (*http://www.eci.org/*).

- The RGB PROFILE defines GIMP's internal color space. Unless you have very specific requirements, consider using the Adobe RGB color space, which has a larger gamut than that of a display monitor or a four-color printer but whose gamut is not excessively large. Many people prefer to stick with the sRGB color space, which is closer to a printer color space.

- The CMYK PROFILE is not used in GIMP, which does not handle CMYK internally. This could change in a future version of GIMP.

- The MONITOR PROFILE likely uses the sRGB color space. If you check the following box, GIMP uses the color profile provided by the operating system and used in its own color management.

- The DISPLAY RENDERING INTENT option allows you to choose among four ways to convert from one color space to another. The methods differ in the way they present colors in the initial color space but not in the final color space. The default, PERCEPTUAL intent, uses an interpolation system that is almost reversible (no important information is lost) and does not clip out the most saturated colors. It is well suited to work with photographs. The SATURATION intent converts saturated input colors to saturated output colors and is well suited to colorizing or similar work. You can safely ignore the two other intents, RELATIVE COLORIMETRIC and ABSOLUTE COLORIMETRIC. (See also "Using Color Management" on page 254.)

- The PRINT SIMULATION PROFILE is used for print preview if you choose print simulation mode. Use a CMYK common profile, such as Fogra27L CMYK Coated Press or your printer's specific profile.

- The SOFTPROOF RENDERING INTENT is used for print preview. The choices are the same as those for DISPLAY RENDERING INTENT, but you can also check the MARK OUT OF GAMUT COLORS and then, in the small box to the right, choose the color to be displayed in place of out-of-gamut colors.

- The FILE OPEN BEHAVIOUR option specifies what GIMP has to do when loading an image with an embedded color profile that differs from the internal sRGB space. GIMP can KEEP THE EMBEDDED PROFILE and thus not convert the image, which will still be displayed correctly using this profile. CONVERT

TO RGB WORKSPACE uses the embedded profile but forgets it afterward. ASK WHAT TO DO is probably the safest option.

Input Devices

The options on the INPUT DEVICES tab, shown in Figure 22.14, are mainly for configuring graphics tablets. This tab has only three buttons and one checkbox; all but the first are self-explanatory.

Clicking CONFIGURE EXTENDED INPUT DEVICES opens the dialog shown in Figure 1.41 on page 22. The menu on the left lists all known devices, but those unavailable are grayed out.

A Wacom tablet is considered to be four different devices: the stylus, the eraser, the mouse (called a cursor), and the pad (the small touchpad(s) present on some tablets).

After selecting a device, you can choose from three modes: DISABLED, SCREEN, and WINDOW. The best choice is generally SCREEN, which allows you to use the stylus or tablet mouse across the entire screen. Choosing DISABLED makes the device act as a simple mouse, without sensitivity to pressure or tilt. You can safely ignore KEYS and most of AXES, except Pressure, which you may find useful for adjusting a tablet that isn't responding properly. It offers an answering curve similar to that of the paint dynamics.

The ADDITIONAL INPUT CONTROLLERS tab, shown in Figure 22.15, is part of the Input Devices tab in the Preferences dialog. It displays available controllers on the left and active controllers on the right. Click an item on one list to move it to the other list using one of the arrow buttons.

When you've selected an item in the right column, you can edit its parameters by double-clicking or by clicking the small icon in the bottom row of the right column. Figure 22.16 shows a part of the dialog that appears when you select MAIN MOUSE WHEEL. A similar dialog pops up when you move a controller from the available to the active list.

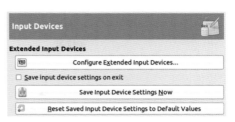

Figure 22.14 *The Preferences dialog, Input Devices tab*

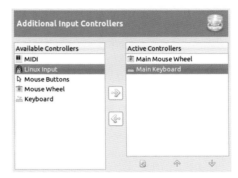

Figure 22.15 *The Preferences dialog, Additional Input Controllers tab*

In the dialog shown in Figure 22.16, you can specify actions that will be triggered by using the mouse wheel. Several predefined actions deal with selecting brushes, patterns, gradients, and fonts and the opacity of the current painting tool. To add a new action, select the event and click the EDIT button at the bottom to open a dialog similar to Figure 22.17.

Figure 22.18 shows the dialog that appears when the active controller is the main keyboard. Notice that several predefined events are available, but none are used by default and you can even redefine these shortcuts to whatever you're familiar with.

Window Management

The WINDOW MANAGEMENT tab, shown in Figure 22.19, controls the way GIMP manages the numerous windows onscreen when you are not in single-window mode.

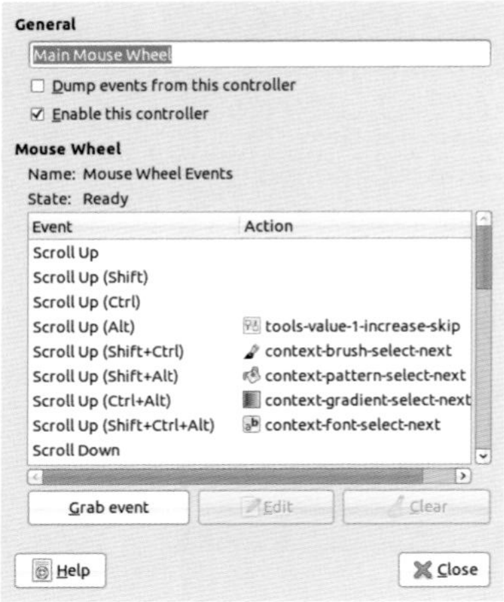

Figure 22.16 *Configuring the main mouse wheel*

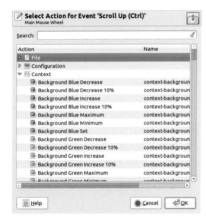

Figure 22.17 *Selecting the action for an event*

WINDOW MANAGER HINTS tells the window manager how to handle the Toolbox and the other dock windows. You can choose from three possibilities:

- UTILITY WINDOW is the default. When this is selected, the Toolbox and dock windows are raised on top of all others as soon as you activate any GIMP window, and they stay there until you raise another window on top of them.

- NORMAL WINDOW makes the Toolbox and dock windows behave like normal windows.

Figure 22.18 *Configuring the main keyboard*

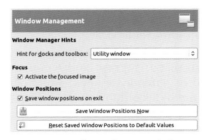

Figure 22.19 *The Preferences dialog, Window Management tab*

- KEEP ABOVE keeps the Toolbox and dock windows on top of any other window.

Your choice of behaviors is a matter of personal taste, but note that some window managers (such as the Windows operating system) don't handle these options correctly, so your actual results may vary. The TAB key may be useful in such cases. Changes you make here are effective only after you restart GIMP.

The ACTIVATE THE FOCUSED IMAGE button, if unchecked, disconnects the fact that a window has *focus* (is active as far as the window manager is concerned) from the fact that it's active as far as GIMP is concerned. This option can be helpful if you set up your window manager so the window under the pointer automatically has focus, but you want to determine which Image window is active.

The checkbox and two buttons under WIN-DOW POSITIONS should be self-explanatory. You can save the screen layout you define or reset it to the default.

Folders

The FOLDERS tab, shown in Figure 22.20, heads up a long list of possible folders, as shown in Figure 22.21. GIMP finds the information and data that it needs in folders, some of which are system-wide, while others belong to the user. On the Folders tab, you can specify the location of the TEMPORARY FOLDER where GIMP stores files that will be automatically deleted upon shutdown. Normally this folder belongs to the user, but you can change it to a system-wide temporary folder that will be cleaned every time the operating systems boots.

The SWAP FOLDER is used for the temporary storage of internal data that does not fit in memory. The default folder is in your personal space, but consider choosing a folder on another disk to improve performance.

The other Folder tabs mention at least two folders: one personal and one system-wide. You can write to your personal folder, that is, add new objects or remove or edit existing ones. Normally, you can't write to the system-wide folder, but if you intend to install new brushes, paint dynamics, patterns, palettes, or gradients, making the corresponding system-wide folder writable (something that is not possible for the other object types) may prove useful.

When you click one of the folder names, the buttons in the top row become active, as shown in Figure 22.22. Here you can move a folder up or down the list, which changes the order in which that folder is searched. You can also re-move a folder from the list, add a new one, or change an existing name. The round button to the left of the folder's name is green if the folder already exists; otherwise, it is red.

Figure 22.20 *The Preferences dialog, Folders tab*

Figure 22.21 *Possible folders*

Figure 22.22 *Brush folders*

22.2 Additional Preferences in the Edit Menu

You can access additional preference dialogs from the **Image: Edit** menu. **Image: Edit > Input devices** opens the same dialog covered in "Input Devices" on page 569. We cover the others here.

Keyboard Shortcuts

We covered keyboard shortcut preferences in "User Interface" on page 562. Here we cover how to define, edit, and erase shortcuts.

Image: Edit > Keyboard Shortcuts opens the dialog shown in Figure 22.23, which is the same as the one accessed from the Preferences dialog. Here, you can define an unlimited number of

Figure 22.23 *The Configure Keyboard Shortcuts dialog*

Figure 22.24 *Configuring the Edit actions*

Figure 22.25 *The Module Manager*

shortcuts, provided you have sufficient imagination to invent them!

The list of actions is divided into submenus. Figure 22.24 shows the Edit actions, including existing shortcuts and the action's internal name, useful when writing a script (see Section 21.3).

To define a new shortcut, select the corresponding action, click in the shortcut field, and then type the shortcut. If the shortcut is already assigned to another action, a dialog opens allowing you to either reassign the shortcut or cancel the definition.

You can also erase existing shortcuts here. If the checkbox at the bottom of the dialog is checked, all new commands will be saved in the gimprc file and be available for future sessions.

Because the number of existing commands is huge, a SEARCH field allows you to find a specific command, as long as you know at least part of its name. The long list of actions that follows the CONTEXT entry allows you to control the tool parameters from the keyboard, as shown in part

in Figure 22.17 on page 570. Consider browsing the various lists of actions in the dialog shown in Figure 22.23, as they offer a peek inside GIMP.

Modules

Image: Edit > Modules opens the dialog shown in Figure 22.25, which lists the various extension modules. Use this dialog to control whether a

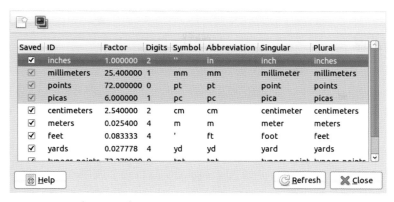

Figure 22.26 *The Unit Editor*

module is loaded. Any changes you make take effect only after you restart GIMP.

When you select a module in the dialog, you should see some information about it. Many of the modules deal with color profiles and color selection, whereas others deal with event controllers. If a module is not loaded, its features are not included in GIMP.

Units

Image: Edit > Units opens the dialog shown in Figure 22.26. This Unit Editor displays information about the various units defined and used in GIMP and allows you to create new ones. You can create a completely new unit or duplicate and then edit an existing one. In Figure 22.27, we've added the fathom unit. The most important field in the Units Editor is FACTOR, which indicates how many of your chosen units make up an inch. The DIGITS field specifies how many decimal digits the input field must have to provide approximately the same accuracy as 1/100th of an inch.

Back in the Unit Editor, the SAVED checkbox, when checked, specifies the unit will be saved when GIMP terminates. The first four units are highlighted to show that they are always saved.

Figure 22.27 *Adding a new unit*

22.3 Customizing Image Views

Figure 22.28 shows the full **Image: View** menu, which allows you to control image views. We cover here only the entries not covered in Chapter 10.

Display Filters

Image: View > Display Filters opens the dialog shown in Figure 22.29. Here, you can choose which filters to apply when an image is displayed. Available filters are shown on the left and the active ones on the right. If you select a filter in the left column, you can copy it to the right column with the corresponding arrow.

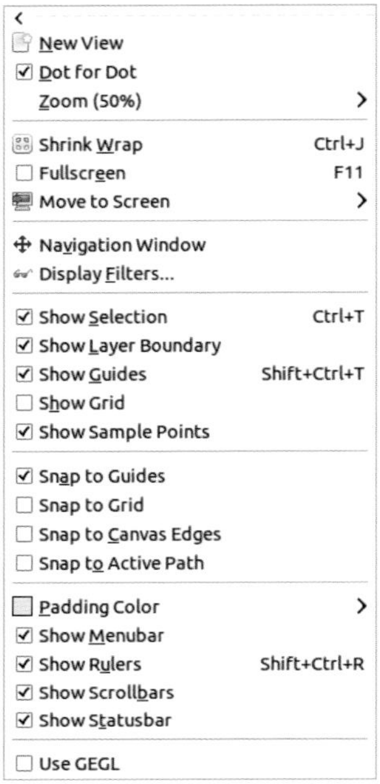

Figure 22.28 *The Image: View menu*

Figure 22.30 *Configuring the Color Deficient Vision filter*

Figure 22.31 *Applying the Deuteranopia filter*

Figure 22.29 *The Configure Color Display Filters dialog*

Uncheck the checkbox next to an active filter to deactivate it without removing it. Initially, only the COLOR MANAGEMENT filter is active, assuming you activated it in the Preferences dialog. Remember, these filters affect only the way an image is displayed; they don't change the image itself.

In Figure 22.30, we chose the COLOR DEFICIENT VISION filter in the left column, copied it to the right column, and selected it. A new field appears that allows us to select the type of

deficient vision: protanopia, deuteranopia, or tritanopia (as described in "Color Blindness" on page 593). Figure 22.31 shows the result when we apply the Deuteranopia filter. The goal is to show us the image as it would look to a person with this type of color blindness. You may find this tool particularly useful when designing a website.

The CONTRAST filter shows the image as it would appear to those suffering from cataracts or retinal disease. It lets you transform the image so they are able to see it correctly. As Figure 22.32 shows, the default value of 1.0 for the number of contrast cycles is too high and creates useless artifacts. A value of 0.3 would yield a usable result.

The GAMMA filter allows you to apply a systematic gamma correction to all displayed

Figure 22.32 *Applying the Contrast filter*

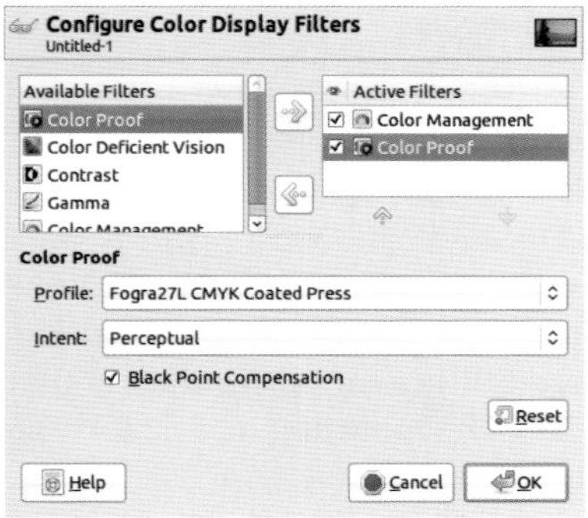

![Configure Color Display Filters dialog]

Figure 22.33 *Configuring the Color Proof filter*

images. This tool is handy when compensating for the distortions of a damaged screen. The filter shows the image aspect under those conditions.

The COLOR PROOF filter, whose configuration dialog appears in Figure 22.33, controls the printer preview. The printer preview displays images to simulate their appearance when printed. You should only use color proofing when preparing to print an image, because the printer will apply a color filter to the image in the form of an ICC profile. Here, you choose the profile and intent to be used when printing an image. Figure 22.34 shows the result of using the parameter values shown in Figure 22.33. The BLACK POINT COMPENSATION button, if checked, improves the representation of dark colors,

Figure 22.34 *Applying the Color Proof filter*

especially blacks. (For more information, see "Color Management" on page 567.)

Hiding or Revealing Parts of the Image Window

The rest of the **Image: View** menu contains numerous checkboxes. We review them here and in the next section:

- SHOW SELECTION ($\boxed{\text{CTRL+T}}$) toggles the visibility of the "marching ants" that show the outline of the current selection. Remember, this outline is in the middle of the selection fuzziness; hiding it can lead to surprises when you find yourself trying to paint in an image without realizing that you are painting outside the current selection.

- SHOW LAYER BOUNDARY is useful when the boundaries of the current layer differ from those of the canvas. The dashed line appears in yellow and black.

- SHOW GUIDES ($\boxed{\text{SHIFT+CTRL+T}}$) is handy for temporarily hiding guides that you want to keep. The dashed line is blue and black.

- SHOW GRID shows or hides the grid.

- SHOW SAMPLE POINTS controls the Sample Points dockable dialog, which is created from the **Image: Windows > Dockable Dialogs** submenu. To create a sample point, $\boxed{\text{CTRL}}$-click in one of the rulers and drag the pointer

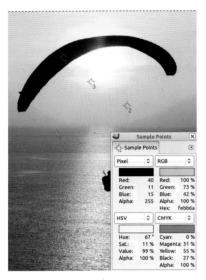

Figure 22.35 *Sample points*

Figure 22.36 *Padding Color*

to the pixel you want to sample. You can create as many sample points as you want, but only the first four are described in the dialog, shown with the points themselves in Figure 22.35. As you can see, you can choose to move a point by dragging it and delete it by dragging it back to a ruler. Note that you can only move these sample points if you have selected the Color Picker tool ([O]).

This feature, when combined with the Levels tool or Curves tool, is especially useful. If you're trying to fix the color balance in an image, place the sample points in areas where you know what the color should be—like a green tree leaf or the blue sky. Then, as you change all the colors with one of the previously mentioned tools, you can simultaneously compare the values in the sample points to make sure the colors of key objects are still accurate.

- The last four checkboxes in the **Image: View** menu let you toggle the visibility of parts of the Image window, including the menu bar, rulers, scroll bars, and status bar. These options are great when you're short on screen space. (Remember, you can access menus by

right-clicking in an image or clicking the image menu button at the top-left corner of the rulers.) The Toggle Quick Mask button disappears if you hide the scroll bars, but you can always access it from the **Image: Selection** menu or by pressing $\boxed{\text{SHIFT+Q}}$.

Padding Colors and Snapping

We still have a few more options to review in the **Image: View** menu.

Image: View > Padding Color opens the menu shown in Figure 22.36, with options similar to those on the Image Window Appearance tab in the Preferences dialog (shown in Figure 22.10 on page 566). One difference is that here we can select the padding color for the active Image window only.

Other customizations available in the **Image: View** menu all relate to *snapping*: Snapping describes the way the mouse pointer is attracted to a feature in the Image window. Snapping is active, by default, for the guides. Select SNAP TO GRID for drawing schema precisely. Select SNAP TO CANVAS EDGES when you want to begin a selection exactly on an edge. Select SNAP TO ACTIVE PATH when working with paths.

22.4 Building New Brushes

GIMP has four kinds of brushes:

- *Ordinary brushes* have no specific name. They are shown in the Brushes dialog as small grayscale images called *pixmaps*. When painting with the ordinary brushes, the current foreground color is used, with the intensity of

Figure 22.37 *Building an ordinary brush*

the color represented by the intensity of black in the pixmap.

- *Color brushes* are represented by a color pixmap in the Brushes dialog. Internally, they are represented by this pixmap, as well as by a grayscale copy of this pixmap, which serves as a mask. When used with paint dynamics without any box checked in the Color row (see "Drawing Tool Options" on page 330), a color brush uses the colors of the pixmap and ignores the foreground color. If at least one box is checked in the Color row of the current paint dynamics, the mask is used, and brushes paint with a gradient.

- *Animated brushes* (also called *image hoses*) apply a series of grayscale or color pixmaps to an image. (A small red triangle appears near the pixmap in the Brushes dialog.) Animated brushes paint with several different pixmaps, depending on the pointer movement. For example, when using a graphic tablet, an animated brush may change its behavior depending on the pressure and tilt of the tablet pen and the current paint dynamics settings.

- *Parametric brushes* are created using a simple graphical interface.

Defining an Ordinary Brush

To define an ordinary brush, first build a grayscale image as shown in Figure 22.37. When you're satisfied with the brush, export it to the GIMP brush .gbr file format, and the dialog

Figure 22.38 *Exporting an ordinary brush*

shown in Figure 22.38 opens. Once in this dialog, you can add a short description of the brush and define its default spacing. Export the brush to your personal brushes folder and refresh the Brushes dialog by clicking the double arrow at the lower right, and you should be able to use your new brush just like any other.

Defining a Color Brush

To define a color brush, first create an image in RGB mode, draw a new brush, and add an Alpha channel. Alternatively, you can create a transparent image and then draw the brush. The brush is drawn in color, and the new brush paints with its own colors.

Note that as soon as you copy or cut a selection, it appears in the Brushes dialog as the first brush. You can use this selection as either an ordinary or color brush, depending on the color mode of the image from which you made the selection. You can also select **Image: Edit > Paste as > New Brush** to immediately export the new brush.

Defining an Animated Brush

To build an animated brush, first build an image containing all of the brush's components. You can build a multilayer image (similar to an animation) using the same techniques described in Chapter 18 so that each layer contains one of the brush's components. You can also build an image with only one layer, containing all components arranged in rows and columns. Finally, you can build an image that mixes these two methods, with several layers and several brush images in each layer.

When you use an animated brush with the Paintbrush tool, the brush image changes as you draw according to the direction of the stroke, the pressure applied on the graphic tablet, or simply the distance traveled. The animated brush's effect differs depending on the tool (such as the Pencil) and its inherent properties. You can combine these conditions so the effects of an animated brush change along several dimensions.

Note, however, that this mechanism is different from and incompatible with paint dynamics: When you use an animated brush, the current paint dynamics setting is ignored.

For example, say we want to build a three-dimensional brush that changes depending on three conditions:

- The shape of the brush (a small arrow) changes along the direction of the stroke. The arrow points 90 degrees clockwise from the direction of the stroke, so if we draw a circle in the clockwise direction, the arrows will point to the center.

- The size of the brush depends on the pressure of the stylus on the graphic tablet: The more pressure, the smaller the arrow.

- The color of the brush varies randomly.

We first define eight directions for the arrow. The first direction points vertically, and the rest each rotate counterclockwise 45°.

We then define four sizes and four colors, producing a total of $8 \times 4 \times 4$ different brushes. We organize the brushes in four differently colored layers, with each layer containing four rows of eight shapes.

First, we draw an arrow in a new 200×200 image, as shown in Figure 22.39. We then scale this image to 40×40 (the size of our brush), and by successively rotating it, we build a row of arrows in a new 320×40 image. To orient the arrow layers precisely, we place vertical guides separated by 80 pixels, as shown in Figure 22.40.

Now we build three more rows of arrows, with brush images of decreasing size. We scale down

Figure 22.39 *The model brush*

Figure 22.40 *Building a row of shapes*

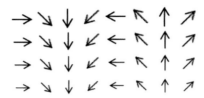

Figure 22.41 *A set of four rows of decreasing size*

each layer individually so it remains in the same place in the row; in other words, we don't scale the entire row at once. In addition to the first row with brush size 40×40, we build three more rows with sizes 35×35, 30×30, and 25×25. For each row, we delete the background layer and merge the other layers to produce a one-layer image. We also extend this layer to the image size for all but the first row.

Each layer of the multilayer image must contain a copy of the four rows that we just defined. So we create a new 320×160 image and copy the four rows as new layers in this image. (A horizontal guide helps us place the rows correctly, as shown in Figure 22.41.) Now we build four different layers in four different colors:

1. Delete the background layer of the image.

2. Merge the four layers.

3. Select the black arrows with the Select by Color tool, using a high threshold.

4. Choose a 100% red color (hue = 0, saturation = value = 100) and fill the selection ($\boxed{\text{CTRL}+,}$).

5. Save the image.

Now we repeat the final two steps for the three remaining colors; for example, choosing hue values 90, 180, and 270 to produce a

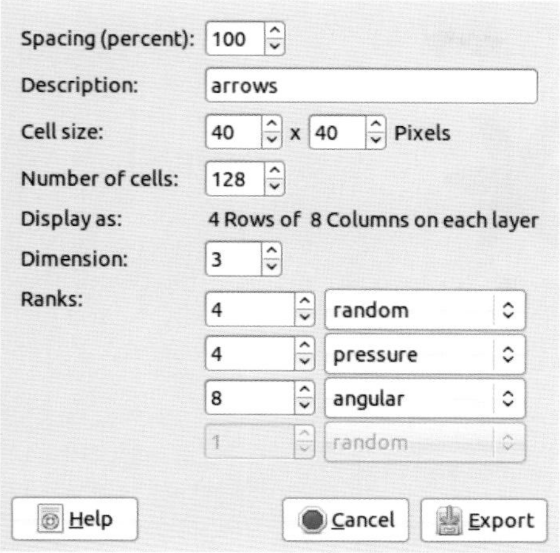

Spacing (percent): 100

Description: arrows

Cell size: 40 x 40 Pixels

Number of cells: 128

Display as: 4 Rows of 8 Columns on each layer

Dimension: 3

Ranks:
4 random
4 pressure
8 angular
1 random

Help Cancel Export

Figure 22.42 *Exporting the animated brush*

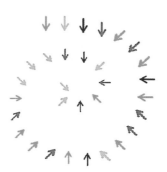

Figure 22.43 *Testing the new dynamic brush*

green, blue, and purple. Then we build the final 320 × 160 image containing the four layers defined earlier. This image has no background layer, and the layers are red, blue, green, and purple, in order from top to bottom.

To export a brush, choose your personal Brushes folder and the .gih suffix. The dialog shown in Figure 22.42 opens. Change all fields as follows:

1. Push the SPACING to 100% to separate the brush images clearly. The user can change this setting when using the brush.

2. Add a description in the DESCRIPTION field. Brushes are listed alphabetically by description in the Brushes dialog.

3. Set the CELL SIZE to 40 × 40.

4. Change the NUMBER OF CELLS to 128. GIMP displays the organization of each layer, so you can check your work.

5. Vary the first dimension at random. (This brush has three DIMENSIONS.) The four layers are the first dimension, which corresponds to the brush's color.

6. Vary the second dimension with stylus pressure. The four rows in each layer are the second dimension, which corresponds to the brush's size.

7. Finally, vary the third dimension with the angle of the stroke. The eight brush images in each row are the third dimension, which corresponds to the brush's orientation. You could vary this third dimension with velocity or tilt instead. Feel free to experiment with your new animated brush!

When you're done, click EXPORT. The brush is now in your personal Brushes folder. Refresh the Brushes dialog by clicking the double arrow at the bottom right to see this new brush in the list.

To test this new brush, select it from the list, create a new 400 × 400 white image, and then draw a clockwise spiral with the tablet stylus, increasing the pressure as you move toward the center. The result is shown in Figure 22.43.

Note that you can easily change the export parameters without changing the brush itself—if the brush is saved as an XCF file. You could, for example, remove the color variations or change them incrementally according to the stylus's tilt.

Defining a Parametric Brush

To define a parametric brush, use the Brush Editor, which appears when you create a new brush, duplicate a brush, or edit a brush. The Brush Editor dialog is shown in Figure 22.44.

Below the dialog menu, you'll see a text field for naming the new brush. The large box shows a preview of the brush. The preview is not

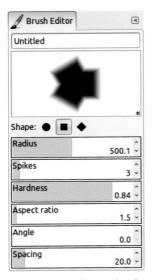

Figure 22.44 *The Brush Editor*

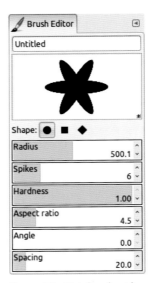

Figure 22.45 *A brush with a round shape, aspect ratio greater than 1, and six spikes*

proportional to the size of the brush, however, because you can build brushes with a radius from 0.1 pixel to 1000 pixels.

When creating a new brush, you can choose from three SHAPES: circular, square, or diamond. The RADIUS is a measure of the distance between the center and the edge of the brush and is, therefore, half the brush size. Spikes extend from the center like flower petals; the tips of the petals are the selected shape (round, square, or pointed). SPIKES don't appear on circles unless the ASPECT RATIO is greater than 1, but shapes with corners exhibit spikes at any aspect ratio. The ASPECT RATIO [1 to 20] controls the relationship between height and width and interacts in interesting ways with the number of spikes to determine the brush's final shape. The minimum number of spikes is two. If you have more than two spikes, you'll get a star polygon when the shape is a diamond. If the aspect ratio is 1 and the shape is a square, then if you have more than three spikes, you'll get a shape with as many sides as there are spikes. Eight spikes yields an octagon, for example. Three spikes yields a bizarre polygon, shown in

Figure 22.44. If the aspect ratio is greater than 1 and the shape is square, you get a star with square tips. Figure 22.45 shows a round shape with an aspect ratio of 4.5 and six spikes.

HARDNESS ranges from 0.0 (completely blurred) to 1.0 (completely sharp). ANGLE [0 to 180] allows you to rotate a brush around its center. Finally, as with other brushes, the SPACING option is the distance between two instances of the brush when you use it to draw.

Once you are satisfied with the brush, close the dialog, and your new brush is saved in your personal Brushes folder with your chosen name and the suffix .vbr.

22.5 Building New Patterns

In Chapter 4, you learned how to define new textures. If you export a texture (or a part of it) to your personal Patterns folder and then refresh the Patterns dialog, the pattern is available immediately. You can export the pattern with the .pat suffix (a specific pattern format), or in GIMP 2.2 or later, you can also save image files

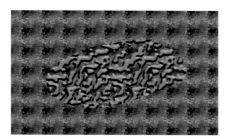

Figure 22.46 *Using a semitransparent pattern*

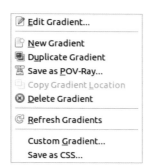

Figure 22.47 *The Gradients dialog menu*

to the Patterns folder as PNG, JPEG, BMP, GIF, or TIFF.

As soon as you copy or cut a selection, the copy becomes available as the first pattern in the Patterns dialog. If you then make another copy or close GIMP, this temporary pattern is lost. You can select **Image: Edit > Paste As > New Pattern** to save the temporary pattern.

Patterns are not necessarily opaque. For example, if you save the top layer of the texture in Figure 4.69 on page 107, copy from it a 200×200 pixel square, and save it as a pattern, the new pattern will be semitransparent. Figure 22.46 shows the result of applying this new pattern to a selection made in an image filled with another pattern.

22.6   Building New Gradients

Whereas brushes and patterns are basically images, gradients are something different. The only way to build a new gradient is with the Gradient Editor (**Gradients: Gradient Menu > Edit Gradient**) or by clicking the bottom-left icon in the Gradients dialog. As with brushes, you cannot edit a gradient that does not belong to you. To edit an existing gradient, you first need to duplicate that gradient, and then you can edit the duplicate.

All of the gradient editing actions are available as buttons at the bottom of the Gradients dialog. Or you can select **Gradients: Gradient Menu** or right-click a gradient to open the Gradients dialog menu (see Figure 22.47). You can

copy the path to the gradient in the clipboard and paste it in a text file. Choose CUSTOM GRADIENT to create an image containing only the current gradient. You can set the height and width of this image, which is useful for testing complicated gradients. And you can export the gradient to POV-Ray format if you're working with Persistence of Vision Raytracer.

The gradients you build are exported with the suffix .ggr (for GIMP Gradient), a GIMP-specific format.

The Gradient Editor

To try out the Gradient Editor, open the Gradients dialog, choose the gradient Caribbean Blues, and click Duplicate Gradient (or select **Gradients: Gradients Menu > Duplicate Gradient**). The dialog shown in Figure 22.48 opens. If you click a color in the gradient, the bottom of the window displays these options:

- POSITION: Horizontal position within the gradient (0.0 = far left, 0.5 = center, 1.0 = far right)

- RGB: The values in the red, green, and blue channels (with the range [0 to 1])

- HSV: The hue (an angle in degrees) and the saturation and value (both as percentages)

- LUMINANCE and OPACITY as percentages

The small rectangle displays the color of the gradient. The four buttons at the bottom of the dialog let you save the gradient, zoom in or

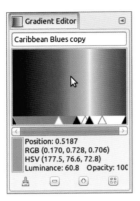

Figure 22.48 *The Gradient Editor*

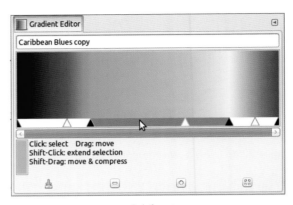

Figure 22.49 *Moving and deforming segments*

out, or return to a set zoom factor such as Fit in Window.

Click the gradient image to set the foreground color or CTRL-click to set the background color. You can click and drag from the Toolbox color swatch to the Gradient Editor to change its colors in real time, but only the RGB values are displayed in the dialog.

At the top of the Gradient Editor dialog, you can change the name of the gradient. Gradients are made up of a sequence of segments. Each segment is a smooth transition from the color on the left (marked by a black triangle) to the color on the right (marked by the next black triangle). The white triangles are similar to the Gamma triangle in the Levels tool: They don't change the first and last colors, but they do change how the transition is done. In other words, the white triangle changes the shape of the answer curve.

To perform simple transformations on the gradient being edited, first widen the window. Next, double-click a segment between two black triangles to select it and make it blue. (To select a sequence of segments, SHIFT-click on the last one.)

Once you've selected a segment, you can move the black triangles to extend, reduce, or move the segment. You can also move the white triangle to deform the answer curve in the segment or move the entire selected segment by

adjusting its two black triangles simultaneously to compress or expand the neighboring segments, as shown in Figure 22.49. When you check the INSTANT UPDATE button, the effect is immediate; otherwise, it shows up when you release the mouse button.

The Gradient Editor Menu

You can open the Gradient Editor menu (Figure 22.50) from the dialog menu or by right-clicking in the gradient in the dialog. This menu allows you to change the two colors that define a gradient segment. Figure 22.51 shows the menu that opens when you choose LEFT COLOR TYPE (the RIGHT COLOR TYPE menu is identical). FIXED mode is the default, and you select the endpoint color using one of the two entries in the Gradient Editor menu. Alternatively, you can choose to attach the color of one of the endpoints to the foreground or background color. The gradient you're building then depends on these colors—like the first four (FG to BG) gradients that come with GIMP.

The endpoint color can have an Alpha channel. If you check an entry that includes "(Transparent)," the Alpha channel is 0 at the first endpoint and increases as it moves toward the other endpoint. Alternatively, click LEFT ENDPOINT'S COLOR (or RIGHT ENDPOINT'S COLOR) in the

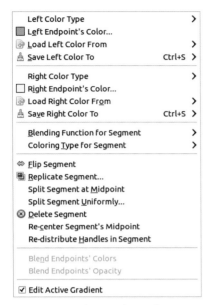

Figure 22.50 *The Gradient Editor menu*

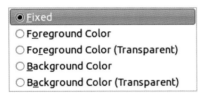

Figure 22.51 *The Left (or Right) Color Type submenu*

Gradient Editor menu, and you can use the Color chooser to change the value of the Alpha channel as you desire.

Selecting LOAD LEFT COLOR FROM (or RIGHT COLOR) in the Gradient Editor menu opens the menu shown in Figure 22.52. Here you can select neighboring colors in the gradient or choose from a set palette of 10 colors, which you can customize. To change to one of the colors on the preset palette, select SAVE LEFT COLOR TO (or RIGHT COLOR) to choose one of those 10 colors.

Alternatively, you can change gradient colors to colors in an image:

1. Select the Color picker tool ([O]).
2. Click a color in an open image.

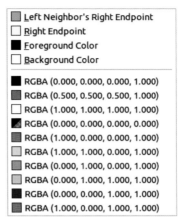

Figure 22.52 *The Load Left (or Right) Color From submenu*

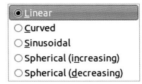

Figure 22.53 *The Blending Function for Segment submenu*

3. Drag the color from the foreground color and drop it into the Gradient Editor at the position in the gradient where you want it.

The next entry in the Gradient Editor menu, BLENDING FUNCTION FOR SEGMENT, opens the menu shown in Figure 22.53. Here, you can choose from five different left-to-right transitions for the current segment:

- LINEAR is the default. The color changes steadily, and the point over the white triangle is a blend of the starting and ending color. For example, if the segment transitions from red to yellow, the point over the white triangle is orange.

- CURVED makes the changes in color faster on the ends of the segment.

- SINUSOIDAL, on the contrary, makes the color change faster in the middle (as set by the white triangle).

- SPHERICAL (INCREASING) makes the color change faster on the left than on the right.

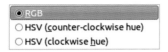

Figure 22.54 *The Coloring Type for Segment submenu*

- SPHERICAL (DECREASING) is the same, but the change is faster on the right.

The next entry, COLORING TYPE FOR SEGMENT, opens the menu shown in Figure 22.54, where you can decide whether the transition between colors is made along the RGB or HSV space. If you look at the first four gradients when the foreground and background colors are actual colors, say blue and red, you can observe the difference between a gradient transitioning along the HSV model versus the RGB model.

The next entries in the Gradient Editor menu are as follows:

- FLIP SEGMENT is the only action that can be reversed because the Gradient Editor does not have any undo capability.

- REPLICATE SEGMENT makes a number of copies of the segment.

- SPLIT SEGMENT AT MIDPOINT creates two segments from the current segment. The segments are split at the white triangle, and a new white triangle is placed at the center of each resulting segment.

- SPLIT SEGMENT UNIFORMLY does the same, but it ignores the white triangle in the segment to be split, and you can choose the number of new segments.

- DELETE SEGMENT deletes the whole segment or a selection within the segment. The segments on both sides of the deleted segment are enlarged to fill the space.

- RE-CENTER SEGMENT'S MIDPOINT places the white triangle exactly in the middle of the segment.

- RE-DISTRIBUTE HANDLES IN SEGMENT makes all triangles equidistant and is only useful when you're selecting several segments.

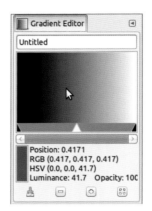

Figure 22.55 *The Gradient Editor's initial dialog*

- BLEND ENDPOINTS' COLORS is active only when several segments are selected. An average of the right color of one segment and the left color of the other replaces the colors on all boundaries in the selection.

- BLEND ENDPOINTS' OPACITY works the same as BLEND ENDPOINTS' COLORS but with opacity instead of color.

Building a Gradient

To help you understand the Gradient Editor's many features, here's an example showing how you can define a gradient with four segments.

Suppose the foreground and background colors are set to their defaults. In the Gradients dialog, click NEW GRADIENT, and the window shown in Figure 22.55 opens.

To define a gradient with four segments, select SPLIT SEGMENT UNIFORMLY from the dialog menu and change the slider value to 4. Then click SPLIT to get the result shown in Figure 22.56. This dialog is narrow, but you can enlarge it. You can also use the zoom icons at the bottom to magnify the dialog, but you won't be able to see the entire gradient.

After splitting, all of the segments are selected. Carefully select the first segment from the left. Applying the LEFT COLOR TYPE and RIGHT COLOR TYPE, set the left endpoint type to

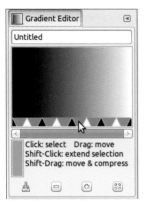

Figure 22.56 *After splitting the gradient into four segments*

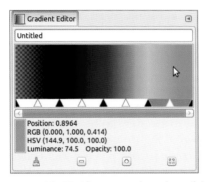

Figure 22.57 *After setting the colors of the four segments*

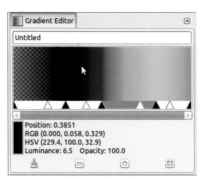

Figure 22.58 *The finished four-segment gradient*

Figure 22.59 *Using the new gradient*

FOREGROUND (TRANSPARENT) and the right endpoint to FOREGROUND. Now the first segment is entirely determined by the foreground color.

Next we change the colors of the three other segments. For each, set the left endpoint color to that of the LEFT NEIGHBOR'S RIGHT ENDPOINT and select any color you like for the right endpoint. The result is smooth transitions between the segments, as shown in Figure 22.57.

Now we'll change the blending function for the segments: linear for the first, sinusoidal for the second, spherical (increasing) for the third, and spherical (decreasing) for the fourth. Finally, move the white and black triangles slightly, as shown in Figure 22.58. Remember, you can't move the triangles independently in a selected segment.

To test the new gradient, change the foreground color to purple, hexadecimal value 8f14e5. Create a new, white 400×400 image and apply to it, from the middle, a radial gradient in normal mode, without repetition. The result is shown in Figure 22.59.

22.7 Building New Palettes

GIMP has two kinds of palettes. One is the colormap, also called an *indexed palette*, which is included with all GIF files, containing a maximum of 256 different colors. Indexed palettes can be automatically defined when you change the image mode from RGB to indexed, but you can also use a "custom palette" that has already been defined.

You can use any palette as a custom palette when converting an image to indexed mode. Working with palettes is like making a tapestry

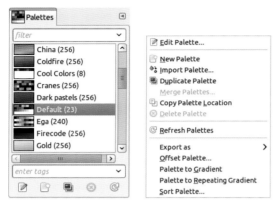

Figure 22.60 *The Palettes dialog and Palettes menu*

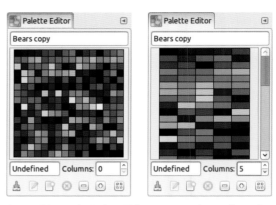

Figure 22.61 *The Palette Editor, as a grid or in five columns*

using a finite set of colors and interspersing those few colors to get the effect of a larger array.

You'll find many GIMP palettes in the system-wide Palettes folder; they have the suffix .gpl (GIMP Palette). The GPL file format contains a short heading followed by the values in the three channels, R, G, and B, as well as an optional name for each color. The order of the values is unimportant.

To see all the existing palettes, open the Palettes dockable dialog (**Image:Windows > Dockable Dialogs > Palettes**), which is shown in Figure 22.60 (left). Figure 22.60 (right) shows the Palettes menu, which you can select from the dialog menu or access by right-clicking inside the dialog. Use this menu to work with palettes directly or access the options by right-clicking the palette you want to edit. You can also use the buttons at the bottom of the Palettes dialog. Like other GIMP objects, palettes have a system-wide and a personal Palettes folder, and you can only edit palettes you create or duplicate.

The Palette Editor

In the Palettes dialog, double-click any palette to open the Palette Editor (Figure 22.61, left).

Clicking any color in the Palette Editor copies it to the foreground color, and $\boxed{\text{CTRL}}$-clicking

copies it to the background color. You can also use the Palette Editor for painting by using the Palette tab of the Color chooser (see "The Color Chooser" on page 254).

One important property in this dockable dialog is the COLUMNS field: If this field is 0, the palette colors are displayed in an optimized way. But you can force them to be displayed in columns, as shown in Figure 22.61 (right).

To change a color in the palette, right-click and select EDIT COLOR (or double-click the color) to open the Color chooser dialog. Using the dialog menu, the bottom buttons, or the right-click menu, you can also delete a color or add the foreground or background color to the palette. You can name the new palette and save it without closing the dialog. Even if you don't explicitly save it, when you close the new palette, it's saved in your personal Palettes folder.

Importing Palettes

Another way to define a new palette is to import it from a gradient, an image, or another palette by selecting **Palettes: Palettes Menu > Import Palette**. When you select this option, the dialog shown in Figure 22.62 opens.

In this dialog, you can select the source and name of the palette. You can also choose the number of different colors for the palette, which cannot be greater than 10,000. But if you import

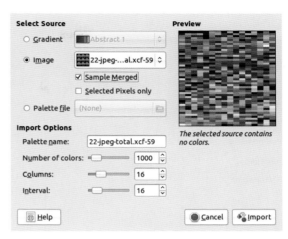

Figure 22.62 *Importing a new palette*   Figure 22.63 *Importing from an RGB image*

the palette from an RGB image, the number of different colors is generally much greater than the maximum, so you'll need to increase the IN-TERVAL, meaning that neighboring colors will be grouped using this vicinity factor. For example, in Figure 22.63, we imported from the base image of Figure 20.5 on page 535, pushed the number of colors to 1000, and set the interval to 16.

Exporting and Duplicating Palettes

Now, let's discuss the remaining entries in the Palettes dialog menu.

- DUPLICATE PALETTE is fairly self-explanatory. The Palette Editor is opened automatically for the new palette.

- EXPORT AS helps you build a table of colors to use in various contexts. The available formats are CSS Style Sheet, Java map, PHP or Python dictionary, and text file. Depending on the palette, the colors may have names. Depending on the output format, the color notation uses various conventions.

- OFFSET PALETTE opens a small dialog where you set the offset value. The number of palette colors that you choose are moved from the end of the palette to the beginning.

This doesn't effect the palette's function, but it does let you rearrange the colors if you're using them to paint, for example.

Palette to Gradient and Sort Palette

The next two entries in the Palettes dialog menu let you use palettes when building gradients. The final entry lets you sort a palette.

- PALETTE TO GRADIENT: Use this option to build and save immediately a new gradient containing all the colors of the present palette, in order. Each color will have the same width in the gradient. This option is best with small palettes because the gradient is easier to edit.

- PALETTE TO REPEATING GRADIENT: The only difference between this option and the previous one is that the first color is repeated at the end of the gradient.

- SORT PALETTE: This opens a dialog for sorting the palette colors based on color model (RGB or HSV) and channel in ascending or descending order. This option is handy when you want to generate a gradient from a palette or when using a palette for painting.

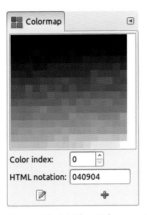

Figure 22.64 *The Colormap Editor*

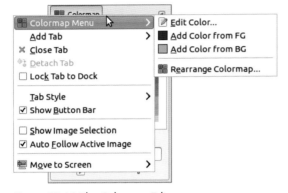

Figure 22.65 *The Colormap Editor menus*

Indexed Palettes

When working on an indexed image, you can edit its indexed palette using the Colormap Editor. The Colormap Editor, shown in Figure 22.64, is a dockable dialog that you access from **Image: Windows > Dockable Dialogs > Colormap**. The menus available are shown in Figure 22.65. As you can see, you can change a color, add new colors from the foreground or background colors (if some space is left in the colormap), or rearrange the indexed palette. Choosing to rearrange the indexed palette opens the window partly shown in Figure 22.66, which also shows the right-click menu.

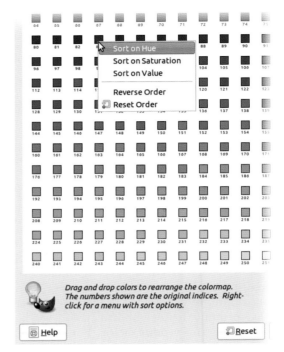

Figure 22.66 *Rearranging an indexed palette*

When you click a color, its index in the colormap appears at the bottom of the dialog, along with its hexadecimal value in the RGB color space (called *HTML notation*). You can change either field: The colormap field selects a color; the hexadecimal field changes the color.

Part III
Appendices

A Vision and Image Representation

In this appendix, we'll explore the nature of vision, image perception, and the re-creation of images in print and on screen. This subject is complicated and technical, but we'll try to present it in an intuitive and easy-to-follow way.

A.1 The Physiology of Vision

An image does not really exist if we can't see it. We're able to see things thanks to the complex and precise organ known as the eye. Our eyes produce the images we see by interpreting a small range of the electromagnetic spectrum known as the *visible spectrum*.

How the Human Eye Works

Figure A.1 is a diagram of the human eye, showing its main components. Light enters the eye through the pupil and is focused by the crystalline lens, and an image is formed in the back of the eye on the retina. The lens is flexible, and small muscles around it allow it to deform to change its focal length. This allows us to focus on objects at various distances. The diameter of the pupil is also variable, which provides a way to regulate the amount of light that enters the eye.

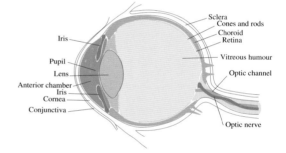

Figure A.1 *The human eye*

Figure A.2 shows a cross section of the retina. Its structure is a very complicated network of sensitive nerve cells. The cells that sense color and light are the *rods* and the *cones*. The main bodies of these cells are buried inside the retina. Light within the visible spectrum is received by the tail ends of the cells, shown on the far right of the cross section in Figure A.2.

The rods in each eye number from 120 to 150 million and are located primarily on the periphery of the retina. Cones number only 6 to 7 million and are located primarily in the center of the retina, in the area called the *fovea*. Figure A.3 shows this variable distribution. It also shows the *blind spot*, which is the place in the retina where the optic nerve emerges from the eye.

Light

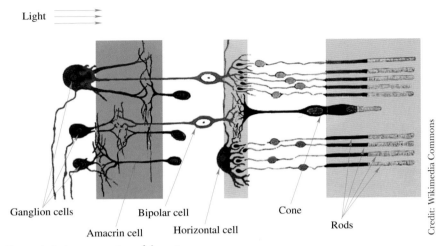

Ganglion cells   Bipolar cell   Cone

Amacrin cell   Horizontal cell   Rods

Credit: Wikimedia Commons

Figure A.2 *A cross section of the retina*

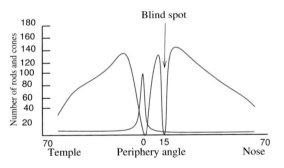

Figure A.3 *Distribution of rods (dark red) and cones (blue) on the retina*

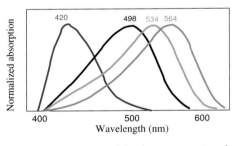

Figure A.4 *Sensitivity of the three categories of cones*

Color Perception

Rods and cones differ in another very important way. Rods are quite sensitive to brightness but not to differences in wavelength. On the other hand, cones just need enough light to work, but they're really sensitive to wavelength. Cones are divided into three categories, depending on the wavelength they're sensitive to. As Figure A.4 shows, blue cones are most sensitive to a wavelength of around 420 nanometers (nm), which corresponds to the color blue. Green cones are most sensitive at around 534 nm, and red cones are most sensitive around 564 nm (which is actually yellow, not red). Also, blue cones represent only 1/50 of the total number; green cones represent approximately 2/5 of the total, and red cones represent approximately 3/5. The black

You're probably not aware of the blind spots that exist in your field of vision. Try this experiment to observe their effect: Close one eye, and look at a fixed point in front of you. Place a small object (such as your forefinger) in front of you at eye level and on the same side as your open eye (the distance between this object and your eye should be between 12 and 20 inches). Now slowly move the object toward your nose. When the angle between the fixed point in front of you and the moving object is about 15°, the object should disappear. Note that your perceptual and cognitive systems usually keep you from noticing this blind spot—your brain can reconstitute the missing information and fill in the gap.

curve in Figure A.4 illustrates the sensitivity range of rod cells.

This distribution of rods and cones has some interesting consequences:

- When not enough light is available, we can't distinguish different colors. For instance, imagine that you're sitting in a garden just before dawn. Several cats are prowling around, and they all appear to be gray. When dawn arrives, the cats slowly regain their color—brown and orange—and the grass grows progressively greener as the sky brightens.

- Only the center of the retina can perceive colors. But our cognitive system infers the colors in the periphery of our vision and adds them, so we don't usually notice this limitation.

- We have very few cones that are sensitive to blue (only 1/50 of the total), yet these cones are responsible for a relatively large range of wavelengths. This means that looking at a picture or landscape whose colors are primarily purple or blue is more tiresome for the eye, especially if the image contains a lot of fine detail. Distinguishing differences in brightness in a scene that contains a lot of blue is also more difficult.

So our perception of color results from the differences among signals sent to the brain by cones sensitive to different wavelengths of light. The color range we can see is defined by the wavelength range our cones are sensitive to. As you will see later, most colors are not defined by a single wavelength; such *monochromatic* colors can be generated by artificial devices, but natural colors are generally a mixture of various wavelengths. We can only sense monochromatic colors that correspond to one of the three cone types. For example, our eyes can't distinguish a monochromatic yellow from a yellow made by combining red and green light. Because we don't have cones specifically sensitive to yellow, the resulting signals from our red and green cones are the same regardless of whether the

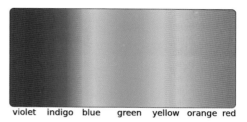

violet indigo blue green yellow orange red

Figure A.5 *The visible spectrum (traditional view)*

yellow is made from red and green light or from pure yellow light.

If we consider the visible spectrum as it's traditionally represented (see Figure A.5), we might get the impression that it's precisely bound on both sides and that it contains seven discrete colors. This overly simple view is not based on science. A more accurate illustration is shown in Figure A.6. The visible spectrum is a tiny subrange of the electromagnetic spectrum, without a blunt beginning or end. The visible spectrum has no real indigo color, and the red area is much larger than the others. The limits of the visible spectrum are fuzzy because the violet color disappears into ultraviolet, and the red color disappears into infrared. Additionally, the visible spectrum differs for some species: Birds and some insects can see ultraviolet.

Light coming from the sun is absorbed by Earth's atmosphere at rates that vary depending on the wavelength. The visible spectrum is the segment of the electromagnetic spectrum that is best able to navigate through Earth's atmosphere and reach its surface and the objects on it. But the atmosphere does scatter blue light more than red light, which explains why the sky looks blue to us (weather permitting).

Color Blindness

Our perception of colors depends on a lot of factors, including our cognitive system. As we see in Figure A.6, red colors cover almost half of the visible spectrum, and red light has the longest wavelength of the visible colors. But our eye's cones that are sensitive to the long wavelengths

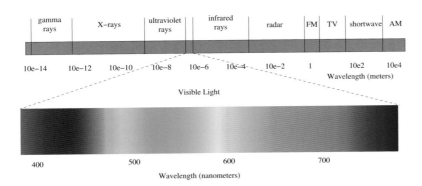

Figure A.6 *The visible spectrum in the electromagnetic spectrum*

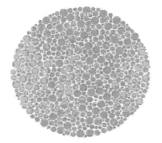

Figure A.7 *A test for color blindness*

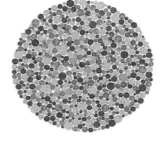

Figure A.8 *Another test for color blindness*

mainly perceive yellow. Despite this, we are normally able to distinguish a variety of different reds as well as orange and yellow.

Thus we see that our perception of colors is not simply a reception of signals emitted by the retina cells but rather a complex interpretation that occurs in the brain. When it works normally, this process allows us to differentiate colors and appreciate the effect of various color combinations.

The most common abnormality of visual perception is called *color blindness*. You may have seen tests for color blindness before, such as those in Figures A.7 and A.8.

The human eye normally contains three types of cones. But sometimes one or more of these is missing. (Many animals have only two types of cones.) If the red cones are missing, a person has a disorder called *daltonism*, also known

Figure A.9 *The traditional color rainbow*

as *protanopia*. Figure A.9 shows the colors of the rainbow as most people see them, and Figure A.10 shows how someone with protanopia sees them. This is the most frequent type of color blindness and is characterized by the dark appearance of the color red.

Missing green cones result in a disorder called *deuteranopia* (illustrated in Figure A.11). This type of color blindness is about as common as protanopia. Missing blue cones result in *tritanopia* (illustrated in Figure A.12). Tritanopia is extremely rare.

Figure A.10 *The rainbow as seen by a person with protanopia*

Figure A.11 *The rainbow as seen by a person with deuteranopia*

Figure A.12 *The rainbow as seen by a person with tritanopia*

Figure A.13 *The rainbow as seen by a person with monochromacy*

Anomalies also occur when all three types of cones are present but some of them are malformed and, as a result, inactive. Because they're inactive, the malformed cones result in the same types of color blindness that missing cones do. There is also a very rare disorder called *monochromacy*, or total color blindness, which occurs when all the cones are missing or inactive. Figure A.13 shows what

a rainbow would look like to someone with monochromacy.

Be aware of these abnormalities because they can affect the accessibility of images, books, and websites. For example, an image that depends entirely on the contrast between orange and green would be meaningless to a person with protanopia or deuteranopia. These two types of color blindness are present in 2% of all males, which is a significant number of people.

Optical Illusions

Whereas color blindness is a deficiency that affects a minority of the population, an optical illusion works on the majority of people. Optical illusions occur when our perception system partially fails and causes us to interpret something in a way that contradicts reality. Optical illusions are interesting for several reasons:

- They provide hints that help us understand how our cognitive processes work.

- They have inspired many artists to create fascinating pictures, for example, M.C. Escher, Salvador Dalí, Giuseppe Arcimboldo, and Victor Vasarely.

- They are fun to create and experience and can be made with the help of GIMP.

A *literal optical illusion* occurs when we see an image other than the one that was created. One of the best examples of this is Adelson's checker-shadow illusion, shown in Figure A.14. The square labeled A appears to be much darker than the square labeled B, but they are actually the exact same shade of gray. We interpret the color of the second square based on the fact that it lies in the shadow of the green cylinder. The only way for most people to see the reality of the image is to create (using GIMP, of course) a parallelogram that links squares A and B and to fill in the parallelogram with the common shade of gray (see Figure A.15).

Credit: Wikimedia Commons

Figure A.14 *Adelson's checker-shadow illusion*

Figure A.15 *Demystifying the illusion*

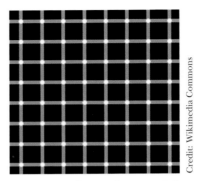

Credit: Wikimedia Commons

Figure A.16 *The scintillating grid illusion*

Credit: Wikimedia Commons

Figure A.17 *An ambiguous illusion*

Physiological illusions occur due to excessive stimulation of some type, either of the eye itself or of the brain. For example, Figure A.16 shows the scintillating grid illusion. The intersections of the gray lines are white dots, but if you look at the center of the grid, you see black dots in distant intersections, appearing and disappearing quickly and at random. The Hermann grid is a similar illusion, but the white dots at the intersections are absent.

A third type of optical illusion is the *cognitive illusion*, which occurs due to unconscious inferences resulting from our assumptions about the world. Cognitive illusions can be divided into four categories.

Rubin's vase, illustrated in Figure A.17, is an example of the cognitive illusion known as an *ambiguous illusion*. This image can appear to be a vase or two facing profiles, depending on what the viewer perceives as the subject versus the background. The representation of a cube as a line drawing is another example of an ambiguous illusion. When you draw a simple cube, telling for certain which side is closest to the viewer and which is farthest away is impossible.

The café wall illusion, illustrated in Figure A.18, is a striking example of another type of cognitive illusion: a *distorting illusion*. The variable positions of the black squares create the illusion that the horizontal lines are curved, rather than parallel. To check that they are actually parallel, hold a ruler up to the image, with the zero at the top line, and move it along the lines. The distance between the lines is the same all the way across.

Fraser's spiral, shown in Figure A.19, is another distorting illusion. Although it looks like a spiral, the image is actually composed of a set

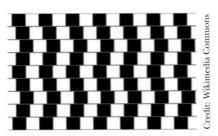

Figure A.18 *The café wall illusion: a distorting illusion*

Figure A.19 *Fraser's spiral: another distorting illusion*

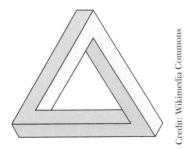

Figure A.20 *Penrose's triangle: a paradox illusion*

of concentric circles. If you're skeptical, follow the outline of one of the circles with a pencil or place a circular object on top of the image.

Penrose's triangle, illustrated in Figure A.20, is an example of the cognitive illusion known as a *paradox illusion*. A paradox illusion appears to represent a three-dimensional solid form, but the form that it represents is actually impossible. M.C. Escher created some celebrated artwork that relied on this idea, like the impossible

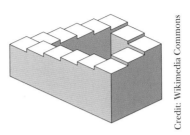

Figure A.21 *The impossible stairs: another paradox illusion*

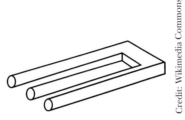

Figure A.22 *The blivet: yet another paradox illusion*

staircase shown in Figure A.21. The blivet, shown in Figure A.22, is another example of a paradox illusion.

A.2 Image Representation

Now that you've seen how colors and images in the real world are perceived by your visual and cognitive systems, we'll discuss how they're represented on the computer.

Discretization

Although it seems counterintuitive, all images are represented discretely, rather than continuously. This is referred to as *discretization*. Images are composed of a large number of tiny, discrete dots, all very close to each other. Because they're so small and so close, we can't distinguish these dots, and so they create the illusion of a continuous image. Consider the following image representations:

- *A visual image:* When an image is focused in our eye, the wavelength and intensity of light

Figure A.23 *A digital image*

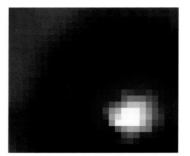

Figure A.24 *Zooming in on part of the image*

are sensed by the rod and cone cells in the retina. Although these cells are extremely small and close together, they are discrete receptors.

- *A digital image:* In a digital camera, an image, like the one in Figure A.23, is focused on a matrix of photoreceptors. These photoreceptors are very similar to the retina, although the density of receptors is much lower than the density of cones in the fovea.

- *A photograph:* On photographic paper, the image is represented with crystals of silver salt, which are very small but discrete. In fact, you can see the grain on a traditional photograph with a good magnifying glass.

- *A printout:* On a printed document, discretization is represented by carbon grains (for a laser printer) or by ink spots (for an inkjet printer).

- *A computer screen:* On a computer screen, the pixels that constitute the screen surface are discrete. You can clearly see this in Figure A.24, which shows an extreme close-up of a small part of Figure A.23.

Color is also discretized:

- The *eye* has specialized cones that each perceive a single color of light.

- The *digital camera* has three types of photoreceptors, and each is sensitive to a specific color (red, green, or blue).

- *Photographic paper* is made up of three layers, one for each fundamental color (red, green, and blue), and each layer is partially transparent.

- *Printers* juxtapose colored dots, sometimes in layers with partial transparency. A printer must have at least three different ink colors but usually has more, for reasons we discuss in "The Subtractive Model" on page 606.

- On a *computer screen*, each pixel is actually composed of three subpixels in the three fundamental colors: red, green, and blue.

No image is truly continuous, although many appear as though they are, so all representations are only approximations of reality and our perception relies strongly on the capabilities of our cognitive system.

Digitalization

In the previous section, we discussed five different situations in which an image is discretely represented. In the eye and the digital camera, each receptor generates a number to represent the intensity of the received signal. (Admittedly, this isn't exactly the case with the retina, but the signal can be measured and quantified.) On photo paper, printed documents, and computer screens, the dots (or pixels) emit light according to some signal strength, which, in turn, can be represented with a number.

Using one number to represent signal strength is enough as long as we're only dealing with grayscale images, for example, if we only consider the signal of rod cells or if we're printing in black and white. If we introduce color, we need at least three values for each pixel or three types of cones in the retina.

An image on a computer requires one number per pixel to represent a grayscale image or (at least) three numbers per pixel to represent a color image. To keep the representation of a pixel from taking up too much space, all representations use integer numbers in a limited subrange. The subrange for pixel values is [0 to 255]. This subrange was chosen because it fits exactly into 1 byte of memory, which means a single color pixel will occupy 3 bytes.

So in a grayscale image, you have 256 possible gray levels for each pixel. In a color image, you have 256 possible values for each color, so you have $256 \times 256 \times 256$, or $16,777,216$ different color values. But professional photographers often prefer to use 2 bytes for each pixel, which results in the value subrange [0 to $65,536$]. Recall that 1 byte results in $2^8 \times 256$ possible values, so 2 bytes leads to 2^{16} or 65,536 values. Whether our eyes can even distinguish such an enormous range of different values is open to debate.

Although most images can be stored in 3 bytes (one for each fundamental color), a pixel frequently uses 32 bits (or 4 bytes) because that size is more natural for a computer; it's the size of the main processor's registers (for most machines), and it's a power of 2 (think binary). The extra byte may be used to represent other things, such as transparency.

Now you know that color pixels are represented by three numbers, but does this really allow you to represent all visible colors? Although this question is actually very complicated, the answer is—unfortunately—no.

Color	Range
Violet	380–440
Blue	440–490
Green	490–565
Yellow	565–590
Orange	590–630
Red	630–780

Figure A.25 *Color Wavelengths*

A simple (or *monochromatic*) color is characterized by its wavelength, and the wavelength ranges in the visible spectrum have common names. In Figure A.25, they are given in nanometers (nm). Note that these ranges are arbitrary approximations and are irregular: For instance, the range for violet is 60 nm, for yellow it's 25 nm, and for red it's 150 nm.

In addition, our visual perception system is not designed to distinguish between simple colors and complex colors. For example, pure light at 580 nm is yellow. But the eye cannot distinguish this pure yellow from a yellow obtained by a specific blend of red and green. Also, most colors in nature are not simple colors. You can't find pink, brown, or purple in the rainbow. And white, black, and all shades of gray are also "colors" that appear in images because we can perceive them.

So most real colors are not monochromatic, and our perception system can't distinguish between a monochromatic and a properly blended color anyway. The problem is that the representation using three numbers in a limited subrange does not allow us to represent all visible colors. For example, imagine these three numbers as coordinates in three-dimensional space. Because the coordinates are limited to the subrange [0 to 255], every point will lie inside a cube whose sides are 256 units long. The sides and corners of this cube have different meanings depending on the model used, as we'll discuss in the next section. But points outside of the cube simply cannot be represented.

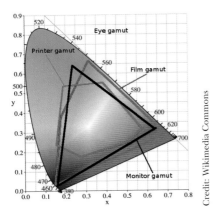

Credit: Wikimedia Commons

Figure A.26 *The CIE chromaticity diagram*

The full subset of colors that can be represented in a given system is called a *(color) gamut*. The Commission Internationale de l'Éclairage (CIE; the International Commission on Illumination) defined a model for the visible colors, represented in Figure A.26. Along the horseshoe curve we find the fully saturated colors of the rainbow, with blue numbers that indicate the corresponding wavelengths in nanometers [400-700]. The straight line at the bottom is the purple boundary. The content of the diagram is the whole set of visible colors based on normal human vision.

Material colors, obtained by mixing colored paints, for example, have more possibilities (a larger gamut) because black or white can be mixed with the colors. They would, therefore, require another dimension with values from black to white in the diagram.

This diagram is actually impossible to represent with complete accuracy, especially in a printed book. (It gives too much prominence to green and not enough to yellow, and the white point, located somewhere in the center, is not really white.) But the chromaticity diagram can be used to show the color gamuts of devices (also shown in Figure A.26). Some devices have a larger gamut than others, but all of them are smaller than the full visible gamut. The smallest one is that of the common inkjet printer, which

is especially bad at representing vivid colors. The black triangle corresponds to cathode ray tube (CRT) monitors, but the gamut of a liquid crystal display device is very similar.

Compression

Being aware of the size of an image file is important, whether the image is stored in memory, on a disk, on a CD, or on a USB stick. Excessively large files can fill up a small storage space or slow down a processor. But even more important is to be aware of the size of the image that will be displayed on a screen, or printed, because an image file is created to be displayed.

For example, suppose we have an image that's 1024×768 pixels (i.e., the size of a rather small computer screen). This image contains 786,432 pixels. If the image is grayscale (sometimes improperly called monochrome or black and white), its file size in bytes is the same as the number of pixels (around 768KB). If the image is in color, you need at least 3 bytes for each pixel, and the file size would be about 2.3MB.

On an LCD screen with a definition of 100 pixels per inch, this image displays as an approximately 10×8 inch rectangle. But on a laser printer with a definition of 600 pixels per inch, the image will be only 1.7×1.28 inches.

The definition of the representation device (such as a printer) is fundamental, and to make nice prints that are larger than a thumbnail, you must build rather large files. Modern digital cameras can capture 10 million pixels or more for a single image. A color image taken with one of these cameras is at least 30MB. At that size, only 25 photos would fit on a normal CD, and fewer than 150 would fit on a DVD. That's also too large a file to send easily to friends and family via email.

Because of this, compressing images is necessary. There are two main compression techniques: *lossless compression*, where no data is lost and the image maintains its exact initial state, and *lossy compression*, where some data loss

Figure A.27 *An image with continuous color variation*

Figure A.28 *The same image reduced to 256 colors*

occurs and the resulting image is lower quality than the original.

Lossless compression reduces the image size in a meaningful way only if the image contains a large amount of redundant information. This typically occurs if the image file uses *indexed representation*. The number of different colors in an indexed image is limited, and these colors are stored in a *colormap*. The pixels are represented as indexes in this colormap, which results in an image with many identical pixels. The advantage of indexing is that the lossless compression rate is excellent, although the overall image quality is inherently worse than with direct representation. For example, Figure A.27 shows an image with a continuous color variation. Figure A.28 shows the same image after converting it to indexed mode with 256 colors (the maximum). For more information on indexing and colormaps, see Chapters 12 and 20.

Many image compression formats are available, but we cover only three here:

- GIF is an indexed format with all the drawbacks that implies. It provides lossless compression, but if an image with continuous color variation is exported as a GIF, information is lost during indexing. GIF images also cannot contain continuous transparency. The format is best suited for diagrams, line drawings, and simple animations.

- JPEG is a nonindexed format that uses a lossy compression technique, with a compression rate that the user can adjust. JPEG is the format of choice for photographs and is used as an output format by most digital cameras.

- PNG can be used for both indexed and nonindexed images. With indexing, PNG has the same properties as GIF but with a better compression rate and the capability to represent continuous transparency. But PNG cannot represent animations. With nonindexed images, it provides lossless compression, which leads to a higher-quality final image than JPEG compression but at a lower compression rate.

File formats can have a major impact on image size and quality. Here's some general advice for choosing the right format for an image:

- If you've created the image yourself and it's composed mostly of lines, text, and flat colors, use indexed PNG. Build the colormap with care.

- If you create a simple animation, store it as a GIF.

- If the image is a photograph, choose JPEG in most cases. But if you need to add text to the photograph, choose PNG. Do not increase the quality rate to more than 85 because doing so increases the file size without visible effect. Also, don't convert the same image to JPEG multiple times because deterioration is cumulative.

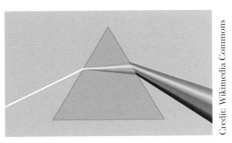

Figure A.29 *The decomposition of light by refraction*

A.3   Color Representation

In nature, things are either translucent, reflective, or opaque, and they have a unique hue. Here's a simple explanation of color: When sunlight strikes an object, the object absorbs a part of the solar spectrum and reflects the rest back at the viewer. The color that the object does not absorb—the color it reflects—is the color that you see. But not all of the visible light that we see comes from the sun. Lightning, fire, and phosphorescent organisms all produce their own light. Additionally, many other natural phenomena lead to visible color.

How Colors Are Produced

Color can be generated in the following ways:

- *Color by refraction:* When light passes through a refractive material, it is split in a pattern that depends on its wavelength. Because white light is made up of a combination of all visible wavelengths, it is split into a rainbow of colors. You've probably seen this happen as light passes through a prism whose nonparallel faces increase the light's refraction (see Figure A.29). But when light passes through a parallelepipedic piece of glass, which has parallel faces, the first face refracts the light, and the second face refocuses it back into white light.

- *Rainbows:* A unique case of color by both reflection and refraction is the rainbow. Solar light is refracted by a large number of tiny water drops. These droplets are

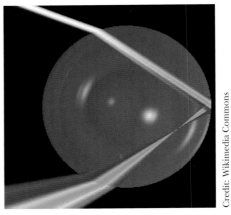

Figure A.30 *Direct light propagation in a droplet*

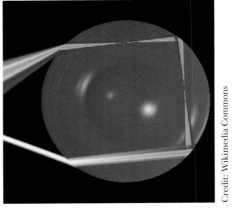

Figure A.31 *Indirect light propagation in a droplet*

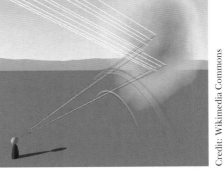

Figure A.32 *Propagation of light rays and reflection and refraction in cloud droplets*

spheres, which disperse the colors in a uniform way, as shown in Figures A.30 and A.31. The direct refraction creates the primary rainbow. A secondary rainbow forms when light that's reflected on the bottom of a droplet is then indirectly refracted. A double rainbow is illustrated in Figure A.32.

- *Color by diffusion:* When light passes through a space that contains many small particles, such as the atmosphere, it's diffused. The dynamics of the diffusion depend on the size of the particles and on the wavelength of the light passing through. Some wavelengths are diffused and reflected in random directions, some are absorbed, and some will pass through. One of the most common cases of color diffusion is the blue sky. As light moves through the atmosphere, most of the longer wavelengths, such as red, orange, and yellow, pass straight through. Much of the shorter-wavelength blue light is absorbed by the gas molecules, however. The absorbed blue light is then radiated back out and scattered in every direction. That scattered light fills the sky, making it look blue.

- *Color by interference:* Light is partially reflected by the first face of a thin, semitransparent material, and the remaining light passes through and is reflected by the second face at the far side of the material. The reflected light from both faces combines, and depending on the depth of the material (the distance between faces), wavelengths are either amplified or canceled out. The resulting phenomenon is called *interference* and can be seen on soap bubbles, mother of pearl (see Figure A.33), puddles covered with oil, and other shimmery surfaces. The color appears to change depending on the angle of observation and can cause iridescence if the material is barbed. The striking colors of a peacock's tail (see Figure A.34) are produced by interference, as are those on a butterfly's wing. Peacock feathers and butterfly wings are both barbed surfaces, so they exhibit iridescence.

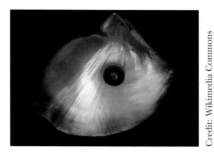

Figure A.33 *Color by interference on a shell and a black pearl*

Figure A.34 *Color by interference on a peacock's tail*

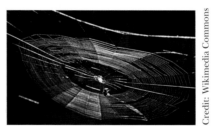

Figure A.35 *Color by diffraction on a spider web*

- *Color by diffraction:* When light moves around an object, or passes through a very small hole or slot, its path changes, like water flowing around rocks or passing from a narrow creek into a lake. The path that the light takes as it moves past the obstacle depends on the wavelength. White light is split into a rainbow of colors. The effect is often subtle, but you can see colors by diffraction on the threads of a spider web in certain conditions (see Figure A.35).

The main characteristic of colors by refraction, diffusion, interference, or diffraction is that they're passive and so can yield only a *subrange* of colors from the solar spectrum. If light of a single color undergoes one of these four processes, the result is the same color. No other colors are produced during the process.

When we artificially create an image to represent something we've seen, we can't use these phenomena because we couldn't easily produce all the colors we would need. Instead, we use color emitters, like the phosphor on a cathode ray tube, or bodies that are only transparent to certain colors, like the liquid crystals on an LCD screen. We can also use opaque materials, such as paint or mosaic tiles, that reflect only certain colors. Ultimately, the color of a material is determined in one of three ways:

- *Color by emission:* The sun appears white because it emits light in all visible frequencies (and many invisible frequencies, too). An incandescent light bulb or a fluorescent tube has a wavelength spectrum similar to that of the sun. A phosphor pixel on a CRT screen emits light at one specific wavelength.

- *Color by reflection:* The wavelengths reflected are the only ones that are visible—the others are all absorbed by the material. The color of the material depends on the light it receives: In normal sunlight, a piece of chalk or a sheet of paper looks white because it receives white light and reflects all wavelengths in the visible range. But in red light, they would appear red.

- *Color by absorption:* For semitransparent materials, such as water and ice, only the wavelengths that pass through the material are visible—the rest are absorbed. For example, if a piece of sea ice absorbs green wavelengths less than other wavelengths, it appears to be green. Once again, a given frequency can only be visible if it's present in the light that strikes the material.

The colors we see are created differently in the three examples just given. With color by reflection, a material that reflects all wavelengths is white, and a material that reflects nothing (absorbs all wavelengths) is black. With color by absorption, a material that absorbs all wavelengths is opaque, and a material that absorbs no wavelengths is transparent. Blue paint reflects the blue frequencies and absorbs the others. Blue glass also absorbs frequencies other than blue, but unlike blue paint, the blue light that gives glass a color passes through the glass to reach us. These concepts lead to the different models of color representation: additive, subtractive, and HSV.

The Additive Model

The *additive model* is not the most intuitive, but it is the most natural. It corresponds to color by emission and to the way our eyes perceive colors.

We already saw that the retina contains three types of cones that are sensitive to red, green, and blue light. These are the three fundamental colors of the additive model. They are also used on computer screens (both CRTs and LCDs): Each pixel contains three subpixels that emit red, green, or blue light.

This model is commonly referred to as *RGB*. On the screen, the relative intensity of light in each subpixel determines what color is produced. If the three subpixels are all at maximum intensity, white light is produced. If they're all at minimum intensity, they produce "black light" (i.e., no light). If they're all at equal levels somewhere between the minimum and the maximum, gray light is produced. A lower intensity results in a darker final color.

Note that although the white light emitted by the sun contains the full wavelength range of visible light, we still perceive a white color when only three wavelengths are present. Whenever all three of the cone types are fully stimulated, we perceive something to be white.

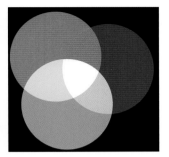

Figure A.36 *The additive model*

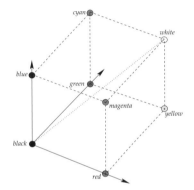

Figure A.37 *The RGB cube*

If light is emitted only by the subpixels of one of the fundamental colors, we see that color. If two different subpixels emit light, we get a *complementary color*, as shown in Figure A.36. Red and green produce *yellow*, red and blue produce *magenta*, and green and blue produce *cyan*. The three complementary colors also exist as monochromatic colors: They're present in the solar spectrum as single wavelengths.

Because the three fundamental color values are in a limited subrange (usually [0 to 255]), the points they define in three-dimensional space are limited to a cube, as shown in Figure A.37. The corners of this cube are labeled with the fundamental colors, the secondary colors, and black and white. The diagonal that links the black corner (coordinates 0,0,0) to the white

Figure A.38 *Decomposition into the RGB channels*

corner (coordinates 255,255,255) is the *diagonal of grays*. Each point is opposite the point of its *complementary color*.

The RGB cube defines the gamut of all colors that can be represented on a computer screen. This gamut is smaller than the visible gamut of colors that we can perceive, as shown in Figure A.26 on page 600.

Figure A.38 shows an image decomposed into its three RGB *channels*. Brighter areas indicate areas where the corresponding channel is more active.

The RGB model is not intuitive: It requires a leap of faith or some serious thought to accept that adding red to green produces yellow. Most people think of color as pigments. When you mix red and green paint, you get something closer to brown, and if you mix the three fundamental colors, red, green, and blue, you get some darker color, not white. Pigment doesn't follow the additive model.

Another challenge of the RGB model is that matching a particular color is difficult. For example, how do we get the color of a pink rose, clean copper, or mahogany wood? The answer could be 248,192,236 for the pink rose; 198, 113,76 for copper; and 100,0,0 for mahogany. All three of these materials appear to be dominated by red, yet pink and copper require a surprising amount of green and blue. (And the mahogany requires only a small amount of red.) Clearly, a more intuitive model would make image creation easier.

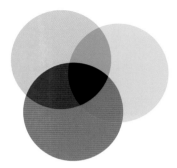

Figure A.39 *The subtractive model*

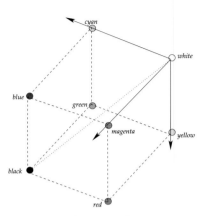

Figure A.40 *The CMY cube*

The Subtractive Model

The *subtractive model* (also known as the *CMY model*) is used to produce color by absorption, as pigments do. Its three fundamental colors are the complementary colors in the RGB model: cyan, magenta, and yellow. Each fundamental color absorbs light of a certain wavelength. If the three colors are all at maximum value, they produce black. If they're all at zero, they produce white. This model assumes that we're adding color to a white surface.

Figure A.39 shows the three fundamental colors and their combinations. The complementary colors of the CMY model are the fundamental colors of the RGB model: Cyan plus magenta is blue, cyan plus yellow is green, and magenta plus yellow is red. When the intensity of all fundamental colors is low, the color is washed out.

The CMY cube (shown in Figure A.40) is complementary to the RGB cube: The same colors are in the corners, but the coordinate values are the complement to the RGB coordinates. The gamut is the same because the cube is the same.

Figure A.41 shows the same image as Figure A.38 but decomposed into its three CMY channels. As before, the lighter areas indicate more active channels, but in this case, when all channels are active, an area is darker, which gives the channels a negative appearance.

The CMY model is the native model for printing. Microscopic dots of the fundamental colors are printed on paper, and their juxtaposition

Figure A.41 *Decomposition into the CMY channels*

Figure A.42 *Decomposition into the CMYK channels*

produces the effect of the subtractive method. Transparent inks can also be used in overlapping layers to produce a similar result. But generating a good black color using the three fundamental colors is difficult, and black ink is relatively cheap, so most printers also include black and use the *CMYK model* (K stands for black).

The values of these four channels are easily computed from the CMY values: K is the minimum (lowest value) across the three channels in a given pixel, and the other channels are replaced with their value minus K. Sometimes the printer requires a lower value for K, with corresponding changes in the other three channels to avoid overly dark, wet prints. In those cases, the values of the other channels are computed in a way that preserves the colors as best as possible.

Figure A.42 shows the same image as Figure A.41 but decomposed into the four CMYK channels. We see the CMY channels are much darker than in Figure A.41, which means that much less ink is needed for printing this image.

Low-cost inkjet printers use only the four ink colors of the CMYK model. As the quality and cost of printers increase, the number of ink colors generally increases as well. Midrange printers frequently add a light cyan and a light magenta ink. High-cost printers, intended for professional photography, add several gray and black inks, which enhance unsaturated colors.

The HSV Model

Neither the RGB model nor the CMY models are very intuitive to work with. Determining the purity, intensity, or hue of a given color when using those models is difficult because each color is represented abstractly as three coordinates.

In fact, some research has indicated that our visual system doesn't simply transmit the three signals emitted by the three types of cones to the brain. The R, G, and B signals are first combined into $R + G$, $R - G$ and $B - (R + G)$. The $R + G$ signal corresponds to what is called *luminance*. Luminance is equivalent to the value dimension in pigment colors, which goes from black to white. The blue component doesn't contribute to the perceived lightness or darkness of a given color, possibly because of the very small proportion of blue cones present in the retina. The two other values ($R - G$ and $B - (R + G)$) represent the *chrominance*, or the hue of the color. These concepts contributed to the CIE standards and the chromaticity diagram shown in Figure A.26 on page 600.

The *HSV model* is based on these concepts and is designed to be a more intuitive way to

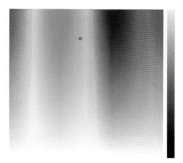

Figure A.43 *The HSV model*

represent colors. Conversions are required to switch between HSV and the other two models, but any modern computer can easily handle the computations needed. This model is the best one to use when you want to choose a color or build a color scheme for a project. The CMYK model is useful only for printing, and, in fact, most software tools for printing make the necessary conversion at the last minute, using information specific to the printer being used. The RGB model is a very important model because all images are internally represented using it. To sum up, images are stored as RGB, the HSV model provides an intuitive way to choose colors, and printing software usually converts an image to CMYK just before printing it.

Now let's look more closely at the HSV model, which is shown in Figure A.43. It contains three coordinates:

- H is the *hue*. The hue is a value on a color wheel that ranges from 0 to 360 degrees. Red is $0°$, and the hue wavelength decreases as the angle increases.

  Figure A.43 represents the color wheel as an unrolled cylinder. The "angle" increases from 0 on the left to 360 on the right. Most of the colors shown are monochromatic, except for purple, which is present at the transition between red and violet.

- S is the *saturation*. Saturation is represented as a percentage: Full saturation (pure color) is 100%, and white (no color) is 0%. As the percentage decreases, the color becomes more

Figure A.44 *Decomposition into the HSV channels: From the top left, you see the original image, and its H, S, and V channels.*

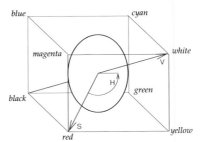

Figure A.45 *The HSV model in the RGB cube*

washed out. In Figure A.43, the saturation is represented by the vertical dimension of the unrolled cylinder and goes from 0 (at the bottom) to 100 (at the top).

- V is the *value*. Value is also a percentage: Fully luminous is 100%, and black (no luminance) is 0%. When the percentage decreases, the color darkens. In Figure A.43, the value is the vertical bar on the right, from 0 (at the bottom) to 100 (at the top).

The small circle in Figure A.43 specifies a precise color (a slightly desaturated cyan hue). The value bar shows this hue at the top and darkens it as it goes down.

Figure A.44 shows the decomposition of an image into the three channels of the HSV model. Because the H and S channels are represented here as grayscale images, they aren't really meaningful. But the V channel is a good representation of the image in grayscale.

Graphically representing the relationship between the HSV model and the RGB model is not easy. Figure A.45 shows the HSV circle and its vectors inside the RGB cube.

The space defined by the three values of the HSV model is represented as a cylinder. But black fills the cylinder's entire bottom. The conical representation, shown in Figure A.27 on page 601, eliminates that redundancy by representing black as the point of the cone and white as the center of the top circle.

A.4 Exercises

So far, we've only presented theoretical information. But the illustrations in this appendix are good examples of what you can do with a tool like GIMP. We created some of these illustrations with a vector graphics program, rather than with GIMP. This is the case, for example, for Figure A.1 on page 591 and Figure A.37 on page 605. We found other images in the Wikimedia Commons collection. We did, however, build or edit several of the images with GIMP. You can begin to explore the potential of GIMP through the following exercises, although you may not be able to complete them until you've read some of the other chapters in this book.

Exercise A.1. We created Figures A.10 through A.13 on page 595 in GIMP using Figure A.9 on page 594 as a starting point. How would you do this?

Exercise A.2. We found the CIE chromatic diagram on Wikimedia Commons. How could you use this original image to make an image similar to Figure A.26 on page 600?

Exercise A.3. Figures A.36 on page 605 and A.39 on page 606 were entirely created with GIMP. Try to re-create them.

Exercise A.4. Using a photograph or picture of your own, try to reproduce the figures that show the decomposition of an image into channels, such as Figure A.38 on page 605.

B Tips and Hints for Selected Exercises

This appendix contains tips to help you complete some of the exercises at the end of the chapters in the first part of this book, as well as in Appendix A.

Chapter 1

Exercise 1.5 The main problem with using the tablet's stylus for signing is that you must look at the screen while signing. Essentially, you're signing on the screen with the stylus. Fortunately, it gets easier with practice. (To practice, try using the stylus as the controller for a video game.)

Exercise 1.6 Process your photograph at a large resolution. Once you've finished processing, select **Image: Filters > Map > Small tiles** to generate the final sheet.

Chapter 2

Exercise 2.1 The five eyedropper buttons are explained in "Levels" on page 258.

Exercise 2.5 The Sharpen filters are explained in Section 17.3.

Chapter 3

All of the tools needed for the various exercises are explained in detail in Chapter 15.

Chapter 4

Exercise 4.1 The following filters manage tilability:

- **Image: Filters > Distort > Ripple**
- **Image: Filters > Render > Clouds > Solid Noise**
- **Image: Filters > Render > Pattern > Maze**
- **Image: Filters > Render > Pattern > Sinus**

The filters in the **Image: Filters > Render** menu are especially useful for generating textures. See Chapter 17 for more details.

Exercise 4.2 Oilify was used the second time to soften the curve. If you skip it, edge detection generates an angular pattern. You could try using artistic filters other than Oilify and Cubism in GIMPressionist. For example, you could replace IWarp with another distort filter, such as Waves, to create a pattern with strong central symmetry that disappears if you then apply a filter like Cubism.

Exercise 4.4 You'll find a good tutorial on the GIMP User Group website: *http://gug.criticalhit. dk/tutorials/ronq1/*. This tutorial uses an old version of GIMP, but adapting the instructions for later versions is not difficult.

Exercise 4.7 The image generated by the script contains three layers above a white background. The logo is on the top layer, the shadow is on the second layer, and the reflection is on the third layer. This third layer also contains a layer mask with a horizontal gradient, which is used to make the reflection paler. To create the shadow, use the technique described in "Proper Shade vs. Cast Shadow" on page 109. To create the reflection, simply flip a copy of the logo horizontally and move it into place. The relief on the logo itself can be added by using a combination of the Emboss and Bump Map filters.

Chapter 5

Exercise 5.1 Try using a simple image and blending it with an image that has a uniform neutral color. You could also try creating an image with four different layers: two for the top layer and two for the background. Then try different combinations of the top and background layers.

Exercise 5.2 Take a nice sky from another photograph, one with interesting clouds. When you add the sky to the panorama, the clouds are stretched out horizontally, but clouds come in all shapes and sizes, so the result should look fine.

Exercise 5.3 Include the leaves in the selection to be cut to create the opening with the Fuzzy Select tool because the leaves contrast with the background. As you can see on the right, however, the tool doesn't work so well due to the flower pot. To address this issue, leave out the pot or use the Quick Mask.

Chapter 6

Exercise 6.1 To fade out progressively, reduce the opacity of the logo layer, merging each new layer with an unchanged background. Copy the resulting layers in reverse order.

Exercise 6.4 A solution is given in "The IWarp Tool" on page 478.

Exercise 6.6 First, build the flickering logo, as in Exercise 6.1 or 6.2. Next, build the animation with the Move Path tool. The logo should pass horizontally from one side to the other during the full animation. Successive layers are taken from the first multilayer animation, if you choose the STEPMODE LOOP.

Chapter 7

Exercise 7.1 The **Image: Colors > Threshold** tool is difficult to use well, and, unfortunately, it generates a black and white image. But you can choose a subrange that preserves the most significant part of the image. And you can often get interesting results by choosing a short subrange to produce something similar to an inverted etching.

Exercise 7.2 Screen mode is a good candidate when combined with an opacity reduced to 40% or less. Normal mode with a very reduced opacity can also be handy.

Chapter 8

Exercise 8.1 This exercise reminds you that pencil and paper are still very convenient tools. You'll work by trial and error, so print several copies of the 960 Grid System sketch sheet. The first layout of a web page is always made this way, and using sketch sheets helps you place your blocks correctly. To use the template, select **Image: File > New** and choose the TEMPLATE menu in the dialog that opens.

Exercise 8.3 You don't need to create extremely precise areas because users will not click their mouse far from the middle of a natural area. To make text appear when the mouse hovers over an area, use the `title=...` tag, as suggested in the third part of the Area Settings dialog.

Appendix A

Exercise A.1 Figure A.13 is a special case. The simplest solution here is to select **Image: Colors > Desaturate** and to choose AVERAGE. For the three other figures, the best solution is to correct each color stripe by hand, using the Fuzzy Select tool to select exactly one stripe and using the **Image: Colors > Hue-Saturation** tool to change the color of the stripe as you wish.

Exercise A.2 First, create a new white layer and place it under the image layer. Select the top layer, and reduce its opacity to 50%. Next, add a transparent layer above this layer, and draw the polygons on it with the Pencil tool, using the SHIFT key to draw straight lines. Add the text on as many new layers as necessary.

Exercise A.3 Create a new square image, for example, 1200 × 1200 pixels, with a black background. Build a circular selection of diameter 600 pixels, using the Ellipse Select tool, and press SHIFT and CTRL after the initial click on the circle's center. (Save this selection as a channel in case you lose it.) Create a transparent layer, and fill the selection with pure red. Then create another transparent layer, move the circular selection, and fill it with pure green. Do the same with a third layer but fill it with pure blue. Now set the three layers with colored circles in Addition mode and move them until you are satisfied. This process builds Figure A.36 on page 605. For Figure A.39 on page 606, proceed in the same way, but use white for the layer background and create the other layers in Multiply mode.

Exercise A.4 Build each figure component using **Image: Colors > Components > Decompose**, and choose not to decompose to layers. The corresponding images are then colorized using **Image: Colors > Colorize**. Finally, gather these components in an image twice the width and height of the original image.

C Resources

This appendix is a commented list of the websites dealing with GIMP, its components, its users, and related matters. Like any such list, it is up-to-date as this book goes to press, but six months from now, some sites may have disappeared and new ones may have been created. In all the URLs that follow, the initial *http://* has been omitted.

C.1 Official GIMP Pages

Here are the main parts of the official GIMP website.

www.gimp.org is the official GIMP site. If you know only one site, it must be this one, especially because it contains links to many other important sites. On the front page, you'll find news about the latest releases and links to pages where you can download them. The rest of the site contains the major pages mentioned in this section.

wiki.gimp.org is the GIMP Developer wiki, a collaborative website about GIMP. It's intended for developers but helpful to anyone who wants to know about developers' projects.

bugs.gimp.org is a somewhat esoteric page. It does not explain how to report bugs, but only enumerates the current list of bugs in various versions of GIMP. This page lets you look at the

work of the developers and get to know who is working on what. To file a bug, take a look at *www.gimp.org/bugs/*.

developer.gimp.org is about GIMP development. It is not really updated presently, and its main interesting feature is the tutorial about writing a plug-in at *developer.gimp.org/writing-a-plug-in/1/*.

gui.gimp.org is a working wiki about the GIMP graphical user interface (GUI). This site explains how the work for this GUI is done and in what direction it is progressing.

docs.gimp.org, surprisingly, is not the same as *www.gimp.org/docs/*. In fact, the first link leads to a page that contains links to the manuals of preceding versions, together with the present one, which is currently a work in progress. The second link leads to the current (finished) documentation and can be accessed directly from GIMP itself. It will point to the documentation of version 2.6 until the documentation of version 2.8 is finished. The documentation is currently available in English, Dutch, French, German, Italian, Norwegian, Korean, Russian, Spanish, and Swedish. For 2.8 it will also include Greek and Japanese.

registry.gimp.org is the GIMP Plugin Registry, where all plug-ins and scripts built by GIMP users are filed and available for download. The GIMP Plugin Registry takes the form of a blog, with the most recent entries appearing on the front page. You'll also find forums, where you can read and leave comments, and most useful of all, a search engine for hunting for a precise plug-in. This website is probably the second most useful site, after *www.gimp.org*.

C.2 Related Official Sites

Here, we mention websites dealing with software projects or similar sites used as frameworks for GIMP or in its construction.

www.gnu.org is the official site of the GNU project. The GNU project is the oldest free software project in the world, and, in fact, this project founded the concept of free software. Initiated in 1983 by Richard M. Stallman, who desired a Unix-like operating system without any constraint regarding its freedom of use, change, and distribution, the project began by building all the necessary components but the kernel. This last has since been supplied by the Linux kernel. The intended GNU kernel, called Hurd, is still in alpha state. Remember that GIMP is an acronym for GNU Image Manipulation Program.

www.gtk.org is the official site of the GTK+ project. This software was initially the GIMP Toolkit, the widget toolkit used in implementing GIMP. Since its beginning, it has developed to the point of being one of the most important toolkits in GNU/Linux. For example, it is the basis of the GNOME desktop environment and is now object oriented (hence the name GTK+), and it has been ported to other operating systems like Windows and Mac OS X.

www.gimp.org/about/COPYING is the GNU General Public License (GPL), the most widely used license in the world of free software. A software product licensed using the GPL offers the four fundamental freedoms: freedom to run the program for any purpose, freedom to study how the program works and adapt it to your own needs, freedom to redistribute copies so you can help your neighbor, and freedom to improve the program and release your improvements to the public so the whole community benefits. Importantly, these freedoms cannot be denied by somebody redistributing the program.

www.gegl.org is the official site of the Generic Graphic Library, a graph-based image-processing framework. In the current version of GIMP, images are represented as arrays of pixels. When you edit an image, you change the pixels, and there is no way to return to the unchanged image other than opening a previously saved copy: This is called *destructive editing*. With GEGL, images are represented as graphs, in which the edges are image components and nodes are operations on these components. By changing the structure of the graph, you can perform nondestructive editing. Moreover, this representation offers provisions for representing images in higher bit depth than the current 8 bits. GEGL operations are already usable in GIMP 2.8, but only GIMP 2.10 or 3.0 will fully benefit from the incorporation of GEGL.

C.3 Tutorials

Many tutorial sites are available for GIMP, but their quality varies. Moreover, many are too old to be useful, since they deal with versions of GIMP older than 2.4. Finding a relevant tutorial is mostly a matter of luck. Here are some interesting and generally useful sites.

www.gimp.org/tutorials/ offers an interesting set of tutorials, although most of them are several years old. No recent additions have been made.

www.ghuj.com is rather slow and complicated to use, but it contains many tutorials.

www.pixel2life.com/tutorials/gimp/ is also slow and complex, but it's supposed to be the largest collection of GIMP tutorials on the Web.

www.gimpusers.com/tutorials/ offers many tutorials, classified in categories.

gimps.de is in English as well as in German and offers tutorials among other content.

gimpology.com is a large tutorial site that is frequently updated.

www.tutorialized.com/tutorials/Gimp/ has a good number of usefully categorized tutorials, especially about photo effects.

gimpguru.org contains tutorials that are old but good.

meetthegimp.org offers video tutorials.

C.4 Communities and Blogs

Although several of the GIMP developers have had blogs, only one is presently "active," at the rate of nine entries in one year: *www.chromecode.com* is the blog of Martin Nordholts, who spends much less time on it than on GIMP. On this blog, he features some of the most spectacular changes he has made to the GIMP graphic interface.

Other interesting community sites include the following:

libregraphicsworld.org is mainly authored by its maintainer, Alexandre Prokoudine, and is organized as a blog. It's a very interesting website about all graphics applications in the world of free software, with announcements, short tutorials, reviews, and so on. Certainly you should have it in your bookmarks!

www.gimpusers.com is a rich site with news, tutorials, and many other features. Beware, however, of its forums, which, for the most part, are simply transcripts of the corresponding mailing lists (see later). If you want to send and read messages on the GIMP users list, for example, use the list directly and avoid the corresponding pseudoforum on this site.

gimp-brainstorm.blogspot.com is a rather unusual site. Everybody can contribute with an idea about the GIMP user interface, but the contributions can be only graphic. You must keep silent, and you must remain anonymous. These ideas can be used by the GIMP UI redesign team or entirely ignored.

www.gimptalk.com is another rich site, with news, tutorials, forums, and other resources like brushes, photographs, and plug-ins.

www.gimpgallery.net has about the same purpose as the preceding site, but it is slightly more complicated to use.

www.graphics-muse.org is the blog of Michael J. Hammel, author of the excellent book *The Artist's Guide to GIMP, 2nd Edition* (No Starch Press).

blog.mmiworks.net/ is the blog of Peter Sikking, principal interaction architect at m+mi works and responsible for the GIMP UI redesign.

www.ramonmiranda.com is the blog of Ramón Miranda. He is the creator of GPS, the Gimp Paint Studio, and a contributor of the new presets in GIMP 2.8. His blog is written in English and Spanish.

groups.google.com/group/gimp-brushmakers-guild is the site of the GIMP Brushmakers Guild. Though not very active this group is trying to fulfill a very important purpose for GIMP.

gimper.net is another community site with news, help, forums, resources, and so on.

gimpmagazine.org is a brand new GIMP magazine, already downloaded ten thousand times during the first 24 hours of its availability. The first number is really promising.

C.5 Brushes and Plug-ins

Many people contribute to GIMP in various ways. We include here only contributions, not deviations.

Brush Sets

code.google.com/p/gps-gimp-paint-studio/ is the site of the GIMP Paint Studio, which is a cleverly built collection of brushes, together with a collection of predefined tool presets. See Chapter 15 for more about this site.

www.pgd-design.com/gimp/ offers a collection of GIMP brushes and patterns.

ljfhutch.blogspot.com.au is the blog of L.J.F. Hutch, a professional 2D painter. The site offers a large collection of brushes.

Plug-in Sets

The following sites contain important and specific plug-ins or plug-in sets:

- *ftp://ftp.gimp.org/pub/gimp/plug-ins/v2.6/gap/* is not a website but an FTP site for the GAP plug-in. For more about GAP, look at the GIMP documentation or read Chapters 6 and 18 of this book.

- *gmic.sourceforge.net* is the G'MIC site.

- *liquidrescale.wikidot.com* is the site for the Liquid Rescale GIMP plug-in.

- *sites.google.com/site/elsamuko/* is the site for the Elsamuko plug-in set.

C.6   Mailing Lists and IRC Channels

GIMP has five official mailing lists, hosted by *lists.xcf.berkeley.edu* (don't try to access this website directly). Use these rather than their corresponding forums on *www.gimpusers.com*. Take a look at *www.gimp.org/mail_lists.html* first if you are not familiar with list etiquette.

- GIMP User (*https://mail.gnome.org/mailman/ listinfo/gimp-user-list*) is an active mailing list for GIMP users. Despite what the official site states, it is not especially Unix based. You can ask anything you want, but please first look at the documentation as well as the list archives.

If your question is well formulated, you will get several useful answers.

- GIMP Developer (*https://mail.gnome.org/ mailman/listinfo/gimp-developer-list*) is also an active mailing list. Despite its name, this list is not used only by developers. It is aimed at them, however, so don't use this list to ask a simple user question. Use it for suggestions you feel are of general interest or to prepare a bug report.

- GIMP Web (*https://mail.gnome.org/mailman/ listinfo/gimp-web-list*) deals with the GIMP website and has been somewhat dormant for a while.

- GIMP Docs (*https://mail.gnome.org/mailman/ listinfo/gimp-docs-list*) deals with GIMP documentation. The people who build and translate the documentation are the primary users, but you can use it to point to an error, for example.

Two IRC channels are available, called #gimp and #gimp-users. Avoid them if you are not accustomed to using IRC. They can be completely dormant sometimes and very active at other times.

C.7   Other Graphics Applications

Of course, we mention here only free software applications.

www.imagemagick.org is the ImageMagick site. This application is described in Appendix F.

krita.org presents Krita, an application with aims similar to those of GIMP. It is embedded in the KDE-based Koffice suite but also works under GNOME. Its main advantage over GIMP is that it accepts 16-bit color depth and multiple color spaces. But it is much less developed in all other aspects, and this advantage will disappear as soon as the next version of GIMP is published.

www.inkscape.org presents Inkscape, a vector graphics editor. Its aim is different from GIMP's, which is a raster graphics editor. These two applications can, in fact, be considered complementary.

www.blender.org is the official site of Blender, an extremely powerful 3D graphics application, with capabilities for modeling, simulating, animating, and so on. Raster images built with GIMP are frequently loaded into Blender as part of a new project.

al.chemy.org presents Alchemy, an open drawing project. Alchemy is a simple application aimed at exploring new ways of sketching and drawing. A first sketch built with Alchemy can be loaded into GIMP for further development.

mypaint.intilinux.com presents MyPaint, a drawing application available for GNU/Linux and Windows. Its most salient feature is the many possibilities of defining new brushes, to be used only with a graphic tablet.

C.8 Related Graphics Software Projects

Here, again, we mention only free software applications.

hugin.sourceforge.net presents the Hugin panorama photo stitcher, which can be used for building panoramas much larger than GIMP can build.

www.sane-project.org is the official site of the Scanner Access Now Easy (SANE) project, which provides standardized access to most raster scanners.

ufraw.sourceforge.net is the UFRaw website. This project aims at reading and manipulating raw images from digital cameras. We recommend using it from the corresponding GIMP plug-in, but it can also be used as an independent application.

www.darktable.org describes Darktable, a photography workflow application and RAW developer with many more features than UFRaw. It works on GNU/Linux and Mac OS X.

www.mplayerhq.hu describes MPlayer, a general-purpose movie player that can also be used as a batch command for converting between different animation formats. Its library is used in some GAP commands.

cinelerra.org presents Cinelerra, a video editor and compositor application. A similar application is PiTiVi (*www.pitivi.org*).

C.9 Other Graphics Sites

The following sites are sources for interesting examples of computer graphics.

www.cgsociety.org is the site of The Computer Graphics Society (CGSociety). Without being a member, you can browse the galleries and portfolios and get a good overview of the current work of computer artists.

art.gnome.org has a different purpose. It is a gallery of icons, backgrounds, and other artwork for changing, and hopefully improving, the visual appearance of your GNOME desktop.

D Frequently Asked Questions

In this section, we answer some of the questions that we've encountered most often. Much of this information is also found in this book and in the GIMP documentation, but this appendix provides a quick reference.

Some common questions are not covered because the problems that led to those questions have been solved in the latest version of GIMP. For example, you can no longer lose your layers, paths, channels, selections, guides, layer masks, and so on when saving an image because you can no longer save it in any other format than XCF, which saves all these image components. You are no longer forbidden to export an image to GIF format, even if it is not in indexed representation, because the transformation will be automatically (and silently) done. You can now add a layer mask to a layer even if it has no Alpha channel. Wrapping text is easy, too, thanks to the Fixed Box option for the new and improved Text tool.

Other frequently asked questions dealt with missing features, and many of those features have been added to GIMP 2.8 (they are mentioned in the Introduction). Of course, some users will find that the features they've been waiting for haven't yet been added, and they'll have to wait for GIMP 3.0. Some of the commonly requested features that have not yet been added are covered in the following answers to questions.

D.1 What Does the Future Hold?

The next major step in GIMP development is the full inclusion of GEGL, which is only partly used in the current version and is mostly invisible to normal users. When GIMP is fully GEGL-capable, it will include the following features:

- Support for 16-bit representation per channel.

- Nondestructive editing, which allows transformations to be made without changing the original content (this is called *adjustment layers* in some raster graphics applications and *node-based workflow* in others).

- Direct use of CMYK color representation.

Other features that are in the works include a combined transform tool, which will replace the five existing transform tools (Scale, Rotate, Shear, Flip, and Perspective); an interactive deform tool similar to the IWarp filter and included in GIMP's core; and better support for sophisticated graphic tablets, which will allow users to work with several styluses and customize them for a given painting tool.

D.2 How...?

How can I draw a straight line?

GIMP has no specific tool for drawing a straight line, but you can draw one with any painting tool. After choosing the drawing tool and setting the parameters, click the first point of the line and then press the $\boxed{\text{SHIFT}}$ key and place the endpoint. You can even draw a polygon in this way, by pressing $\boxed{\text{SHIFT}}$ and clicking at each corner of the shape.

How can I draw a circle?

We explain this in detail in "Drawing Ellipses and Rectangles" on page 85. The simplest solution is to stroke a circular selection, but you can create a ring-shaped selection and fill it or transform it to a path and stroke it.

How can I create an outline around text?

The most direct solution is to create a path from the text (use the layer menu of the text layer) and then to stroke this path with the painting tool and whatever options you want.

How do I save a selection within an image to a file?

Suppose you build a complicated selection and want to save it as a new image. Copy it and then select **Image: Edit > Paste As > New Image** or press $\boxed{\text{SHIFT+CTRL+V}}$. Then save this new image.

How do I merge an image from another file with the current image?

Select **Image: File > Open as layers** or press $\boxed{\text{CTRL+ALT+O}}$. You can also drag the image thumbnail from a file manager or a browser to the current image, and it will be added to it as a new layer.

How do I get small fonts to look as nice as large fonts?

As a rule, using small fonts in a raster image is not a good idea. Building a larger image with proportionate fonts and then scaling it to the proper size is a better idea. Either way, always check the ANTIALIAS checkbox in the Text tool options and choose anything other than NONE for HINTING.

How do I set keyboard shortcuts?

You can set keyboard shortcuts using two methods. The safer method is to select **Image: Edit > Keyboard Shortcuts**. You can then select the command you want to define a shortcut for and type the shortcut.

The other method is to open **Image: Edit > Preferences**, choose the INTERFACE page, and check the option USE DYNAMIC KEYBOARD SHORTCUTS. Once you've checked this option, you can define a new shortcut by selecting the menu entry corresponding to the command and typing the desired shortcut. Do not leave this option checked, however, because accidentally changing an existing shortcut is easy.

How do I set up GIMP so a layer becomes active when I click an element in that layer?

One way is to select **Image: Edit > Preferences**, choose the TOOL OPTIONS page, and check the option SET LAYER OR PATH AS ACTIVE. Once you've done this, moving a layer with the Move tool makes it active. Note that working this way can become confusing.

How do I fill a layer or selection with transparency?

First, the layer you want to add transparency to must have an Alpha channel, which you can add from the layer menu or in **Image: Layer > Transparency**. If an Alpha channel is present, cutting or deleting a selection, or using the Erase tool, replaces the color with transparency. For example, if you use the Select by Color tool and then cut the selection, all the pixels of the selected color are replaced with transparency.

Another way to do this is to apply **Image: Colors > Color to Alpha**.

How do I draw in a different color?

The color of the brush is the only painting tool option that is not chosen in its option dialog. A brush paints with the foreground color, which you can change by clicking the color swatch in the bottom-left part of the Toolbox to open the Color chooser dialog. From here, you have several ways to choose the new color.

How do I add a blur to my image?

If you want to blur a selection or layer, open the **Image: Filters > Blur** submenu and select one of the available filters. If you want to blur a small part of the image, use the Blur/Sharpen tool (SHIFT+U).

How can I paint along the outline of a rectangle?

First use the Rectangle Select tool (R) to build the outline of the rectangle. Then select **Image: Edit > Stroke Selection**, which allows you to choose all the details of the stroke.

How do I move existing guides?

Select the Move tool (M), and click and drag the guide you want to move. If this moves the active layer, change the TOOL TOGGLE option or press SHIFT.

How do I get rid of a floating selection?

You can get rid of a floating selection in three ways: Delete it, if you don't need it; anchor it to the previously active layer or channel; or create a new layer with it. All these actions are available in the Layers menu, which you can access by right-clicking the Layers dialog. You can also access them directly from the **Image: Layer** menu or by clicking the buttons at the bottom of the Layers dialog.

How do I paint in a transparent area?

The LOCK ALPHA CHANNEL button must be unchecked. This button is the second button from left on the line beginning with LOCK in the Layers dialog.

How can I see the marching ants and know whether my selection has been made?

Make sure the **Image: View > Show Selection** option is checked. CTRL+T toggles this visibility.

How can I add color to a black and white image?

Change the mode of the image to RGB using **Image: Image > Mode > RGB**.

How do I resize my photo to a precise size, say 5 × 7 cm?

The short answer is that this is done when printing the image, using your printing software, rather than through GIMP.

You can easily adjust the size of your photo on the screen, but that won't change its size on a website or its size when printed.

The photo's size on a website depends on its dimensions in pixels and on the definition of the screen used for viewing it, which you can't control. The photo will be a different size on a smartphone, an LCD screen, and a CRT screen, for example.

The printed photo size is chosen in the printing interface. You can change the printing definition to change the printed size, or you can change the final size of the print, which changes the definition. In any case, the printing size is generally very different from the viewing size on a screen.

How do I set the foreground color to a color in my image?

The easiest way is to CTRL-click the image with one of the paint tools, which makes the color you clicked the new foreground color.

How can I keep text sharp when scaling it down?

Text should scale without any loss of quality as long as it is not rasterized, so don't merge the text layer with the underlying layer until your image is finished.

How do I copy a layer mask to another layer mask?

Just as you would any other component (or *drawable* in GIMP jargon): Make the layer mask active (by clicking its thumbnail in the Layers dialog), select it (using any selection tool), copy it (CTRL+C), make the layer mask of the destination layer active, paste (CTRL+V), and anchor (CTRL+H).

How can I search for a specific font, brush, or pattern?

If the list is long and you know the name of the font, brush, or pattern, press CTRL+F (or sometimes CTRL+S), and then type the first letters of the name. You can also use tags to restrict the size of the list, for example, when selecting a brush in the Texture category.

How do I erase with a tool other than the Eraser?

Let's assume that by "erasing" you mean replacing with transparency. The active layer must have an Alpha channel (its name does not appear in boldface in the Layers dialog). Choose your painting tool, its brush, and all its options but change the tool mode to COLOR ERASE. You then replace the pixels of the foreground color with transparency. **Image: Colors > Color to Alpha** replaces the foreground color with transparency throughout the entire layer or selection.

How can I use the Scale tool to enlarge an image?

The Scale tool enlarges the current selection or layer. To enlarge the image, apply **Image: Image > Scale Image**. Or, if you only want to see the image with more detail on your screen, choose a zoom tool instead.

How can I find a dialog I closed by accident?

All the dialogs can be opened via **Image: Windows > Dockable Dialogs**. If you closed a dock with several dialogs inside, select **Image: Windows > Recently Closed Docks**.

Some dialogs can also be accessed directly with a keyboard shortcut: CTRL+B opens the Toolbox; CTRL+L opens the Layers di-

alog; CTRL+G opens the Gradients dialog; SHIFT+CTRL+B opens the Brushes dialog; and SHIFT+CTRL+P opens the Patterns dialog. Double-clicking a tool icon in the Toolbox opens the tool options dialog with the options for that tool.

How can I invert grayscale values without changing the colors?

Duplicate the layer. Then invert the colors on the lower layer and set the layer mode of the upper (unchanged) layer to Color.

How do I crop with a defined aspect ratio?

Look at the tool options for the Crop tool. Check the FIXED box, and choose ASPECT RATIO in the field on the right. Then enter an aspect ratio, like 4:3 or 5:8, in the field below.

D.3 Why...?

Why are some of the filter names grayed out?

Most filters apply only to RGB images. Check the status of **Image: Image > Mode** and change it to RGB if needed. A few filters have other requirements. For example **Image: Filters > Enhance > NL filter** is grayed out if the current layer has an Alpha channel.

Why is nothing happening?

If you're trying to edit an image and your actions seem to have no effect, check the following points:

- Is there a floating selection? If so, you need to either delete the floating selection or place it into a layer before doing anything else.

- Is the layer you want to change the active layer? The active layer is emphasized in the Layers dialog.

- A selection may not be visible either because it is too small or because it is not shown. Try pressing CTRL+T to toggle selection visibility or $\boxed{\text{SHIFT+CTRL+A}}$ to cancel any existing selection.

- Does your current layer have an active layer mask? If so, you'll see a thumbnail of this layer mask framed in white in the layer line of the Layers dialog. Click the layer thumbnail to make the layer active.

- Is your current layer opaque and in normal mode? Check its OPACITY slider and its mode in the Layers dialog. If needed, push the slider to the right or change the mode.

- Is there an active Paint Dynamics? For example, Basic Dynamics correlates Opacity with Pressure, and if you're using the mouse, the pressure is very low pressure. Depending on what you intend to do, either switch to Dynamics Off or use the tablet stylus.

Why doesn't anything happen when I try to cut, paste, or apply a filter to a selection?

You're probably changing an invisible layer. An invisible layer can still be active, which is indicated by the emphasis on the layer in the Layers dialog. Any action you take is performed on the active layer. Visibility is indicated by the eye icon on the left of the layer line in the Layers dialog. If the eye is not shown, the layer is invisible. Click the icon to restore layer visibility.

Why can't I modify the channel I built by saving a selection?

The selection is probably still active. If so, you won't be able change the channel areas that are outside of the selection. Make it inactive by pressing $\boxed{\text{SHIFT+CTRL+A}}$ or selecting **Image: Select > None**.

Why can't I change my image after I saved a selection to a channel?

The channel is now active, so you have no active layer. In the Layers dialog, select the layer you want to change.

Why do my paint strokes appear on the image when I try painting on a layer mask?

Because the layer is active and the layer mask is not. Click the layer mask thumbnail in the Layers dialog, and ensure it is framed in white, which means it's active.

Why did the size of my file increase when I exported it to JPEG with 100% quality?

The quality of a JPEG is actually not a percentage; it simply happens to have a range from 0 to 100. Saving at a quality level greater than 85 (the default in GIMP) is generally pointless. Digital cameras often save images at a higher level, so saving the image at 85 can decrease its size without a visible loss of quality.

Why can't I draw in the color I chose?

If you choose a deep blue, for example, but the line is drawn in black or white, your image is probably in indexed mode and that shade of blue isn't in the current indexed palette. Generally, you want to work in RGB mode and change to indexed mode, if necessary, only when the image is finished. The major exception to this rule is when you are preparing an image like a textile design that's restricted to a very limited color set.

E   Installing GIMP

Installing GIMP on your computer is no longer difficult. Thus, this appendix will be rather short, and if you run into trouble, you will find help on the websites mentioned in Appendix C. The official GIMP website (*http://www.gimp. org/*) is the best way to obtain instructions for downloading and installing GIMP and its components.

Although the GPL license does not forbid the selling of GIMP distributions, buying a commercial distribution of GIMP is useless and possibly even harmful: It will have no added value other than some elaborate packaging, and some commercial distributions are known to contain viruses. Do not download GIMP from sites that are not the official GIMP site or that are not directly pointed to by the GIMP website.

E.1   GNU/Linux and Unix

GIMP was initially designed for GNU/Linux, and most of its developers work on this operating system. Therefore, installing it on this system is especially easy. Moreover, the main GNU/Linux distributions provide automated tools for installing GIMP (if it's not already installed by default). Of course, if your distribution was installed some months ago, and you do not regularly update it, most likely the version of GIMP on your system is not the latest one (i.e., 2.8), so you need to update your software. In most cases, simply updating your installation is enough.

Debian

With Debian, the simple command

    apt-get install gimp

run as the `root` user installs GIMP and all its dependencies. But installing some additional packages can be handy. Here are the main ones:

- `gimp-gap` is the GIMP Animation Package, described in Chapter 18.
- `gimp-plugin-registry` contains many handy plug-ins and scripts, as described in Chapter 21.
- `gimp-gmic` is the G'MIC plug-in set, also described in Chapter 21.
- `gnome-xcf-thumbnailer` allows the GNOME desktop environment to display thumbnails of XCF files.
- `gtkam-gimp` links GIMP to `Gtkam` for accessing photographs from a digital camera.
- `gimp-gutenprint` links to `Gutenprint` for a powerful and flexible interface to many printers.

- `gimp-ufraw` links GIMP to `Ufraw` for handling raw photographs taken from most digital still cameras.

- `gimp-data-extras` offers additional sets of brushes, palettes, and gradients.

These packages are simple to install using the synaptic graphic tool.

Ubuntu

Because Ubuntu is a derivative of Debian, the installation instructions are the same. The only real differences are that, by default, Ubuntu has no `root` user and the installation command is

```
sudo apt-get install gimp
```

Since Ubuntu version 10.04, GIMP is no longer part of the installation CD, so you have to install it separately.

Mint

Mint is a relatively new GNU/Linux distribution that comes in two versions. Linux Mint 12 is based on Ubuntu and Linux Mint Debian on Debian. Thus the instructions for installing GIMP on Mint are the same as for these distributions, respectively.

Fedora

With Fedora, the concepts are similar, but the commands are different. Run

```
yum install gimp
```

as the `root` user to install GIMP. The Fedora package database also contains the following packages:

- `gimp-data-extras` plays the same role as in Debian.

- `gimpfx-foundry` provides a set of additional plug-ins.

- `gimp-help` gives you access to GIMP help in a separate package.

The other plug-ins, including GAP, must be installed manually using the GIMP Plugin Registry.

OpenSUSE

With OpenSUSE, run

```
zypper install gimp
```

as the `root` user (if you are using the latest version of OpenSUSE). You must install all additional data or plug-ins manually.

Mandriva

With Mandriva, run

```
urpmi gimp
```

as the `root` user. Additional packages include the following:

- `gimp-data-extras` plays the same role as in Debian.

- `gimp2-gap` is the GAP plug-in set.

- `gimpfx-foundry` offers you a set of additional plug-ins.

- `gimp-help` gives you access to GIMP help in separate packages, depending on the language.

Other Unix-like Operating Systems

With other Unix-like operating systems, such as BSD versions or less well-known distributions of GNU/Linux, already compiled packages are not available, and your only solution is to compile GIMP and all the needed libraries from source text. This experience can be painful, although all this software is free and the source text freely available. Go to *http://www.gimp.org/downloads/* and follow the instructions. Choose a mirror site near your location: This way you avoid overloading the main website and increase your download speed.

E.2 Windows

Although most GIMP developers are users of GNU/Linux, they know that the outside world is still dominated by various versions of the Windows operating system. As explained on *http://www.gimp.org/windows/*, Jernej Simončič contributed a GIMP installer for Windows and updates it for every new version. From the website *http://gimp-win.sourceforge.net/stable.html*, you can download the package and install it immediately. It contains everything you will need and installs smoothly on Windows XP SP2 and later versions. The installation process is similar to that of most applications and is not detailed here. Once GIMP is installed, download and install any additional plug-ins from the GIMP Plugin Registry (*http://registry.gimp.org/*).

Beware, however, that the online help is a separate package, available in several languages. We also recommend that, if you already have a previous version of GIMP installed, you first uninstall it before trying to install GIMP 2.8.

If you perform these simple actions correctly, you should not encounter problems. Of course, the Windows desktop environment is different from the various available GNU/Linux environments, and it is generally less convenient for using GIMP. With Windows, you do not have the advantage of several workspaces, which means all windows are on the same screen, and handling several applications at the same time, or even a single application with several windows, can be cumbersome.

Windows users will probably prefer the single-window mode GIMP interface, described in Chapter 9. This does not mean that the multi-window interface is not available, but Windows users will have to change some of their habits to use it. Moreover, such an interface is handy only if you can change the window manager's behavior so a window becomes active as soon as your mouse pointer is on it. Having to click twice every time you change from the Toolbox to the Image window (one click activates the window; the second click triggers the intended action) can be very annoying.

Do not try to use GIMP on Windows versions previous to Windows XP SP2. And don't forget that installing a GNU/Linux distribution on your computer, in addition to Windows, is easy, as is sharing the same data with the two operating systems. For more details, see *http://en.wikipedia.org/wiki/Multiboot*.

E.3 Mac OS X

The number of GIMP developers using OS X is still less than the number using Windows. But the websites *ftp://ftp.gimp.org/pub/gimp/v2.8/osx/gimp-2.8.2-dmg-2.dmg* and *http://gimp.lisanet.de/* offer OS X users good tools for installing GIMP as easily as on Windows. It's no longer necessary to first install the X11 environment. Do not install GIMP on an older version of Mac OS.

As with Windows, the GIMP help is in a separate package, but it is available only in English, German, Spanish, and French.

Other interface problems, due to the Mac interface, have all been solved recently, and GIMP on the Mac now behaves in exactly the same way as on other operating systems. Even the menu bar uses the GIMP style, not the Mac style, so the top bar on your screen will not be very useful. Mac users will probably prefer the single-window mode interface for the same reasons that Windows users do.

F Batch Processing

At some point, you may want to edit several images simultaneously to, for example, convert them from one format to another, change their size, or apply a filter. If you want to do the same thing to dozens of images, repeating the process over and over would be tedious and time consuming. Thankfully, computers excel at automating repetitive processes. Remember: If you're doing something repetitive on a computer, there's probably a better—and faster—way to do it!

Automatically applying changes to a series of images, one after another, is called *batch processing*. Here, we'll discuss three ways to transform multiple images at the same time. The first one is done from a command line and can be used only in rather simple situations. The second one uses a plug-in, but it works only for a small set of simple operations. The last one uses an independent application.

F.1 GIMP Batch Mode

The command line is used for typing textual commands and gives users full access to all the capabilities of their operating system. Many graphical interfaces are complicated ways to access simple textual commands. To use the command line, you open a terminal window in which you type commands. A *terminal* is a text-only window in a graphical interface. Type a command, and after you press ENTER, you get results or answers. Some commands are interactive and ask questions and display answers. Others simply execute what you ask.

The capabilities of the command line have a lot to do with the *shell*, the interactive program that opens a terminal window in which you type commands in GNU/Linux. The shell accepts a command language with many capabilities. Certain shell commands can be used to apply the same process to several files (in our case, image files), including a command to call another command over and over, on all the files in a folder, or on a subset of files using just one command with a *wildcard*. Wildcards are symbols that can stand in for one or more characters.

Mac OS X users enjoy exactly the same capabilities because Mac is a Unix-based system. With Windows, however, the command language is rather poor, so the usefulness of the command line is more limited than in GNU/Linux or on a Mac.

When you work with GIMP from the command line, you use options and arguments. The *options* specify actions or parameters. The *arguments* are the names of the files to which the actions are applied.

When using GIMP in batch mode from the command line, you need to specify the following options: -b for batch processing and -i for running without the user interface. The -b option needs an argument, which is the command to execute. A complete call has the following form:

```
gimp -i -b 'command' files
```

The command is written using the Script-Fu language, presented in "Scheme" on page 554. If you want to write a short script on the command line one line at a time, you can use the following form instead:

```
gimp -i -b - files
commands
```

and then type the script on the following lines.

You can also define a new Script-Fu function and call it from the command line. In this context, the file-glob plug-in is useful: Given an encoded pattern that specifies the files, it returns the list of filenames matching this pattern. To see an example, look at *http://www.gimp.org/tutorials/Basic_Batch/*.

F.2   David's Batch Processor

Calling GIMP from the command line and controlling it using the Script-Fu language might be daunting unless you have some experience in programming.   David's Batch Processor, also called DBP, is an alternative for people less inclined to write code.   For Debian and Ubuntu GNU/Linux distributions, David's Batch Processor plug-in is included in the package called gimp-plugin-registry. Otherwise, visit *http://members.ozemail.com.au/~hodsond/dbp.html* to download the plug-in.   Once it's installed, you can access the plug-in via **Image: Filters > Batch > Batch Process**.   Its dialog is shown in Figure F.1.

This dialog contains nine tabs. The first one is where you select the files to process, the next six

Figure F.1 *The DBP dialog, Input tab*

tabs are where you specify the various processes to apply to these files, the eighth tab is where you change the filenames and specify global changes to the images, and the ninth tab is where you specify the final format and a few other global parameters.

The INPUT tab is fairly self-explanatory. Clicking ADD FILES opens the file manager window. You can select several files at the same time by pressing CTRL or SHIFT when clicking the filenames. When you click ADD, all the selected files are added to the list. Once the list has files, you can select and remove files or clear the whole list.

The tool dialog is inactive while the file manager window is open, which is unusual behavior for a GIMP dialog. After the file manager window is closed, you can make adjustments on the tool dialog tabs. On each transformation tab, the ENABLE box must be checked for the transformation to be active. The TURN tab (Figure F.2) lets you rotate the images only by a multiple of 90°.

The BLUR tab (Figure F.3) applies a Gaussian blur with the specified radius.

Figure F.2 *The DBP dialog, Turn tab*

Figure F.3 *The DBP dialog, Blur tab*

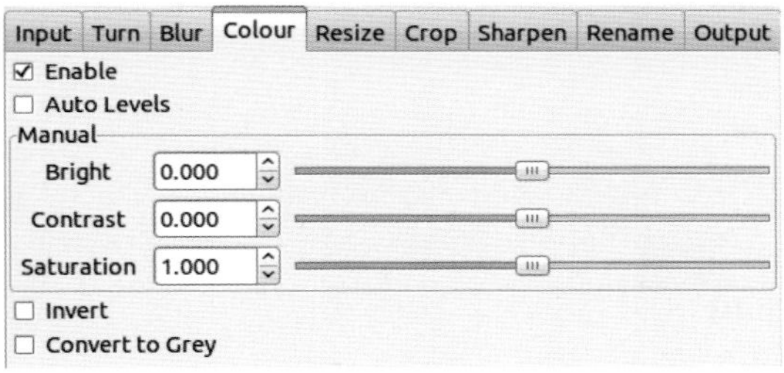

Figure F.4 *The DBP dialog, Colour tab*

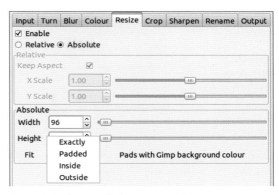

Figure F.5 *The DBP dialog, Resize tab*

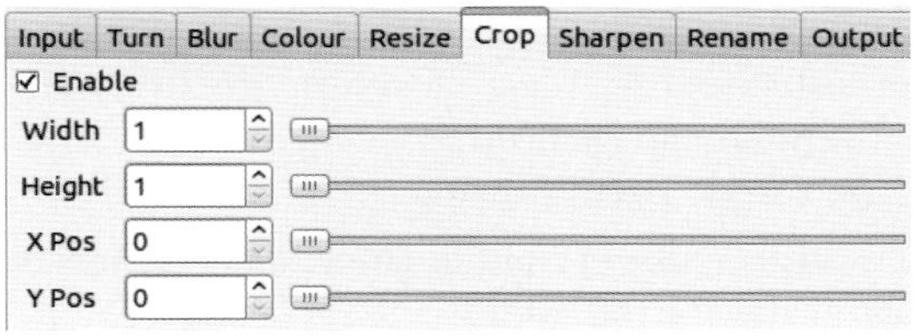

Figure F.6 *The DBP dialog, Crop tab*

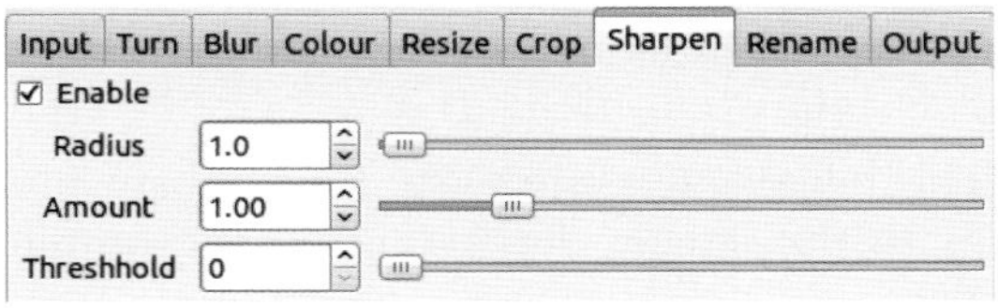

Figure F.7 *The DBP dialog, Sharpen tab*

The COLOUR tab (Figure F.4) transforms the colors in several ways: level equalization; adjusting brightness, contrast, and saturation; inverting colors; and converting to grayscale. This tab is useful if you want to correct a systematic color distortion in a series of photographs, for example.

The RESIZE tab (Figure F.5) does what its name implies. You can choose between relative resizing, where the sliders change by a scaling factor, and absolute resizing, where you choose the final width and height. The FIT drop-down menu, shown in Figure F.5, lets you choose how the new dimensions are applied:

- EXACTLY: The dimensions chosen are used, regardless of how the aspect changes.

- PADDED: The aspect is maintained, and the resulting empty space is filled with the background color.

- INSIDE: The aspect is maintained, and the image may be smaller than the specified dimensions.

- OUTSIDE: Same idea, but the image can be larger than the specified dimensions.

The CROP tab (Figure F.6) is where you crop the images. You can specify the origin (top-left corner, for example) of the cropping rectangle, as well as its width and height.

The SHARPEN tab (Figure F.7) works the same as the **Image: Filters > Enhance > Unsharp Mask** filter and has the same parameters. See Section 17.3.

Be careful when using the RENAME tab (Figure F.8)—it's easy to accidentally invert your file- naming scheme. This tab lets you choose how the new files will be named, but it won't

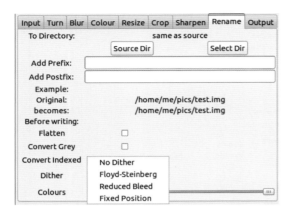

Figure F.8 *The DBP dialog, Rename tab*

overwrite existing files. Attempts to overwrite the originals are ignored.

You can do the following:

- Choose a target folder (directory) different from the source folder.

- Append a prefix or a suffix to all filenames to prevent replacing existing files and to label the files with the new characteristics (thumb, gray, improved, etc.).

This tab also lets you make final transformations to the image, depending on the output format:

- Flatten the image (merge into one layer).

- Convert it to grayscale.

- Convert it to indexed mode, with or without dithering, with a specified number of colors.

Note that you can convert to both grayscale and indexed mode.

The OUTPUT tab (Figure F.9) is mainly used to select the output format and its parameters. The available output formats are shown in Figure F.10, and Figure F.9 shows the parameters for PNG. For BMP, MIFF, PAT, TIFF, and XCF, no parameters are available.

When you've selected all the actions you want to perform and set all the parameters, click TEST to preview the result for the first picture,

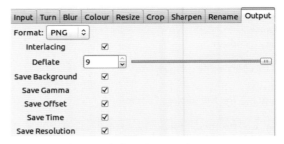

Figure F.9 *The DBP dialog, Output tab*

Figure F.10 *Available output formats*

or click START and go grab a beverage while GIMP processes your images.

F.3   ImageMagick

ImageMagick is a free software project (with an Apache-like license) that supports about 100 image formats and format conversions. ImageMagick is also capable of doing a number of sophisticated things to images. For more details, check out its home page (*http://www.imagemagick.org/*).

Calling ImageMagick

ImageMagick is normally called from a terminal or command line, but its functionalities can also be accessed from other programs. When using it to process many files, you'll find the *filename globbing* facilities of GNU/Linux extremely useful. For example, the command

```
convert *.jpg animation.gif
```

converts all the files in the current folder with a `.jpg` suffix to a single GIF animation called `animation.gif`. The asterisk is a wildcard, which matches any character or string. The Windows command language does not support globbing, but ImageMagick adds support, so you can use the same commands in Windows.

ImageMagick contains 10 different programs, the most useful being `convert`, which we used in the previous example. Among the myriads of possible usages, we describe just a few to give you a taste of this powerful application. These examples use GNU/Linux shell notation, but Windows users can refer to the detailed page *http://www.imagemagick.org/Usage/windows/*. But this first example is given in both notations.

Suppose we have a folder with a lot of photographs—called `img001`, `img002`, and so on—in TIFF format, and we want to convert all of them to the PNG format. The input files do not have a file extension, so we have to tell the `convert` command what their format is. We do this with the prefix `tiff:`. With GNU/Linux, here is how we write it:

```
for i in img*
do convert tiff:$i $i.png
done
```

With Windows and the DOS shell, we write it as

```
FOR %a in (img*) DO ^
  convert tiff:%a %a.jpg
```

The caret is used to continue the command on the next line.

Another solution is to use the `mogrify` command, which does not check whether the target files already exist and happily overwrites files when asked. The following command would work in both GNU/Linux and Windows:

```
mogrify -format png tiff:*
```

But avoiding this command is best because accidentally erasing files is very easy.

Building Thumbnails

One of ImageMagick's main purposes is to generate thumbnails. ImageMagick makes generating uniform-looking thumbnails for a whole set of images easy. You can use thumbnails on a web page, for example, as links to the actual images. Because thumbnails are normally small images, say 200×200 at most, generate them in GIF format, which compresses well. At this size, the limitation to 256 colors is not a problem.

The following example generates the thumbnail image `thumbnail.gif` from the source image `image.jpg`:

```
convert -define jpeg:size=500x180
   image.jpg  -auto-orient
   -thumbnail 250x90 -unsharp 0x.5
   thumbnail.gif
```

The command is written here on four successive lines, but, in fact, you type it on one line only.

The `-define` option is not necessary, but it may accelerate the process if the source image is very large. The JPEG library must enlarge the (compressed) image when it loads, and this option sets the approximate size that the image is enlarged to. The `-auto-orient` option uses the EXIF information provided by the camera and rotates the image if necessary. The `-thumbnail` option sets the final dimensions of the thumbnail and can be used to discard any useless information from the image, such as comments. The aspect ratio is maintained: The resulting thumbnail is 90 pixels high, but its width is 250 pixels or less. Finally, the `-unsharp` option is used to sharpen the image because resizing always results in a slight blur.

To generate thumbnails for several images at the same time, you could use the `mogrify` command, but calling `convert` in a loop is safer. One challenge of generating thumbnails from source images is getting thumbnails with names like `img0567.jpg.gif`. mogrify can solve the problem with its -format option. If you need to use convert, with GNU/Linux you can use the shell capabilities for discarding a file extension:

```
for i in *
do convert $i ${i%jpg}gif
done
```

The notation ${i%jpg}gif discards the jpg extension from the filename and replaces it with the gif extension, which also tells ImageMagick which conversion to perform.

Many other additions could be made to the simple example just given. Review *http://www.imagemagick.org/Usage/thumbnails/*.

Labels and Transformations

ImageMagick can be used to add labels to images:

```
convert image.jpg -background Khaki
   label:'Label' -gravity Center
   -append labeled-image.jpg
```

In this example, a fixed label with a khaki background is added to the bottom center of the image. If you want to label many images, use the following example (with the GNU/Linux shell):

```
for i in *
do convert $i -background Khaki
   label:"${i%.jpg}" -gravity
   Center -append labeled-$i
done
```

Here, the images are labeled with their name minus the extension, and the labeled image name is prefixed with `labeled-`.

Use ImageMagick to perform many of the transformations that GIMP does but on lots of images consecutively. For example, decide which transformations you want to perform, as well as the parameter values. Then you can use the convert command with many options and parameters to reproduce the GIMP transformation over and over. Test it on the first image.

Then embed this command in a loop, start it, and have a beverage while the computer works.

Once again, the ImageMagick website is an invaluable source of really sophisticated examples.

Index

More no-nonsense books from **NO STARCH PRESS**

THE ARTIST'S GUIDE TO GIMP, 2ND EDITION

Creative Techniques for Photographers, Artists, and Designers

by MICHAEL J. HAMMEL
JUNE 2012, 320 PP., $39.95
ISBN 978-1-59327-414-6
full color

THE BOOK OF INKSCAPE

The Definitive Guide to the Free Graphics Editor

by DMITRY KIRSANOV
SEPTEMBER 2009, 472 PP., $44.95
ISBN 978-1-59327-181-7

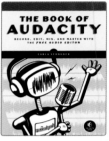

THE BOOK OF AUDACITY

Record, Edit, Mix, and Master with the Free Audio Editor

by CARLA SCHRODER
MARCH 2011, 384 PP., $34.95
ISBN 978-1-59327-270-8

UBUNTU MADE EASY

A Project-Based Introduction to Linux

by RICKFORD GRANT *with* PHIL BULL
JULY 2012, 480 PP. W/CD, $34.95
ISBN 978-1-59327-425-2

THE BOOK OF CSS3

A Developer's Guide to the Future of Web Design

by PETER GASSTON
MAY 2011, 304 PP., $34.95
ISBN 978-1-59327-286-9

THE LINUX COMMAND LINE

A Complete Introduction

by WILLIAM E. SHOTTS, JR.
JANUARY 2012, 480 PP., $39.95
ISBN 978-1-59327-389-7

PHONE:
800.420.7240 OR
415.863.9900

EMAIL:
SALES@NOSTARCH.COM
WEB:
WWW.NOSTARCH.COM